MIDDLESBROUGH

A Complete Record

MIDDLESBROUGH
A Complete Record

Harry Glasper

The Breedon Books
Publishing Company
Derby

First published in Great Britain by
The Breedon Books Publishing Company Limited
44 Friar Gate, Derby, DE1 1DA
1993

© Harry Glasper 1993

ISBN 1 873626 46 0

Printed and bound by Hillmans Printers, Frome, Somerset.
Covers printed by BDC Printing Services Limited of Derby.

Contents

Photographic Acknowledgements

The photographs in this book have been supplied mostly by the *North-Eastern Evening Gazette* in Middlesbrough and thanks go to the newspaper's editor, Mr Ranald Allan, and also to the staff who searched out those pictures. Other photographs have come from the Hulton-Deutsch Picture Library, the EMPICS agency in Nottingham, and Colorsport of London.

Introduction & Acknowledgements

THE six months spent updating this 'Complete Record' history of Middlesbrough Football Club has been for me another labour of love and a most enjoyable one at that. Things were done at a more leisurely pace this time, for there were fewer all-night typing sessions, and it has been a real pleasure to compile.

Every effort has been made at the proof-reading stage to eliminate all known errors but, because of the sheer amount of statistical data contained and, despite every attempt to eradicate them, these errors do occasionally slip through the net and make it to the final print and I apologise for those that do in advance.

The publication of *Middlesbrough: A Complete Record 1876-1989* was so well received by the club's many fans that I would like to thank all those who were so kind and complimentary regarding my project. Since the book's publication in November 1989, many changes have taken place at Ayresome Park. Amazingly, in each of the four seasons the club was either fighting relegation, suffering relegation itself, winning promotion or involved in the Play-off Finals — life has never been dull for us Middlesbrough fans of late.

Also for the first time in the club's 117-year history, Middlesbrough's fans experienced Wembley with the Zenith Data Systems Cup Final in March 1990. Bruce Rioch ended an era when he and 'Boro parted company just before the club's trip to Wembley and since then Colin Todd and Lennie Lawrence have guided Middlesbrough through Football League waters.

Coincidentally, when the first history of the club in Breedon Books' excellent series was published in 1989, Middlesbrough were relegated from the First Division.

Uncannily, this publication has coincided with Middlesbrough's relegation from the FA Premier League — perhaps if I had not attempted this project the club would have remained in the Premier League!

In closing I would like to thank the following for the help, active support and co-operation given in the compilation of this book, the new history of Middlesbrough FC: John Davis, George Harris, David Larry, Matty Lamb, Dave Allan and Mike McGeary of the fanzine *Bread 'n Boro*, Brian Ayre, Peter Barnett, Ken Jackson, Derek Ferguson, Brian McNeil, Michael Batey, my son Richard Glasper and both Joyce Chesney and Mick Clark of Stockton Library.

One of my regrets is that in the acknowledgments in the last book, I inadvertently omitted the name of the man who was responsible for my initial acceptance to the Sports Desk at the *Evening Gazette* to look through their files in the mid-1970s — the late Cliff Mitchell. I sincerely hope that I have redressed that omittance with this insertion.

I would like to re-dedicate this book to the memory of my late father, Ernest Glasper, who would have been so very proud of what has been achieved with the publication of this and the first book on the history of his beloved Middlesbrough Football Club, and to all other Middlesbrough fans, past, present and future. Enjoy the book.

Up the 'Boro!

HARRY GLASPER
New Marske, Redcar
24 June 1993

The 'Boro Story

THE STORY of Middlesbrough Football Club runs parallel with the story of soccer in the North-East. The origin of the 'Boro club goes back to the very beginnings of the game in that part of England and Middlesbrough FC are the oldest of today's major clubs in the area. Indeed, Middlesbrough is one of the oldest names in the history of football.

Many of today's Football League clubs owe their birth either to Victorian church, chapel or works sides. The origins of Middlesbrough Football Club appear to be strongly linked with the town's amateur cricket club, when some of their players wanted to train together during the winter months. A decision was made to embrace the infant game of Association Football as a practical way of operating as a team and a physical means of keeping fit.

In the early 1870s, the game of cricket had long been an established part of the national sporting scene and local games were well covered by the newspapers. Certain names which appeared for the town's cricket team in the summer months more often than not turned up in the winter months with the football team.

The new club, called Middlesbrough Association, was formed in the Commercial Room of the old Talbot Hotel (affectionately known as 'the Old Dog') in the Old Market Place, with James Greenwood appointed the first secretary-treasurer, the club thus today being the oldest football club in the North-East.

The story that the Middlesbrough club was formed at a tripe supper has never been corroborated — nor disproved for that matter — but does appear to have been the work of an imaginative journalist. At the turn of the century, John Wood, who was one of the people in at the very beginning of the club, printed his version of the club's early days and, significantly, does not mention a tripe supper.

The council parks committee was approached and permission was given for the newly-formed club to play their matches at the Archery Ground in Albert Park (opposite where Nazareth House now stands). With no available dressing-room facilities at Albert Park, the players had to dress at home ready for the match and then walk through the town to the Archery Ground, then on the outskirts of the town, carrying their football boots underarm, all of which caused great merriment along the way.

The historic first match is reported to have taken place against Tees Wanderers, local Rugby Union side, and both Jim Greenwood and Fred Hardisty substantiated this in later years. The game ended in a 1-1 draw with Jackson Ewbank claiming the club's first-ever goal.

The *Weekly Exchange* dated 1 March 1877 reported the first game ever played by the Middlesbrough club thus:

FOOTBALL MATCH

On Saturday afternoon last a match (Association rules) was played between the eleven of the Tees Wanderers and eleven of the Middlesbrough Football Club, on the archery ground at Albert Park. There was a good attendance of visitors. The ball was kicked-off by Mr Harvey (captain of the Middlesbrough club). A very strong wind was blowing against the Wanderers, but, notwithstanding this, some excellent play was witnessed. The ball was taken towards the Wanderers' goal, and kept near the whole of the half with one exception, when it was taken back in very good play by Jenkins; and a goal kicked by Ewbank. In the second half the Wanderers, who, after showing some excellent play, succeeded in making a goal, thus making a tie, both sides having one goal each. The playing of Lees, Ewbank, Jenkins and Hildreth for the Middlesbrough club was very good, as was also that of Logan Dickens and Wilson. The sides were as follows:
Middlesbrough club: Harvey (captain) goalkeeper; Windross, Hardisty, backs; Charles Booth, Parkin, half-backs; Frank Lees, Jackson Ewbank, Greenwood, Jenkins, Harrison, Hildreth, forwards.
Wanderers: E. Wilson, goalkeeper; Brewster, Wilson, backs; Dickens, Addyman, half-backs; Bell (captain), Child, Napier, Brewster, Logan, W. Richardson, forwards.

It does seem strange, however, that the club's first recorded match took place a full year after 'Boro were officially formed on 18 February 1876.

Although nationally the formation of the new club did not attract much interest — the stronghold of soccer in the industrial north in the 1870s was rooted firmly in Sheffield — the applications to join Middlesbrough FC came in thick and fast from local young men. The early Middlesbrough club had a problem in finding opponents but gradually, more soccer clubs in the North-East sprang up and in 1877-78, Middlesbrough played what is thought to be their first-ever away match when they went down 1-0 at Barnard Castle on 22 December 1877. Three weeks later they scored a fine 4-0 win over older-established South Bank and on 26 January 1878, the visit of the Newcastle club, Tyne Association, drew 150 spectators to Albert Park to see the sides draw.

A month later, in Newcastle, the sides drew again — this time in a match played in four separate periods — and when first Loftus, and then Eston, were beaten at Albert Park, Middlesbrough's home attendances had reached the 200 mark. The result of this new-found success meant that the club had to change grounds. The local Parks Committee, mindful of the fact that the ever-growing number of spectators were spilling on to the pitch and damaging the turf, told Middlesbrough to find another venue for their home matches.

In October 1878, it was reported that the team would play on a rented field behind Jim Windross' house in Grove Hill. Later in the season, during March 1879, the club moved to Breckon Hill Road, where they rented a field from a Mr Kemp, charging threepence admission to help pay the rent. Small boys paid a penny and what few women chose to see the matches were let in free. An old man collected the 'gate money' in a white basin and average takings were under £3. At the same time, 'Boro began to run a reserve team.

Middlesbrough still found matches hard to come by and it was November before the first match of 1878-79 was played, when Billy Pickstock — later to become a great Middlesbrough favourite — made his debut at South Bank. Pickstock was bald and always wore a cap when he was playing because he did not want to head the ball with his hairless pate.

Later that month, Tyne Association were beaten 3-2 at Breckon Hill and Middlesbrough eventually wound up their season with a 2-0 win over Redcar, played on 'the famous Redcar beach'.

The following season saw Middlesbrough move home again, this time to an old cricket field in Linthorpe Road, and the 1879-80 season also saw the club play in front of their first-ever four-figure attendance when visitors Sheffield Exchange drew a crowd of 1,000. Although they were beaten 1-0, Middlesbrough had much to be pleased about that season. Jackson Ewbank was chosen to play for a representative Sheffield Association side against a Scottish team and the club signed two fine players in Albert Borrie and Dicky Peel. Peel, a ball-playing half-back, made his debut at Loftus in November and Borrie later served Middlesbrough with distinction as an administrator.

The club's success meant that soccer was taking a real hold in the area and other teams came into being. Redcar were Middlesbrough's greatest rivals and in October 1880, some 2,500 packed Linthorpe Road to see the sides meet in a Sheffield Cup game. After a draw, Middlesbrough won the replay 3-1 and Ewbank established his personal prowess as one of the North-East's leading players with two goals. Thus confirmed as a first-class side, Middlesbrough invited Scottish sides Govan and Athole to Linthorpe Road and, in the space of three days, beat both Glasgow teams.

On 5 February 1881, the Cleveland Association was formed in the Swatters Carr Hotel and in a pipe-opening representative game against Northumberland and Durham, Cleveland won 10-0 with five Middlesbrough players in their side. Redcar supplied four players to underline the superiority of the two clubs, but Middlesbrough were clearly the top side in the North-East.

They dominated the Cleveland Association Challenge Cup

for the first five years of that competition's existence before making way for other teams in 1886. In October 1881, Jack Thompson made the first of many appearances for the club as a menacing outside-right and Middlesbrough scored convincing victories over many of their visitors. Whitby were hammered 13-0, Guisborough 9-0, Newcastle Rangers 8-1, North Ormesby 7-1, Sheffield Albion 6-0 and Loftus and Tyne 5-0 each, although Glasgow Rangers Swifts won 6-2 on New Year's Day in what was to become an annual fixture.

On 10 November 1883, Middlesbrough played their first-ever FA Cup-tie when the Derbyshire mining team of Staveley travelled north and inflicted a 5-1 defeat on 'Boro in the first round of the competition. Staveley were 'a bruising, physical side and many of Middlesbrough's players needed subsequent hospital treatment'.

The following season, Middlesbrough did better in reaching the fourth round where they lost 5-2 to Old Etonians.

A win would have given 'Boro a bye into the last eight but, even so, the mere fact that they were now playing such teams as Old Etonians, six times FA Cup Finalists and twice winners of the trophy, meant that Middlesbrough had arrived as a force in English soccer.

Redcar, too, were also making their way and in the fifth round of the 1885-86 FA Cup, the Yorkshire rivals met at Redcar Cricket Field. Middlesbrough had beaten Grimsby Town 2-1 in the third round and then, like Redcar, received a bye into the fifth. Amid the snow and sleet of 23 January 1886, some 1,000 people saw Redcar win 2-1, but they were then knocked out 2-0 by Small Heath (later to become Birmingham City) in the quarter-finals.

That season Middlesbrough and Redcar were also due to meet in the Cleveland Association Challenge Cup Final — Middlesbrough had won the previous four Finals against Redcar — and on 13 March 1886, over 5,000 spectators packed the Saltburn ground to see the two North-East giants draw 0-0 after extra-time. The match was stopped short of the full period when Redcar's Paul broke a leg. The replay was set for 3 April and, as their opponents were short of their two best players, Middlesbrough agreed to the Final being staged at Redcar. It made little difference as 'Boro romped home 8-1 before withdrawing from the competition.

Season 1885-86 was a magnificent one for Middlesbrough — that FA Cup defeat by Redcar excepted. They twice drew with Blackburn Olympic, FA Cup winners in 1883, and beat Nottingham and District 2-1. Individual players turned out for Cleveland against Northumberland with Oswald Cochrane captaining the side. Jack Thompson was a reserve in the North v South game and Albert Borrie played centre-forward for the North-East team which met the famous Corinthians on Tyne's ground.

Two seasons later, in 1887-88, 'Boro played their first game against Sunderland, who were rising stars and challenging Middlesbrough's place at the top of the North-East soccer ladder. This first-ever encounter between sides who were to become great rivals was fraught with incident. The match was in a qualifying round of the FA Cup and at half-time, Sunderland led 2-0 at Linthorpe Road. In the second half, Middlesbrough tore their way back into the game and earned a 2-2 draw before 8,000 spectators. Each club received £34 7s 9d and by the time the teams met at Newcastle Road for the replay, they knew that the winners would receive a bye into the last 16, where they would entertain the London side, Old Foresters.

This time it was Middlesbrough's turn to take a 2-0 lead and Sunderland's to fight back. The Wearsiders won 4-2, but Middlesbrough immediately protested about the professionalism of three Scotsmen in the Sunderland side. On 27 December 1887, at the North-Eastern Hotel, Darlington, an inquiry suspended the three players, booted Sunderland out of the Cup and gave their place to Middlesbrough, who gratefully went through to the quarter-finals with a 4-0 win over Old Foresters.

Even that game was soured by controversy. The London side complained about the state of the Linthorpe Road pitch, hoping for a home replay. When the FA upheld their protest but ordered the game to be replayed at Middlesbrough, Old Foresters withdrew rather than face another trip north. In the quarter-finals, Crewe Alexandra won 2-0 before 6,000 fans at Linthorpe

Road. Amazingly, as 1994 dawned, Middlesbrough were still waiting to play in their first FA Cup semi-final.

In 1888, the Football League was formed and that development, plus the obvious need for professional players, led to a split in Middlesbrough football. The club's officials and supporters were divided as to whether they should adopt professionalism and, eventually, those who wanted to pay players and stay in touch with the clubs which were now taking over the stage, broke away from the old club.

They formed a team called Ironopolis Football Company (see also *The Other Middlesbrough*) which had its headquarters at the Swatters Carr Hotel in Linthorpe Road, a stone's throw from Middlesbrough's HQ. The new club's colours were maroon and green stripes and three Middlesbrough first-teamers switched camps, being joined by players from Scottish clubs, Arthurlie and Dundee Strathmore. Ironopolis' chairman was Alfred Mattison.

The old club now knew that they had to turn professional as well, if they were to avoid becoming second-best. After a brief attempt to bring in legislation allowing players to be paid expenses while retaining their amateur status, Middlesbrough joined the professionals and, indeed, played their first game as a professional club one week before Ironopolis. On 7 December 1889, Sunderland won 3-0 at Linthorpe Road. That Saturday, Ironopolis drew 1-1 with Gainsborough Trinity before 5,000 spectators. The battle for soccer supremacy in Middlesbrough was joined.

Both teams were now members of the newly-formed Northern League. In its first season of 1889-90, the competition had been won by Darlington St Augustine's before Ironopolis took the next three championships. Other clubs in the Northern League at that time were Bishop Auckland, Birtley, Darlington, Elswick Rangers, Newcastle East End, Newcastle West End, South Bank and Stockton.

Middlesbrough ('The Scabs') and Ironopolis ('The Washers' or The Nops') vied for position. Ironopolis arranged top friendlies against Preston, Everton and Sunderland at their ground — their dressing-rooms and headquarters were now at the County Hotel, Newport Road — and Middlesbrough finished runners-up in the Northern League and reached the second round of the FA Cup, where they lost 2-1 at home to Preston, who had beaten Ironopolis 6-0 in the previous round.

Although both clubs had been successful in 1891-92, officials from both camps knew that only amalgamation would be the answer to mounting a serious challenge in the Football League which was now four seasons old. On 7 May 1892, a meeting was held to discuss such a merger and it was agreed to make an application to the Football League annual meeting in Sunderland later that month, under the name of Middlesbrough & Ironopolis Football and Athletic Co Ltd.

Newcastle East End also applied, but the clubs received only one vote each and although they were later invited to form part of the new Second Division, both declined on the grounds that many of their prospective opponents would not be sufficiently attractive to warrant the increased travel.

With admission to the Football League not now an issue, the Middlesbrough clubs again went their separate ways. In the 1892-93 FA Cup, Middlesbrough were knocked out 2-1 by Wolves, the eventual Cup winners, whilst Ironopolis reached the next round before being trounced 7-0 at home to Preston after drawing 2-2 in Lancashire.

In the close season of 1893, Ironopolis made the decision to go it alone in a bid to join the Football League and when the League decided to extend the Second Division to 15 clubs, Ironopolis were in. Bootle resigned from the Second Division, Accrington failed to gain election after finishing next to the bottom of the First Division, and Ironopolis — along with Newcastle United, Rotherham United, Arsenal and Liverpool — stepped up to take their places alongside existing Second Division clubs like Walsall, Burton Swifts, Grimsby, Northwich Victoria, Lincoln City, Crewe Alexandra and Manchester City.

The first-ever Football League match in Middlesbrough took place on 2 September 1893, when Liverpool visited the Paradise Ground and won 2-0. Ironopolis lost their next two games — away to Manchester City (6-1) on 9 September and away to Burton (5-0) on 20 September — before beating Manchester City (then Ardwick) 2-0 on 23 September.

Middlesbrough pictured with the FA Amateur Cup in 1894-95. Back row (left to right): Gettins, Wilson, Cooper, Piercy, Murphy. Front row: Nelmes, Morren, Bach, Allport, Johnson, Mullen.

From a playing point of view, Ironopolis' only season in the Football League was not a disaster. True, they lost all but one away game, but they totalled 20 points from 28 games, which kept them out of the re-election zone. The real problems had been financial. At the end of the season Ironopolis folded, underlining the argument that if the combined sides had taken up the invitation to join the Second Division a season earlier, they would have had the undivided support of all the town's football enthusiasts. As it was, support was too fragmented to sustain two top clubs and Ironopolis' name faded, not from the Football League alone, but from the story of English soccer altogether.

Middlesbrough, meanwhile, had reverted to amateur status during Ironopolis' Football League season and the town was in exactly the same position as it had been before the breakaway club was formed. The amateur Middlesbrough now asserted themselves with the Northern League championship in 1894, 1895 and 1897 and the FA Amateur Cup in 1895 and 1898.

The Amateur Cup was inaugurated in 1893-94, when Old Carthusians became the first winners of the new trophy. The following season Middlesbrough beat Bishop Auckland, Darlington (after two drawn games) and Old Brightonians, who they hammered 8-0, before meeting the Lancaster Regiment (Portsmouth) in the semi-final at Derby. Middlesbrough won 4-0 and met Old Carthusians in the FA Amateur Cup Final on 27 April 1895. The Charterhouse old boys' side took a second-half lead at Headingley before 4,000 people saw Dave Mullen level the scores and then 'Happy' Nelmes hit the winner.

At Middlesbrough railway station a band led the triumphant team to the celebrations at the Masham Hotel, kept at that time by Tom Bach, the Middlesbrough skipper. Alas, there was no trophy to present. Old Carthusians had considered the result such a formality that they had not bothered to bring the FA Amateur Cup with them. It was some days before the new winners laid hands on their prize.

This success had its drawbacks. Players were suddenly thrust into the limelight and professional clubs were soon flocking to offer terms to Middlesbrough's amateurs. Tom Morren moved to Sheffield United, where he went on to win an international cap for England, and Phil Bach did the same when he moved on to Sunderland, although he returned to give great service to Middlesbrough as chairman. Despite losing some of their best players, Middlesbrough remained a force and in 1898 they won the FA Amateur Cup again after reaching the semi-finals the previous season, where they were beaten by Royal Artillery (Portsmouth).

Middlesbrough's path to their second Final was bizarre to say the least. After beating Leadgate Park, Thornaby Utopians and Casuals, Middlesbrough faced a semi-final tie against Thornaby at Darlington. At that time there was a smallpox epidemic in the lower Teesside area and Darlington people protested strongly about supporters of two semi-finalists bringing the disease into their town. The FA arranged for the semi-final to be played in secret in the Cleveland hill village of Brotton, two miles from the sea.

Middlesbrough won this eccentric semi-final and took their place in the Amateur Cup Final against Uxbridge at the Crystal Palace. It was a hot, humid day as Middlesbrough, skippered by left-back Robert Piercy, took control of the game and won 2-1 with goals from Bishop and Kemplay. The date was 23 April 1898 and it was Middlesbrough's last cup win until their Anglo-Scottish Cup triumph 78 years later.

Middlesbrough's days in the unpaid ranks were almost over.

The players were at the top of the amateur tree and there was really nothing more that they could achieve. In addition they could see that fellow players — some not nearly so talented — were making money at other clubs. The end of the old-fashioned opposition to professionalism was also in sight and Middlesbrough played only one more season as an amateur club. In the FA Cup they beat Darlington 6-2 in the qualifying competition before going out 1-0 at home to Hebburn Argyle.

Apart from the FA Cup, the only time Middlesbrough fans saw top-class professional opposition was when Middlesbrough arranged friendlies against teams like Preston, Millwall, Burnley, Spurs and Southampton, paying the visiting clubs guarantees of between £10 and £40 to visit Teesside. The breach with the people who had broken away to form Ironopolis was healed and the way was now clear for Middlesbrough to assume professional status once again. On 28 February 1899, at a meeting presided over by the club chairman, R.H.Forrester, Middlesbrough FC rejoined the ranks of the professional clubs.

'Boro's next ambition was to join the Football League and after raising 1,000 £1 shares, they applied, with the backing of Sunderland, Newcastle United and Harry Walker, North Riding FA's representative on the FA Council. The Football League annual meeting was held on 19 May 1899, at the Old Boar's Head Hotel in Manchester, and there were nine applicants for three vacant places in the Second Division. Middlesbrough received 17 votes to Blackpool's 15 (Blackpool were seeking re-election) and League football returned to Middlesbrough after a gap of five seasons. Next-to-bottom Loughborough were re-elected with 28 votes and newcomers Chesterfield (27 votes) came in at the expense of the bottom club, Darwen, who had conceded 141 goals and won only nine points in 34 games.

Middlesbrough did just enough in their first season as a Football League club. The first game was on 2 September 1899, when they lost 3-0 at Lincoln. There followed two more defeats before Middlesbrough won their first League point with a 1-1 draw at New Brighton on 16 September. A week later they recorded their first League win by beating Grimsby Town 1-0 at Linthorpe Road. On 11 November, Middlesbrough crushed Burton Swifts 8-1 at home. Although there were several defeats at Linthorpe Road, it was their home form which kept them alive. They failed to win a single away match in finishing 14th out of 18 clubs.

Unlike Ironopolis, Middlesbrough's debut in the Football League was successful in terms of finance and they finished the season with a profit of £176. Near the end of the season they signed Newcastle United's left-winger, Willie Wardrope, to underline their arrival as a serious force in professional football under manager John Robson.

Middlesbrough's colours in those early days of the Football League were white shirts and blue shorts with a change strip of black shirts and white shorts. Even in those times, vandalism was a problem and a report to the June board meeting told of damage to the ground. The members' entrance had been broken by carthorses and it was resolved 'that horses shall not be allowed on the field in future'. Shares were offered to local tradesmen and one proprietor of a local boot and shoe firm offered 11 pairs of boots — which were gratefully accepted.

Once settled into the Football League, Middlesbrough lost little time in making their presence felt and in the 1900-01 season they shot up the table to finish in sixth place. After winning their first match of the season, 2-0 at home to Lincoln, they went down 4-0 at Newton Heath (later Manchester United) and then drew 2-2 at home to Glossop North End. On 22 September, however, Middlesbrough recorded their first-ever away win in the Football League when they beat Chesterfield 3-2.

On 9 March 1901, Middlesbrough crushed Gainsborough 9-2 at Linthorpe Road and at the end of the season they had climbed up the table and had almost doubled their gate receipts to £8,347. If 'Boro fans felt that their team was on the verge of greater things, they were not going to be disappointed. In only their third season in the Football League, Middlesbrough stormed to promotion, finishing runners-up to West Bromwich Albion and nine points clear of third club Preston North End.

From the moment they won their opening game of the season, beating Stockport County 3-1 at Edgeley Park, Middlesbrough looked set for the First Division. Only West Brom managed

to win at Linthorpe Road — a 2-1 defeat for 'Boro on 12 October 1901 — and Middlesbrough's final goals for and against tallies of 90-24 were each the best of any club in the Football League. In 17 home matches, Middlesbrough dropped only three points and scored 58 goals with just seven against.

The Middlesbrough side had undergone a complete transformation. Of the old guard, only Ramsay remained at left-back. The club's half-backs in that promotion season were Dave Smith, 'Bullet' Jones and Andy Davidson — a half-back line which supporters talked about for years afterwards.

On 19 April 1902, Middlesbrough entertained Bristol City and beat them 2-0. In that game, manager John Robson gave a debut to a young goalkeeper, 18-year-old Tim Williamson. Less than 5ft 10in tall, Williamson became known as 'Tiny' and went on to establish himself as one of the best goalkeepers of his day. When he appeared against Ireland at Ayresome Park in February 1905, he became the first player to be capped for England while playing for Middlesbrough. Williamson was capped seven times in all and there could have been no one in the crowd for that match against Bristol City who realised that they were watching the start of an illustrious career. When he left the club in 1923, Williamson had played a record 602 games for Middlesbrough (563 League and 39 FA Cup). He is part of the Middlesbrough legend.

Season 1902-03 was not only Middlesbrough's first in the First Division. It also signalled the beginnings of their present home at Ayresome Park. Even before the season began there was tremendous interest in 'Boro's fortunes and crowds of 12-15,000 turned up to see their pre-season practice matches. On 1 September 1902, Middlesbrough played their first match in the First Division and 'Sandy' Robertson gave them the best possible start to their career in the top-flight when he scored the only goal of their match at Blackburn Rovers. One week later Robertson was on target again when he scored the only goal against Everton as Middlesbrough recorded their first home win in the First Division. The crowd at Linthorpe Road that day was around 20,000.

Middlesbrough also had their first taste of local derby games at the highest level. On 18 October 1902 they beat Newcastle United 1-0 at St James' Park. When they met Newcastle in the return at Linthorpe Road on 14 February, Middlesbrough won by the same score. The games against Sunderland, however, were a different tale. On 20 December, the Wearsiders won 1-0 at Middlesbrough and late in the season — on 18 April 1903 — Sunderland won 2-1 in a match played at Newcastle after Roker Park had been closed due to crowd trouble.

Middlesbrough finished their first season in the First Division in 13th place, seven points clear of relegated Grimsby Town. Ten of their 14 wins were at Linthorpe Road, where they scored 27 of their 41 goals. Newcastle finished on level points with 'Boro but an inferior goal average pushed them into 14th place.

In the FA Cup, Middlesbrough went out in the first round, losing 3-1 at Bristol City. Indeed, 'Boro's progress in the Cup had been painfully slow. After their quarter-final appearance of 1888 they had to wait 13 seasons before appearing in the last 16 again. In 1900-01 they fought through the preliminary competition for the right to meet Newcastle at Middlesbrough and won the local derby 3-1. In the next round an easy home tie with Kettering was won 5-0 and Middlesbrough fans were thinking of a semi-final place when West Brom upset their plans by winning 1-0 at Linthorpe Road.

Throughout the 1902-03 season preparations had been underway to move from Linthorpe Road to Ayresome Park. The last game played on the old ground which had served Middlesbrough so well was the 1-1 draw against Stoke on 25 April 1903. Then 'Boro moved lock, stock and barrel to their new home. Early in September 1903, Glasgow Celtic took part in the first game at Ayresome Park and were beaten 1-0. But the official opening came a few days later, on 12 September 1903 when Sunderland were the visitors for a First Division match.

Once settled into their new ground — their first League win at Ayresome Park was on 26 September 1903, when they beat Small Heath (later Birmingham City) 3-1 — Middlesbrough began to consolidate themselves in the First Division and finished a respectable tenth. In addition, 'Boro had the added bonus of a profit of £3,314 on the season.

'Boro team for the match against Sunderland which saw the official opening of Ayresome Park in September 1903. Seated (left to right, players only): White, Williamson, Hogg, Smith, Davison, Brown, Cassidy, Atherton, Blackett. On ground: Gettins, Jones.

Official Ayresome Opening

MIDDLESBROUGH 2   SUNDERLAND 3

THE first game played at Ayresome Park was on Saturday, 5 September 1903, Glasgow Celtic providing the attractive Scottish opposition in a friendly game as a pipe-opener to the imminent 1903-04 season. Ayresome Park itself was designed by Scottish architect Archibald Leitch who had built many football grounds. New boy Willie White scored the only goal of the game in front of 7,000 spectators, who were more interested in giving the new ground the critical once over. Although the builders toiled many long hours to complete the outstanding work, parts of the new North Stand were not finished and were therefore closed to the public for the opening day ceremony. The old wooden stand was transported, plank for plank and nail for nail from the old Linthorpe Road ground to its new home opposite the newly-constructed North Stand.

James Clifton Robinson, president and managing director of Imperial Tramways, and also a shareholder of the club, performed the official opening ceremony of Ayresome Park on Saturday, 12 September 1903 to coincide with Middlesbrough's first home game of the new season against neighbours Sunderland, Local MPs Pike Pease and Herbert Samuel, ever keen to make their presence felt in the community, led the procession of local dignatories as Mr Robinson was handed a golden key to perform the event.

The opening ceremony was a brief affair, Mr Robinson said a few auspicious words, wishing the club good fortune in its new location and turned the key, unlocking the huge gates. Club chairman R.W.Williams hoisted the Union Jack, and the attendant band played the National Anthem, the eager crowd of 30,000 paid almost £908 at the turnstile, and the impressive new ground and enclosure was open to the paying public.

Middlesbrough's first-half display was irrepressible and Sunderland's Scottish international full-backs Andy McCombie and Jimmy Watson were sorely pressed to stop the Middlesbrough forwards attack on goal. The inevitable happened four minutes before the half-time whistle when Joe Cassidy, Middlesbrough's captain, became the first man to score at Ayresome Park, putting the ball into the net from a scrimmage.

Sunderland revved up the pace at the start of the second half and Gemmell equalised from Bridgett's pass early on but within 30 seconds Brown had restored Middlesbrough's one-goal lead. Hogg equalised for Sunderland and Robinson ensured two points for the Roker brigade before the final whistle to spoil Middlesbrough's party.

Middlesbrough: Williamson; Hogg, Blackett, D.W.Smith, A.Jones, Davidson, E.Gettins, White, A.Brown, Cassidy, Atherton.
Sunderland: Doig; Watson, McCombie, Jackson, McAllister, Farquhar, Bridgett, Gemmell, Hogg, Robinson, Craggs.
Attendance: 30,000

In the FA Cup that year, they equalled their best run with a trip to the quarter-finals. In the first round proper they went to Millwall and beat the London club 2-0. 'Sandy' Brown scored both goals against a Millwall side which included Joe Gettins, who had played for 'Boro in the 1895 FA Amateur Cup Final and who was an amateur on the books of both clubs. In the second round Middlesbrough visited Preston and another two goals from Brown helped them on their way to a sensational 3-0 victory over that season's Second Division champions. It was Preston's only defeat of the season.

'Boro were in the quarter-finals for the third time in their history and when they managed a goalless draw at Manchester City there were many Middlesbrough fans who thought that 1904 might be their year. But when the sides met at Ayresome Park for the replay, the Lancashire club cruised to a 3-1 win — a big disappointment to the thousands of Teesside youngsters who had been given the Wednesday afternoon off school to watch their favourites battle for the right to meet Sheffield Wednesday in the semi-final.

All was not well in the Middlesbrough camp, despite the satisfactory performances of 1903-04, and the following season 'Boro found themselves in the relegation zone. By February

Middlesbrough on the attack at White Hart Lane in February 1905, when they lost 1-0 to Tottenham Hotspur in a first-round FA Cup replay.

1905, they were next-to-bottom of the First Division and had not won an away game in the League for two years. The club knew that they had to do something out of the ordinary to revive the fortunes of their flagging side. Middlesbrough had already moved into the transfer market with the signing of Stockport County's centre-forward Tom Green. In the New Year they also approached Sunderland and asked the Roker Park directors about the possible transfer of forward Alf Common.

The deal took some time to set up but by the end of February, Common was a Middlesbrough player and destined to become one of the most famous names in the history of soccer, not for what he achieved in the game, but for the fact that at a transfer fee of £1,000, he became the first 'four-figure footballer'. Although it was perfectly acceptable for a club to buy players to win titles, it was considered almost immoral to spend money on avoiding relegation. And when such extravagance was shown by one of the Football League's newest clubs *The Athletic News* commented: 'As a matter of commerce, ten young recruits at £100 apiece might have paid better, and as a matter of sport, the Second Division would be more honourable than retention of place by purchase.'

Whatever the morals of the transfer, Common proved his worth immediately. On 25 February, Middlesbrough went to Bramall Lane to play Sheffield United and won 1-0, Common scoring the only goal of the game from the penalty-spot. It was 'Boro's first away win since their 3-1 victory against the same club on 7 March 1903. Middlesbrough's fortunes picked up and when they won 2-0 at Blackburn on 15 April 1905, they were safe. Even a 3-0 home defeat at the hands of Newcastle on the last day on the season could not harm them and they finished 15th.

In the FA Cup, Middlesbrough could only draw 1-1 with Tottenham Hotspur, who were then a Southern League side. In the replay at White Hart Lane, the Londoners won 1-0. Perhaps the greatest measure of 'Boro's mediocre season was the fact that their leading scorer for 1904-05 was Tom Green,

the centre-forward signed midway through the season from Stockport. Green headed 'Boro's scorers with just four goals.

Even after relegation had been avoided the club's troubles were not over and during the course of the following season — when 'Boro again fought to avoid the drop to the Second Division — the Football Association fined the club £250 and suspended 11 of the 12 directors, including the chairman R.W.Williams, for allegedly making irregular bonus payments to players.

In 1905-06, Middlesbrough came nearer to relegation than the previous season, saved only perhaps by the Football League's decision to retain the bottom two clubs of 1904-05 — Bury and Notts County — and extend the First Division to 20 clubs. Alex Mackie, the former Sunderland boss, was now manager in place of John Robson. In the end it was Mackie's swoop into the transfer market which once again saved 'Boro's First Division status. Again the deals involving Middlesbrough were little short of sensational. In March 1906, the club amazed the football world with three signings.

The legendary Steve Bloomer — already an established England international — came from Derby County, a move which was as much a shock to his devoted fans at the Baseball Ground as it was to Ayresome Park supporters; Billy Brawn arrived from Aston Villa after winning two England caps and playing for Villa against Newcastle in the 1905 FA Cup Final; and Fred Wilcox moved from Birmingham to Ayresome Park. In addition, Middlesbrough also brought Bloomer's teammate, full-back Emor ('Jack') Ratcliffe from Derby, although he was only a makeweight which enabled Derby to obtain a more realistic fee for Bloomer under the transfer regulations then in force.

Unlike Alf Common, there was to be no story-book debut for Bloomer. He played his first game for 'Boro against First Division leaders Liverpool at Anfield on 17 March 1906 and saw his side humiliated by the Merseysiders, who were on their way to their second Championship. The last day of the season arrived with Wolves already relegated. Middlesbrough and Bury had 30 points each, Nottingham Forest 31. Bury won 3-0 at

Sunderland, Forest went down 4-1 at Everton and Middlesbrough managed a 1-1 draw at Blackburn to escape the drop by virtue of a better goal-average than Forest, who joined Wolves in the Second Division.

The years leading up to the start of World War One were memorable more for the controversy surrounding the club's financial dealings than for anything Middlesbrough achieved on the field. In the FA Cup, they never progressed beyond the third round. In fact, they had to wait until 1936 for their next quarter-final appearance. In the First Division they rose to fourth in 1914, but for most of the time hovered around mid-table.

The financial problems were highlighted on 4 January 1906, when the FA suspended the club because the £250 fine imposed for irregular payments had not been paid. So that Middlesbrough could play Derby County at the Baseball Ground the following Saturday, 'Boro's new chairman, Lieutenant-Colonel T. Gibson Poole, sent his personal cheque to clear the debt and Middlesbrough duly went to Derby and drew 1-1 with a goal from Alf Common. The club also owed Stoke £155 for the transfer of Coxon and this was also settled in due course.

Middlesbrough's March 1906 transfer dealings had made the club unpopular — as had the £1,000 signing of Alf Common, who finished 1905-06 as 'Boro's leading scorer with 19 goals — and soon rumours were rife that several clubs, wishing to see Bury relegated, had assisted Middlesbrough in the purchase of Bloomer, Brawn and Wilcox. Football's ruling body could hardly ignore such accusations and in May 1906 a commission met in Manchester to examine Middlesbrough's books and question officials from Derby, Villa and Birmingham.

A later meeting at Blackburn cross-examined chairman Poole and manager Mackie and reported that 'Boro had paid Bloomer an improper bonus of £10 to re-sign for 1906-07. In addition, they said, 'Boro's books were not properly kept. Middlesbrough were fined £50 and two members of the League Management Committee would visit the club twice before the end of April 1907 — at 'Boro's expense — to ensure that the books were kept in order. By now the FA considered Middlesbrough's accounts to be in such a mess that a special commission was set up to investigate the entire financial running of the club.

The commission found, among other things, that the club chairman sometimes retained takings himself, paying the club's bills out of his personal account, and that he owed Middlesbrough £500. The chairman paid the balance into the club's bank and escaped public censure. But Alex Mackie, who had already resigned, was suspended. Steve Bloomer was also banned for two weeks.

On the field things were going just as badly and 'Boro started 1906-07 with only two points from their first eight games, losing two home games to Sheffield Wednesday (1-3) and Manchester City (2-3). In late October, they appointed a player-manager in the shape of Andy Aitken, a Scottish international centre-half and great favourite at St James' Park. Although Middlesbrough were bottom of the First Division by Christmas, under Aitken they rallied to finish the season in 11th place, thanks mainly to the inspiring example of their new manager and the splendid Williamson in goal. Before the end of the season, Middlesbrough made another important signing when Sunderland's left-back, Jimmy Watson, arrived at Ayresome Park.

With their defence strengthened by the inclusion of Aitken, Watson and the fast-improving Williamson, Middlesbrough set out on the 1907-08 season in more confident mood and, although they again failed in the FA Cup, losing 2-0 to Notts County in the first round, they climbed up the First Division to finish in what was then their best-ever position of sixth.

'Boro were only two points behind runners-up Aston Villa and had it not been for a poor start to the season — 17 points from their first 21 games — they would have finished second to champions Manchester United. Bloomer was leading scorer with 12 League goals to add to the 18 which had seen him in first place the previous season.

In the close season, Aitken left the club for Leicester Fosse, who had just won promotion to the First Division and in 1908-09 'Boro finished in ninth place. Their FA Cup run again ended in the first round, this time at Preston.

In 1909-10, Middlesbrough found themselves at the wrong end of the table and by New Year they were second from bottom. Into the side had come George Elliott, a Sunderland-born

youngster who teamed up with Steve Bloomer, Common having been tried at centre-half in a bid to plug the gap left by the departure of Aitken.

Elliott was an immediate success with the Ayresome Park fans. Like Tim Williamson he was to give great service to 'Boro and when he left in 1925, he had played 364 League and FA Cup games and scored 208 goals. When one considers that World War One robbed Elliott of four seasons, they are awesome figures indeed.

Four victories in March 1910 saved Middlesbrough from relegation. Wins over Bolton (home 5-0), Bristol City (home 2-1), Sheffield United (home 1-0) and Nottingham Forest (away 1-0) edged 'Boro to 31 points, level with Arsenal and two more than relegated Chelsea, who went down with bottom club, Bolton Wanderers.

But still there were dark clouds off the field. After the 1-1 draw with Newcastle at Ayresome Park on 9 April, the referee alleged that 'Boro and the FA Cup Finalists had come to an arrangement over the result. A joint FA-Football League inquiry reported: 'There was no proof of any arrangement between clubs or players to influence the result.' Nevertheless, Middlesbrough's name had cropped up again in connection with alleged irregularities.

The club's gate receipts were £1,000 down on the previous season and Lieutenant-Colonel Poole offered Alf Common a free transfer if he did not claim the £250 benefit which the club had promised him. Common agreed and soon the history-making footballer was on his way to Arsenal. It was ironic that the game's first four-figure footballer should be given away to save the club from financial embarrassment. Bloomer went back to Derby in September 1910 and Watson became assistant trainer before joining non-League Shildon shortly afterwards.

Despite losing three star names, Middlesbrough began 1910-11 well. Manager Andy Walker introduced a Scottish lad, Andy Jackson, at centre-half and at last the gap created by Aitken's departure was filled, although Robert Young, who had joined Everton in the close season for £1,200, had done well enough. Young Jackson's performances made him a firm favourite at Ayresome Park. But for his tragic death in World War One, he may well have become one of the game's great players.

On 17 December 1910, Middlesbrough beat Bradford City 3-2 at Ayresome Park to put themselves only a point from the top of the First Division after a superb run which had given them 23 points from their first 16 games. From that moment the side took only nine points from their remaining 22 games. What happened to halt this 'Boro side in its tracks? Again it was an off-the-field scandal.

This time the row centred around the visit of League leaders Sunderland on 3 December 1910. At that time the Wearsiders were the only unbeaten side in the Football League and nearly 28,000 fans packed into Middlesbrough's ground for what they saw as the match of the season. At the same time, the Middlesbrough Parliamentary election was only two days away and Lieutenant-Colonel Poole was standing as Tory candidate. Some of the 'Boro players had spoken on his behalf and, amazing though it may seem today, the result of the First Division match became tied up with the election result as the Liberals forecast a Sunderland victory.

All this may, on the face of it, seem harmless enthusiasm. But it had sinister overtones. Before the game 'Boro manager Andy Walker offered Sunderland's skipper Charlie Thomson £30 (£10 for himself and £2 for each of the other Sunderland players) to let Middlesbrough win the game, 'so as to help the chairman win the election.' Thomson told Sunderland's trainer, Billy Williams, and Williams told Mr Fred Taylor, the Wearsiders' chairman. Taylor and another Sunderland director reported the matter to the Football Association.

Even though Sunderland could not have been trying harder, Middlesbrough won the game 1-0, through a goal from outside-left Nichol. Despite the result, the 'Boro chairman lost the election by 3,749 votes and once again Middlesbrough were before a commission of inquiry. In addition, Walker was also in trouble for making an illegal approach to an Airdrieonians player. He was suspended for four weeks on that charge and the 'Boro club fined £100.

On 16 January 1911, the commission reported they were

Middlesbrough in 1908. Back row (left to right): Heslop, J.C.Brown (assistant secretary), Campbell, A.E.Forbes (director), Hasell, F.France (director), Gordon, T.R.Bell. Second row: Jack Bingley (trainer), T.Burdon (director), Groves, Andy Aitken (manager), Watson, J.H.Gunter (director), McKenzie, C.G.Hunt (director), Pentland, J.R.Smiles (vice-chairman). Seated: Wilcox, Hall, Jones, S.Aitken (captain), Col T.G.Poole VD, JP (chairman), Bloomer, Wilson, Cail, Verrill. Front row: Haxby, Kent, Orobin, Miller, Thackeray, Barker, Dixon, McClure.

satisfied that an offer of money to influence the result had been made and both Walker and Poole were suspended permanently. Poole received little sympathy, but over 12,500 people signed a petition asking the FA to reinstate Walker, without success.

Middlesbrough's name was now bad news to both the FA and the Football League and at the club's annual meeting, the League president told shareholders that any further malpractices would result in Middlesbrough losing their place in the competition. The affair probably cost the club the First Division title because the players never recovered from the scandal and the jibes that they had tried to buy victory.

Two players seemingly unaffected by the scandal were Tim Williamson and George Elliott. Williamson won his second cap, against Ireland at Derby on 11 February 1911, thus breaking Sam Hardy's seemingly permanent hold of the position, and went on to play in six of the next seven England games. Elliott became Middlesbrough's leading goalscorer with ten goals out of 'Boro's total of 49. Elliott held the top 'Boro goalscoring spot for the next three seasons and for several seasons after the war.

For season 1911-12, Middlesbrough had a new set of directors and a new manager. Andy Aitken applied for his old job but the post went to Tom McIntosh, the Darlington boss. For the first few weeks of the season, the North-East took the First Division by storm. In November, 'Boro topped the table with Newcastle second and Sunderland third. Eventually, only Newcastle finished in the top three and Middlesbrough had to be content with seventh place, one ahead of Sunderland.

Alf Common led Arsenal to a 3-1 win over 'Boro at Highbury on 16 December and when the Gunners came to Ayresome Park in February, they won again, this time 2-0. But the highlight of the season was the visit of Newcastle on 11 November. The clubs stood first and second in the table and a record 30,000 crowd packed Ayresome Park to see the 1-1 draw. It was the final confirmation that the bad old days of relegation worries and scandals were over for the time being.

The splendidly-named George Washington Elliott continued

to bang home the goals — although in the last season before the shutdown for World War One, he made way for Walter Tinsley, who scored 23 League goals.

The Carr brothers joined the club around this time. Willie Carr, a centre-half and the eldest of the three, signed in November 1910; three months later, Jackie, who was to go on to make 466 first-team appearances and score 78 goals, signed; later, younger brother George also pulled on a Middlesbrough shirt.

In 1912-13, 'Boro finished 16th but Williamson continued to perform wonders in goal and was now club skipper, whilst Elliott played his first game for England, against Ireland in Belfast. In that same game, incidentally, Williamson won his last cap.

In 1913-14, Middlesbrough achieved their best position in the First Division when they finished third behind Blackburn and Aston Villa. Elliott's 31 goals made him the top scorer in the First Division, despite the fact that he had missed six games, and Walter Tinsley, who came from Sunderland in December 1913, managed 19 goals in only 23 games. 'Boro had now found their goalscoring touch with 77 goals. Only champions Blackburn (with 78) hit more.

'Boro's last season before World War One saw them drop to 12th place after averaging a point a game. In their match with Oldham at Ayresome Park on 3 April 1915, 'Boro were leading 4-1 after 55 minutes when the Oldham full-back, Billy Cook, refused to leave the field after being sent off. The referee abandoned the game and the League ordered the result to stand.

The outbreak of war meant the end of many potentially illustrious football careers. Besides those players who were too old to resume when war ended in 1918, Middlesbrough lost four players killed in the fighting — Andrew Jackson, Archie Wilson, Harry Cook and the former Celtic player, Don McLeod. Ayresome Park became a military training centre and the club closed down for the duration.

In January 1919, Middlesbrough, Newcastle and Sunderland were the mainstays of the Northern Victory League, introduced as a preliminary to the return of the Football League. 'Boro

Middlesbrough players pictured at Ayresome Park before the start of the 1912-13 season.

No Ref — Match Abandoned!

MIDDLESBROUGH 4   OLDHAM ATHLETIC 1

OLDHAM Athletic were first promoted to Division One at the end of the 1909-10 season and were pressing for the League Championship in season 1914-15 when the clubs first met at Boundary Park on 28 November 1914. Middlesbrough were routed as Oldham turned on the style and ran out 5-1 winners, Jackie Carr scoring 'Boro's solitary goal.

Revenge was uppermost in Middlesbrough's mind when the return fixture was enacted at Ayresome Park on 3 April 1915, no one realising the historic footballing precedent that was about to be witnessed. 'Boro went into the lead as early as the first minute through Walter Tinsley and on ten minutes the potential champions were reeling when Tommy Urwin beat Matthews to make the score 2-0. On 20 minutes Oldham took umbrage when referee Mr H.Smith of Nottingham refused to award a penalty, waved play on and Tom Storey broke away and set up a scoring chance for Tinsley, who clinically finished the move to put the game beyond Athletic's reach. Oldham took great indignation at Middlesbrough's scoring audacity and immediately adopted unsporting tactics. The ball was kicked off the centre-spot three times before the referee warned several Oldham players regarding their conduct. Oldham settled down again to try and play themselves back into the game, and things looked hopeful when Kemp pulled a goal back.

Bill Cook, the Oldham full-back was judged to have fouled Carr in the penalty area. Cook protested his innocence but the referee would not waive from his penalty decision and

Tinsley calmly scored from the kick. Carr had won his club many penalties by verbally goading an opposing defender into committing a foul, and this appears to have been the case in this incident. Shortly after, on 55 minutes, Cook up-ended Carr and Mr Smith ordered the offending full-back to leave the field. Obviously feeling badly done by, the player refused point-blank to leave the pitch. Charlie Roberts, Oldham's captain, and one-time chairman of the Players' Union, played his part in attempting to get Cook to leave the field, but the player remained adamant that he was going to remain on the pitch.

The referee, with his options fast running out, then gave Cook a final ultimatum, one minute to leave the field. Again the player refused to leave, so the referee walked off the pitch, and with no official to control the game the match was abandoned when both teams followed the referee to the dressing-rooms.

Oldham played Cook in League games following the Ayresome Park incident but, following an FA inquiry, he was suspended from 16 April 1915 to 30 April 1916. The score of 4-1 at the time of the abandonment was ordered to stand.

Middlesbrough: Davies; Holmes, J.Walker, Davidson, A.Jackson, Malcolm, Storey, J.Carr, Wilson, Tinsley, Urwin.
Oldham Athletic: Matthews; Hodson, Cook, Moffat, Roberts, Wilson, Tummon, Pilkington, Gee, Kemp, Walters.
Attendance: 5,000

took the title, three points ahead of the Wearsiders, and the club looked forward to the first proper football since 1915.

Willie Carr had taken over from Jackson at centre-half and under Tom McIntosh — the man who guided Middlesbrough to their highest-ever First Division position in 1913-14 — 'Boro looked forward to their first game of the season in a First Division now extended to 22 clubs. Their first post-war match took place at Hillsborough on 30 August 1919, when 'Boro won 1-0 against Sheffield Wednesday, the side which finished seventh in the last season of peace.

But the intervening years had done much to change the face of football and at the end of the season, Wednesday were relegated, finishing bottom of the table, 13 points adrift of the next club, Notts County. Middlesbrough floundered after

their promising start. Although George Elliott was still finding the net regularly — 31 League goals in the season — and despite the fact that Williamson was performing as well in goal as he had done almost two decades earlier, 'Boro's play lacked the consistency to make them Championship contenders. They finished 13th and were knocked out of the FA Cup in the second round, going down 1-0 at Notts County.

For the next two seasons, 'Boro's League position maintained a steady improvement. They finished eighth in both 1920-21 and 1921-22. In the latter season, Middlesbrough had the added bonus of their Scottish international, Andrew Wilson, returning to the fold. Wilson was injured during the war and played with a glove over a paralysed hand. He went 'on loan' to Dunfermline, then playing in a 'rebel' Central League in

Jogging around Ayresome in the early 1920s, 'Boro players are led by Walter Holmes (far left) and George Elliott (second left).

Scotland, but 'Boro refused to transfer him and he returned to Ayresome Park in August 1921, to a hero's welcome.

Elliott moved to inside-forward to accommodate the Scottish international centre-forward and, despite his reluctance to return, Wilson repaid 'Boro with 32 goals in his first season as the side maintained eighth place in the First Division, with exactly the same number of points — 46.

Middlesbrough's forward line read: Jackie Carr, Billy Birrell (from Raith Rovers), Andy Wilson, George Elliott and Tommy Urwin. It is a front line which still rolls easily off the tongues of the most senior of today's 'Boro supporters.

A measure of Elliott's talent was the fact that on 8 April 1922, when Wilson was scoring the winning goal for Scotland against England at Birmingham, Elliott deputized at centre-forward and netted a hat-trick in the 4-2 win over Arsenal at Ayresome Park. And the following season Elliott was back as 'Boro's leading scorer with 23 goals.

But if 1922-23 was a good one for Elliott, it was a bad one for the 'Boro team, who slipped to 18th place in the First Division, albeit six points clear of relegation. Off the field the club lost over £7,000 and it was clear that a crisis was at hand. It broke the following season.

The 1923-24 season was Middlesbrough's 18th in the First Division since winning promotion in 1902. It also proved to be their last for three seasons. The side won only seven games and finished bottom of the table with 22 points — ten fewer than Chelsea, who went down with them. 'Boro won only one game away from home (a 1-0 victory at Sheffield United on 29 December) and Andy Wilson was leading scorer with only eight goals, five of which had been scored in one game against Nottingham Forest when 'Boro had a purple patch and won 5-2. Manager Jim Howie, who had replaced Tom McIntosh in 1921, left Ayresome Park early in the relegation season to be replaced by Herbert Bamlett. But the former referee could not halt the slide.

After his five goals against Forest, Wilson was transferred to Chelsea for £6,000; Tim Williamson was missing from the Middlesbrough side for the first time since 1902; and George Carr had been transferred to Leicester City, then a mid-table Second Division side. 'Boro themselves were busy in the transfer market. Bamlett brought full-backs Reg Freeman from Oldham Athletic, Alf Maitland from South Shields and Owen Williams, Clapton Orient's English international outside-left. Williams and Freeman settled into the 'Boro side, but Maitland was soon on his way to Newcastle. A deficit in the transfer market saw 'Boro lose £8,000 on the season, making their total loss for two seasons some £15,000 and they were fined £50 for an illegal approach to a player of another club.

'Boro's first season back in the Second Division was one of consolidation and they finished 13th and scored only 36 goals, of which Owen Williams and Ian Dickson bagged seven each. At the back, their defence held out match after match to restore the balance, although when George Carr returned to Ayresome Park with Leicester City on 3 January 1925, 'Boro conceded five goals as City continued their romp towards the Second Division title. Before the season began, Tommy Urwin was transferred to Newcastle United, who were already looking to strengthen the side which had just won the FA Cup.

Season 1925-26 started off in glorious style. Beating Portsmouth 5-1 at Fratton Park on the opening day, 'Boro won 11 of their first 14 games. But the rot set in and 'Boro lost six games on the trot to finish ninth. There were individual triumphs, however. Jimmy McClelland, signed from Raith Rovers, scored a club record 38 goals (32 in the League) and in the FA Cup third round game against Leeds United at Ayresome Park he netted all the goals as 'Boro romped home 5-1. In the next round, Owen Williams had an unhappy return to his old club as Clapton Orient beat 'Boro 4-2.

The 1926-27 season opened disastrously for Middlesbrough with a 3-0 defeat at Chelsea, followed by a 2-1 reverse at Southampton two days later. When Preston went to Ayresome Park for 'Boro's first home game of the season, the Lancashire

Middlesbrough goalkeeper Jimmy Mathieson clears from Arsenal's Charlie Buchan at Highbury in November 1927.

side won 2-0. A goalless draw at South Shields meant that 'Boro had started the season with only one point and one goal from four games. Yet by the end of that season, they had romped away with the Second Division championship, eight points clear of Portsmouth. Their 122 goals is a Second Division record which will surely never be beaten.

What was the reason for this transformation? It is always dangerous to attribute a side's success to one player, but consider the facts. For that fourth game of the season at South Shields, McClelland was injured and 'Boro brought in George Camsell, who had been signed from Third Division North side Durham City the previous season. Camsell finished the 1926-27 campaign as 'Boro's leading scorer with a record League 59 goals, including nine hat-tricks.

After he came into the side, 'Boro won nine out of the next ten games and from mid-November to mid-April they were unbeaten in the League. Over Christmas, Camsell scored 14 goals in four games including five at Manchester City on Christmas Day. 'Boro scored seven goals three times — against Portsmouth and Swansea at home and at Grimsby.

Camsell was just the player to exploit Middlesbrough's style. Wingers Billy Pease and Owen Williams repeatedly got round the backs of defences and slung over crosses which Camsell converted into goals; and Jackie Carr schemed away and released the ball at just the right time for the centre-forward to run on to and take through to goal. Pease was a close-season signing from Northampton and, with new goalkeeper Jimmy Mathieson from Raith Rovers also establishing himself in the illustrious boots of Williamson, the new-look 'Boro side were on the crest of the wave. Camsell would be 'Boro's leading goalscorer for each of the next ten seasons. In fact, he would become the club's greatest scorer of all-time.

Middlesbrough romped back to the First Division, although they went out in the fifth round of the FA Cup when Millwall won 3-2 at The Den. Incredible though it may seem, both Camsell and Pease (who scored a record 23 goals from the wing that season) both missed penalties.

In January 1927, Middlesbrough had suddenly decided to change their manager, even though Herbert Bamlett was in

the middle of a fine run with the side. In the New Year, former Spurs manager Peter McWilliam took charge at a salary reported to be £1,500 a year — the highest in the country for a soccer manager at that time.

But disaster was just around the corner. Within one season Middlesbrough were back in the Second Division, finishing bottom of the table with the doubtful consolation of having the highest number of points — 37 — ever gained by a relegated club. Tottenham, too, went down with the same number, although they were on a foreign tour when they heard their fate.

'Boro started off reasonably well and in most seasons that number of points would have ensured a position away from the relegation zone. But there was little to choose between the teams and on the last day of the season, Middlesbrough met Sunderland at Ayresome Park. Both clubs had the same number of points. Each needed a win to be safe. The date was 5 May 1928, when nearly 42,000 fans crammed into the Middlesbrough ground. After a bright start 'Boro faded and Wright gave Sunderland a half-time lead. In the second half Halliday and then the aptly-named Death sealed 'Boro's fate at 3-0.

Middlesbrough bounced back. It took them only one season to win the Second Division title again, this time with 55 points. Camsell continued to score the goals, Pease broke the record for a winger when he had netted 105, and Bobby Bruce, from Aberdeen, and Jackie Carr, now 37, all contributed much to 'Boro's quick return. On 9 February 1929, Middlesbrough beat Wolves 8-3 at Ayresome Park and Pease scored four.

Middlesbrough's return to the First Division was not met by another disaster. The side managed to finish 16th, beating Sunderland 3-0 at Ayresome Park in November 1929 and reaching the fifth round of the FA Cup before going out 2-0 to Arsenal after wins over Chesterfield (after a replay) and Charlton (after two replays). Camsell was still finding the net and finished the season with 30 League goals.

In 1930-31, Middlesbrough finished seventh and on 18 April that season, at Blackburn, Camsell scored his 200th League goal in helping 'Boro to a 5-4 win. That score epitomised much of 'Boro's season — 98 goals for and 90 against.

Second Division Champions

MIDDLESBROUGH 3   GRIMSBY TOWN 0

BOTH Grimsby Town, managed by Wilf Gillow, and Middlesbrough were assured of promotion to Division One, but the winners of the game would take the Second Division championship shield waiting in the North stand. The League table showed on the morning of the game that both teams had played 41 games and both had 53 points, but Middlesbrough's slightly better goal average placed them first. A draw would be sufficient for Boro and Grimsby needed to win, what a game was in prospect.

A superb performance by Jimmy Mathieson in 'Boro's goal denied shots from Prior, Coleman and Coglin in quick succession. On the half-hour 'Boro finally broke away and scored the opening goal. It started on the right wing with Bob Ferguson finding George Emmerson, and the young reserve player fed George Camsell who rammed the ball into the back of the net.

Grimsby seemed a different side after the break, having expended so much first-half energy attempting to break down 'Boro's resolute defence, and fine defensive work by full-backs 'Jock' Smith and Reg Freeman further denied the Town forwards.

With five minutes to go Camsell headed 'Boro's decisive, second goal and Tommy Poskett, Town's debutant goalie made a blunder in the dying seconds of the game, allowing Owen Williams the opportunity to score from the wing.

Charles E. Sutcliffe, vice-president of the Football League, presented the Second Division Shield to 'Boro skipper Joe Peacock, congratulating both sides for playing 'Good, clean attractive football.'

Middlesbrough: Mathieson; Freeman, J. Smith, Miller, Ferguson, Peacock, Emmerson, J. Carr, Camsell, Bruce, O. Williams.
Grimsby Town: Poskett; C. Wilson, Jacobson, Priestley, Wrack, Caldewood, Prior, Bestall, Coleman, Coglin, Wright.
Attendance: 36,503

Middlesbrough, Second Division champions 1928-29. Back row (left to right, players only): Miller, Jarvis, Mathieson, Freeman, Peacock. Front row: Pease, Carr, Camsell, Bruce, Williams, Ferguson.

Middlesbrough were now settled in the First Division and they finished just out of the relegation zones in 1931-32 and 1932-33. In 1933-34, came one of the most sensational games in the club's history when they met Sheffield United at Ayresome Park. Only 6,461 people turned up on a miserable, rain-sodden day, but they were rewarded with 'Boro's record win of 10-3, with Camsell netting four. In the Reserves, young Micky Fenton played well enough to warrant three first-team games that season — the first of many.

In 1934-35, Middlesbrough again found themselves in deep water when they won only ten games and finished in 20th position, missing relegation by only one point. Ralph Birkett,

Arsenal's right winger, was signed in mid-March but returned to Highbury to see his old teammates crush 'Boro 8-0 on 19 April 1935. The relegation issue was not decided until the very last day of the season when goals from Yorston and Warren saw Middlesbrough draw 2-2 with Chelsea and the Ayresome Park club squeezed home. Fenton played in half the games, but Camsell missed half the season through ill health.

Things looked different for 1935-36 when 'Boro won their first two away matches — 5-0 at Preston and 7-2 at Aston Villa with Camsell scoring five. Middlesbrough continued to crack in the goals — four against League leaders Huddersfield, six against Everton and Blackburn and five against Grimsby and

St Valentine's Day Massacre

NEWCASTLE UNITED 0   MIDDLESBROUGH 5

PETER McWilliam, Middlesbrough's manager, was not at St James' Park to watch his boys beat Newcastle United on St Valentine's Day, 1931. No official reason was given for McWilliam's absence, but it was widely rumoured that he would sometimes feel physically sick before an important game and so stayed away.

Billy Pease passed a fitness test and so 'Boro kept an unchanged side from the team that drew 2-2 with newly-promoted Chelsea the week before.

The first goal came after 11 minutes after Johnny McKay found Pease, who put over a low centre. George Camsell and United defender Fairhurst both missed the ball, but Welshman Freddy Warren made it 1-0, evading a strong challenge from Jimmy Nelson.

After 38 minutes Kenny Cameron received the ball direct from a throw-in. United full-back Nelson slipped at the critical moment, and Cameron moved in for the kill, scoring with a rising shot.

Syd Jarvis, 'Boro's left-back, dropped the ball perfectly on Pease's toe and his shot hit the underside of the crossbar.

Camsell, following up, pounced to smash goal number-three past Albert McInroy without a Newcastle player touching the ball.

Three minutes later 'Boro were four-up when Pease took a free-kick, passing to Camsell, whose fierce shot was pushed out by McInroy, McKay moving in to score.

Five minutes from time the Pease-Camsell combination clicked into gear again. From Pease's centre Camsell hooked the ball past McInroy to complete the scoring and guarantee a well-deserved double over the Geordies.

The Press reported that Middlesbrough had: 'extra speed in tackling' and: 'splendid ball distribution,' and were: 'meritorious winners'.

Newcastle United: McInroy; Nelson, Fairhurst, Naylor, Davidson, Weaver, Boyd, Bedford, Hutchinson, Starling, Wilkinson.
Middlesbrough: Mathieson; Jennings, Jarvis, Macfarlane, Elkes, Forrest, Pease, McKay, Camsell, Cameron, Warren.
Attendance: 31,945

Middlesbrough in 1933-34. Back row (left to right): Brown, Cole (trainer), Jennings, Gibson, Jarvis, Baxter, Martin. Front row: Williams, Bruce, Griffiths, Camsell, Fenton, Warren.

Joe Hillier is challenged by Arsenal's Alex James during a match at Highbury in April 1935.

Champions Hit For Six

MIDDLESBROUGH 6   SUNDERLAND 0

IN late March 1936, Sunderland were League leaders, six points clear of second-placed Derby County, but had been spluttering of late having gone four games without a win. Members of the Scottish FA selection committee came to Ayresome Park to assess three Sunderland players, Hastings, Connor and Gallacher with a view to international selection, but must have left the game more impressed with 'Boro's Scottish duo, Bob Baxter and Benny Yorston.

After 16 minutes 'Boro forged into the lead through an Arthur Cunliffe goal when he cut in from the left to beat Matt Middleton. Middleton, who starred for the 'Boro as a guest player during the wartime Regional games, was again beaten, this time by Ralph Birkett who broke through on the half-hour to make it 2-0.

George Camsell scored his customary goal three minutes into the second period and ten minutes later Yorston, 'Boro's pocket dynamo, was entrusted with a penalty-kick, and it must have been an enjoyable moment for him when the ball smacked into the net, to score against the club that had discarded him earlier in his career. On 70 minutes Norman Higham, playing in only his second game for Middlesbrough, scored the fifth.

With the match at the three-quarter stage an unsavoury incident led to the dismissal of two of Sunderland's star players. Billy Brown, 'Boro's right-back, received a nasty kick from Raich Carter, and with the Sunderland star pleading innocence, experienced referee Bert Fogg of Bolton ordered Carter from the field. Baxter, the 'Boro captain, attempted to defuse the situation but the referee remained adamant that Carter must go. Brown had to leave the field for treatment but later returned to complete the game.

Within a minute, Davis, Carter's wing partner, said something that did not meet with Mr Fogg's critical approval and joined this teammate in the dressing-room.

Higham completed the rout three minutes from time with his second and Middlesbrough's final goal. The dismissals in no way affected the outcome of the game, for 'Boro were leading 5-0 before the double sending-off, and as the contemporary Press reported: 'Sunderland were not beaten, they were thrashed.'

It was Middlesbrough's first victory over Sunderland in five seasons, and the 6-0 defeat was to be Sunderland's heaviest of the season, whilst it was 'Boro's most decisive victory. The Roker Park club held on to clinch the Championship at the end of the season, beating Derby County by eight points.

At the subsequent FA inquiry at Darlington, Raich Carter was still insisting that the kick that Brown received was accidental, but he was found guilty and received a seven-day suspension. Davis received a 12-day suspension and a five guinea (£5.25) fine.

Middlesbrough: Gibson; Brown, Stuart, Martin, Baxter, Forrest, Birkett, Higham, Camsell, Yorston, Cunliffe.
Sunderland: Middleton; Murray, Hall, Thomson, Johnston, Hastings, Davis, Carter, Gurney, Gallacher, Connor.
Attendance: 29,990

Sheffield Wednesday. Camsell took his season's total to 28 and 'Boro netted 84 goals in finishing 14th.

Perhaps the most controversial event of the season was the visit of champions-elect Sunderland on 28 March 1936. 'Boro thrashed them 6-0 and the Wearsiders lost Carter and Davis, both sent off. Other milestones were left-back Bobby Stuart's 100th consecutive appearance for 'Boro in November 1935 and Camsell's first England cap, against Scotland. In the FA Cup, 'Boro reached the quarter-finals for the first time since 1904. Southampton, Clapton Orient and Leicester were all beaten at home before Grimsby Town beat 'Boro 3-1 at Blundell Park to earn themselves a semi-final tie against Arsenal.

Season 1936-37 saw the emergence of a player destined to become one of the most famous in English football, when a fair-haired youngster called Wilf Mannion, who Middlesbrough had signed from local club South Bank St Peter's, arrived on the scene. Seventeen-year-old Mannion made his debut in a 2-2 draw with Portsmouth at Ayresome Park on 2 January 1937. He played once more that season, but 'Boro had already seen enough to know that they had an international in the making.

During the same season, another face appeared at Middlesbrough in the shape of full-back George Hardwick. Hardwick came from South Bank East End and he, too, was to become a Middlesbrough and England giant in the years after World War Two. Middlesbrough, with Aberdeen-born Dave Cumming now in goal, finished seventh in 1936-37, when Arthur Cunliffe broke Camsell's monopoly of the leading scorers' position with 22 goals. Camsell netted 18.

In 1937-38, Middlesbrough finished fifth, with Micky Fenton now established. Fenton was leading scorer with 24 goals and became the fourth Middlesbrough centre-forward to play for England between the wars, when he appeared in the 1-0 defeat by Scotland at Wembley on 9 April 1938.

The following season — the last full one before World War Two — 'Boro climbed up a place to fourth, their highest in the First Division since 1913-14. Fenton was again top scorer, this time with 34 goals, but the real revelation was the young Mannion. He had come to everyone's notice the previous season but now he began to score goals and finished second-highest scorer with 14 — including four in the 9-2 win over Blackpool on 10 December 1938. Camsell played only 11 games but scored ten goals and Milne appeared on either wing with equal skill.

There was a potentially epic tussle in the fourth round of the FA Cup when 'Boro met Sunderland at Ayresome Park. A record 51,080 paid just under £4,000 and saw Middlesbrough go down 2-0. Again their Wembley hopes were sealed for another season, yet the team assembled under former Grimsby boss, Wilf Gillow, who had succeeded McWilliam in 1934, looked good enough to take the title in 1939-40. Mannion and Hardwick were coming into their own and Fenton, too, was fulfilling the rich, early promise he had shown.

In fact, Middlesbrough were next-to-the-bottom of the First Division when war was declared on 3 September 1939, having lost the opening game of the season, 2-0 at Aston Villa on 26 August, and going down 4-1 at Liverpool the following Wednesday before earning their first point with a 2-2 draw at home to Stoke on what was the second — and last — Saturday of the season.

Whether or not they would have recovered is idle speculation, but certainly Middlesbrough had potentially their finest-ever side. For the next seven years football took on a bizarre aspect with guest players and regional leagues. Both Hardwick and Mannion played in wartime internationals, as did Ralph Birkett, who turned out against Scotland in 1940-41.

Middlesbrough started the first season of peacetime football with a new manager. Wilf Gillow died in 1944 and was replaced by David Jack of 'White Horse Cup Final' fame. He scored the first goal in a Wembley Cup Final, for Bolton in 1923. Jack led 'Boro into the 1945-46 FA Cup — it was played on a two-legged basis up to and including the quarter-final — with a side containing old heads from pre-war days and youngsters who had made their way during the hostilities.

In the third round, 'Boro drew 4-4 at Leeds in the first leg before completing the job with a 7-2 win at Ayresome Park. Blackpool then took 'Boro to a third game before the Ayresome club ran out 1-0 winners in the replay. In the fifth round, Bolton won 1-0 at Burnden Park and then held on 1-1 at Ayresome Park. Middlesbrough were out of the Cup again.

In 1946-47, League football returned and 'Boro finished 11th with Mannion and Fenton each scoring 18 goals. Hardwick had blossomed into a fine player and behind him, Dave Cumming, the pre-war goalkeeper, was also performing well. Again 'Boro had a good run in the FA Cup. It started with a 1-1 draw at QPR before Rangers went down 2-1 at Middlesbrough. Then 42,250 fans saw Chesterfield beaten

Middlesbrough, 1939-40. Back row (left to right): Cole (trainer), McKenzie, Laking, Cumming, Stuart, Forrest, N.Fowler. Front row: J.Milne, Fenton, Yorston, Wilf Gillow (manager), Baxter, Mannion, Chadwick.

'Boro Hit Seven at Ewood Park

BLACKBURN ROVERS 1   MIDDLESBROUGH 7

GEOFF Walker had recovered from a pulled leg muscle picked up in midweek, so Middlesbrough trainer Charlie Cole reported no injuries to the weekly Thursday board meeting and, for the sixth successive game, the directors named an unchanged team for the trip across the Pennines to play Blackburn Rovers on 29 November 1947. With winter only just around the corner, traces of frost could be seen on the bone-hard Ewood Park pitch as the teams took the field.

On 13 minutes, Johnny Spuhler collected a throw-in from Harry Bell and manoeuvred the ball forward to Cec McCormack, who beat Blackburn 'keeper George Marks to register the first goal. The lead was increased on 34 minutes when a Micky Fenton 'special' was partially stopped by the Rovers defence, but the loose ball was whacked home by Geoff Walker.

Seven minutes before half-time, Spuhler's centre dropped nicely into the goalmouth for McCormack to lash the ball past Marks to make the half-time score 3-0 in 'Boro's favour.

Rovers had injured left-back Bob Tomlinson on the left wing for the whole of the second half, yet John Oakes managed to pull a goal back for the home side after 56 minutes. Ten minutes from the end, Rovers' hopes of salvaging a point were in tatters as 'Boro's eager forwards stretched their beleaguered opponents even further, scoring another four goals.

Fenton cleverly ran over the ball, leaving Walker in the clear to score 'Boro's fourth goal. Two minutes later, Fenton himself beat Marks with a stinging shot and then scored another three minutes before full-time, when veteran Rovers defender Bob Pryde failed to clear a dangerous situation.

Middlesbrough managed to squeeze one more goal out of the 90 minutes when Fenton's strong shot was partially cleared out to McCormack, who registered his hat-trick, his second of the season, with two minutes still showing on the referee's watch.

The many delighted Middlesbrough fans at Ewood Park started singing "1-2-3-4-5-6-7" and this was taken up by those Rovers fans who were still in the ground at the final whistle.

The 7-1 defeat (Middlesbrough also had two goals disallowed for offside infringements) was Blackburn's heaviest home defeat for 57 years and the seven goals took 'Boro's tally to 16 in the last three games (two of them away games), with the defence conceding only one goal.

The players were given a five-day break at Scarborough, apart from Harry Bell and Cec McCormack, who could not get leave from the RAF.

Blackburn Rovers: Marks; Cook, Tomlinson, Baldwin, Pryde, Miller, Oakes, Graham, Weir, Campbell, Langton.
Middlesbrough: Goodfellow; Robinson, Hardwick, Bell, Whitaker, Gordon, McCormack, Spuhler, Fenton, Mannion, Walker.
Attendance: 26,506

Middlesbrough, 1946-47. Back row (left to right): David Jack (manager), Bell, Robinson, Cumming, Cole (trainer), Hardwick, Gordon, Murphy. Front row: Spuhler, Mannion, Fenton, Dews, Walker, Shepherdson.

2-1 in the fourth round and, although Mannion scored an own-goal to help Nottingham Forest draw 2-2 at the City Ground, the same player netted a hat-trick at Ayresome Park as Forest crashed 6-2 in the replay.

Yet again, 'Boro could not get past the quarter-final stage. A crowd of 53,025 saw Second Division Burnley draw 1-1 with an equaliser in the last ten minutes. At Turf Moor, a hotly-disputed goal by Billy Morris gave the Lancashire side a semi-final place against Liverpool. Middlesbrough's Wembley dreams were over again. At the end of the season Hardwick and Mannion played for the Great Britain side against the Rest of Europe, with Hardwick captaining the British side to a 6-1 win.

Jimmy Hartnett rises high to head the ball towards the Chelsea goal at Stamford Bridge in October 1951.

In 1947-48, 'Boro transferred McCabe to Leeds for £10,000, Dews (£7,000) to Plymouth and Stuart (£4,000) also to Plymouth, during which time they finished 16th in the League and went out of the FA Cup in the fifth round when Derby beat them 2-1 at Ayresome Park. That day the Rams had third-choice goalkeeper Frank Payne playing what was to be his only game for them.

Mannion had been reluctant to sign for that season and in the close season of 1948, he moved his home to Oldham, intending to set up a business and play for the Third Division North side. But Oldham could not afford the £25,000 fee and Mannion would go to no other club. In January 1949, Mannion returned to Ayresome Park to find his side struggling again.

'Boro had tried to buy Jackie Milburn from Newcastle, instead settling for United's reserve-team centre-forward Andy Donaldson, for what was then a big fee of £17,000. Donaldson scored six vital goals as 'Boro avoided the drop by one point to finish in 19th place.

Mannion was playing well enough to have re-established himself in the England team but, before the start of 1949-50, 'Boro received a blow when Donaldson broke his ankle in a practice match and was soon on his way to Peterborough United, then in the Midland League.

On 27 December 1949, Middlesbrough's present ground record was set when 53,802 saw them beat Newcastle United 1-0. With Jamaican-born Lindy Delapenha, signed from Portsmouth, playing well on the wing, 'Boro climbed to ninth in the First Division. In the FA Cup, Second Division Chesterfield beat them 3-2 in the fourth round at Saltergate.

Middlesbrough headed the First Division towards the end of 1950, but a 1-0 defeat in the FA Cup at Leeds seemed to affect the players and after that they took only 13 points from 19 games to finish in sixth position. Midway through the season, George Hardwick had left the club to become player-manager of Oldham Athletic. From that moment 'Boro began to falter, finishing 18th the following season and 13th in 1952-53 before the dreaded blow of relegation fell once more in 1953-54.

Walter Rowley had taken over as manager from David Jack in 1952 and the 'Boro side now contained Rolando Ugolini, Mannion and Bill Harris, who was signed from Hull City and made his debut against Chelsea on 6 March 1954. Two months later Harris was playing his first game at wing-half for Wales against Austria in Vienna.

'Boro gained only 12 points from their first 19 games. It was a start too bad to overcome and they went down with Liverpool, although five draws in a row, followed by a shock 4-2 win over champions-elect Wolves, gave them some hope of staving off the drop. But after losing 5-2 to Manchester City, Middlesbrough dropped four points in their two Easter games with Liverpool and, in the end, it was their fellow strugglers who pulled them down. Only Delapenha, with 18 goals, could look back on the season with any satisfaction.

Walter Rowley retired in the close season and his place was taken by Bob Dennison, the former Newcastle, Forest and Fulham player, who was in charge of Northampton Town. Dennison had the worst possible start. First Mannion refused to sign and, then after a 2-2 draw at Plymouth on 21 August 1954, 'Boro lost their next eight games.

It was not until 25 September, when they beat Lincoln 2-1 at Middlesbrough, that 'Boro came to terms with the Second Division. That was the start of a run of ten points from six games, including a 6-0 win against West Ham United. A week later, Middlesbrough went to Blackburn and crashed 9-0. It says much for the character of the side that they recovered to finish in 12th position.

Wilf Mannion had played his last game for Middlesbrough in their relegation season, refusing terms for the following season before being transferred to Hull City, where he played a handful of games before being suspended over some newspaper articles which appeared under his name. Eventually the greatest ball-player ever to pull on a Middlesbrough shirt disappeared into non-League soccer.

Middlesbrough now began a 20-year spell outside the First Division. Yet, on the horizon was another in the long line

Wilf Mannion leads 'Boro out at Ayresome Park in November 1951.

Middlesbrough, 1954-55. Back row (left to right): Harold Shepherdson (trainer), Harris, Barnard, Ugolini, Robinson, Brown, Dicks, Bob Dennison (manager). Front row: Delapenha, Scott, Wayman, Fitzsimons, Mitchell.

of great Middlesbrough centre-forwards. Brian Clough made his debut in 1955-56 and played nine games, scoring his first goal at home to Leicester on 8 October as 'Boro won 4-3. The young centre-forward took over from former Preston player, Charlie Wayman, who was injured in training. He showed a flair for goals and Dennison surely knew he had a great striker in the making.

Another player to make his debut that season was Billy Day and with Delapenha knocking home 17 goals, 'Boro finished in 14th place. The following year belonged to Clough. He scored 38 League goals as 'Boro climbed up to sixth in the Second Division, taking 15 points from their last nine games, including a 7-2 win over Huddersfield and a 6-2 win against Swansea. Peter Taylor, one day to become Clough's managerial

Brian Clough, the former ICI clerk who became a prolific goalscorer for the 'Boro and then went on to become one of the greatest managers in the game.

Bob Appleby's dive is too late and Roger Hunt scores an equaliser for Liverpool at Ayresome Park in August 1960.

'twin', took over in goal from Ugolini and Wayman signed for Darlington.

For the next four seasons, Clough rattled in the goals — 40 in 1957-58, 43 in 1958-59, 39 in 1959-60 and 34 in 1960-61. He played two England matches in 1959-60 — it is still a mystery as to why he was never selected again — and scored five goals for the Football League in Belfast in September 1959.

In that time, Middlesbrough maintained reasonable progress in the Second Division without ever looking as if they would win promotion. New players like Alan Peacock and Edwin Holliday came into the team. Peacock, an 18-year-old reserve centre-forward, came into the Middlesbrough side in December 1957, when a run of five defeats sent 'Boro plunging from third place in the table. Clough was now the inevitable target for opposing defenders and Peacock came in and took some of the weight off the prolific goalscorer's shoulders.

'Boro began the 1958-59 season in tremendous style, beating newly-promoted Brighton 9-0. Clough hit five and Peacock two as the South Coast team were destroyed. There followed a run of nine games without victory and, after trying to persuade Don Revie — a native of Middlesbrough — to join the club, Dennison went to Glasgow Celtic and brought back Willie Fernie for £17,000. But Middlesbrough could only finish 13th.

The era had also seen Middlesbrough's trainer, Harold Shepherdson, take over in that role with the England party — the start of another illustrious career. Shepherdson served his country for many years and was trainer when they won the World Cup in 1966. On 13 December 1958, Ray Yeoman made his debut in the 2-0 defeat at Hillsborough. He was still in the side 215 matches later, ending his record run when 'Boro beat Norwich 6-2 at Ayresome Park in the final game of 1962-63.

After finishing fifth in consecutive seasons in 1959-60 and 1960-61, 'Boro slipped to 12th place in 1961-62. In July 1961, Brian Clough went up the coast to Sunderland for £40,000. Never far from controversy, even in those days, Clough's departure from Ayresome Park was perhaps inevitable but sad. He became Sunderland's top scorer, whilst the gap he left at Middlesbrough was never filled.

Alan Peacock took over the leading goalscoring spot with 24 League goals and followed this up with 31 in 1962-63, when Middlesbrough finished fourth. Sunderland were third and

another four points for 'Boro would have seen them back in the First Division.

Yet from that moment on, the only way for 'Boro was down. Slowly they slid towards the bottom of the Second Division until in 1965-66, the unthinkable happened and Middlesbrough FC were a Third Division club. Bob Dennison had resigned in 1963 and his place was taken by Raich Carter, the former Sunderland idol.

The drop hinged on the last match of the season with 'Boro needing to draw at Ninian Park against Cardiff City, who needed both points to be safe. 'Boro converted centre-half Dickie Rooks to centre-forward and the makeshift striker responded magnificently with a hat-trick. But there was to be no *Boys' Own Comic* finish. Cardiff won 5-3 to stay up. 'Boro plunged down into Division Three. Carter had resigned just before the end of the season, his place taken by skipper Stan Anderson. It was now Anderson's job to get the side back into the Second Division.

He did so at the first attempt. 'Boro finished second in the Third Division. After the brief interlude of some World Cup matches at Middlesbrough, the team won their first match of the season at Colchester United. There followed a slump of nine League games which produced only one win and the more despondent 'Boro supporters saw their side already down into the Fourth Division.

But new signings were on the way. John O'Rourke came as a centre-forward from Luton Town, winger Dave Chadwick from Southampton and goalkeeper Willie Whigham from Falkirk. Sheffield Wednesday full-back John Hickton joined 'Boro, who were now skippered by Gordon Jones. Jones, a former apprentice, was to set a post-war record of 523 games for the club.

O'Rourke soon began to find the back of the net and with six games left, Middlesbrough were in seventh place. A thrilling win at Peterborough started a winning run which took the club to fourth place with 53 points and one game to play. On 16 May 1967, 'Boro met Oxford United at Ayresome Park before 39,683 spectators. Queen's Park Rangers were already champions, Watford were second with 54 points and Reading third with 53. Both Watford and Reading had completed their fixtures.

'Boro had to win and they did so in style, beating Oxford 4-1 to bring Second Division soccer back to Ayresome after

Middlesbrough in 1966. Back row (left to right): Davidson, Wilson, Myton, Worthington, Gates, McPartland, Appleby, O'Rourke, A.Smith, Chapman, Garbett. Second row: G.Wright (trainer), Lakey, Spraggon, Masson, Horsfield, Butler, Horner, Lawson, D.Smith, Rooks, Chadwick, J.Hedridge (trainer). Seated: Directors Messrs G.Wood, G.Kitching, A.King, E.Varley and H.Thomas, Jones, directors Messrs J.E.Thomas, C.Amer, G.Winney and Dr U.N.Phillips, H.Green (secretary), Stan Anderson (manager). On ground: Downing, Allen, Lugg, Congerton, Laidlaw, McMordie.

only one season in the Third. John O'Rourke had finished the season with 27 goals and Arthur Horsfield with 22. In the FA Cup, 'Boro had the strange experience of going into the hat for the first-round draw. After hammering Chester 5-2 at Sealand Road, they went out in the very next round, 2-0 at Mansfield's Field Mill.

For Middlesbrough fans, the experience of seeing their once proud club with its long traditions, floundering for a time in the Third Division had been a traumatic one. Now they had witnessed 'Boro's first promotion triumph since they won their way to the First Division in 1929. Anderson set about strengthening the side for a concerted push towards the Second Division championship and one of his first signings was Manchester City's Irish international midfielder, Johnny Crossan, whose curious career had taken him to Ayresome Park via a controversial spell in the comparative backwaters of Irish soccer, Dutch and Belgian League football with Sparta Rotterdam and Standard Liege, Sunderland and Maine Road.

In the other direction Anderson transferred full-back Geoff Butler to Chelsea for a Middlesbrough record fee of £57,500, after Tommy Docherty's First Division side had met 'Boro in the Football League Cup. In the FA Cup there was a marathon third-round tie with Hull before 'Boro won the second replay at York, only to go down in the next round at Bristol City. The season ended with Middlesbrough in sixth place — a satisfactory placing after winning promotion.

The following season, 'Boro again moved up the table to finish in fourth place. Indeed, two away wins at Sheffield United and Oxford at the end of October saw 'Boro on top of the table. But a 'flu bug which hit the club in February meant the postponement of the game with Blackburn and, although they were still in second place with ten games to play, 'Boro fell away badly in the run-in to the season.

One of the real revelations of 1967-68 was the form of John Hickton, who was moved up to the attack with devastating effect. He finished top scorer with 24 goals and as 'Boro vied for the title in 1968-69, it was Hickton again who led the way with 18 goals. Hickton had played the occasional game in attack for Wednesday, but when Anderson found him a regular place up front, the powerful defender responded in fine style. Crossan played only two games in 1969-70 before moving to Belgium, but his short career at Ayresome Park had been reasonably successful.

As 'Boro finished fourth again, Anderson brought Carlisle's Hugh McIlmoyle to play alongside Hickton. Once again

Middlesbrough reached the quarter-finals of the FA Cup, only to find their path to the semi-final barred. Derrick Downing and Hugh McIlmoyle gave them a third-round win over First Division West Ham; York City were removed 4-1 and then 'Boro went to their 'bogey' ground of Brunton Park, where they managed their first-ever win over Carlisle United, 2-1, thanks to goals from Hickton and Downing.

Middlesbrough now faced First Division Manchester United. The first game at Ayresome Park ended 1-1 and 'Boro fans could already see their chances of following their team into the semi-finals for the first time, receding. Sure enough, the task of beating United at Old Trafford proved too much and 'Boro went down 2-1. The two games were watched by a total of 100,000 people. Willie Maddren and David Mills made their debuts during the season. Both would become important parts of Middlesbrough's machine in the coming years.

'Boro stayed in the promotion race for much of 1970-71. But their last win of the season came at home to Luton on 27 March 1971, after which a run of eight drawn games left them in seventh position and far behind promoted clubs Leicester City and Sheffield United. In the FA Cup, Middlesbrough had revenge over Manchester United, beating them in a third-round replay at Ayresome Park through McIlmoyle and Downing. In the fourth round, however, 'Boro crashed 3-0 to Everton at Goodison Park.

For 1971-72, Middlesbrough's team took on a new look. During the close season, Manchester United's former World Cup star Nobby Stiles, Newcastle's John Craggs and Mansfield's Stuart Boam were signed. Maddren and Mills, together with Laidlaw, were now regulars and Jim Platt had taken over in goal. David Armstrong was brought in for his first game.

The team was taking shape but it was not ready to make the supreme effort and had to be content with ninth place. In the FA Cup, 'Boro fought through to the fifth round with replays against Manchester City and Millwall. It was Manchester United who again stood in their way. This time it was United's turn to win a replay. After doing the difficult bit by drawing 0-0 at Old Trafford, 'Boro collapsed at home and went down 3-0.

On the opening day of the 1972-73 season, Middlesbrough beat old rivals Sunderland 2-1 at Ayresome Park with both goals coming from Malcolm Smith, who had been on the club's books as a junior. A win over Wrexham in the second round of the Football League Cup set 'Boro up for a tie with Spurs which they surrendered only after a second replay on the London club's ground.

Middlesbrough's 1971 first-team squad, minus Gordon Jones who was still on holiday. Back row (left to right): Gates, Smith, Moody, Boam, Whigham, Hickton, Maddren, Vincent. Front row: McMordie, Stiles, Downing, Mills, Spraggon, Laidlaw.

Eyes closed! Willie Maddren and Millwall's Derek Possee leap high for a ball neither can apparently see at The Den in February 1972, during an FA Cup fourth-round tie.

Things looked set for another fine season, this time with the possibility of a return at last to the top flight. But 'Boro's goals tally was still worrying Anderson and in October he moved for ex-Newcastle striker, Alan Foggon, who was playing with Cardiff. Two months later, Graeme Souness, Spurs' reserve midfielder, was on his way north and Anderson said that he now had the team which could win promotion.

But there were black clouds on the horizon. In January, 'Boro suffered a shock defeat at the hands of Plymouth Argyle in the third round of the FA Cup. Stan Anderson had seen enough. He resigned his post and for the rest of the season Harold Shepherdson took charge of the side which finished in fourth place, losing only three of the last 16 games.

Middlesbrough needed a 'name' to take over and they plumped for Jackie Charlton, Leeds United's distinguished England international centre-half. Charlton made only one change. Stiles joined Charlton's brother, Bobby, at Preston and was replaced by Scottish international midfielder, Bobby Murdoch, from Celtic. For the rest of the team which he had inherited, Charlton elected to give them all a run.

What a season the 1973-74 campaign turned out to be. After winning their opening game at Portsmouth, 'Boro lost a home game to Fulham 2-0 and people began to doubt Jack Charlton's ability to get the side back into the First Division. But Charlton knew better. 'Boro remained unbeaten until the New Year. They went to the top of the table in October and stayed there for the rest of the season, ensuring promotion as early as 23 March. And with eight games of the season still to play, Middlesbrough became runaway champions of the Second Division with victory at Luton.

In storming to the title Middlesbrough had achieved the following:

Their highest-ever number of points — 65.

A run of 20 home games without defeat.

Their longest unbeaten League run — 24 games.

Their best defensive record of 30 goals against.

The biggest-ever points margin — 15 — in the Second Division.

Going Up in Style

MIDDLESBROUGH 8   SHEFFIELD WEDNESDAY 0

MIDDLESBROUGH clinched the 1973-74 Second Division championship as early as 30 March when a goal from David Mills at Luton meant that the title was bound for Teesside for only the third time in the club's history. However, the 1-0 away victory at Kenilworth Road did not please manager Jack Charlton too much. He had hoped that the team would draw the game, which meant that the championship would be decided at Ayresome Park against Oxford United the following week, before the club's home fans.

With two games left, three points were needed to break the post-war Division Two points record of 63, held jointly by Derby County and Leeds United. The first of the two games was at Ayresome Park, in the final home game of the season, against Steve Burtenshaw's Sheffield Wednesday on 20 April. With the season wrapped up as far as promotion was concerned, Jack Charlton shuffled his team for the game at Burnden Park, but reverted to the usual line-up for the Owls' visit. Jim Platt was back in goal, to the exclusion of Pat Cuff; John Craggs displaced Peter Creamer at right-back. Regulars John Hickton and Frank Spraggon had both recovered from leg injuries picked up in the rare defeat at Bolton and were back in the 'Boro team.

Before the game kicked-off, League president Len Shipman presented the Second Division championship trophy to club chairman Charles Amer and individual championship medals to the players.

The avalanche of goals started on five minutes when Alan Foggon moved out to the left wing and made enough space to flight over a superb cross from John Hickton to latch on to and the former Wednesday player showed Springett no mercy, his header bulging the net. Nine minutes later Foggon laid off a perfect ball for David Mills to dash through the middle before lobbing the ball over Springett. 'Boro were firing on all cylinders now.

There were two quick bookings for Eddie Prudham and John Holsgrove, for fouls on David Armstrong and David Mills respectively, before 'Boro struck again. A long pass out of defence reached Hickton and it did not take him long to measure a centre to Foggon waiting at the far post. With the Owls' defence anticipating a shot, Foggon flicked

the ball on for Bobby Murdoch to lash it into the roof of the net from close range.

The second half started as the first half ended, with two goals, both from Graeme Souness. The first came when John Craggs collected the ball from Platt and found Hickton with one sweeping movement. In a moment, it was with Souness and the Scottish Under-23 star trapped the ball, looked up, picked his spot — simple as that, 4-0!

The same player clocked up the fifth goal minutes later when he picked up a loose ball on the edge of Wednesday's box. There was no holding this rampant Middlesbrough side now. On the hour, Murdoch was brought off and substitute Harry Charlton was pushed on to give the young player some match action following a long injury lay-off. Eight minutes later it was 6-0 to 'Boro when a David Armstrong corner was half cleared to Graeme Souness and, sure enough, the ball bulged the net in an instant.

Souness claimed his first, and only, hat-trick for the club shortly after from an unselfish pass from Mills. The final and eighth scoring success for 'Boro came on 87 minutes when Foggon cut in from the left wing and tried a screw shot which Springett could only help into the net. Wednesday's demoralised 'keeper claimed that the ball had not crossed the line, but the linesman signalled and a goal was given.

Such was 'Boro's dominance that the crowd were urging goalkeeper Platt to get up with the forwards, for he was the only squad member not to have found the net so far that season.

Jack Charlton's first season as Middlesbrough manager ended with a 4-2 win at Deepdale over brother Bobby's Preston North End. Preston were already relegated but offered little resistance to the Second Division champions.

Middlesbrough: Platt; Craggs, Spraggon, Souness, Boam, Maddren, Murdoch(Charlton), Mills, Hickton, Foggon, Armstrong.
Sheffield Wednesday: Springett; Rodrigues, Shaw, Mullen, Holsgrove, Coyle(Eustace), Potts, Prudham, Joicey, Craig, Cameron.
Attendance: 25,287

Middlesbrough fans salute their champions in April 1974. From left to right are Souness, Hickton, Armstrong, Maddren, Murdoch, Boam, Brine (half-hidden), Mills, Charlton and Foggon.

Celebrations for a jubilant 'Boro from John Hickton and John Craggs (running up) who congratulate goalscorer David Mills against crestfallen Leicester City in the third round of the League Cup in October 1974.

Every player except the goalkeeper had found himself on the score-sheet.

In their first season back in the First Division since 1953-54, Middlesbrough relied on the players who had won them promotion, plus Charlton's old Leeds teammate, full-back Terry Cooper. It was a satisfactory blend as 'Boro climbed to seventh place — a good performance from any newly-promoted side. Alan Foggon, the man brought back to the North-East, responded in the promotion season with 19 League goals, thus ending Hickton's run of six seasons as 'Boro's top scorer, and in the first season back at the top the ex-Newcastle striker finished top again, this time with 16.

Until their return to the First Division, Middlesbrough's progress in the Football League Cup — they first entered the competition in 1960-61 — was parallel in many ways with their lack of success in the FA Cup. But in 1974-75, 'Boro not only reached the sixth round of the FA Cup, they also went to the quarter-finals of the League Cup, where their old Cup adversaries Manchester United beat them 3-0 after yet another replay.

The following season 'Boro went one step further and reached the semi-finals of the League Cup. Their run started with a second-round match at Bury, where they won 2-1. There followed a good win over League Champions Derby County at the Baseball Ground; an easy fourth-round tie with Peterborough United at Ayresome Park; and a 2-0 victory at Burnley which put them into the last four against Manchester City. In the first leg on 13 January 1976, Hickton gave 'Boro a slender 1-0 lead. 'Boro fans feared that it may not be enough and they were right. Eight days later, Keegan, Oakes, Barnes and Royle sent City through to Wembley with a 4-0 win.

But Middlesbrough did win their first cup as a professional side in 1975-76. They lifted the Anglo-Scottish Cup in a two-legged Final with Second Division Fulham. After winning a qualifying competition involving Sunderland, Newcastle and Carlisle, 'Boro beat Aberdeen in the quarter-finals and Mansfield Town in the semi-final before Dave Armstrong's goal in the first leg at Ayresome Park on 26 November set them up for a goalless draw at Craven Cottage. They finished the season 13th in the League.

One again 'Boro almost reached the semi-finals of the FA Cup in 1976-77. Spurs had knocked them out of the League

West Ham's Billy Bonds and Frank Lampard try to dispossess Middlesbrough's David Armstrong at Upton Park in December 1976.

Cup as early as the second round, but after a scare at non-League Wimbledon — who were later to be elected to the League partly as a result of holding 'Boro to a 0-0 draw at Plough Lane — Middlesbrough put four goals each past Hereford and Arsenal to earn a quarter-final place with Liverpool at Anfield. Liverpool, though, were on their way to Wembley and goals from Keegan and Fairclough sent 'Boro spinning out again before 55,881 fans.

Another mid-table spot, 12th, was all that 'Boro could manage in the First Division and on 21 April 1977, Jack Charlton resigned after some four years at Ayresome Park. On 19 May, John Neal, after just failing to lift Wrexham into the Second Division, became the new boss of Middlesbrough. The former Hull, Swindon, Aston Villa and Southend player had steered the Welsh club to promotion from the Fourth Division in 1970 and taken them to the quarter-finals of the European Cup-winners' Cup in 1976.

In his first season at Ayresome Park, Neal saw 'Boro into 14th place and to the quarter-finals of the FA Cup once again. This time 'Boro really should have made that elusive semi-final. Their opponents in the last 16 — after eliminating Coventry, Everton and Bolton — were Second Division Orient, a side struggling in the bottom half of the table. Middlesbrough should have finished the job at Ayresome Park, but the London club held on to draw 0-0 and 'Boro faced the unenviable task of visiting Brisbane Road three days later. The Londoners' tails were up and, although Armstrong scored for Middlesbrough, goals from Kitchen and Mayo saw Orient through to the last four.

David Mills finished the season as top scorer with ten goals in the League, four in the FA Cup and two in the League Cup. The Whitby-born striker had also passed his 250th match for 'Boro. John Hickton, the defender turned striker, had his contract cancelled in April 1978. Hickton had played well over 400 games for 'Boro and in League matches alone he netted 159 goals to put him up with the great Middlesbrough strikers of yesteryear.

'Boro's 1978-79 season never really got off the ground. They were knocked out of both the FA Cup and the League Cup

at the first hurdles and never rose above tenth in the table, finally finishing in 12th place. The real bright spot of the season was the form of Micky Burns, who arrived at Ayresome Park via Blackpool, Newcastle and Cardiff and who finished leading scorer with 14 League goals, including four in one match against Chelsea when 'Boro hammered the soon-to-be-relegated Londoners 7-2.

Burns continued his goalscoring in 1979-80, when he scored ten as 'Boro edged back up the table to ninth place. But he was overtaken as the club's leading scorer by David Armstrong who netted 11 in the League and made his first appearance in a full England shirt when he played against Australia — the first time the countries had met in a full international. Northern Ireland's Jim Platt continued his fine run in Middlesbrough's goal, taking his League appearances to 296 by the end of the season.

'Boro's 1980-81 season was one of contrasts. The club might have reached their first-ever FA Cup semi-final when they played Wolves in the quarter-final at Ayresome Park. In the end, only the brilliance of the ever-reliable Jim Platt kept 'Boro in the game and they lost the replay to the Midlanders.

Then South African-born Craig Johnston was sold to Liverpool for £750,000 after he alleged that 'Boro's fans had ultimately driven him away from Teesside when he and the club disagreed over money. Finally, 'Boro settled the First Division championship on the last Saturday of the season when they beat contenders Ipswich 2-1 — with both goals from Jankovic — and allowed Villa through, despite the fact that they had lost at Highbury. But for Middlesbrough, a major honour still eluded them and at the season's end, John Neal became the game's latest managerial casualty.

The 1981-82 season saw former 'Boro player, Bobby Murdoch, take over as manager at Ayresome Park, but he saw two of his star players leave the club. David Armstrong was on his way to Southampton and Mark Proctor moved to Nottingham Forest.

Three players — Joe Bolton, Mick Baxter and Heine Otto — made their debuts in the first game of the season, at home

Craig Johnston scores one of Middlesbrough's five goals against Arsenal at Highbury in May 1980.

'Boro Rout the Gunners' Hopes

MIDDLESBROUGH 5   ARSENAL 0

BY mid-May 1980, Arsenal's long season (the match at Ayresome Park would be the London club's 70th of the season) had fallen apart. The Gunners had lost to West Ham in the FA Cup Final and they were losers in a midweek penalty shoot-out against Valencia in the European Cup-winners' Cup Final in Brussels, Graham Rix failing with his penalty kick. Arsenal's last hope of securing a UEFA Cup qualification lay in winning at both Molineux and Middlesbrough in their final League games of the season.

Because of the importance of the remaining two games, Arsenal manager Terry Neill felt he had no option but to pull goalkeeper Pat Jennings and defenders Pat Rice and Sammy Nelson out of the Northern Ireland squad about to enter the Home International championships. Ironically, Jennings' exclusion meant that Middlesbrough's Jim Platt would play for Northern Ireland in goal.

Arsenal produced the necessary result at Molineux, beating Wolves 2-1 to leave the Gunners needing a win, by any score, at Ayresome Park three days later — a defeat against the 'Boro would hand the final UEFA Cup place to Ipswich Town.

Billy Ashcroft was handed the central defender's role by manager John Neal as Alan Ramage had just been released by the club so he could resume his county cricket career with Yorkshire. The game was a personal milestone in the career of David Armstrong, for it was his 350th consecutive League and Cup game for the club.

Middlesbrough took the lead on 11 minutes when David Hodgson headed John Craggs' pass forward and Craig Johnston scored from the edge of the area. Nine minutes later Ian Bailey 'nutmegged' Arsenal's David Price, only to see Jennings miraculously palm the ball out, but Dave Shearer headed it back into the goal area and Dave Hodgson scored. Six minutes before half-time, Shearer, looking suspiciously offside, collected a crossfield pass from Mark Proctor and dummied Jennings for Graeme Hedley to almost walk the ball into an empty net.

Early in the second half Hodgson chipped the ball over the static Gunners' defence for Armstrong to beat Jennings. 'Spike' Armstrong celebrated his record-making 350th consecutive appearance with another goal, Proctor's centre was headed on to the crossbar by 'Sheik' Shearer, and Armstrong was 'Boro's man on the spot, scoring the fifth and final goal of the game.

Two minutes from full-time, Middlesbrough captain Tony McAndrew tripped Frank Stapleton but Alan Sunderland missed the penalty, or rather Jim Stewart correctly guessed the direction of Sunderland's spot-kick and managed to smother the ball. The Middlesbrough team received a standing ovation as it left the field, an excellent end to the club's League campaign.

The 5-0 reverse was Arsenal's worst defeat for six and a half years (Sheffield United turned them over by the same score at Bramall Lane in September 1973.) It is to date, 'Boro's best-ever win over the Londoners. The next night Middlesbrough players Jim Platt and Terry Cochrane both played for Northern Ireland at Wembley against England and it was Cochrane who scored the late equaliser for Northern Ireland in a 1-1 draw. They remained at home to play in the remaining Home championship games whilst the rest of the 'Boro team jetted off to compete in the Japan Cup.

Middlesbrough: Stewart; Craggs, Bailey, Hedley, Ashcroft, McAndrew, Johnston(Askew), Proctor, Hodgson, Shearer, Armstrong.
Arsenal: Jennings; Rice, Nelson, Talbot, Walford (Vaessen), Young, Brady, Sunderland, Stapleton, Price, Rix.
Attendance: 15,579

Armstrong and Johnston watch as Jankovic scores one of his two goals against Norwich City at Ayresome in October 1980.

to Tottenham Hotspur. Otto scored for 'Boro, but it was Spurs who won the game, 3-1.

The first victory, three games later, was at Ayresome Park against Birmingham City, Otto and David Hodgson scoring in a 2-1 win. John Craggs started the season as captain, but eventually conceded the job to Tony McAndrew.

In October, a 2-1 home victory against Plymouth Argyle in the second round of the Milk Cup was sufficient to carry Middlesbrough through the Home Park leg, which ended 0-0. The third round brought sterner opposition in the shape of Liverpool and the Merseysiders coasted through to the next round with a 4-1 victory at Anfield.

'Boro did not progress beyond the third round of the FA Cup, yet they started well enough with a goalless draw at Loftus Road, always a difficult venue for Middlesbrough, on 2 January. Bad weather meant that the much-postponed replay eventually took place on 18 January, when Rangers took the tie in extra-time, winning 3-2.

In February 1982, Middlesbrough chairman Charles Amer and his son Kevin, a director, resigned from the board, stepping aside for George Kitching to move in. The 100th Tees-Wear derby game on 3 April saw a rare victory for Middlesbrough at Roker Park, but the attendance was a disappointing 19,006.

Escape from relegation had been a mathematical possibility right up until the home game against Arsenal, but the London club sealed Middlesbrough's fate by winning 3-1 at Ayresome Park in May 1982. The penultimate game of the disappointing season brought a rare away victory, the eighth win of the season, at Vetch Field against First Division debutants Swansea City. Middlesbrough's last First Division game was against eventual champions Liverpool and 'Boro pulled off a creditable draw against the Reds.

Although only 34 League goals were scored, Middlesbrough ended the season with more points (39) than the previous season, but finished bottom of the Division. The juniors winning the Northern Intermediate League was one of the few bright spots of the campaign.

Jim Platt, the only ever-present of the season, took part in the World Cup Finals in Spain, appearing once for Northern Ireland, but Terry Cochrane, originally selected, had to

withdraw from the squad through injury. Graeme Hedley, Colin Blackburn, Jeff Peters and Andy McCreesh, all players with limited League appearances, were released and at the 90th annual meeting, held in December 1982, a loss of £307,718 was reported to shareholders.

With Bobby Murdoch still in the managerial hot seat and Jim Platt as captain, Middlesbrough kicked off the 1982-83 season at Hillsborough, against Jack Charlton's Sheffield Wednesday. David Currie and Mick Kennedy made their Middlesbrough debuts as Wednesday won 3-1.

In September, Tony Mowbray made his Middlesbrough debut at outside-right in front of 27,986 (the season's highest League attendance) at St James' Park, Newcastle, where a Darren Wood goal earned 'Boro a point.

Three successive 4-1 home defeats plunged 'Boro into hot water in September. Third Division champions Burnley, Fulham (Tony Mowbray's home debut) and Grimsby Town (Ray Hankin's debut game in which he was sent off) all put four past a disheartened defence. The Middlesbrough board had little option and manager Murdoch was asked to resign. Harold Shepherdson again filled the breach until a successor could be recruited.

A Garry Macdonald goal gave 'Boro their first win of the season, against Bolton Wanderers in October. Then George Kitching relinquished the chair and Mike McCullagh stepped up with Keith Varley being named as vice-chairman.

McCullagh introduced Malcolm Allison, Murdoch's successor, to the crowd before the start of the home game against Queen's Park Rangers and goals from Nattrass (penalty) and Otto took 'Boro to a 2-1 win.

Middlesbrough's fortunes seemed to have turned the corner as Allison's first game in charge brought a precious away point against Rotherham United — but then Blackburn Rovers won 5-1 at Ayresome Park.

In January 1983, non-League Bishop's Stortford proved to be bonny FA Cup fighters in forcing a 2-2 draw at Ayresome Park. A sensational Cup exit was on the cards and in the replay at the George Wilson Stadium on 11 January, Lynch put the non-League club into the lead on the stroke of half-time. David

Shearer saved Middlesbrough from further embarrassment by scoring two second-half goals, but it had been a close shave.

Notts County were the fourth-round visitors on 29 January, before an Ayresome Park crowd of 17,114. A first-half goal by Rankin was consolidated by a Beattie penalty in the second half and together they earned 'Boro a home tie against First Division Arsenal.

At Ayresome Park, an Otto goal helped Middlesbrough to a 1-1 draw against the Gunners but a spirited display and two goals from David Shearer were not enough to stop the Londoners winning 3-2 at Highbury.

In January, Charles Amer, who had joined the Middlesbrough board in the early 1960s, severed his long association with the club by resigning his directorship.

In early March 1983, Queen's Park Rangers, on their way to the First Division, tore Middlesbrough apart, winning 6-1 at Loftus Road. *Match of the Day* cameras showed Clive Allen securing a hat-trick, with Middlesbrough playing in borrowed bright orange shirts.

Goals from Sugrue, Hamilton and Otto saw Middlesbrough notch their first away win of 1983 at Grimsby Town, avenging the earlier reverse at Ayresome Park. And one defeat in the last six games of the season ensured that the club finished in a respectable 16th in Division Two.

A long-awaited testimonial game was played at Ayresome Park on 17 May 1983, when two of Middlesbrough's most famous sons shared a benefit. Wilf Mannion and George Hardwick, names synonymous with the club's immediate post-war period, were honoured when a Middlesbrough XI played an England XI. England starlet Paul Walsh scored two goals as 'England' won 2-1.

Jim Platt had returned to Ireland in April 1983 and with no new players in the side Middlesbrough won the opening game of 1983-84 at Fratton Park with a Heine Otto goal, despite Portsmouth protests that their goalkeeper had been fouled.

The joy was short-lived, however, as Chesterfield won 1-0 at Ayresome Park in the first leg of the Milk Cup. Two important League games followed immediately. David Currie scored twice in a pulsating 2-2 home draw against Leeds United and, three days later, the season's highest home crowd saw Middlesbrough pull off a thrilling 3-2 win over Newcastle United, Currie scoring two and Gary Hamilton the third.

Otto scored the only goal in the second leg of the Milk Cup tie at Chesterfield to take the game into extra-time. With no further goals, there was a sudden-death penalty shoot-out, which Chesterfield won 5-3.

Middlesbrough's League form, meanwhile, was excellent, and they won three of the first four games. Then five successive defeats followed. The rot was checked in late October with a confidence-boosting 4-0 home win against Rotherham United and promotion-winning form returned in November with only one defeat — a 1-0 reverse at Derby.

In the home game against Cardiff City, Stephen Pears, on loan from Manchester United, made his debut as 'Boro beat the Welshmen 2-0. Only one win came in December, a 2-0 success at Hillsborough against that season's Second Division champions.

An early opportunity to avenge the previous season's FA Cup exit at Highbury came on 7 January, when Arsenal were the opposition at Ayresome Park for a third-round tie and goals from Garry Macdonald, Paul Sugrue and Mick Baxter carried Middlesbrough through.

On the last day of the month it was Bournemouth's turn to be dumped out of the Cup, two goals from Sugrue doing the job at Ayresome Park. However, a fifth-round journey to Notts County ended Middlesbrough's Wembley dreams for another season.

As usual, the biggest attendances of the season centred around the derby games and on 17 March at St James' Park, a crowd of 30,421 saw Newcastle United win 3-1.

With serious financial problems staring Middlesbrough in the face, Malcolm Allison was being pressured into off-loading the club's star players to keep the 'Boro afloat financially. Matters came to a head in late March 1984, when he claimed

that it was 'better for the club to die than to linger slowly on its deathbed'. This statement was the kiss of death for extrovert Allison and out he went. Jack Charlton agreed to steer the club through its temporary crisis and, assisted by Willie Maddren, he stayed until the end of the season. Middlesbrough struggled through, finishing in 17th place.

Middlesbrough's 1984-85 season began at Fratton Park but, even with new boys Mick Buckley and the prodigal David Mills in Willie Maddren's side, the team could not repeat the success of 1983-84 and lost 1-0.

Middlesbrough went out of the Milk Cup on aggregate to Bradford City and then Darren Wood, one of the club's major playing assets, was transferred to Chelsea in a deal that saw cash change hands and the return of former Middlesbrough stalwart, Tony McAndrew, to the 'Boro side. The club then reached their highest League position of the season beating Manchester City 2-1 at Ayresome Park, to complete a sequence of three victories in October.

Tony Mowbray, now established in the side, was sent off at Leeds on 27 October and David Currie was dismissed in November, at home to Blackburn Rovers. Paul Sugrue joined Portsmouth on a free transfer in early December and over Christmas, 'Boro picked up three useful points at Carlisle.

The FA Cup meeting with neighbours Darlington at Ayresome Park in early January 1985 attracted a crowd of 19,084 and Middlesbrough were fortunate to escape with a 0-0 draw. The Feethams replay three days later was deservedly lost 2-1, despite a late goal from Tony McAndrew, in front of a 14,237 crowd. The victory must have been doubly sweet for the Skernesiders, for it was their first-ever success over Middlesbrough.

An abysmal sequence of the ten League games without a win had started on New Year's Day, with a 1-0 home defeat against Oxford United, the eventual Second Division champions. Middlesbrough's next victory was a 1-0 win over Sheffield United, on the day that 'Archie' Stephens signed for 'Boro.

The highest home and away attendances of Middlesbrough's season were recorded in successive games in March. The visit of Yorkshire rivals Leeds United attracted only 8,817, yet it was still the highest home 'gate'. And the following week, 'Boro played in front of a crowd of 22,399 at Maine Road against Second Division leaders Manchester City.

Needing three points to ensure a further season of Second Division football, Middlesbrough pulled off a fine 2-0 win at Gay Meadow on the last day of the season, but a double dismissal was recorded when Gary Hamilton and Peter Beagrie were sent off.

David Mills ended the 1984-85 season as the club's highest scorer on 15 goals, but again Middlesbrough floundered and this time finished in 19th place.

They released regular goalkeeper Kelham O'Hanlon, who quickly got fixed up with Rotherham United, and Mick Buckley. Heine Otto, who had scored some valuable goals for the club, turned down an extension on his contract, returning home to sign for Den Haag, a Dutch Second Division side.

On the recommendation of Jack Charlton, Middlesbrough chairman Mike McCullagh offered the vacant manager's job to Willie Maddren. The new boss named four debutants — Steve Corden, Gary Pallister, Don O'Riordan, Gary Rowell — in the side that lost 3-0 on the opening day of the 1985-86 season, at Plough Lane, Wimbledon. Defender Corden, son of director Dick Corden, broke a leg just before half-time and never played for the club again.

The Milk Cup first round paired Middlesbrough with Mansfield Town, with the first leg at Field Mill. The Stags won 2-0 and a week later, at Ayresome Park, Middlesbrough's leaky defence helped Mansfield to draw 4-4 and go through on aggregate. 'Boro, once renowned as 'bonny Cup fighters', were now getting knocked out of the competition with alarming regularity in the early rounds.

The club's luck in the Full Members' Cup, however, was holding out and a 2-0 home victory over Carlisle United in early October meant a visit to Hull City in the Northern Area semi-final.

The Elland Road fixture on 12 October is a red-letter day

Don O'Riordan (5) outjumps a packed defence to head home for Middlesbrough against Southampton in the third round of the FA Cup in January 1986.

in the history of Middlesbrough Football Club. The game marked the debut of Bernie Slaven in the forward line. He did not score — indeed, Leeds won 1-0 — but he made his mark on his home debut, against Bradford City. That day, Slavin scored the first of many goals for 'Boro, in a match that ended 1-1.

On 2 November a double sending-off occurred at Ayresome Park, in the goalless draw against Blackburn Rovers. David Currie went for a 'double-booking' and Blackburn's Northern Ireland international Noel Brotherston followed for a similar reason.

Middlesbrough's 3-2 home victory over Oldham Athletic in mid-November ended a sequence of eight League games without a win, but hopes of a Cup victory disappeared as 'Boro went out of the Full Members' Cup Northern Area semi-final, losing 3-1 at Boothferry Park.

Middlesbrough desperately needed cash but the board was split over plans to raise £1 million by a public share issue. On 2 December, chairman Mike McCullagh and director Peter Cook resigned over the matter and Alf Duffield stepped into the breach.

The highlight of the Christmas games was an excellent 2-0 victory over Sunderland at Ayresome Park. Goals from Tony Mowbray and Tony McAndrew sent the crowd of 19,701 (the highest home attendance of the season) home delighted.

The month of January saw Middlesbrough relinquish any FA Cup dreams that they may have cherished, as they tamely submitted 3-1 to Southampton at Ayresome Park in the third round.

A spell of bad weather bit deeply into the February programme and Middlesbrough played only one game during the month, another home defeat, this time against Charlton Athletic.

Willie Maddren had left the club and coach Bruce Rioch was in charge of team affairs when, in March 1986, 'Boro went down with all guns blazing at Ayresome Park, losing 2-1 to Sheffield United. Such was the team's commitment to the game that, despite the loss of three desperately-needed points, they were accorded a standing ovation as they walked off the pitch.

Bruce Rioch received a midnight call from chairman Duffield offering him the manager's job and, to the relief of Teesside fans, he accepted.

In April 1986, the club, now fighting for its very existence, had to borrow £30,000 from the Professional Footballers' Association to pay the players and things were looking very black indeed.

It was a case of *déjà vu* for the final game of the season. The venue was again at Gay Meadow and Middlesbrough needed to win to stay in the Second Division. Archie Stephens scored for 'Boro and Gary Pallister was sent off as Shrewsbury won 2-1 and down Middlesbrough went.

On 21 May 1986, the worst fears of 'Boro's fans were realised. With crippling debts, rumoured to be approaching £2 million, the club called in the Provisional Liquidator and shortly afterwards, Middlesbrough Football Club's pulse ceased to beat.

In late July 1986, the Inland Revenue took the club to court, claiming £115,156 in tax arrears and the judge issued a winding-up order. On 2 August, Bruce Rioch and 29 other non-playing staff were sacked by the Official Receiver and the gates to Ayresome Park were padlocked.

Some players decided to leave the club and were now free to do so, arranging new contracts with other clubs and duly moving on. The ones that stayed, all unpaid, became more resolute in their determination to see the thing through and, led by Bruce Rioch and coach Colin Todd, they changed in the backs of cars and trained on any piece of turf that was available.

The club re-formed under the name of 'Middlesbrough Football and Athletic Company (1986) Limited' and, chaired by Colin Henderson, intended to carry on playing football, no matter what class of soccer they ended up in.

In order to continue under the auspices of the Football League, stringent rules had to be adhered to and with the first game of 1986-87, at home to Port Vale, fast approaching, frantic behind-the-scenes talks meant that the re-formed club could stay in the League, provided they could fulfill the Port Vale fixture.

Hartlepool United offered Middlesbrough (no longer on the football coupons) the use of the Victoria Ground and the gracious

Panic stations in the Port Vale defence as Tony Mowbray causes problems. This Middlesbrough 'home' game was played at Hartlepool United's Victoria Ground as 'Boro struggled to survive and return to Ayresome Park.

Middlesbrough players celebrate in the Ayresome Park bath after regaining their Second Division place in May 1987.

gesture was gratefully accepted. Port Vale complained to the Football League over the intended venue, but the League overruled Vale's complaint. Hartlepool were also at home on the first day of the season, so the League sanctioned Middlesbrough's game as an evening kick-off.

Archie Stephens scored two cracking goals to put Middlesbrough into a 2-0 lead, but 'Boro had not played any pre-season practice games and Vale, a fitter and better-prepared side, forced a 2-2 draw.

Three days later, in the first round of the Littlewoods Cup, the long arm of coincidence threw Hartlepool and 'Boro together for the first competitive meeting between the two clubs. At the Victoria Ground, a crowd of 7,735 saw the sides play out a 1-1 draw with Bernie Slaven netting for 'Boro.

The next League fixture was a 2-0 win at Wigan Athletic and the players and supporters made an emotional return to Ayresome Park for the second leg of the Littlewoods Cup on 2 September. Hartlepool offered little resistance as 'Boro won 2-0 with goals form Stuart Ripley and Gary Hamilton, who also missed a penalty.

Middlesbrough recovered from their traumatic start to the season and remained unbeaten in the League until Blackpool won 3-1 at Ayresome Park on 11 October. The Seasiders were back at Ayresome Park in November, for the first round of

the FA Cup, but this time a Bernie Slaven hat-trick saw Middlesbrough through to the next round.

The first local derby of the season was at Feethams against Darlington, also in November, when a goal from Stephens was enough to ensure victory for 'Boro. December yielded an excellent points return as Middlesbrough went through the month unbeaten, winning four of their five games. One of those victories was at Notts County in the second round of the FA Cup.

York City halted Middlesbrough's League progress at Bootham Crescent on New Year's Day, with an impressive 3-1 win, and further disappointment followed nine days later when Fourth Division Preston North End scored the only goal of the FA Cup third-round game at Ayresome Park.

On 7 February, 'Boro lost the services of Brian Laws when he stepped up to take a penalty against Bristol Rovers at Ayresome Park. He severely damaged his knee ligaments in his run-up and was ruled out for the rest of the season.

In April and May, seven successive wins kept Middlesbrough in the promotion frame and a point was needed at Ayresome Park in the last home match of the season to guarantee promotion to the Second Division. Wigan proved to be unyielding in defence but, more important, failed to score. At the end of the game the Ayresome Park crowd were in raptures. The 'impossible'

A Double Over Villa
— But They Laughed Last

MIDDLESBROUGH 2   ASTON VILLA 1

IN recent seasons there have been some memorable clashes between Middlesbrough and Aston Villa, and this was one of those matches. The Second Division game between Middlesbrough and Villa on Valentine's Day 1988 was the first match outside the First Division to be televised live (on ITV) nationally. Because of this it was played on a Sunday.

Graham Taylor's Villa, clear leaders at the top of the Second Division, had to wait until the fifth game of the season before winning their first League match, at Leicester City. By February 1988, though, Villa had 11 away victories to their credit and with them the best away record in the entire Football League, needing only two more away wins to equal the all-time record for the division.

This was the fourth time that the sides had met in that season. Villa had won 1-0 in both games in the League Cup whilst 'Boro had won 1-0 at Villa Park in the League in early September. Three days before the game, Colin Cooper became the first Middlesbrough player to be chosen as the Barclay Young Eagle of the Month for the North-East region.

Early in the game Stephen Pears' head met the full force of Garry Thompson's elbow which necessitated him leaving the field for six minutes to have eight stitches inserted in a nasty head wound, Cooper going in goal. Pears returned to a great reception and Cooper could boast that he had handled the ball quite safely three times.

On 35 minutes, Thompson's blistering pace deceived Tony Mowbray on the North Stand side of the pitch, and he swept past 'Boro's star defender. Worse was to follow for 'Boro, for his cross was swept home by Tony Daley from close in.

Late in the second half, manager Bruce Rioch pushed both his substitutes on, Alan Kernaghan replaced former Villa player Paul Kerr and another Villa player, Mark Burke, substituting for the injured Stuart Ripley. The double substitution had the desired affect. On 81 minutes, Kernaghan headed the ball down to Bernie Slaven, whose shot produced a scintillating save from Nigel Spink, but Kernaghan himself was on hand to tap the rebound over the line.

It was now Villa's turn to absorb the pressure as the home club stepped up a gear, looking for the winning goal. It came three minutes later. Brian Laws swung over a high cross and captain Tony Mowbray, totally unmarked on the 18-yard line and with only Spink in front of him, deftly placed his diving header into the net: 2-1 to 'Boro!

Now it was 'Boro's turn to hang on to a slender lead as the home crowd started whistling for the referee to end the game. What cheers greeted the final whistle and what a worthy game it had been, an excellent advertisement for Second Division football.

'Boro were 6th before the game and leapfrogged over Bradford City, Millwall and Crystal Palace into third place. The top of the table now looked like this:

Aston Villa	32	17	10	5	51	27	61	1st
Blackburn Rovers	31	17	9	5	45	28	60	2nd
Middlesbrough	31	16	8	7	43	25	56	3rd

The attendance of 16,958 was the club's second-highest League crowd of the season, despite the game being televised. And who else but 'Boro captain Tony Mowbray won the bottle of champagne for his performance as 'Man of the Match'.

So Middlesbrough recorded a League double over Villa, only Second Division champions Millwall managing to equal that feat, later in the season. It was Villa who had the last laugh over Middlesbrough, though. After 44 League games, a twist of fate saw both 'Boro and Villa on the same number of points and with identical goal-differences of 27, but Villa scraped through to the First Division by virtue of scoring five more goals, 68 compared to Middlesbrough's 63.

Middlesbrough: Pears; Glover, Cooper, Mowbray, Parkinson, Pallister, Slaven, Ripley(Burke), Hamilton, Kerr(Kernaghan), Laws.
Aston Villa: Spink; Gage, Gallacher, Gray, Evans, Keown, Birch, Lillis, Thompson, Daley(Gray), McInally.
Attendance: 16,957

Aston Villa goalkeeper Nigel Spink comes under pressure from a Middlesbrough attack.

The jubilation is on Paul Kerr's face for all to see as he celebrates with goalscorer Bernie Slaven and the Holgate End fans. 'Boro are on their way to the First Division Play-off Final and a game against Chelsea after this victory over Bradford City in May 1988.

had happened — not only were Middlesbrough FC still alive, they were back in Division Two.

Bruce Rioch returned to his old club, Aston Villa, to buy defender Dean 'Dino' Glover in the summer of 1987 and Glover made his debut at right-back at Ayresome Park against Millwall on 15 August. Archie Stephens scored for Middlesbrough as Millwall forced a 1-1 draw before a crowd of 11,471.

Glover, who quickly became a favourite at Middlesbrough because of his commitment and 'hard man' image, hit the headlines three days later at Roker Park. In the Littlewoods Cup game against Sunderland he incurred the wrath of the referee when he struck Gary Bennett and received his marching orders after only 12 minutes on the pitch. Sunderland won the match 1-0. A week later, Middlesbrough wrapped up the second leg when goals from Bernie Slaven and skipper Tony Mowbray carried the club through on aggregate.

Bradford City won 2-0 at Valley Parade on 3 October but this defeat launched Middlesbrough on a run of 14 unbeaten games which ended in a 2-0 defeat at Elland Road on 28 December before a crowd of 34,186. The match was soured

by the double dismissal of 'Boro's Stuart Ripley and United's Ian Snodin in the 43rd minute.

Middlesbrough's name was paired with non-League opposition for the third round of the FA Cup and underdogs Sutton United, cheered on by the nation, almost took 'Boro's scalp. A Gary Pallister goal put 'Boro ahead after 63 minutes, before Golley's equaliser ten minutes from time meant an Ayresome Park replay.

It took a goal from Paul Kerr in extra-time of that replay to extinguish brave Sutton's Cup dreams and earn Middlesbrough a fourth-round game against First Division Everton at Goodison Park. This time 'Boro were the underdogs and the game's two goals came either side of the interval. Graeme Sharp put the Blues ahead with almost the last kick of the half. Paul Kerr equalised almost from the second-half kick-off.

The Ayresome Park replay was a stamina-sapping cracker. Dave Watson put the Merseysiders ahead inside 66 minutes and Tony Mowbray equalised in the dying seconds of normal time. Alan Kernaghan put 'Boro ahead for the first time in the tie, after 99 minutes, but Trevor Stevens equalised with the last kick of the game. A second replay took place at Everton and this

Trevor Senior heads a goal for Middlesbrough in the first-leg of the 1988 Play-off Final against Chelsea at Ayresome Park.

We're going up! Middlesbrough players celebrate, for despite a 1-0 defeat at Stamford Bridge they won the Final on aggregate.

time the Merseysiders took command on a blustery night, winning 2-1.

Bruce Rioch took Watford striker, Trevor Senior, to Ayresome Park and the player contributed with two goals as 'Boro crushed Sheffield United 6-0 on his home debut.

Middlesbrough needed to beat Leicester City at Ayresome Park in the last game of the season to ensure a second promotion success, but City turned 'Boro's impending celebrations into a funeral wake by winning 2-1. 'Boro's players were asking the crowd how other results had gone as they walked off the pitch and learned that Aston Villa — on the same number of points and with the same goal-difference — had achieved promotion by virtue of winning more games, leaving Middlesbrough to try for the First Division through the play-off system.

Gary Pallister outjumps the Norwich City attack at Carrow Road in December 1988. The 'Boro number-nine is Dean Glover.

Four play-off games stood between Middlesbrough and the First Division and the first one kicked-off at Valley Parade on Sunday 15 May, against Bradford City. The match yielded three goals, all scored in a three-minute second-half spell. City went ahead after 67 minutes, then Senior scored 'Boro's equaliser two minutes later. City's captain, Stuart McCall, restored Bradford's lead within a minute and set the scene for an interesting game at Ayresome Park three days later.

A goal by Bernie Slaven took the scores level on aggregate and with no further goals the match went into 30 minutes' extra-time. Within the first minute, Gary Hamilton ended City's aspirations by scoring the conclusive goal.

Chelsea now stood between Middlesbrough and Division One and the first game of the play-off 'Final', at Ayresome Park, took place on Wednesday 25 May. Despite Chelsea's obvious class, Middlesbrough took the game 2-0 with goals from Trevor Senior and Bernie Slaven.

At Stamford Bridge the following Saturday, Pat Nevin was in inspiring form and set up Chelsea's goal, Gordon Durie scoring after 19 minutes. Middlesbrough's defence, with Mowbray and Pallister twin towers of resistance, thwarted every Chelsea raid and they held on to take the tie 2-1 on aggregate. Chelsea's fans, unable to take defeat with dignity, marred the afternoon with ugly scenes which were later shown on television. It was half an hour before the Middlesbrough players were allowed back on to the pitch to celebrate promotion with their fans.

For Middlesbrough's return to the First Division, manager Bruce Rioch went into the transfer market to bring Mark Brennan to Ayresome Park. Brennan was given his debut on the opening day of the 1988-89 season, at Derby where a Paul Goddard goal was enough to give the Rams victory.

With this semi-final goal against Aston Villa, Bernie Slaven sets Middlesbrough on the way to a Wembley Final in the 1990 Zenith Data Systems Cup.

'Boro also lost the next two games. Their first win eventually came on 17 September, when Gary Hamilton's goal gave them victory over Wimbledon. It was an unhappy match, however, for striker Trevor Senior was booed off the pitch and within a matter of days had been transferred back to Reading.

Once again, Middlesbrough were dumped out of the Littlewoods Cup by a team in the lower reaches of the Football League. Tranmere Rovers forced a draw at Ayresome Park and deservedly won the Prenton Park game 1-0.

Sandwiched between the Littlewoods games, Bernie Slaven and David Speedie both scored hat-tricks at Highfield Road, where 'Boro just held on to beat Coventry City 4-3. At the end of October, however, Middlesbrough suffered a humiliating 3-0 defeat at Newcastle. Three days later, Middlesbrough beat a slick Millwall side 4-2 and everyone was happy again.

Later that month, Peter Davenport agreed to sign for Middlesbrough and, although he struggled to find his scoring touch, he did have the satisfaction of netting against his old club, Manchester United, on 2 January, helping 'Boro to end a sequence of seven games without a win.

There was another shock just around the corner, however, and Fourth Division Grimsby Town lowered 'Boro's FA Cup colours at Ayresome Park. Middlesbrough went ahead but then the Mariners' substitute, Marc North, scored twice.

In March 1989, Mark Proctor was surprisingly re-signed by Middlesbrough when Rioch paid £300,000 to buy him from Sheffield Wednesday. Proctor and Mark Barham made their debuts in a 1-1 draw at Wimbledon, although for Proctor, of course, it was his second League bow for the club.

Middlesbrough were now slipping deeper into trouble and a run of 12 games without a win saw them slump into the relegation zone. Then late goals by Slaven at West Ham earned 'Boro a 2-1 win and gave rise to hopes of a climb to safety.

Yet there was still much work to be done and when Arsenal kept their League Championship hopes alive with a 1-0 win at Ayresome Park on 6 May, they also left Middlesbrough needing victory at Hillsborough in their last match of the season. But Sheffield Wednesday were also desperate for the points and they scored the only goal of the game to send 'Boro back to the Second Division.

After the heady climb from the brink of oblivion to the First Division, relegation was disappointing, but not as disastrous as the alternative facing Middlesbrough in 1986.

'Boro began 1989-90 with a 4-2 win over Wolves at Ayresome Park, 21,727 turning up to see Bernie Slaven hit two more goals, but the inevitable happened on 29 August when England defender Gary Pallister joined Manchester United for £2.3 million, then a record between two British clubs.

Simon Coleman was signed from Mansfield Town to replace Pallister, but after a Mark Proctor goal beat Hull in September, Middlesbrough went ten League games without victory until Alan Kernaghan hit a hat-trick at Ewood Park in a surprise 4-2 win over promotion-chasing Blackburn.

By this time, Wimbledon had ended 'Boro's interest in the League Cup with a 2-1 win over two legs. In the League, Middlesbrough were hovering in the lower reaches of the table and Rioch signed Ian Baird from Leeds for £500,000 to inject more power in attack. Initially it proved fruitless and after an FA Cup exit, after three games with Everton, and four consecutive League defeats, Bruce Rioch was sacked on 9 March with the club in 20th position.

Colin Todd was asked to take over and the position worsened as Blackburn won 3-0 at Ayresome Park to make further relegation a real possibility. Todd signed left-back Jimmy Phillips from Oxford United and a 2-1 win at Plymouth, followed by a Slaven goal to beat Oldham at home, eased them up to 19th.

However, three defeats in four home games put Middlesbrough into the last remaining relegation slot as the final game of the season, at home to Newcastle approached. 'Boro had to win to ensure survival, and if Bournemouth beat Leeds even that would be to no avail. In front of 18,484 northern fans (Newcastle were already assured third-place and a play-off chance) Middlesbrough turned it on as two goals each for Slaven and Baird made Owen McGee's own-goal irrelevant. News filtered through that Bournemouth had lost 1-0 to Second Division champions Leeds, and 'Boro were safe.

Slaven's 21 League goals had been crucial because the club had been on the brink of a return journey to Division Three — for many Middlesbrough fans, too awful to contemplate.

For 1990-91, Todd signed striker Robbie Mustoe from Oxford United and John Hendrie from Leeds United. John Wark, at 32 years old, came from Ipswich to add steel in midfield.

Inconsistent early results were forgotten on 29 September as 'Boro hammered Leicester City 6-0, four goals coming in in the first half. A Slaven hat-trick at the Goldstone Ground in late October set up a 4-2 win, and six wins in seven games pushed Middlesbrough to third — an automatic promotion position in this particular season.

Progress in the League Cup was steady, 'Boro beating Tranmere, Newcastle and Norwich before losing 3-2 at Villa Park, despite another two goals from Slaven. The FA Cup challenge, however, ended in a disappointing 2-0 defeat at the hands of Third Division leaders Cambridge United.

Middlesbrough were always in a play-off slot, as seventh place would ensure this, but a run of only two wins in nine games in March and April set a few hearts fluttering. Wolves and Brighton were both beaten 2-0 at Ayresome Park and although

Here we go . . .Bernie Slaven scores Middlesbrough's first goal past Newcastle's John Burridge.

'Boro Stay Up

MIDDLESBROUGH 4   NEWCASTLE UNITED 1

THIS was the 84th derby meeting between Tees and Tyne and it was also a crucial match for both sides. Jim Smith's Newcastle United, with an impressive nine-match unbeaten run behind them, came to Ayresome Park on 5 May 1990 looking for the points to bolster their claims to an automatic promotion place to the First Division.

The match was just as crucial to Middlesbrough, but for a different reason. Colin Todd's side needed to win to have any realistic chance of staying in the Second Division and, even then, safety was not guaranteed, for it all hinged on whether Bournemouth beat Leeds United at Dean Court.

Newcastle, despite their fanatical support, received only just over 1,000 tickets for the game, so huge TV screens were hastily erected at St James' Park for all the fans who could not get a ticket and 14,000 United fans watched the game back in Newcastle.

Playing the brinkmanship game, Todd ordered the touchlines on the pitch to be narrowed, hoping to curtail United's free-flowing style of play. It appeared to do the trick because Mark McGhee and Mick Quinn, who between them had scored 51 League goals for the Magpies during the season, failed to find the net in this game.

The tension proved too much for both sides and there were six bookings in the game, three on each side. For 'Boro, Colin Cooper and Simon Coleman were cautioned for dissent, and Mark Brennan for a foul. United's bad boys were Kevin Dillon, Ray Ranson and Kevin Scott — all booked for fouls.

There was disheartening half-time news for both sets of fans: Leeds United were holding Bournemouth to a goalless draw at Dean Court, but the news from Filbert Street was worse for Newcastle's fans because Sheffield United were leading Leicester City 4-2.

All five goals came in the second half and Middlesbrough scored every one. They achieved the vital breakthrough on the hour, just after news had filtered through that Bournemouth had fallen behind to Leeds. United 'keeper John Burridge was at fault for the first goal, hesitating before coming out to meet Paul Kerr's cross from the left. Bernie

Slaven showed no hesitancy as he rifled the ball into the net with the help of the right-hand post.

Six minutes later, Magpies' full-back John Anderson sold his 'keeper short with a disastrous back-pass. Again it was predator Slaven who capitalised to leave Ian Baird the easiest of tasks to tap the ball past Burridge. Within three minutes, Newcastle had pulled one back with a little help from 'Boro defender Owen McGee, who got his head in the way of a Kevin Brock header and the ball was diverted past Pears to give the Geordies fresh hope.

However, it was Middlesbrough who ended the game with a powerful flourish. On 75 minutes, Baird finished off a superb build-up with a magnificent goal. In the last minute, Mark Proctor's shot glanced off Burridge's left-hand post and there was Slaven to steer the ball into the net.

Despite the 4-1 thrashing of United, it would have counted for nothing had Bournemouth beaten Leeds. After the final whistle, thousands of fans stayed behind at Ayresome Park waiting for news of the other games.

The heartening news (for Middlesbrough fans) from Dean Court was that Leeds had won 1-0, condemning Bournemouth to the Third Division and ensured Middlesbrough's survival in the Second. The news of Bournemouth's misfortune signalled great rejoicing on the pitch and on the terraces, almost as though Middlesbrough had won promotion rather than only just avoiding relegation.

It was less inspiring news for Newcastle fans at the other end of the ground — Sheffield United had slaughtered Leicester City 5-2 at Filbert Street to claim the second promotion place, leaving Newcastle to face the agony of the Second Division play-offs. After defeat by Sunderland at St James' Park, Newcastle stayed in the Second Division, like Middlesbrough.

Middlesbrough: Pears; Cooper, Phillips, Kernaghan, Coleman, McGee, Slaven, Proctor, Baird, Kerr, Brennan.
Newcastle United: Burridge; Scott(Bradshaw), Stimson, Aitken, Anderson, Ranson, Brock, Dillon, Quinn(O'Brien), McGhee, Kristensen.
Attendance: 19,484

Phillips (centre, mostly hidden, arm raised) scores Middlesbrough's equaliser against Notts County in the 1991 Play-off semi-final first leg.

Jimmy Phillips celebrates Slaven's equaliser in the second leg of the 1992 Rumbelows Cup semi-final against Manchester United.

the programme ended with defeats at champions Oldham and at Barnsley 'Boro duly finished seventh and met Notts County (who finished fourth with 11 points more) in the first play-off.

County had finished the season with seven straight victories and Turner gave them a first-half lead. Indeed, only four minutes remained when Jimmy Phillips crashed in a vital equaliser. Notts won by a single goal at Meadow Lane and 'Boro would have to wait a year for another promotion.

A month later Colin Todd dropped a bombshell, resigning as manager and citing 'board interference' as his reason. On 10 July, Charlton Athletic's Lennie Lawrence was appointed as Todd's successor, after nine turbulent years with the London club, who had, amongst other problems, lost their Valley ground and, like 'Boro, been on the brink of extinction.

For 1991-92, Lawrence moved to bring Watford centre-forward Paul Wilkinson to Ayresome Park. Willie Falconer also arrived from the Vicarage Road club, whilst Wark returned to Ipswich.

The new manager seemed loathe to find a place for the supporters' hero, Bernie Slaven, as 'Boro began well, for despite losing at Derby and Ipswich they won seven of their opening nine League matches to go top of the table, a position which they held until Bonfire Night.

Slaven scored twice after coming on as a second-half substitute at Oxford and after this was given an extended run in the side. Wilkinson was also finding the net regularly and the League Cup campaign was hotting up. After steady passage to the fourth round, First Division Manchester City were beaten

Robbie Mustoe clashes with Wimbledon's John Fashanu in March 1993 during an FA Premier League game.

2-1 at Ayresome Park with goals from Mustoe and Wilkinson on 3 December. A month later, City were put out of the FA Cup by the same score at the same venue, this time Kernaghan and Wilkinson scoring.

In the fourth round 'Boro went to Hillsborough and came back with another 2-1 triumph, and also disposed of Peterborough in the League Cup quarter-final, but League form was suffering. At Ayresome Park, things went well but only one win in nine away matches had left Middlesbrough as low as seventh until well into April.

Through to only their second semi-final in a major domestic tournament, Middlesbrough entertained mighty Manchester United at Ayresome Park, where 25,572 saw a goalless draw. The replay was a thriller with Slaven's goal taking the tie into extra-time, in which 'Boro fell to a Ryan Giggs goal. But the game had been a turning point and Middlesbrough now knew that they could match top-class opponents.

In the League, Brighton were hammered 4-0 with Slaven's sixth (and last) hat-trick for the club. Middlesbrough hauled themselves back up to fourth with one game left at Molineux on 2 May. Ipswich were already up, second-placed Leicester were at home to struggling Newcastle, and third-placed Derby at home to Swindon. The permutations were myriad and with 20 minutes to go at Wolverhampton, all looked bleak for 'Boro. Wolves were 1-0 up and Nicky Mohan had been sent off. Although Leicester were losing, Derby were 2-0 up and would be promoted if 'Boro could not find two goals.

They did so triumphantly with Jon Gittens' equaliser followed by jubilant Paul Wilkinson's 77th-minute winner to

bring Premier League football to Ayresome Park after Lennie Lawrence's first season

The 1992-93 season was supposed to herald the new FA Premier League. In reality, however there was little change and it proved to be still the 'First' Division much as before.

Despite a 2-1 defeat at Coventry on 15 August, Middlesbrough began quite well. Two Slaven goals accounted for Manchester City and three days later, reigning League Champions Leeds United were thrashed 4-1 at Ayresome Park with goals from Wilkinson, Tommy Wright, a £650,000 signing from Leicester, and Hendrie.

An away win at Maine Road on 12 September saw 'Boro stand sixth in the League — the highest they were to achieve as things began to change. After a home defeat by Aston Villa, Manchester United — the eventual Champions — attracted the season's highest League attendance of 24,172 to Ayresome Park. The crowd didn't know it then, but Bernie Slaven's second-half equaliser was to be his last goal for the club.

On 7 October, after a goalless first leg at St James's Park, Middlesbrough crashed 3-1 to a home League Cup exit at the hands of Kevin Keegan's high-flying Newcastle, who were sweeping all before them in the new First Division.

In the Premier League, form deserted Lawrence's side, who lost 4-1 at both Liverpool and Oldham, despite the capture of Craig Hignett, the highly-rated Crewe Alexandra winger, financed by the pre-season sale of Stuart Ripley to Blackburn for £1.3 million. The only highspot of a barren winter was coming from behind to beat Blackburn 3-2, thanks to a John Hendrie hat-trick. Heavy away defeats at Aston Villa (5-1), Leeds

The Champions Hammered

MIDDLESBROUGH 4   LEEDS UNITED 1

MIDDLESBROUGH'S FA Premier League match against the old First Division champions, Leeds United, on 22 August 1992 was made an all-ticket game. The long-awaited encounter drew the pre-match comment from 'Boro manager Lennie Lawrence that this game was to be the 'ultimate test' for his side.

Two Middlesbrough players — John Hendrie and Tommy Wright — were former Leeds men. Both players had something to prove that afternoon and they did just that. The match started with Gary Speed receiving a sixth-minute booking for a foul on Republic of Ireland international Chris Morris, then 'Boro sprung to life on a slippery surface with two goals in as many minutes from their ace striker Paul Wilkinson.

'Boro took the lead on seven minutes when Tommy Wright was allowed generous space down the left flank and his cross was met by Wilkinson's outstretched right foot. Chris Whyte failed to intercept Wright's cross and Wilkinson flicked the ball past John Lukic — 'Boro were in the lead.

Two minutes later, Wright and Wilkinson combined again and the end product was the same — another goal for 'Boro. It was Chris Fairclough who misjudged Tommy Wright's cross and Wilkinson's full-length diving header flashed into the net from eight yards out.

Both teams made substitutions at the start of the second half. Wilkinson, who had limped off with strained ankle ligaments, failed to reappear for Middlesbrough with Robbie Mustoe coming on. United full-back Jon Newsome was taken off and veteran Gordon Strachan was pushed on with Gary Speed moving to full-back, but not even the introduction of Strachan could spark United into life.

Two minutes after half-time, Tommy Wright, one of the smallest players on the pitch, continued his outstanding contribution to the match as he rose, unchallenged, to head in a corner from Jimmy Phillips. There was no way back for the champions now.

Still Middlesbrough kept pressing forward, looking for further goals, and their persistence paid off on the hour.

'Reject' Tommy Wright chipped the ball over Gary Speed for John Hendrie to cut inside Chris Whyte and Chris Fairclough to plant the ball in the far corner of the net.

Eight minutes later Frenchman Eric Cantona gave United's travelling army of fans a faint glimmer of hope with a consolation goal from Wallace's centre, but the match had already been won and lost. Two minutes later, United's David Batty went into the referee's book for a heavy foul on Andy Peake and was immediately substituted by Steve Hodge. Lennie Lawrence also made a substitution, pushing Jamie Pollock into the fray for Bernie Slaven.

The Times headline on the match read: 'Middlesbrough humble inept champions', and even the *Yorkshire Post* reported: 'Boro were simply magnificent. Hendrie and Wright oozed confidence, running at the Leeds defence with guile, pace and purpose.'

United manager Howard Wilkinson, a little lost for words, attempted to apologise for his team's ineffective display. He said: "I am angry, bemused and upset. We were simply beaten by a better team; we were turned over . . .you name it, they did it; you name it, we didn't!"

His opposite number, Lennie Lawrence, commented with pride "It was the most professional performance I have been involved with in my ten years as a football manager."

Middlesbrough were relegated at the end of the season, whilst Leeds United never won a match all season away from Elland Road, so the combination of both probably dilutes the retrospective significance of this match, but at the time it was a most emphatic victory for Middlesbrough over the champions of the Football League.

Middlesbrough: Ironside; Morris, Phillips, Kernaghan (captain), Whyte, Peake, Slaven(Pollock), Falconer, Wilkinson(Mustoe), Wright, Hendrie.
Leeds United: Lukic; Newsome(Strachan), Dorigo, Batty (Hodge), Fairclough, Whyte, Cantona, Wallace, Chapman, McAllister, Speed.
Attendance: 18,649

Paul Wilkinson scores for 'Boro against Leeds United as the champions are hammered on the opening day of the new FA Premier League.

Derek Whyte of Middlesbrough and Darren Ferguson of Manchester United in action at Ayresome Park in October 1992.

John Hendrie goes for a bouncing ball as Oldham's Neil Pointon challenges him at Ayresome Park in March 1993.

and Manchester United (3-0 each), Chelsea (4-0) and Crystal Palace (4-1) condemned 'Boro to relegation, despite two wins and a draw to end the season. FA Cup hopes had been ended in the fourth round with a 3-0 home thumping by fellow relegation companions Nottingham Forest, after a 1-1 draw at the City Ground.

So 1993-94 will see Middlesbrough once again in the second flight of League football and without some familiar names. Slaven, forced out of the club on a free transfer to Port Vale in March 1993, Gary Parkinson, rejoining Rioch at Bolton, and Mark Proctor, also released.

The history of Middlesbrough Football Club has, like the story of all clubs, had its fair share of ups and downs. From amateur giants in the gaslit days of the last century to a First Division side that has boasted the likes of Camsell, Mannion and Hardwick, 'Boro have contributed to football's rich tapestry. After the trials and tribulations during the 1980s, when the club's very existence was in doubt, their supporters, were grateful that they had a club at all. Thus, when subsequent relegations are set within that context, it does not seem quite such a disaster. At least the 'Boro live to fight another day.

The Other Middlesbrough — Middlesbrough Ironopolis

MIDDLESBROUGH Ironopolis Football Club was formed in 1885 because of a split amongst the members of Middlesbrough FC over whether or not the club should adopt professionalism. Alf Mattison, a director with Middlesbrough, became club chairman and the Nops hold a little piece of football history because they became the first football club to be registered as a Limited Liability Company at Companies House.

It was around this time that the old Middlesbrough club became known as the 'Scabs' and Ironopolis the 'Washers'. The 'Scabs' nickname was allegedly accorded to the team that returned from playing a Northern League game at Newcastle East End on a 'ground that was covered in ashes and clinkers' and scabs later developed over the wounds received on the East End pitch. George Waller, a Middlesbrough player of the period, offered this much later as the reason for the clubs' nicknames.

Ironopolis became known as the 'Washers' because the new club was wealthier than the old one and, soon afterwards, the club's followers supported badges made from washers.

Ironopolis played all their home games at the quaintly-named Paradise Ground, which today is part of Ayresome Park. Rivalry between the two clubs was as intense then as is that in the cities of Manchester, Liverpool, Sheffield and Nottingham today, the rancour being further heightened by Ironopolis luring away Middlesbrough's better players with professional offers. Billy Hopewell, Jack Taylor and Tom Cronshaw were all lured to the Paradise Ground with Hopewell becoming the Nops' first captain.

As a professional club Ironopolis quickly grew in size and soon became the strongest and usually the best-supported in the area. It seems that the club's first playing strip was maroon and green shirts with dark blue shorts, but this strip had changed by the time the club was elected to the Football League.

Nops' historic first game was on 14 December 1889 at the Paradise Ground against Gainsborough Trinity, the advertisement placed in the *North Eastern Daily Gazette*, to entice prospective spectators to the new club, read:

'Grand Opening Match
Opposite (Royal Albert) Park Gates
kick-off 2.30pm
Gentlemen 6d, Boys 3d.'

It was reported that the 'new stands would hopefully be finished in time for Christmas and that the new road leading to the ground would also be finished soon'. The playing field itself, once the home of the rugbyites in the town, 'was not yet in the best playing condition but, at least it had been drained and would subsequently be levelled.' Not much is recorded about the new club's ground, but it was further reported that 'substantial barricades had been erected to prevent the encroachment of spectators on to the pitch' and that 'boarded paths had been laid around the playing area.' Near to the ground was a large, deep pond that was later used by Nops' followers who sometimes steered the visiting supporters towards after the game, especially if Nops lost.

The players had gathered together for the first time for match practice only three days before the game against Gainsborough but, after a public training session it was anticipated that all signings would prove useful to the club. The game, which attracted an inquisitive 4,000 crowd, was kicked-off by chairman J.H.Boolds and ended in a convenient 1-1 draw with Tommy Seymour scoring the Nops' first-ever goal. The team which represented the infant club was: G.Smart (ex-Birtley), T.Anderson (ex-Arthurlie), J.Matthew (Dundee Strathmore), J.A. (Jimmy) Elliott, W.Hopewell (captain, ex-Middlesbrough), T.Cronshaw (ex-Middlesbrough), J McGregor (ex-Dundee), T.J.Morrissey (ex-Dundee Harp), J.Taylor (ex-Middlesbrough) and T.Seymour (ex-Arthurlie).

On the same day as Ironopolis' baptism, Middlesbrough were away to Darlington in a Northern League fixture and lost heavily, 7-0.

The Northern League was formed in 1889 and its formation put football on a formal footing in the North-East with a rigid fixture list and league tables being based on the format initiated by the Football League the year before. Unfashionable Darlington St Augustine won the first championship but when Ironopolis, with many imported Scottish players, joined the League for the start of the 1890-91 season, the 'Nops' immediately became the dominant force in the infant league, winning the championship for the next three seasons. Such was the Nops' playing strength that they lost only four games in their three years' Northern League history.

On 8 February 1890, Ironopolis sent a deputation headed by club secretary A.Sanderson with an offer to the Middlesbrough committee members proposing an amalgamation of the two clubs. The Nops' deputation suggested the amalgamation, also offering the idea that a limited liability company be formed to bring fresh money into the new club. The 'Boro committee opposed the suggestion, advising the deputation that the 'old club was in a good financial condition'.

Two days later there was a further meeting at the King's Head Hotel in the town and it was at this meeting that the Ironopolis directors demanded £650 from the Middlesbrough committee as a compensation for the proposed amalgamation. The Middlesbrough committee immediately ended the meeting and the rift between the clubs was still as wide as ever.

The club's new colours of cherry and white striped shirts and white shorts were presented to chairman J.H.Boolds by Alderman Richard Weighell, who was the owner of the Oxford Music Hall and the Cleveland Bay Hotel. The new colours were first worn at the Paradise Ground in a 2-1 victory over crack Scottish side Cambuslang on 3 January 1891.

It looked as though the disagreements between the two clubs were to be finally healed in 1892, when both clubs agreed to meet, with the local Press acting as mediators, to discuss an amalgamation before applying to join the Football League. But there were two main issues of contention. The first concerned the name for the new club. Many names were put forward, with Middlesbrough County and Middlesbrough United being the most favoured. After geat debate, the accepted name was to be Middlesbrough and Ironopolis Football and Athletic Company.

The remaining issue hinged on which ground the new club would play at. Naturally, Ironopolis wanted the Paradise Ground as the headquarters, but Middlesbrough felt that the Linthrope Road Ground was the better venue, so again the meeting broke up in discord. Both clubs separately applied for entry into the newly-formed Second Division of the football League but each club's attempt proved unsuccessful. The town, of course, could not support two Football League clubs and as Ironopolis grew in strength, Middlesbrough's flame flickered and almost extinguished. In an attempt to revive the old club's fortunes, it was agreed that 'Boro should revert to amateur status for the 1893-4 season.

Football League founder members Accrington resigned and the Nops were elected to an extended Second Division in 1893-4, along with other League newcomers Liverpool and Arsenal. Indeed, the first Football League game played in the town was against Liverpool at the Paradise Ground in September 1893, the visitors winning 2-0. The Nops lost six of the opening seven games and did not record their first success until 23 September 1893, against Ardwick (later Manchester City) at the Paradise Ground. Ever so gradually the club's fortunes started to improve, Rotherham Town were beaten 6-1 at the Paradise Ground in December, in a sequence that saw the club lose only one game out of eight played.

The Nops even made it to the last 16 of the FA Cup before losing to Nottingham Forest, but it was becoming increasingly difficult for the directors to find the money to travel to away matches. In December 1893, with the club almost £1,500 in debt, the directors called an extraordinary meeting with the

players and asked them to turn out as amateurs until the end of the season. The players' retort was not reported, but the club did manage to see the season out. The campaign ended with four successive defeats, including a 4-1 reverse at Rotherham Town on 14 April 1894, with the club's final League analysis reading:

P	W	D	L	F	A	Pts	Pos
28	8	4	16	37	72	20	11th

There would have been no danger of having to apply for re-election, even more so when the League was extended to 16 clubs for the following season, but the club submitted a letter of resignation from the Football League. Upon receipt of Nops' written withdrawal, the Football League looked upon Nops' misfortunes most sympathetically and promised to 'look favourably' on any future application to rejoin the League but it was the end of the road for Middlesbrough Ironopolis Football Club.

Strangely, as Ironopolis' fortunes waned, Middlesbrough went from strength to strength. They won their first Northern League championship in 1893-4, the FA Amateur Cup twice — in 1895 and 1898 — before winning Football League status in May 1899.

Middlesbrough Ironopolis
Division Two (1893-4)

Sep	2	(h)	Liverpool	L	0-2
Sep	9	(a)	Ardwick	L	1-6
Sep	18	(a)	Burslem Port Vale	L	0-4
Sep	23	(h)	Ardwick	W	2-0
Sep	30	(a)	Crewe Alexandra	L	0-5
Oct	7	(a)	Liverpool	L	0-6
Oct	21	(a)	Walsall Town Swifts	L	0-1
Oct	28	(h)	Burton Swifts	W	2-1
Nov	4	(a)	Notts County	L	0-3
Nov	11	(h)	Grimsby Town	L	2-6
Nov	25	(h)	Small Heath	W	3-0
Dec	2	(h)	Rotherham Town	W	6-1
Dec	16	(h)	Notts County	D	0-0
Dec	23	(a)	Small Heath	L	1-2
Dec	25	(h)	Newcastle United	D	1-1
Dec	26	(a)	Lincoln City	W	3-2
Dec	30	(h)	Walsall Town Swifts	D	1-1
Jan	1	(h)	Burslem Port Vale	W	3-1
Jan	2	(a)	Newcatle United	L	2-7
Jan	6	(h)	Crewe Alexandra	W	2-0
Jan	13	(h)	Lincoln City	D	0-0
Feb	3	(a)	Grimsby Town	L	1-2
Feb	24	(h)	Royal Arsenal	L	3-6
Mar	3	(h)	Northwich Victoria	W	2-1
Mar	10	(a)	Royal Arsenal	L	0-1
Mar	17	(a)	Burton Swifts	L	0-7
Apr	7	(a)	Northwich Victoria	L	1-2
Apr	14	(a)	Rotherham Town	L	1-4

	P	W	D	L	F	A	Pts	
Home	14	7	4	3	27	20	18	
Away	14	1	0	13	10	52	2	
	28	8	4	16	37	72	20	11th

Ironopolis' playing analysis (1889-1894)

	P	W	D	L	F	A
1889-1890	36	20	8	8	95	56
1890-1891	53	36	4	12	162	73
1891-1892	50	34	6	10	140	65
1892-1893	56	33	8	15	116	78
1893-1894	40	15	7	18	55	84
	234	138	33	63	568	356

Top: Bill Whittaker shows some local lads a few tips outside Ayresome Park in November 1951. **Bottom:** Former Middlesbrough player Cliff Chadwick is off to a new life in Australia in 1989, at the ripe old age of 75. Chadwick, who made 97 League and Cup appearances for 'Boro, went to live near Melbourne.

Middlesbrough's Grounds

Ayresome Park, pictured in 1905, not long after the ground opened.

IN MAY 1875, Middlesbrough Cricket Club moved to its new home at the junction of Linthorpe Road and Southfield Road, at what is now Princes Road, and the ground's perimeter extended up to what is currently Clifton Street and as far west as Pelham Street.

Albert Borrie, Fred Hardisty (both later secretaries of the cricket club) and Jackson Ewbank were all accomplished members of the town's cricket club and they, and other cricketers, were prominent players in Middlesbrough Association's early days, so the strong link between the two clubs was clearly self-evident.

Middlesbrough Association's initial football was played, with the Parks Committee's permission, on the Archery Ground in a busy corner of Albert Park, near to where Nazareth House is currently situated, the Archery Ground running parallel to Park Road.

As local enthusiasm for the game of soccer grew and the Archery Ground began attracting larger crowds, the Parks Committee expressed concern about the deteriorating condition of the grassed area along the perimeter of the pitch. An extraordinary meeting was hastily convened and the committee regrettably ordered that the club must find another site on which to play future games.

In March 1879 an agreement was struck between the club and a certain Mr Kemp, who owned a field in Breckon Hill (now at the back of Longlands College and later owned by Middlesbrough High School). For a stipulated ground rent it was agreed that the club could use the field in the pursuit of football and charge interested spectators admission. As the team quickly grew in stature, attendances increased dramatically and within a very short time Mr Kemp decided to capitalise on the club's increasing popularity and advised the club that he was about to increase the ground rent and also demanded a cash bond. The club decided not to comply with Mr Kemp's overtures for more money and immediately started to look for yet another new home.

It is around this time that certain sources quote that the club played on the Swatters' Carr field which was situated at the intersection of Linthorpe Road and Southfield Road, near to the cricket club. All contemporary newspaper reports of Middlesbrough's home games that actually mention the ground refer only to the game being played on the cricket field.

During the 1879-80 season, Middlesbrough Association played its first competitive cup game, in the Sheffield Challenge Cup, recording its first 1,000 attendance against Sheffield Albion.

The football club had moved lock, stock and barrel from the Breckon Hill field to play its first full season on the cricket field in the 1882-83 season, the football club occupying a pitch that was adjacent to the southern boundary of the cricket field.

In 1885 professionalism was legalised but there was turbulent discord at the football club amongst the 400 or so club members. Certain factions felt that the club's long-term future lay with the professional game and pressed that the club adopt the professional code but the opposing faction wished the club to remain amateur. Such was the intensity of feeling that a meeting to 'clear the air' was held at the Oddfellows' Hall on 25 February 1886.

Alf Mattison urged the retention of amateur status but so close was the vote, it was reported that there was a 'forest of hands for professionalism', that it became necessary for club chairman Oswald Henry Cochrane (Ossie was an Oxford graduate and former player and captain of the club who later became coroner in the town) to exercise his casting vote and he gave his vote to the amateur following.

The closeness of the vote only agitated the professional faction even more and they soon after broke away and formed Middlesbrough Ironopolis under the chairmanship of Alf Mattison (a former player with North Ormesby and Middlesbrough) who had, apparently, changed his allegiance since the meeting at the Oddfellows' Hall.

Ironopolis' new ground was situated opposite the main gates to Albert Park and was called the Paradise Ground and has been erroneously recorded over the years as being situated in Milton Street. Today, the Paradise Ground is now part of Ayresome Park and is situated in the south-east corner of the ground currently allocated to visiting supporters.

The Cleveland Association was formed in February 1881 and the Linthorpe Road Ground, being the top playing surface in the area, was used for many representative games that Cleveland County played against other county sides.

Exhaustive research on the author's part which would have hopefully revealed what the Linthorpe Road Ground looked like during the 20 years that Middlesbrough called it home, failed to produce much of note. One little point of interest that was noticed was that the popular end of the ground was called The Plantation End. Another item was found from 1887, reporting that the Grandstand, which accommodated 300 patrons, was to be increased in size to allow another 600 spectators and the additional work was to cost £160.

Middlesbrough Cricket Club moved to the Breckon Hill Field during the 1893-4 season and the football club became the senior occupiers of the Linthorpe Road Ground. It was around this time that a baseball club was formed in the town by the committee club members of Middlesbrough Football Club and the baseball club, for a brief while, flourished. Middlesbrough were now the top amateur soccer side in the area and the club won the Northern League championship for the first time.

Middlesbrough also won the FA Amateur Cup twice in the mid-1890s and, in keeping with the club's growing stature,

the Linthorpe Road Ground was awarded the prestigious FA Amateur Cup Final between Stockton and Harwich & Parkeston on 25 March 1899. Stockton, one of Middlesbrough's arch-rivals of the period, won the game 1-0.

In July 1899, Alf Mattison, was back at the club as chairman as the club prepared for its Football League batism. Middlesbrough Football and Athletic Company's League debut was in early September, 1899 and the first Football League game was played at the Linthorpe Road Ground before 10,000 spectators against Small Heath (later Birmingham City) on 9 September 1899. Mick Murphy scored the first League goal on the ground but Small Heath won 3-1.

At the initial annual general meetings, the board of directors reported healthy working profits to the shareholders and it was felt that the ambitious club should now seek a ground more in keeping with their growing Football League stature. In January 1901 much of the Ayresome Grange Estate, which contained part of the Ironopolis' Old Paradise Ground, was drained with the intention of moving to the new venue some time in 1904. Part of the new land was to be used as a training pitch and also as a playing surface for the reserve side. The pitch intended for Football League games was carefully rolled flat and grassed in readiness for the club's move in 1904. After careful consideration the name of the new ground was decided upon as Ayresome Park because the ground was situated in the Ayresome ward of the town.

The architect of Ayresome Park was Archibald Leitch of Glasgow, who had successfully built many similar football stadia throughout the length and breadth of Britain, and the cost of the ground was £10,436.16. The cost to erect a new North Stand and its fittings was an estimated £1,521 and the total expenditure, approaching £12,000 would prove to be a costly venture for the club for almost a decade. A delightful coloured sketch of Mr Leitch's vision of Ayresome Park is on view at the main entrance to the general office at the club.

Season ticket prices for the promotion winning season 1901-02 at the Linthorpe Road Ground were:

Enclosure
Gentleman £1 1s 0d (£1.05)
Ladies and boys 10s 6d (52.5p)

Entrance to the Ground and covered stand
Shareholders 12s 6d (62.5p)
Non-Shareholders 15s 0d (75p)
Ladies and boys 7s 6d (37.5p)

Entrance to the Ground and open stand
Boys 5s 0d (25p)

In January 1903, Middlesbrough's board of directors failed to extend the tenancy of the Linthorpe Road Ground from the Owners of the Middlesbrough Estate for another year and the intended move to Ayresome Park was hastily brought forward to coincide with the start of the 1903-04 season.

The last game on the old Linthorpe Road Ground, which had served the club so well for 21 years, was on 25 April 1903 — a 1-1 draw against Stoke — a 10,000 crowd was present to see Bob Currie score the last Middlesbrough goal on the old ground.

Fortunately, the club's opening fixture of the 1903-04 season was away to Sheffield Wednesday, which gave the workmen another week's grace to get Ayresome Park ready for League football. However, the board had pre-arranged an attractive friendly against Glasgow Celtic at Ayresome Park on 7 September, possibly to defray part of the cost of the new ground. It must have felt strange for the faithful Middlesbrough fans as they filed past the old and empty Linthorpe Road Ground on the way up Linthorpe Road to the new ground, wondering what the future seasons would bring. New boy Willie White scored the first goal at Ayresome Park with Middlesbrough beating Celtic 1-0 before an inquisitive 7,000 crowd.

Five days later, on 12 September 1903, James Clifton Robinson, managing director and chief engineer of the Electric Tram Company, officially opened the gates at the front of the club with a huge golden key (he was to die, rather fittingly, in a tram whilst in New York years later). Neighbours and rivals Sunderland won the game 3-2 before a huge crowd approaching 30,000. The ground had a capacity of 33,000 but part of the main North Stand was partitioned off from

the public, for the workmen were still frantically working behind the scenes to complete the project.

Opposite the sparkling, brand new North Stand, which ran the full length of the pitch, was the dimunitive 50ft long old slated stand that had been the main stand at the Linthorpe Road Ground for nearly 20 years. The stand itself had been carefully disassembled, nail by nail, plank by plank and transported the half mile up Linthorpe Road to be painstakingly reassembled at the new ground. Almost like David and Goliath the two vastly contrasting stands silently kept each other company for another 32 years.

The first of three full England international games was played at Ayresome Park against Ireland in February, 1905 and Middlesbrough's popular goalkeeper Reginald 'Tim' Williamson won his first cap in the game to become the youngest England debutant, at that time. 'Tim', however, blotted his copy book by dropping the ball into his own net (He was also the first England goalkeeper to concede an own-goal!) and the game ended all square at 1-1 before a crowd of 24,000, who had paid £1,070 to watch the game.

In August 1911 the ground in front of the main stand had railway sleepers laid to accommodate standing, at a cost of £2,500. It had previously been a slope of ashes.

On 2 May 1912, the club proudly reported that the ground, after almost nine years' occupancy, had now been purchased and now belonged to the club. On St Valentine's Day 1914, another 24,000 crowd turned up for the second international to be played at the ground. Like the first game nine years earlier, Ireland were the international opposition, only this time they went one better and won the game 3-0. Middlesbrough's centre-forward George Elliott won his first cap that day and trainer Charlie Cole was England's 'sponge man'.

It was at Ayresome Park in April 1915 that a little piece of football history was created when Oldham Athletic's Bill Cook refused to leave the field when he was dismissed. The referee eventually abandoned the game, the League subsequently ruling that the score of 4-1 would stand as the final score.

During World War One, League football was suspended with only a few clubs playing infrequent regional football in the period. Like the majority of clubs, Middlesbrough wound down and most of its players enlisted and went to fight for King and Country. Ayresome Park itself was requisitioned by the Army and was used as an assembly and training centre for the troops.

In September 1919 the *North-Eastern Daily Gazette* briefly reported that, for the second time in as many months, one of the Ayresome Park's stand had been extensively damaged by fire and that arson could not be ruled out.

In the summer of 1920 it was reported that two new turnstiles were added at the Linthorpe Road end of the Grandstand, one to feed the back of the stand, the other to feed the front. Also, at the East End of the ground the 'Tannerites' area, had half of the earth bank removed and concrete steps put in. These steps, it was reported, began about 3ft from the railings running around the playing pitch and went upwards to half the height of the earth bank, some 14 steps in all. A new flight of wooden steps had also been built leading from the top of the bank down to the exit gates and it was confirmed that they would only be used as exit steps.

The report continued that the wind problems in the West Stand had been resolved. There had been many complaints from those who sat at the back of the stand that a strong draught of wind blew through the stand all through the games causing great discomfort to the spectators. This had been remedied by the addition of felt strips along the length of the stand. The complaints concerning the long queues to the turnstiles of the 1s 9d stand (the old South Stand) had been resolved by the opening of four turnstiles in Clive Road.

A year later, in the summer of 1921, the press box was moved from the rear to the front of the North Stand (then called the Grandstand.)

First Division status was regained in the record-breaking Golden Jubilee season of 1926-7 and, in anticipation of increased attendances, loads of clay were tipped at the shilling end of the ground in June, 1927 to enlarge the spectator's accommodation area.

On 15 June 1936, the club announced that Dorman, Long & Co would erect the new South Stand which was to be 250ft

Aerial view of Ayresome Park, Middlesbrough, in the 1980s.

long, 58ft deep and 25ft above ground level and further work was to be carried out by putting a roof over the West End terracing. The new stand, which would accommodate 9,000 fans, was built to replace the faithful 'little slated roof' stand which had been brought to Ayresome Park from the old Linthorpe Road Ground in 1903. The work on the new South Stand took a full year and was completed in 1937.

A club announcement on 30 June 1939 that the club was soon to cover 'the Boys' End' (the East End) was soon forgotten as Europe was plunged into World War Two less three months later. As war enveloped Europe, the government decided that, for public morale, it would be beneficial to continue football on a regional basis. Middlesbrough played during World War Two but the new South Stand, however, was closed from 1939 to September 1945.

The immediate post-war period saw record crowds flood into British football grounds and Middlesbrough was no exception to this. In 1947 the East End was restructured and anti-crush barriers were erected, another £20,000 was spent on East End improvements the following season. It was on 29 December 1949 that Middlesbrough's record ground attendance of 53,802 was set at Ayresome Park. The opposition was Newcastle United and 'Boro won 1-0. In the present climatic swing to all-seater stadiums, this record attendance is never likely to be surpassed.

In 1950, eight and a half acres were purchased at Hutton Road in the Longlands area of Middlesbrough and the club used this ground as a training pitch and it was also used by the club's Northern Intermediate League side for many years. The ground, until only recently, had been allowed to deteriorate, through vandalism and neglect, into a dilapidated condition but it has recently received a much-needed face-lift.

In 1954 a new roof on the South Stand coincided with the club's relegation to Division Two after a quarter of a century of First Division football.

New floodlights, costing £20,119, were installed in the summer of 1957. A series of floodlit friendlies were played during the season to defray the cost of the floodlights, some of the games attracting crowds well in the excess of 30,000.

In 1963, club chairman Eric Thomas agreed to a social club opening under the South Stand and the social club flourished for many years. On 11 August 1964, the club announced that Ayresome Park had been chosen as one of the two North-East World Cup venues in July 1966, after Newcastle United had been forced to pull out following problems with Newcastle City Council. The government of the day allocated a grant of £49,200 towards the overall cost of £125,000 with the club receiving a £30,500 loan repayable over five years for the

remainder. The pitch was to be lengthened by one yard to 115 yards (in fact, the current dimensions are 115 yards by 75 yards) to comply line with World Cup requirements. In April 1965, at the end of the season, the vision-blocking stanchions in the North Stand were removed and it was at that time that a 9in sewer was found that nobody knew about.

The draw was held in January 1965 and, like Sunderland, Middlesbrough were allocated three matches — USSR v North Korea, Chile v North Korea and Italy v North Korea in the Group Four games. In May 1966 the East End was covered for the three World Cup games and 4,000 seats were installed in the 'Bob End' reducing the ground capacity to some 42,000, but by then the club had been relegated to Division Three. The three World Cup games attracted a disappointing aggregate crowd of just over 56,000, but the North Koreans, wearing red shirts (just like Middlesbrough) won the hearts of the Ayresome Park crowds with their spirited displays against supposedly stronger opponents.

The controversial sports hall at the club was built in 1981, apparently without planning permission from the local council and has, over the years, proved to be an embarrassment to the club.

With the 'Boro club heavily in debt and in its final death, throes the ground was padlocked by the Official Receiver's agent on 1 August 1986 and it looked as though Ayresome Park would not stage any more Football League games. At the last moment a consortium saved the club from extinction but the opening home game of the 1986-7 season against Port Vale was played at the Victoria Ground, Hartlepool.

In 1989, the 284ft x 82ft roof of the North Stand went into the *Guinness Book of Records*, all 23,228 square feet of it, for it carried the largest advertising hoarding in the world. The ground capacity was now 32,000 and was reduced even further in 1990 to 26,400, when seating was installed in the South Stand terracing.

The chief groundsmen at Ayresome Park have been Charlie Flintoff, Wilf Atkinson and the current groundsman, David Rigg. Under the supervision of Wilf Atkinson, who served the club for more than 30 years and who sadly died in May 1993, the pitch surface deserved and received many accolades from visiting teams and was for many years rated the best playing surface in the country, second only to Wembley.

In almost 90 years of League football at Ayresome Park, the crowd has never experienced the joy of winning a Football League championship, nor a victorious FA Cup winning team parading the trophy around the cinder track, but hope springs eternal as Ayresome Park moves ever closer to the 21st century.

Big Games at Ayresome Park

1966 World Cup Games

ENGLAND staged the 1966 World Cup Finals and the Group Four North-East matches were originally scheduled for Roker Park, Sunderland and St James' Park, Newcastle. United were not the owners of the ground and had to have the blessing of Newcastle City Council in order to stage the matches. A dispute between both parties meant that Middlesbrough, as a Third Division side, was offered the chance to stage the games and, at the 11th hour the World Cup came to Ayresome Park in July 1966.

12 July 1966
USSR 3   **North Korea 0**
USSR: Kavasashvili; Ponomarev, Shesterniev, Khurtsilava, Ostrovski, Sabo, Sichinava, Chislenko, Malafeev, Banichevski, Khusainov.
Scorers: Malafeev 2, Banichevski
North Korea: Chan-myung; Li-sup, Yung-kyoo, Zoong-sun, Bong-chil, Seung-zin, Seung-hwi, Bong-jin, Doo-ik, Byong-woon, Seung-il.
Att: 22,568
Ref: Juan Gardeazabal Garay (Spain)

15 July 1966
Chile 1   **North Korea 1**
Chile: Olivares; Valentini, Cruz, Figueroa, Villanueva, Prieto, Marcos, Fouilloux, Landa, Araya, Sánchez.
Scorer: Marcos (pen)
North Korea: Chan-myung; Li-sup, Yung-kyoo, Zoong-sun, Yoon-kyung, Seung-zin, Seung-hwi, Bong-jin, Doo-ik, Dong-woon, Seung-il.
Scorer: Seung-zin
Att: 15,887
Ref: Ali Kandil (Egypt)
19 July 1966
Italy 0   **North Korea 1**
Italy: Albertosi; Landini, Facchetti, Guarneri, Janich, Fogli, Perani, Bulgarelli, Mazzola, Rivera, Barison.
North Korea: Chan-myung; Zoong-sun, Yung-kyoo, Yung-won, Yoon-kyung, Seung-hwi, Bong-jin, Doo-ik, Seung-zin, Bong-hwan, Seung-kook.
Scorer: Doo-ik
Att: 18,727
Ref: Pierre Schwinte (France)

FINAL GROUP POSITIONS

	P	W	D	L	F	A	Pts
USSR	3	3	0	0	6	1	6
North Korea	3	1	1	1	2	4	3
Italy	3	1	0	2	2	2	2
Chile	3	0	1	2	2	5	1

Full England International Matches

25 Feb 1905
England 1   **Ireland 1**
England: Williamson (Middlesbrough); Balmer (Everton), Carr (Newcastle U), Wolstenholme (Everton), Roberts(Manchester U), Leake (Aston V), Bond (Preston NE), Bloomer (Derby C), Woodward (Tottenham H), Harris (Corinthians), Booth (Manchester C).
Scorer: Bloomer
Ireland: Scott (Linfield); McCracken (Newcastle U), McCartney (Everton), Darling (Linfield), Connor (Belfast C), Nicholl (Belfast C), Sloan (Bohemians), Sheridan (Stoke), Murphy (QPR), Shanks (Brentford), Kirwan (Tottenham H).
Scorer: Williamson (own-goal)
Att: 24,000
Referee: T.Robertson (Scotland)

14 Feb 1914
England 0   **Ireland 3**
England: Hardy (Aston V); Crompton (Blackburn R), Pennington (WBA), Cuggy (Sunderland), Buckley (Derby C), Watson (Burnley), Wallace (Aston V), Shea (Blackburn R), Elliott (Middlesbrough), Latheron (Blackburn R), Martin (Sunderland).

Ireland: McKee (Belfast C); McConnell (Bohemians), Craig (Morton), Hampton (Bradford C), O'Connell (Hull C), Hammill (Manchester C), Rollo (Linfield), Young (Linfield), Gillespie (Sheffield U), Lacey (Liverpool), Thompson (Clyde).
Scorers: Gillespie, Lacey 2
Att: 24,000
Referee: A.Jackson (Scotland)

17 Nov 1937
England 2   **Wales 1**
England: Woodley (Chelsea); Sproston (Leeds U), Barkas (Manchester C), Crayston (Arsenal), Cullis (Wolves), Copping (Arsenal), Matthews (Stoke C), Hall (Tottenham H), Mills (Chelsea), Goulden (West Ham U), Brook (Manchester C)
Scorers: Hall, Matthews
Wales: Gray (Chester); Turner (Charlton A), Hughes (Birmingham), Murphy (West Brom), Hanford (Sheffield W), Richards (Brentford), Hopkins (Brentford), L.Jones (Coventry C), Perry (Doncaster R), B.Jones (Wolves), Morris (Birmingham).
Scorer: Perry
Att: 30,608
Referee: W.E.Webb (Scotland)

England Trial Game

Wednesday, 8 Feb 1928
England 8
England: Brown (Sheffield W); Goodall (Huddersfield T), Osborne (Leicester C), Edwards (Leeds U), Kean (Sheffield W), Bishop (Leicester C), Hulme (Arsenal), Kelly (Huddersfield T), Dean (Everton), J.Carr (Middlesbrough), W.H.Smith (Huddersfield T).
Scorers: Dean 5, W.H.Smith, Hulme 2
Rest 3
Rest: Hufton (West Ham U); Finch (West Bromwich A), Silcock (Manchester U), Andrews (Sunderland), Matthews (Sheffield U), Storer (Derby C), Burton (Burnley), Hine (Leicester C), Camsell (Middlesbrough), Stephenson (Derby C), Tunstall (Sheffield U).
Scorers: Tunstall, Hine, Camsell.
Att: 18,000
Ref: A.Josephs

Football League Representative Games

17 Feb 1912
Football League 2   **Scottish League 0**
Football League: Williamson (Middlesbrough); Crompton (Blackburn R), Pennington (WBA), Duckworth (Manchester U), Boyle (Burnley), Fay (Bolton W), Wallace (Aston V), Buchan (Sunderland), Freeman (Burnley), Holley (Sunderland), Mordue (Sunderland).
Scorers: Freeman, Mordue
Scottish League: Brownlie (Third Lanark); Blair (Clyde), McNair (Celtic), Galt (Rangers), McAndrew (Clyde), Mercer (Hearts), Brown (Celtic), Cunningham (Kilmarnock), Quinn (Celtic), McMenemy (Celtic), Bennett (Rangers).
Att: 24,149
Ref: H.S.Bamlett (Gateshead)

22 Mar 1950
Football League 3   **Scottish League 1**
Football League: Williams (Wolves); Ramsey (Spurs), Aston (Manchester U), Wright (Wolves), Franklin (Stoke C), Dickinson (Portsmouth), Hancocks (Wolves), Mannion (Middlesbrough), Mortensen (Blackpool), Baily (Spurs), Langton (Blackburn R).
Scorers: Mortensen 2, Baily
Scottish League: Brown (Rangers); Cox (Rangers), Young (Rangers), Hewitt (Partick T), Woodburn (Rangers), Evans (Celtic), Reilly (Hibs), Brown (East Fife), Bauld (Hearts), Mason (Hibs), Smith (Hibs).
Scorer: Young (pen)
Att: 39,352
Ref: H.Holt (Rochdale)

20 Mar 1968
Football League 2   **Scottish League 0**
Football League: Stepney (Manchester U); K.Newton (Blackburn R), Knowles (Spurs), Stiles (Manchester U), Labone (Everton), Moore (West Ham), Ball (Everton), Hunt (Liverpool), R.Charlton (Manchester U), Hurst (West Ham), Peters (West Ham).
Scorers: Hunt, Newton
Scottish League: McCloy (Motherwell); Callaghan (Dunfermline), Gemmell (Celtic), Greig (Rangers), McKinnon (Rangers), D.Smith (Rangers), Johnstone (Celtic), Murdoch (Celtic), Stein (Hibs)[J.Smith (Aberdeen)], Lennox (Celtic), Hughes (Celtic).
Att: 34,190
Ref: J.E.Carr (Sheffield)

15 Mar 1972
Football League 3   **Scottish League 2**
Football League: Clemence (Liverpool); Lawler (Liverpool), Nish (Leicester C), Doyle (Manchester C), Blockley (Arsenal), Moore (West Ham), Hughes (Liverpool), Macdonald (Newcastle U), Currie (Sheffield U), Hurst (West Ham), Wagstaffe (Wolves).
Scorers: Currie 2, Doyle
Scottish League: Hunter (Kilmarnock); Brownlie (Hibs), Forsyth (Partick T), Jardine (Rangers)[Graham (Aberdeen)], Connelly (Celtic), Blackley (Hibs), McQuade (Partick T), Phillips (Dundee), Stein (Rangers), Hay (Celtic), Ford (Hearts).
Scorer: Stein 2
Att: 19,996
Ref: P.Partridge (Middlesbrough)

UEFA Youth Tournament

5 Oct 1983
England Under-16 3   **Scotland Under-16 1**
England: Digby (Manchester U); Ratcliffe (Manchester U), Crane (Ipswich T), Keen (West Ham), Adams (Arsenal), Anderson (Coventry C), Carr (Blackburn R), Moulden (Manchester C), Beckford (Manchester C), Beresford (Manchester C), Kilner (Burnley).
Scorers: Beckford, Moulden, Carr
Scotland: Donaldson (Dundee U); Traynor (Celtic), McGee (Celtic), Robertson (Aberdeen), Riddell (Aberdeen)[McLeod (Dundee U)], Winnie (St Mirren), Shepherd (Celtic), Ferguson (Rangers), Gray (Aberdeen), Miller (Aberdeen), Wright (Aberdeen)[Fraser (Celtic)].
Scorer: Winnie
Att: 929

Other Representative Games
Amateur Internationals
27 Jan 1923 England 4 Wales 4
15 May 1951 England 2 Norway 1
10 May 1963 England 0 West Germany 1

Youth Internationals
6 Feb 1954 England 2 Scotland 1
22 Feb 1964 England 1 Scotland 1

Schoolboy International
22 April 1993 England 2 Austria 1

Amateurs Cup Finals

1898-99	Stockton..........1	Harwich & Parkeston 0	
1911-12	Stockton..........0	Eston United 0	
	Stockton..........1	Eston United 0	
1920-21	Bishop Auckland...4	Swindon Victoria ...2	
1921-22	Bishop Auckland...5	South Bank 2	
1927-28	Leyton 3	Cockfield 2	
1934-35	Bishop Auckland...0	Wimbledon 0	
1953-54	Crook Town 1	Bishop Auckland ...0	
1955-56	Bishop Auckland...4	Corinthian Casuals 1	
1961-62	Crook Town 4	Hounslow Town 0	

Aggregate Attendances
(1925-1993)

HOME

*Ground attendance record. †Played at Victoria Ground, Hartlepool.

Season	Pld	Agg	Ave	High	Opponents	Low	Opponents
				DIVISION TWO			
1925-26	42	278,442	13,259	31,045	Darlington	6,672	Bradford C
1926-27	42	458,563	21,836	*43,754	Manchester C	8,680	Portsmouth
				DIVISION ONE			
1927-28	42	475,335	22,635	41,997	Sunderland	13,922	Bury
				DIVISION TWO			
1928-29	42	393,201	18,724	36,503	Grimsby T	9,541	Bristol C
				DIVISION ONE			
1929-30	42	402,604	19,172	40,538	Newcastle U	5,370	Burnley
1930-31	42	354,025	16,858	30,307	Sunderland	7,471	Sheffield U
1931-32	42	291,696	13,890	28,006	Aston Villa	5,410	Leicester C
1932-33	42	255,290	12,157	22,137	Arsenal	6,572	Preston NE
1933-34	42	265,322	12,364	28,915	Sunderland	4,758	Leicester C
1934-35	42	301,906	14,376	29,171	Arsenal	6,572	Preston NE
1935-36	42	394,198	18,771	38,107	Brentford	7,206	Derby C
1936-37	42	470,194	22,390	*44,523	Arsenal	11,790	Manchester U
1937-38	42	509,469	24,260	*46,747	Sunderland	12,905	West Brom A
1938-39	42	444,945	21,188	33,534	Birmingham	6,116	Portsmouth
1946-47	42	754,143	35,912	45,336	Leeds U	27,106	Everton
1947-48	42	711,912	35,901	45,145	Sunderland	20,892	Aston Villa
1948-49	42	720,141	34,292	44,780	Blackpool	21,184	Aston Villa
1949-50	42	743,541	35,407	*53,802	Newcastle U	21,764	Bolton W
1950-51	42	758,579	36,123	52,764	Sunderland	24,423	Bolton W
1951-52	42	604,279	28,775	44,434	Manchester U	16,899	Preston NE
1952-53	42	568,608	27,077	42,159	Cardiff C	13,176	Aston Villa
1953-54	42	567,037	27,002	39,416	Blackpool	17,144	West Brom A
				DIVISION TWO			
1954-55	42	443,272	21,108	45,271	Leeds U	7,944	Bury
1955-56	42	375,191	17,866	26,275	Fulham	8,298	Lincoln C
1956-57	42	443,657	21,127	31,513	West Ham U	11,147	Barnsley
1957-58	42	512,358	24,398	31,771	Blackburn R	14,879	Notts C
1958-59	42	522,401	24,876	42,866	Sheffield U	12,019	Grimsby T
1959-60	42	536,554	25,550	47,297	Sunderland	13,044	Leyton O
1960-61	42	333,038	15,859	27,458	Sunderland	8,736	Stoke C
1961-62	42	332,011	15,810	35,666	Sunderland	9,955	Leyton O
1962-63	42	347,094	16,528	43,509	Sunderland	7,626	Norwich C
1963-64	42	394,512	18,786	43,905	Sunderland	8,472	Cardiff C
1964-65	42	306,855	14,612	38,194	Newcastle U	8,627	Charlton A
1965-66	42	282,452	13,450	21,107	Leyton O	9,582	Portsmouth
				DIVISION THREE			
1966-67	46	380,321	16,540	39,683	Oxford U	8,126	Swindon T
				DIVISION TWO			
1967-68	42	397,027	18,906	29,217	Bolton W	10,181	Norwich C
1968-69	42	442,332	21,063	29,824	Aston Villa	10,417	Bury
1969-70	42	416,966	19,856	29,703	Carlisle U	13,859	Cardiff C
1970-71	42	389,224	18,534	30,682	Leicester C	12,802	Birmingham C
1971-72	42	376,794	17,943	34,446	Sunderland	9,539	Hull C
1972-73	42	218,774	10,418	24,145	Sunderland	6,816	Brighton
1973-74	42	472,459	22,498	37,030	Sunderland	14,742	Aston Villa
				DIVISION ONE			
1974-75	42	600,696	28,605	39,500	Leeds U	21,478	Luton T
1975-76	42	487,687	23,223	32,959	Leeds U	14,764	Ipswich T
1976-77	42	451,074	21,840	31,451	Aston Villa	14,500	QPR
1977-78	42	417,349	19,874	30,805	Liverpool	13,247	West Ham U
1978-79	42	387,648	18,459	32,214	Liverpool	12,822	QPR
1979-80	42	393,522	18,739	30,587	Manchester U	11,789	Bolton W
1980-81	42	345,076	16,432	35,065	Sunderland	11,076	Brighton
1981-82	42	281,668	13,413	21,019	Sunderland	9,403	West Brom A
				DIVISION TWO			
1982-83	42	210,380	10,018	25,184	Newcastle U	5,521	Bolton W
1983-84	42	177,930	8,473	19,807	Newcastle U	4,720	Charlton A
1984-85	42	107,827	5,135	8,817	Leeds U	3,364	Notts C
1985-86	42	131,400	6,257	9,701	Sunderland	4,061	Shrewsbury T
				DIVISION THREE			
1986-87	46	234,010	10,174	18,523	Wigan A	†3,690	Port Vale
				DIVISION TWO			
1987-88	44	319,621	14,528	27,645	Leicester C	9,344	Swindon T
				DIVISION ONE			
1988-89	38	379,989	19,999	25,197	Liverpool	16,065	Charlton A
				DIVISION TWO			
1989-90	46	352,067	15,307	23,617	West Ham U	11,428	Leicester C
1990-91	46	391,482	17,020	22,869	Sheffield W	13,846	Bristol C
1991-92	46	337,987	14,695	19,424	Sunderland	9,664	Southend U
				FA PREMIER LEAGUE			
1992-93	42	351,199	16,724	24,152	Manchester U	12,290	Oldham A

NB — The play-off games of seasons 1987-88 and 1990-91 are not included in analysis.

AWAY

‡Played at Maine Road, Manchester, Old Trafford bomb damaged.

Season	Pld	Agg	Ave	High	Opponents	Low	Opponents
				DIVISION TWO			
1925-26	42	304,344	14,493	25,522	Chelsea	8,361	Barnsley
1926-27	42	351,782	16,752	44,077	Manchester C	7,519	South Shields
				DIVISION ONE			
1927-28	42	525,584	25,028	46,432	Everton	12,017	Derby C
				DIVISION TWO			
1928-29	42	369,200	17,581	48,775	Chelsea	8,837	Nottingham F
				DIVISION ONE			
1929-30	42	461,047	21,955	38,922	Newcastle U	8,234	Huddersfield T
1930-31	42	421,568	20,075	48,935	Chelsea	3,969	Manchester U
1931-32	42	425,502	20,262	41,569	Newcastle U	8,795	Blackburn R
1932-33	42	327,769	15,608	37,748	Arsenal	4,992	Huddersfield T
1933-34	42	431,041	20,526	35,800	Tottenham H	1,980	Leicester C
1934-35	42	435,557	20,741	45,936	Liverpool	5,729	Birmingham
1935-36	42	470,708	22,415	58,902	Sunderland	4,366	Huddersfield T
1936-37	42	521,006	24,810	56,227	Manchester C	7,022	West Brom A
1937-38	42	488,904	23,281	56,717	Sunderland	8,254	West Brom A
1938-39	42	485,805	23,134	39,440	Sunderland	11,717	Grimsby T
1946-47	42	682,203	32,486	‡65,279	Manchester U	13,376	Grimsby T
1947-48	42	752,903	35,853	57,557	Arsenal	14,812	Grimsby T
1948-49	42	811,226	38,630	64,381	Newcastle U	16,413	Huddersfield T
1949-50	42	723,668	34,460	62,487	Sunderland	12,367	Burnley
1950-51	42	811,226	38,630	63,038	Arsenal	11,329	Charlton A
1951-52	42	691,428	32,925	59,364	Newcastle U	10,567	Derby C
1952-53	42	675,160	32,151	51,512	Cardiff C	15,041	West Brom A
1953-54	42	614,931	29,282	44,911	Tottenham H	18,909	Preston NE
				DIVISION TWO			
1954-55	42	409,955	19,522	29,189	Blackburn R	8,368	Lincoln C
1955-56	42	395,782	18,847	35,213	Liverpool	5,670	Doncaster R
1956-57	42	380,371	18,113	38,890	Liverpool	8,601	Lincoln C
1957-58	42	396,618	18,887	39,246	Liverpool	8,901	Lincoln C
1958-59	42	422,625	20,125	45,954	Sunderland	10,234	Leyton O
1959-60	42	410,535	19,549	39,000	Liverpool	9,780	Lincoln C
1960-61	42	373,517	17,787	53,254	Sunderland	5,115	Lincoln C
1961-62	42	318,225	15,154	48,428	Sunderland	6,037	Rotherham U
1962-63	42	365,541	17,407	48,106	Sunderland	6,431	Luton T
1963-64	42	338,157	16,103	56,918	Newcastle U	6,148	Bury
1964-65	42	361,245	17,202	54,750	Newcastle U	6,143	Bury
1965-66	42	285,238	13,583	25,278	Manchester C	2,286	Leyton O
				DIVISION THREE			
1966-67	46	188,285	8,186	18,144	Darlington	4,053	Scunthorpe U
				DIVISION TWO			
1967-68	42	330,685	15,747	28,885	Birmingham C	9,040	Plymouth A
1968-69	42	373,647	17,793	43,781	Crystal P	7,193	Blackburn R
1969-70	42	330,013	15,715	26,528	Leicester C	9,496	Oxford U
1970-71	42	332,213	15,820	42,617	Sunderland	6,690	Leyton O
1971-72	42	306,651	14,602	37,202	Birmingham C	7,372	Leyton O
1972-73	42	244,469	11,641	30,345	Aston Villa	4,688	Portsmouth
1973-74	42	359,962	17,141	41,658	Sunderland	6,958	Swindon T
				DIVISION ONE			
1974-75	42	574,823	27,372	52,590	Liverpool	10,464	Luton T
1975-76	42	558,954	26,617	58,527	Manchester U	13,548	Wolves
1976-77	42	548,650	26,126	56,712	Manchester U	12,893	Coventry C
1977-78	42	538,496	25,643	49,305	Manchester U	12,925	QPR
1978-79	42	496,425	23,639	45,402	Manchester U	9,899	QPR
1979-80	42	476,216	22,677	51,015	Manchester U	10,613	Bolton W
1980-81	42	463,676	22,080	54,394	Manchester U	11,847	Stoke C
1981-82	42	386,764	18,417	38,342	Manchester U	6,707	Notts C
				DIVISION TWO			
1982-83	42	218,726	10,416	27,984	Newcastle U	2,573	Cambridge U
1983-84	42	220,776	10,513	30,421	Newcastle Uf	2,819	Cambridge U
1984-85	42	157,808	7,515	22,399	Manchester C	2,338	Wimbledon
1985-86	42	149,287	7,109	20,541	Sunderland	2,844	Wimbledon
				DIVISION THREE			
1986-87	46	134,498	5,848	13,855	Bournemouth	2,788	Newport C
				DIVISION TWO			
1987-88	44	236,651	10,757	34,186	Leeds U	5,603	Shrewsbury T
				DIVISION ONE			
1988-89	38	370,399	19,495	40,442	Manchester U	5,275	Wimbledon
				DIVISION TWO			
1989-90	46	262,870	11,429	25,004	Leeds U	5,504	Brighton
1990-91	46	261,928	11,388	30,598	Sheffield W	5,262	Oxford U
1991-92	46	258,862	11,254	26,563	Newcastle U	4,229	Oxford U
				FA PREMIER LEAGUE			
1992-93	42	406,356	19,350	36,251	Manchester U	5,821	Wimbledon

NB — 40,550 attended the play-off with Chelsea (a) on 28 May 1988.

Middlesbrough Managers

John Robson
(May 1899-May 1905)

JOHN Robson was born at Gainford in Durham and, as a young boy, moved with his family to Middlesbrough. He played in goal for Middlesbrough Swifts, the club's reserve side, and when the 'Boro sampled professionalism, the Swifts team retained its amateur status. Robson's natural flair for administrative matters surfaced and he became secretary of the Swifts' committee soon afterwards. When Middlesbrough reverted to amateur status he became assistant secretary to Albert Borrie.

In May 1899, Middlesbrough Football and Athletic Club Limited successfully applied to join the Football League as a Second Division side and, at the club's annual general meeting convened shortly after, a bombshell was dropped when it was announced that 'Boro secretary Herbert W. Winney, a schoolteacher, had regretfully offered his resignation because of health reasons. So, with League football only three months away, the club turned to Robson in a moment of crisis.

He reluctantly accepted the position of secretary-manager at a salary of £156 per annum. Apparently one of the conditions of his appointment was that, as an economy measure, he was not to accompany the team to away games. His response was magnificent and in the space of three months he moulded the Northern League club into a side ready for the Second Division.

John Robson was left untarnished by the irregular payments to players scandal which shook the football world in 1905. He had the foresight to have a document signed by the club chairman, totally absolving him of any dubious involvement in the unsavoury episode.

Robson ran a tobacconist's shop in Wilson Street for a while, but the urge to return to football proved too strong and, after 17 years with the Middlesbrough club, he moved south to become Crystal Palace manager for the start of the 1905-06 season, where he stayed for two seasons. Such was the esteem that his old club and its grateful supporters held for Robson, at a 'smoker evening' held in his honour, he was presented with a handsome gold watch and chain, whilst Mrs Robson received a silver tea service and both were assured of the good wishes of the townspeople.

He took charge of team duties at Manchester United on 28 December 1914, whom he joined from Brighton. When John Chapman became United team manager in 1916, Robson became his assistant. Ill health had dogged Robson, eventually forcing his early retirement in October 1921. A heavy cold led to pneumonia which claimed his life on 11 January 1922.

Middlesbrough, along with the rest of the football world, paid its final respects to a loyal friend and servant at his funeral. On the practical side, Manchester United staged a benefit game for his widow and family when Jackie Carr, 'Boro's England international, represented John Robson's old club.

Alex Mackie
(June 1905-May 1906)

ALEX Mackie was born in 1870, in Banffshire, and played his early football for Aberdeen and

then joined Glasgow Association before becoming club secretary at Inverness.

Mackie then spent seven seasons at Sunderland as player-manager in one of the Wearsiders' most productive playing periods, although his involvement in the 'Andy McCombie Scandal' brought him a suspension imposed by the Football Association.

He was one of 70 applicants for the Middlesbrough job vacated by John Robson and his achievements at Roker Park convinced the 'Boro board that he was the man for the job, which he took on in the summer of 1905.

Whilst Robson had shown perspicacity in securing a letter of absolution in the irregular payments scandal, Mackie had failed to insure himself in a likewise manner and, for his part in the incident, he received a ban forbidding him from any active participation in football. He was, however, already disillusioned with the game and its ruling body and pre-empted the ban by voluntarily severing his interests in football. He took over the Star and Garter Hotel in Marton Road, Middlesbrough, in June 1906.

Andy Aitken
(October 1906-February 1909)

ANDY Aitken's first job was as a grocer's assistant, but he later admitted that, more often than not, when he should have been delivering groceries he was kicking a football around a field. He became apprenticed to a trade and played as a forward for his local side, Elmbank. After a couple of seasons, he moved to Ayr Parkhouse, where he stayed for one season. He was 17 when Manchester United and Preston North End showed a positive interest in him, but he decided to finish his apprenticeship in Scotland.

Newcastle United made the first firm offer

after his appenticeship was completed and, in July 1895, he became an adopted Geordie, signing for the Magpies as an inside-forward. His first full Scotland cap came in 1901-02 and he made over 300 appearances in a Newcastle career that lasted 11 years and took in two FA Cup Finals and a League Championship, although he was to miss their greatest days of the later 1900s.

At the age of 30, Aitken joined 'Boro on 31 October 1906, as the club's first player-manager. The transfer deal cost Middlesbrough £500. Within a fortnight of joining his new club, he was also appointed secretary and his brilliance as a pivotal defender for 'Boro won him a further three international caps.

Aitken later said that the Middlesbrough job had given him the most satisfaction in his career, but that there was one particular person at Ayresome Park with whom he could not get on. He diplomatically refused to disclose that person's identity, but the clash of personalities forced him to leave and he joined Leicester Fosse as player-manager in February 1909.

Again he was chosen to play for his country, eventually taking his total of Scottish caps to 14 caps. After two and a half seasons at Leicester, Aitken returned to his native Scotland to play for Dundee in May 1911 and then turned out for Kilmarnock before a groin injury ended his playing career.

Shortly afterwards he managed Gateshead Town for a spell, then became a licensee and acted as a scout for Arsenal in the 1930s. He once said that he was never fast and felt that his best work was done as a centre-half, his playing strength being the effective use of his head to clear the ball. He was born at Ayr in 1877 and died on Tyneside in 1955.

Andy Walker
(June 1910-January 1911)

FOLLOWING the departure of Andy Aitken to Leicester Fosse, the Middlesbrough board approached Airdrie manager Andy Walker and he accepted the job on 27 June 1910. Soon afterwards, however, Walker was in trouble for illegally approaching an Airdrie player to induce him to sign for Middlesbrough. The manager was suspended for four weeks and the 'Boro club was fined £100.

In December 1910, Middlesbrough chairman Thomas Gibson-Poole, the local Tory Parliamentary candidate, thought that if Middlesbrough beat Sunderland in the 'derby' game at Ayresome Park two days before the election, it would enhance his chances of becoming an MP for the town. Before the game, Andy Walker offered Sunderland skipper Charlie Thomson £30 to 'throw' the match, but Thomson reported the matter to his chairman, Fred Taylor, who promptly notified the FA. Jimmy Nichol ensured a Middlesbrough victory, but Gibson-Poole lost the election by over 3,000 votes.

On 16 January 1911, an FA Commission decided that money had been offered and Walker and Gibson-Poole were permanently suspended from football. Certain factions believed that the manager had simply been used as the pawn of a scheming chairman and, bearing this in mind, the FA should view his case sympathetically. A petition containing 12,500 signatures was presented to the FA for Walker's reinstatement, but without success.

Tom McIntosh
(August 1911-December 1919)

TOM McIntosh began his career as a right-half with Darlington in 1895. In July 1902, the Darlington board offered him the secretary's job at Feethams and he began his association with football administration which was to last for more than 20 years.

The bribery scandal of 1910-11 saw the suspension of secretary-manager Andy Walker and chairman Thomas Gibson-Poole. Phil Bach, the new chairman, was given the task of reforming the Middlesbrough board of directors and McIntosh accepted the post of 'Boro secretary-manager on 1 August 1911.

He was at Ayresome Park to see the club achieve its highest League placing of third in Division One in 1913-14 but, with a potential League Championship-winning team shaping under his guidance, his plans were abruptly shelved with the outbreak of World War One, although the League continued until the end of 1914-15.

Middlesbrough released their players and closed down, whilst Ayresome Park was used by the Army as a storage depot. At the start of the war in August 1914, McIntosh had joined the Teesside Pioneers and later saw active service as a sergeant in France.

At the beginning of 1919, the war over, he guided Middlesbrough to the Northern Victory League title and prepared the club for 'normal' football, with Herbert Glasper now acting as secretary. In December that year, however, Everton offered McIntosh the opportunity to steer the Goodison side into the 1920s and he left with the full blessing of the Middlesbrough board. Tom McIntosh died, aged 56, on 29 October 1935.

Jimmy Howie
(April 1920-July 1923)

JIMMY Howie, who was born at Galston, Ayrshire, on 19 March 1878, became the second ex-Newcastle United player to become manager of Middlesbrough, when he succeeded Tommy McIntosh in April 1920.

His playing career began with his home-town club, Galston Athletic, and he moved to Kilmarnock in 1899 before travelling south to play for Kettering Town. In 1902 he was transferred to Bristol Rovers, but his career really took off upon his arrival at Newcastle United in May 1903.

At St James' Park he won League Championship medals in 1905, 1907 and 1909, although Newcastle's failure to win the FA Cup Final in 1905, 1906 and 1908 (he scored a goal against Wolves that year) meant runners-up medals for 'Gentleman Jim'. In 1910, he finally gained a winners' medal when Newcastle needed a replay at Everton to beat Barnsley 2-0. By the time his Newcastle United career ended in December 1910, with a £675 transfer to ambitious non-League Huddersfield Town, he had clocked up 198 League appearances, 67 goals and three full Scotland caps, mainly as an attacking inside-forward.

In November 1913, with his League career behind him, he successfully applied for the job of manager at Queen's Park Rangers, then in the Southern League. He was named as Tommy McIntosh's successor in April 1920, and stayed at Ayresome Park until July 1923. He later became a tobacconist in the London area and died in January 1963.

Herbert Bamlett
(August 1923-March 1927)

WHEN 32-year-old Herbert Bamlett took charge of the 1914 FA Cup Final between Burnley and Liverpool, he became the youngest man to referee the Cup Final. For Bamlett, who was born at Gateshead on 1 March 1882, it was his last game as a referee and the following month he took over as manager of Oldham Athletic.

Those were difficult times and within a few weeks of his appointment at Boundary Park, war broke out. However, despite the problems of finding a regular team, Bamlett steered Oldham to what is still their best-ever League position of runners-up in Division One, a

considerable feat in the face of selection problems and severe financial restrictions.

Called up for military service in 1916, Bamlett was demobbed in 1919 and set about re-building the team for the first peacetime season. After two indifferent seasons, though, he left for Wigan Borough, becoming manager for their first two seasons in the new Third Division North.

Wigan finished 17th and then fifth and on 12 August 1923, Bamlett was appointed manager of Middlesbrough. With the inevitable retirement of Tim Williamson and the ageing George Elliott's loss of form, he saw his new club relegated to Division Two — 'Boro's first-ever taste of relegation — at the end of his first season in charge at Ayresome Park.

The Middlesbrough board did not, as expected, sack him and their faith in his potential was realized two seasons later, in the club's golden jubilee year. A disastrous start to that eventful 1926-7 season saw the team lose the opening three games, before the first point was wrested in a bruising game at South Shields. Injuries to Maurice Webster and Jimmy McClelland prompted Bamlett to try Walter Holmes at centre-half, whilst one of the directors suggested playing young George Camsell at centre-forward for the home game against Hull City.

The team went on to win their next six matches, scoring 16 goals with Camsell bagging seven of them. Middlesbrough quickly became the talk of the country as they rattled in goal after goal. They scored 122 goals, still a Second Division record, and Camsell's personal tally was a record 59 as 'Boro steam-rollered their way out of Division Two.

Herbert Bamlett, though, was not at Ayresome Park to see the culmination of that triumphant season. Three years earlier the 'Boro board had kept him on after relegation. Now, on the brink of promotion, they dismissed him.

He became manager of Manchester United and the opening game of the 1927-8 season saw his old team take on his new side at Old Trafford. Bamlett must have been extremely satisfied when United ran out 3-0 winners. He stayed at Old Trafford for four seasons, until United suffered relegation at the end of 1930-31, conceding 115 goals along the way.

Peter McWilliam
(April 1927-March 1934)

PETER McWilliam was born in Inverness in 1882 and played for Inverness Thistle in 1899 before signing for Newcastle United in August 1902. He was nicknamed 'Pat' by his teammates at St James' Park and 'Peter the Great' by his adoring Geordie fans. A contemporary pen-picture of the likeable Scot described him as 'popularly believed to possess India-rubber legs . . .he developed a body wriggle that was annoyingly deceptive'.

Football folklore records that he was so relaxed before a game that he would occasionally take a half-hour nap before the kick-off but, as a manager, he was sometimes so nervous that he could not bear to watch his team in action.

His League and Cup successes were identical to his friend and Newcastle teammate Jimmy

Howie, even matching Howie on 198 League appearances for United. He won eight full Scottish caps whilst on Tyneside, but a knee injury suffered against Wales ended his playing career in 1911.

McWilliam made a successful transition from player to manager with Tottenham Hotspur, whom he joined in 1912. His team experienced relegation to the Second Division at the end of 1914-15, before war intervened, but in 1920 promotion was achieved with a remarkable 70 points (a Second Division record in the days of two points for a win). McWilliam's team were triumphant in winning the FA Cup in 1921, beating Wolves 1-0 in the Final, and he was Tottenham's longest-serving manager until Bill Nicholson.

The Middlesbrough board had made several furtive attempts to wrench McWilliam from Spurs three years earlier, but had failed at every attempt. His eventual 'appointment' as Middlesbrough manager broke in the Press in early January 1927, but was initially strenuously denied by the Tottenham board. He was on a salary of £850 per annum at Spurs and later admitted that he would have stayed at White Hart Lane 'if Spurs had offered another £3 a week'.

Middlesbrough had no such reservations about paying the man they wanted and offered him £1,500 a year, then a phenomenal sum for a manager, and he moved north. His wife hailed from Redcar and she probably played an influential part in his decision to accept the post at Ayresome Park.

McWilliam was to be given total control in team selection without any interference from the board, but he never won the hearts of the Middlesbrough public whose sympathy lay with Herbert Bamlett. His time at the club was very much an up and down period. He enjoyed the tail-end of promotion in 1927 but the following season 'Boro dropped back into Division Two. In 1928-9, with McWilliam still at the helm, they won the Second Division title again.

McWilliam kept them in Division One until his retirement in March 1934 and he then had a spell as chief scout for Arsenal before he made a sentimental return to manage Tottenham Hotspur in 1938. He remained at White Hart Lane for little more than a year, although in that short time he began to promote the famous Northfleet nursery which was to produce so many fine players for Tottenham.

Peter McWilliam returned to the North-East but, when the war was over, he decided he was too old to remain in football. He died at his home in Corporation Road, Redcar, on 1 October 1951, aged 72 and was buried at nearby Kirkleatham cemetery. Representatives from all his former clubs attended his funeral.

Wilf Gillow
(March 1934-March 1944)

WILF Gillow was born in Peston on 8 July 1892 and first played for Lancaster Town in the West Lancashire League when he was 15. He was on Preston's books without making a League appearance and then signed for Fleetwood before moving to Blackpool in 1912. He made 26 League appearances for the Seasiders and then returned to Deepdale, where he played three League games before joining the Army upon the outbreak of World War One.

Gillow played briefly for Preston in 1918-19 and then made another four League appearances in the first proper peacetime season before signing for Grimsby Town in

February 1920. He played 80 games for them, mostly at right-half, and then rejoined Fleetwood, only to return to Grimsby in 1923. A year later he became player-manager of the Mariners and older Grimsby supporters rate him amongst the top three Town managers of all time.

Under Gillow the Blundell Park club achieved promotion to Division One in May 1929, for the first time in 26 seasons, and when Middlesbrough and Grimsby met at Ayresome Park in the final game of that season, both clubs were already assured of promotion, but 'Boro pipped the Mariners to the Second Division championship.

Town's flirtation with First Division football was brief and within two seasons they were back in the Second Division. In April 1932, Wilf Gillow relinquished the manager's job and left football management until March 1934, when he replaced Peter McWilliam at 'Boro. The Ayresome club just escaped relegation in his first season, but every season after that showed an improvement.

The quietly spoken pipe-smoker was much respected by players and fans alike and, under his guidance, Middlesbrough finished fourth at the end of season 1938-9. Many thought that, with the emergence of bright young stars like Wilf Mannion, Micky Fenton, George Hardwick and the older heads of Bobby Stuart, George Camsell, Billy Forrest, the elusive League Championship was only a season or two away.

War spoiled that dream, but football was allowed to continue on a regional basis. Gillow, too old for active service, worked in Middlesbrough Council treasurer's department during the day, serving as 'Boro manager on a part-time basis at evenings and weekends. He died in his early 50s, on 11 March 1944 in a County Durham Hospital after complications set in following an operation. He is buried in Thornaby cemetery.

Gillow, incidentally, was also a good cricketer and he turned out for Middlesbrough CC in the North Yorkshire and South Durham League until well into his 40s. An earlier spell on the Lancashire groundstaff had seen him field as a substitute for England against Australia at Old Trafford.

David Jack
(November 1944-April 1952)

DAVID Jack was born on 3 April 1899, in Bolton where his father, Bob Jack, was playing for the Trotters. When Bob Jack became manager of Plymouth Argyle in 1910, young David also went south and eventually signed for Argyle (after playing in Southend junior football when his father had a spell as manager there). During World War One he guested for Chelsea whilst on leave from the Royal Navy and played in the Home Park club's final Southern League season of 1920-21.

After only 14 Football League appearances for Plymouth, Jack was transferred to Bolton Wanderers in December 1920, for £3,500 (a record for both clubs). He has a permanent spot in the football history books as the first player to score a goal in a Wembley Cup Final. Indeed, he scored both goals when Bolton beat West Ham 2-0 in that historic 1923 game.

He also played for Bolton in the 1926 Final before being transferred to Arsenal for a record fee of £10,340 in October 1928. He had five successful seasons at Highbury and played in the 1930 and 1932 FA Cup Finals for the Gunners, won three League Championship medals (1930-31, 1932-3 and 1933-4) and won a total of nine England caps with Bolton and Arsenal. At the end of a playing career during which he became known as the 'prince of centre-forwards', he had scored well over 250 goals in just over 500 games.

His first position as a League club manager was with Southend United in May 1934, a post he held until 1940. On the untimely death of Wilf Gillow he relinquished his job as manager of Sunderland Greyhound Stadium to become manager at Ayresome Park on 1 November 1944, when 'Boro was playing wartime League North football.

The 1950-51 season was David Jack's best with Middlesbrough. 'Boro and Spurs were

vying with each other at the top of the First Division but injuries and loss of form saw the Ayresome club slip away after Christmas and eventually they finished sixth. One criticism of pipe-smoking David Jack was that he was too 'relaxed' and lacked the forceful personality needed to motivate his players.

Because of his wife's health, he resigned his position as manager in April 1952 and, disillusioned, left the game to become a publican in Islington, London. He soon discovered, however, that the game meant too much to him and he needed little persuasion to return to management with League of Ireland club Shelbourne, in August 1953. He stayed there until April 1955 and then took a job with the Air Ministry. He died in St Thomas' Hospital, London, on 10 September 1958.

Walter Rowley
(June 1952-February 1954)

WALTER Rowley spent all his working life in football, including 38 years with Bolton Wanderers, as a half-back, coach and manager. He was born at Little Hulton in 1891 and spent two years with Oldham Athletic Reserves before signing for the Trotters in August 1912, aged 21.

Rowley missed the 1923 Cup Final because he had only just finished a six-week suspension and in May 1925 he was forced to retire through injury and was appointed coach to Bolton's reserve team. In August 1944 he became secretary-manager at Burnden Park and at the end of his first season in charge, Bolton won the Football League War Cup. In his second they reached the FA Cup semi-finals. Ill health forced him to resign in October 1950 and Bolton made him a life member of the club.

Fully recovered, he succeeded David Jack as Middlesbrough manager in June 1952. 'Boro finished 13th in his first full season as manager, but worse was to come the following season. It was a frustrating time for Rowley. The team were struggling in the relegation zone and his doctors advised him to undergo hospital treatment for a stomach ulcer. On 3 February 1954, before entering hospital, he proffered his written resignation, stating that a football club fighting for survival in the First Division should have a fully fit man at the helm.

On 10 March, the Middlesbrough board announced that they had reluctantly parted company with their manager but, by then, Rowley had recovered sufficiently to withdraw his resignation.

'Boro's directors, though, had begun to canvas for a new manager and, although their first choice, Alec Stock of Leyton Orient, eventually turned down their offer because his wife did not wish to leave London, there was now no place for Walter Rowley in the board's plans. He spent three seasons as manager of Shrewsbury Town before leaving football in 1957.

Bob Dennison
(July 1954-January 1963)

BOB Dennison was born in Amble, a village on the Northumbrian coast, on 6 March 1912. He played junior football for Radcliffe United before joining Newcastle United as an inside-left in May 1929, but his appearances in the famous black and white striped shirt were restricted to 11 League games in five seasons because, in his own words, he was 'just an ordinary player'.

In May 1934 Dennison was transferred to

Nottingham Forest but, a year later, moved to Fulham. At Craven Cottage he was converted to centre-half and during the war guested for Northampton Town after working in the timber business in that town. Dennison eventually signed for the Cobblers and was appointed their manager in 1948.

In July 1954, Northampton released him from his contract and he joined Middlesbrough for the start of the club's first season back in the Second Division. He assumed the secretarial duties at Ayresome Park from August 1955 until the arrival of Harry Green in 1961.

Bob Dennison spent nine eventful years as Middlesbrough manager as, season after season, the club narrowly missed out on promotion, even with Brian Clough, Alan Peacock, Billy Day and Eddie Holliday in the team. It was Dennison who 'discovered' Clough and who also took Peter Taylor to Ayresome Park, thus bringing together the men who would later form one of the most famous and successful managerial partnerships in football.

On 10 January 1963 Dennison was told that his contract, which still had 19 months to run, would be terminated forthwith. The board issued a Press statement to the effect that the parting was by mutual consent, but Dennison subsequently took the club to the High Court, where he won damages of £3,200 for 'unfair dismissal'.

Undaunted, in December 1963 he went into non-League management with Southern League Hereford United and later served Coventry City, as chief scout from December 1967 and then as assistant manager from December 1968. He was caretaker manager at Highfield Road for a brief spell in 1972, between the reigns of Noel Cantwell and Gordon Milne, before retiring in 1978. Dennison went to live in Kent, continuing his Coventry links as a part-time scout.

Raich Carter
(January 1963-February 1966)

RAICH Carter — real name Horatio Stratton Carter — was born the son of a professional footballer on 21 December 1913, in Sunderland. He was a natural sportsman and a prolific scorer in junior football with Hendon Boys' School, Whitburn St Mary's, Sunderland Forge and Esh Winning, before collecting England Schoolboy honours in 1927.

He had trials with Leicester City but was turned down as being 'too small'. Sunderland, his home-town club, realized his potential, however, and his career blossomed at Roker Park. By the time he was 24, Carter had won every major honour then open to a footballer — England caps, League Championship and FA Cup winners' medals. During the war he joined, first the fire brigade, then the RAF. It was whilst at RAF Loughborough that he teamed up with another great inside-forward of the day, Peter Doherty, and the two of them guested for Derby County and helped the Rams win the FA Cup in 1945-6.

By then Carter had joined Derby officially and he stayed with them until April 1948, when he signed for Hull City as player-assistant manager. He was a naturally left-footed player who was renowned for his ability to split defences with unerringly accurate passes. His style made him appear slow, but he could quickly switch into top gear and leave opponents standing. He was also a fine cricketer who played for Minor Counties side, Durham, and made three first-class appearances for Derbyshire in 1946.

Carter became manager at Boothferry Road and helped Hull win the Third Division North title in 1948-9. He retired as manager in September 1951 and as a player in 1952, although he played for Cork Athletic in the League of Ireland from January to May 1953, when he took over from Major Frank Buckley

as manager of Leeds United. Five years earlier he had taken over from Buckley at Hull.

Carter shrewdly guided the Yorkshire club back into the First Division in 1956, having built his team around the brilliant John Charles, but was surprisingly sacked on 10 May 1958, after Leeds had slipped to 17th place in Division One and his contract was up for renewal. He re-emerged as Mansfield Town manager in February 1960 and laid the foundations for the Stags' return to Division Three before turning his attentions to Ayresome Park in mid-January 1963.

Carter's days at Middlesbrough were the least successful of his football career. 'Boro went to the brink of relegation to Division Three for the first time in their history and he was dismissed on 12 February 1966, with Harold Shepherdson in the role of caretaker manager, selecting the team until a successor could be appointed. Carter became a sports department manager at a large Hull store and today lives in retirement at Willerby on North Humberside, alas not enjoying the best of health.

Stan Anderson
(April 1966-January 1973)

STAN ANDERSON, who was born in Horden on 27 February 1934, had a trial for Middlesbrough, but manager David Jack turned him away because he felt that the club had an abundance of wing-halves. Anderson signed for Horden Colliery Welfare and took a job as an apprentice plumber.

In 1949, however, Sunderland came knocking on his door and he signed junior forms for the Wearsiders. His First Division debut came three seasons later, in 1952-3, when he quickly impressed as a stylish wing-half but took the precaution of playing part-time football and keeping on with his trade until his 19th birthday.

His stylish displays caught the eyes of the England selectors and Anderson won four

Under-23 caps and two full caps during his stay at Roker. Then, to the surprise of Sunderland supporters, he was sold to Second Division Newcastle United for £30,000 in November 1963, after clocking up 402 League appearances for the Wearsiders.

Anderson captained the Magpies to the Second Division championship in 1964-5, but another surprise was on the way and in November 1965, he accepted the position of player-coach with 'Boro, the first such appointment in Middlesbrough's history. His new club, managed by Raich Carter, were attempting to avoid the drop to Division Three and within a short time he became the first player to have captained all three of the North-East's major clubs.

Stan Anderson accepted the job of manager in April 1966, but could not help Middlesbrough avoid relegation. After an indifferent start, however, he led the side to promotion in his first full season as boss, when 'Boro ensured promotion in the last game, at home to Oxford United.

On 25 January 1973, however, following a 1-0 FA Cup defeat at Plymouth, Anderson, a taciturn, deep-thinking man, resigned, despite the directors' attempts to persuade him to change his mind. He was adamant that he was not the man to take the club into the First Division.

As when Raich Carter left the club, Harold Shepherdson looked after team selection until the end of the season. By August 1973, Anderson was named as manager of Greek club, AEK Athens. He later managed Panathinaikos, but returned to England in September 1974, to become assistant manager of Queen's Park Rangers.

In February 1975, he took over from Maurice Setters as manager of Doncaster Rovers and joined Bolton Wanderers in November 1978 as assistant manager to Ian Greaves. He succeeded Greaves as manager in February 1980, but again was unable to prevent relegation, this time from Division One. Despite being allowed to strengthen the Trotters' squad, Anderson could not provide an improvement in results the following season and in May 1981 he was sacked with two years of his contract still to run.

Jack Charlton OBE
(May 1973-April 1977 &
March-June 1984)

JACK Charlton was born at Ashington, Northumberland, on 8 May 1935. His was a footballing family (he is related to the Milburns) and he preceded his brother Bobby into League football, joining Leeds United straight from school.

His uncle, Jim Milburn, then a Leeds full-back, recommended Jack to the Yorkshire club. His made his League debut in April 1953, against Doncaster Rovers, and went on to notch up a record 629 League games for Leeds, spending almost two decades with United.

Middlesbrough-born Don Revie became Leeds' manager in 1961 and within two seasons had moulded Jack Charlton into a commanding centre-half. Leeds returned to Division One and Jack Charlton shared in all their great domestic and European triumphs of the late 1960s and early '70s. He won 35 full England caps and was in the side which lifted the World Cup in 1966. A year later, he succeeded his more famous brother as the Footballer of the Year.

On his retirement in 1973, Jack Charlton

expressed an interest in League management and was offered the job at Middlesbrough. He accepted the post on 7 May 1973, saying that he would not stay longer than four years in the job. The pre-season tour of Scotland proved to be the ideal scenario for the new manager to get to know the strengths and weaknesses of his playing staff and the players knew from the start that Charlton was the boss.

The manager and the team got off to a flying start, winning all three friendlies. His managerial League baptism also proved to be a successful one, a 1-0 victory at Fratton Park against promotion hopefuls Portsmouth. The first home game was against Fulham but the Cottagers won 2-0. At the final whistle, Jack Charlton was heard to comment, "Unbelievable . . .they'll do it my way now!" And they did.

His first managerial master-stroke was persuading Celtic legend Bobby Murdoch to come to Ayresome Park on a free transfer. The Scot proved to be the missing link that had eluded Stan Anderson for so long.

Charlton took a team, basically the side built by Anderson, blended the experience of Murdoch and piloted the club into Division One in his first season. Once back in the top flight, the quality of the team was emphasized by the impressive final placing of sixth — all done without further recourse to the transfer market.

The transition from successful player to successful manager was instantaneous and Charlton was voted Bell's Manager of the Year for his achievements at Ayresome Park. Yet the first Second Division manager to lift the title was unwilling to accept any contract from the Middlesbrough board.

On 12 November 1974, Jack Charlton had an important date in a London — an 11am appointment at Buckingham Palace to receive

his OBE. Later that day he was at Anfield for a League Cup tie and diplomatically refused to comment on which occasion gave him more satisfaction, for his team beat Liverpool 1-0.

In 1976 he steered the club to within 90 minutes of the League Cup Final. It would have been the first Wembley appearance in 'Boro's history, but in the semi-final second-leg, Manchester City won 4-0 at Maine Road and 4-1 on aggregate.

True to his word, Charlton resigned as 'Boro manager at the end of April 1977, saying that after 26 years in football and with his financial security guaranteed, it was about time he had a rest and was looking forward to some fishing, hunting and shooting, some after-dinner speaking and to spending more time with his family.

Yet he was back in managerial harness in late 1977, when he took on the task of rebuilding Third Division Sheffield Wednesday after the departure of Len Ashurst. Again he stipulated that his stay would not be long-term. Within two seasons, the Owls were back in Division Two and in 1982 they missed promotion to the First Division by only one point. He left Wednesday, as promised, in 1983, having laid the foundation for his successor, Howard Wilkinson, to lead Wednesday back into Division One in his first season as Owls' manager. Following Allison's sacking, Charlton briefly returned to Ayresome Park as caretaker manager in 1984.

Shortly afterwards, Charlton became manager of Newcastle United but spent only one mediocre season on Tyneside, quitting after he was booed by the Geordie supporters during a pre-season friendly game. Appointed team manager of the Republic of Ireland, he received much public acclaim in June 1988, when he engineered Eire's famous 1-0 victory over England in the European Championships and in 1990 led his adopted country to the World Cup quarter-finals, where they were beaten by Italy.

John Neal
(May 1977-July 1981)

JOHN Neal, regarded as one of the quiet men in football, was born on 3 April 1932, in Silksworth, County Durham, and supported Sunderland as a boy. He progressed from junior football with Silksworth Juniors to Hull City, signing for the Tigers, then managed by Raich Carter, in August 1949. Despite several seasons on Humberside, Neal played in only 60 League games and in July 1956 he dropped into non-League soccer with King's Lynn.

In July 1957 he was back in League football with Swindon Town and was a regular full-back at the County Ground until Joe Mercer took him to Villa Park in August 1959. He enjoyed most success as a player there. Aston Villa had been relegated to Division Two at the end of 1958-9, but returned immediately as Second Division champions. Neal added a League Cup winners' medal in 1961, when Villa became the first team to win the trophy, beating Rotherham United in a two-legged Final.

A move to Southend United in November 1962 saw Neal spend almost three seasons with the Shrimpers, making over 100 League appearances until, in 1965, he decided to try League management and successfully applied for the vacant manager's job at Fourth Division Wrexham.

He did well at the Racecourse Ground, taking the Welsh club into the Third Division

and to the quarter-finals of the European Cup-winners' Cup. When he moved to Ayresome Park on 19 May 1977, he left behind a strong side which soon went on to win promotion to Division Two for the first time in Wrexham's history.

John Neal caught up with his new club in Australia, on their world tour. Those who thought that he would walk in the shadow of Jack Charlton were quickly silenced with his comment: "I have my own style, my own beliefs and my own principles."

He instilled an attacking flair into the team, but came in for strong criticism when he methodically dismantled the nucleus of Jack Charlton's side. His list of departures included Graeme Souness to Liverpool, David Mills to West Brom, Stuart Boam to Newcastle and Stan Cummins to Sunderland.

The players he brought to Ayresome included Billy Ashcroft (from his old club Wrexham), Welsh international John Mahoney, Micky Burns, Terry Cochrane, Bosco Jankovic, goalkeeper Jim Stewart and club record buy Irving Nattrass from Newcastle United.

Neal left Middlesbrough in the summer of 1981, after disagreeing with the club's decision to sell Craig Johnston to Liverpool, and was snapped up by Chelsea chairman Ken Bates, who saw him as the man to replace Geoff Hurst at Stamford Bridge. Neal soon returned to Teesside, but only to lure 'Boro favourite Tony McAndrew to Chelsea.

Neal took the Londoners back to Division One at the end of 1983-4, but his health was not robust after heart surgery and in 1986 he was replaced by long-serving Chelsea player John Hollins.

Bobby Murdoch
(June 1981-October 1982)

BOBBY Murdoch was one of Scotland's most influential post-war players and spent 14 good years at Celtic where he shared in seven consecutive League Championship wins as well as success in the Scottish FA Cup and League Cup. In addition, Murdoch was capped 12 times for Scotland and was voted Scotland's Player of the Year in 1969, two years after he was a member of the Celtic team which became the first British club to win the European Cup.

At the beginning of the 1973-4 season, one of Jack Charlton's first jobs as 'Boro manager was to persuade Bobby Murdoch to join him at Ayresome Park. Murdoch made his debut in a Middlesbrough shirt at Halifax in a North Midlands League game in September 1973. His League debut followed soon afterwards and he marked his first appearance with a superb goal against Bristol City.

Murdoch, who was born in Bothwell, Lanarkshire, on 17 August 1944 and began with Cambuslang Rangers, had forged his reputation as an attacking inside-forward and, although not as mobile as in his Parkhead days, he nevertheless proved an effective signing for 'Boro. His vision in the midfield helped take the Ayresome club back to Division One in his first season with 'Boro.

In 1975, his first-team playing days over, Murdoch was appointed youth-team coach at Middlesbrough and when John Neal left Ayresome Park in the summer of 1981, the former Celtic man took over the side, even though he had no previous managerial experience.

He was unfortuate to become manager at a time when 'Boro were suffering from the loss of several fine players. Mark Procter, Craig Johnston and David Armstrong had all left the club and the team was not strong enough to survive in the top flight.

After relegation at the end of Murdoch's first season as manager, many people thought he would be dismissed. In fact, he held the job until early the following season but could not survive a dreadful 'Boro performance against Grimsby Town at Ayresome Park in September 1982. The Mariners won 4-1 and Murdoch was soon on his way. For the fourth time in his 45-year career at Middlesbrough, Harold Shepherdson took over as caretaker manager whilst the board looked around for a more permanent successor to Murdoch.

Malcolm Allison
(October 1982-March 1984)

MALCOLM Allison is one of the most colourful characters to emerge in post-war football. The flamboyant manager, with his fedora hat, cigar and champagne in hand, livened many a Press conference at the peak of his managerial career, whilst his personal life sometimes put him on the front pages, rather than the sports pages, of the national newspapers.

Indeed, his image as a manager has overshadowed the fact that Allison was a fine centre-half in his playing days. He was born at Dartford on 5 September 1927 and his first League club was Charlton Athletic, for whom he signed in 1944. He made only two League appearances for Charlton but his career took off after he joined West Ham United in February 1951. By the time he was forced to retire in 1958 because of a serious illness — he had a lung removed after contracting tuberculosis — Allison had made 238 League appearances for the Hammers.

He had been a member of a fine West Ham team, several of whose members later became prominent coaches and managers, and Allison also took up coaching after his playing days had ended. He worked with the Cambridge University side, then in Toronto and with Southern League Bath City before entering Football League management with Plymouth Argyle in 1964.

In his one season at Home Park, Allison took Argyle to the semi-final of the Football League Cup — admittedly, then a lack-lustre competition — but their League form was patchy and before the campaign was over, he was at loggerheads with the directors over team selection and left.

In July 1965, he joined Joe Mercer at Maine Road and the two men took Manchester City to some of that club's greatest successes. By 1972, though, Allison felt that his contribution was such that he deserved more than the title of assistant manager. Mercer left to manage Coventry City and Allison had his wish. Before the end of his first season, however, he was

off to manage Crystal Palace, saying that he could no longer motivate the City players.

There followed another spell at Plymouth and then periods coaching in Istanbul and in North America before he returned to Maine Road in July 1979. Despite spending huge sums of money on players, there was no return to the glory days and early in the 1980-81 season both Allison and general manager Tony Book were dismissed.

Again Allison was on his travels. He returned to Crystal Palace briefly and worked as an advisor to non-League Yeovil Town before Sporting Lisbon offered him a job. Allison repaid them by taking Sporting to the Portuguese League and Cup double before being controversially sacked in July 1982.

Three months later he broke a pledge never to return to Football League management by signing a two-year contract with Middlesbrough. Teesside's football fans, starved of success, looked upon the appointment of this colourful character as the arrival of a 'Messiah', who would lead their club from the wilderness of the Second Division.

They warmed to him still further when 'Boro beat table-topping QPR, but there was no money to buy new players and the club was limping along on meagre attendances. When he did sign a player — former England man Kevin Beattie, who came from Colchester United in November 1982 — bad luck followed. Beattie was injured after only two games and sidelined until January.

In his first season, Allison saw Middlesbrough finish in 16th place and reach the last 16 of the FA Cup. He showed himself determined to hang on to young talent by signing Stephen Bell on a four-year contract.

Allison also signed a new contract, for two years from March 1983, but the club was being sucked into the maelstrom of financial disaster and he was coming under intense pressure to sell the best players. His response was typically controversial — "It's better for the club to die than linger on" — and on 28 March 1984 he was dismissed, the gap between directors and manager now too wide to overcome.

He later worked in such diverse places as Willington, County Durham, and Kuwait. In the summer of 1989, Malcolm Allison was back in the news again, this time as manager of GM Vauxhall Conference club, Fisher Athletic, promising that he would take them into the Football League inside two years, but spending only five months in the job. He reappeared most recently in November 1992 as a consultant to Bristol Rovers, who were on their way down from the new First Division.

Willie Maddren
(June 1984-February 1986)

WILLIE Maddren, who was born at Haverton Hill on 11 January 1951, had an unlucky start to his football career. He was playing for Port Clarence Juniors and broke his ankle just two days before he was due to have a trial with Leeds United. Leeds never followed up his progress and that was to Middlesbrough's good fortune, for Maddren went on to become one of the club's finest players.

He was recommended to 'Boro by local scout Freddie Barnes and signed professional forms in June 1968, at the same time as David Mills. He made his League debut as a forward in the last home game of that season, against Bury at Ayresome Park, but had been on the pitch for only ten minutes when he broke his nose. Maddren soon returned to the fray and scored

a goal, but his heroics were in vain as 'Boro eventually went down 3-2.

He was voted Player of the Year by Middlesbrough supporters in 1971 and proved his versatility by appearing in seven different positions. It was as a central defender, though, that he made real progress. After Bill Gates broke his jaw in an FA Cup game at Old Trafford, Maddren stepped up and established himself.

His emergence as a defender of the highest quality coincided with the signing of Stuart Boam. The two forged a marvellous understanding and, although the selectors ignored Boam, Maddren was rewarded with five England Under-23 caps.

His playing career, during which he made over 300 appearances for 'Boro, ended after a serious injury to his right knee in 1977. After a spell as coach at Hartlepool United, he returned to Ayresome Park as a coach and physiotherapist. He came back on the recommendation of Jack Charlton, who was at Ayresome for a short spell following the dismissal of Malcolm Allison.

The fans wanted Charlton to stay but he was adamant that the arrangement should be only short-term. Chairman Mike McCullagh offered Maddren the manager's job and the former 'Boro player took it on, commenting that the task of resurrecting the club's playing fortunes would take at least three years' hard work.

David Mills returned and ended the 1983-84 season as 'Boro's top scorer, but things were far from rosy. Middlesbrough were already £1.2 million in debt and the chances of rebuilding the team with quality players were negligible. Mills was injured the following season but Maddren resisted pressure to blood youngsters at this traumatic time in 'Boro's history.

In October 1985, he threatened to resign but stayed on. Early in 1986, Maddren appointed Bruce Rioch as coach. In February, the manager was sacked and Rioch took over.

Willie Maddren now runs three successful sports outfitters shops, but he has never returned to the ground that he graced with so many superlative displays for nine years.

Bruce Rioch
(February 1986-March 1990)

BRUCE Rioch, the son of a Scottish RSM, was born in Aldershot on 6 September 1947 and was brought up in Luton. He joined the Hatters on leaving school and became a professional in September 1964.

Luton were relegated to the Fourth Division for the first time in 1965, but Rioch's goals helped them to the Fourth Division title in 1968 and Tommy Docherty parted with £100,000, a record for a Third Division player, to take him to Second Division Aston Villa in July 1969. Again, Rioch experienced relegation when Villa slipped into the Third Division for the first time in their long history.

Rioch, an aggressive, attacking wing-half, was prone to cartilage trouble throughout his playing career, having cartilages removed from both knees during 1971-2. But he made a remarkable recovery and played an active part in Villa winning the Third Division championship and reaching the Football League Cup Final the same season.

Dave Mackay paid £200,000 to take him to Derby County in February 1974 and Rioch was ever-present in the Rams' League Championship side of 1974-5, ending the season as Derby's leading scorer. The first of his 24 full Scotland caps came in Glasgow in May 1975, against Portugal.

Rioch was on the move again in December 1976, this time to Everton, but was back at the Baseball Ground after only 11 months on Merseyside. He had two loan spells whilst on Derby's books, with Birmingham City and Sheffield United.

The highlight of his playing career was his captaincy of Scotland in the 1978 World Cup Finals in Argentina, when he created history by becoming the first English-born player to skipper the Scots.

He played with Seattle Sounders in the North American Soccer League before returning to England on a free transfer in October 1980. He joined Fourth Division Torquay United, progressing from player to coach and ultimately replaced manager Frank O'Farrell in July 1982.

Rioch joined Middlesbrough as first-team coach in January 1986, but on the departure of Willie Maddren the following month, chairman Alf Duffield offered Bruce the job, although it was too late to stop the club's slide into the Third Division.

'Boro's spluttering demise in the summer of 1986 meant that the non-playing staff, which numbered 30 including Rioch and coach Colin Todd, lost their jobs as the gates were closed at Ayresome Park. But Rioch and Todd stayed on, even more determined to see the job through.

A dramatic last-minute reprieve saw a new Middlesbrough club rise from the ashes of liquidation and Bruce Rioch, who had turned down the opportunity to move to a First Division club that summer, steered 'Boro back to the Second Division. He became the first Middlesbrough manager to take the club to two successive promotion successes, even though the route back to the First Division was via the exciting play-offs against Bradford City and Chelsea in May 1988.

For a man who had worked so hard for success and who had achieved so much personal glory in his football career, relegation at the end of the 1988-9 season must have been a bitter pill to swallow.

The following season was an even greater disappointment as 'Boro continued to struggle in the Second Division and in March 1990, Rioch was sacked, being replaced by his assistant, Colin Todd.

There was a feeling that the 'Boro board had short memories considering all that Rioch had achieved for their club. He became manager of Millwall and, despite a fairly unhappy time at The Den, proved himself once more when he took over as manager of Bolton Wanderers, leading the Totters to promotion to the new First Division in 1993 as well as seeing them enjoy an impressive FA Cup run which accounted for Liverpool along the way.

Bruce Rioch is certainly regarded as one of British football's progressive, bright young managers.

Colin Todd
(March 1990-June 1991)

BORN at Chester-le-Street on 12 December 1948, Colin Todd joined Sunderland from school, becoming a full-time professional in December 1966. Derby County manager Brian Clough paid a record fee for a defender when he spent £170,000 to take Todd to the Baseball Ground in February 1971.

Todd enjoyed the best days of his career at Derby, winning two League Championship medals, playing in a European Cup semi-final and winning 27 England caps. He was also the PFA Player of the Year in 1975.

He was that rarity, a defender who could excite the crowds with his brilliant tackling and breathtaking cross-field passes of 40 yards and more.

Todd later had spells with Everton, Birmingham City (with whom he won promotion to the First Division), Oxford United and

Division, but in 1990-91 he had a successful, albeit ultimately disappointing, season when 'Boro reached the Second Division play-offs before losing to Notts County.

In June 1991, Todd surprisingly resigned, citing 'board interference' as the reason. A year later he rejoined Rioch at Bolton and so began another successful partnership.

Lennie Lawrence (July 1991-)

ROBIN Michael 'Lennie' Lawrence was born in Brighton on 14 December 1947. His playing career could not have been more contrasting to that of his immediate predecessor, for where Colin Todd had enjoyed great success at club and international level, Lawrence had never played League football, representing Croydon, Carshalton and Sutton United before assistant managers' jobs at Plymouth Argyle and Lincoln City.

He was in charge of Charlton Athletic Reserves when, in November 1983, he was promoted to manager following the departure of Ken Craggs.

Larwence's eight years as Charlton boss saw despair, triumph and turmoil as the Valiants nearly went out of business, lost their ground at The Valley, were promoted and then eventually relegated from Division One.

In a superb first season at Middlesbrough, he took the club to runners-up in the Second Division and thus into the new FA Premier League. 'Boro also reached the Littlewooods Cup semi-finals before losing on aggregate to Manchester United.

Lawrence signed Paul Wilkinson from Watford for £550,000 — he led the way with 22 goals — but also sold Tony Mowbray to Celtic and repeatedly dropped crowd favourite Bernie Slaven. Middlesbrough struggled in the

Luton Town before retiring after a career which spanned almost 750 senior games.

He was managing Whitley Bay when Bruce Rioch, a former Derby County colleague, asked him to become his assistant at Middlesbrough. Todd succeeded Rioch in March 1990, far too late to help stave off relegation to the Second

Premier League and in 1993 Lawrence tasted his second relegation in three years when 'Boro finished next to bottom of the table.

Lennie Lawrence is chaired by the fans after 'Boro's promotion in 1992.

Middlesbrough Stars A-Z

DAVID ARMSTRONG

Midfielder David Armstrong, who was born at Durham City on Boxing Day 1954, began his long association with Middlesbrough when he was only nine. George Wardle brought him from his native city and 'Boro watched the lad develop into an England Schoolboy international. He signed as an amateur in September 1968, became an apprentice in June 1970 and a full-time professional on New Year's Eve 1971. A natural left-sided midfielder, Armstrong made his first-team debut as a 17-year-old substitute against Queen's Park Rangers in March 1972. He won England Under-23 and 'B' international caps and gained full recognition against Australia in May 1980. Middlesbrough manager Jack Charlton called him his 'little gem' and he was only 25 when 'Boro awarded him a testimonial match in October 1980, against the club's 1973-74 promotion-winning team. He is the current holder of Middlesbrough's consecutive appearances record (356 League and Cup games) and altogether made 413 full senior appearances, plus three as a substitute, and scored 73 goals. In the 1981 close season, Armstrong was transferred to Southampton for a record £600,000 and went on to win three further full England caps. After 222 League games for the Saints, he ended his playing career with Bournemouth and is currently a soft-drinks salesman on the South Coast, although desperately keen to get into football management. Armstrong quit as manager of non-League side Andover Town and is currently Hampshire Schools' sports liaison officer.

BILLY ASHCROFT

Liverpool-born Billy Ashcroft represented his home city at both athletics and swimming, but football was his first love. As a centre-half he signed for Blackpool on associate schoolboy forms before asking Wrexham for a trial. Ashcroft signed for the Welsh side in October 1970 and in seven seasons at the Racecourse Ground he made almost 200 League appearances, earning the nickname of the 'Bear of Bruges' when Wrexham played Anderlecht in the quarter-finals of the European Cup in Belgium. When Wrexham manager John Neal became Middlesbrough's new boss in May 1977, he returned to his former club to persuade Wrexham's new manager, Arfon Griffiths, to part with Ashcroft. Griffiths would not release the player until he had found a replacement, so Neal had to wait some weeks before he got his man. When he did sign Ashcroft, for £135,000 in September 1977, it was the second time in as many weeks that Neal had paid a club record fee: he had just paid Stoke City £90,000 for John Mahoney. With his long hair and full beard, Ashcroft was once called 'the caveman in a Middlesbrough shirt'. He made a scoring home debut against Birmingham City but 'Boro lost 2-1. After the transfer of Stuart Boam to Newcastle United, he played some games for the club at centre-half but was often barracked by the fans when he was going through a bad spell. Ashcroft was released at the end of the 1981-82 season and, on the recommendation of Middlesbrough's Dutch international Heine Otto, was picked up by Dutch club, Twente Enschede. He returned to England in August 1985 to play one season for Tranmere Rovers and now runs the Derby Arms pub in Halewood village, near Liverpool. For Middlesbrough he made 157/22 League and Cup appearances scoring 25 goals.

DON ASHMAN

Staindrop-born Don Ashman, a cool, unruffled half-back, worked as a coal-miner and played part-time football for Cockfield Albion. Middlesbrough manager Herbert Bamlett brought him to Ayresome Park on 5 May 1924, for a £10 fee and a guaranteed friendly match at Cockfield's ground. Ashman was soon pushed into Middlesbrough's reserve team in the North-Eastern League and made his first-team debut six months later, at Coventry City on 1 November 1924. He was an established member of the promotion winning sides of 1926-27 and 1928-29, clocking up 174 League and Cup games before his £500 transfer to Queen's Park Rangers in May 1932. He returned to the North-East to play for Darlington before the outbreak of World War Two.

IAN BAILEY

Ian Bailey was born in Middlesbrough on 26 October 1956 and played his early football as a centre-forward at Easterside Junior School. He was an outside-left by the time he had reached Bertram Ramsey School and played for Middlesbrough Boys and Yorkshire Boys in that position. When his team was short of a left-back, Bailey played some games in that berth and thus found his natural position. Like his brother, he signed for Middlesbrough as an apprentice in October 1972, becoming a full-time professional on his 18th birthday and making his first-team debut at left-back against Tottenham Hotspur in December 1974. He was loaned to Stan Anderson's Doncaster Rovers, and to Bob Moncur's Carlisle United early in 1977. A serious cartilage injury kept him out of the game

for almost five months, but he made a full recovery and appeared on loan for Bolton Wanderers. Like many Football League players, he tried his luck in the North American Soccer League, playing for Minnesota Kicks in the summer of 1977. In July 1980, Bailey was in contractual dispute with 'Boro, but still trained regularly at Ayresome Park without the security of a contract. After further talks with manager John Neal he was taken off the transfer list at his own request and signed a one-year contract. Sheffield Wednesday manager Jack Charlton returned to his former club in an attempt to sign Bailey for the Owls. 'Boro valued the player at £300,000, but Charlton offered only £80,000. A Football League tribunal was asked to resolve the problem, but just as it was about to sit, Middlesbrough announced that they had accepted Wednesday's original offer. Charlton had apparently threatened to pull out of the transfer if the tribunal ruled that Bailey was worth more than his original estimate, and the player signed a three-year contract on 3 August 1982. At Hillsborough he was loaned to Blackpool in October 1984, but a leg injury prematurely ended his playing career. However, he is still actively involved in football after becoming a physiotherapist at Sheffield United in 1987. For Middlesbrough he made 163/7 League and Cup appearances.

IAN BAIRD

Rotherham-born Ian Baird played football in the same Hampshire schoolboys team as Paul Kerr and represented England as a midfielder at schoolboy level. He was also an accomplished cricketer and represented his home town. Baird joined Southampton upon leaving school but, despite making his League debut at the age of 18, against Sunderland in 1982, he found it difficult to get a regular game with the Saints and was loaned to both Cardiff City and Newcastle United. He played five games for

the Geordies and looked at one point to be signing for the club, but Lawrie McMenemy and Jack Charlton could not agree on a transfer figure. He eventually left The Dell to sign for Leeds United, managed by Eddie Gray, in a £75,000 transfer. Gray bought him without seeing him play, on the recommendation of Joe Jordan, a teammate of Baird's at The Dell. He later turned down possible moves to both Celtic and Aberdeen, to join Alan Ball's Portsmouth, but had a disappointing seven months at Fratton Park, scoring only one goal in over 20 games as Pompey made an unsuccessful attempt to stave off relegation. He willingly agreed to a return to Leeds United and was voted Player of the Year by the Elland Road fans in 1989, although disappointed when new Leeds manager Howard Wilkinson brought Lee Chappman from Nottingham Forest. Baird was one of Bruce Rioch's last signings for Middlesbrough when he agreed to a move from Leeds in February 1990 for a £500,000 fee. He missed 'Boro's Zenith Data Systems Cup run and eventual first Wembley appearance because he was cup-tied, having played for Leeds in the competition that season. He would have missed the Final anyway, for he was suspended at the time. He played nine games before he struck his first goal for his new club, but scored two of 'Boro's goals in a 4-1 thrashing of Newcastle United on the last day of the season to help keep Middlesbrough in the Second Division. He won a Second Division promotion medal as a Leeds United player, even though he was at Middlesbrough because he figured in more than 20 games for United. A sometimes volatile striker (he had been sent off five times previously in his career) he was voted Middlesbrough supporters' Player of the Year in 1990, but it was a huge surprise to everyone when he was transferred to Hearts in July 1991, upon the arrival of new manager Lennie Lawrence at Ayresome Park. For Middlesbrough, Baird scored 20 goals in 70/4 League and Cup games.

BOB BAXTER

When Middlesbrough manager Peter McWilliam went to Scotland on a scouting mission and found the game he intended to watch had been cancelled, he switched to another match and discovered Bob Baxter. A coal-miner, Baxter was playing for Bruntonian Juniors and supplemented his wages by running a dance band in the evenings. 'Boro took him away from all that and he made his League debut in October 1932, at inside-left against Birmingham at St Andrew's. In November 1935, after centre-half and captain Tom Griffiths was transferred to Aston Villa, Baxter was tried at pivot and held the position until the outbreak of war, winning three Scottish caps. He was a constructive player, but was sometimes inclined to overdo the fancy stuff. During his Middlesbrough career, which spanned 266 League and Cup games in which he scored 20 goals, he played in nine different first-team positions and was rated by many as the club's best-ever captain. At the outbreak of war he returned to Scotland and resumed his occupation as a miner. He also ran a newsagent's and tobacconist's shop and guested for Hibernian and Heart of Midlothian. Released by Middlesbrough in August 1945, he was transferred to Hearts. Baxter later managed Leith Athletic and Edinburgh Monarchs speedway team. He later lived in retirement in Billingham. Bob died on 5 April 1991 at a Middleton St George nursing home.

HARRY BELL

Harry Bell was spotted by Sunderland whilst playing junior football with Hylton Colliery and signed amateur forms for his home-town club in 1943. Bell, who was born in Sunderland on 14 October 1924, remained at Roker Park until his transfer

to Middlesbrough in September 1945. It was David Jack who noticed Bell, when Jack was manager of Sunderland Greyhound Stadium and Bell was playing in a five-a-side competition there. Bell was signed as a full-time professional at Ayresome Park and his fee set at £1,250. He arrived there as an inside-forward, but was switched to right-half as an emergency measure and became an immediate success in his new position. Bell proved a brave performer and this was highlighted during a game at Huddersfield in November 1948, when he broke his nose early on but continued to the final whistle. In September 1955, after 315 League and Cup appearances for 'Boro, he moved to Darlington and spent one season as a full-timer and four as a part-timer at Feethams. Bell, who was also a professional cricketer with Middlesbrough and Crook, now lives in Gosforth and has a top job with Tetley Breweries.

STEPHEN BELL

Big things were expected of Stephen Bell, the player, whose skill and ball control excited everyone who saw him play and he was hailed as the 'next Wilf Mannion'. Bell was born in the town on 13 March 1965, played for Middlesbrough Schoolboys when they won the ESFA Shield and also represented England at Youth international level. Middlesbrough were pleased when he signed a lucrative four-year contract with the club at the tender age of 17 and the football world was apparently at his feet. Bell equalled the club record previously held by Sam Lawrie, of being the club's youngest debutant player in January 1982 when he made his first full appearance

against Southampton (his only game that season). Alas he had only made 87 League and Cup appearances before the club announced in 1985 that his contract had been cancelled at the age of 20. Later, Bell confessed: "I mixed with the wrong crowd and it was a classic example of having too much too soon and not being able to handle it." Portsmouth manager Alan Ball offered him the chance to resurrect his career at Fratton Park but he walked out on them. Darlington caretaker-manager Paul Ward, a former Ayresome Park colleague of Bell's, gave him yet another chance and it looked, at last, as though he had learned his lesson. He was offered a contract at Feethams but again he failed. In 1986-7 he was reported to be playing for North Ormesby Institute. With Stephen Bell it was definitely a case of . . .if only!

RALPH BIRKETT

Speedy winger Ralph Birkett, the son of a Middlesbrough man, was born in Ashford, Kent, on 9 January 1912 and first played junior football with his local side, Dartmouth United, while he followed employment as a clerk. In August 1929, Birkett signed for Torquay United, spending almost four seasons at Plainmoor and scoring 15 goals in 95 appearances. In March 1933, he moved into the big time with a £2,000 transfer to First Division Arsenal. However, Arsenal's resources were hugely talented and he made only 19 appearances, scoring seven goals, in two years at Highbury. In March 1935 he moved to Middlesbrough for £5,900 and made an immediate impact, his four goals in seven League games helping keep 'Boro in the First Division. In October 1935, Birkett was capped for England against Ireland but missed the game against Germany two months later due to a pulled leg muscle.

Back to full fitness, he finished the season with 21 goals. Teesside fans were dismayed when Middlesbrough agreed to sell the popular Birkett to Second Division Newcastle United in July 1938, for £6,000. He had made 101 League and Cup appearances for the Ayresome Park club, scoring 36 goals. One year later, his football career was drastically curtailed by the outbreak of war. He became an Army PT instructor and served in India.

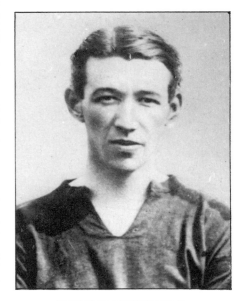

BILLY BIRRELL

Considering his experiences during World War One, Billy Birrell did well to enjoy such a successful football career when peace was restored. In 1915, whilst serving with the Black Watch, he suffered a foot injury soon after arriving in France. And in 1918, shortly before the Armistice was signed, he was captured and spent the remaining weeks of the war as a PoW. After the war he played for Raith Rovers, but decided that his future would be brighter on the other

side of the world. In January 1921, he had completed his plans to emigrate to America when Middlesbrough stepped in with an offer of £2,100. 'Boro manager Jimmy Howie saw Birrell as a replacement for Jackie Mordue, but little did Howie realise that his new signing would become one of Middlesbrough's most influential midfield generals. In his early days at Ayresome Park, Birrell was still troubled by his war wound but the injury cleared up after a period of rest. He was one of Middlesbrough's shrewdest captains and skippered the side which stormed out of the Second Division in 1926-27. He owned a cafe near the ground but found that his long-term interests lay in football and was keen to try League management. The Middlesbrough board reluctantly agreed to release him if a job came up and in November 1927, after making 235 League and Cup appearances in which he had scored 63 goals, Birrell returned to Raith Rovers as player-manager, with full-back Syd Jarvis travelling south in an exchange deal. Birrell became secretary-manager of Third Division South club Bournemouth in 1930, staying five seasons at Dean Court before accepting the manager's job at QPR in 1935. By the outbreak of World War Two, he was managing Chelsea, linking up with his old Middlesbrough colleague, Stewart Davidson, who was assistant manager. They led Chelsea to two wartime Cup Finals. Billy Birrell retired as manager in 1952 and died in November 1968.

their great favourite had been sold. In fact, Bloomer's debut for his new club was something of a disaster, for 'Boro went down 6-1 at Liverpool. But by the end of his time at Ayresome Park, he had made a valuable contribution to 'Boro's First Division survival and scored over 60 League and Cup goals for the club. Born at Cradley Heath on 20 January 1874, Bloomer began with Derby Swifts and Tutbury Hawthorn before signing for the Rams in April 1892. He soon established himself as a goalscorer, knocking them in from all angles, from close range and from long distance. He was Derby's leading scorer in 14 seasons (altogether he scored 332 League and Cup goals in 525 games for them) and won 23 caps with his two clubs. One contemporary critic said he was 'as slippery as an eel and much given to dealing electric shocks to goalkeepers'. He returned to Derby in September 1910, after a chance meeting with Rams manager Jimmy Methven on a railway station, and skippered his old club to promotion from Division Two in 1911-12. In 1914 he went to coach in Germany and was caught up in World War One, being interned for the duration. After the war he coached at Derby and in Spain before returning to the Baseball Ground as a general assistant. Bloomer's health had been failing for some years and in 1938 he was sent on a cruise. In April, three weeks after returning, he died and was buried in Nottingham Road cemetery, Derby. For Middlesbrough he scored 62 goals in 130 senior appearances.

Stiles, the man he was to replace as team captain, made their 'Boro debuts in August 1971, at Portsmouth. Boam was appointed captain on the arrival of new manager Jack Charlton in the summer of 1973, although in Charlton's early days at Ayresome Park, the player was not happy with the manager's forthright criticism of his style. Boam settled down, however, and developed an almost 'telepathic' understanding with Willie Maddren that confounded many opposing forwards. Boam captained the First Division promotion side but, unlike Maddren, did not win international honours. After 378 League and Cup games for Middlesbrough, he moved to Newcastle United in August 1979, for £100,000, and made 69 League appearances for the Magpies before returning to Mansfield as player-manager in July 1981. Towards the end of his League career he played some games for Fourth Division Hartlepool United, before a spell as player-manager at Guisborough Town in August 1983. He returned to the Mansfield area and is working in the Kodak factory there, but is still an occasional visitor to Ayresome Park.

BILLY BRAWN

Few players can have been so aptly named as Billy Brawn, who, despite being an outside-right, stood over 6ft 1in tall and tipped the scales at well over 13st. Brawn's Middlesbrough career was relatively brief — he joined them from Aston Villa in March 1906 and was transferred to Chelsea in November 1907 — but he was one of the leading players of the day. Born at Wellingborough on 1 August 1878, Brawn played for Wellingborough Town and Northampton Town before entering League football with Sheffield United in January 1900. He moved to Villa Park in December 1901 and, although injured on his debut, he recovered to enjoy a fine career in the Midlands. Brawn won an FA Cup medal in 1905 and two England caps before signing for 'Boro. He made his debut against his old club, Sheffield United, and helped 'Boro preserve their First Division status that season, going on to make 58 League and Cup appearances altogether. After Chelsea he played for Brentford and ran a pub in that area after hanging up his boots. From July 1919 until June 1921, he acted as an advisor to Brentford, who were regrouping after the war. Brawn was reported dead in 1931.

STEVE BLOOMER

Middlesbrough caused quite a stir when they signed Derby County's prolific goalscorer Steve Bloomer in March 1906. Bloomer was an established England international and the Derby fans were incensed that

STUART BOAM

Stuart Boam was born at Kirkby-in-Ashfield on 28 January 1948 and played his early football for Kirkby Boys' Club. He signed for Mansfield Town in July 1966 and over the next four seasons missed only ten matches for the Stags. A commanding centre-half, Boam made over 170 appearances — 162 of them consecutively — for Mansfield. When 'Boro manager Stan Anderson signed Boam in May 1971, he had to part with a reported £50,000 for the Mansfield skipper. Both Boam and Nobby

BILLY BROWN

Billy Brown was working as a miner and playing football as a part-timer with West Stanley, where he was born, when Middlesbrough manager Peter McWilliam paid a £225 fee to sign the young wing-half in December 1928. McWilliam guaranteed the West Stanley club a further £100 when Brown had made 12 first-team appearances but after three years, with their former player still waiting to make his League debut, West Stanley must have thought they would never receive their money. However, after finally making his bow against Leicester City in August 1931, Brown went on to make 274 League and Cup appearances and Middlesbrough certainly had good value for their modest outlay. Although primarily a right-half, Brown did extremely well at right-back after being switched there when Jack Jennings was injured. During World War Two, the former miner guested for Watford and, after being released by Middlesbrough at the end of the 1945-46 season, he made 80 League appearances for Hartlepools United in the Third Division North before retiring in 1948.

BOBBY BRUCE

Bobby Bruce, was born in Paisley on 29 January 1906 and played for St Anthony's (Glasgow) before signing for Aberdeen in the 1924 close season. Bruce, who stood only 5ft 6in tall, was equally at home at centre or inside-forward and proved an elusive opponent who could pass the ball accurately, even when running at top speed. Despite his youth, Bruce quickly became a regular Dons first-teamer. He toured South Africa with Aberdeen in 1927 and, just before joining Middlesbrough for £4,500 in January 1928, he created history by becoming the first player to score a hat-trick in a Scottish Cup tie and still finish on the losing side. He made his 'Boro debut in a 5-2 defeat at Burnden Park and was a member of the Middlesbrough side which

won the Second Division championship the following season. In April 1930, Bruce asked for a transfer after being barracked by a section of the Ayresome Park crowd, but manager Peter McWilliam refused the request. One of Bruce's faults, which riled the crowd so much, was that he sometimes liked to try long-range shots rather than pass to a better-placed colleague. He was described as 'consistently inconsistent' and the crowd never took to his style of play. Despite this, he was capped against Austria in November 1933. After seven seasons on Teesside, during which he made 253 League and Cup appearances, scoring 71 goals, Bruce was transferred to Sheffield Wednesday in October 1935 for £2,500. He made only five League appearances for the Owls before signing for non-League Ipswich Town in July 1936 and ended his career with Mossley, whom he joined in the close season of 1938.

MICKY BURNS

Micky Burns was born in Preston on 21 December 1946 and began his football career as an amateur with Chorley. He joined Skelmersdale United and won an FA Amateur Cup runners-up medal with them in 1967 as well as being capped for the England Amateur side. Burns turned professional with Blackpool in May 1969 and made a scoring League debut against Portsmouth the following August. His goals helped the Seasiders back to the First Division that season, but relegation followed at the end of the 1970-71 campaign. In July 1974, Newcastle United paid £166,000 for the former schoolteacher, who has a degree in economics from Manchester University, and he ended that season with a Texaco Cup-winners' medal. Burns and Irving Nattrass were in the Newcastle team

that lost to Manchester City in the 1976 League Cup Final. He left St James' Park in August 1979, after over 150 appearances, and became player-coach at Cardiff City. Burns could not settle in Wales, however, and two months later he moved to Middlesbrough for £72,000, the same figure that Cardiff had paid for him. He scored on his debut for 'Boro, at Old Trafford in October, but missed some of the season because of a back injury. When his playing career ended after 67 senior appearances for Middlesbrough, in which he scored 24 goals, Burns coached the juniors at Ayresome Park but, working without a contract, he was sacked in November 1982, as part of the club's economy drive. He was later involved in a YTS football training scheme in Darlington.

GEORGE CAMSELL

Centre-forward George Camsell will always be remembered as the man who scored a record 59 League goals when Middlesbrough stormed away with the Second Division championship in 1926-27, a figure which stands second only to Dixie Dean's 60 for Everton the following season. Camsell was born at Framwellgate Moor, County Durham, on 27 November 1902 and made 21 Third Division North appearances for Durham City before joining Middlesbrough in October 1925, for £600. In his early days he was an outside-left but made little impression and might have joined Barnsley for £200, but the Colliers found it difficult to raise the money. Camsell's career as a centre-forward at Ayresome Park took off after he came into the side for the fifth game of 1926-27, when 'Boro were struggling after a disastrous start. Middlesbrough won nine of their next ten games and by the end of the season they were back in Division One and Camsell had his astonishing record. He was a brave, two-footed centre-forward and it is surprising that he won only nine full England caps, especially as he responded with 18 goals in those international

appearances. He possessed excellent ball-control and would try a shot from any angle if he could see a half-chance. In a long line of great 'Boro centre-forwards — Common, Elliott and Clough to name but three — George Camsell surely stands at the top of the list. He won a second Division Two championship medal with 'Boro in 1928-29 and also represented the Football League. Camsell retired during World War Two and between 1944 and 1963 served Middlesbrough as chief scout, coach and assistant secretary respectively. He died, after a long illness, in Middlesbrough General Hospital on 7 March 1966. His overall career figures for Middlesbrough are truly monumental — 345 goals in 453 League and Cup matches.

GEORGE CARR

One of the four Carr brothers to play League football for Middlesbrough, George Carr was the only one not to begin his career with South Bank. Mostly an inside-forward, he signed for Bradford in 1916 and when 'Boro tried to tempt him from Park Avenue, it was rumoured that he would not consider the matter until they awarded his brothers, Jackie and Willie, benefit games. Only the Football League could sanction such games and George eventually signed for 'Boro in June 1919. Jackie and Willie got their reward in April 1922, when they shared a

£650 benefit game with Andy Wilson. George Carr's time at Ayresome Park was not a particularly happy period of his career and he was often barracked by the crowd. In March 1924 he moved to Leicester City for £2,300 and spent 11 happy years at Filbert Street, three as captain. He won a Second Division championship medal in his first season, missing only one game. Despite breaking a leg against Leeds United in 1925, he recovered and ended his League career with a move to Stockport County in 1932. Carr later played for Nuneaton Town and spent seven years as manager of Cheltenham Town before returning to Teesside as a Leicester City scout. He managed the Black Lion Hotel in North Ormesby for a spell and coached South Bank in the late 1940s. For 'Boro he made 70 senior appearances, scoring 23 goals.

JACKIE CARR

John 'Jackie' Carr was the most famous of five footballing brothers, four of whom played League soccer. Born at South Bank on 26 November 1891, he was playing for South Bank East End when Sunderland rejected him as being too small. In 1910, South Bank reached the FA Amateur Cup Final and Jackie Carr, with brothers Harry and Willie, were in their team which lost to Royal Marine Light Infantry at Bishop Auckland. Jackie, a tee-totaller and non-smoker, joined Middlesbrough in 1910. Offered £3 per week, he said he could earn more by following his trade as a gas-fitter. 'Boro upped his wages by 10s (50p) and he signed. Carr scored twice on his debut, against Nottingham Forest at Ayresome Park in January 1911, although that was the only game he played that season. Local folklore has it that Carr, who weighed only 9st, had his jersey and shorts 'tightened' with safety pins for the big occasion. During World War One he served in the Royal Engineers and in the first post-war season he was capped by England against Ireland. Injured in his second, and last, international, against Wales in 1923, he contracted pneumonia later that year but recovered and was a key figure in 'Boro's two Second Division titles of the 1920s. In 1929, after 19 years at 'Boro in which he had scored

81 goals in 449 League and Cup games, he moved to Blackpool for £500 and helped the Seasiders win promotion to Division One in 1930. A year later he became player-coach of Hartlepools United and managed them from 1932 to 1935. Carr also managed Tranmere Rovers and Darlington before World War Two. During the war he worked at Head Wrightson, but died suddenly on 10 May 1942 and is buried in Normanby cemetery.

BRIAN CLOUGH

Brian Clough made his name in two very distinct phases of his career, first as a goalscoring centre-forward with Middlesbrough and Sunderland, then as one of the game's most successful post-war managers. Clough was born in Grove Hill, Middlesbrough, on 21 March 1935, one of nine children. He worked as a clerk with ICI and played for Billingham Synthonia and Great Broughton before joining Middlesbrough as an amateur in November 1951. Clough, 'oozing confidence to shoot from every angle,' became a full-time professional in May 1952 and made his League debut in September 1955, against Barnsley, when 'Boro were in the middle of an injury crisis. Despite an impressive season, he put in the first of many transfer requests, but manager Bob Dennison turned them all down flat. Despite being the Second Division's leading scorer for three seasons in a row, Clough could not help Middlesbrough to promotion, but his tally of 254 goals in 271 games for 'Boro and Sunderland is still a post-war

TOM COCHRANE

Outside-left Tom Cochrane served Middlesbrough for the last three seasons before the Football League was suspended upon the outbreak of World War Two. Those were relatively heady days for 'Boro, who finished seventh, fifth and fourth respectively in Division One, and Cochrane played his part in a side which might have gone on to enjoy even greater success had war not intervened. Born at Newcastle upon Tyne on 7 October 1908, he began with St Peter's Albion in the Tyneside League and had trials with Hull City and Sheffield Wednesday before joining Leeds United in August 1928. Once he had won over Leeds' fickle fans, Cochrane performed like a world-beater at Elland Road and was one of the keys to their promotion to Division One in 1932. After 244 League appearances for United he was transferred to 'Boro in October 1936 and made his League debut at home to Liverpool, scoring in a 3-3 draw. In May 1939, his job at Middlesbrough done, with 16 goals in 81 League and Cup games, he moved to Bradford but retired after a few wartime games with the Park Avenue club. Tom Cochrane died in Cleveland in 1976.

ALF COMMON

Alf Common will always be known as the first footballer to be transferred for a four-figure fee, when he moved from Sunderland to Middlesbrough for £1,000 in February 1905. Common, who was born in Millfield, Sunderland, played for South Hylton Juniors and Jarrow before joining the Wearsiders. In 1901 he was transferred to Sheffield United for £325 and won an FA Cup-winners' medal with the Blades in 1902 and two England caps in 1903-04. In the 1904 close season he returned to Sunderland, joining the Roker club for a record fee of £520. Seven months later, Middlesbrough broke the transfer record by paying Sunderland what was then the remarkable sum of £1,000 for Common's signature. 'Boro were denounced for 'buying' their way out

record. For 'Boro alone he netted a remarkable 204 goals in only 222 games. It was strange that he was capped only twice for England, though he failed to score on either occasion. In November 1959 came the infamous 'round robin' incident when nine of his teammates signed a petition asking for Clough to be relieved of the captaincy. Again, a transfer request was denied. In July 1961, however, Clough finally left Ayresome Park for Sunderland, although the £45,000 move upset many 'Boro fans. In two seasons with Second Division Sunderland he scored 53 goals, before an injury suffered against Bury on Boxing Day 1962 virtually ended his playing career. After a spell on Sunderland's coaching staff, Clough became manager of Hartlepool United. He rejuvenated that club before taking Derby County from Division Two to League Champions, with his old 'Boro colleague Peter Taylor as his assistant. There followed a spell at Brighton and 44 unhappy days as manager of Leeds United before Clough took over Nottingham Forest and guided them from the Second Division to European Cup winners. He was the first British manager to pay £1 million for a player — Trevor Francis — and took Forest to two League Cup Final successes as well as their League Championship and European victories, although an FA Cup Final win always eluded him. In May 1993, with Forest dropping out of the FA Premier League along with Middlesbrough, Clough resigned in controversial circumstances amidst newspaper accusations about his private life. It was a sad end to a truly magnificent career in football.

TERRY COCHRANE

Terry Cochrane was born in Killyleagh, Northern Ireland, on 23 January 1953 and became a labourer in a tannery when he left school, playing part-time football for Derry City in the Irish League. At the age of 17 he had a trial with Nottingham Forest but failed to impress and, two years later, suffered a similar rejection by Everton. He was laying electric cables and supplementing his wages by playing for another Irish League club, Linfield, when the Linfield boss, Bertie Peacock, switched Cochrane from his usual midfield position to the wing. Thereafter, Cochrane's fortunes improved and his form so impressed Burnley that the Turf Moor club paid £38,000 for his signature in October 1976. After 67 League appearances (13 goals) for the Clarets, he was transferred to Middlesbrough in October 1978, when manager John Neal paid a club record fee of £238,000. Neal rated Cochrane as one of the top wingers in the League and he showed great form at Ayresome Park, teasing and tormenting defenders with his tricky ball skills. In October 1983, he moved to Gillingham and later played for Millwall and Hartlepool on a non-contract basis before helping Billingham Synthonia to win the Northern League title in 1988-89. Cochrane won 19 of his 26 Northern Ireland caps when he was with 'Boro, for whom he scored 12 goals in 128 senior appearances (12 of those games as a substitute).

of the relegation zone and a transfer-fee limit was enforced. Common, meanwhile, scored a penalty at Bramall Lane to help Middlesbrough achieve their first away win for two years. Capped again whilst with 'Boro, Common was an aggressive forward, once described as 'brawny and full of stamina'. He weighed around 13st, yet was deceptively quick. He lost the Middlesbrough captaincy in September 1907 and was fined £10 by the club for 'drunkenness and violent behaviour'. In August 1910, Common moved to Woolwich Arsenal for £100 before being transferred to Preston in December 1912. He won a Second Division championship medal with Preston and later took a pub in Darlington. Common retired in 1943 and died in the town on 3 April 1946. For 'Boro he scored 65 goals in 178 League and Cup games.

COLIN COOPER

Colin Cooper, born in Middlesbrough on 28 February 1967, is a former apprentice who joined 'Boro on the YTS scheme. As a schoolboy he played for Kelloe Under-11s and Bishop Auckland Boys and had trials at Ayresome Park as well as for Newcastle United and Crystal Palace, but it was Middlesbrough who won the race for his signature. Making his first-team debut in the 1985-86 season, Cooper gave some impressive performances as the club's regular left-back, although a naturally right-footed player. Winner of three Barclay's Young Eagle of the Month awards, he was capped several times by England Under-21s and played for his country in the first-leg of the European Championship semi-final in France. Cooper suffered with stress fractures to his right foot, before moving to Millwall in July 1991 for £300,000, to rejoin Bruce Rioch after 223 senior games for Middlesbrough. New Millwall manager Mick McCarthy successfully converted Cooper into a central defender and immediately his transfer value rocketed almost to the £1 million mark, attracting the attention of clubs like Arsenal and Chelsea before Frank Clark spent £1.5 million to take him to Nottingham Forest in June 1993.

TERRY COOPER

Castleford-born Terry Cooper was an attacking left winger as a schoolboy and played for Ferrybridge Amateurs whilst he served his apprenticeship as a colliery fitter. He failed to impress in a trial at Wolves before joining Leeds United as a 16-year-old apprentice. He signed full-time professional forms in July 1962 and it was Don Revie who converted him into an attacking full-back. Cooper played a great part in Leeds' success story. He won the first of 20 full caps in 1969 and was one of England's stars in the 1970 Mexico World Cup Finals. In April 1972, he broke a leg but returned to action and won another cap. Cooper made 350 appearances for Leeds and scored 11 goals, including the winner in the 1967 League Cup Final. He joined his former Leeds teammate, Jack Charlton, at Middles-

brough in March 1975, for £50,000, but things turned sour when he refused to accompany the club on their Norwegian tour in 1978. 'Boro suspended him and he asked to go on the transfer list with a year of his contract still to run. After 123 first-team appearances for Middlesbrough, Cooper joined another Leeds United old boy, Norman Hunter at Bristol City but stayed only one season before moving to Bristol Rovers, first as a player, then as player-manager. Controversially dismissed from Eastville, Cooper teamed up with Billy Bremner, yet another former Leeds player, at Doncaster before returning to Bristol City as player-manager. Cooper guided City to two Wembley appearances in Freight/Rover Trophy Finals. He joined the board at Ashton Gate (he was English football's first player-director) but eventually left the club to manage first Exeter City, then Birmingham City from 1991, leading them to promotion from the Third Division.

JOHN CRAGGS

Stan Anderson returned to his former club, Newcastle United, to bring stocky John Craggs to Ayresome Park in August 1971 for £60,000, a sizeable fee for a player who was not even a regular in United's senior side. Craggs, a former England Youth international, joined United in December 1965 but found his progress checked by the consistency of the brilliant David Craig, who limited Craggs to 50 appearances in six years at St James' Park. When Jack Charlton took over as 'Boro manager he called Craggs 'the best attacking right-back

in the business'. He was, indeed, a polished defender who liked to make penetrative, overlapping runs into the opponents' half and, as a result, he scored some spectacular goals for 'Boro. One critic described him as playing 'with a calm assurance, indulging in delightful precision passing'. He was called 'Ted' by his teammates after someone spotted a letter arrive at the club addressed to him and quoting his full name of John Edward Craggs. A keen sportsman, he plays golf, cricket, table-tennis and snooker and is also an accomplished guitarist. With over 400 League appearances to his credit, he was awarded a benefit game against his old club, Newcastle United, before returning to St James' Park on a free transfer in the summer of 1982. In December 1988, after a spell with Darlington, he teamed up again with his old Newcastle teammate, Bobby Moncur, the manager of Hartlepool United. Craggs went to the Victoria Ground as youth-team coach. For Middlesbrough he made 473 first-team appearances, scoring 13 goals. He is now working for his former playing colleague, Willie Maddren, at Maddren's sports shop in the Teesside Park shopping complex.

JOHNNY CROSSAN

Johnny Crossan first caught the headlines when he was alleged to have been paid whilst an amateur with Irish League club, Coleraine. Peter Doherty brought him to England to sign for Bristol City, but when his registration forms were sent to the Football League for approval, they were refused and Crossan returned to his Londonderry home — he was born there on 29 November 1938 — and was later banned from playing football in England. Determined to seek a higher grade of soccer, Crossan signed for the Dutch club, Sparta Rotterdam, and later played Belgian League football with Standard Liege, for whom he also appeared in the European Cup. The

Football League ban was eventually lifted and in October 1962, Crossan signed for Sunderland, for £27,000. He was in the side which clinched promotion to Division One for the Wearsiders in 1964 and in January 1965, Manchester City paid £40,000 for his midfield skills. He skippered City back to the First Division but, after one season in the top flight, he found his place threatened by Bell and Young. City sold him to Middlesbrough for £35,000 — 'Boro's record fee — in August 1967. During 1968-69 he suffered so badly from insomnia that he received hospital treatment and later had major abdominal surgery, so his stay at Ayresome Park was not altogether successful, although he managed nine goals in 63 senior games for Middlesbrough. Winner of 24 Northern Ireland caps, Crossan was released by 'Boro at the end of the 1969-70 season and returned to Belgium to play for Tongren FC.

DAVE CUMMING

Early in the 1936-37 season, Middlesbrough tried to buy Grimsby Town goalkeeper Jim Tweedy as a replacement for Fred Gibson, but Tweedy was happy to stay at Blundell Park. 'Boro switched their attentions to Arbroath's Dave Cumming, who signed for the Ayresome club in October. Cumming, who was born on 6 May 1910, started in junior football with Hall Russell in his home town and joined Aberdeen in 1929. He spent four seasons at Pittodrie before going to Arbroath on a free transfer. He enjoyed immediate success at Gayfield Park and Middlesbrough had to pay £3,000 to sign him, which made Cumming the most expensive goalkeeper to leave Scotland. Cumming and Tom Cochrane, newly transferred from Leeds United, made their debuts in a 3-3 draw against Liverpool at Ayresome Park. Cumming soon adapted to the English game and was capped for Scotland against England in 1938. He won several wartime caps and was the only 'Boro player to guest for Newcastle United. In December 1947, he was sent-off for striking Arsenal's Leslie Compton. Cumming handed his jersey to Johnny Spuhler and

walked off before the referee could dismiss him. He played his last game, at home to Blackpool, that month when he dislocated a kneecap. Cumming made 157 League and FA Cup appearances for Middlesbrough.

DAVID CURRIE

David Currie was born in Stockton on 27 November 1962 and played for Mandale Juniors before having trials with Southampton. But it was 'Boro who signed him as a professional in February 1982. He made his debut as a playing substitute at the end of the season, against Swansea at Ayresome Park. Middlesbrough won 2-1 but other results confirmed their relegation into Division Two. Currie went on to score 30 goals in the next four seasons at Ayresome Park but he was released by Bruce Rioch, to be eagerly snapped up by neighbours Darlington on 17 June 1986. In two seasons at Feethams, he upped his goals return to 33 and immediately attracted interest from other clubs. Barnsley manager Allan Clarke, himself a renowned goalscorer at all levels, realised Currie's potential and paid out a club record figure of £150,000 to take him to Oakwell in February 1988. He repaid a huge chunk of the transfer fee by finishing that season as Barnsley's top scorer. A handsome return of 23 goals in 56 League games at Oakwell interested Nottingham Forest manager Brian Clough and the player duly signed for First Division Forest in January 1990. Alas, he never hit the big-time with Forest, for he was to spend only seven frustrating months at the City Ground, starting only four League games in that period. Languishing in Forest's reserve side he was grateful when Oldham Athletic manager Joe Royle came in with a £450,000 offer — a record outgoing transfer fee for the Latics — and Currie moved to Boundary Park in August 1990. He spent only one full season with Oldham before one of his former clubs, Barnsley, took him on again in September 1991. He was loaned to Rotherham United during 1992-93. He made 105/20 League and Cup appearances for 'Boro.

STEWART DAVIDSON

Stewart Davidson, who was born in Aberdeen on 1 June 1889, was a legal clerk by profession. He first played for Aberdeen Shamrocks and was signed by Middlesbrough manager Tom McIntosh from Aberdeen on 17 April 1913, for £675. Davidson made his 'Boro debut at right-half — the position in which he played most of his games for the club — on 6 May 1913, against Manchester City at Hyde Road. During World War One he guested for Chelsea before joining up. Although wounded in action, he was able to resume his football career when the war ended in 1918 and took over as club captain from George Elliott in 1920. His loyal service to Middlesbrough was rewarded with a benefit match against Derby County on 20 November 1920. He was capped for Scotland against England in 1921 but in May 1923, 'Boro felt they could release him. Davidson appealed against the £500 fee which the club wanted and the Football League reduced it to £250. His former club, Aberdeen, stepped in and Stewart returned home. He was later player-manager of Forress Mechanics and coached for the Kent County FA before joining his former Middlesbrough colleague, Billy Birrell, who was then manager at Chelsea. Davidson remained as assistant manager at Stamford Bridge until his retirement in July 1957. He died on Boxing Day 1960. For Middlesbrough, Davidson made 216 first-team appearances.

BILLY DAY

Billy Day, who was born in Middlesbrough on 27 December 1936, was an amateur with Sheffield Wednesday but made no first-team appearances for the Owls before signing professional forms for 'Boro in May 1955.

Day, who had been playing for South Bank Juniors, made his League debut at outside-right against Leicester City on 8 October 1955 and went on to serve Middlesbrough well for 131 League and FA Cup games, scoring 21 goals. When he was posted to Germany with the Army on National Service, manager Bob Dennison considered him so vital a member of the team that he arranged for the club to pay for Day to be flown home for matches every week. After making over 100 League appearances for 'Boro, Day had the misfortune to break his leg in a practice match at the club's training ground in Hutton Road. Eager to

get back into action, his return to League duty was a little premature and he did not allow the leg sufficient time to heal. Dennison eventually agreed to his transfer request and Newcastle United paid £12,000 for Day in March 1962. He scored on his League debut for the Magpies, at home to Scunthorpe United, but it was his only League goal for them. Still dogged by leg trouble, he moved to Peterborough United in April 1963. However, after only 17 League games for Posh he signed for Cambridge United, then in the Southern League. He recovered his form, but a bout of pneumonia ended his playing career and, at the age of 29, he returned to Teesside and became a successful bookmaker.

LINDY DELAPENHA

Lindy Delapenha was one of those footballers whose name was always being misspelt, but the player himself confirms the above as the correct version. Delapenha, whose first name was really Lloyd, was born in Jamaica on 25 May 1927 and, after being demobbed from the RAF, he had a trial with

Arsenal. He did not impress the Highbury management, however, and in April 1948 was allowed to move to Portsmouth. At that time Pompey had probably the best side in their history and Delapenha was restricted to only seven League appearances. In April 1950, Portsmouth were happy to let him go to Middlesbrough and it was at Ayresome Park that his career really took off. As a fast, clever and powerful winger or inside-forward, playing in the same front line as Wilf Mannion, he soon impressed. He was Middlesbrough's leading scorer in 1952-53, 1953-54 and 1955-56 and his sturdy physique — he was a stocky 5ft 7in tall — made him particularly effective in the rough and tumble around the penalty area. He enjoyed a good strike rate for 'Boro — he was also something of a penalty expert — and netted 93 goals in 270 senior games before joining Mansfield Town in June 1958 and he also gave the Stags good service with 27 goals in 115 League appearances before retiring from League soccer in 1960. He later played for Burton Albion and Heanor Town before returning to Jamaica, progressing to a senior position with the sports department of the Jamaican Broadcasting Corporation.

RONNIE DICKS

Ronnie Dicks was once described as 'a barrel-chested 90-minute footballer'. Born in Kennington on 13 April 1924, Dicks first played for Dulwich Hamlet and signed as an amateur for Middlesbrough in April 1943, whilst doing military service on Teesside. A month later he became a professional and played his early games for the club as a winger. Despite making many wartime appearances, he had to wait until August 1947 — the second season after the resumption of the League — for his senior debut in peacetime. He impressed in that first game, against Manchester United at Ayresome Park, and it was the start of an

illustrious career with 'Boro. He developed into something of a utility player — David Jack called him, 'The Handyman of Ayresome Park' — but settled down at wing-half or full-back. A long throw-in specialist, he had 'speed, a deceptive swerve and the ability to kick with either foot'. He did chase the ball but preferred to 'loiter' until it came his way. A chipped ankle-bone against Derby in 1949-50 kept him out for a month and an Achilles tendon injury later cost him a place in the Football League side. Yet another injury saw Dicks miss an England 'B' cap. He retired in 1958 and still lives in Middlesbrough. Younger brother, Alan, played League football for Chelsea, Southend and Brighton and managed Bristol City. Ronnie Dicks made 334 League and Cup appearances for Middlesbrough, scoring ten goals.

DERRICK DOWNING

Derrick Downing was born in Doncaster on 3 November 1945 and worked as a clerk after leaving school. He played some games at junior and reserve level for Doncaster Rovers before signing for Frickley Colliery and then joining Middlesbrough, where Raich Carter was manager, in February 1965. Downing had plenty of success as a forward with 'Boro and also made something of a name for himself as a long throw-in expert. He could reach the far post with the ball when taking throw-ins and also scored several goals with brave, diving headers. A prime example of this was the one he netted against West Ham in the FA Cup in 1970. In May 1972, Downing found himself surplus to manager Stan Anderson's requirements and was transferred to Orient. He made exactly 100

full League appearances for the Brisbane Road club, who converted him to full-back. In July 1975 he returned to his native Yorkshire to play for York City (47 League appearances and two goals) before ending his career with Hartlepool United, whom he joined in July 1977. He made 40 League appearances and scored four goals for United. For 'Boro he made 199/12 senior appearances, scoring 48 goals.

GEORGE ELLIOTT

George Washington Elliott, one of a long line of Middlesbrough international centre-forwards, was born at Sunderland in 1889, the son of a seafaring captain. His father later set up in Middlesbrough with a tugboat company and, later still, managed the American Oil Company in the town. Young George was a brilliant student at Middlesbrough High School but, although his family wanted him to go to Cambridge University, the boy was a compulsive sportsman (he boxed under an assumed name) and after playing for Redcar Crusaders, he helped South Bank win the Northern League title in 1908. Late on 3 May 1909, Elliott was awakened from his bed and signed for Middlesbrough in a nearby hotel. He played his first few games for 'Boro as an inside-right. The first of three full England caps came in 1913-14, against Ireland at Ayresome Park, and that season his 31 goals made him Division One's leading scorer. He still holds the club record for most goals in a single game (11 for the Reserves in a 14-1 win over Houghton Rovers) and during World War One he guested for Bradford, Fulham and Celtic. Starting in 1910-11, Elliott was 'Boro's leading scorer in seven out of nine peacetime seasons. His last appearance was at Southampton in 1924-25 after which, despite offers from Sunderland and Newcastle, he retired. He had made 365 senior appearances for 'Boro, scoring 213 goals. George Elliott resumed his job as a cargo superintendent at Middlesbrough docks. He

died, aged 59, in Middlesbrough General Hospital in November 1948 and is buried in Acklam cemetery.

MICKY FENTON

Micky Fenton, who possessed a 'powerful shot with both feet' and was 'a very strong header of the ball', was born at Portrack, Stockton, on 30 October 1913 and Middlesbrough was his only professional club. He first played for Princess Street Juniors, then moved to South Bank East End. Offered a

month's trial with Wolves, he returned after one day. Fenton signed professional forms for Middlesbrough in March 1933, making a scoring debut in 'Boro's 4-0 home win against Blackburn Rovers. One of his weaknesses was that he was 'guilty of fiddling with the ball' in the opponents' penalty area and, when confronted with too much to do, he would try a shot instead of passing. He played once for England, against Scotland in 1938, and toured South Africa with the FA in 1939. During the war, Fenton served in the RAF and played in one unofficial international before resuming normal football in August 1946, when he was 33. Two months later, Everton manager Theo Kelly tried to sign Fenton as the replacement for Tommy Lawton, who had been transferred to Chelsea. The Middlesbrough team left for Derby and manager David Jack fuelled speculation that Fenton was about to leave by dropping him and playing Alex Linwood at centre-forward. Billy Kelly, 'Boro's chairman, said that the player should decide and Fenton remained at Ayresome Park. Altogether he scored 162 goals in 269 League and Cup games for Middlesbrough.

ance, against West Brom at The Hawthorns, he went on to play in 231 League and Cup games for the club, scoring 51 goals, and won 25 caps altogether as a Middlesbrough player. He was born in Dublin on 16 December 1929 and had played for the League of Ireland before joining 'Boro. An inside-forward, he would often jink around two or three defenders in the penalty area before sometimes skying the ball over the bar. It is alleged that on one occasion, an exasperated Brian Clough told him: "You make the bloody goals — I'll do the scoring." Fitzsimons moved to Lincoln City in March 1955 and made seven League appearances, winning his last cap, before a transfer to Mansfield Town at the beginning of the 1959-60 season. He retired in 1961, after 61 League games for the Stags. Fitzsimons later coached the League of Ireland representative side.

week suspension, but soon proved his worth. Foggon ended the 1973-74 promotion season as 'Boro's leading scorer with 19 League goals, many of them coming as a result of his deceptive turn of speed. He was a lethal finisher, bursting through from deep positions. During the club's 1975 world tour, Foggon asked for a transfer, claiming that he did not fit in with 'Boro's style. Manchester United manager Tommy Docherty flew to Montreal to see Foggon play for Hartford Bi-Centennials in the NASL and the player joined United for £27,000. By September 1976, however, he was with Sunderland. After only seven League games for the Wearsiders he moved to Southend in June 1977, but returned to the North-East for a loan spell with Hartlepool before going to non-League Consett in August 1978. He scored 49 goals in 136 senior games (12 as a substitute) for Middlesbrough. Foggan, who now lives in Jarrow, ran a pub in Spennymoor for five years before becoming a contracts manager with a North-Eastern security firm.

ARTHUR FITZSIMONS

Arthur Fitzsimons and Peter Desmond hit the football headlines in September 1949, when they played for the Republic of Ireland against Finland in a World Cup qualifying game in Dublin, even though they had still to make their first-team debuts for Middlesbrough. Four months earlier, 'Boro manager David Jack had signed both players from Irish club Shelbourne, paying £18,000 for Fitzsimons. Yet, even after winning his first cap, Fitzsimons had to wait a further eight months before making his League debut. After that first appear-

ALAN FOGGON

Alan Foggon was born in West Pelton, County Durham, on 23 February 1950. A former England Youth international, he signed for Newcastle United in November 1967 and played a major part in their Fairs Cup win in 1969, scoring a spectacular goal in the second leg of the Final against Újpesti Dózsa. Foggon made 54 League appearances for Newcastle, scoring 13 goals, before being transferred to Cardiff City in August 1971. Cardiff were fighting to avoid relegation to the Third Division and he played only 14 times for them before signing for Middlesbrough in October 1972, for £10,000, after a week's wrangling between the clubs. He returned to the North-East under a three-

BILLY FORREST

Billy Forrest, the eldest of seven brothers and three sisters, played his early football for Haddington and Musselborough Juniors, then turned out for Edinburgh St Bernard's. Middlesbrough were one of several clubs alerted to his potential and in March 1929, 'Boro manager Peter

McWilliam met Forrest, who was a cooper by trade, and his father in the North British Hotel, Edinburgh, where the young player signed for the Ayresome Park club. He made his debut as a left-half against Manchester United in January 1930 and played most of his games for 'Boro in that position. McWilliam later asked Forrest's opinion of a youngster called Bob Baxter, who had just scored five goals in a Scottish junior game, and Forrest played an active part in Baxter signing for Middlesbrough. The two Scots became firm friends and married sisters, Forrest 'eloping' to Gretna Green to be wed. When he retired in 1945, Billy Forrest coached the juniors at Middlesbrough until his appointment as Darlington manager. He left the Skernesiders at the end of the 1949-50 season and later ran the Station Hotel, Billingham. In 1956, he was partially paralysed as the result of an accident which led to his early death. For 'Boro he made 333 first-team appearances.

REG FREEMAN

Reg Freeman, a native of Birkenhead, was starring as a full-back with Northern Nomads, one of the leading amateur clubs of the day, at the end of World War One. He joined First Division Oldham Athletic in 1920, becoming captain of the side during the 1922-23 season, and his sterling displays saw him play in an England trial. He was also named as reserve for the Football League against the League of Ireland. Middlesbrough paid £3,600 for Freeman in May 1923 and he proved to be an excellent purchase. In a Middlesbrough career that spanned seven seasons — which included two Second Division championships — he was a key figure. Freeman was transferred to Rotherham United on 5 September 1930, for £150, and was appointed player-manager at Millmoor in January 1934. He had no money to buy experienced players but moulded untried youngsters into a team which took Rotherham to the League North Third Division championship during the war. In May 1951, the Millers clinched promotion from the Third Division North with seven points to spare. Freeman later managed Sheffield United, signing a five-year contract in August 1952, but after an illness lasting several months he died on 4 August 1955. His appearances for Middlesbrough totalled 186 in League and Cup.

BILL GATES

Bill Gates, was born at Ferryhill on 8 May 1944 and captained England Youth before joining Middlesbrough as an amateur in October 1959. He made headlines by playing for 'Boro's first team when he was a 16-year-old and still at Spennymoor Grammar School, but was initially torn between professional football and following a career as an accountant. Football won, although he continued his studies, and he made his debut against Swansea Town in 1961 before turning professional later that year. During his 13-year stay with Middlesbrough, he experienced some fluctuating fortunes, sometimes winning a place only when other players were injured. Nevertheless, he made over 300 appearances, mostly at centre-half, although he could play in a number of other positions. Gates suffered a double fracture of his jaw during a League Cup tie against Manchester United, but recovered to maintain his 'tough guy' image. He enjoyed a testimonial game against League Champions Leeds United in May 1974, when over 30,000 fans came to support him, and in July that year he was released after making 329 senior appearances for the club. He played cricket for Normanby Hall and went into business after his retirement from football, concentrating on running his sports outfitting shops, the sale of which in 1989 made him a wealthy man. His younger brother, Eric, played for Ipswich Town and England.

JIMMY GORDON

Jimmy Gordon began his career with Wishaw Juniors — he was born at Fauldhouse on 23 October 1915 — and broke into the Football League with Newcastle United, for whom he signed in April 1935. Gordon, a hard-tackling, constructive right-half, made 132 League appearances for the Magpies before his transfer to Middlesbrough in November 1945. Like so many

players of his generation, Gordon lost valuable years of his career to the war, but Newcastle certainly made a mistake in releasing him, even though one of their directors called him 'only a 20-minute footballer'. His move to 'Boro extended Gordon's career by nine years and he gave the club wonderful service as a tenacious, ball-player who commanded the midfield. In all he made 253 League and Cup appearances for the club. In the early 1960s he was given charge of Middlesbrough's junior side before joining Blackburn Rovers as the Ewood Park club's reserve-team trainer. When Brian Clough and Peter Taylor took over at Derby County, they remembered Gordon, who was the Rams' trainer when they won the League Championship in 1972. Gordon later shared in Nottingham Forest's European Cup success — again with Clough and Taylor — and he was allowed to lead Forest out at Wembley for a League Cup Final.

TOM GRIFFITHS

Welsh international centre-half Tom Griffiths was born in Wrexham in 1906 and joined his local league club in 1922. In 1929 he moved to Everton and spent five seasons at Goodison as a playing contemporary of Dixie Dean, although he managed only 78 League and Cup appearances for the Merseysiders. In December 1931, Griffiths joined Bolton Wanderers for a transfer fee of more than £5,500, but the following season Bolton were relegated from Division One. 'Boro manager Peter McWilliam persuaded the Trotters to part with Griffiths for £4,500 in May 1933. His move to Ayresome Park saw him embark upon the best period of his career and 50 years later, there are still those who regard Tom Griffiths as the best centre-half to have played for the club. When he challenged for a ball he seemed to 'hang in the air a little longer than his opponent' and he 'rarely failed in a tackle.' One weakness, though, was poor distribution of the ball. After injury to regular full-back Jack Jennings, Griffiths played right-back for six games and won rave reviews. In November 1935, Aston Villa — who were spending heavily in a bid to avoid relegation — signed

Griffiths for nearly £6,000. But Villa still went down and he was thus relegated with three different clubs in seven seasons (he was in the Everton side which dropped into Division Two in 1929-30.) Towards the end of his playing days, the former Welsh international skipper — he was capped 21 times altogether — joined Wrexham as player-coach and became a publican in the town. An accomplished celloist, he was later appointed a director at the Racecourse Ground and died in Wrexham on Christmas Day 1981. He made 92 senior appearances for Middlesbrough.

GARY HAMILTON

Winger Gary Hamilton, who was born in Glasgow on 27 December 1965, attended All Saints' School in that city and played for the Eastercraigs youth team, the side which produced Tony McAndrew and Everton's Graeme Sharp. Middlesbrough's Scottish scout recommended Hamilton for a day's trial at Ayresome Park in 1981 and he was asked to return for a fortnight's trial period before 'Boro signed him as an apprentice professional in January 1982. Malcolm Allison gave him his first chance of League football, against Bolton Wanderers and he became a full-time professional in May 1983. The following year, Hamilton toured Russia with the Scotland Youth side and went on to win seven caps altogether. He had a brief spell on the transfer list in May 1986 and when Middlesbrough dropped into the Third Division, Charlton Athletic offered him a two-year contract, but he decided to ride out 'Boro's troubles. Hamilton suffered with knee injuries in the late 1980s and had not played in 'Boro's first team since May 1989 when he was loaned to Darlington in September 1991. Sadly, the best part of his career had come before his 25th birthday. He retired in March 1992 after making 260 appearances for 'Boro (12 as a substitute) and scoring 27 goals. He played

some games on loan to Darlington but he announced his enforced retirement from the game at the Manchester United League Cup semi-final at Ayresome Park in March 1992. He later played some games for non-League Billingham Town and is due a testimonial game during 1993-94 season.

GEORGE HARDWICK

George Hardwick was one of the game's best-known post-war players. Capped 13 times for England and captain of the Great Britain side which met the Rest of Europe in 1947, Hardwick was a fine left-back who served Middlesbrough in the years immediately after World War Two. He was born in Saltburn on 2 February 1920, into a footballing family, for his grandfather, Frank Hardwick, had played for Middlesbrough Ironopolis in the early 1890s. George first played for South Bank East End Juniors and when he left school he began work as a costing clerk with Dorman Long. He signed amateur forms for Middlesbrough in October 1935 and became a full-time professional in April 1937. Arsenal and Rangers had also shown an interest, but young Hardwick's sole ambition was to play for 'Boro. He scored an own-goal in the first minute of his debut game, at home to Bolton in December 1937, but made only a handful of appearances before the outbreak of war, during which he served as a sergeant in RAF Bomber Command. He appeared in two wartime Wembley Cup Finals as a Chelsea guest and recovered from injuries to both legs, suffered during an air-raid on his RAF base on the Isle of Sheppey, to play in 17 wartime internationals. He skippered England in every one of his full internationals. In November 1950, after 166 senior games for 'Boro in peacetime, he joined Oldham Athletic as player-manager for £15,000 (after turning down a player-coach's job with Everton). He took Oldham into Division Two but they dropped back into Division Three North and in April 1956 he quit after Oldham had slumped still

further and there was no money to strengthen the team. Later, Hardwick worked as a coach to the US Seventh Army's soccer team in Stuttgart and with PSV Eindhoven and the Dutch FA. From August 1961 to November 1963 he was youth-team coach at Ayresome Park. In November 1964 he took over as Sunderland manager but was ousted after only 169 days at Roker, having helped the Wearsiders achieve their highest post-war League position. From 1968 to 1970 he managed Gateshead. In May 1983, Middlesbrough finally gave Hardwick and Wilf Mannion a joint testimonial.

BILL HARRIS

Wing-half Bill Harris was on the books of Swansea Town — he was born in that town

on 31 October 1928 — but was released by the Welsh club after completing his National Service. Anxious to stay in football, he tried his luck with Llanelli and shone well enough in the Southern League to attract the attention of Hull City, who signed him for £2,000 in March 1950. The Tigers agreed to pay Llanelli an extra £250 if Harris won international honours and they eventually had to pay up, although by then Harris had moved to Middlesbrough. He made 145 League and Cup appearances for Hull before joining 'Boro for £15,000 in March 1954 and it was at Ayresome Park that he was converted to inside-forward. Middlesbrough were soon relegated but, as a cultured Second Division performer, Harris won six full caps. In March 1965, after 378 first-team appearances and 72 goals for Middlesbrough, he was transferred to Bradford City and was manager at Valley Parade before returning to the North-East to manage Stockton FC. Bill Harris died in 1989.

JOHN HENDRIE

Born in Lennoxtown on 24 October 1963, John Hendrie joined Coventry City as an apprentice in June 1980, making his League debut at 18. His opportunities during four years at Highfield Road were limited and he moved to Bradford City on a free transfer in June 1984. Hendrie was a favourite at Valley Parade, missing only one match in four seasons (173 consecutive League appearances) and winning a Third Division championship medal before a £500,000 move to Newcastle United. Alas, United were relegated in his season at St James' Park and following an unspectacular year at Leeds, where he struggled for regular

first-team football — although he played enough games to gain a Second Division championship medal in 1989-90 — he moved again (the third successive June transfer) to Middlesbrough for £550,000. Hendrie immediately settled down at Ayresome Park and became a great crowd pleaser with darting runs and accurate shooting. In 1991-92 he was briefly out of the side but returned in the New Year to play his part in both the thrilling League Cup run to the semi-final and to promotion. Hendrie scored nine goals in 'Boro's relegation season of Premier League soccer. Always an entertainer, on 5 December 1992 he scored the second senior hat-trick of his career as Middlesbrough recovered to beat high-flying Blackburn Rovers 3-2. By the end of that season, Hendrie, a former Scottish Youth international, had made 136 League and Cup appearances for 'Boro, four of them as sub, and scored 18 goals. He was voted Middlesbrough's Player of the Year for 1992-93.

JOHN HICKTON

John Hickton was born in Birmingham but moved with his family to Chesterfield as a boy and signed for Sheffield Wednesday in January 1962. He scored eight goals from centre-forward in an FA Youth Cup game, but it was at left-back that he made his League debut, against Aston Villa in March 1964. Hickton began to score regularly in

the Central League and was promoted to the first-team forward line when Wednesday were having problems up front. He responded with 21 goals in 52 appearances — he scored a hat-trick of headers against Arsenal in 1965-66 — but eventually lost his place to Jim McCalliog. He might have played at centre-half for Wednesday against Everton in the 1966 FA Cup Final. Vic Mobley had been injured in the semi-final and Hickton deputised for five games, but conceded his place to Sam Ellis for the Wembley game. The Sheffield club sold him to Middlesbrough for £20,000 in September 1966 and lived to regret their decision. Hickton was 'Boro's leading scorer for six consecutive seasons and headed the Second Division scoring list three times. In 1974, he scored 'Boro's first goal in Division One for almost 21 years and then began the second phase of his Middlesbrough career, becoming a 'target man' rather than an out and out scorer. By the time he announced his intention to retire at the end of 1976-77, he had been loaned to Hull City in January and his appearances in a Middlesbrough shirt were diminishing as he played only the occasional game as a utility man. In his testimonial game, against Sunderland in April 1977, he scored three goals in a 6-1 win for Middlesbrough and ended his League career with 185 goals in 458 senior games. Hickton later broke a leg playing in the NASL for Fort Lauderdale and then turned down a chance to return to League soccer with Hartlepool United. He played for Whitby Town in September 1979 before finally hanging up his boots. Hickton, who now lives in Chesterfield, works in insurance as well as owning some property in the Derbyshire town.

DAVID HODGSON

David Hodgson, the son of a former Northern League footballer, was born in Gateshead on 6 August 1960. He had trials with Ipswich Town, Bolton Wanderers and Sheffield Wednesday, but opted for Middlesbrough and signed apprentice forms on his 16th birthday. He was playing for 'Boro's reserve side when he was 17 and made an occasional substitute appearance in the first team before establishing himself in 1978-79, although he missed some games late in the season due to a broken toe. When he was out of action, Hodgson would delight the Holgate End crowd by standing with them to watch the team. He netted a marvellous hat-trick against Spurs in December 1980, when Middlesbrough won 4-1, and although he did not score as many goals as was perhaps expected of him, he used his speed to get past defenders and set up chances for others. In 1981, Hodgson won the first of six England Under-21 caps with Middlesbrough, but in August 1982 he followed in the footsteps of Graeme Souness and Craig Johnston, joining Liverpool for £450,000. After only 28 League appearances for the Merseysiders, however, Hodgson returned to the North-East in a £125,000 transfer to Sunderland. Norwich City signed him, also for £125,000, in July 1986, but his first-team opportunities were even more restricted at Carrow Road and he was loaned to Middlesbrough in February 1987. Alas, his old sparkle was missing and his second spell was marred by being sent off against Bristol City (he

a schoolmaster in 1912 and in the 1913-14 football season helped Willington Athletic, his home-town club, to win the Northern League championship. Holmes signed amateur forms for 'Boro in October 1912 and became a professional in April 1914, although the club allowed him to continue as a teacher. During World War One he saw active service in France as an RAMC officer and recovered from bronchial pneumonia to continue his football career. He became a schoolmaster in Middlesbrough in 1921, the same year that he was awarded a benefit by the club. Given a free transfer at the end of 1927-28, Holmes served Darlington for a further season until his retirement in 1929. In the late 1940s he was headmaster of South End School in Middlesbrough. A teetotaller and a Methodist lay preacher, he always considered football an 'interesting sideline'. Until his death in the summer of 1978, he was a regular spectator at Ayresome Park, along with Maurice Webster, his old friend and playing colleague of the 1920s. He made 174 senior appearances for 'Boro.

for whom he made 56 League appearances, and Peterborough United in the close season of 1969. He managed only 16 League games for Peterborough before retiring in 1970 after breaking a leg. His uncle, Colin Grainger, played for Sheffield United and England. For Middlesbrough, Eddie Holliday made 169 first-team appearances, scoring 25 goals.

had earlier been dismissed against Manchester City in 1980). After an unhappy spell with the Spanish club, Jerez, Hodgson returned to the Football League with Sheffield Wednesday in July 1988. In 1989 he was the subject of a £25,000 bid from Japanese club, Mazda, but later had a spell with FC Metz in the French League and in 1992 made a handful of appearances for Swansea City. For 'Boro he made 141 senior appearances (nine as sub), scoring 20 goals.

EDDIE HOLLIDAY

Outside-left Eddie Holliday was a key member of Middlesbrough's explosive attack of the late 1950s, when Billy Day, Brian Clough and Alan Peacock wrought havoc amongst Second Division defences. Holliday, who was born near Barnsley on 7 June 1939, joined Middlesbrough in June 1956. He was a fast, tidy winger whose ability to send over hard, accurate crosses brought a hatful of goals for his colleagues and earned him three full England caps as well as Under-23 and Football League representative appearances. In March 1962, Holliday was transferred to Sheffield Wednesday, but after only 55 League appearances for the Owls he rejoined 'Boro in the close season of 1965. Holliday never recaptured the heights of his first spell at Ayresome Park and in the summer of 1966 he went into the Southern League with Hereford United. He returned to League soccer with Workington in February 1968,

WALTER HOLMES

Walter 'Squire' Holmes played his early football as an outside-right, establishing a record of 38 goals for Bede College, where he was training to be a teacher. He became

BILLY HORNER

Billy Horner was once described as 'a no-nonsense, stylish wing-half'. He was born in Middlesbrough on 7 September 1942 and joined 'Boro's groundstaff in 1957, becoming a full-time professional in the autumn of 1959. He made his League debut at left-half against Leyton Orient at Brisbane Road in March 1961. Horner served 'Boro in 217 League and Cup games before being transferred to Darlington in June 1969. Many supporters thought that 'Boro manager Stan Anderson had made a mistake in allowing Horner to leave Ayresome Park, for it appeared that the player had several good years still ahead of him. He spent five

years at Feethams, making a further 200-plus appearances and then managing Darlington for a while. In 1976 he began a seven-year association with Hartlepool and was voted Fourth Division Manager of the Month in January 1980. After leaving the Victoria Ground in 1983, he had a spell as coach with York City before returning to Hartlepool for a second time in 1984. In September 1986, however, he went the way of all 'Pool managers and paid for a continued lack of success by losing his job. He was coach at GM Vauxhall Conference club, Gateshead, in December 1991.

ARTHUR HORSFIELD

England Youth international Arthur Horsfield was born in Newcastle upon Tyne on 5 July 1946 and 'Boro beat off all opposition to sign him as an apprentice on 30 July 1962; he became a full-time professional on 5 July 1963. Horsfield's breakthrough into Middlesbrough's first team came with a scoring debut against Grimsby Town in a 6-0 victory at Ayresome Park in early September 1963. His best season at the club, from a goalscoring point of view, was when his 22 League goals helped to lift 'Boro back into the Second Division at the end of the 1966-67 season. Indeed, only leading scorer John O'Rourke scored more goals in that promotion-winning season. Newcastle United manager Joe Harvey persuaded Stan Anderson to part with the player in January 1969, with only £17,550 being paid. Horsfield signed a one-year contract but played only seven League games for the Geordies before moving to Swindon Town in June 1969. At the County Ground, he reclaimed his scoring flair and in just over a century of League appearances for Town averaged a goal every other game. A move to Charlton Athletic followed in June 1972 and he spent two happy seasons at The Valley. His final League club was Watford, for whom he signed in September 1975 and stayed with them until the end of the season. He left to play for Dartford with over 150 League goals to his credit. For Middlesbrough he scored 56 goals in 121/7 League and Cup games.

JIM IRVINE

Scottish schoolboy international Jim Irvine, affectionately tagged 'Big Jim' by the fans at Ayresome Park, was born in Whitburn, Scotland, on 17 August 1940. He started on an injury-prone playing career with Dundee United as a centre-forward before signing for Middlesbrough manager Raich Carter on 26 May 1964, Carter parting with £25,000 to bring the big, burly striker to Ayresome Park. Irvine found instant success on Teesside, ending his first two seasons as the club's leading scorer. He lost his place, initially through appendicitis, then cartilage trouble and, as a consequence, was in and out of the team. Despite his goals, 'Boro were relegated to Division Three for the first time. He was in the team for the start of the following season, but lost his place and, as the side began to win, he found it difficult to regain his place. Without him, Middlesbrough regained Second Division status under new manager Stan Anderson. On 9 May 1967, Irvine was suspended for a week and put on the transfer list for an undisclosed breach of club discipline. Whilst the club was still celebrating its return to the Second Division, Irvine quietly slipped out of Ayresome Park with a £10,000 transfer to Hearts on 18 May 1967, only two days after 'Boro had clinched promotion. At Tynecastle he helped Hearts reach the Scottish Cup Final but he collided with another Hearts player in a training session and missed the Final. Three years later, he was back in English football when he signed for Fourth Division Barrow, where he enjoyed moderate success, scoring 17 goals in 67 League appearances. For Middlesbrough he hit 43 goals in 99/1 League and Cup games.

ANDY JACKSON

Andy Jackson, who was born at Cambose Mount, Scotland, joined Middlesbrough in 1910, when manager Andy Walker signed him to take the place of centre-half Bob

Young, who had been transferred to Everton. Walker made his League debut for 'Boro on 3 September 1910, against Everton at Ayresome Park. The Merseysiders, who had Young in their ranks, won 1-0. Jackson stood only 5ft 8in tall but, of course, these were not the days of the 'stopper' centre-half and his determined displays as the pivot of the Middlesbrough team eventually earned him the captaincy, when he took over from Tim Williamson. Jackson was a close friend of 'Boro centre-forward George Elliott and the men were similar in many respects, always well-groomed and smartly dressed when they went out on the town. Jackson guested for Chelsea before enlisting in the Army during World War One. He soon reached the rank of sergeant but, within days of arriving at the front line in France, he was killed in action. His death surely robbed Scotland of a future international star, who might have graced the game for some years. For Middlesbrough he played in 137 League and Cup games.

BOSCO JANKOVIC

A Yugoslav international with five caps, Bosco Jankovic was born in Sarajevo and trained as a civil lawyer. He was originally spotted by Zeljeznicar as a 13-year-old and eventually helped that club win the Yugoslav League championship in 1972. 'Boro manager John Neal sent Harold Shepherdson and Jimmy Greenhalgh to Yugoslavia to assess the player and on Shepherdson's recommendation he was offered a fortnight's trial, eventually signing from Zeljeznicar in February 1979 (Yugoslav law stipulated that players could not sign for a foreign club before the age of 28). Because of the Yugoslav season, he had an enforced winter break and it took two months to get him into shape before he was blooded into English football, the player making his First Division debut at Burnden Park. He scored some vital goals for the club — 18

in 52/10 appearances all told — and Ipswich Town will remember him for his two goals against them at Ayresome Park in early May 1981 which denied Ipswich the First Division title. John Neal, by then manager of Chelsea, tried to sign him from French club Metz, without paying Middlesbrough a fee, but 'Boro stepped in and blocked the deal. Both clubs were summoned to a Football League tribunal with secretary Harry Green and Harold Shepherdson representing Middlesbrough. 'Boro had offered Jankovic a new contract in the summer of 1981, which the player had declined with the statement that he wished to pursue his career as a civil lawyer in Yugoslavia. The tribunal ruled that if the player did return to English football, Middlesbrough, who held his Football League registration, would receive £60,000. Chelsea lost interest and pulled out of the attempted transfer.

JACK JENNINGS

Full-back Jack Jennings was a railway fireman before becoming a professional footballer. He started with Wigan Borough before joining Cardiff City and toured Canada with the FA party in 1926. Jennings hit the football headlines when he was one of three Cardiff players transferred to Middlesbrough in January 1930. Chairman Phil Bach and manager Peter McWilliam travelled to Ninian Park and after making an offer for Jennings, they were told that goalkeeper Joe Hillier and reserve winger Fred Warren were also available. A fee of £850 secured all three and each player made a firm contribution to Middlesbrough's team. Jennings made his debut at Filbert Street in a 4-1 defeat by Leicester City on 1 February 1930. He overcame a cartilage operation whilst he was at Middlesbrough to become club captain, a job he held until the arrival of Tom Griffiths. In February 1934 he was named as 12th man for the Football League team to play the Scottish League at Ibrox. His goals tally was exceptionally high for a defender because he was 'Boro's regular penalty-taker, half of his ten goals coming from the spot. In

September 1936 he was transferred to Preston North End and ended his career at Northampton Town, where he became trainer. In January 1949, he was appointed trainer to the England Amateur international team. During his time with the Cobblers, his manager at Northampton was future Middlesbrough boss, Bob Dennison. He made 205 senior appearances for 'Boro.

CRAIG JOHNSTON

Craig Johnston was born in Johannesburg on 8 December 1960, but lived most of his life in Australia, where he first saw Middlesbrough play. 'Boro were in New South Wales during their 1975 world tour, and Johnston, keen to break into League football, later wrote to Middlesbrough for a trial, along with Manchester United, Chelsea, Bolton and Fulham. 'Boro were the first to reply but, after paying his own air-fare to England, he was rejected and returned home. The following year, however, his persistence paid off and when he repeated the journey, Middlesbrough were sufficiently impressed to sign him on. Johnston, a ball-winning midfielder who liked to move forward for a crack at goal, worked hard and damaged a pelvis in his bid to reach peak fitness. He was qualified to play international football for Australia, England and Scotland but chose England and was rewarded with two Under-21 appearances. He followed Graeme Souness to Liverpool in April 1981, for a reputed £580,000 fee, and shared in some of the Merseysiders' greatest triumphs in Europe and at home. However, in 1988, with a year of his contract still to run, he caused quite a stir by announcing his retirement because of family problems. Johnston returned to Australia, where he now works as a sports journalist. In 1989 he was on Merseyside helping to comfort the families of Hillsborough victims. For Middlesbrough he made 77 League and Cup appearances (seven as sub), scoring 16 goals.

GORDON JONES

Since World War Two, no player has made more appearances for Middlesbrough than full-back Gordon Jones, who clocked up 528 in League and Cup, only five of them as a substitute. Born at Sedgefield on 6 March 1943, he signed amateur forms for 'Boro in August 1958 and became a full-time professional in March 1960. In January 1961, Jones made his first League appearance (he had played in a League Cup match against Cardiff on 3 October 1960) against Southampton when he travelled as 12th man. Some 20 minutes before the kick-off, Jones was told that he was to play as 'Boro had decided not to risk Derek Stonehouse, who had been taken ill overnight. His first appearance came at right-back, but when the regular left-back, Mick McNeil, was transferred to Ipswich, Jones switched over to replace him. Within weeks he had won the first of nine England Under-23 caps and he was later considered to have a chance of making the 1966 World Cup squad, although Ray Wilson claimed the position before him. Jones had been chosen for the imminent Under-23 tour, but a cracked left fibula ruled him out. He made a full recovery and took over the captaincy when Ian Gibson left. Jones skippered 'Boro to promotion from Division Three in 1967 and two years later he was awarded a testimonial. In February 1973, after 12 years with Middlesbrough, he was transferred to Darlington, for whom he made 85 League appearances. He later played for Crook Town on a tour of India and became a successful Teesside businessman.

ARTHUR KAYE

At only 5ft 3½ins tall, Arthur Kaye was one of the smallest players in the Football League. Born in Barnsley on 9 May 1933, he played for England Schoolboys before joining Barnsley straight from school and signed professional forms for the Oakwell club in May 1950, on his 17th birthday. Despite the fact that Barnsley were by no means one of the game's 'glamour' clubs,

he was soon capped by England Under-23s and played for the Football League. After 265 appearances for the Colliers, Kaye moved to Blackpool in May 1959, as an eventual replacement for the legendary Stanley Matthews. But as Matthews just kept going, Kaye moved on after 48 League appearances for the Seasiders. He arrived at Middlesbrough in November 1960, for £10,000, and quickly recovered the form he had shown at Barnsley. In five years with 'Boro he was a regular goalscorer until his final move, to Colchester United in June 1965. They had just been relegated to Division Four and Kaye stayed at Layer Road for a season and a half, making 49 League appearances. For 'Boro he played in 185 League and Cup games, scoring 44 goals.

ALAN KERNAGHAN

Alan Kernaghan was born in Otley on 25 April 1967 and arrived at Ayresome Park in September 1981 as an associate schoolboy player. He rose through the ranks and made his League debut at centre-forward in a 1-0 home defeat against Notts County in February 1985. His appearances were limited up front and in 1989-90 he was switched to the centre of defence, although in November 1989 he scored a hat-trick at Ewood Park when injuries required him to revert to attack. In December 1990 he lost his place to Simon Coleman and was allowed to join Charlton Athletic on loan. Amusingly, Lennie Lawrence, then manager of Charlton, tried frantically to sign Kernaghan permanently in the close season of 1991. Once he was appointed Middlesbrough manager, negotiations were suspended and Lawrence had to persuade his new player to remain at Ayresome Park! From then on, his place at the heart of defence has been assured as he starred in the 1991-92 promotion campaign and the League Cup run to the semi-final. Appointed club captain following Tony Mowbray's departure, Kernaghan was injured for the vital game at Molineux on which promotion hinged. Watching from the bench, the pressure was too great and at half-time he left the ground to buy a sandwich and newspaper; when he returned 'Boro were losing and had a player sent off, but two late goals clinched a Premier

League place in a dramatic finale. Kernaghan, a Northern Ireland schoolboy international, has so far made 198 full appearances for 'Boro, plus 52 as sub, and scored 19 goals. Now an established Republic of Ireland international, he refused to sign a new contract and was poised to leave Ayresome Park in 1993, following relegation.

CYRIL KNOWLES

Cyril Knowles, the son of a West Riding miner, was born in the Yorkshire pit village of Fitzwilliam, near Pontefract, on 13 July 1944. He played his early football for South Elmshall District Boys before becoming a miner, driving a pit-pony at nearby Monckton Colliery and turning out for the colliery's football team. He was turned down by both Wolves, where his brother Peter was on the playing staff, and Manchester United before writing to Harold Shepherdson at Middlesbrough. He was taken on as an amateur, playing for the club as an outside-left but he was on the point of leaving when manager Bob Dennison offered him professional terms in October 1962. He got his lucky break when regular full-back Mick McNeil picked up an injury and, in desperation, manager Bob Dennison played Knowles at left-back. From then, he never looked back. In May 1964 he was signed by Bill Nicholson, joining Tottenham Hotspur for £45,000, a record fee for a full-back. Nicholson wanted him as a right-back replacement for a player who had

emigrated to South Africa. After losing confidence following a bad playing spell, Knowles asked to be switched to left-back and went on to become, arguably, the best in Tottenham's history. At White Hart Lane, he quickly developed into a 'strong, stylish attacking full-back who had an excellent left foot and could accurately cross the ball on the run'. Six Under-23 caps were followed by four full England caps. He had a special rapport with supporters at all his clubs and was the subject of the hit song *Nice One, Cyril* (of which he did not approve because it was done without his permission). He made over 500 appearances for Tottenham Hotspur in his 11 seasons, picking up FA Cup, League Cup and UEFA Cup winners' medals along the way at White Hart Lane before a knee injury ended his playing career in 1975 at the age of 31. Staying in football, he became Billy Bremner's assistant at Doncaster Rovers before Bobby Murdoch, whom Knowles had met on a coaching course, offered him the job of reserve-team trainer-coach at Ayresome Park in 1981. He managed Darlington from May 1983 until May 1987, guiding the Quakers to a rare promotion success. Then it was on to Torquay United where he won the Bell's Manager of the Month award, also taking Torquay to the 1988-89 Sherpa Van Trophy Final at Wembley. He parted company with Torquay in October 1989, returning to the North-East to manage Hartlepool United. When Knowles arrived, 'Pool were in serious danger of dropping out of the Football League but he guided them to safety and then led the side to the brink of clinching promotion to the Third

Division when he was struck down by a brain tumour in March 1991. Hartlepool reluctantly terminated his contract in the summer and Cyril Knowles died, following an operation, in Middlesbrough General Hospital on 31 August 1991. For 'Boro he made 39 League and Cup appearances.

BRIAN LAWS

Brian Laws was born in Wallsend on 14 October 1961 and played for Wallsend Boys' Club before joining First Division Burnley as an apprentice. He stayed at Turf Moor for six seasons and saw the Clarets drop down two divisions before helping them win back their Second Division place. After John Bond replaced Brian Miller as Burnley manager, Laws was transferred to Huddersfield Town in 1984 for £10,000, after making more than 120 League appearances for the Turf Moor club. 'Boro boss Willie Maddren took him to Ayresome Park in March 1985 for £30,000 and he scored some spectacular goals with long-range shots from midfield. His 1986-87 season ended prematurely when he injured knee ligaments at home to Bristol Rovers in March and, at one stage, there was concern that his career might be over. But he recovered and earned a first-team recall in October 1987. Brian Clough took him to Nottingham Forest in the summer of 1988, when his fee was fixed at £120,000 by a Football League tribunal. At the City Ground, Laws took a little while to break through into the first team but won Littlewoods Cup and Simod Cup-winners' medals, although his own-goal helped Liverpool to an FA Cup Final place and cost Forest the chance of recording a Wembley treble, although he did come on as substitute when Forest lost to Spurs in the 1991 FA Cup Final. He was still at Forest in 1993. For Middlesbrough he made 124 League and Cup appearances, scoring 14 goals.

TONY McANDREW

Tony McAndrew was born at Lanark on 11 April 1956 and won Scottish Youth international honours after joining Middlesbrough in July 1971. He made his first-team debut in November 1973, deputizing for the injured Graeme Souness against Luton Town. It was McAndrew's solitary appearance in that record-breaking season. He scored the only hat-trick of his League career against Sheffield United in the last home game of 1975-76, his only other hat-trick being in the North Riding Senior Cup Final against South Bank. In 1976, he played for Vancouver Whitecaps in the North American Soccer League. In his own words, he was 'a naturally aggressive player'. Manager John Neal handed him the captaincy when Stuart Boam was transferred to Newcastle United in August 1979. In 1982, McAndrew rejected the contract offered by Middlesbrough and in the August of his testimonial season he joined Chelsea, who were now managed by Neal. 'Boro asked for £300,000 but the fee decided by a Football League tribunal was £92,500. Willie Maddren took him back to Teesside in September 1984 and he bolstered the defence for another two seasons, playing his last season as the club slipped into the Third Division. He looked after the juniors in March 1986, but took up an appointment as a brewery representative before the year ended, playing part-time football with

Willington. He made a surprise return to League football with Hartlepool in March 1989, staying at the Victoria Ground until the end of the season. He was assistant manager to Frank Gray at Darlington. For Middlesbrough he made 349 senior appearances, plus five as sub, and scored 18 goals. Then he became youth-team coach at Hartlepool United under new manager Alan Murray. He was still playing football at the age of 37, with Northern League side Billingham Synthonia.

JIMMY McCLELLAND

Dysart-born Jimmy McClelland was an old-fashioned, centre-forward who liked nothing better than to run with the ball. Long-legged, fair-haired McClelland played for Raith Rovers before his transfer to Southend United just before World War One. Middlesbrough manager Herbert Bamlett took McClelland to Ayresome Park in March 1925, in a player exchange which saw Morris Hick go to Southend. He scored all Middlesbrough's goals in their 5-1 FA Cup victory over Leeds United in January 1926 and was chaired off the pitch by his colleagues at the end of that marvellous feat. He had another reason to remember that day, for his son Charles, who played post-war football for Blackburn Rovers, was born. In the same season, McClelland established a new individual club scoring record of 32 goals, beating George Elliott's 31, although Elliott's were in the First Division. In September 1926, McClelland was injured in a bruising game against South Shields and for the next game, George Camsell took his place and began his magnificent career in earnest. McClelland returned to the team later that season but was now mostly a reserve (he was a prolific scorer for 'Boro's second string). In March 1928, after scoring 48 goals for Middlesbrough in only 85 senior games, he was happy to agree to a transfer to Bolton Wanderers, where he won an FA Cup-winners' medal in 1929.

ALEX McCRAE

Alex McCrae played for Haddington Juniors before signing for Heart of Midlothian in 1941. He joined Charlton Athletic in May 1947, for a reported fee of £7,500, but his style did not fit in at The Valley and he made only 43 League appearances for the London club. McCrae turned down the chance of joining Sheffield United, a few days before Middlesbrough stepped in with an offer of £10,000 in October 1948. In his early days at Ayresome Park he could not find his best form and after a few games he was dropped from the side. He won back his place after some sterling displays for the Reserves in the North-Eastern League. McCrae, who was born in Stoneyburn on 2 January 1920, was described as 'a natural left-footed player with a lethal shot' and favoured 'the short, ground pass'. He also possessed 'quick acceleration and will play anywhere in the forward line but inside-left is his favourite position'. After five years at Ayresome Park, during which time he scored 49 goals in 130 League and Cup games, McCrae was transferred to Falkirk in March 1953 and became player-coach of Ballymena United in September 1957. He returned to Scotland as manager of Stirling Albion in January 1960. Within two months, however, he was back at Falkirk, where he stayed until April 1965. In November 1966, he was appointed a Middlesbrough scout in Scotland.

JOHN McKAY

Curly-haired Johnny McKay was born in Glasgow at the end of the last century and was first spotted by Glasgow Celtic. He then played for First Division Blackburn Rovers before new Middlesbrough manager, Peter McWilliam, made him his first signing for his new club. McKay made his debut for 'Boro against Darlington at Ayresome Park on 19 March 1927 and managed seven League appearances that memorable season, scoring one goal, at Blackpool. Back

in the First Division for the start of the 1927-28 season, he experienced great difficulty breaking into the Middlesbrough side and made only eight appearances at inside-forward. In the next three seasons McKay made regular appearances on the wing, but lost most of 1932 through injury and appeared only once, against Leicester City at Filbert Street. He had accepted the job of coaching the club's junior players but Bolton Wanderers took him away from Ayresome Park, although he did not appear in their Football League side before returning to Scotland and signing for Hibernian. For Middlesbrough he scored 20 goals in 109 first-team games.

ERIC McMORDIE

Alexander McMordie, always known as Eric, was born in Belfast on 12 August 1946

and played local soccer before having a trial with Manchester United — at the same time as George Best — when he was 15. Homesick, both lads went back to Ulster and, although Matt Busby asked both to return to Old Trafford, only Best obliged, whilst McMordie turned out as an amateur with the Dundela club. When McMordie was 18, Middlesbrough's Irish-based scout, Matt Willis, recommended him to 'Boro manager Raich Carter. In 1964, McMordie was signed as a professional and made his debut, as an inside-forward, during the club's relegation season of 1965-66. The team bounced back into the Second Division, but he made less than 20 appearances and in 1967-68, although he started the season in the team, he did not establish himself as a regular until December. First selected for Northern Ireland for a match against Israel, his international debut was delayed when the Israelis asked for a late postponement. The first of 21 full caps eventually came against Israel in Jaffa in September 1968. In 1972-73, he lost his place in Middlesbrough's team due to a stomach complaint. When Jack Charlton arrived during the summer of 1973, the new manager was not impressed by McMordie's style and the Irishman made only seven appearances in 'Boro's successful promotion push of 1973-74. He was loaned to Sheffield Wednesday in October 1974 but, despite six goals in nine League games, nothing permanent came from his stay at Hillsborough. He signed for York City in May 1975, then Hartlepool United in December 1976, playing almost 50 games for each club. McMordie quit the game in 1977 and went into business on Teesside. For 'Boro he scored 25 goals in 273 games, 11 of his appearances coming as a substitute.

MICK McNEIL

Mick McNeil, who was born in Middlesbrough on 7 February 1940, played inside-left for Middlesbrough Boys. After leaving school he turned out for the works' team of Cargo Fleet, where he was studying to

be an analytical chemist. Jimmy Gordon, who was then 'Boro's coach, spotted his potential and McNeil signed professional forms for the club in May 1957. His League debut was at left-half against Brighton, but he lost his place upon the arrival of Ray Yeoman from Northampton Town. Bill Harris was switched to right-half to accommodate Yeoman and McNeil went back to the Reserves. Injury to centre-half Bryan Phillips earned him a brief recall before he established himself at full-back, the position in which he would be capped for England. Picked for an FA XI against the Army at Newcastle, McNeil followed this up with Under-23 caps. He made an impressive debut against France at Roker Park and then went on tour to East Germany, Israel and Poland. He was a forceful defender who could carry the ball through to set up attacks and his gritty displays earned him his full England debut in Belfast. Eight further full caps quickly followed. McNeil moved to Ipswich Town in July 1964 and was in the Suffolk club's side which won promotion to Division One in 1968. He retired in 1971 to run a successful sports outfitting business in Suffolk. For Middlesbrough he appeared in 193 League and Cup games.

JOHN MAHONEY

John Mahoney, the son of a professional Rugby League player, was born in Cardiff on 20 September 1946 but he spent his early life in Manchester. Although he was born on Welsh soil, he was ignored by the Welsh selectors for a long while because they thought that he was not qualified for that country. He joined Fourth Division Crewe Alexandra from non-League Ashton United in March 1966. He received international recognition at Gresty Road with Welsh

Under-23 caps. A year later, in March 1967, First Division Stoke City dug deep to pay the Railwaymen a club record receipt of £17,000 to take Mahoney to the Victoria Ground. It was rumoured that with the money, Crewe were able to pay off the outstanding debt on the Gresty Road ground. In the spotlight of the First Division, he won his first full cap, against England during the following season. He missed the first three months of the 1970-71 season with ankle ligament trouble but made a complete recovery to play a vital part in helping Stoke City to their first-ever Wembley appearance in 1972, where he won a League Cup winners' medal as a playing substitute against Chelsea. In August 1977, Middlesbrough manager John Neal spent a club record £90,000 to bring the Welshman to Ayresome Park, Mahoney making his 'Boro debut in the 1-1 home draw against Liverpool, although his first game was overshadowed by Kenny Dalglish's debut for Liverpool. He won a further 13 caps in his stay with the club before joining John Toshack at Swansea City on 23 July 1979, after 90 League and Cup games for Middlesbrough. At Vetch Field he continued to make regular international appearances for Wales, lifting his final total to 51 caps as the Swans claimed First Division status for the first time in club history in 1981. A triple stress fracture of the left ankle ended his League career and he moved to non-League Bangor City as player-manager in 1985.

WILF MANNION

Wilf Mannion is undoubtedly the most famous player in the history of Middlesbrough Football Club. Born at South Bank on 16 May 1918, Mannion played in the Teesside League with South Bank St Peter's

before signing for 'Boro in September 1936. During the war he served in the Auxiliary Fire Service before being called up for military service and it was in 1941 that he played his first game in an England shirt, against Scotland in an unofficial international. Demobbed in 1946, Wilf Mannion went on to become one of the finest inside-forwards of the post-war period. In the days of Carter, Hagan and Shackleton, many critics reckoned that Mannion, the 'Golden Boy' of football, was the best. He had a marvellous sense of anticipation and one contemporary description called him 'a ball-playing genius with a classic body-swerve, who has the ability to work in a confined area'. Altogether he won 26 full England caps and scored twice for Great Britain when they beat the Rest of Europe 6-1 in 1947. At the start of 1947-48 he refused to re-sign for 'Boro and made plans to move to Oldham, to go into business there and play for Oldham Athletic. Middlesbrough, realizing Mannion's determination, agreed but placed a £25,000 transfer fee on his head. Oldham could find only £15,000 and the player eventually returned to help 'Boro avoid relegation. He retired after Middlesbrough eventually dropped into Division Two at the end of 1953-54 — he had totalled 110 goals in his 368 League and Cup appearances for the Ayresome Park club — but was persuaded to return to League football with Hull City. Hull paid £5,000 for Mannion's signature and when he made his debut on Boxing Day 1954, the Booth-ferry Park attendance doubled from the average figure to nearly 40,000. He spent only one season at Hull and, during that time, trouble was brewing over newspaper articles he had written during his 'retirement'. The Football League ordered him to explain stories of alleged illegal payments to players but Mannion declined and in June 1955 the League suspended him until he complied. Instead, Mannion went to play for non-League Poole Town and later turned out for King's Lynn, Haverhill Rovers and Earlstown until his final retirement in 1962. For his two major clubs he made a total of 360 League appearances and was later awarded a joint benefit game with former Middlesbrough and England skipper, George Hardwick.

JOCK MARSHALL

Immediately after World War One, John Marshall — he was always known as Jock — was hailed as 'the best right-back in the world.' He first played for Shettleston and signed for Middlesbrough from St Mirren in November 1919 for a fee of £1,800. He was also known as the 'ferro-concrete back' and was certainly a tough character. It was alleged that he could kick the ball almost the length of the field, without taking a run at it. In 1922, with six full Scottish caps to his name (and one Victory international appearance), he asked for a transfer but 'Boro would not release him and he was suspended by the Football League after taking part in a five-a-side game in Scotland. Towards the end of 1922-23, he was also suspended by the club for leaving the district without permission when he returned to Scotland. The suspension was eventually lifted but the rift between club and player was too great and he was finally given a transfer in April 1923, after making 121 League and Cup appearances. After

declining to join Preston North End, Marshall opted for Llanelly and became the only player this century to win a Scottish cap whilst with a non-League club. He later set up in business in New York and in 1926 was playing for Belmont FC.

JACK MARTIN

Fair-haired Sunderland-born Jack Martin had trials at Portsmouth but was turned down by the Fratton Park club. Despite this set-back, he pursued his ambition to become a professional footballer and was turning out for Horden Colliery Welfare as a 'natural ball-playing wing-half' when Middlesbrough manager Peter McWilliam spotted his potential. McWilliam signed Martin in March 1932, giving the Horden club a £10 donation. The player had to wait a year for his League debut for 'Boro, playing in a 4-0 home victory over Blackburn Rovers on 6 May 1933, a game which also heralded the debut of Micky Fenton. Martin was a first-team regular until the outbreak of war in September 1939 and was one of the mainstays of a makeshift 'Boro team during the days of wartime regional football. He was injured at Bradford on 28 October 1944 and took almost a year to recover. In September 1945 he had to undergo an operation on his knee and was then unfortunate enough to tear a leg muscle. Fully recovered, however, Martin was re-signed as a professional in October that year, but was freed at the end of the season, when he was 33, after making 121 senior appearances for the club. He later became trainer of Huddersfield Town and then Doncaster Rovers.

JIMMY MATHIESON

Methil-born goalkeeper Jimmy Mathieson was playing for Raith Rovers when he was recommended to Middlesbrough by Peter McWilliam, before McWilliam became manager at Ayresome Park. The Middlesbrough board took Mathieson on without even seeing him play, signing him for £1,200 in June 1926, and he proved to be good value with 264 senior appearances. In the next five years he missed only seven games after making his League debut at Stamford Bridge in August 1926, a game which Chelsea won 3-0. Mathieson was 'Boro's regular goalkeeper as Middlesbrough experienced promotion, relegation and promotion in successive seasons. In the early 1930s, Third Division Brentford swooped for several Middlesbrough players — Johnny Holliday, Bill Scott, Ernie Muttitt etc — and Mathieson was one of those to go to Griffin Park when he joined the Bees in May 1934. Brentford, with several former 'Boro players in their side, won promotion to the First Division and remained there for five seasons. Mathieson, meanwhile, returned to Scotland and signed for Queen of the South in June 1938.

DAVID MILLS

David Mills was born in Whitby on 6 December 1951 but was brought up in Thornaby. An England Schoolboy international, he attracted several clubs, including Hull City, Stoke City, Manchester United, Burnley and Middlesbrough, but a back injury kept him out of football for almost a year. Fully recovered, he signed for Middlesbrough in July 1968, joining the club at the same time as Willie Maddren. His first-team debut was as a substitute towards the close of 1968-69 and he scored on his full debut, at Swindon in 1969-70. Capped eight times by England Under-23s, he first came to the attention of the selectors during 'Boro's 1973-74 Second Division championship season, when he showed his flair as a speedy forward. In December 1976, Mills asked for a move and was transfer-listed at £200,000. He remained at the club for a further two years before becoming Britain's first half-million pound footballer on his transfer to West Brom in January 1979. He scored on his first full appearance for Albion but, despite the huge sum invested in him, he was not given many opportunities to prove himself at The Hawthorns and was loaned to Newcastle United. Sheffield Wednesday paid only £30,000 for Mills, but he stayed only briefly

at Hillsborough, before returning to Newcastle on a permanent transfer. In June 1984, Willie Maddren re-signed him for 'Boro on a free transfer and he stayed for one season, finishing top scorer with 14 goals. After coaching Middlesbrough's juniors, Mills went to play a handful of games for Darlington before joining Northern League Whitby Town. He was seriously injured in a car crash on Tyneside, which claimed the life of his father. When recovered David Mills worked as a representative for a printing firm. For Middlesbrough he had made 381 League and Cup appearances, including 20 as sub, and scored 108 goals. He is now a commentator on TFM Radio.

NEIL MOCHAN

It was Scottish international inside-forward Billy Steele who unearthed the talent of Neil Mochan. Mochan, who was born at Larbert, Stirlingshire, on 6 April 1927, was turning out for a junior club called Dunipace Thistle when Steele was playing for Morton. Small, but solidly built, Mochan had superb ball-control and possessed a snap shot which often surprised goalkeepers. He joined Morton in April 1944 and 'Boro paid £14,000 for his signature in May 1951. He played for the club against Partizan Belgrade in that year's Festival of Britain match, but made only 38 League appearances before being transferred to Celtic in May 1953 for £8,000. Despite his relatively few appearances for 'Boro, he had a good strike rate of 14 goals. He won three full Scottish caps, against Norway, Austria and Hungary in 1954, and one 'B' cap, as well as lifting Scottish League, Scottish Cup and Scottish League Cup-winners' medals at Parkhead. He was something of a utility player at Parkhead and even played at left-back before moving to Dundee United in November 1963. He later played for Raith Rovers and was Celtic's trainer when they won the European Cup in 1967. He scored 14 goals in 39 League and Cup games for 'Boro. He now lives in retirement in Falkirk.

TONY MOWBRAY

Tony Mowbray was born at Saltburn on 22 November 1963 and as a boy he stood on the Holgate End at Ayresome Park and cheered his hero, John Hickton. Mowbray captained the Langbaurgh and Cleveland Under-15 sides, when Steve Smelt was in charge of the team, and also turned out for Grangetown Boys, Nunthorpe Athletic and Guisborough Town as well as playing rugby for his school. In 1978, his most cherished dream came true when he signed schoolboy forms for Middlesbrough and two years later he became an apprentice. The youngster had enjoyed a fine career as a schoolboy and was called up for an England trial, but broke a leg in the first practice game. Mowbray, a 6ft 1in tall central defender, made his League debut for 'Boro in September 1982, in a 1-1 draw at St James' Park, and thereafter shared in many of Middlesbrough's ups and downs. In the summer of 1989 he received international recognition when he was chosen for the England 'B' tour, along with his Middlesbrough colleague, Gary Pallister.

Mowbray played in all three games, against Switzerland, Norway and Iceland. After over 400 senior appearances for Middlesbrough he was sold to Celtic for £1 million in November 1991. There is a clause in the contract which stipulates that Middlesbrough have first refusal if Mowbray leaves Celtic. He has spent much of his time at Parkhead on the treatment table.

IRVING NATTRASS

Fishburn-born Irving Nattrass joined Newcastle United as an apprentice and became a full-time professional in July 1970, his first-team debut coming as a substitute against Derby County in March 1971. The highlight of his career at St James' Park was a Wembley appearance in the 1976 League Cup Final, when United lost to Manchester City. While at Newcastle, Nattrass missed out on several England Under-23 caps, due to injury, and was also forced to miss England's trip to South America in 1977, when he might have won a full cap. He also missed out on United's run to the 1974 FA Cup Final, due to a knee-ligament injury. When Newcastle lost their First Division status in 1979, Nattrass wanted to stay in the top flight and an independent tribunal fixed his fee at £475,000, a 'Boro club record at the time. An Achilles tendon injury delayed his debut and in the following six months he suffered three hair-line fractures of the leg. Despite all this, Nattrass still managed 220 League and Cup games in six years with Middlesbrough and played in nine different positions for the club.

MEL NURSE

Centre-half Mel Nurse was born in Swansea on 11 October 1937 and won Welsh Schoolboy international honours. Linked to Swansea Town via the juniors, he signed professional forms for the Swans in June 1955. Nurse spent seven years at Vetch Field, during which time he won two Welsh Under-23 caps, five full caps and played in over 150 League games. Middlesbrough paid £25,000 for the 6ft, 13st defender in September 1962 and Nurse made his debut in a 4-3 victory at Grimsby Town. He 'added stability to any defence and instilled confidence amongst his fellow defenders'. Seven full Welsh caps followed whilst with Middlesbrough and as a commanding figure in the defence he was soon appointed 'Boro skipper. One of his biggest regrets must have been scoring the goal which sent his previous club, Swansea, crashing into Division Three. His wife wanted to return nearer to Wales and in August 1965 he was transferred to Swindon Town for £15,000. Nurse renewed his association with Swansea in June 1968 and in 1970 he went into non-League football with the Suffolk club, Bury, before finishing his career with Merthyr Tydfil, for whom he was playing when he suffered a broken leg. He made 124 League and Cup appearances for Middlesbrough. He now owns and runs a country hotel in Wales.

KELHAM O'HANLON

Republic of Ireland goalkeeper Kelham O'Hanlon was born in Saltburn on 16 May 1962 and attended Southlands school. He had trials with Derby County and Aston Villa but chose to sign for First Division Middlesbrough, becoming a professional in May 1980. He waited patiently for three years for his first senior game before replacing Jim Platt in goal against Sheffield Wednesday on 15 January 1983. Manager Malcolm Allison rewarded the player by keeping him in the side for the rest of the season, a campaign that took him to the fringe of Under-21 honours. Platt returned to Ireland at the end of the season and

Allison made O'Hanlon number-one 'keeper at Ayresome Park until he was displaced by the arrival of Steve Pears, on loan from Manchester United in November 1983. He was eventually released by manager Willie Maddren in May 1985, but quickly found another club when Rotherham United moved in for him three months later. He spent five full seasons at Millmoor and finally received international recognition in 1988 when he was awarded his only Eire cap so far, against Israel. That season, United clinched the Fourth Division championship with Kelham as the Millermen's regular goalkeeper. He was transferred to Carlisle United in 1992 and is still doing a good job for the Brunton Park side.

JOHN O'ROURKE

John O'Rourke was born in Northampton on 11 February 1945 and after a spell as an amateur with Arsenal and then some time on Chelsea's books, the centre-forward signed for Luton Town in December 1963. O'Rourke scored goals galore in a struggling Hatters side and after an impressive 64 goals in only 84 League games, he was signed by Stan Anderson as an attacking spearhead as Middlesbrough prepared for their first-ever season in the Third Division. O'Rourke began to deliver immediately, scoring twice on his debut in a 3-2 win over Colchester United at Layer Road on 20 August 1967. He found the net regularly that season with 30 League and Cup goals as 'Boro clinched promotion. His goals included three hat-tricks, crucially one in the final match of the season, against Oxford United, which Middlesbrough had to win to go up. In June 1967, O'Rourke won his only England under-23 cap, scoring in a 3-0 victory over Turkey in Ankara, and had added 11 more goals for 'Boro in 1967-68 before Bobby Robson swooped to take him to First Division Ipswich Town in February 1968. Leading scorer once more in his brief stay at Portman Road, O'Rourke was transferred to Coventry City in November 1969, followed by spells at QPR and Bournemouth before leaving League football in 1975. O'Rourke scored goals for all his clubs. His tally for Middlesbrough was 42 in 72 League and Cup games and overall he netted 165 in 322/5 games.

BRYAN ORRITT

Bryan 'Taffy' Orritt was born in the small Welsh village of Cwm-Y-Glo on 22 February 1937 and was one of the few Welsh-speaking players in the Football League. As a boy he attended Caernarfon Grammar School and his first club was the one with the longest name in the game, now shortened to Llanfair PG FC. At the age of 17 he was playing for Bangor in the Cheshire League and was twice chosen as reserve for the Welsh international youth team. Orritt turned professional with Birmingham City in January 1956 and went on to make exactly 100 League appearances for them. He won three Welsh Under-23 caps, played for the Army during his National Service and appeared for Birmingham in the 1960 and 1961 Inter-Cities Fairs Cup Finals. He was serving a seven-day suspension, following an incident whilst playing for Birmingham City Reserves, when he was

transferred to Middlesbrough on 1 March 1962. Orrittt was Middlesbrough's first playing substitute, perhaps a fitting honour for a utility man who played in all 11 positions for the club. He emigrated to South Africa to play for Johannesburg and still lives in that country, although he is a frequent visitor to Britain. He scored 23 goals in 128 League and Cup games for Middlesbrough.

HEINE OTTO

Heine Otto, who was born in the Netherlands on 24 August 1954, worked for his father-in-law in the gold business, and then in a whisky distillery before becoming a professional footballer. Otto played for Twente Enschede, replacing Arnold Muhren who had left for Ipswich Town. Capped several times for Holland Under-23s, Otto won one full cap, playing the last 20 minutes of a game against Yugoslavia after coming on as a substitute. In the summer of 1981, he played in three friendly games for Middlesbrough with a view to a permanent transfer and impressed 'Boro manager Bobby Murdoch enough to be signed on a two-year contract in August that year. He made a scoring debut in the Football League, against Spurs at Ayresome Park, although 'Boro lost 3-1. A midfielder-cum-striker, Otto was the club's top scorer with a meagre five goals when 'Boro dropped into the Second Division in 1982. He turned down an extension of his existing contract in May 1985 and returned to Holland the following month, to play for Den Haag, a Dutch Second Division side. He had made 188 senior appearances for 'Boro, scoring 28 goals. In May 1990, he set a new Dutch consecutive appearance record with Den Haag. In February 1993 he was appointed an executive at ADO Den Haag.

GARY PALLISTER

Gary Pallister, who was born in Ramsgate on 30 June 1965, was a fine all-round schoolboy sportsman, who played basketball for Cleveland and cricket for Stockton. Football, though, was his first love and he signed as a junior for Billingham Town in the Northern League. He went to Middlesbrough for a trial when Malcolm Allison was manager but played only one Central League game before being released. Willie Maddren, 'Boro's coach at the time and Allison's eventual successor, kept in touch with his progress and a year later, Pallister, now a stronger, fitter player rejoined Middlesbrough. Richard Corden, a local businessman and later a Middlesbrough director, paid Pallister's wages for a year during Middlesbrough's financial crisis, affording the club the opportunity to hang on to the tall defender. Early in his career, he made seven League appearances on loan to Darlington. Pallister was the first player from Division Two to be chosen by Bobby Robson for the full England squad, but Bruce Rioch pulled him out of the party in order to prepare for the play-off games. He eventually won his first full England cap in March 1988, against Hungary. After Middlesbrough dropped into Division Two, speculation increased as to whether they could hold on to such a talented player. He ended the 1988-89 season on England's 'B' tour, with Middlesbrough skipper Tony Mowbray, before Manchester United paid £2.3m for his signature. He had made 180 League and Cup appearances for Middlesbrough. Pallister had a nightmare debut for United, at home to Norwich who won 2-0, but he ignored the boo-boys, soon settled down and was named PFA Player of the Year in 1992. He won a championship medal at Old Trafford in 1992-93, the first year of the FA Premier League, adding that to his European Cup-winners' Cup winners' medal gained in 1991, and his Littlewoods Cup winners' medal a year later. Pallister returned to England duty in 1993 and was one of the few successes on the summer tour to the United States.

GARY PARKINSON

Gary Parkinson was born at Thornaby on 10 January 1968 and played for St Patrick's School and graduated to the Cleveland and Stockton Boys teams before joining Everton as an apprentice. The youngster soon became homesick on Merseyside and returned home within three weeks of arriving at Goodison. In 1983-84, however, he was given a second chance of League football when he joined Middlesbrough as an apprentice on the Youth Training Scheme. He soon fitted in and was a key figure in the Reserves' successful bid to win promotion to the First Division of the Central League. Parkinson made his Football League debut as a raw recruit in the 'off-on' game against Port Vale at Hartlepool's Victoria Ground, at the start of 'Boro's Third Division championship-winning season. He made a major contribution to that success and in 1987-88 regained his place, after being suspended, to play another vital role in another Middlesbrough promotion. In January 1989 he missed two games through injury and was then dropped for the Coventry game. He recovered from a knee injury in March to return to the team and became the regular penalty-taker. Parkinson benefited by having skipper Tony Mowbray alongside him in defence and made 243 senior appearances for 'Boro, although he played only four times in 1992-93. In April 1993 he was transferred to Bolton Wanderers, managed by Bruce Rioch. His Ayresome Park chances had become very limited since the arrival of Eire international full-backs Chris Morris and Curtis Fleming. He had a month's loan spell with Southend United, but still could not find a place in the first-team on his return to Ayresome Park in November 1992. Reluctantly, he finally moved out of the club, accepting a free transfer in 1993.

ALAN PEACOCK

Alan Peacock, 6ft tall and an immaculate header of a football, was born in North Ormesby on 29 October 1937 and attended Lawson Street School. He signed professional forms for Middlesbrough in November 1954 but did not make his League debut until a year later — the same season as Brian Clough's first game — in a 7-2 defeat at Bristol Rovers. Awarded England Youth honours in 1956, Peacock starred at inside-left for three seasons (National Service interrupting his career) and then formed a twin spearhead with goalscoring sensation, Clough. Their partnership produced many goals but the two players did not get on well with each other. After Clough's departure to Sunderland, Peacock

was switched to centre-forward and the move proved so successful that he was chosen for England's 1962 World Cup party. Selected to play against Austria, he suffered a fractured cheekbone only 90 seconds into the derby game at Roker Park in March 1962. The injury jinx continued when he damaged his knee before joining the World Cup party but he succeeded in making his full England debut in the World Cup Finals in Chile. In December 1963, Peacock lost his 'Boro place through injury but was fit enough to join Leeds United in February 1964, for £55,000, after scoring 141 goals in 238 senior games for 'Boro. With Leeds he won a Division Two championship medal, played in the 1965 FA Cup Final and won two more caps. A move to Plymouth followed in November 1967, but a troublesome knee injury forced his retirement in March 1968. He returned to Teesside, became a successful businessman and now lives in Carlton.

STEPHEN PEARS

Goalkeeper Stephen Pears was born at Brandon on 22 January 1962 and played schoolboy football for Ushaw Moor. He had trials with Middlesbrough before joining Manchester United as a 14-year-old on associate schoolboy forms and spent nine

years at Old Trafford, where he was understudy to England goalkeeper Gary Bailey. Pears won his first-team chance at Old Trafford when Bailey broke a finger in training, but opportunities were few and in November 1983, Malcolm Allison took him to Second Division Middlesbrough on a month's loan. An appeal was made to raise the £80,000 to make the transfer permanent, but the target was not reached and Pears returned to United and was offered a two-year contract. Willie Maddren eventually secured Pears for 'Boro in June 1985 but his fine displays could not prevent the club falling into Division Three. Pears, though, was one of the mainstays of Middlesbrough's fight-back before injury and loss of form saw him lose his place to Kevin Poole. Following a hernia operation in 1989, both Poole and Dibble kept Pears out of the side but he battled back to appear in all but the final match of the 1991-92 promotion season. His consistency impressed Graham Taylor who called him into the full England squad but, alas, Pears was forced to withdraw because of a cracked cheekbone sustained in a clash with Cambridge United striker Dion Dublin. He lost his Middlesbrough place through injury in 1992-93 and so far has made 341 senior appearances for 'Boro. He also runs a successful landscaping business. He was voted Hennessey North-East Footballer of the Year for 1990-91.

BILLY PEASE

Billy Pease served with the Royal Northumberland Fusiliers in World War One, then joined Leeds City, his home-town club, as an amateur. After City were expelled from the Football League in October 1919, Pease signed for Northampton Town, who gained entry into the newly-formed Third Division in 1920. He was a speedy winger who could run hard with the ball before surprising

opponents by cutting inside to try a shot at goal. Middlesbrough manager Herbert Bamlett bought his services for £2,000 on 18 May 1926 and Pease made his debut at outside-right on the opening day of the new season in Middlesbrough's 3-0 defeat at Stamford Bridge. During the Second Division championship-winning season of 1926-27, he confided in his pal, Jacky Carr, telling him that he had a date with a girl and would like to get away from the game early, so he would feign injury. Sure enough, during the game against South Shields, Pease was helped off the field — but he had broken his collarbone and was out for the rest of the season. As a Second Division player he was capped for England against Wales in February 1927 and he toured South Africa with the FA team in 1929. Transferred to Luton Town in June 1933 for £500, he became a publican in Middlesbrough after his retirement from the game, then worked at nearby ICI Wilton in the late 1940s and coached Redcar Albion in his spare time. Billy Pease was 56 when he died on 2 October 1955 and is buried in Redcar cemetery. For Middlesbrough he scored 103 goals in 239 League and Cup appearances.

FRED PENTLAND

Fred Pentland was born in Wolverhampton on 18 September 1883 and played for Avondale Juniors before graduating to the Football League with Small Heath (later Birmingham City) in August 1900. He moved to Blackpool in 1903 before returning to First Division football with Blackburn Rovers the same year. He moved to Brentford in May 1906, but only a year later he found himself at Queen's Park Rangers, then a force in the Southern League.

Pentland joined 'Boro towards the end of the 1907-08 season, for £350, a record receipt for QPR. He won five England caps during his stay at Middlesbrough, the last three coming during a tour of Hungary and Austria. He moved to Halifax early in February 1913, before joining Stoke in the same year. He was coaching in Germany when World War One broke out in August 1914 and was interned for the duration, along with another former Middlesbrough player, Steve Bloomer. A telegram received in England via the Netherlands FA stated that he was allowed to 'go about as he likes, but he cannot leave Germany'. After the war, he coached in France and then spent 15 years in Spain, coaching Athletic Bilbao until the outbreak of the Civil War in 1936. On his return to England he joined the coaching staff at Brentford, then managed Barrow from January 1938 until World War Two was declared in September 1939. For Middlesbrough he made 96 senior appearances, scoring 11 goals.

JIMMY PHILLIPS

Cultured left-back Jimmy Phillips was born in Bolton on 8 February 1966, signing for his home-town club as an associate schoolboy in August 1981. He made the number-three shirt his own at Burnden Park before Glasgow Rangers signed him in March 1987, for £95,000. He managed 25 Scottish League games and four European Cup ties at Ibrox, but often found himself in Rangers Reserves and moved to Oxford United in August 1988, for £110,000, where he missed only two matches in 18 months. Signed by Colin Todd for 'Boro in March 1990, this time in a £250,000 move, he helped stave off relegation and missed only five games in the next two seasons as Middlesbrough were transformed into a side challenging for promotion. Phillips continued to perform admirably as they battled for

survival in the FA Premier League, albeit that the struggle eventually proved unsuccessful. By the end of the 1992-93 season he had made 167 senior appearances for Middlesbrough.

JIM PLATT

Jim Platt comes from a footballing family. His father played for Ballymena United and his brother, John, was with Cliftonville. Jim, who was born at Ballymoney on 26 January 1952, was a wing-half at school but had turned to goalkeeping by the time he was 16 and playing for Ballymena. He had a three-week trial at Liverpool but the Reds had just signed Ray Clemence from Scunthorpe United. Platt won Irish Amateur caps and an Irish FA Cup runners-up medal before joining Middlesbrough for £7,000 in May 1970. After ten League appearances, 'Boro had to give Ballymena a further £3,000 but Platt soon established himself as one

of the best post-war goalkeepers to come from Ireland. He displaced out-of-form Willie Whigham, making his League debut in a 1-0 home victory over Blackpool, and overcame homesickness to make the position his own for almost eight seasons. In 1971-72 he was voted 'Boro's Player of the Year. He was almost ever-present in the Middlesbrough side that won the 1973-74 Second Division championship. When promotion was assured, Jack Charlton blooded Pat Cuff, who had waited patiently for six years for his first chance. The first of 20 Northern Ireland caps won with Middlesbrough came in March 1976, when he came on as substitute against Israel in Tel Aviv. After a much-publicised row with Jack Charlton over tactics, Platt eventually lost his place and with the arrival of Jim Stewart from Kilmarnock in May 1978, he must have thought his first-team days were numbered. Stewart was the regular 'keeper for the start of 1978-79 and Platt did not return to the side until the following March. In August he was loaned to Billy Horner's Fourth Division Hartlepool United, playing 13 League games. He had a further loan spell in November, with Cardiff. Platt was unfortunate to have played at the same time as Pat Jennings and Willie McFaul but he was in goal in 1980 when Northern Ireland clinched the Home International Championship for the first time since 1914. Back in the Middlesbrough side, he was voted the North-East's Player of the Year for 1980-81 and was was awarded a testimonial game against Sunderland in September 1981. Alas, things had turned sour between the player and club towards the end of the season, but his transfer request was turned down by the Middlesbrough board. He played once in the 1982 World Cup finals in Spain and with Middlesbrough back in Division Two, was named club captain for his last full season of 1982-83. Kelham O'Hanlon replaced Platt in the Middlesbrough goal and he was appointed junior coach after a marvellous record of 468 senior appearances for Middlesbrough. In August 1983 he returned to Ballymena United on a three-year contract as part-time player-manager. He runs a printing business in Belfast and is an occasional visitor to Ayresome Park. In May 1990 he was sacked by Coleraine, with Willie McFaul replacing him. He then became full-time manager with Ballyclare Comrades.

MARK PROCTOR

Mark Proctor, born in Middlesbrough on 30 January 1961, played for St Gabriel's and then St Anthony's Schools before having a trial with Leeds United when he was 14. Homesick, he returned to Teesside after only three days at Elland Road and signed for Middlesbrough on associate schoolboy forms in August 1975, playing some games for Nunthorpe Athletic along the way. Proctor captained the England Youth side in an international tournament in Las Palmas before becoming a full-time professional with 'Boro in September 1978. The first of his two England Under-21 caps as a Middlesbrough player came as substitute against the Republic of Ireland at Anfield in March 1981. After a further cap, against Switzerland in May, he signed for Nottingham Forest for £440,000 in August 1981. As a Forest player, he won two more Under-21 caps and was loaned to Sunderland,

playing five League games before the Wearsiders signed him permanently. He made more than 120 League appearances for the Roker club before First Division Sheffield Wednesday paid £275,000 for his signature during the 1987-88 season. After 59 League appearances for the Owls, Proctor made a surprise return to Middlesbrough for £300,000, but, despite some stylish displays in midfield, he arrived too late to save 'Boro from relegation. In 1991 he played for them in the play-offs, then helped them into the FA Premier League as runners-up the following season. He started only six games when 'Boro were relegated again in 1992-93 and was loaned to Tranmere, appearing for them in the play-offs before being released by Middlesbrough after 263 League and Cup appearances for them (26 as sub) and 20 goals.

ARTHUR RIGBY

Arthur Rigby was born in Chorlton in 1900 and became an electrician by trade. His father had played as a full-back for Ardwick (now Manchester City) but young Arthur did not take up the game until he was in his late teens, playing his initial football as a goalkeeper in the Manchester Amateur League with Crossley Gas Engine Works. He had converted to an outside-left, playing for Stafford YMCA, when he had a trial period with Stockport County but was not taken on at Edgeley Park. He signed for Crewe Alexandra, then moved to First Division Bradford City in a £1,200 transfer deal. His transfer fee had more than doubled when he moved to Blackburn Rovers in April 1925 and it was at Ewood Park that he won five full England caps, and an FA Cup winners' medal in 1928. He lost his place and was put on the transfer list before

attracting Everton's attention in November 1929. He helped the Toffees reclaim First Division status before Middlesbrough manager Peter McWilliam brought him and George Martin (Everton's left wing) to Ayresome Park on 6 May 1932, in a combined £900 transfer deal, but Rigby was not to stay too long on Teesside. Just over a season later he was on his travels again, this time for £150 to Clapton Orient for whom he signed on 22 August 1933. His last League club was also his first club, for he returned to Crewe Alexandra in August 1935. He helped Crewe to win the Welsh Cup in 1936 before he eventually retired in 1937 and he was still living the town when he died, aged 59, on 25 March 1960.

STUART RIPLEY

Stuart Ripley's first honour in football came when he was a member of the Middlesbrough

Boys team that shared the English Schools FA Trophy with Sunderland. He was born at Middlesbrough on 20 November 1967 and had trials with Manchester City and Chelsea before joining his home-town club as an apprentice professional. Ripley was with the England Youth team in China when he heard of Middlesbrough's relegation to the Third Division and then played five games on loan to Bolton Wanderers — he scored on his debut for the Trotters — before making his first appearance in 'Boro's League side. He really established himself at Ayresome Park during the 1986-87 season and in April 1988 scored the first League hat-trick of his career when Middlesbrough hammered Sheffield United 6-0 at Ayresome Park. His six goals in as many games at the close of that season did much to push 'Boro to the brink of the First Division, and he won eight England caps at Under-21 level into the bargain. Ripley remained loyal to Middlesbrough after relegation in 1989 and helped them into the FA Premier League in 1992 before moving to Blackburn Rovers, who went up with 'Boro, albeit via the play-offs. Ripley had made 295 senior appearances for Middlesbrough (a remarkable 42 as sub) and scored 30 goals.

DICKY ROBINSON

Reliable, stylish Richard 'Dicky' Robinson was spotted by 'Boro manager David Jack playing football with his local side, Marsden Juniors, in the Sunderland district and was looked upon as a promising forward. Robinson, who was born at Whitburn on 19 February 1927, worked down the mines as a 'Bevin Boy' in Dunfermline during the war and guested for Dunfermline Athletic. He signed for Middlesbrough, aged 18, on 9 April 1945 and played at right-back in the club's first

post-war League game, on 31 August 1946 at Villa Park, when a Wilf Mannion goal won 'Boro maximum points. Robinson's outstanding displays over the next four years earned him Football League representative honours and he also went on tour with an FA party. Alas, he lost confidence after a string of niggling injuries and a badly pulled muscle, suffered at White Hart Lane in December 1951, kept him out for the rest of that season. Although most of his games were at full-back, he was also tried at centre-half and, occasionally, in the forward line. In June 1959, at the age of 32, he was transferred to Barrow, then a Football League club. He spent three full seasons at Holker Street before retiring in 1962 with over 500 League games to his credit. He had made 416 senior appearances for 'Boro alone, managing just one goal.

DICKY ROOKS

Centre-half Dicky Rooks was born at Sunderland on 29 May 1940 and for many seasons was understudy to Charlie Hurley at Roker Park, his appearances restricted to 34 League games. Desperate for regular first-team football, he agreed to a £17,000 transfer to Ayresome Park in late August 1965. Raich Carter saw Rooks as the natural successor to Mel Nurse, following the Welshman's transfer to Swindon Town. Rooks made his debut at Huddersfield Town on 28 August 1965, but it was hardly a happy start as Middlesbrough were hammered 6-0. Although he wore the number-five shirt, he played at centre-forward and scored a memorable hat-trick (one goal from the penalty-spot) in 'Boro's dramatic 5-3 defeat at Cardiff City which sent the club plummeting to Division Three. In July 1966, he asked for a transfer but stayed as 'Boro clawed their way back to Division Two, when he competed with Bill Gates for the centre-half spot. He was extremely disappointed when Stan Anderson dropped him for the home game against Bury in 1968-69, which cost him the chance of being an ever-present that season. A £17,000 move to Bristol City in June 1969 caused great consternation amongst Mid-

dlesbrough fans but Anderson felt that he had a natural replacement in utility player Gates. Rooks joined Scunthorpe United as manager in 1974 and stayed two seasons at the Old Show Ground. He later had a spell at Willington as player-coach. He played in 150 senior games for 'Boro.

GARY ROWELL

Seasoned League traveller Gary Rowell was born in Seaham on 6 June 1957. He joined Sunderland straight from school, becoming a Roker Park apprentice in July 1974. He was capped at Under-21 level against Finland but, surprisingly, it was his only representative honour. Rowell was transferred to Norwich City in August 1984, after nearly a century of goals at Roker Park, but his career did not progress as expected at Carrow Road. He welcomed a return to the North-East when Willie Maddren brought him to Ayresome Park in mid-August 1985 for only £25,000. He finished the season as the club's leading scorer, although his goals failed to prevent Middlesbrough's relegation to Division Three. He was out in the cold under new manager Bruce Rioch and was on his way to Brighton in August 1986, but again he failed to find a regular place in the Seagulls' first team. He tried his luck north of the border with Dundee, but played in only one game before returning to English football with Fourth Division Carlisle United in March 1988. Burnley picked him up on a free transfer in August 1988, but most of his games at Turf Moor have been as substitute. With Middlesbrough he scored 12 goals in 30 League and Cup appearances.

TREVOR SENIOR

Trevor Senior wrote to Bristol City as an aspiring 15-year-old but was played out of position when he had a trial at Ashton Gate and was not kept on. Senior, who was born at Dorchester on 28 November 1961, went into non-league football with Dorchester Town before Portsmouth snapped him up for £35,000, in December 1981. He made only 11 League appearances at Fratton Park, scoring two goals, but had more success in a loan spell at Aldershot, where he scored seven goals in ten games. Reading manager Maurice Evans spotted Senior's potential and paid £30,000 for him in August 1983. At Elm Park, Senior quickly found his scoring touch and netted 123 goals in 186 League and Cup appearances. Desperate to play in a higher division, he was on the transfer list for eight months before Watford gave him a chance in the First Division. Senior moved to Vicarage Road in October 1987, for £325,000, but the dream turned sour and he managed only one goal for them in the top flight. In late March 1988, Middlesbrough stepped in with a £200,000 offer and the 6ft 1in striker signed on the eve of the transfer deadline. He made his debut two weeks later, in a 1-1 draw against Birmingham City, and scored twice in a 6-0 home defeat of Sheffield United, but his goals against Bradford City and Chelsea in the play-off games proved the most important in 'Boro's successful bid to reach Division One. Back in the First Division, he again failed to score. Booed off the pitch after being substituted in one game, Senior was transfer-listed. Reading, by now in the Third Division, bought him and he resumed his goalscoring habits at Elm Park, notching another 51 League goals for them. For Middlesbrough he had managed four goals in 14 games. He was released by Reading at the end of the 1991-92 season and accepted an offer to join GM Vauxhall Conference side, Woking.

DAVID SHEARER

David Shearer, nicknamed 'Sheik', was born in Caol on 16 October 1958 and worked as a labourer on a building site after leaving school, playing part-time football with Inverness Clachnacuddin. Middlesbrough beat Hearts for the young Scot's signature but he played in a trial match before the club would sign him for a nominal £5,000 fee, eventually doing so in January 1978. He made a sensational debut when he scored both goals in a 2-0 home win over Chelsea on 4 April 1978. A badly damaged ankle in the 1980-81 season kept out of football for the rest of the season. Restored to full fitness, he was loaned out to Football League new boys Wigan Athletic in March 1980, where he again found his scoring touch with a vengeance, scoring nine goals in his two months' loan spell at Springfield Park. He was allowed to leave for Grimsby Town on 17 June 1983, but he played in only one full League game at Blundell Park in his season there. He had better success following his move to Gillingham in August 1984, averaging a goal in every two League games for the Gills. He then spent four months at Bournemouth when they were in the Second Division but moved to Scunthorpe United in February 1986. In December 1988, he returned to the North-East in a £10,000 transfer to play for his last League club, Darlington, but only made a handful of appearances at Feethams. His brother, Duncan, is the Chelsea, Huddersfield Town, Swindon Town, Blackburn Rovers and Aberdeen player. For 'Boro, David Shearer scored 30 goals in 102/15 League and Cup games.

HAROLD SHEPHERDSON MBE

Harold Shepherdson became best-known as England's trainer and held that position when the World Cup was won in 1966, but he also gave great service to Middlesbrough for almost 50 years, although he made only 17 senior appearances. He was born in the town on 28 October 1918 and played football and cricket for Middlesbrough Boys and Yorkshire Boys. He signed as an amateur for 'Boro in 1932 and became a full-time professional four years later. First-team opportunities were hard to come by, however, because of the wealth of talent at Ayresome Park. During the war, Shepherdson served as an Army PTI staff sergeant and made the occasional appearance for 'Boro in the regional leagues. He was transferred to Southend United in May 1947 but before he made his League debut he suffered a knee injury which ended his playing career. Charlie Cole, 'Boro's trainer, recommended him for the post of assistant trainer at Middlesbrough and in 1949, Shepherdson was promoted after Tom Mayson, Cole's successor, had retired. He became England's trainer in 1957 and served under Walter Winterbottom and Sir Alf Ramsey. Awarded the MBE in 1969, Shepherdson served four periods as caretaker manager of 'Boro. In May 1973 he was awarded a testimonial by the FA and he

retired in October 1983, when he was Middlesbrough's chief executive (football) and covered football for BBC Radio Cleveland. When news broke of Bobby Moore's death early in 1993, one daily newspaper erroneously reported in Moore's obituary that former England trainer Harold Shepherdson was also dead. Like Mark Twain before him, Harold said that reports of his death were 'greatly exaggerated'.

BERNIE SLAVEN

Bernie Slaven, self-confessed junk food addict, who was born in Paisley on 13 November 1960, was affectionately known as 'The Wolfman' by colleagues and supporters. A non-smoker and teetotaller, Slaven played for Morton, Airdrie, Queen of South and Albion Rovers and enjoyed his biggest success with Albion, completing the 1984-85 season as Scotland's top scorer with 31 goals, which won him the Golden Shot Trophy. Despite this, he spent that summer in dispute with his club, refusing to re-sign, and did not play competitive football for three months. In a desperate bid to salvage his career, he wrote to every English First and Second Division club,

asking for a trial. Slaven was a part-time gardener on a short-term contract with Glasgow Corporation and playing part-time football when 'Boro boss, Willie Maddren, offered him a trial at Ayresome Park. In October 1985, Maddren signed Slaven, at a £15,000 bargain price, with a further £10,000 to be paid to Albion Rovers after a certain number of first-team appearances. It later transpired that Maddren had moved at just the right time, for Leeds United were showing an interest in the player. Maddren agreed to buy Slaven without club chairman Alf Duffield's approval, but when Duffield saw Slaven play, he was soon won over. Slaven became a favourite, scoring on his home debut against Bradford City. He experienced relegation in his first full season and almost returned to Scotland amidst the trauma of the club's bankruptcy. Happily, he remained to help 'Boro back and proved he could thrive in the First Division. Slaven went on to become Middlesbrough's leading League scorer for six consecutive seasons but surprisingly was not favoured by new boss Lennie Lawrence. Yet despite starting only 28 games, he was second-highest scorer when 'Boro regained their place in the top flight. In 1993, 15 clubs came in for Slaven — Nottingham Forest, Aston Villa and Blackburn Rovers were all willing to take him on until the end of the season — but he was looking further ahead and rejected them all. He took a free transfer to John Rudge's Port Vale, but made an inauspi-

cious debut by being sent off at Leyton Orient. He scored a goal and made another for former 'Boro player Paul Kerr in Vale's first-ever appearance at Wembley as they won the Autoglass Trophy in late May 1993. He returned a week later in the Second Division Play-off Final against West Brom, but the Baggies won, thus preventing a double celebration. A Republic of Ireland international by grandparental qualification, Bernie Slaven is seventh in the list of all-time Middlesbrough goalscorers. Altogether he scored 134 goals in 334/26 senior games.

GEORGE SMITH

Wing-half George Smith, a midfield dynamo and a player in the Billy Bremner mould, was born in Newcastle upon Tyne and signed for Newcastle United in September 1963. He went on to play for seven other League clubs in his career. From United, it was on to Barrow in March 1965 and he stayed two years in Cumbria where he had his most successful scoring return of 11 goals in 91 League appearances. Second Division Portsmouth was his next port of call under his new boss, also called George Smith. Stan Anderson parted with £50,000 to bring Smith to Ayresome Park in January 1969. He quickly became a favourite with the fans and was elected Player of the Year at the end of his first season. After 82 League and Cup appearances for Middlesbrough, he was involved in a player-exchange deal in March 1971 which brought Birmingham City's Johnny Vincent to Teesside. But Smith's stay at St Andrew's was brief, for he was soon on his way to Cardiff City, where Vincent also ended up after Middlesbrough. Two seasons later, he was still in Wales, now playing for Swansea Town. He was transferred to Hartlepool United in October 1977, as player-coach.

GRAEME SOUNESS

Graeme Souness, an elegant player with a lethal shot, was born in Edinburgh on 6 May 1953, the son of a glazier. A Scottish Schoolboy and Youth international, he signed apprentice forms for Spurs in 1969 and became a professional the following year. He was a member of the Tottenham

side which won the FA Youth Cup but was homesick and returned to Scotland. He went back, but was unable to make much impression as there was fierce competition for places at White Hart Lane. In December 1972, Souness became one of Stan Anderson's last signings for Middlesbrough, joining the club for £32,000. Capped by Scotland Under-23's in his first full season in the Middlesbrough side, he was a member of the Second Division promotion team and, with 'Boro back in Division One, he won his first full cap. His 'skilful, silky style' disguised the aggression that was always just under the surface and he had a gritty determination to win. A Middlesbrough club record receipt of £352,000 took him to Liverpool in 1978, after 204 senior appearances and 23 goals for 'Boro, and he spent seven seasons at Anfield, sharing in some great domestic and European triumphs and captaining both club and country. In June 1984, after making more than 350 first-team appearances for the Reds, he was transferred to Sampdoria for a reputed £600,000 fee. Souness later returned to Britain to resurrect the flagging fortunes of Glasgow Rangers, replacing Jock Wallace at Ibrox. As player-manager of a side which contained several English-born players, Souness took Rangers to several honours and became Britain's first player-manager-director, when he bought a stake in the Ibrox club. In April 1991, Souness was appointed manager of Liverpool and, despite an FA

Cup win in 1992, has not enjoyed the success of his illustrious predecessors. He underwent a heart by-pass operation in April 1992 and after speculation about his future, he was given a vote of confidence by the Liverpool board in May 1993.

FRANK SPRAGGON

Frank Spraggon, son-in-law of Harold Shepherdson, was born at Marley Hill on 27 October 1945 and joined Middlesbrough in 1962, when Bob Dennison was in charge. He signed professional forms in November that year and progressed through the junior and reserve ranks before making his first-team debut in a League Cup tie against Bradford in October 1963. Spraggon went on to become Middlesbrough's regular left-half for several seasons, although a cartilage operation and then trouble with blurred vision combined to keep him out of the game for seven months of the 1971-72 season. With the emergence of Willie Maddren in the number-six position, Spraggon made a successful switch to left-back. He was not a flamboyant player but could always be relied upon to give 100 per cent. After a testimonial game against Dinamo Zagreb in 1975, Spraggon went to play for Minnesota Kicks in the North American Soccer League and made 24 appearances for them in the summer of 1976. He returned to England and signed for Hartlepool but, after only one League appearance for them, he was forced to retire in December 1976 because of a knee injury. He made 318/4 appearances in League and Cup games for 'Boro.

JOHNNY SPUHLER

Johnny Spuhler, born in Sunderland on 18 September 1917, won England Schoolboy honours in 1931 and was taken on as an office boy at Roker Park after he left school. After a while he decided to become a joiner but then Sunderland offered him professional terms and he signed for the Wearsiders in September 1943. During World War Two he guested for Middlesbrough and manager David Jack persuaded him to sign for 'Boro in October 1945, for £1,750. Quickly nicknamed 'Sulpher' by his teammates, he was playing well enough at one time to keep Andy Donaldson, an £18,000 centre-forward, out of the team. Not renowned for intricate ball-skills, Spuhler was most effective when he sprinted into good positions and he was also a fine header of the ball. Occasionally he would drift into offside positions, much to the annoyance of 'Boro's fans. In 1950, he broke his nose against Blackpool but played for several more games before agreeing to go into hospital. In 1954, after 'Boro were relegated, he joined Darlington for £1,000 and by 1956 was player-manager of Spennymoor United. He then had a spell as Shrewsbury Town manager and was full-time coach to Stockton FC but lost the job through economic cut-backs. For eight years he ran a Post Office at Yarm and later lived in Barnard Castle. He scored 81 goals in 241 senior games for Middlesbrough.

ARCHIE STEPHENS

'Archie' Stephens, a superb header of a ball, was born in Liverpool on 19 May 1954 and was baptised Arthur Stephens. He was discovered by Bristol Rovers manager Clive Middlemass playing non-League football for Melksham Town in the Western League. Middlemass offered him a two-game trial with Rovers and, on the strength of those

games, he was offered a one-year contract under new manager Terry Cooper, Melksham Town benefiting by some £3,000. That was in August 1981 and Stephens went on to register 40 League goals in 100 League appearances for Rovers in the lower divisions of the Football League. He signed, in a theatrical manner, on the pitch at half-time in a £20,000 transfer to 'Boro during the home game against Sheffield United on 16 March 1985. In the club's Third Division season of 1986-87, he struck up a good understanding with Bernie Slaven and the twin strike force netted 33 goals between them which took the club back into the Second Division at the first attempt. Stephens was on the transfer list for over two months when Clive Middlemass, now manager of Carlisle United, took him to Brunton Park on 23 December 1987 for £12,000, but his appearances were restricted because of a leg injury. He had a loan spell at Darlington in late April 1989 but the Quakers lost their Football League status when they dropped into the GM Vauxhall Conference. His appearances at Feethams were now rapidly diminishing as Darlington regained their League status at the first attempt. His own Football League career ended in May 1990 at the age of 36, when he left Darlington and played part-time football for Guisborough Town. For Middlesbrough he scored 25 goals in 98/6 League and Cup games.

JIM STEWART

James Stewart, the goalkeeper with the film star's name, was born in Kilwinning on 4 March 1954. He progressed from Troon Juniors to Kilmarnock, where he was capped at Youth, Under-21 and Under-23 levels for Scotland. He won his first full cap as a substitute 'keeper against Chile in 1977. John Neal brought him to Ayresome Park in a £100,000 transfer in May 1978, as cover and competition for Northern Ireland international Jim Platt. Stewart started off the next season as the club's number-one but Platt regained his place in March 1979. At Middlesbrough he won another Under-21 cap, against Portugal and, more importantly, his second full cap was awarded against Norway in 1978. He gained another Under-21 against Portugal as an over-age player. On 15 March 1981, with three years of his contract left, Stewart made a sudden and surprise move to Glasgow Rangers. Their manager John Greig paid Middlesbrough £115,000 to beat the transfer deadline by one day. Middlesbrough manager John Neal wanted him to stay at the club, but said that he would not stand in the player's way if his mind was set on leaving. He made a competent debut three days later, against Dundee United at Ibrox, but was on the losing side, Rangers going down 4-1. Consolation, and revenge against Dundee United, came at the end of the season when he won a Scottish Cup winners' medal at United's expense. United were again the victims at the end of the next season when Stewart picked up a League Cup winners' medal. Jock Wallace became Rangers' manager in November 1984 and immediately Jim Stewart's appearances for Scotland's premier club were curtailed. He was loaned to Dumbarton later in the season, before going to St Mirren on a free transfer as understudy to Campbell Money. He now works as a policeman for the Ministry of Defence and is a part-time goalkeeping coach with Kilmarnock.

NOBBY STILES

Norbert 'Nobby' Stiles was born in Colly-hurst, Manchester, on 18 May 1942, the son of a football-mad undertaker. Stiles captained Manchester Boys and played for England Schoolboys in 1957, joining the Old Trafford groundstaff shortly after leaving school. The Munich air disaster of February 1958 thrust him into United's reserve side, but he did not secure a regular first-team place until the 1964-65 season. But what a season that was for Nobby Stiles. He won a League Championship medal and made his full England debut against Scotland at Wembley in April 1965. He was a star of England's 1966 World Cup Final win — who will ever forget his toothless grin as he danced around Wembley? — and altogether he gained 28 full caps and travelled with the 1970 squad to the World Cup Finals in Mexico. He picked up another League Championship medal and a European Cup-winners' medal in 1968 and after 14 years at Old Trafford, he was transferred to Middlesbrough in May 1971 for a nominal £20,000 fee. Immediately appointed captain by Stan Anderson, injuries and loss of form restricted his appearances in a Middlesbrough shirt. Not fitting into Jack Charlton's plans, he joined Bobby Charlton's Preston North End as player-coach and was manager when they won promotion to Division Two in 1977. He assisted Johnny Giles at Vancouver Whitecaps and was in charge of West Bromwich Albion's youth team until his dismissal at the end of 1988-89. Manchester United stepped in with an offer for Stiles to help Brian Kidd coach the youngsters at Old Trafford. For 'Boro he made 69 appearances.

BOBBY STUART

Full-back Bobby Stuart started his football at Victoria Road School, Middlesbrough, before joining South Bank Juniors. He won an England Schoolboy cap and was signed on amateur forms with Middlesbrough in 1928, when Peter McWilliam was manager. Director John Pallister found Stuart a job as a motor mechanic in his Oxford Road garage before he signed professional forms on 7 January 1931. The player suffered a dislocation of the shoulder in his first game in 'Boro's reserve team, but made a quick recovery. He held the unenviable record of conceding five own-goals in a Middlesbrough shirt. Stuart saw RAF service in Iceland in World War Two but still managed to skipper Middlesbrough for much of the wartime period. On 28 October 1947, David Jack transferred Stuart and striker George Dews to Second Division Plymouth Argyle for a combined fee reported to be £11,000. Stuart, who made 268 senior appearances for 'Boro, had asked for a transfer in March 1947, because George Hardwick had recovered his fitness and the younger Dicky Robinson was waiting in the wings. He coached Whitby in 1951, but an accident in 1953 ended his active participation in football. Stuart died in hospital on 25 August 1987.

PETER TAYLOR

Peter Taylor is perhaps best known as Brian Clough's managerial partner at Derby County and Nottingham Forest in the late 1960s and 1970s. But Taylor also enjoyed a good career as a goalkeeper, primarily with Middlesbrough. He was born at Nottingham on 2 July 1928 and was on Forest's books as an amateur before signing for Coventry City in May 1946. After 86 League appearances for the Highfield Road club, Taylor was signed by Middlesbrough in August 1955 and eventually replaced Rolando Ugolini as 'Boro's first-choice

'keeper. At Ayresome Park he became a close friend of Clough and that partnership later took both Derby and Forest to League Championship wins. In June 1961, Taylor was transferred to Port Vale after making 146 senior appearances for Middlesbrough, but he played only one League game for Vale before retiring. He became manager of Southern League Burton Albion, whilst teaching PE on a part-time basis at a local school, and then rejoined Clough at Hartlepool United, where the former 'Boro centre-forward was manager. The pair moved to Derby in 1967 but in 1974, after Derby had enjoyed the greatest success in their history, both men resigned amidst huge controversy. They continued their partnership at Brighton, but when Clough was tempted to Leeds, Taylor stayed at the Goldstone Ground. He joined up with Clough again at Nottingham and shared in the Reds' European Cup triumphs before an acrimonious split with Clough. Taylor later returned to Derby as manager, but when the Rams were on their way to Division Three, he was dismissed. He went to live in retirement near Nottingham and died whilst on holiday in Majorca on 4 October 1990.

KEN THOMSON

Ken Thomson was born in Aberdeen on 25 February 1930 and signed for the Dons from the Banks O'Dee club in January 1947, when he was just 17 years of age. He joined First Division Stoke City on 5 September

1952, the £22,000 fee being a club record receipt for Aberdeen. He was signed just in time to make his debut, coincidentally against Middlesbrough, at the Victoria Ground. City won that game 1-0, but Thomson experienced relegation in his full season with the Potters. However, with a balanced, determined side, Stoke regained First Division status at the first attempt. City manager Frank Taylor and 'Boro boss Bob Dennison agreed on a £9,000 transfer to Middlesbrough on 10 December 1959, but only on the proviso that 'Boro did not play him against Stoke City at the Victoria Ground the next day. 'Boro agreed and promptly won the match 5-2! Thomson made his debut nine days after signing for the club in a 6-3 defeat by Portsmouth at Fratton Park. He soon displayed his leadership qualities and was named team captain when Brian Clough relinquished the role in the summer of 1960. In September 1962, Dennison brought Welsh international centre-half Mel Nurse to the club and within a month Ken Thomson was on his way to Hartlepool United, on 12 October 1962 but he was suspended *sine die* for illegal activities after playing only 28 games for 'Pool. He died of a heart attack whilst playing golf at Maiden Castle.

ROLANDO UGOLINI

Rolando Ugolini, nicknamed 'Ugo' upon his entry into League football, was born in Lucca, home of Italy's olive oil industry, in June 1924. In 1925 his family moved to Scotland and he became a naturalised Briton. With his Glasgow background it is no surprise that he speaks with a pro-

nounced Scottish accent. Ugolini earned a big reputation in junior football and was on Hearts' books before being snapped up by Celtic in April 1944, although the form of Scottish international Willie Miller kept 'Ugo' out of the first team. The young reserve 'keeper turned down a move to Chelsea, but in May 1948 he was ready to join 'Boro for £7,000 and soon established himself as first choice, despite conceding seven goals on his first appearance, in a pre-season practice game. The following week's programme notes gave this summary on Ugolini's League debut at Stamford Bridge: 'This lithe young man, who possesses all the acrobatics of the Continental 'keeper plus the reliability associated with those who play for British teams'. Ugolini could send a dead ball well into his opponents' half, his handling was safe and he liked to keep the game flowing. Known as 'Rolando the Cat', he was a great character — a bit like today's Bruce Grobbelaar — and was 'Boro's regular goalkeeper for almost nine years, helping them finish sixth in Division One in 1950-51. Eventually he was replaced by Peter Taylor for the last game of 1955-56, at Doncaster. He spent the whole of the following season in the Reserves and in June 1957, aged 33, was transferred to Third Division Wrexham after making 335 League and Cup appearances for Middlesbrough. He spent two seasons in their first-team before leaving English football in 1959 with over 400 League appearances to his credit. He later played for Dundee United, sold his betting shops and now lives in retirement in Scotland.

TOMMY URWIN

Tommy Urwin played for all three big North-East clubs and was awarded benefit games with all of them. He starred for England Schoolboys in 1910 and his first tentative steps in senior football were with Fulwell, then Lambton Star and Shildon in 1913, as he collected County Durham representative honours along the way. He signed for Middlesbrough as an amateur in February 1914, then professional in May, and made his League debut at outside-left

against Sunderland in January 1915. He was awarded his Middlesbrough benefit during 1921-22 and toured with the England party, winning two full caps against Sweden in May 1923. Urwin would not accept the terms offered by Middlesbrough when the club suffered their first relegation at the end of 1923-24 and he signed for Newcastle United in August 1924, after exactly 200 first-team appearances for Middlesbrough. When 'Boro won the Second Division championship in 1927, Newcastle United clinched the League Championship. With Newcastle he earned Football League representative honours in 1927. In February 1930, Urwin moved to Sunderland, where he ended his League career in 1936 and took up a position as youth-team coach. In 1948 he was acting as a scout for the club and working as an accountant at Sunderland Royal Infirmary. He once owned a tailor's shop in that town.

GEOFF WALKER

Geoff Walker was a speedy winger whose fierce shots from the wing and hard, dangerous centres terrorised opposing defences. He was born in Bradford on 29 September 1926 and during World War Two he played for Bradford in the regional league. Middlesbrough manager David Jack signed Walker from Park Avenue in June 1946, in time for the first peacetime Football

League season, and he went on to score over 50 goals for the club in League football. In February 1949, Walker asked for a transfer but came off the list when no other club showed an interest. It was not until December 1954, with Middlesbrough now a Second Division side, that he finally moved from Ayresome Park, joining Doncaster Rovers who were also in Division Two. In almost two seasons at Belle Vue, Walker made 84 League appearances and scored 15 goals. In 1957 he moved back to his home town, this time to sign for Bradford City, but made only two League appearances for them. In August 1963, aged 36, he was playing for Clacton Town in the Southern League and was a sports master at a nearby public school. For Middlesbrough he netted 53 goals in 259 senior games.

JOHN WALKER

John Walker played junior football as an outside-left in Beith, where he was born, but switched to left-back when kicking about in a makeshift game during a dinner-break when he was a factory worker. After moving to Burnbank Athletic, he was spotted by Raith Rovers and signed for the Scottish Second Division club. Dogged by a persistent leg injury and concerned that the attentions of the Raith trainer were not improving matters, he sought the advice of the Celtic trainer, who advised complete rest. Raith found out about his visit and suspended him. Walker swore that he would never play for Rovers again and returned to Beith. When he was fit again, Rangers signed him for £60 in the 1905-06 season but in the close season of 1907 he switched to Southern League Swindon Town. In 1911, he won the first of nine caps for Scotland, and toured Argentina with Swindon, who had just won the Southern League championship. In 1913, Middlesbrough manager Tommy McIntosh paid £1,000 to sign the man who was regarded as the best full-back in the Southern League and Walker served 'Boro either side of World War Two, playing in 109 peacetime games altogether. He was transferred to Reading in 1921 and retired from the game a year later. He later ran a fish shop in Swindon for some years.

JOHN WARK

Glaswegian John Wark was born on 4 August 1957 and played his early football with Drumchapel Amateurs. After winning Scottish Youth international honours, he joined Ipswich Town as a centre-half in August 1974. The holder of eight Under-21 caps, he picked up an FA Cup winners' medal in 1977 when Ipswich beat Arsenal in the Wembley Final. Wark's goals helped Ipswich win the UEFA Cup in 1981 and two successive Football League runners-up spots, to Aston Villa and Liverpool. However, his disappointment was dispelled with a fine display in the 1982 World Cup finals in Spain in 1982. he won a total of 26 caps during his stay at Portman Road. A £450,000 transfer to Liverpool followed in 1984 and he picked up his first League championship success at Anfield along with another three Scottish caps. Wark missed a full season at Anfield with a broken ankle, which was followed by some damage to his Achilles tendon. Ipswich Town manager John Duncan took him back to Portman Road in January 1988 and at the end of the season he was voted Town's Player of the Year. New manager John Lyall offered him a fresh contract in the close season, but Wark felt the terms were derisory. He was approached by Norwich City, Hull City, West Bromwich Albion and Middlesbrough before deciding to throw in his lot with Colin Todd at Ayresome Park, signing a two-year contract in the summer of 1990, Ipswich receiving a nominal £50,000 fee. Todd and Middlesbrough parted company in June 1991, but new manager Lennie Lawrence decided to release Wark with a year of his contract still to run. He turned down an offer from First Division Coventry

City and also rejected an opportunity to join Colchester United in the GM Vauxhall Conference, instead returning to Ipswich Town for the third time, on a one-year contract. He proved that there was still life in the old dog by helping Ipswich clinch the Second Division championship, claiming that his Football League career had lasted so long because he slept so much when not playing football. For Middlesbrough he made 38/1 League and Cup appearances.

FREDDY WARREN

Frederick Windsor Warren was born in Cardiff on 23 December 1909 and joined his home-town club Cardiff City, then a First Division side, after playing in local football. Middlesbrough manager Peter McWilliam caused quite a stir in the football world when he signed three players from the same club, Cardiff City, on the same day — 29 January 1930. The three Cardiff players were goalkeeper Joe Hillier, defender Jack Jennings and outside-left Freddy Warren. Of the three signings, Jennings and Warren, who already a Welsh cap each to their credit, were to make the most impact on Teesside. All three made their League debuts for Middlesbrough in the same match — a 4-1 defeat at Leicester on 1 February 1930. Warren was sent off in 'Boro's game against Sheffield Wednesday at Hillsborough on 29 December 1930 and was suspended by the FA for a fortnight for misconduct. He was prone to injuries which often cost him his place in the 'Boro side for most of the 1931-32 season, but on his making a complete recovery the Welsh selectors remembered the speedy winger and he won a further three caps as a Middlesbrough player. Injury again forced him to miss a lot of games during 1932-33, but again, following an operation, he made a complete recovery, so

much so that he played in the first Welsh side to play international football abroad when he was picked to play against the French in Paris in 1933, a game that ended 1-1. Playing in a North-Eastern League game against for Middlesbrough Reserves against Durham City on Christmas Day 1933, he wrenched a muscle behind the knee so badly that the injury kept him out of the game for three months. He was transferred to Hearts in a £650 deal on 9 May 1936, after nearly seven seasons with Middlesbrough, during which he had scored 50 goals in 164 League and Cup appearances. His playing career ended with a fifth and final cap as a Hearts player.

JIMMY WATSON

Jimmy Watson, veteran of 107 senior games for Middlesbrough, was born on 4 October 1877 and started his football career with Burnbank, a Lanarkshire junior side. He declined an offer from Hearts, on the grounds that Edinburgh was too far from his native Motherwell, and then failed to impress in two trial games at Sheffield United. Eventually he signed for Clyde and his displays at full-back quickly brought him to the attention of Sunderland, where he spent eight successful seasons, winning a League Championship medal in 1902 and four full Scotland caps, against England (three games) and Wales. His transfer to Middlesbrough came towards the close of the 1906-07 season and he was ever-present the following season. In 1909 he won two further caps, against England and Ireland, and the following year was appointed 'Boro's assistant trainer for a spell before ending his career with Shildon. He managed the Leviathan Hotel in Sussex Street, Middlesbrough, before emigrating to Canada and in the 1920s was coaching in that country. Watson had the nickname of 'Daddy Long Legs' because he 'threw' his legs and arms all over the place in his relentless pursuit of an opponent. He was instantly recognizable in team photographs because of his dark hair, parted down the middle and his 'circus strongman' moustache.

CHARLIE WAYMAN

Centre-forward Charlie Wayman was a natural goalscorer who did well for all his clubs. Born at Bishop Auckland on 16 May 1921, Wayman worked as a miner and played for Spennymoor United before signing for Newcastle United in September 1941. He scored four of Newcastle's goals in their 13-0 Second Division rout of Newport County in 1946-47, but the headlines centred on United's debutant Len Shackleton, who rattled in six goals against the Welsh side. After scoring 32 goals in 47 League games, Wayman was allowed to move to Southampton (the team against whom he had scored an FA Cup hat-trick the previous season) in October 1947. He led the Saints' attack for three memorable seasons, scoring 73 goals in 100 League games. His wife could not settle in the area, however, and in September 1950 he moved to Preston. Wayman continued his spectacular scoring for the Deepdale club with 104 goals in 157 League games. He also netted one of Preston's goals in the 1954 FA Cup Final. Bob Dennison paid £8,000 to take Wayman to Ayresome Park in September

1954 and his goals played a vital part in keeping 'Boro in the Second Division. He spent two seasons at Middlesbrough, with a fine strike rate of 33 goals in only 58 senior games, before moving to Darlington in December 1956, at the age of 35, before a knee injury ended his League career in March 1958. He later became a brewery representative in Bishop Auckland. He revealed that one of the secrets of his goalscoring ability was that he wore Brazilian football boots.

MAURICE WEBSTER

Blackpool-born Maurice Webster played local football in the South Shore & District Wednesday League. He enlisted in the 4th Duke of Wellington's Regiment at the tender age of 17 and saw service in France during World War One. After the war he joined Lytham in the West Lancashire League and then turned out for Fleetwood in the Lancashire Combination. Webster declined the chance to join Blackburn Rovers, after trial games in the Central League, before signing professional forms for Stalybridge Celtic in 1921. Less than a season later, Middlesbrough manager, James Howie, persuaded Stalybridge, then in their brief career in the Football League, to part with Webster for £1,500 and he signed on 27 March 1922. Howie just beat Liverpool manager David Ashworth for Webster's signature and the player made his 'Boro debut in a reserve game at Workington the following week. His Football League debut came at Huddersfield on 1 May 1922. Webster played in an England trial match at Liverpool and was given the task of marking his Middlesbrough colleague, George Camsell. He did so with distinction (his side won 6-1) and gained three England caps in 1930, the first against Scotland in April. He was selected for the England

summer tour and played in Vienna and Berlin, where he had the misfortune to break his nose. After 281 senior games for Middlesbrough, Webster was transferred to Carlisle United on 6 June 1935 and in his 13th game for the Cumbrian side he broke his right leg. He remained at Brunton Park as trainer until war broke out and was trainer, coach and groundsman at Stockton FC from 1948 until 1954. He also worked at Dorman Long's Port Clarence Works and was a regular spectator at Ayresome Park, right up to his death early in 1978.

WILLIE WHIGHAM

Goalkeeper Willie Whigham was born at Airdrie on 9 October 1939 and was a qualified motor mechanic when former

Middlesbrough player, Alex McCrae, signed him for Falkirk. Whigham helped Falkirk to promotion from the Scottish First Division in 1961 and missed only a handful of games in his five seasons at Brockville Park. In October 1966, Middlesbrough manager Stan Anderson paid a bargain £10,000 for Whigham, who went straight into the first team against Watford. Gordon Jones, 'Boro's skipper during that 1966-67 promotion campaign, insisted later that the side would not have gone up without Whigham as their goalkeeper. Yet he was erratic, often playing a 'blinder' one week and letting in a 'soft' goal the next. Always considered something of a rebel, Whigham missed 14 games in 1969-70 because he was dissatisfied with his basic wage and put in a transfer request. He later withdrew it after being offered better terms while he played without a contract. He was dropped after a 4-1 defeat at Sunderland — Jim Platt replaced him — and he moved to Dumbarton. In the summer of 1974 he joined Darlington but made only four League appearances for them. Whigham made 210 first-team appearances for Middlesbrough.

BILL WHITAKER

In April 1942, centre-half Bill Whitaker, who was once described as 'pale-faced and possessor of a lolloping run', was a Bevin Boy down the pit when he signed amateur forms for Chesterfield. Whitaker, who was born in Chesterfield on 7 October 1923, became a professional in the summer of 1942 and soon made his first-team debut in the wartime regional league. He had played in 13 post-war League games when Middlesbrough stepped in to sign him in June 1947, for £9,500, and he went straight into 'Boro's League side to begin a career which saw

him make 184 senior appearances all told. In mid-October 1949, he asked for a transfer after losing his place to Tom Blenkinsopp, but regained his first-team position before anything could develop. Whitaker went on to captain Middlesbrough before losing his place again, this time because of an injury to his knee ligaments. Indeed, throughout his career he had been dogged by knee trouble and it was a cartilage problem that ended his playing days in 1954. Whitaker, who appeared for the Football League representative team at the height of his career, returned to working down the coal-mines.

PAUL WILKINSON

Born in Louth on 30 October 1964, Paul Wilkinson began his Football League career with Grimsby Town, where he netted 33 goals for the Mariners. After spells at Everton (where he gained a League Championship medal although he was at the City Ground by the time Everton clinched the title) and Nottingham Forest, where he failed to make much impact, he became a goalscoring hero at Watford, being leading marksman in his three seasons at Vicarage Road. Middlesbrough signed Wilkinson in August 1991, for £550,000, and he played in all the 58 matches during the subsequent remarkable season, with 22 senior goals including the promotion-clinching winning goal at Wolverhampton. In 1992-93 he continued to thrive despite 'Boro's struggle in the top flight and to date has scored 37 goals in 104 senior appearances. He won four caps as an England Under-21 player.

OWEN WILLIAMS

Owen Williams was born in Ryhope and was once on Sunderland's books, but was allowed to leave the area and signed for Manchester United. Things did not work out for him in Manchester, either, and he returned to the North-East to play non-League football for Easington Colliery Welfare. At the end of World War One, Clapton Orient showed an interest in him and that was the beginning of a successful League career. Williams spent five good years with Orient, making over 160 appearances before being transferred to Middlesbrough in February 1924. He made his debut

for 'Boro, against West Bromwich Albion, three days later, but at the end of the season found himself in Division Two as Middlesbrough were relegated. He was, though, a member of the famous forward line – Birrell, Pease, Camsell, Jack Carr and Williams – which took 'Boro to the championship in 1926-27. At the end of 1929-30, after another relegation and promotion for the club, he was placed on the transfer list and signed for Southend United in August 1930, for £250. His 194 senior games for Middlesbrough yielded 44 goals.

TIM WILLIAMSON

Reginald Garnet Williamson, known as 'Tim' throughout his footballing life, was born at North Ormesby on 6 June 1884.

His early football career was spent with Coatham Grammar School, Redcar Juniors and Redcar Crusaders before he kept goal as a 17-year-old for Middlesbrough in a friendly against Cliftonville. 'Boro wanted to sign him as a professional but he agreed only after they allowed him to continue his interest in becoming a qualified draughtsman. Williamson's first competitive game for the club was against Crook Town in the Northern Alliance on New Year's Day 1902. His League debut came against Bristol City at Linthorpe Road on 19 April that year — the first of 602 League and Cup appearances which stands as a club record to this day. After initially understudying Scottish international Rab Macfarlane, he gained a regular place in 1903-04 and never looked back. The first of seven full England caps came in February 1905 in the first international to be played at Ayresome Park (he scored an own-goal for Ireland) but his second appearance was delayed for six years, due to the brilliance of Sam Hardy. A reserved occupation meant that Williamson was exempt from military service in World War One but later, the Football League refused to sanction his benefit on the grounds that those war years did not contribute towards his Middlesbrough service. He retired at the end of 1922-23 but continued to keep goal for a works team. Not interested in watching football, he spent his free time playing golf and taking his sporting gun to Teesmouth. On 1 August 1943, Tim Williamson died at North Ormesby Hospital, after an operation, and is buried in Coatham Churchyard.

of £4 per week. He played a full season with his new club before enlisting in the 6th Highland Light Infantry in August 1915. Posted to France with the 16th Royal Scots, he lost his lance-corporal's stripe at Arras in what he described as 'a disagreement' with another soldier. It was at Arras, early in 1918, that a shell fragment shattered his left hand. 'Boro still held his Football League registration but, after being invalided home, he was allowed to play for Hearts and also scored four goals for Scotland in two Victory international wins over England and Ireland. He won his first six full caps whilst with Dunfermline Athletic in the 'rebel' Scottish Central League (for whom he netted 104 goals in two seasons) and was a prolific scorer for Scotland on a goodwill tour of North America, before rejoining Middlesbrough in August 1921. Wilson was the leading First Division scorer in 1921-22 and in late November 1923 he moved to Chelsea for a record £6,000. At the end of that season Chelsea and 'Boro were relegated and Wilson was leading scorer for both clubs. He became a favourite at Stamford Bridge and later played for QPR and in France before managing Clacton Town, Walsall and Gravesend & Northfleet. His son, Jimmy, played for Chelsea in the 1950s. He scored 57 goals in only 90 senior games for 'Boro. Despite the physical handicap of the hand injury, he was a most accomplished sportsman and won the London and Southern Counties gold badge at bowls. His death was reported in October 1973.

League appearances before moving to 'Boro for £3,750. He went into the Reserves before making his Football League debut in a 2-0 defeat at Hillsborough in December 1958. That was the start of a fine career at Ayresome Park and in May 1963 Yeoman ended a remarkable spell of 207 consecutive League and Cup appearances. Altogether he made 227 senior appearances. In June 1964, aged 30, he was transferred to Darlington and made 103 League appearances for them before being appointed manager in 1968. He left Feethams in 1970 and joined Sunderland as youth-team manager that summer. Now in business on Teesside, Ray Yeoman is a frequent visitor to Ayresome Park in his capacity as a scout for Everton.

BENNY YORSTON

Diminutive Benny Yorston — he stood only 5ft 5in tall — was Middlesbrough's pocket-sized dynamo of a centre-forward who served the club in the years leading up to World War Two. Born at Nigg, Aberdeen, on 14 October 1905, the son of a trawler skipper, Yorston played junior football with Mugiemoss whilst working as an office boy for Aberdeen. After a few games in the Dons' third team, Yorston was allowed to sign for Richmond. He later played for Montrose, where he was capped as a Scottish junior international, before Aberdeen took him on again. He first showed his paces on Aberdeen's 1927 tour of South Africa and responded with goals galore. In 1929-30 he set a still unbeaten club record with 38 goals and was capped by Scotland in 1931. In January 1932, Sunderland snapped him up for £2,000 and in March 1934 he moved to Middlesbrough for £1,184. 'Boro wanted Raich Carter, but the Wearsiders offered 29-year-old Yorston instead. A broken leg at Blackpool in December 1937 checked his progress but he recovered to play regularly until war was declared. He joined the Army Physical Training Corps in 1940 and ended his playing days during the war. Yorston served Bury, then Barnsley, as chief scout after the war before going into business in South Kensington, London, where he let flats. In November 1977, he died at his London home, aged 72. He scored 54 goals in 159 League and Cup games for Middlesbrough.

ANDY WILSON

At Christmas 1913, Andy Wilson played for Cambuslang, a Glasgow junior team, in a friendly at Roker Park against Sunderland Reserves. After the game Middlesbrough chairman Phil Bach offered Wilson £10 to sign for 'Boro and the player agreed, although he returned to Scotland that day. On 20 February 1914, manager Tommy McIntosh travelled north and completed the formalities, Wilson joining 'Boro for the maximum wage

RAY YEOMAN

Ramon Yeoman, who was known as 'Ray' throughout his football career, was born in Perth on 13 May 1934 and played for St Johnstone before moving to Northampton Town in September 1953. Bob Dennison was then managing the Cobblers and he was impressed by Yeoman, an inside-forward who was described as having 'an honest style . . .a player of integrity, dedication and determination'. Dennison moved to Middlesbrough in 1954 but it was some years later, in November 1958, that he signed Yeoman for a second time. Yeoman had been converted to wing-half at the County Ground and had made 168

Middlesbrough's Record in the League 1899-1993

		HOME					AWAY						
Season	P	W	D	L	F	A	W	D	L	F	A	Pts	Pos
DIVISION TWO													
1899-1900	34	8	4	5	28	15	0	4	13	11	54	24	14th
1900-01	34	11	4	2	38	13	4	3	10	12	27	37	6th
1901-02	34	15	1	1	58	7	8	4	5	32	17	51	2nd
DIVISION ONE													
1902-03	34	10	3	4	27	16	4	1	12	14	34	32	13th
1903-04	34	9	3	5	30	17	0	9	8	16	30	30	10th
1904-05	34	7	3	7	21	24	2	5	10	15	32	26	15th
1905-06	38	10	4	5	41	23	0	7	12	15	48	31	18th
1906-07	38	11	2	6	33	21	4	4	11	23	42	36	11th
1907-08	38	12	2	5	32	16	5	5	9	22	29	41	6th
1908-09	38	11	2	6	38	21	3	7	9	21	32	37	9th
1909-10	38	8	4	7	34	36	3	5	11	22	37	37	17th
1910-11	38	9	5	5	31	21	2	5	12	18	42	32	16th
1911-12	38	11	6	2	35	17	5	2	12	21	28	40	7th
1912-13	38	6	9	4	29	22	5	1	13	26	47	32	16th
1913-14	38	14	2	3	55	20	5	3	11	22	40	43	3rd
1914-15	38	10	6	3	42	24	3	6	10	20	50	38	12th
1919-20	42	10	5	6	35	23	5	5	11	26	42	40	13th
1920-21	42	10	6	5	29	21	7	6	8	24	32	46	8th
1921-22	42	12	6	3	46	19	4	8	9	33	50	46	8th
1922-23	42	11	4	6	41	25	2	6	13	16	38	36	18th
1923-24	42	6	4	11	23	23	1	4	16	14	37	22	22nd
DIVISION TWO													
1924-25	42	6	10	5	22	21	4	9	8	14	23	39	13th
1925-26	42	14	1	6	56	28	7	1	13	21	40	44	9th
1926-27	42	18	2	1	78	23	9	6	6	44	37	62	1st
DIVISION ONE													
1927-28	42	7	9	5	46	35	4	6	11	35	53	37	22nd
DIVISION TWO													
1928-29	42	14	4	3	54	22	8	7	6	38	35	55	1st
DIVISION ONE													
1929-30	42	11	3	7	48	31	5	3	13	34	53	38	16th
1930-31	42	13	5	3	57	28	6	3	12	41	62	46	7th
1931-32	42	12	3	6	41	29	3	6	12	23	54	38	18th
1932-33	42	8	5	8	35	33	6	4	11	28	40	37	17th
1933-34	42	13	3	5	51	26	3	4	14	17	51	39	16th
1934-35	42	8	9	4	38	29	2	5	14	32	61	34	20th
1935-36	42	12	6	3	56	23	3	4	14	28	47	40	14th
1936-37	42	14	6	1	49	22	5	2	14	25	49	46	7th
1937-38	42	12	4	5	40	26	7	4	10	32	39	46	5th
1938-39	42	13	6	2	64	27	7	3	11	29	47	49	4th
1946-47	42	11	3	7	46	32	6	5	10	27	36	42	11th
1947-48	42	8	7	6	37	27	6	2	13	34	46	37	16th
1948-49	42	10	6	5	37	23	1	6	14	9	34	34	19th
1949-50	42	14	2	5	37	18	6	5	10	22	30	47	9th
1950-51	42	12	7	2	51	25	6	4	11	25	40	47	6th
1951-52	42	12	4	5	37	25	3	2	16	27	63	36	18th
1952-53	42	12	5	4	46	27	2	6	13	24	50	39	13th
1953-54	42	6	6	9	29	35	4	4	13	31	56	30	21st
DIVISION TWO													
1954-55	42	13	1	7	48	31	5	5	11	25	51	42	12th
1955-56	42	11	4	6	46	31	5	4	12	30	47	40	14th
1956-57	42	12	5	4	51	29	7	5	9	33	31	48	6th
1957-58	42	13	3	5	52	29	6	4	11	31	45	45	7th
1958-59	42	9	7	5	51	26	6	3	12	36	45	40	13th
1959-60	42	14	5	2	56	21	5	5	11	34	43	48	5th
1960-61	42	13	6	2	44	20	5	6	10	39	54	48	5th
1961-62	42	11	3	7	45	29	5	4	12	31	43	39	12th
1962-63	42	12	4	5	48	35	8	5	8	38	50	49	4th
1963-64	42	14	4	3	47	16	1	7	13	20	36	41	10th
1964-65	42	8	5	8	40	31	5	4	12	30	45	35	17th
1965-66	42	8	8	5	36	28	2	5	14	22	58	33	21st
DIVISION THREE													
1966-67	46	16	3	4	51	20	7	6	10	36	44	55	2nd
DIVISION TWO													
1967-68	42	10	7	4	39	19	7	5	9	21	35	46	6th
1968-69	42	13	7	1	36	13	6	4	11	22	36	49	4th
1969-70	42	15	4	2	36	14	5	6	10	19	31	50	4th
1970-71	42	13	6	2	37	16	4	8	9	23	27	48	7th
1971-72	42	16	4	1	31	11	3	4	14	19	37	46	9th
1972-73	42	12	6	3	29	15	5	7	9	17	28	47	4th
1973-74	42	16	4	1	40	8	11	7	3	37	22	65	1st
DIVISION ONE													
1974-75	42	11	7	3	33	14	7	5	9	21	26	48	7th
1975-76	42	9	7	5	23	11	6	3	12	23	34	40	13th
1976-77	42	11	6	4	25	14	3	7	11	15	31	41	12th
1977-78	42	8	8	5	25	19	4	7	10	17	35	39	14th
1978-79	42	10	5	6	33	21	5	5	11	24	29	40	12th
1979-80	42	11	7	3	31	14	5	5	11	19	30	44	9th
1980-81	42	14	4	3	38	16	2	1	18	15	45	37	14th
1981-82	42	5	9	7	20	24	3	6	12	14	28	*39	22nd
DIVISION TWO													
1982-83	42	8	7	6	27	29	3	8	10	19	58	48	16th
1983-84	42	9	8	4	26	18	3	5	13	15	29	49	17th
1984-85	42	6	8	7	22	26	4	2	15	19	31	40	19th
1985-86	42	8	6	7	26	23	4	3	14	18	30	45	21st
DIVISION THREE													
1986-87	46	16	5	2	38	11	12	5	6	29	19	94	2nd
DIVISION TWO													
1987-88	44	15	4	3	47	16	7	8	7	19	20	78	3rd
DIVISION ONE													
1988-89	38	6	7	6	28	30	3	5	11	16	31	39	18th
DIVISION TWO													
1989-90	46	10	3	10	33	29	3	8	12	19	34	50	21st
1990-91	46	12	4	7	36	17	8	5	10	30	30	69	7th
1991-92	46	15	6	2	37	13	8	5	10	21	28	80	2nd
FA PREMIER DIVISION													
1992-93	42	8	5	8	33	27	3	6	12	21	48	44	21st

*From 1981-82 three points awarded for a win.

1899-1900
Division 2

Player columns (left to right): Smith EG, Shaw TW, Ramsey A, Allport HG, McNally J, McCracken JP, Wanless R, Longstaffe G, Gettins JH, Page R, Pugh CE, Osborne F, Hughes M, Redfern J, Callaghan J, Murphy M, Bell FW, Pratt R, Eglington R, Stott J, Lamb TJ, Piercy FR, Gray R, Raisbeck L, Clark E, Reid G, Murphy J, Cowan J, McCorquodale D, Jones J, Piercy HR

Date	Opponent	Result	Scorers	Att.	Sm	Sh	Ra	Al	McN	McC	Wa	Lo	Ge	Pa	Pu	Os	Hu	Re	Ca	MuM	Be	Pr	Eg	St	La	PiF	Gr	Rai	Cl	Rd	MuJ	Co	McCq	Jo	PiH
Sep 2 (a)	Lincoln C	L 0-3			1	2	3	4	5	6	7	8	9	10	11																				
Sep 4 (a)	Port Vale	L 1-3	Page	1,800	1	2	3	4	5	6	8	7		10	11	9																			
Sep 9 (h)	Small Heath	L 1-3	M.Murphy	10,000		2	3	4	5		7		9		11		1			6	8	10													
Sep 16 (a)	New Brighton	D 1-1	Eglington			2	3	4	5		7				11		1				8		6				9	10							
Sep 23 (h)	Grimsby T	W 1-0	Eglington	4,000		2	3	4	5		7				11		1					9	10				6	8							
Sep 30 (a)	W Arsenal	L 0-3		5,000		2	3	4	5	6	7				11		1					9	10					8							
Oct 7 (h)	Barnsley	W 3-0	Longstaffe, Lamb 2		1	2	3	4	5	6	7	9			11								10		8										
Oct 14 (a)	Leicester F	L 1-4	Lamb		1	2	3	4	5		7				11								9		8	6		10							
Oct 21 (h)	Luton T	D 0-0			1	2	3	4	5		7				11	9									8		6	10							
Nov 4 (h)	Walsall	D 1-1	Lamb		1	2	3	4	5	6	7	8			11										10			9						
Nov 11 (h)	Burton S	W 8-1	J.Murphy 3, Longstaffe, Pugh 2, Reid 2		1		3	4		6	7	8			11													5		2	9				10
Nov 25 (h)	Gainsborough T	D 0-0		6,000	1		3	4		6	7	8			11													5		2	9				10
Dec 2 (a)	Bolton W	L 0-3		3,156			3	4		6	7	8			11		1											5		2	9				10
Dec 9 (h)	Loughborough T	W 3-0	Raisbeck, M.Murphy, J.Murphy	3,000			3	4		6	7	8			11		1			10								5		2	9				
Dec 16 (a)	Newton Heath	L 1-2	Reid	4,000			3	4		6	7	8			11		1					10						5		2	9				
Dec 23 (h)	Sheffield W	L 1-2	Reid				3	4		6	7	8			11		1					10						5		2	9				
Dec 30 (h)	Lincoln C	D 1-1	J.Murphy	6,000			3	4		6	7	8			11		1					11						5		2	9	10		3	4
Jan 6 (h)	Small Heath	L 1-5	Pratt			2					7					6	1					10			8			5		9	11	3		4	
Jan 13 (h)	New Brighton	W 5-2	Page, Longstaffe, Lamb 2, Pugh	4,000			4	3			7	8		10	11	6	1											5		9		2			
Jan 20 (a)	Grimsby T	L 0-2		3,500			4	3			7	8			11	6	1					10						5		9		2			
Jan 27 (a)	Chesterfield	L 1-7	Pugh	1,000			4	3			7	8			11	6	1					10						5				2			
Feb 3 (h)	W Arsenal	W 1-0	Pugh	5,000			4	2			7	8			11	6	1											5		9		3			
Feb 10 (a)	Barnsley	L 2-5	Reid, H.Piercy			3	4	2				8				6	1					10								9		5			
Feb 17 (a)	Leicester F	L 0-1		8,000		2	3	4		2	7				11		1								8			5		9		6			
Feb 24 (a)	Luton T	D 1-1	Osborne	1,000			3	4		2					11	6	1					7			8		5								
Mar 3 (h)	Port Vale	W 1-0	Pugh				3	4		2	7				11	6	1					10			8										
Mar 10 (a)	Walsall	D 1-1	Pugh	1,000			3	4		2	7			10	11	6	1								8			5							
Mar 17 (a)	Burton S	L 0-5					3	4		2	7			10	11	6	1								8			5							
Mar 24 (h)	Chesterfield	L 0-1		5,000			3	4		2	7				11	6	1								8				10	5					
Mar 31 (a)	Gainsborough T	L 0-5					3	4			5				11	6	1					10			8				7		2			
Apr 7 (h)	Bolton W	L 0-3		8,000			3	4	5				9	6			1					10								7	11	2			
Apr 14 (a)	Loughborough T	D 1-1	Niblo	500			3	4		6				10	11	6	1								8				7		2				
Apr 21 (h)	Newton Heath	W 2-0	Niblo, Osborne	8,000	1		2	4		3					6	11	8					10										2			
Apr 28 (a)	Sheffield W	L 0-3		3,000	1		3								6	11	7					10										2			
Apps					10	12	27	31	2	33	10	19	3	14	31	12	24	3	2	2	1	16	5	1	23	1	3	19	1	15	6	17	2	2	8
Goals												3		2	7	2				2		1	2	6			1		5	5				1

FA Cup

Date	Opponent	Result	Scorers	Sh	Ra	Al	McN	Wa	Pu	Hu	Pr	Eg	La	Gr	Round
Oct 28 (h)	Jarrow	L 1-2	Eglington	2	3	4	5	7	11	1	9	10	8	6	Q1
Apps				1	1	1	1	1	1	1	1	1	1	1	
Goals												1			

In the League S.Buckley played number 9 against Chesterfield (a); G.Madden played number 10 against Woolwich Arsenal (h), number 11 against Barnsley (a) and number 9 against Burton Swifts (a); R.W.Evans played number 10 against Leicester Fosse (h) and Luton Town (a); T.Linton played number 9 against Luton Town (a), Port Vale (h), Walsall (a) and Chesterfield (h); J.Clark played number 8 against Bolton Wanderers (h); J.Ostler played number 5 against Loughborough Town (a), Newton Heath (h) and Sheffield Wednesday (a); T.B.Niblo played number 9 against Loughborough Town (a), scoring once, Newton Heath (h), scoring once, and Sheffield Wednesday (a); W.Wardrope played number 7 against Newton Heath (h) and number 8 against Sheffield Wednesday (a).

1900-01
Division 2

Date		Opponent	Res	Scorers	Att	Frail J	Dow MJ	Ramsay A	Millar J	Higgins W	Davidson A	Moran M	Wardrope W	Robertson A	Wilkie J	Brown, James	Brown, John	McCowie A	Eckford J	Carrick C	Jones J	Doig T	Hodgson G	Smith DW	Gettins JH	Macfarlane T	Thompson A	McNally J	Cochrane M	Brearley J
Sep	1 (h)	Lincoln C	W 2-0	Wardrope, A.Robertson	10,088	1	2	3	4	5	6	7	8	9	10	11														
	8 (a)	Newton Heath	L 0-4		5,500	1	2	3	4	5	6	7	8	9	10		11													
	15 (h)	Glossop	D 2-2	Moran, A.Robertson	12,000	1	2	3	4	5	6	7	11	9	10		8													
	22 (a)	Chesterfield	W 3-2	John Brown 2 (1 pen), Moran	4,000	1	2	3	4	5	6	7	11	9	10		8													
	29 (a)	Burnley	L 0-2			1	2	3	4		6	7	11	9	10	5	8													
Oct	6 (h)	Port Vale	W 4-0	A.Robertson, Wardrope 2, John Brown	8,000	1	2	3	4	5	6	7	11	9	10		8													
	13 (a)	Leicester F	L 0-1		5,000	1	2	3	4	5	6	7	11	9	10		8													
	20 (h)	New Brighton	W 2-1	John Brown (pen), Wardrope	8,500	1	2	3	4	5	6	7	11	9	10		8													
	27 (a)	Gainsborough T	D 1-1	Wardrope	2,000	1	2	3	4	5	6	7	11	9	10		8													
Nov	10 (a)	Burton S	D 0-0		5,000	1	2	3	4	5	6	7	11	9			8	10												
	24 (a)	W Arsenal	L 0-1		8,000	1	2	3		5	6	7	8					4	9	10	11									
Dec	1 (h)	Blackpool	W 3-1	Moran, Wardrope, Higgins	10,000	1	2			5	6	7	8		10		9		11	3	4									
	15 (h)	Small Heath	L 0-1		12,000	1	2			5	6	7	8		10		9		11	3	4									
	22 (a)	Grimsby T	L 0-2		8,000		2	3		5	6	7	8		10		9	11		4			1							
	26 (h)	Barnsley	W 3-0	A.Robertson 2, Moran	8,000		2	3		5	6	7	8	11				10					1	4	9					
	29 (a)	Lincoln C	W 2-1	A.Robertson, J.H.Gettins	5,000		2	3		5	6	7	8	11				10					1	4	9					
Jan	1 (h)	Newton Heath	L 1-2	Wardrope	12,000		2	3		5	6	7	8	11	10		9						1	4						
	12 (a)	Glossop	L 0-2		4,000	1	2	3		5	6	7	8	11	10									4	9					
	19 (h)	Chesterfield	W 2-0	Moran, D.W.Smith*	8,000	1	2	3	5		6	7	11		10		9	8						4						
Feb	16 (h)	Leicester F	W 2-1	Wardrope 2	8,000	1	2	3		5	6	7	11	9			10	8						4						
Mar	2 (h)	Gainsborough T	W 9-2	Wilkie 5, Davidson, A.Robertson, McCowie 2	6,000	1	2	3			6	7	11	9	10		5	8						4						
	9 (h)	Walsall	W 2-1	McCowie, Wilkie	8,000	1	2	3			6	7	11	9	10		5	8						4						
	11 (a)	Port Vale	W 2-0	A.Robertson, Davidson	4,000	1	2		5		6	7	11	9	10									4		3	8			
	14 (a)	Barnsley	L 1-3	Wardrope		1		3	6	4			11	8	10					7		2				5		9		
	16 (h)	Burton S	W 3-1	McCowie 2, D.W.Smith (pen)		1	2	3		5	6	7	11	9	10			8						4						
	25 (a)	New Brighton	L 1-3	Goldie (og)		1	2	3		5	6	7	11	9	10			8						4						
	30 (h)	W Arsenal	D 1-1	A.Robertson	6,000	1		3		5	6	7	11	9	10			8						4					2	
Apr	5 (a)	Stockport C	W 1-0	Wilkie	4,000	1	2	3		5	6	7	11	9	10			8						4						
	6 (a)	Blackpool	L 0-3		2,000	1	2			5	6	7	11		10		9	8						4					3	
	9 (h)	Burnley	D 0-0		6,000	1		3		5	6	7	11	9	10			8						4					3	
	13 (h)	Stockport C	W 2-0	John Brown, Wilkie		1		3		5	6	7	11	9	10		8							4					2	
	20 (a)	Small Heath	L 1-2	Wardrope	8,000	1	2	3		5	6	7	11	9	10			8						4						
	22 (a)	Walsall	D 0-0		1,000	1		3		5	6	7	11	9	10			8						4					2	
	27 (h)	Grimsby T	D 0-0		6,000	1	2			5	6	7	11	9				10						4					3	8
			Apps			30	29	29	19	24	32	33	33	29	28	2	21	17	3	2	2	3	4	19	3	2	2	1	6	1
			Goals							1	2	5	11	9	8		5	5						2	1					

*Some sources credit own-goal but club credit D.W.Smith

1 own-goal

FA Cup

Date		Opponent	Res	Scorers	Att	Frail J	Dow MJ	Ramsay A	Millar J	Higgins W	Davidson A	Moran M	Wardrope W	Robertson A	Wilkie J	Brown, James	Brown, John	McCowie A	Eckford J	Carrick C	Jones J	Doig T	Hodgson G	Smith DW	Gettins JH	Macfarlane T	Thompson A	McNally J	Cochrane M	Brearley J	Round
Nov	3 (h)	Willington A	D 3-3	John Brown, Wardrope, Higgins	6,000	1	2	3	4	5	6	7	11		10		9	8													Q1
	7 (a)	Willington A	D 0-0		2,000	1		3	4		6	7	8	9	10	5			11							2					R
	12 (h)	Willington A	W 8-0	Moran, Carrick 2, Wardrope, A.Robertson 2, Higgins 2	4,000	1	2	3		5	6	7	8	9			4		10	11											2R
	17 (h)	Jarrow	W 3-0	Carrick 2, A.Robertson	8,000	1	2	3		5	6	7	8	9			4		10	11											Q2
Dec	8 (h)	Bishop Auckland	W 4-0	John Brown 4	9,000	1	2			5	6	7	8	10			9	11		3	4										Q3
Jan	5 (a)	Grimsby T	W 1-0	Wilkie	8,000	1	2	3	4	6		7	8	10	11	9									5						1
Feb	9 (h)	Newcastle U	W 3-1	A.Robertson, McCowie, Wardrope	16,000	1		3			6	7	11	9	10		5	8		2				4							2
	23 (h)	Kettering T	W 5-0	McCowie, Wilkie, A.Robertson 3	12,000	1	2	3			6	7	11	9	10		5	8						4							3
Mar	23 (h)	West Brom A	L 0-1		20,000	1	2	3			6	7	11	9	10		5	8						4							4
			Apps			9	7	8	3	5	8	9	9	7	7		9	4	3	3	2	1		3		1		1			
			Goals							3		1	3	7	2		5	2		4										

1901-02
Division 2

Date	Opponent	Res	Scorers	Att	Frail J	Dow MJ	Ramsey A	Smith DW	Jones A	Davidson A	Wardrope W	Brearley J	Cassidy J	Turner P	Tennant J	Jones J	Leslie J	Blackett J	Robertson J	Moran M	Crawford J	Thompson A	Watson R	Robertson A	Williamson RG
Sep 7 (a)	Stockport C	W 3-1	Wardrope, Cassidy, Tennant	5,000	1	2	3	4	5	6	7	8	9	10	11										
14 (h)	Newton Heath	W 5-0	Davidson, Brearley 2, Cassidy, Turner	12,000	1	2	3	4	5	6	7	8	9	10	11										
21 (a)	Glossop	L 0-1		3,000	1	2	3	4	5	6	7	8	9	10	11										
28 (h)	Doncaster R	W 6-0	A.Jones, Wardrope, Brearley 2, Turner, Tennant	10,638	1		3	4	5	6	7	8	9	10	11	2									
Oct 5 (a)	Lincoln C	L 1-2	Tennant	4,000	1		3	4	5	6	7	8	9	10	11	2									
12 (h)	West Brom A	L 1-2	D.W.Smith	15,000	1		3	4	5	6	7		9	10	11	2	8								
19 (a)	W Arsenal	W 3-0	D.W.Smith (pen), Brearley, Cassidy	8,000	1		3	4	5	6		8	9	10	11			2	7						
26 (h)	Barnsley	W 2-1	Brearley 2	5,000	1		3	4	5	6	7	8	9	10	11			2							
Nov 2 (a)	Leicester F	W 2-0	Brearley, Tennant	6,000	1		3	4	5	6	7	8	9	10	11			2							
9 (h)	Preston NE	W 2-1	Brearley, Turner	12,000	1		3	4	5	6	7	8	9	10	11			2							
16 (a)	Burnley	D 2-2	Brearley, Tennant		1		3	4	5	6		8	9	10	11			2		7					
23 (h)	Port Vale	W 3-0	Turner, Cassidy, Tennant	9,000	1		3	4	5	6		8	9	10	11			2		7					
30 (a)	Chesterfield	D 0-0			1		3	4	5	6	7	8	9	10	11			2							
Dec 7 (h)	Gainsborough T	W 3-1	D.W.Smith (pen), Brearley, Tennant	7,000	1		3	4	5	6		8	9	10	11			2	7						
14 (a)	West Brom A	L 0-2		6,868	1		3	4	5	6	11	8	9	10				2			7				
21 (a)	Bristol C	L 0-1		6,000	1		3	4	5	6		8	11	10				2		9	7				
28 (h)	Blackpool	W 2-1	Thompson 2	6,000	1		3		5	6		4	8	10	11			2			7	9			
Jan 1 (h)	Burton U	W 5-0	A.Jones, Cassidy 3, Turner	10,000	1		3		5	6	11	4	8	10				2			7	9			
4 (a)	Stockport C	W 6-0	A.Jones, Turner, Wardrope, Brearley, Cassidy, D.W.Smith	7,000	1		3	4	5	6	8	11	9	10				2			7				
18 (h)	Glossop	W 5-0	D.W.Smith, A.Jones, Wardrope 2, Cassidy	9,000	1		3	4	5	6	8	11	9	10				2			7				
Feb 1 (h)	Lincoln C	D 0-0		8,000	1		3	4	5	6	8	11	9	10				2			7				
15 (h)	W Arsenal	W 1-0	Cassidy	7,000	1	2		4	5	6	8	9	11	10				3			7				
22 (a)	Barnsley	W 7-2	Davidson, Wardrope, Brearley 4, Leslie	2,000	1		3	4	5	6	11	9	10				8	2			7				
Mar 1 (h)	Leicester F	W 5-0	D.W.Smith (pen), Cassidy 2, Leslie, Crawford	10,000	1		3	4	5	6	11	9	10				8	2			7				
8 (a)	Preston NE	W 3-0	A.Jones, Brearley, Leslie		1		3	4	5	6	11	9	10				8	2			7				
15 (h)	Burnley	W 3-0	Cassidy, Brearley 2	10,000	1		3	4	5	6	10	9	11				8	2			7				
22 (a)	Port Vale	D 1-1	Ramsey		1	2	3	4	5	6	10	9	11				8				7				
28 (a)	Doncaster R	D 0-0		7,000	1		3	4	5	6	10	9	11				8	2			7				
29 (h)	Chesterfield	W 7-1	Wardrope, Cassidy 2, A.Robertson 3, R.Watson	7,000	1		3	4	5	6	10		11					2			7		8	9	
Apr 5 (a)	Gainsborough T	W 4-1	Wardrope, Brearley, A.Robertson 2	500	1		3	4	5	6	10	8	11					2			7			9	
7 (h)	Newton Heath	W 2-1	A.Jones, A.Robertson	2,000	1		3	4	5	6	10	8	11					2			7			9	
12 (a)	Burton U	L 2-3	Brearley 2	3,000	1		3	4	5	6		8		10	11			2			7			9	
19 (h)	Bristol C	W 2-0	Wardrope 2	12,000			3	4	5	6	10	8	11					2			7			9	1
26 (a)	Blackpool	W 2-0	A.Robertson 2				3	4	5	6	10		11					2			7		8	9	1
Apps					32	5	33	32	34	34	27	31	32	23	17	3	7	27	2	3	20	2	2	6	2
Goals							1	6	6	2	10	22	15	6	7		3				1	2	1	8	

FA Cup

Date	Opponent	Res	Scorers	Att	Frail J	Dow MJ	Ramsey A	Smith DW	Jones A	Davidson A	Wardrope W	Brearley J	Cassidy J	Turner P	Tennant J	Jones J	Leslie J	Blackett J	Robertson J	Moran M	Crawford J	Thompson A	Watson R	Robertson A	Williamson RG	Round
Jan 25 (h)	Bristol R	D 1-1	Cassidy	13,000	1		3	4	5	6	8	11	9	10				2			7					1
29 (a)	Bristol R	L 0-1		7,600	1		3	4	5	6	8	11	9	10				2			7					R
Apps					2		2	2	2	2	2	2	2	2				2			2					
Goals													1													

1902-03

Division 1

Date	Opponent	Res	Scorers	Att	MacFarlane R	Blackett J	Ramsey A	Smith DW	Jones A	Davidson A	Crawford J	MacAulay W	Robertson A	Cassidy J	Muir J	Robertson J	Hogg J	Watson R	Carrick C	Muir W	Thompson A	Millar J	Goodson L	Godley W	Gettins JH	Williamson RG	Piercy FR	Douglas H	Currie R
Sep 1 (a) Blackburn R	W 1-0	A.Robertson	3,000	1	2	3	4	5	6	7	8	9	10	11														
6 (h) Everton	W 1-0	A.Robertson	20,000	1	2	3	4	5	6		8	9	10	11	7													
13 (a) Sheffield W	L 0-2		20,000	1		3	4	5	6		8	9	10	11	7	2												
20 (h) West Brom A	D 1-1	Cassidy	22,420	1	2	3	4	5	6		8	9	10	11	7													
27 (a) Notts C	L 0-2		10,000	1	2	3	4	5	6	8			10		7		9	11										
Oct 4 (h) Bolton W	W 4-3	R.Watson 2, Cassidy 2	8,000	1	2	3		5	6			9	10		7		8	11	4									
11 (a) Derby C	L 2-3	A.Jones (pen), R.Watson	10,000	1	2	3		5	6			9	10		7		8	11	4									
18 (a) Newcastle U	W 1-0	Carrick	26,000	1		3	4	5	6			9	10		7	2	8	11										
25 (h) Wolves	W 2-0	Cassidy, Carrick	15,000	1		3	4	5	6			9	10		7	2	8	11										
Nov 1 (a) Liverpool	L 0-5		15,000	1		3	4	5	6			9	10		7	2	8	11										
8 (h) Sheffield U	L 0-2		14,000	1		3	4	5	6			9	10		7	2	8	11										
15 (a) Grimsby T	D 2-2	Carrick, A.Jones (pen)	5,000	1		3	4	5	6			9	10		7	2	8	11										
22 (h) Aston Villa	L 1-2	J.Robertson	15,000	1		3	4	5	6				10		7	2	8	11		9								
29 (a) Nottingham F	L 0-1		5,000	1		3	4	5				9	10		7	2	8	11	6									
Dec 6 (h) Bury	D 1-1	Carrick	18,000	1		3	4	5	6	9			10		7	2	8	11										
20 (h) Sunderland	L 0-1		15,000	1		3	4	5	6		8	9			7	2		11				10						
26 (a) Wolves	L 0-2		16,000	1		3	4	5	6		8			11	7	2						10	9					
27 (h) Stoke	W 2-0	Carrick, Goodson	7,000	1		3	4	5	6		8				7	2		11				10		9				
Jan 3 (a) Everton	L 0-3					3	4	5			8					2	7	11	6			10		9	1			
10 (h) Sheffield W	W 2-1	D.W.Smith, R.Watson	8,000				4	5	6		8					2	7	11				10		9	1	3		
17 (a) West Brom A	L 0-1		18,033			3	4	5	6			9	10		8	2						11			1	7		
24 (h) Notts C	W 2-1	Cassidy, Thompson	10,000			3	4	5	6				10			2		8		9		11			1	7		
31 (a) Bolton W	L 1-2	A.Davidson	14,000			3	4	5	6				10		7	2		8			9	11			1			
Feb 14 (h) Newcastle U	W 1-0	Cassidy	20,000			3	4		6	7			10			2						11			1	5	8	9
28 (h) Liverpool	L 0-2		15,000				4	5	6				10		8	2						11			1	3	7	9
Mar 7 (a) Sheffield U	W 3-1	A.Robertson 2, Goodson	10,000			3	4	5	6			9	10		7	2		8				11			1			
14 (h) Grimsby T	W 2-0	D.W.Smith, Carrick	12,000			3	4	5	6			9	10		7	2		11						8	1			
28 (h) Nottingham F	W 2-0	A.Robertson, Goodson	10,000			3	4	5	6			9	10		7	2		8				11			1			
Apr 4 (a) Bury	L 1-3	A.Davidson	7,000			3	4	5	6			9	10		7	2		8				11			1			
11 (a) Blackburn R	W 4-0	McAulay (pen), Cassidy, J.Robertson, A.Robertson	7,000			3	4	5	6		8	9	10		7	2						11			1			
13 (h) Derby C	W 3-1	A.Robertson, MacAulay (pen), D.W.Smith	15,000			3	4	5	6		8	9	10		7	2						11			1			
18 (a*) Sunderland	L 1-2	J.Robertson	25,000			3	4	5	6		8	9		11	7	2						10			1			
25 (h) Stoke	D 1-1	Currie	10,000			3	4		6		8			11	7	2				5		10			1			9
27 (a) Aston Villa	L 0-5		9,000			3	4	5	6		8	9		11	7	2						10			1			
Apps				18	8	30	32	32	32	4	21	13	26	9	30	28	14	22	4	3	1	16	1	4	16	3	4	3
Goals							3	2			2	7	7		3		4	6		1		3						1

*Played at St James' Park, Newcastle.

FA Cup

Date	Opponent	Res	Scorers	Att	MacFarlane R	Blackett J	Ramsey A	Smith DW	Jones A	Davidson A	Crawford J	MacAulay W	Robertson A	Cassidy J	Muir J	Robertson J	Hogg J	Watson R	Carrick C	Muir W	Thompson A	Millar J	Goodson L	Godley W	Gettins JH	Williamson RG	Piercy FR	Douglas H	Currie R	Round
Dec 13 (a) Bristol C	L 1-3	A.Robertson	8,000	1		3	4	5	6			7	10			2	8	11		9									1
Apps				1		1	1	1	1			1	1			1	1	1		1									
Goals												1																

1903-04
Division 1

Date	Opponent	Result	Scorers	Att	Williamson RG	Hogg J	Ramsey A	Smith DW	Jones A	Davidson A	Gettins E	White W	Brown A	Cassidy J	Atherton RH	Blackett J	Goodson L	Carrick C	Aitken S	Suddick J	Muir J	McGuigan A	Godley W	Page R	Boddington H	Roberts RJ	Featherstone T
Sep 5 (a)	Sheffield W	L 1-4	A.Brown	20,000	1	2	3	4	5	6	7	8	9	10	11												
Sep 12 (h)	Sunderland	L 2-3	Cassidy, A.Brown	*30,000	1	2	3	4	5	6	7	8	9	10	11												
Sep 19 (a)	West Brom A	D 0-0		14,130	1	2		4	5	6	7	8	9	10	11	3											
Sep 26 (h)	Small Heath	W 3-1	Cassidy 2, A.Brown	18,000	1	2		4	5	6	7	8	9	10	11	3											
Oct 3 (a)	Everton	L 0-2		15,000	1	2		4	5	6	7	8	9	10	11	3											
Oct 10 (h)	Stoke	W 2-0	Cassidy, E.Gettins	15,000	1	2		4	5	6	7		9	10	8	3	11										
Oct 17 (a)	Derby C	D 2-2	Cassidy, E.Gettins	7,000	1	2		4	5	6		7	9	10	8	3	11										
Oct 24 (h)	Manchester C	W 6-0	Atherton 2, Cassidy, Goodson, A.Brown, D.W.Smith	15,000	1	2		4	5	6	7		9	10	8	3	11										
Oct 31 (a)	Notts C	L 2-3	A.Brown, Blackett (pen)	8,000	1	2		4	5	6	7		9	10	8	3	11										
Nov 7 (h)	Sheffield U	W 4-1	Goodson, A.Davidson, Atherton 2	25,000	1	2		4	5	6	7		9	10	8	3	11										
Nov 14 (a)	Newcastle U	L 1-2	A.Brown	28,000	1	2			5	6	7		9	10	8	3	11		4								
Nov 21 (h)	Aston Villa	W 2-1	Cassidy, Blackett (pen)	20,000	1	2			5	6	7		9	10	8	3	11		4								
Nov 28 (h)	Wolves	L 1-2	Atherton	8,000	1	2			5	6	7		9	10	8	3	11		4								
Dec 12 (h)	Bury	W 1-0		10,000	1	2			5	6	7		9	10	8	3	11		4								
Dec 19 (a)	Blackburn R	D 1-1	Cassidy	15,000	1	2			5	6	7		9	10	8	3	11		4								
Dec 26 (h)	Nottingham F	D 1-1	Atherton	14,000	1	2			5	6	7		9	10	8	3	11		4								
Dec 28 (a)	Stoke	D 0-0		10,000	1	2			5	6	7		9	10	8	3	11		4								
Jan 1 (a)	Manchester C	D 1-1	A.Brown	30,000	1	2			5	6	7		9	10	8	3	11		4								
Jan 2 (h)	Sheffield W	L 0-1			1	2			5	6	7		9	10	8	3	11		4								
Jan 9 (a)	Sunderland	L 1-3	Suddick	15,000	1	2			5	6			9	10	8	3	11		4	7							
Jan 16 (h)	West Brom A	D 2-2	A.Brown, Goodson	18,021	1	2			5	6	7		9	10	7	3	11	4	8								
Jan 23 (a)	Small Heath	D 2-2	Blackett (pen), Atherton	10,000	1		3		5	6	7		9	10	8	2	11		4								
Jan 30 (h)	Everton	W 3-0	A.Brown, E.Gettins, Cassidy	12,000	1	2			5	6	7		9	10	8	3	11		4								
Feb 13 (h)	Derby C	D 0-0		10,000	1	2			5	6	7		9	10	8	3	11		4								
Feb 22 (a)	Liverpool	L 0-1		15,000	1	2			5	6	7		9	10	8	3			4		11						
Feb 27 (h)	Notts C	W 1-0	A.Brown	6,000	1		3		5	6	7		9	10	8	2			4			11					
Mar 12 (a)	Newcastle U	L 1-3	Cassidy	20,000	1		3		5	6	7		9	10		2		8	4		11						
Mar 19 (a)	Aston Villa	L 1-2	Atherton	10,000	1	2		4	5	6	7		9	10	8	3					11						
Mar 26 (a)	Wolves	D 2-2	A.Brown, Atherton	4,000	1	2		4		6	7		9	10	8	3					11			5			
Mar 28 (a)	Sheffield U	L 0-3			1	2		4		6	7		9	10	8	3								5	11		
Apr 2 (h)	Liverpool	W 1-0	Roberts	12,000	1	2			5	6	7		9	10	8	3			4							11	
Apr 9 (a)	Bury	D 1-1	Roberts	3,000	1	2		4	5		7	8		10	6	3										11	9
Apr 16 (h)	Blackburn R	L 0-2		12,000	1	2		4	5	6	7		9	10	8	3										11	
Apr 23 (a)	Nottingham F	D 1-1	Cassidy	5,000	1	2		4		6	7		9	10	8	3	5									11	
Apps					34	31	5	17	31	33	30	7	33	34	33	32	18	2	19	1	4	1	1	2	1	4	1
Goals								1		1	3		12	11	9	3	3		1							2	

*Official opening of Ayresome Park

FA Cup

Date	Opponent	Result	Scorers	Att	Williamson RG	Hogg J	Ramsey A	Smith DW	Jones A	Davidson A	Gettins E	White W	Brown A	Cassidy J	Atherton RH	Blackett J	Goodson L	Carrick C	Aitken S	Suddick J	Muir J	McGuigan A	Godley W	Page R	Boddington H	Roberts RJ	Featherstone T	Round
Feb 6 (a)	Millwall	W 2-0	A.Brown 2	12,000	1	2			5	6	7		9	10	8	3	11		4									1
Feb 20 (a)	Preston NE	W 3-0	A.Brown 2, Atherton	15,000	1	2			5	6	7		9	10	8	3			4		11							2
Mar 5 (a)	Manchester C	D 0-0		35,000	1	2			5	6	7		9	10	8	3		11	4									3
Mar 9 (h)	Manchester C	L 1-3	A.Brown	†34,000	1	2			5	6	7		9	10	8	3		11					4					R
Apps					4	4			4	4	4		4	4	4	4	1	2	3		1		1					
Goals													5		1													

†Ground attendance record

1904-05
Division 1

Date	Opponent	Res	Scorers	Att	Williamson RG	Hogg J	Agnew WB	Aitken S	Jones A	Davidson A	Astley H	Atherton RH	Brown A	Cassidy J	Roberts RJ	Blackett J	Smith DW	Page R	Gettins E	Goodson L	Thackeray J	Bell J	Craig T	McCallum D	Davies WF	Hewitt C	Green T	Phillipson TF	Frail J	Common A
Sep 3 (h)	Sheffield W	L 1-3	Atherton	18,000	1	2	3	4	5	6	7	8	9	10	11															
Sep 10 (a)	Sunderland	D 1-1	E.Gettins	16,000	1	2			5			9	8	10	11	3	4	6	7											
Sep 17 (h)	W Arsenal	W 1-0	A.Brown	15,000	1	2			5	6		8	9	10	11	3	4		7											
Sep 24 (a)	Derby C	L 2-4	A.Brown, Davidson	8,000	1	2			5	6	10	8	9		11	3	4		7											
Oct 1 (h)	Everton	W 1-0	E.Gettins	10,000	1	2		4	5	6		8	9	10		3			7	11										
Oct 8 (a)	Small Heath	L 1-2	Atherton	12,000	1	2		4		6		8	9	10	11	3	5		7											
Oct 15 (h)	Manchester C	L 0-1		20,000	1	2	3	4	5	6		8	9	10					7		11									
Oct 22 (a)	Notts C	D 0-0		8,000	1		3	4	5			10	9		2			6	7		11	8								
Oct 29 (h)	Sheffield U	L 0-1		14,000	1		3	4	5			10	9		2			6	7		11	8								
Nov 5 (a)	Newcastle U	L 0-3		23,262	1	2		4	5	6		9	8	10		3			7		11									
Nov 12 (h)	Preston NE	D 1-1	Jones	12,000	1	2		4	5			10	9	6					7		11	8	3							
Nov 19 (a)	Stoke	L 1-3	A.Brown	8,000	1		3	4	5			8	9	6	7	10					11		2							
Nov 26 (a)	Wolves	L 3-5	Bell, Blackett (pen), R.J.Roberts	8,000	1		3	4	5		9			6	10	2			7		11	8								
Dec 3 (h)	Bury	D 2-2	Astley 2	9,000	1		3	4	5		9			6	10	2			7		11	8								
Dec 10 (a)	Aston Villa	D 0-0		8,000	1		3		5		9	10		6	7			4			11	8		2						
Dec 17 (h)	Blackburn R	W 2-1	Bell 2	10,000	1		3		5		9	10		6	7			4			11	8		2						
Dec 24 (a)	Nottingham F	D 1-1	Astley		1		3		5		9	10		6				4			11	8		2	7					
Dec 26 (h)	Small Heath	L 0-1		20,000	1		3		5		9	10		6				4			11	8		2	7					
Dec 31 (a)	Sheffield W	L 0-5			1		3		5		9	10		6				4			11	8		2	7					
Jan 7 (h)	Sunderland	L 1-3	Agnew (pen)	12,000	1		3	4	5		8	9		6	11						10			2	7					
Jan 14 (a)	W Arsenal	D 1-1	Thackeray	16,000	1		3	4	5	6	8	9			11						10			2	7					
Jan 21 (h)	Derby C	W 2-0	Astley, Atherton	12,000	1		3	4			9	8		6	11		5				10			2	7					
Jan 28 (a)	Everton	L 0-1		20,000	1		3	4	5		9	8		6	11				7		10			2						
Feb 11 (a)	Manchester C	L 2-3	Phillipson, Atherton	16,000	1		3		5			8		6				4			11			2	7		9	10		
Feb 25 (a)	Sheffield U	W 1-0	Common (pen)	10,000			3	4	5			10		6							11			2	7		9		1	8
Mar 4 (h)	Nottingham F	D 0-0		12,000	1		3	4	5					6							11			2	7		9	10		8
Mar 11 (a)	Preston NE	L 0-2		5,000	1		3	4	5			10		6							11			2		9	7			8
Mar 18 (h)	Stoke	W 2-1	Common, R.J.Roberts	6,000	1		3	4	5	6				10	11									2		9	7			8
Mar 25 (h)	Wolves	W 3-1	Common, Green 2	7,000	1		3	4	5	6				10	11									2		9	7			8
Apr 1 (a)	Bury	L 0-1		5,000	1		3	4	5	6				10	11									2		9	7			8
Apr 8 (h)	Aston Villa	W 3-1	Hewitt, R.J.Roberts, Common	13,000	1		3	4	5	6				10	11									2		9	7			8
Apr 15 (a)	Blackburn R	W 2-0	Hewitt 2	4,000	1		3	4	5	6				10	11									2		9	7			8
Apr 24 (h)	Notts C	L 2-5	Green, Phillipson	10,000	1	2	3	4	5	6					11										7		9	10		8
Apr 29 (h)	Newcastle U	L 0-3		12,000	1		3	4	5	6		8			11									2			7	10		9
Apps					33	8	29	30	27	15	14	27	11	28	19	11	8	6	13	1	22	10	2	19	10	6	11	3	1	10
Goals							1		1	1	4	4	3		3	1			2		1	3				3	3	2		4

FA Cup

Date	Opponent	Res	Scorers	Att	Williamson RG	Hogg J	Agnew WB	Aitken S	Jones A	Davidson A	Astley H	Atherton RH	Brown A	Cassidy J	Roberts RJ	Blackett J	Smith DW	Page R	Gettins E	Goodson L	Thackeray J	Bell J	Craig T	McCallum D	Davies WF	Hewitt C	Green T	Phillipson TF	Frail J	Common A	Round
Feb 4 (h)	Tottenham H	D 1-1	Astley	20,340	1		3	6	5		9	8		10		4					11			2	7						1
Feb 8 (a)	Tottenham H	L 0-1		23,000	1		3	6	5		9	8				4					11	10		2	7						R
Apps					2		2	2	2		2	2		1		2					2	1		2	2						
Goals											1																			

1905-06
Division 1

Date	Opponent	Result	Scorers	Att	Williamson RG	McCallum D	Agnew WB	Aitken S	Jones A	Davidson A	Hewitt C	Common A	Green T	Reid GT	Cassidy J	Hogg J	Thackeray J	Murray T	Coxon T	Duffy CF	Hedley GT	Henderson GH	Thompson WT	Walker RH	Barker WC	Trechman OL	Hunter H	Worrall WE	Bloomer S	Brawn WF	Wilcox FJ	Ratcliffe E
Sep 2 (a)	Everton	L 1-4	Common	25,000	1	2	3	4	5	6	7	8	9	10	11																	
9 (h)	Derby C	L 0-1		10,000	1		3	4	5	6		8	7	9	10	2	11															
16 (a)	Sheffield W	L 0-3		20,000	1	3		4	5	6		8	7	9	11	2		10														
23 (h)	Nottingham F	W 2-0	Murray, Reid	15,000	1		3	4	5	6	7	8		9	11	2		10														
30 (a)	Manchester C	L 0-4		15,000	1		3	4	5	6	7	8		10		2			9	11												
Oct 7 (h)	Bury	W 5-1	Reid 3, Hewitt, Common	10,000	1		3	4	5	6	7	8	9	10		2				11												
14 (h)	Wolves	W 3-1	Green 3	10,000	1		3	4	5	6	7	8	9	10		2				11												
21 (a)	Preston NE	L 1-2	Common	10,000	1		3	4	5	6	7	8	9	10		2				11												
28 (a)	Newcastle U	L 1-4	Hewitt	35,000	1	2	3	4	5	6	7	8	9	10						11												
Nov 4 (a)	Aston Villa	L 1-4	Reid	15,000	1		3		5		7	8	9	10	6		11					2	4									
11 (h)	Liverpool	L 1-5	Hewitt	8,000	1		3	4	5		7	8	9	10	6		11					2										
18 (a)	Sheffield U	L 0-1		5,000	1		3	4	5	6		8	9	7	10	2						11										
25 (h)	Notts C	W 4-1	Reid, Green 2, Hewitt	8,000	1		3	4	5	6		8	9	7	10	2						11										
Dec 2 (a)	Stoke	D 1-1	Common	5,000	1	2	3	4	5	6			9	7	10				8			11										
9 (h)	Bolton W	D 4-4	Hewitt, Thompson 2, Green	12,500	1		3	4	5	6		8	9	7			11					2	10									
16 (a)	W Arsenal	D 2-2	Hewitt, Common	12,000	1		3	4	5	6		8	9	7		2	11		10													
23 (h)	Blackburn R	D 1-1	Coxon	12,000	1		3	5		6		8	9	7		2	11		10			4										
25 (h)	Birmingham	W 1-0	Common	20,000	1		3	5		6		8	9	7		2	11		10			4										
26 (a)	Birmingham	L 0-7		15,000	1		3	5		6			9	7	8	2	11		10			4										
30 (h)	Everton	D 0-0		15,000	1	2	3	5		6		8	9	7			11		10			4										
Jan 1 (a)	Sunderland	L 1-2	Common	24,000	1	2	3	5		6		8	9	7			11		10			4										
6 (a)	Derby C	D 1-1	Common	2,000	1		3	5		6		8	9	7		2	11		10			4										
20 (h)	Sheffield W	D 2-2	Hewitt 2	10,000	1		3	5		6		8	9	7		2	11		10			4										
27 (a)	Nottingham F	L 1-2	Common	12,000	1		3	5		6		8	9	7		2	11		10			4										
Feb 10 (a)	Bury	D 1-1	Hewitt	4,000	1		3	5				8	9	7	6	2	11		10					4								
17 (a)	Wolves	D 0-0		6,000	1		3	5		6		8		7		2	11		10			4		9								
Mar 3 (h)	Newcastle U	W 1-0	R.H.Walker	20,000			3	5		6	7		9			2	11					4	10	8			1					
10 (h)	Aston Villa	L 1-2	Common	12,000			3	5		6		8	9	7		2	11					4	10				1					
14 (h)	Preston NE	L 1-2	R.H.Walker	25,000			3	5		6		8	9	7		2	11					4	10				1					
17 (a)	Liverpool	L 1-6	Agnew	25,000			3	5		6	7		9			2	11					4	10				1	8				
24 (h)	Sheffield U	L 0-1		12,000	1		3	5		6			9			2	11					4							8	7	10	
31 (h)	Notts C	D 1-1	Bloomer	15,000	1		3	5		6			9				11					4							8	7	10	2
Apr 7 (h)	Stoke	W 5-0	Common 3 (1 pen), Brawn, Bloomer	20,000	1		3	5		6		9					11					4							8	7	10	2
13 (h)	Sunderland	W 2-1	Bloomer, Common	14,000	1		3	5		6		9					11					4							8	7	10	2
14 (a)	Bolton W	L 1-2	Common	20,000	1		3	5		6		9					11					4							8	7	10	2
17 (h)	Manchester C	W 6-1	S.Aitken, Bloomer 2, Thackeray, Common 2	15,000	1		3	5		6		9					11					4							8	7	10	2
21 (h)	W Arsenal	W 2-0	Common 2	16,000	1		3	5		6		9					11					4							8	7	10	2
28 (a)	Blackburn R	D 1-1	Bloomer	5,000	1		3	5		6		9					11					4							8	7	10	2
Apps					34	6	37	37	16	35	27	36	26	24	6	23	21	3	11	4	3	10	6	9	7	1	3	1	9	8	8	7
Goals							1	1			9	19	6	5			1	1	1				2	2					6	1		

FA Cup

Date	Opponent	Result	Scorers	Att	Williamson RG	McCallum D	Agnew WB	Aitken S	Jones A	Davidson A	Hewitt C	Common A	Green T	Reid GT	Cassidy J	Hogg J	Thackeray J	Murray T	Coxon T	Duffy CF	Hedley GT	Henderson GH	Thompson WT	Walker RH	Barker WC	Trechman OL	Hunter H	Worrall WE	Bloomer S	Brawn WF	Wilcox FJ	Ratcliffe E	Round
Jan 13 (h)	Bolton W	W 3-0	Common, Hewitt, Thackeray	22,000	1		2	5		4	10	9	11			3	7					6	8										1
Feb 3 (a)	Brighton & HA	D 1-1	Hewitt	7,462	1		3	5		6	7	8	9			2	11		10			4											2
7 (h)	Brighton & HA	D 1-1	Common	15,000	1		3	5		6		8	9	7		2	11		10			4											R
12 (n*)	Brighton & HA	W 3-1	Common 3	11,528	1		3	5		6		8	9	7		2	11		10			4											2R
24 (a)	Southampton	L 1-6	R.H.Walker	12,000	1		3	5		6		8	9	7		2	11					4		10									3
	*Played at Bramall Lane, Sheffield			**Apps**	5		5	5		5	5	5	5	2		5	5		3			3	5										
				Goals							2	5					1							1									

1906-07
Division 1

Date	Opponent	Res	Score	Scorers	Att	Williamson RG	Ratcliffe E	Campbell A	Shand H	Aitken S	Barker WC	Brawn WF	Bloomer S	Common A	Wilcox FJ	Thackeray J	Hickling W	Hanlon E	Priest F	Barker FM	Murray T	Priest AE	Tomlin J	O'Hagan C	Tyldesley J	Tucker WH	Harkins J	Roberts J	Roberts WS	Aitken A	Cail SG	Brown JR	Watson J
Sep 1 (h)	Everton	D	2-2	Wilcox, Barker	20,000	1	2	3	4	5	6	7	8	9	10	11																	
8 (a)	W Arsenal	L	0-2		20,000	1	2		4		6	7	8		10	11	3	5	9														
15 (h)	Sheffield W	L	1-3	Thackeray	17,000	1		3		4	6	7	8	5	10	11								9	2								
22 (a)	Bury	D	1-1	Bloomer		1		3		4	6	7	8		9	11								2	5	10							
29 (h)	Manchester C	L	2-3	Wilcox, O'Hagan	22,000	1		3		4	6	7	8		9	11								5	10	2							
Oct 6 (a)	Derby C	L	0-1		10,000	1		3		4	6	7	8		9	11								5	10	2							
13 (a)	Preston NE	L	2-4	Tucker, Brawn		1		3		4	6	7	8		10	11								5	2	9							
20 (h)	Newcastle U	L	0-3		17,000	1		3		4	6	7	8		10							2			9					5		11	
27 (a)	Aston Villa	W	3-2	Bloomer 2, Common	20,000	1		3		4	6	7	8	9	10							2								5		11	
Nov 3 (h)	Liverpool	L	0-1		18,000	1		3		4		7	8	9	10							2					6		11	5			
10 (a)	Bristol C	L	0-3		12,000	1		3		4		7	8		10	11						2			9		6			5			
17 (h)	Notts C	W	2-0	Wilcox 2	12,000	1				4		7	8	9	10	11	3					2					6			5			
24 (a)	Sheffield U	D	1-1	Bloomer		1		3		4		7	8	9	10	11						2					6			5			
Dec 1 (h)	Bolton W	D	0-0			1		3		4		7	8	9	10	11						2					6			5			
8 (a)	Manchester U	L	1-3	Bloomer	12,000	1		3		4		7	8	9	10	11						2					6			5			
15 (h)	Stoke	W	5-0	Wilcox, Common 2, Bloomer 2		1		3		4		7	8	9	10	11						2					6			5			
22 (a)	Blackburn R	L	1-4	Bloomer		1		3		4		7	8	9	10	11						2					6			5			
25 (h)	Sunderland	W	2-1	Wilcox, Brawn	25,000	1		3		4		7	8	9	10	11						2					6			5			
26 (a)	Birmingham	D	0-0		32,000	1				4	6	7	8	9	10	11						2								5		3	
29 (a)	Everton	L	1-5	Brawn		1				4	6	7	8	9		11					10	2								5		3	
Jan 1 (h)	Birmingham	W	1-0	Bloomer	16,000	1				4		7	8	9	10	11	3								2		6			5			
2 (a)	Manchester C	L	1-3	Murray	7,000	1				4		7	8		10	11	3				9				2		6			5			
5 (h)	W Arsenal	W	5-3	Bloomer 4, Wilcox	15,000	1				4		7	8	9	10	11	3								2		6			5			
19 (a)	Sheffield W	W	2-0	Common, Wilcox		1		3		4		7	8	9	10	11									2		6			5			
26 (h)	Bury	W	3-1	Bloomer 2, Common		1		3		4		7	8	9	10	11									2		6			5			
Feb 9 (h)	Derby C	W	4-1	Brawn, Bloomer, Thackeray 2	10,000	1		3		4		7	8	9	10	11									2		6			5			
16 (h)	Preston NE	W	2-1	Common 2		1		3		4		7	8	9	10	11									2		6			5			
23 (a)	Newcastle U	L	0-4		47,000	1				4	6	7	8	9	10	11	3								2					5			
Mar 2 (h)	Aston Villa	W	1-0	Wilcox	20,000	1		3		4		7	8		10	11									2		6			5	9		
16 (h)	Bristol C	W	1-0	Thackeray	14,000	1		3		4		7	8	9	10	11									2		6			5			
30 (h)	Sheffield U	L	0-1		20,000	1		3		4		7	8	9	10	11									2		6			5			
Apr 1 (a)	Sunderland	L	2-4	Bloomer, Common (pen)	30,000	1		3		4		7	8	9	10										2		6		11	5			
6 (a)	Bolton W	L	0-1			1			8	5	4	7			10	11					9							3		6		2	
10 (h)	Notts C	D	2-2	Common, Wilcox	6,000	1				4		7	8	9	10	11	3								2		6			5			
13 (h)	Manchester U	W	2-0	Wilcox 2	15,000	1				4		7	8	9	10	11											6			5		2	3
17 (a)	Liverpool	W	4-2	S.Aitken, Common 3	8,000	1				4		7	8	9	10	11	3										6			5		2	
20 (h)	Stoke	W	2-0	S.Aitken, Bloomer		1				4		7	8	9	10	11											6			5		2	3
27 (h)	Blackburn R	L	0-1			1				5	4	7	8	9	10	11											6					2	3
Apps						38	2	24	2	35	17	37	34	29	37	28	5	1	1	1	9	12	4	5	23	4	30	1	3	27	1	5	3
Goals										2	1	4	18	12	12	4					1			1		1							

FA Cup

Date	Opponent	Res	Score	Scorers	Att	Williamson RG	Ratcliffe E	Campbell A	Shand H	Aitken S	Barker WC	Brawn WF	Bloomer S	Common A	Wilcox FJ	Thackeray J	Hickling W	Hanlon E	Priest F	Barker FM	Murray T	Priest AE	Tomlin J	O'Hagan C	Tyldesley J	Tucker WH	Harkins J	Roberts J	Roberts WS	Aitken A	Cail SG	Brown JR	Watson J	Round
Jan 12 (h)	Northampton T	W	4-2	Bloomer 2, Common, Brawn*	15,000	1		3		4		7	8	9	10	11									2		6			5				1
Feb 2 (a)	Brentford	L	0-1		22,000	1		3		4		7	8	9	10	11									2		6			5				2
Apps						2		2		2		2	2	2	2	2									2		2			2				
Goals												1	2	1																			

*Some sources credit Cooch (og) but club credit Brawn

1907-08
Division 1

Date	Opponent	Result	Scorers	Att	Williamson RG	Groves JA	Watson J	Aitken S	Aitken A	Harkins J	Roberts WS	Bloomer S	Common A	Wilcox FJ	Brawn WF	Brown JR	Thackeray J	McCulloch A	Barker WC	Hasel AA	Verrill E	Dixon T	Urquhart A	Campbell A	Cail SG	Wilson TT
Sep 4 (h)	Birmingham	W 1-0	Bloomer	20,000	1	2	3	4	5	6	7	8	9	10	11											
7 (a)	Nottingham F	W 3-0	Wilcox, Common, Bloomer	12,000	1		3	4	5	6	7	8	9	10		2	11									
9 (a)	Manchester U	l 1-2	Wilcox	20,000	1		3	4	5	6		8	9	10	7	2	11									
14 (h)	Manchester U	W 2-1	S.Aitken, Wilcox	25,000	1		3	4	5	6	11	8	9	10	7	2										
21 (a)	Blackburn R	L 0-2		20,000	1		3	4	5	6	10	8		9	7	2	11									
28 (h)	Bolton W	L 0-2		18,000	1		3	4	5	6		8		10	7	2	11	9								
Oct 5 (a)	Birmingham	W 4-1	Bloomer, Wilcox 2, Common	20,000	1		3	4	5		11	8	9	10	7	2			6							
12 (h)	Everton	L 0-2		17,000			3	4	5		11	8	9	10	7	2			6	1						
19 (a)	Sunderland	D 0-0		28,600	1		3	4	5		11	8	9	10	7	2			6							
26 (h)	W Arsenal	D 0-0		15,000	1		3	4	5			8	9	10	7	2	11		6							
Nov 2 (a)	Sheffield W	L 2-3	Common 2 (1 pen)	18,000	1		3	4	5			8	9	10	7	2	11		6							
9 (h)	Bristol C	L 0-1		18,000	1		3	4	5			8	9	10	7	2	11		6							
16 (a)	Notts C	L 0-2		8,000	1		3	4	5		7		8	10		2	11	9	6							
23 (h)	Manchester C	W 2-0	Thackeray, Dixon	10,000	1		3	4	5	6			9	10		2	11				7	8				
30 (a)	Preston NE	D 1-1	McCulloch	9,000	1		3	4	5	6			9	11		2		10			7	8				
Dec 7 (h)	Bury	L 0-2		14,000	1		3	4	5	6		8	9	11		2					7	10				
14 (a)	Aston Villa	L 0-6		10,000	1		3	4	5			8		10		2			6		11	9	7			
21 (h)	Liverpool	W 3-1	Bloomer 2, Wilcox	14,000	1		3	4	5			8	9	10				11			6		7	2		
25 (a)	Sheffield U	D 0-0		25,000	1		3	4	5		11	8	9	10							6		7	2		
26 (a)	Chelsea	L 0-1		45,000	1		3	4	5			8	9	10		2					6	11	7			
28 (a)	Newcastle U	D 1-1	Thackeray	20,000	1		3	4	5			8	9	10		2	11				6	7				
Jan 1 (h)	Chelsea	W 3-1	Dixon 2, Bloomer	30,000	1		3	4	5			8	9	10		2	11				6	7				
4 (h)	Nottingham F	D 1-1	Cail	15,000	1		3	4	5			8		10		2	11				6	7			9	
18 (h)	Blackburn R	W 3-0	Bloomer, Common, Cail	15,000	1		3	4	5			7	8	10			11				6			2	9	
25 (a)	Bolton W	D 1-1	Cail	12,000	1	2	3	4	5			7	8	10			11				6				9	
Feb 1 (h)	Sheffield U	W 2-0	Cail, Common		1	2	3	4	5			7	8	10			11				6				9	
8 (a)	Everton	L 1-2	Cail	15,000	1	2	3	4	5			8		10			11				6	7			9	
15 (h)	Sunderland	W 3-1	Cail, Thackeray, A.Aitken	25,000	1	2	3	4	5			7	8	10			11				6				9	
22 (a)	W Arsenal	L 1-4	Cail	7,000	1	2	3	4	5			7	8	10			11				6				9	
Mar 7 (a)	Bristol C	W 1-0	Bloomer	10,000	1	2	3	4	5			7	8	10			11				6				9	
14 (h)	Notts C	W 3-1	Cail 2, Common	15,000	1	2	3	4	5			7	8	10			11				6				9	
21 (a)	Manchester C	L 1-2	Cail	30,000	1	2	3	4				7	8	10			11		5		6				9	
28 (h)	Preston NE	W 1-0	Common	20,000	1		3	4	5				9	10			11				6	7		2	8	
Apr 4 (a)	Bury	W 4-1	Wilcox 2, Cail, Bloomer	11,000	1		3	4				8	7	10			11				6			2	9	5
8 (h)	Sheffield W	W 6-1	Wilcox, Bloomer 2, Common, Cail, Thackeray		1		3	4				8	7	10			11				6			2	9	5
11 (h)	Aston Villa	L 0-1		15,000	1		3	4				8	7				11				6	10		2	9	5
18 (a)	Liverpool	W 1-0	Thackeray	8,000	1		3	4				8	5				11				6	7		2	9	10
20 (h)	Newcastle U	W 2-1	Dixon, Bloomer	20,000	1		3	4				8	5				11				6	7		2	9	10
Apps					37	9	38	38	32	9	9	34	34	34	11	20	28	3	9	1	25	13	4	9	16	5
Goals							1	1				12	9	9			5	1				4			12	

FA Cup

Round

Date	Opponent	Result	Att	Williamson RG	Groves JA	Watson J	Aitken S	Aitken A	Harkins J	Roberts WS	Bloomer S	Common A	Wilcox FJ	Brawn WF	Brown JR	Thackeray J	McCulloch A	Barker WC	Hasel AA	Verrill E	Dixon T	Urquhart A	Campbell A	Cail SG	Wilson TT	
Jan 11 (a)	Notts C	L 0-2	16,000	1		3	4	5			8	9	10		2	11				6	7					1
Apps				1		1	1	1			1	1	1		1	1				1	1					
Goals																										

1908-09
Division 1

Date	Opponent	Result	Scorers	Att	Williamson RG	Groves JA	Watson J	Aitken S	Aitken A	Verrill E	Pentland FB	Bloomer S	Hall JH	Wilcox FJ	Thackeray J	Common A	Gordon D	Kent H	Cail SG	Campbell A	Wilson TT	McLeod D	Dixon T	Young RT	Barker WC	Jones JL
Sep 5 (h)	Bradford C	W 1-0	Bloomer	19,000	1	2	3	4	5	6	7	8	9	10	11											
9 (h)	Sunderland	L 0-3		18,000	1	2	3	4	5	6		8	9	10	11	7										
12 (a)	Manchester U	L 3-6	Bloomer 2, Hall	25,000	1	3		4	5		7	8	9	11			2	6	10							
19 (h)	Everton	L 2-3	Bloomer 2	18,000	1		3	4	5	6	7	8		11		9			10	2						
26 (a)	Leicester F	D 1-1	Wilcox	20,000	1	2	3	4	5	6	7	8		10	11				9							
Oct 3 (h)	W Arsenal	D 1-1	Cail	8,000	1		3	4	2	6	7	8	10	11					9		5					
10 (a)	Notts C	L 2-3	Bloomer 2 (1 pen)	10,000	1		3	4		6		8	10	11		7		5	9			2				
17 (h)	Newcastle U	D 0-0		20,000	1		3	4	5			8	10	6	11	7			9			2				
24 (a)	Bristol C	D 1-1	Common	12,000	1		3	4	5			8	10	6	11	7			9			2				
31 (h)	Preston NE	W 4-2	Hall 2, Bloomer, Cail	17,000	1		3	4				8	10	5	11	7			9		6	2				
Nov 7 (a)	Sheffield W	L 2-3	Cail, Thackeray	15,000	1		3	4				8		5	11	7			9		6	2	10			
14 (a)	Manchester C	D 0-0		15,000	1		3	4	5		9	8		6	11	7						2	10			
21 (h)	Liverpool	W 1-0	Bloomer	15,000	1		3	4	5	6	7	8	10		11	9						2				
28 (a)	Bury	L 1-2	Common	10,000	1		3	4	5	6	7	8	10		11	9						2				
Dec 5 (h)	Sheffield U	L 1-2	Bloomer	9,000	1		3	4	5		7	8	10	6	11	9						2				
12 (a)	Aston Villa	W 3-0	Hall, S.Aitken, Bloomer	20,000	1		3	4	5		7	8	9	6	11	10						2				
19 (h)	Nottingham F	W 4-0	Cail, Hall 2, Common	15,000	1		3	4	5		7		9	6	11	10			8			2				
25 (a)	Blackburn R	D 0-0		25,000	1		3	4	5		7		9	6	11	10			8			2				
26 (a)	Sunderland	L 0-2		20,000	1		3	4	5		7		9	6	11	10			8			2				
Jan 1 (h)	Chelsea	L 1-4	Common	25,000	1		3	4	5		7		9	8	11	10						2	6			
2 (a)	Bradford C	W 2-0	Hall, Pentland	30,000	1		3			6	7		9	5	11	10			8			2	4			
9 (h)	Manchester U	W 5-0	Cail, Common 2, Hall 2	15,000	1		3			6	7		9	5	11	10			8			2	4			
23 (a)	Everton	D 1-1	Common	25,000	1		3			6	7		9	5	11	10			8			2	4			
30 (h)	Leicester F	W 6-2	Hall 3, Hedley (og), Thackeray, Cail	10,000	1	3				6	7		9	5	11	10			8			2	4			
Feb 13 (h)	Notts C	L 1-2	Pentland	12,000	1	3				6	7		9	5	11	10			8			2	4			
27 (h)	Bristol C	W 4-0	Hall 2, Cail, Bloomer	10,000	1		3	4		6	7	8	9	5	11				10			2				
Mar 6 (a)	Preston NE	D 1-1	Thackeray	6,000	1		3	4		6	7	8	9	5	11	10						2				
13 (h)	Sheffield W	W 2-1	Hall, Cail	8,000	1		3	4		6		8	9	5	11	7			10			2				
17 (a)	W Arsenal	D 1-1	Cail	15,000	1			4		6		8		11	10				9			2	7	5	3	
20 (h)	Manchester C	W 3-0	Common 2, Bloomer	12,000	1		3	4		6	7	8			10			5				2	9			11
27 (a)	Liverpool	W 2-1	Common, Bloomer	10,000	1			4		6	7	8	9		10			5				2		3		11
31 (a)	Newcastle U	L 0-1		45,000	1	3		4		6		8	9		10			5	7			2				11
Apr 4 (h)	Bury	L 0-1		10,000	1	3		5		6		8	9	11	10				9			2	7	4		
9 (a)	Chelsea	L 0-3		50,000	1	3		5		6	7	8	9	11	10							2		4		
10 (a)	Sheffield U	L 0-2		9,000	1	3		5		6	7			11	10							2	8	4		
12 (h)	Blackburn R	W 1-0	Hall	12,000	1	3		4		6	7	8	9	11	10			5				2				
17 (h)	Aston Villa	W 1-0	Hall	8,000	1		3	4		6	7	8	9	11	5				10			2				
24 (a)	Nottingham F	L 1-4	Hall	7,000	1	3		4		6	7	8	9	11	5				10			2				
Apps					38	12	27	33	17	26	28	28	30	26	31	33	1	6	25	1	3	32	6	10	2	3
Goals								1			2	14	18	1	3	10			9							

1 own-goal

FA Cup

Date	Opponent	Result	Att	Williamson RG	Groves JA	Watson J	Aitken S	Aitken A	Verrill E	Pentland FB	Bloomer S	Hall JH	Wilcox FJ	Thackeray J	Common A	Gordon D	Kent H	Cail SG	Campbell A	Wilson TT	McLeod D	Dixon T	Young RT	Barker WC	Jones JL	Round
Jan 16 (a)	Preston NE	L 0-1	9,000	1		3			6	7		9	5	11	10			8			2	4				1
Apps				1		1			1	1		1	1	1	1			1			1	1				
Goals																									

1909-10
Division 1

Date		Opponent	Result	Scorers	Att	Williamson RG	McLeod D	Watson J	Aitken S	Common A	Verrill E	Pentland FB	Elliott GW	Hall JH	Cail SG	Thackeray J	Bloomer S	Dixon T	Jones JL	Wilcox FJ	Young RT	Groves JA	Barker WC	Wilson TT	Burton G	Beaton S	Flint WA	Boardman H
Sep 1	(h)	Sheffield U	L 0-2		8,000	1	2	3	4	5	6	7	8	9	10	11												
4	(a)	Sheffield W	W 5-1	Dixon, S.Aitken, Hall 2, Bloomer	10,000	1	2	3	4	5	6	7		9			8	10	11									
11	(h)	W Arsenal	W 5-2	Dixon 2, Bloomer (pen), Hall 2	12,000	1	2	3	4	5	6	7		9			8	10	11									
18	(a)	Bristol C	L 1-4	Bloomer	10,000	1	2	3	4	5	6	7		9			8	10	11									
25	(h)	Bolton W	L 1-2	Bloomer	12,000	1	2	3	4	5	6	7		9			8	10	11									
Oct 2	(a)	Bury	L 1-2	Hall	10,000	1	2	3	4	5	6	7	10	9		11	8											
9	(h)	Chelsea	L 0-1		12,000	1	2	3	4		6	7	10	9		11	8		5									
16	(a)	Tottenham H	W 3-1	Groves 2, Common	25,000	1	2	3	4	8	6		10			11	9				5	7						
23	(h)	Blackburn R	L 1-3	Bloomer	5,000	1	2	3	4		6	7	10			11	9				5	8						
30	(a)	Preston NE	L 0-1		8,000	1	2	3	5	10	6	7		9		11	8					4						
Nov 6	(h)	Nottingham F	W 2-1	Hall, Cail	10,000	1	2	3	4		6	7	10	9		11	8			5								
13	(a)	Notts C	L 1-2	Cail	9,000	1	2	3	4		6	7	10	9		11	8				5							
20	(h)	Sunderland	W 3-2	Common, Verrill, Hall	20,000	1	2	3	4	8	6	7	10	9		11					5							
27	(a)	Newcastle U	L 0-2		28,000	1	2	3	4	8	6	7	10	9		11					5							
Dec 4	(h)	Everton	D 1-1	Common	10,000	1	2	3	4	8	6		10	9		11	7				5							
11	(a)	Liverpool	D 0-0		20,000	1	2		4	8	6		10		11		7				5	3	9					
18	(h)	Manchester U	L 1-2	Hall	10,000	1	2	3	4	8	6	7		10	11	9					5							
25	(h)	Bradford C	L 3-7	Hall, Bloomer 2	25,000	1	2	5	4	8	6	7		10	11		9	3										
27	(a)	Bradford C	L 1-4	Bloomer (pen)	35,000	1	2	3	5		6	7	10	8		11	9					4						
Jan 1	(a)	Sheffield U	L 0-2		12,000	1		3			6	7	8	10	9	11					5		2	4				
8	(h)	Sheffield W	W 4-0	Elliott, Thackeray, Cail 2	10,000	1	2	3	4		6	7	8	10	9	11					5							
22	(a)	W Arsenal	L 0-3		6,000	1	2	3	4		10	9	11	8	7						5	6						
Feb 5	(a)	Bolton W	D 1-1	Bloomer	10,000	1	2	3	4		6	7	10	9		11	8				5							
12	(h)	Bury	L 0-5		8,000	1	2	3	4		6	7	10	9		11	8				5							
19	(a)	Chelsea	L 1-2	Hall	12,000	1	2	3			6		8	10		11					5		9	4	7			
26	(h)	Tottenham H	W 4-3	Young, Verrill, Cail, Pentland	7,000	1		3		8	6	7		10	9	11					5		4					2
Mar 5	(a)	Blackburn R	D 1-1	Young (pen)	15,000	1		3	4	8	6	7	10	9		11					5							2
12	(h)	Preston NE	W 1-0	Verrill	8,000	1	2		4	8	6	7	10	9		11					5							3
19	(a)	Nottingham F	W 1-0	Young (pen)	5,000	1	2	3	4	8	6	7	10	9		11					5							
25	(a)	Aston Villa	L 2-4	Cail, Common	30,000	1	2	3	4	9	6	7		10	8	11					5							
26	(h)	Notts C	W 2-0	Hall, Pentland	12,000	1	2	3	4	8	6	7		9	10	11					5							
28	(h)	Aston Villa	W 3-2	Young (pen), Cail, Elliott	20,000	1	2	3	4	9	6	7	8		10	11					5							
Apr 2	(a)	Sunderland	D 2-2	Young (pen), Elliott	12,000	1	2	3	4	9	6	7	8		10	11					5							
9	(h)	Newcastle U	D 1-1	Cail	12,000	1	2	3	4	9	6	7	8		10	11					5							
16	(a)	Everton	D 1-1	Thackeray	15,000	1	2	3	4	9	6	7	8		10	11					5							
20	(h)	Bristol C	D 0-0		12,000	1	2	3	4	9	6	7	8		10	11					5							
23	(h)	Liverpool	D 2-2	Elliott, Williamson (pen)	5,000	1	2	3	5	9	6	7	8	10					11				4					
30	(a)	Manchester U	L 1-4	Hall	10,000	1	2		5		6	7	8	9	10	11												3
				Apps		38	35	35	35	26	37	33	15	29	25	27	20	5	11	1	24	6	5	2	2	2	1	4
				Goals		1			1	4	3	2	4	12	8	2	9	3			5	2						

FA Cup

Date		Opponent	Result	Scorers	Att	Williamson RG	McLeod D	Watson J	Aitken S	Common A	Verrill E	Pentland FB	Elliott GW	Hall JH	Cail SG	Thackeray J	Bloomer S	Dixon T	Jones JL	Wilcox FJ	Young RT		Round
Jan 15	(h)	Everton	D 1-1	Thackeray	25,000	1	2	3	4		6	7	8	10		11	9				5		1
19	(a)	Everton	L 3-5	Common, Cail, Bloomer	20,000	1	2	3	4	7	6		10	9	11		8				5		R
				Apps		2	2	2	1	2	1	1	2	1	2	2					2		
				Goals						1					1	1	1						

1910-11
Division 1

Date	Opponent	Result	Scorers	Att	Williamson RG	McLeod D	Weir J	Barker WC	Jackson A	Verrill E	Gibson RJ	Elliott GW	Pentland FB	McClure S	Nichol J	Duguid W	Cail SG	Kelly B	Peggie J	Wardrope A	Davidson W	Carr J	Davies B	Carr H	Dixon T	Crosier J	Best C	Howling E	Leonard HD	James WE	Carr W
Sep 3 (h)	Everton	W 1-0	McClure	17,000	1	2	3	4	5	6	7	8	9	10	11																
10 (a)	Sheffield W	D 1-1	McClure	12,000	1	2	3	4	5	6	7	8	9	10	11																
17 (h)	Bristol C	W 3-0	Pentland, Gibson, Williamson (pen)	20,000	1	2	3	4	5	6	7	8	9	10	11																
24 (a)	Newcastle U	D 0-0		40,000	1	2	3	4	5	6	7	8	9	10	11																
Oct 1 (h)	Tottenham H	W 2-0	Pentland, Elliott	24,000	1	2	3		5	6	7	8	9	10	11	4															
8 (a)	Oldham A	D 1-1	Nichol	20,000	1	2	3	4	5	6	7	8	9		11		10														
15 (a)	Preston NE	D 1-1	Nichol		1	2	3	4	5	6	7	8			11	10	9														
22 (h)	Notts C	W 4-1	Pentland, Cail, Nichol, Elliott	17,000	1	2	3	4	5	6	7	8	9		11		10														
29 (a)	Manchester U	W 2-1	Pentland, Cail	35,000	1	2	3	4	5	6	7	8	9		11		10														
Nov 5 (h)	Liverpool	D 2-2	McClure, Elliott	26,000	1	2	3	4	5	6	7	8	9	10	11																
12 (a)	Bury	L 2-4	Elliott, Gibson	6,000	1	2	3	4	5	6	7	8	9		11		10														
19 (h)	Sheffield U	W 3-1	Cail 2, Elliott	17,000	1		3	4	5	6	7	8			11		10	2	9												
26 (a)	Aston Villa	L 0-5		15,000	1		3	4		6	7		9		11		10	2	8	5											
Dec 3 (h)	Sunderland	W 1-0	Nichol	27,980	1	2	3	4		6	7		9	8	11		10			5											
10 (a)	W Arsenal	W 2-0	Elliott, Nichol	8,000	1	2	3	4	5	6	7	8	9		11		10														
17 (h)	Bradford C	W 3-2	Elliott, Pentland, Nichol	15,000	1	2	3	4	5	6	7	8	9	10							11										
24 (a)	Blackburn R	L 1-5	Verrill	12,000	1	2	3	4	5	6	7	8	9				10				11										
26 (h)	Manchester C	D 0-0		25,000	1	2	3	4		6		8	7				10	9	5		11										
27 (a)	Nottingham F	D 1-1	Elliott	20,000	1	2	3	4		6		8	9	10				7	5		11										
31 (a)	Everton	L 0-2		15,000	1	2	3	4	5			8	9	10		6			7		11										
Jan 2 (h)	Nottingham F	D 2-2	J.Carr 2	15,000	1	2	3	4	5	6			9	10	7						11	8									
7 (h)	Sheffield W	L 0-1			1		3	4	5		7		9	8	10	6				2	11										
21 (a)	Bristol C	L 2-3	Elliott, Wedlock (og)	10,000	1		3	4	5	6	7	8	9				10			2	11										
28 (h)	Newcastle U	L 0-2		25,000	1	2		4	5	6	7	8	9			3	10				11										
Feb 11 (h)	Oldham A	L 1-2	H.Carr	12,000		2	3	4			7	8			11	6	10			5			1	9							
13 (a)	Tottenham H	L 2-6	H.Carr 2	8,000	1	2	3	4							11	6	10			5	7			9	8						
18 (h)	Preston NE	W 2-0	Pentland, Elliott	7,000	1	2	3	4	5	6		8	9		11		10				7										
Mar 4 (h)	Manchester U	D 2-2	Dixon, Gibson	11,000	1	2	3		5	6	7		9		11		10								8	4					
11 (a)	Liverpool	L 0-3		20,000	1	2	3		5	6	7		8			4	10				11			9							
18 (h)	Bury	W 2-1	Cail 2	7,000	1	2	3		5				8	9			10		6		11				4	7					
27 (a)	Sheffield U	L 1-2	Best	6,000	1	2	3	4	5	6			8	9			10				11						7				
Apr 1 (h)	Aston Villa	L 0-1		18,000		2			5		6		8	7			10	3							4			1	9	11	
8 (a)	Sunderland	L 1-3	Pentland		1	2		4			7						10	3	8								5		9	11	
14 (a)	Manchester C	L 1-2	Cail	35,000	1	2	3	4	5	6	7						10				11						8		9		
15 (h)	W Arsenal	D 1-1	Nichol	14,000	1	2	3		5	6	7				11		10			4							8		9		
18 (a)	Notts C	L 0-1		8,000	1	2	3	4		6	7						10										5		8	9	11
27 (a)	Bradford C	L 0-1		10,000	1	2	3	4		6	7						10				11								9		5
29 (h)	Blackburn R	L 2-3	Leonard, Nichol		1	2	3		5	6	7		8		11		10												9	4	
Apps					36	34	35	32	28	33	28	25	30	11	24	9	26	4	6	10	16	1	1	3	3	5	5	1	7	3	2
Goals					1					1	3	10	7	3	8		7					2		3	1		1		1		

1 own-goal

FA Cup

Date	Opponent	Result	Scorers	Att	Williamson RG	McLeod D	Weir J	Barker WC	Jackson A	Verrill E	Gibson RJ	Elliott GW	Pentland FB	McClure S	Nichol J	Duguid W	Cail SG	Kelly B	Peggie J	Wardrope A	Davidson W	Carr J	Davies B	Carr H	Dixon T	Crosier J	Best C	Howling E	Leonard HD	James WE	Carr W	Round
Jan 14 (h)	Glossop	W 1-0	Cail	15,000	1		3	4	5	6	7	8	9				10			2	11											1
Feb 4 (h)	Leicester F	D 0-0		17,000	1	2	3	4	5		7	8		10		6	9				11											2
9 (a)	Leicester F	W 2-1*	Cail, Dixon	14,000	1	2	3	4	5	6	7	8			11		9								10							R
25 (h)	Blackburn R	L 0-3		30,369	1	2	3	4	5	6		8	9		11		10				7											3
Apps					4	3	4	4	4	3	3	4	2	1	2	1	4			1	3				1							
Goals																	2								1						

*After extra-time

1911-12
Division 1

Date		Opponent	Result	Scorers	Att	Williamson RG	McLeod D	Weir J	Barker WC	Jackson A	Verrill E	Stirling J	Elliott GW	Leonard HD	Cail SG	Eyre E	Carr W	Duguid W	James WE	Layton AE	Windridge JE	Pentland FB	Crosier J	Carr J	McRobbie A	Davies B	Hisbent JM	Cook J	Haworth JH	Nichol J	Fraser A
Sep	2 (a)	Sunderland	L 0-1		30,000	1	2	3	4	5	6	7	8	9	10	11															
	9 (h)	Blackburn R	W 2-1	Leonard, Elliott	19,147	1	2	3	4	5	6	7	8	9	10	11															
	16 (a)	Sheffield W	W 2-0	Cail 2	16,000	1	2	3	4		6	7	8	9	10	11	5														
	23 (h)	Bury	D 1-1	Eyre	16,761	1	2	3	4		6	7	8	9	10	11	5														
	30 (h)	Preston NE	W 4-2	Cail, Elliott 2, Leonard	10,000	1	2	3	4		6	7	8	9	10	11	5														
Oct	7 (a)	Notts C	L 1-2	Elliott	20,000	1	2	3		5	6	7	8	9	10	11		4													
	14 (h)	Tottenham H	W 2-0	James, Elliott	15,394	1	2	3	4		6	7	8		10	11	5		9												
	21 (a)	Manchester U	W 4-3	Elliott 2, Cail, Eyre	20,000	1	2	3	4		6	7	8		10	11	5		9												
	28 (h)	Liverpool	W 3-2	Elliott, Eyre, Stirling	13,720	1	2	3	4		6	7	8		10	11	5		9												
Nov	4 (a)	Aston Villa	L 1-2	James	30,000	1	2		4		6	7	8		10	11	5		9	3											
	11 (h)	Newcastle U	D 1-1	Elliott	32,986	1	2	3	4	5	6	7	8		10	11			9												
	18 (a)	Sheffield U	D 1-1	James		1	2	3	4	5	6	7	8		10	11			9												
	25 (h)	Oldham A	W 3-0	Elliott 2, James	14,527	1	2	3	4	5	6	7	8		10	11			9												
Dec	2 (a)	Bolton W	L 0-1		26,000	1	2	3	4	5	6	7	8			11			9	10											
	9 (h)	Bradford C	W 1-0	Windridge	17,020	1	2	3	4	5	6	7	8			11			9		10										
	16 (a)	W Arsenal	L 1-3	James	10,000	1	2	3	4	5	6	7	8						11		10	9									
	23 (h)	Manchester C	W 3-1	Stirling, James 2 (1 pen)	12,000	1	2	3	4	5	6	7	8			11			9		10										
	25 (h)	Everton	D 0-0		22,436	1		3	4	5	6	7	8			11			9		10		2								
	26 (a)	Everton	L 0-1		25,000	1		3	4	5	6	7	8	9		11					10		2								
	30 (h)	Sunderland	D 3-3	Elliott, James, Eyre	18,750	1		3	4	5	6	7	8			11			9		10		2								
Jan	6 (a)	Blackburn R	L 1-2	Elliott	10,167	1	2	3	4	5	6	7	8		10	11			9												
	20 (h)	Sheffield W	D 1-1	Eyre	10,887	1	2	3	4		6	7	8			11	5		9		10										
	27 (a)	Bury	W 2-0	Eyre 2	10,000	1	2				6	7			5	11	6	4	9	3	10			8							
Feb	10 (h)	Notts C	W 4-0	Eyre, Cail 2, Elliott	9,714	1	2		4	5	6	7	8		9	11				10				3							
	17 (a)	Tottenham H	L 1-2	Elliott	22,000		2	3	4	5	6	7	8		9	11				10					1						
	24 (h)	W Arsenal	L 0-2		12,291	1		3	4	5		7	8		9	11											2	10	6		
Mar	2 (a)	Liverpool	D 1-1	Jackson	20,000	1	2	3	4	5	6	7	8		9					10									11		
	9 (h)	Aston Villa	L 1-2	Windridge	13,359	1	2	3	4	5	6	7	8			11			9	10											
	16 (a)	Newcastle U	W 1-0	Cail	8,790	1		3	4				8		9	11	5				10			7			2		6		
	23 (h)	Sheffield U	D 1-1	Windridge	8,790	1		3	4				8		9	11	5				10			7			2		6		
	30 (a)	Oldham A	L 0-2		5,000	1		3	4			7	8		9	11	5				10						2		6		
Apr	5 (h)	West Brom A	W 1-0	Cail	13,000	1		3	4			7	8		9	11	5				10						2		6		
	6 (h)	Bolton W	W 1-0	Cail (pen)	7,000	1		3	4			7	8		9	11	5				10						2		6		
	8 (a)	West Brom A	L 1-3	Elliott	25,027	1		3	4			7	8		9	11	5				10						2		6		
	13 (a)	Bradford C	L 1-2	J.Carr	10,000	1		3				7	8		9	11	5							10			2		6		4
	17 (h)	Manchester U	W 3-0	Cail 3	5,000	1		3	4			7	8		9	11	5							10			2		6		
	22 (a)	Preston NE	W 3-0	Cail, Elliott, Stirling		1		3	4		6	7	8		9	11	5				10						2				
	27 (a)	Manchester C	L 0-2		20,000	1		3	4			7	8		9	11	5				10						2		6		
		Apps				36	24	33	32	18	31	36	35	6	30	32	13	6	19	7	20	1	1	4	1	2	11	1	11	4	4
		Goals								1		3	17	2	13	8			8		3			1							

FA Cup

Date		Opponent	Result	Scorers	Att	Williamson RG	McLeod D	Weir J	Barker WC	Jackson A	Verrill E	Stirling J	Elliott GW	Leonard HD	Cail SG	Eyre E	Carr W	Duguid W	James WE	Layton AE	Windridge JE	Pentland FB	Crosier J	Carr J	McRobbie A	Davies B	Hisbent JM	Cook J	Haworth JH	Nichol J	Fraser A	Round
Jan	13 (h)	Sheffield W	D 0-0		24,700	1	2	3	4	5	6	7	8		9	11					10											1
	25 (a)	Sheffield W	W 2-1	James, Windridge	30,468	1	2	3	4	5	6	7	8						9		10									11		R
Feb	3 (h)	West Ham U	D 1-1	Elliott	12,327	1	2	3	4	5	6	7	8			11			9		10											2
	8 (a)	West Ham U	L 1-2	Elliott*	10,000	1	2		4	5	6	7	8			11			9		10			3								R
		Apps				4	4	3	4	4	4	4	4		1	3			3		4			1						1		
		Goals											2						1		1										

*Some sources credit Verrill but club credits Elliott

1912-13
Division 1

Date		Opponent	Result	Scorers	Att	Williamson RG	McLeod D	Weir J	Fraser A	Carr W	Verrill E	Stirling J	Elliott GW	Brown AS	Windridge JE	Eyre E	Duguid W	Haworth JH	Hisbent JM	Cook H	Cail SG	Crosier J	Carr J	Nichol J	McRobbie A	Barker WC	Malcolm G	Jackson A	James WE	Davies B	Cook J
Sep	4 (a)	West Brom A	L 0-2		15,085	1	2	3	4	5	6	7	8	9	10	11															
	7 (h)	Everton	D 0-0		17,360	1	2	3		5	6	7	8	9	10	11	4														
	14 (a)	Sheffield W	L 1-3	Elliott	25,000	1	2	3		5		7	8	9	10	11	4	6													
	21 (h)	Blackburn R	D 0-0		18,577	1	2	3		5	6	7	8	9	10	11			4												
	28 (a)	Derby C	W 2-0	Cail, Elliott	12,000	1		3		5	6	7	8		10	11					2	4	9								
Oct	5 (h)	Tottenham H	D 1-1	Elliott	14,076	1		3		5	6	7	8		10	11					2	4	9								
	12 (a)	Sunderland	L 0-4		25,000	1		3		5	6	7	8		10	11	4				2		9								
	19 (a)	Notts C	W 3-1	Nichol, Elliott 2	10,000	1		3		5	6	7	9								2	10	4	8	11						
	26 (h)	Manchester U	W 3-2	J.Carr 2, Windridge	9,929	1		3		5	6	7	9		10								8	11	2	4					
Nov	2 (a)	Aston Villa	L 1-5	J.Carr	20,000	1	2			5	6	7			10		3					9	8	11			4				
	9 (h)	Liverpool	L 3-4	J.Carr, Elliott, Nichol	11,973	1		3			6	7	9		10						2		8	11			4	5			
	16 (a)	Bolton W	L 2-3	Elliott, J.Carr	10,000	1		3			6	7	9		10						2		8	11			4	5			
	23 (h)	Sheffield U	W 4-1	Elliott 2 (1 pen), Windridge, J.Carr	10,400	1		3			6	7	9		10						2		8	11			4	5			
	30 (a)	Newcastle U	L 1-3	Elliott	20,000	1		3			6	7	9		10						2		8	11			4	5			
Dec	7 (h)	Oldham A	D 2-2	Windridge, J.Carr	11,259	1		3			6	7	9		10						2		8	11			4	5			
	14 (a)	Chelsea	W 3-2	J.Carr 2, Elliott	15,000	1	2	3				7	9		10							4	8	11			6	5			
	21 (h)	W Arsenal	W 2-0	J.Carr, Windridge	9,568	1	2	3		5		7	9		10							4	8	11			6				
	26 (h)	Bradford C	D 1-1	Elliott	13,013	1	2	3				7	9		10							4	8	11			6	5			
	28 (a)	Everton	L 0-1		25,000	1		3					9		10	11	2			6	8	4	7					5			
Jan	1 (h)	West Brom A	W 3-1	Elliott 2, Eyre	18,222	1	2	3				7	9		10	11						4	8				6	5			
	4 (h)	Sheffield W	L 0-2		13,575	1		3				7	9		10	11					2	4	8				6	5			
	25 (h)	Derby C	W 4-1	Eyre 2, Betts (og), Cail	16,021	1		3			6	7	9			11			2		10	4	8					5			
Feb	4 (a)	Bradford C	W 2-1	Stirling, Elliott	12,000	1		3				7	9		10	11			4		2		8				6	5			
	8 (a)	Tottenham H	L 3-5	J.Carr 2, Elliott	24,000	1						7	9		10	11	3		4		2		8				6	5			
	10 (a)	Blackburn R	L 2-5	J.Carr (pen), Eyre	15,000	1									10	11	3				8	4	7		2		6	5	9		
	15 (h)	Sunderland	L 0-2		13,992			3				7			10	11					2	9	4	8			6	5	1		
Mar	1 (a)	Manchester U	W 3-2	J.Cook, Elliott 2	15,000	1					6	7	9			11	3		4				8		2			5			10
	15 (a)	Liverpool	L 2-4	J.Carr 2	10,000	1		3			6	7	9		10	11					2		8				4	5			
	21 (h)	Manchester C	D 0-0		12,026	1		3			6	7	9		10	11					2		8				4	5			
	22 (h)	Bolton W	W 4-0	Elliott 3, Windridge	10,165	1		3			6	7	9		10						2		8	11			4	5			
	24 (a)	Manchester C	L 0-3		26,000	1		3			6	7	9		10						2	5	8	11			4				
	31 (a)	Sheffield U	L 0-1			1		3				7	9		10						2	4	8	11			6	5			
Apr	2 (h)	Notts C	D 1-1	J.Carr (pen)	6,000	1		3		5	6	7			10	11					2	4	8						9		
	5 (h)	Newcastle U	D 0-0		10,370	1	2			5	6	7			10	11					9	4	8		3						
	9 (h)	Aston Villa	D 1-1	Cail	6,894	1	2			5		7	9			11				3	10	4	8				6				
	12 (a)	Oldham A	L 0-1		4,000	1	2	3				7	9			11				5	10	4	8				6				
	19 (h)	Chelsea	L 0-3		9,000	1	2	3		5	6	7	9		10	11							8				4				
	26 (a)	W Arsenal	D 1-1	Elliott (pen)	6,000	1		3		5		7	9		10	11					2	4	8				6				
		Apps				37	13	32	1	15	21	33	33	4	33	27	8	2	22	5	13	19	30	11	6	1	25	20	2	1	4
		Goals										1	22		5	4					3		16	2							1

1 own-goal

FA Cup

Date		Opponent	Result	Scorers	Att	Williamson RG	McLeod D	Weir J	Fraser A	Carr W	Verrill E	Stirling J	Elliott GW	Brown AS	Windridge JE	Eyre E	Duguid W	Haworth JH	Hisbent JM	Cook H	Cail SG	Crosier J	Carr J	Nichol J	McRobbie A	Barker WC	Malcolm G	Jackson A	James WE	Davies B	Cook J	Round
Jan	11 (a)	Millwall	D 0-0		22,000	1		3				7	9		10						2	4	8	11			6	5				1
	15 (h)	Millwall	W 4-1	J.Carr 3 (1 pen), Elliott	12,780	1		3				7	9		10	11					2	4	8				6	5				R
Feb	1 (h)	Queen's Park R	W 3-2	Elliott 2, Eyre	27,774	1		3				7	9		10	11						4	8		2		6	5				2
	22 (a)	Burnley	L 1-3	Eyre	27,824	1		3				7	9		10	11					2	4	8				6	5				3
		Apps				4		4				4	4		4	3					3	4	4	1	1		4	4				
		Goals											3			2							3									

1913-14
Division 1

Date	Opponent	Res	Scorers	Att	Williamson RG	Walker J	Weir J	Davidson S	Jackson A	Malcolm G	Stirling J	Carr J	Elliott GW	Windridge JE	Nichol J	Verrill E	Cook J	Hisbent JM	Davies B	Cook H	Kirby F	Carr W	Eyre E	Tinsley W	Haworth JH	Crosier J	Storey T	Healey R	Stage W	Wynn R
Sep 6 (a)	Manchester C	D 1-1	Nichol	30,000	1	2	3	4	5	6	7	8	9	10	11															
10 (a)	Derby C	D 2-2	Elliott 2	5,000	1	2	3	4	5	6	7	8	9	10	11															
13 (h)	Bradford C	D 1-1	Windridge	18,748	1	2	3	4	5	6	7	8	9	10	11															
20 (a)	Blackburn R	L 0-6		25,000	1	2	3	4	5		7		9	10	11	6	8													
27 (h)	Sunderland	L 3-4	Elliott 3	26,972	1		3		4	5	6	7	8	9	11	10	2													
Oct 4 (a)	Everton	L 0-2		20,000			3	4		6	7			10	11		8	2	1	5	9									
11 (h)	West Brom A	W 3-0	Stirling, Nichol, Windridge	14,197			3	4		6	7		9	10	11		8	2	1	5										
18 (a)	Sheffield W	L 0-2		15,000			3	4		6	7		9	10	11		8	2	1	5										
25 (h)	Bolton W	L 2-3	Eyre, J.Carr	13,633			3	4		6	7	8	9	10				2	1			5	11							
Nov 1 (a)	Chelsea	L 2-3	J.Carr, Elliott	25,000		2	3	4		6	7	8	9	10	11				1	5										
8 (h)	Oldham A	D 0-0		10,000		2	3	4		6	7	8	9		11		10		1	5										
15 (a)	Manchester U	W 1-0	J.Carr	10,000			3	4			7	8	9	10	11			2	1	6		5								
22 (h)	Burnley	W 2-1	Windridge, Elliott	15,800			3	4			7	8	9	10	11			2	1	6		5								
29 (a)	Preston NE	L 1-4	Nichol				3			6	7	8	9	10	11			2	1	4		5								
Dec 6 (h)	Newcastle U	W 3-0	Elliott 2 (1 pen), Stirling	15,300	1	2	3		5	6	7		9				8			4				11	10					
13 (a)	Liverpool	L 1-2	Elliott	25,000	1	2	3		5	6	7		9				8			4				11	10					
20 (h)	Aston Villa	W 5-2	Tinsley 3, Elliott, J.Carr	13,411	1		3		5	6	7	8	9				11							10	2	4				
25 (a)	Sheffield U	L 1-3	Elliott	30,000	1		3		5	6	7	8	9				11	2						10		4				
26 (a)	Tottenham H	W 1-0	Tinsley	37,055	1		3	4	5	6	7	8	9				11							10	2					
27 (h)	Manchester C	W 2-0	Tinsley, Elliott	12,000	1		3	4	5	6	7	8	9				11							10	2					
Jan 1 (h)	Derby C	W 3-2	J.Carr, Tinsley, Elliott	18,341	1		3	4	5	6	7	8	9				11							10	2					
3 (a)	Bradford C	W 3-2	Tinsley 2, J.Cook	20,000	1		3	4	5	6		8	9				11							10	2		7			
17 (h)	Blackburn R	W 3-0	Elliott 3 (1 pen)	17,000	1		3	4	5	6	7	8	9				11							10	2					
24 (a)	Sunderland	L 2-4	Elliott 2		1		3	4	5	6	7	8	9				11							10	2					
Feb 7 (h)	Everton	W 2-0	Tinsley, Elliott	13,000	1		3	4	5	6	7	8	9				11							10	2					
14 (a)	West Brom A	L 1-2	J.Carr	15,692	1		3	4	5	6	7	8		10			11							9	2					
21 (h)	Manchester U	W 3-1	Stirling, Elliott, Malcolm	12,000	1		3	4		6	7	8	9	10			11					5			2					
28 (a)	Bolton W	D 1-1	Elliott (pen)	18,000	1		3	4	5	6	7	8	9				11							10	2					
Mar 7 (h)	Chelsea	W 2-0	Elliott, J.Carr	14,000	1		3	4	5	6	7	8	9				11							10	2					
14 (a)	Oldham A	L 0-3		7,000	1		3	4	5	6	7	8	9				11							10	2					
18 (h)	Sheffield W	W 5-2	J.Carr, Tinsley, Elliott 3	8,000	1		3	4	5	6		8	9				11							10	2		7			
Apr 4 (h)	Preston NE	W 4-1	Tinsley, Elliott 2 (1 pen), Healey	11,000	1		3	4	5	6	7		9				11							10	2			8		
6 (a)	Burnley	W 2-1	J.Carr, Elliott	6,000	1		3	4	5	6	7	8	9											10	2				11	
10 (h)	Sheffield U	L 2-3	Elliott, Tinsley	16,000	1		3	4	5	6	7	8	9											10	2				11	
11 (a)	Newcastle U	L 0-1		25,000	1		3	4	5	6	7	8	9											10	2				11	
13 (h)	Tottenham H	W 6-0	Stirling, Tinsley 2, J.Carr 2, Wynn	22,000	1		3	4	5	6	7	8	9											10	2					11
18 (h)	Liverpool	W 4-0	Davison, Tinsley 3	13,000	1		3	4	5		7	8				6				9				10	2					11
25 (a)	Aston Villa	W 3-1	Tinsley 2, Elliott	15,000	1		3	4	5	6	7	8	9				11							10	2					
Apps					29	8	35	30	28	35	34	30	32	15	13	6	25	10	9	10	2	7	4	23	21	2	2	1	3	2
Goals								1		1	4	11	31	3	3		1						1	19				1		1

FA Cup

Date	Opponent	Res	Att	Williamson RG	Walker J	Weir J	Davidson S	Jackson A	Malcolm G	Stirling J	Carr J	Elliott GW	Windridge JE	Nichol J	Verrill E	Cook J	Hisbent JM	Davies B	Cook H	Kirby F	Carr W	Eyre E	Tinsley W	Haworth JH	Crosier J	Storey T	Healey R	Stage W	Wynn R	Round
Jan 19 (a)	Blackburn R	L 0-3	25,395	1		3	4	5	6	7	8	9				11							10	2						1
Apps				1		1	1	1	1	1	1	1				1							1	1						
Goals																														

1914-15
Division 1

Date	Match	Result	Scorers	Att	Williamson RG	Haworth JH	Walker J	Davidson S	Jackson A	Malcolm G	Wilson A	Carr J	Elliott GW	Tinsley W	Cook J	Carr W	Davies B	Weir J	Storey T	Wynn R	Healey R	Hisbent JM	Cook H	Verrill E	Urwin T	Davies AE	Wilson AN	Holmes W	Caig H
Sep 1 (a)	Sheffield W	L 1-3	Elliott (pen)	12,000	1	2	3	4	5	6	7	8	9	10	11														
5 (h)	West Brom A	W 2-0	Tinsley, Jackson	12,000	1	2	3	4	5	6	7	8	9	10	11														
12 (a)	Everton	W 3-2	Tinsley, J.Carr, Fleetwood (og)	14,000	1	2	3	4		6	7	8	9	10	11	5													
19 (h)	Chelsea	W 3-0	Elliott, Tinsley, A.Wilson	12,000	1	2	3	4	5	6	7	8	9	10	11														
26 (a)	Bradford C	D 1-1	Tinsley	20,000	1	2	3	4	5	6	7	8	9	10	11														
Oct 3 (h)	Burnley	D 1-1	Elliott	15,000	1	2	3	4	5	6	7	8	9	10	11														
10 (a)	Tottenham H	D 3-3	Tinsley, J.Carr 2 (1 pen)	13,000	1	2	3	4	5	6	7	8	9	10	11														
17 (h)	Newcastle U	D 1-1	Tinsley	18,000		2		4	5	6		8	9	10			1	3	7	11									
24 (a)	Manchester C	D 1-1	Tinsley	25,000		2		4	5	6		8	9	10	11		1	3	7										
31 (a)	Sheffield U	W 1-0	Elliott	12,000		2		4	5	6			9	10			1	3	7	11	8								
Nov 7 (h)	Aston Villa	D 1-1	J.Carr	15,000		2		4	5	6	7	8	9	10			1	3		11									
14 (a)	Liverpool	D 1-1	Elliott	17,000		2	3	4	5	6		8	9	10			1		7	11									
21 (h)	Bradford	L 1-3	Healey	9,000		2	3	4	5	6		8	9				1		7	11	10								
28 (a)	Oldham A	L 1-5	J.Carr	8,300		2		4	5	6		8	9	10	11		1	3	7										
Dec 5 (h)	Manchester U	D 1-1	Elliott	7,000		2	3	4		6	7	8	9	10	11	5	1												
12 (a)	Bolton W	L 0-4				2	3	4		6	7	8	9	10	11	5	1												
19 (h)	Blackburn R	L 1-4	Tinsley	7,000			3	4		7	8		9	10	11	5	1					2	6						
25 (h)	Notts C	W 1-0	Tinsley	9,000	1	2	3	4			7	8	9	10	11								5	6					
26 (a)	Notts C	L 1-5	J.Carr	14,000	1	2	3	4			7	8	9	10	11								5	6					
Jan 1 (h)	Sunderland	L 2-3	Elliott, A.Wilson	12,000	1	2	3	4	5	6	7	8	9	10											11				
2 (a)	West Brom A	L 0-1		10,940	1	2	3	4		6	7	8		10									5		11		9		
16 (h)	Everton	W 5-1	A.Wilson 2, J.Carr, A.N.Wilson 2	7,500	1	2	3		5	6	7	8		10	11								4				9		
23 (a)	Chelsea	D 2-2	Tinsley, A.N.Wilson	9,000	1	2	3		5	6	7	8		10	11								4				9		
Feb 3 (h)	Bradford C	W 3-0	A.N.Wilson, J.Cook, Tinsley		1	2	3	4	5	6		8		10	11				7								9		
6 (a)	Burnley	L 0-4		9,000	1	2	3	4	5	6		8		10	11				7								9		
13 (h)	Tottenham H	W 7-5	J.Carr 2, Storey, Tinsley 3 (1 pen), Elliott	7,000	1	2	3	4	5	6		8	9	10	11				7										
27 (h)	Manchester C	W 1-0	Elliott	8,000			3	4	5	6		8	9	10	11		1		7									2	
Mar 10 (a)	Newcastle U	W 2-1	Elliott 2	10,000		2	3	4		6		8	9	10	11	5	1		7										
13 (h)	Aston Villa	L 0-5		13,000			3	4				8	9	10		5	1		7				6		11			2	
17 (h)	Sheffield U	D 2-2	Elliott 2			2	3	4	5	6		8	9	10			1		7						11				
20 (h)	Liverpool	W 3-0	Tinsley 3	6,000			3	4	5	6		8		10			1		7						11		9	2	
27 (a)	Bradford	L 0-2		10,000			3	4	5	6			9	10			1		7		8				11			2	
Apr 2 (a)	Sunderland	L 1-4	Elliott	18,000			3	4	5	6		8		10			1		7						11		9	2	
3 (h)	Oldham A*	W 4-1	Tinsley 3 (1 pen), Urwin	5,000			3	4	5	6		8	9	10			1		7						11			2	
5 (h)	Sheffield W	W 3-1	Tinsley 2, A.N.Wilson	11,000	1		3	4	5	6	11	8		10					7								9	2	
10 (a)	Manchester U	D 2-2	Tinsley, Jackson	15,000	1		3	4	5	6	11		9	10					7								8	2	
17 (h)	Bolton W	D 0-0		8,000	1		3	4	5	6	11		9	10	8				7									2	
24 (a)	Blackburn R	L 0-4		7,000	1		3	4	5		11		9	10					7				6					2	8
Apps					20	27	33	36	29	34	21	33	29	37	22	6	18	5	21	5	3	1	8	2	7	1	9	10	1
Goals									2		4	9	14	23	1				1		1				1		5		

*Abandoned, see *Abandoned Games* section.

1 own-goal

FA Cup

Date	Match	Result	Scorers	Att	Williamson RG	Haworth JH	Walker J	Davidson S	Jackson A	Malcolm G	Wilson A	Carr J	Elliott GW	Tinsley W	Cook J	Carr W	Davies B	Weir J	Storey T	Wynn R	Healey R	Hisbent JM	Cook H	Verrill E	Urwin T	Davies AE	Wilson AN	Holmes W	Caig H	Round
Jan 9 (h)	Goole T†	W 9-3	J.Carr 3, Elliott 3, Tinsley 3	8,650	1	2		4		6	7	8	9	10		3							5		11					1
30 (a)	Bradford C	L 0-1		26,457	1	2	3		5	6	7	8	9	10	11								4							2
Apps					2	2	1	1	1	2	2	2	2	2	1	1							2		1					
Goals												3	3	3															

† Middlesbrough bought choice of venue.

1918-19
Northern Victory League

					Williamson RG	Dixon C	Weir J	Robinson JW	Fox WV	Carr W	Storey T	Carr J	Elliott GW	Carr G	Cook J	Donaghy P	Malcolm G	Burton†	Chesser†	Forshaw R†	Gallagher J†	Gascoigne†	Holmes W	Evans†	Mines†	Wilson†	Lloyd E	Stage W
Jan 11	(h) Scotswood	D 0-0		6,000	1	2	3	4	5	6	7	8	9	10	11													
18	(a) Sunderland	L 0-2		12,000	1	2	3				7		9	5	10	4	6	8	11									
25	(h) Durham C	W 5-0	Elliott 5		1	2	3		5		7		9	4	8		6		11	10								
Feb 1	(a) Hartlepools U	W 2-1	Elliott 2		1	2			5	6	7	8	9	4	11					10	3							
8	(h) Newcastle U	W 3-0	Elliott 2, Forshaw	15,000	1	2			6	5	7	8	9	4					11	10	3							
15	(h) South Shields	W 2-1	W.Carr, J.Carr	10,000	1	2			6	5	7	8	9	4				10			3	11						
22	(a) Darlington Forge	W 2-0		9,000	1	2			6	5	7	8	9	4		11				10	3							
Mar 1	(h) Hartlepools U	W 8-2	Elliott 6, J.Carr, Forshaw	15,000	1	2			6	5		8	9	4		11				10			3	7				
8	(a) Scotswood	W 2-1	G.Carr, Elliott	12,000	1	2			6	5	7	8	9	4		11				10	3							
15	(h) Sunderland	L 1-2	Elliott	20,000	1	2			6	5	7	8	9	4		11				10	3							
22	(a) Durham C	W 1-0	J.Carr	5,000	1	2			6		7	8	9	4		11				10	3		5					
29	(a) Newcastle U	W 1-0		20,000	1	2			6	5		8	9	4		11				10	3			7				
Apr 12	(a) South Shields	L 1-3	Wilson	10,000	1	3			2	5	11	7	8	4			6			10					9			
19	(h) Darlington Forge	D 0-0		18,000	1	2			6	5	7	8	9			4				3						10	11	
			Apps		14	14	3	1	13	11	12	12	14	13	4	5	8	1	2	10	9	1	1	1	1	2	1	1
			Goals							1		3	20	1						2						1		

NB. The appearances and goals scored in Northern Victory League do not contribute to player career records.

†Guest players, only season with club.

1919-20
Division 1

					Williamson RG	Dixon C	Walker J	Davidson S	Ellerington W	Fox WV	Curtis J	Carr J	Elliott GW	Tinsley W	Urwin T	Butler R	Holmes W	Storey T	Harrison H	Honeyman J	Carr G	Robinson JW	Marshall J	Davison JW	Pender R	Lloyd EW	Carr W	Clarke W	Poulton A	Jennings S	Donaghy P
Aug 30	(a) Sheffield W	W 1-0	Tinsley	20,000	1	2	3	4	5	6	7	8	9	10	11																
Sep 3	(h) Blackburn R	D 2-2	Butler, Fox	25,000	1	2	3	4	5	6		7	8		10	11	9														
6	(h) Sheffield W	W 3-0	Elliott 2, Butler	21,000	1	2	3	4	5	6		7	8		10	11	9														
13	(h) Sheffield U	W 1-0	Butler	20,000	1	2	3	4	5	6		7	8		10	11	9														
15	(a) Blackburn R	W 2-0	Elliott 2	10,000	1	2	3	4	5	6		7	8		10	11	9														
17	(h) Bolton W	L 1-3	Butler	15,000	1	2	3	4	5	6		7	8		10	11	9														
20	(a) Sheffield U	L 1-5	Elliott (pen)	25,000	1	2	3	4	5	6		7	8		10	11	9														
27	(h) Manchester U	D 1-1	Elliott	19,300	1		3	4	5	6		8	9	10	11			2	7												
Oct 4	(a) Manchester U	D 1-1	Davidson	20,000		2	3	4	5			8		10	11	9			7	1	6										
11	(h) Oldham A	W 1-0	J.Carr (pen)	18,359		2	3	4	5	6		8		10	11	9			7	1											
18	(a) Oldham A	W 2-1	Butler 2	10,000		2	3	4	5	6			8	10	11	9			7	1											
25	(h) Aston Villa	L 1-4	Butler	10,000		2	3	4	5	6			8	10	11	9			7	1											
Nov 1	(a) Aston Villa	L 3-5	Elliott 3	45,000	1		3	4	5			8	10		11	9		2	7		6										
8	(h) Newcastle U	L 0-1		30,000	1		3	4	5		7	8	10		11	9	2					6									
22	(h) Chelsea	D 0-0		25,000	1		3	4	5	6	7	8	10		11	9						2									
29	(a) Chelsea	L 1-3	Tinsley	20,000	1		3	4	5		7	8	9	10	11							2	6								
Dec 3	(a) Newcastle U	D 0-0		40,000	1		3	4	5		7	8	9	10	11							2	6								
6	(h) Liverpool	W 3-2	Pender, Elliott, J.Carr	15,000	1		3	4	5			8	9		11		2	7							6	10					
13	(a) Liverpool	L 0-1		30,000	1		3	4	5			8	9		11	10		7							6						
20	(h) Bradford	L 1-2	Elliott	10,000	1		3	4	5			8	9		11			7							6	10					
25	(a) Burnley	L 3-5	Butler, G.Carr, Elliott	25,000	1		3	4	5			7	8		11	9					10				6						
27	(h) Bradford	D 1-1	Elliott	18,000	1		3	4	5			7	8		11	9					10				6						
Jan 1	(h) Burnley	W 4-0	Elliott 3 (1 pen), Pender	25,000	1		3	4			8		7	9	11						10				6	5					
3	(h) Preston NE	W 4-1	Elliott 2, Butler, Urwin	15,000	1		3	4				7	8		11	9	2				10				6	5					
17	(a) Preston NE	L 1-3	Butler	16,000	1		3	4				7	9		8						10	2			6	5	11				
24	(a) Manchester C	L 0-1		28,000	1			4	5	6		7	9		8	2					11	3			10						
Feb 7	(a) Derby C	W 2-1	Urwin, W.Carr	15,000	1			4	6			7	9		11	2					8	3			10	5					
14	(h) Derby C	W 2-0	Pender, Elliott	25,000	1			4	6			7	9		11	2					8	3			10	5					
18	(h) Manchester C	L 0-2		15,000	1			3	4	6		7	9		11	8						2			10	5					
21	(a) West Brom A	L 1-4	Pender	24,995	1			4	6				8		9	2	7					3			10	5	11				
28	(h) West Brom A	D 0-0		30,000	1		3	4	6			7	8		11	9						2			10	5					
Mar 6	(h) Sunderland	L 0-2		21,581	1		3	4	5	6			8		11	9						2			10		7				
13	(a) Sunderland	D 1-1	Elliott	30,000	1		3	4		6		7	8		11	9						2			10	5					
20	(h) Arsenal	W 1-0	Elliott	16,000	1		3	4		6		7	8		11	9						2			10	5					
27	(h) Arsenal	L 1-2	Pender	25,000	1		3	4		6		7	9		11							2			10	5		8			
Apr 2	(a) Notts C	D 1-1	Elliott	20,000	1		3	4		6		7	9		11							2			10	5		8			
3	(h) Everton	D 1-1	Elliott	14,000	1			4		6		7	9		11	2					8	3			10	5					
5	(h) Notts C	W 5-2	Elliott 3, Urwin, G.Carr	22,000	1			4		6		7	9		11	2					8	3			10	5					
10	(a) Everton	L 2-5	Jennings, Butler	20,000	1			4		6		7			11	9	2				8	3				5				10	
17	(h) Bradford C	W 4-0	Elliott 4 (1 pen)	25,000	1			4		6		7	9		11	2					8	3				5				10	
24	(a) Bradford C	W 1-0	Jennings	13,000	1		3	4	5			7			11	9					8	2								10	6
May 1	(a) Bolton W	L 1-2	Elliott	15,000	1		3	4	5				9		11						7	2			10					8	6
			Apps		38	11	34	42	31	23	5	37	38	14	39	27	15	10	4	1	15	1	24	1	23	2	16	3	2	4	2
			Goals			1		1				2	31	2	3	11					2				5		1			2	

FA Cup

					Williamson RG	Dixon C	Walker J	Davidson S	Ellerington W	Fox WV	Curtis J	Carr J	Elliott GW	Tinsley W	Urwin T	Butler R	Holmes W	Storey T	Harrison H	Honeyman J	Carr G	Robinson JW	Marshall J	Davison JW	Pender R	Lloyd EW	Carr W	Clarke W	Poulton A	Jennings S	Donaghy P	Round
Jan 14	(h) Lincoln C†	W 4-1	Elliott 3, W.Carr	17,746	1		3	4				7	9		11	8					10		2		6		5					3
31	(a) Notts C	L 0-1		28,000	1			4	5	6		7	9		11		2				8		3		10							4
			Apps		2		1	2	1	1		2	2		2	1	1				2		2		2		1					
			Goals										3														1					

† Middlesbrough bought choice of venue.

1920-21
Division 1

Date	Result	Scorers	Att	Williamson RG	Marshall J	Walker J	Davidson S	Ellerington W	Donaghy P	Hastie J	Carr J	Elliott GW	Tinsley W	Urwin T	Holmes W	Fox WV	Jennings S	Carr W	Mordue J	Pender R	Chipperfield F	Poulton A	Clarke W	Carr G	Dowson F	Birrell W	Dixon C	Gallagher J	Brown T	Young EW
Aug 28 (h) Oldham A	L 1-2	Elliott	29,000	1	2	3	4	5	6	7	8	9	10	11																
30 (h) Preston NE	D 0-0		20,000	1		3	4	5	11		8	9	10	7	2	6														
Sep 4 (a) Oldham A	D 3-3	Elliott 2, Tinsley	19,951	1	2		4	5			7	9	10	11	3	6	8													
6 (a) Preston NE	L 0-2		20,000	1	2	3	4	5			7	9	10	11		6	8													
11 (a) Burnley	L 1-2	Elliott	28,000	1	2		4		6		8	9		11	3		10	5	7											
18 (h) Burnley	D 0-0		30,000	1	2		4		6		8	9	10	11	3			5	7											
25 (a) Arsenal	D 2-2	Mordue, Pender	45,000	1	2		4		6		8	9		11	3			5	7	10										
Oct 2 (h) Arsenal	W 2-1	Elliott 2	20,000	1	2		4		6		8	9		11	3			5	7	10										
9 (h) Bradford C	W 2-1	Elliott, Ellerington	20,000	1	2		4		6		8	9		11	3			5	7	10										
16 (a) Bradford C	W 1-0	Pender	30,000	1	2		4		6		8	9		11	3			5	7	10										
23 (h) Bolton W	W 4-1	J.Carr 2, Elliott 2	28,947	1	2		4		6		8	9	10	11	3			5	7											
30 (a) Bolton W	L 2-6	Elliott, Urwin		1	2		4		6		8	9	10	11	3				7		5									
Nov 6 (h) Sunderland	W 2-0	Elliott 2	*35,703	1	2		4		6		8	9	10	11	3			5	7											
13 (a) Sunderland	W 2-1	Elliott 2	40,000	1	2		4		6		8	9		11	3			5		7		10								
20 (h) Derby C	W 1-0	Elliott	28,000	1	2		4		6		8	9		11	3			5		7		10								
27 (a) Derby C	W 1-0	Poulton	12,520	1	2		4		6		8	9		11	3			5		7		10								
Dec 4 (h) Everton	W 3-1	Poulton, Elliott 2	4,000	1	2		4		6		8	9		11	3			5		7		10								
11 (a) Everton	L 1-2	Poulton		1	2		4		6		8	9		11	3			5		7		10								
18 (a) Blackburn R	L 2-3	Poulton, Elliott	15,000	1	2		4		6		8	9		11	3			5		7		10								
25 (h) Huddersfield T	W 2-0	J.Carr, Elliott	35,000	1	2		4				8	9		11	3			5	7	6		10								
27 (h) Huddersfield T	W 1-0	Pender	32,430	1	2		4				8	9		11	3			5		6		10	7							
Jan 1 (h) Blackburn R	D 1-1	Tinsley	30,000	1			4				7	9	10		3		2	5		6		8	11							
15 (a) Sheffield U	D 1-1	J.Carr	18,000	1	2		4		6		8	9		11	3			5		7		10								
22 (h) Sheffield U	D 2-2	Elliott 2 (1 pen)	25,000	1	2		4		6		8	9	10	11	3			5		7										
29 (h) West Brom A	L 0-1		28,000	1	2		4		6		7	9			3		8	5	10			11								
Feb 5 (a) West Brom A	W 1-0	Elliott	24,920	1	2		4	5			8	9			3		10	11	6							7				
12 (a) Bradford	L 0-3		15,000	1			4	5				9		11	3	2	10	7	6							8				
19 (a) Bradford	W 2-1	Birrell, Urwin	25,000	1	2		4		6		8	9	10		3			5	11							7				
26 (a) Newcastle U	L 0-2		40,000	1			4		6		8		10		3			5				9	11			7	2			
Mar 5 (h) Newcastle U	D 0-0		38,000	1	2		4		6		8	9		11	3			5				10				7				
12 (a) Liverpool	D 0-0		40,000	1	2		4		6		8			11	3			5				9		10		7				
19 (h) Liverpool	L 0-1		25,000	1	2		4		6		8	9	10	11	3			5								7				
25 (a) Manchester C	L 1-2	Poulton	25,000	1	2		4		6		8	9		11	3			5				10				7				
26 (h) Aston Villa	L 1-4	Elliott	30,000	1	2		4		6		8	9		11	3			5				10				7				
28 (h) Manchester C	W 3-1	Elliott, Dowson 2	29,000	1					6		8	9		11	3	2		5	4						10	7				
Apr 2 (a) Aston Villa	W 1-0	Elliott	35,000	1	2				6		8	9		11	3			5	4						10	7				
9 (h) Manchester U	L 2-4	W.Carr, G.Carr	25,000	1					6		8	9		11		2		5	4			7		10				3		
16 (a) Manchester U	W 1-0	Elliott	15,000	1	2		4		6		7	9		11	3			5	10			8								
23 (h) Chelsea	D 0-0		15,000	1			4	2	6				10	11	3			5	8										7	9
30 (a) Chelsea	D 1-1	Birrell	30,000	1	2		4	5	6					11	3				8						10	9			7	
May 2 (h) Tottenham H	W 1-0	W.Carr	15,000	1	2				6		8			11	3			5	4						10	9			7	
7 (a) Tottenham H	D 2-2	Urwin, G.Carr	27,000	1	2			5	6					11	3				4			8		10		9			7	
Apps				42	36	2	37	34	10	1	38	36	12	39	40	7	6	32	19	18	1	14	5	5	7	14	1	1	4	1
Goals								1			4	26	2	3				2	1	3		5		2	2	2				

*Ground attendance record

FA Cup

Date	Result	Scorers	Att	Williamson RG	Marshall J	Walker J	Davidson S	Ellerington W	Donaghy P	Hastie J	Carr J	Elliott GW	Tinsley W	Urwin T	Holmes W	Fox WV	Jennings S	Carr W	Mordue J	Pender R	Chipperfield F	Poulton A	Clarke W	Carr G	Dowson F	Birrell W	Dixon C	Gallagher J	Brown T	Young EW	Round
Jan 8 (a) Derby C	L 0-2		23,000	1	2		4		6		8	9		11	3			5				10	7								1
Apps				1	1		1		1		1	1		1	1			1				1	1								
Goals																														

1921-22
Division 1

					Williamson RG	Marshall J	Holmes W	Davidson S	Ellerington W	Donaghy P	Birrell W	Elliott GW	Wilson AN	Poulton A	Urwin T	Mordue J	Carr G	Fox WV	Carr J	Pender R	Davison JW	Carr W	Harrison H	Murray W	Webster M
Aug	27 (a) West Brom A	D	0-0	24,880	1	2	3	4	5	6	7	8	9	10	11										
	29 (h) Oldham A	D	1-1	A.N.Wilson	20,000	1	2	3	4	5	6	7	8	9	10	11										
Sep	3 (h) West Brom A	W	3-2	A.N.Wilson 3	30,000	1	2	3	4	5	6	8		9		11	7	10								
	5 (a) Oldham A	W	1-0	A.N.Wilson	18,000	1	2		4	5	6	8		9		11	7	10	3							
	10 (a) Tottenham H	W	4-2	G.Carr, Birrell, A.N.Wilson 2	34,882	1	2		4	5	6	8		9		11	7	10	3							
	17 (h) Tottenham H	D	0-0		18,000	1	2		4	5	6			8	9	11	7	10	3							
	24 (a) Cardiff C	L	1-3	Elliott (pen)	40,000	1	2		4	5	6	8	10	9		11			3	7						
Oct	1 (h) Cardiff C	D	0-0		33,000	1	2		4	5		8	10	9		11			3	7	6					
	8 (a) Bradford C	W	2-0	Pender, A.N.Wilson	25,000	1	2		4	5		8	9			11		10	3	7	6					
	15 (h) Bradford C	L	1-2	G.Carr	25,000	1	2		4	5		8	9			11	7	10	3		6					
	22 (h) Aston Villa	W	5-0	Birrell 2, G.Carr 3	10,000	1	2		4	5		8	9			11	7	10	3		6					
	29 (a) Aston Villa	L	2-6	Elliott, J.Carr	35,000	1	2		4	5			9			11	7	10	3	8	6					
Nov	5 (a) Manchester U	W	5-3	Elliott 2, A.N.Wilson, J.Carr, Urwin	30,000	1	2		4	5			10	9		11	7		3	8	6					
	12 (h) Manchester U	W	2-0	A.N.Wilson, S.Davidson	18,000	1	2		4	5			10	9		11	7		3	8	6					
	19 (a) Liverpool	L	0-4		40,000	1		2	4	5				9		11	7	10	3	8	6					
	26 (h) Liverpool	W	3-1	Birrell 2, A.N.Wilson	24,000	1	2		4	5		8		9			11	10	3	7	6					
Dec	3 (a) Newcastle U	D	0-0		50,000	1	2		4	5		8	10	9		11			3	7	6					
	10 (h) Newcastle U	D	1-1	Birrell	35,000	1		2	4	5		8	10	9		11			3	7	6					
	17 (h) Burnley	W	4-1	A.N.Wilson 2, Elliott, G.Carr	25,000	1		3	4			7	8	9			11	10			6	2	5			
	24 (a) Burnley	L	1-3	A.N.Wilson	25,000	1		2	4		6	7	8	9			11	10	3				5			
	26 (h) Chelsea	L	0-1		35,000	1			4		6	7	8	9		11		10	3			2	5			
	27 (a) Chelsea	D	1-1	A.N.Wilson (pen)	60,000	1			4		6	8		9		11	7	10	3			2	5			
	31 (a) Sheffield U	L	1-6	A.N.Wilson		1			4	5	6	8		9		11	7	10	3			2				
Jan	14 (h) Sheffield U	D	1-1	Urwin	18,000	1	2		4			9				11	7	10	3	8	6		5			
	21 (a) Manchester C	D	2-2	S.Davidson, G.Carr	25,000		2		4			8		9		11		10	3	7	6		5	1		
Feb	1 (h) Manchester C	W	4-1	A.N.Wilson 3, Urwin	20,000		2		4			8		9		11		10	3	7	6		5	1		
	11 (h) Everton	W	3-1	Birrell 2, G.Carr	20,000		2		4			8		9		11		10	3	7	6		5	1		
	18 (a) Sunderland	D	1-1	A.N.Wilson	30,000		2		4	6		8		9		11		10	3	7			5	1		
	25 (h) Sunderland	W	3-0	A.N.Wilson 2 (1 pen), G.Carr	30,000		2		4	6		8		9		11		10	3	7			5	1		
Mar	1 (a) Everton	L	1-4	G.Carr				2	4	6		8		9		11		10	3	7			5	1		
	11 (h) Huddersfield T	W	5-1	A.N.Wilson 2, Elliott 2, Urwin	26,000		2		4	6		8	10	9		11			3	7			5	1		
	18 (h) Birmingham	D	1-1	A.N.Wilson	20,000	1	2		4	6		8	10	9		11			3	7			5			
	25 (a) Birmingham	L	3-4	A.N.Wilson 2, Elliott	20,000	1	2		4	6		8	10	9		11			3	7			5			
Apr	1 (a) Arsenal	D	2-2	A.N.Wilson, Birrell	30,000		2		4	6		8	10	9		11			3	7			5	1		
	8 (h) Arsenal	W	4-2	Elliott 3 (1 pen), Urwin	15,000		3		4			8	9			11		10		7	6	2	5	1		
	14 (a) Preston NE	D	1-1	A.N.Wilson	30,000		2		4	6		8	10	9		11			3	7			5	1		
	15 (h) Blackburn R	L	0-1		15,000		2		4	6		8	10	9		11			3	7			5	1		
	17 (h) Preston NE	W	1-0	A.N.Wilson	20,000		2			6			8	9				10	3	7	4		5	1	11	
	22 (a) Blackburn R	D	2-2	A.N.Wilson, Elliott	20,000		2		4	5			8	9				10	3	7	6			1	11	
	29 (h) Bolton W	W	4-2	G.Carr 3, A.N.Wilson	16,000		2		4	5		8		9		11		10	3	7	6			1		
May	1 (a) Huddersfield T	L	1-2	G.Carr	27,000		2		4	6		8		9		11		10	3	7				1		5
	6 (a) Bolton W	L	2-4	G.Carr, Elliott	15,000		2		4	5		8	9			7		10	3		6			1	11	
	Apps				26	33	9	41	33	11	35	26	35	2	37	16	28	37	28	21	5	19	16	3	1
	Goals						2				9	13	32		5		15		2	1					

FA Cup

																									Round
Jan	7 (a) Hull C	L	0-5	25,000	1	2		4	5		8	10	9		11			3	7	6						1
	Apps			1	1		1	1		1	1	1		1			1	1	1						
	Goals																								

1922-23
Division 1

Date	Opponent	Res	Scorers	Att	Williamson RG	Marshall J	Fox WV	Davidson S	Ellerington W	Pender R	Carr J	Birrell W	Wilson AN	Elliott GW	Urwin T	Holmes W	Carr G	Slade CH	Brown T	Murray W	Webster M	Bottrill WG	Davison JW	Donaghy P	Clough J	Harris J	Cochrane AF	Butler W
Aug 26	(h) Huddersfield T	D 2-2	Birrell, Elliott	20,000	1	2	3	4	5	6	7	8	9	10	11													
28	(a) Manchester C	L 1-2	Elliott	25,000	1	2	3	4	5	6	7	8	9	10	11													
Sep 2	(a) Huddersfield T	W 2-0	Birrell 2	12,000	1	2	3	4	5	6	7	8	9	10	11													
4	(h) Manchester C	W 5-0	Elliott 3, A.N.Wilson 2	15,000	1	2	3	4	5	6	7	8	9	10	11													
9	(a) Chelsea	D 1-1	A.N.Wilson	30,000	1	2	3	4	5	6	7	8	9	10	11													
16	(h) Chelsea	W 2-1	Elliott 2 (1 pen)	20,000	1	2	3	4	5	6	7	8	9	10	11													
23	(a) Aston Villa	D 2-2	Elliott, A.N.Wilson	35,000	1		3	4	5	6	7	8	9	10	11	2												
30	(h) Aston Villa	D 2-2	Elliott 2 (2 pens)	20,000	1	2	3	4	5	6	7	8	9	10	11													
Oct 7	(a) Oldham A	D 0-0		20,000	1		3	4	5	6		7	9	10	11	2	8											
14	(h) Oldham A	W 2-1	Elliott, A.N.Wilson	25,000	1	2	3	4	5	6	7	8	9	10	11													
21	(h) Birmingham	W 2-1	A.N.Wilson 2 (1 pen)	18,000	1	2	3		5	6		8	9		11	10	4	7										
28	(a) Birmingham	L 0-2		30,000	1	2	3		5	6		8	9	10	7		4				11							
Nov 4	(h) Sheffield U	W 3-2	Elliott 3	15,000	1	2	3		5	6	7	8	9	10	11		4											
11	(a) Sheffield U	L 1-4	Birrell		1	2	3		5	6	7	8	9		11	10	4											
18	(a) Preston NE	W 2-1	G.Carr, Elliott	20,000	1	2	3		5	6	7	8	9			10	4				11							
25	(h) Preston NE	D 1-1	G.Carr	16,000	1	2	3		5	6	7	8	9			10	4				11							
Dec 2	(h) Burnley	W 4-1	J.Carr, Birrell, Elliott, Urwin	20,000	1	2	3		5	6	7	8	9		11	10	4											
9	(a) Burnley	L 0-3		15,000	1	2	3	4	5	6	7	8	9		11	10												
16	(h) Stoke	W 3-1	Elliott 2 (1 pen), J.Carr	10,000	1	2	3	4		6	7	8	9		11					10	5							
23	(a) Stoke	D 0-0		15,000	1	2	3	4		6	7	8	9		11					10	5							
25	(a) Newcastle U	D 1-1	Elliott	30,000	1	2	3	4		6	7	9	8	11						10	5							
26	(h) Newcastle U	D 1-1	Pender	30,000	1	2	3	4		6		8	9							10	5	7						
30	(h) Tottenham H	W 2-0	Murray, G.Carr	15,000	1		3	4		6			9		11	2	8			10	5	7						
Jan 6	(a) Tottenham H	L 0-2		30,000	1					6		8	9		11	3	10	4			5	7	2					
20	(h) Liverpool	L 0-2		25,000	1		3	4		6	7	8	9		11	2	10				5							
27	(a) Liverpool	L 0-2		42,000	1		3	4	2	6	7	8	9		11					10	5							
Feb 10	(a) Sunderland	L 1-2	Donaghy	12,000	1			3		6	7	8				2	10	4		11	5			9				
17	(a) Everton	L 2-4	Donaghy, G.Carr	12,000	1		3	2		6		8					10	4		11	5	7		9				
28	(a) Everton	L 3-5	Birrell 3	20,000	1		3	4		6	7	8	9		11	2					5			10				
Mar 3	(h) Arsenal	W 2-0	Cochrane, Elliott	20,000			3			6	7	8		9		2				11	5				1	4	10	
10	(a) Arsenal	L 0-3		25,000			3		5	6	7	9	8	11	2										1	4	10	
17	(a) Cardiff C	L 0-2		22,000			3				7	8		11	2		6				5			9	1	4	10	
24	(h) Cardiff C	L 0-1		20,000	1		3				7	9	8	11	2		6				5					4	10	
30	(a) Nottingham F	L 1-2	Urwin	18,000		2						8	9	10	11	3	6				5			7	1	4		
31	(a) Bolton W	D 1-1	A.N.Wilson	18,000		2						8	9	10	11	3	6				5			7	1	4		
Apr 2	(h) Nottingham F	W 4-0	Elliott, A.N.Wilson 2, Barrett (og)	15,000				4	3			8	9	10	11	2	6				5	7			1			
7	(h) Bolton W	L 1-2	A.N.Wilson	15,000		2	3	4				8	9	10	11		6				5	7			1			
14	(a) Blackburn R	L 0-2		15,000			3		5			8		10	11	2	6				4			9	1		7	
18	(a) Sunderland	W 2-0	Birrell, Elliott	20,000			3				6	8	9	10	11	2	4				5			7	1			
21	(h) Blackburn R	L 1-2	Elliott	12,000			3			6		8	9	10	11	2	4				5			7	1			
28	(a) West Brom A	L 0-1		10,021			3				6	9	8	11	2	10					5				1	4		7
May 5	(h) West Brom A	L 0-1		10,000			3					8	9	10	11	2					5				1	4		7
Apps					30	23	37	22	24	33	24	38	29	33	37	19	13	20	1	12	23	8	1	7	12	8	6	2
Goals										1	2	9	11	23	2		4			1				2			1	

1 own-goal

FA Cup

Date	Opponent	Res	Scorers	Att	Williamson RG	Marshall J	Fox WV	Davidson S	Ellerington W	Pender R	Carr J	Birrell W	Wilson AN	Elliott GW	Urwin T	Holmes W	Carr G	Slade CH	Brown T	Murray W	Webster M	Bottrill WG	Davison JW	Donaghy P	Clough J	Harris J	Cochrane AF	Butler W	Round
Jan 13	(a) Oldham A	W 1-0	Birrell	18,000	1		3	4		6	7	8	9		11	2	10				5								1
Feb 3	(h) Sheffield U	D 1-1	A.N.Wilson (pen)	*38,067	1	2	3	4		6	7	8	9		11					10	5								2
8	(a) Sheffield U	L 0-3		38,500	1		3	4		6	7	8	9		11	2				10	5								R
Apps					3	1	3	3		3	3	3	3		3	2	1			2	3								
Goals												1	1															

*Ground attendance record

1923-24
Division 1

Date	Opponent	Result	Scorers	Att	Clough J	Freeman RV	Maitland AE	Harris J	Ellerington W	Slade CH	Bottrill WG	Birrell W	Wilson AN	Elliott GW	Urwin T	Cochrane AF	Webster M	Pender R	Carr J	Carr G	Carr W	Harrison H	Holmes W	Stevenson AB	Fox WV	Dickson IW	Wainscoat WR	Smith EE	Williams O	Hick WM
Aug 25 (a)	Huddersfield T	L 0-1		20,500	1	2	3	4	5	6	7	8	9	10	11															
29 (h)	Notts C	L 2-3	Elliott, Wilson	10,000	1	2	3	4	5	6		7	9	8	11	10														
Sep 1 (h)	Huddersfield T	W 2-0	Birrell, Cochrane	20,000	1	2	3	4				7	9	8	11	10	5	6												
8 (a)	Tottenham H	L 1-2	Elliott	38,000	1	2	3	4				7	9	8	11	10	5	6												
15 (h)	Tottenham H	L 0-1		25,000	1	2	3	4				7	9	8	11	10	5	6												
22 (a)	West Ham U	D 1-1	Wilson	20,000	1	2	3	4				8	9		11		5	6	7	10										
29 (h)	West Ham U	L 0-1		22,000	1	2	3	4		6		8	9		11		5		7	10										
Oct 4 (a)	Notts C	L 0-1		12,000	1	2	3	4		6		8	9	10	11				7		5									
6 (h)	Nottingham F	W 5-2	Wilson 5 (1 pen)	18,000			3	4		6			9		11	10			7	8	5	1	2							
13 (a)	Nottingham F	L 1-3	Cochrane	17,000			3	4		6			9		11	10			7	8	5	1	2							
20 (h)	Newcastle U	W 1-0	Elliott (pen)	25,000		2	3	4				8	9	10	11			6	7		5	1								
27 (a)	Newcastle U	L 2-3	J.Carr, Cochrane	30,000		2	3	4		6		8	9		11	10			7		5	1								
Nov 3 (a)	Arsenal	L 1-2	Cochrane	25,000	1	2	3	4		6		8	9			10			7		5				11					
10 (h)	Arsenal	D 0-0		13,000	1	2	3	5			7	4	9		11	10				8					6					
17 (h)	Chelsea	W 2-0	Wilson, Elliott	12,000	1	2	3	4					9	8	11	10	5		7						6					
24 (a)	Chelsea	L 0-2		25,000	1	2	3	4					9	8	11	10	5		7						6					
Dec 1 (a)	Aston Villa	D 0-0		20,000	1	2	3	4		6			9		11	10	5		7	8										
8 (h)	Aston Villa	L 0-2		15,000	1	2	3	4		6			9		11	10	5		7	8										
15 (a)	Preston NE	L 0-4		15,000	1	2	3	4		6		8	9			10	5		7					11						
22 (h)	Preston NE	L 1-2	Wainscoat	20,000	1	2	3	4		6	7						5		8					11			9	10		
25 (a)	Burnley	D 0-0		25,000	1		3	4		6	7	8					5						2	11		9	10			
26 (h)	Burnley	W 3-0	Dickson 3	20,000	1		3	4		6	7	8		10			5						2	11		9				
29 (a)	Sheffield U	W 1-0	Dickson	20,000	1		3	4		6	7	8					5						2	11		9	10			
Jan 1 (h)	Cardiff C	L 0-1		33,000	1		3	4		6	7	8					5						2	11		9	10			
5 (h)	Sheffield U	L 0-1		20,000	1		3	4		6	7	8			11		5						2			9	10			
19 (a)	Everton	L 0-1		30,000	1		3	4		6	7	8			11		5						2			9	10			
26 (h)	Everton	D 1-1	Dickson	15,000	1		3	4				8			7	11	6						2			9	10	5		
Feb 2 (a)	Blackburn R	L 0-2		15,000	1		3			4		8			7	11	6						2			9	10	5		
9 (h)	West Brom A	L 0-1		16,000	1		3			4		8			7		6						2			9	10	5	11	
16 (a)	Birmingham	L 1-2	Birrell	22,000	1		3			4		8			7		6						2			9	10	5	11	
23 (h)	Birmingham	L 0-1		15,000	1		3	6		4		8			7		9						2				10	5	11	
Mar 1 (a)	Manchester C	L 2-3	Slade, J.Carr	20,000			3		5	4				10	7		6		8			1	2			9			11	
8 (h)	Blackburn R	W 2-0	Hick, Wainscoat	14,000			3			4					7		6		8			1	2				10	5	11	9
15 (h)	Bolton W	L 1-2	Elliott	22,000			3			4					7		6		8			1	2				10	5	11	9
22 (a)	Bolton W	L 0-2		15,000			3			4					7		6		8			1	2				10	5	11	9
29 (h)	Sunderland	L 1-3	J.Carr (pen)	20,000			3			4					7			6	8			1	2			9	10	5	11	
Apr 2 (h)	Manchester C	D 1-1	Slade	6,000			3			4					7			6	8			1	2			9	10	5	11	
5 (a)	Sunderland	L 2-3	Hick 2	30,000		2	3			4				10	7			6	8			1						5	11	9
9 (a)	West Brom A	D 1-1	Elliott	14,473	1	2	3	4						10	7			6	8								10	5	11	
12 (a)	Liverpool	L 1-3	Elliott (pen)	20,000	1	2	3	4						8	7		5	6									10		11	9
19 (h)	Liverpool	D 1-1	Hick	18,000	1	2	3	4						10	7		5	6	8										11	9
21 (a)	Cardiff C	L 0-1		35,000	1	2	3	4						10	7		5	6									11	8		9
	Apps				31	40	25	32	5	27	9	21	13	25	33	18	32	9	24	6	6	11	19	8	3	16	17	12	13	7
	Goals									2		2	8	7		4			3							5	2		4

FA Cup

Date	Opponent	Result	Scorers	Att	Clough J	Freeman RV	Maitland AE	Harris J	Ellerington W	Slade CH	Bottrill WG	Birrell W	Wilson AN	Elliott GW	Urwin T	Cochrane AF	Webster M	Pender R	Carr J	Carr G	Carr W	Harrison H	Holmes W	Stevenson AB	Fox WV	Dickson IW	Wainscoat WR	Smith EE	Williams O	Hick WM	Round
Jan 12 (h)	Watford	L 0-1		24,192	1	2	3	4		6	7	8			11		5									9	10				1
	Apps				1	1	1	1		1	1	1			1		1									1	1				
	Goals																													

1924-25
Division 2

Date		Opponent	Result	Scorers	Att	Clough J	Bissett JT	Freeman RV	Harris J	Webster M	Slade CH	Carr J	Cochrane AF	Elliott GW	Wainscoat WR	Williams O	Smith EE	Hick WM	Williams JT	Birrell W	Dickinson PE	Good H	Ashman D	Dickson IW	Holmes W	French JP	McAllister W	Ferguson RG	McClelland J	Wilson J
Aug 30	(h)	Barnsley	W 2-0	O.Williams, Elliott	22,000	1	2	3	4	5	6	7	8	9	10	11														
Sep 6	(a)	Leicester C	D 0-0		24,000	1	2	3	4		6	7	8	9	10	11	5													
Sep 10	(h)	Wolves	W 2-0	Elliott 2 (1 pen)	20,000	1	2	3	4		6	7		8	10	11	5	9												
Sep 13	(a)	Port Vale	L 1-2	Wainscoat	8,000	1	2	3	4		6	7		8	10	11	5	9												
Sep 20	(h)	Bradford C	W 1-0	Hick	18,000	1	3	2	6		4	7		8	10	11	5	9												
Sep 27	(a)	South Shields	W 1-0	Hick	10,000	1	2	3	6		4			8	10	7	5	9	11											
Oct 4	(h)	Derby C	L 1-3	Wainscoat	24,000	1	2	3	6		4			10	7		5	9	11	8										
Oct 11	(a)	Blackpool	D 1-1	Elliott	14,000	1	2	3	6		4		8	10	9	7	5		11											
Oct 18	(h)	Hull C	L 0-1		18,000	1	2	3	6		4		8	10	9		5		11		7									
Oct 25	(h)	Stoke	W 1-0	Cochrane	10,000	1	2	3	6		4		8	11	9				10		7	5								
Nov 1	(a)	Coventry C	D 2-2	J.Carr, Dickinson	10,000	1	2	3	4			8		10	9				11		7	5	6							
Nov 8	(h)	Oldham A	D 0-0		14,000	1	2	3	6		4		8	10	9				11		7	5								
Nov 15	(a)	Sheffield W	L 0-2		13,983	1	2	3	6		4		8	10					11		7	5		9						
Nov 22	(h)	Clapton O	D 1-1	Dickson	10,000	1	2		6		4		8	10					11	7	5	9	3							
Nov 29	(a)	Crystal P	D 2-2	Elliott, O.Williams	15,000	1	2		4	5	6		8	10				9	11	7			3							
Dec 1	(a)	Fulham	D 0-0		10,000	1	2		4	5	6		8	9	10				11	7			3							
Dec 6	(h)	Southampton	D 0-0		14,000	1	2	3	4	5	6		8	9	10				11	7										
Dec 13	(a)	Chelsea	L 0-2		22,000	1	2	3	4	5	6		8	10	11			9		7										
Dec 20	(h)	Stockport C	D 1-1	Wainscoat	12,000	1	2	3	4	5	6		8	10	11			9		7										
Dec 25	(h)	Manchester U	D 1-1	J.T.Williams	18,500	1	2	3	4	5	6		8	10				9	11	7										
Dec 26	(a)	Manchester U	L 0-2		44,000	1	2		4	5				10	9				11	7	8	6	3							
Dec 27	(a)	Barnsley	L 0-1		8,000	1		3		6		8		11	10			9	7	4	5		2							
Jan 1	(h)	Fulham	L 1-3	Dickson	14,000	1		3		5	6	7		10				9	11	4				8	2					
Jan 3	(h)	Leicester C	L 1-5	Hick (pen)	12,000	1			4	5	6	7		10					11		9			8	2		3			
Jan 17	(h)	Port Vale	L 0-1		8,000	1	2	3	4		6	7		10			5		11	8	9									
Jan 24	(a)	Bradford C	W 1-0	Dickson (pen)	15,000	1	2	3	4	5		7		10					11	8			6	9						
Jan 31	(h)	South Shields	D 1-1	O.Williams	14,000	1	2	3	4	5		7		10					11	8			6	9						
Feb 7	(a)	Derby C	L 1-3	Birrell	14,000	1		3				7			10	11				8			6	9	2		4	5		
Feb 14	(h)	Blackpool	W 4-1	J.T.Williams 2, O.Williams 2	12,000	1		3		5		7			10	11				8				9	2		4	6		
Feb 28	(a)	Stoke	W 1-0	Dickson	10,000	1		3		5		7	8		10	11								9	2		4	6		
Mar 7	(h)	Coventry C	D 1-1	Dickson	13,000	1		3		5		7			10	11				8				9	2		4	6		
Mar 14	(a)	Oldham A	D 0-0		6,000	1		3		5		7			10	11				8				9	2		4	6		
Mar 19	(h)	Hull C	D 0-0		6,000	1		3		5					10	11				7			6	8	2		4	9		
Mar 21	(h)	Sheffield W	W 2-0	McClelland, O.Williams	6,000	1		3		5					10	11				7			6	8	2		4		9	
Mar 28	(a)	Clapton O	W 1-0	Dickson	8,000	1		3		5					10	11				7			6	8	2		4		9	
Apr 4	(h)	Crystal P	D 0-0		16,000	1				5					10	11				7			6	8	3		4		9	2
Apr 10	(a)	Portsmouth	L 1-3	Dickson	20,000	1		3		5		7			10	11				8			6	9	2		4			
Apr 11	(a)	Southampton	D 1-1	Birrell	10,000	1				5				10	7	11				8			6	9	3		4			2
Apr 12	(h)	Portsmouth	D 1-1	J.T.Williams	17,000	1				5		7		10		11			8				6	9	3		4			2
Apr 18	(h)	Chelsea	D 1-1	Birrell	10,000	1				5		7		11	10					8			6	9	3		4			2
Apr 20	(a)	Stockport C	D 1-1	O.Williams	12,000	1		3		5				11		10			7	8			6	9	2		4			
May 2	(a)	Wolves	L 0-1		10,977	1		3		5		7			10	11				8			6	9	2		4			
Apps						42	24	33	16	37	21	31	23	17	17	30	9	9	27	27	6	8	13	21	22	1	15	5	4	4
Goals												1	1	5	3	7		3	4	3	1			7					1	

FA Cup

Date		Opponent	Result	Scorers	Att	Clough J	Bissett JT	Freeman RV	Harris J	Webster M	Slade CH	Carr J	Cochrane AF	Elliott GW	Wainscoat WR	Williams O	Smith EE	Hick WM	Williams JT	Birrell W	Dickinson PE	Good H	Ashman D	Dickson IW	Holmes W	French JP	McAllister W	Ferguson RG	McClelland J	Wilson J	Round
Jan 10	(a)	Bradford	L 0-1		28,000	1		3		5	6	8	11		10			9	7	4			2								1
Apps						1		1		1	1	1	1		1			1	1	1			1							
Goals																														

1925-26
Division 2

Date	Opp	Res	Scorers	Att	Clough J	Holmes W	Freeman RV	McAllister W	Webster M	Ashman D	Carr J	Birrell W	McClelland J	Thompson N	Williams O	Cochrane AF	Ferguson RG	Jones GW	Gowland N	Camsell GH	Wilson J	Swales N	Williams JT	Good H	Bissett JT	Watson A	Cartwright P
Aug 29 (a) Portsmouth		W 5-1	Birrell, Thompson 2, O.Williams, McClelland	24,108	1	2	3	4	5	6	7	8	9	10	11												
Sep 2 (h) Blackpool		W 3-2	Thompson, Birrell 2	18,108	1	2	3	4	5	6	7	8	9	10	11												
5 (h) Wolves		W 4-1	McClelland 3, Birrell	17,414	1	2	3	4	5	6	7	8	9	10	11												
7 (a) Blackpool		W 3-2	McClelland 3	17,036	1	2	3	4	5	6	7	8	9	10	11												
12 (a) Swansea T		L 0-4		20,289	1	2	3	4	5	6	7	8	9	10	11												
14 (a) Preston NE		L 0-1		13,075	1	2	3	4	5	6	7	8	9		11	10											
19 (h) Sheffield W		W 3-0	Birrell 2 (1 pen), McClelland	13,983	1	2	3		5	6		8	9		11	10	4	7									
23 (h) Preston NE		W 5-1	Cochrane, McClelland 2, Birrell 2	14,252	1	2	3		5	6		8	9		11	10	4	7									
26 (a) Stoke C		L 0-4		9,666	1	2	3		5	6		8	9		11	10	4	7									
Oct 3 (h) Oldham A		W 2-1	Birrell, Jones	14,906		2	3		5	6		8	9		11	10	4	7	1								
10 (a) Stockport C		W 2-1	McClelland, O.Williams	11,762	1	2	3		5	6		8	9		11	10	4	7									
17 (h) Darlington		W 3-2	O.Williams, McClelland 2	31,045	1	2	3	4	5			8	9		11	10	6	7									
24 (a) Hull C		W 2-1	Birrell, McClelland	10,358	1	2	3	4		6		8	9		11	10	5	7									
31 (h) Nottingham F		W 1-0	Birrell (pen)	16,490	1	2	3	4	5			8		10	11		6	7		9							
Nov 7 (a) Southampton		L 1-3	McClelland	12,233	1	2	3	4	5			8	9		11	10	6	7									
14 (h) Barnsley		W 5-0	Cochrane, O.Williams 2, Birrell, McClelland	12,760	1	2		4	5			8	9		11	10	6	7				3					
21 (a) Port Vale		L 0-4		9,336	1	2	3	4	5			8	9	10	11		6	7									
28 (h) Bradford C		L 2-5	McClelland 2	6,672	1	2	3	4	5			8	9		11	10	6	7									
Dec 5 (a) Derby C		L 0-2		14,835	1	2	3	4	5		7	8	9		11	10	6										
12 (h) Chelsea		L 1-2	O.Williams	14,395	1		3		5	6	7	8	9		10	11	4				2						
19 (a) Clapton O		L 0-1		10,955	1		3		5	6	7	8	9		10	11					2	4					
25 (a) Fulham		L 0-2		19,616	1		3		5	6		8	9		11			7			2	4					
26 (h) Fulham		W 4-0	J.T.Williams 2, Birrell, McClelland	17,405	1		3		5	6	10	8	9				4	7			2		11				
Jan 1 (h) South Shields		L 1-2	J.T.Williams	19,007	1		3		5	6	10	8	9				4	7			2		11				
2 (h) Portsmouth		W 4-1	McClelland 3, J.Carr	10,028	1	2	3		5	6	10	8	9		11		4	7									
16 (a) Wolves		L 1-3	McClelland	8,888	1	2	3	4	5	6	10	8	9					7					11				
23 (h) Swansea T		L 0-3		12,134	1	2	3	4	5	6	10	8	9		11			7									
Feb 6 (h) Stoke C		W 3-0	Birrell, McClelland, J.Carr	7,462	1	2	3		5	6	10	8	9		11		4	7									
13 (a) Oldham A		L 1-4	Birrell	14,407	1	2	3		5	6	10	8			11		4			9			7				
20 (h) Stockport C		W 4-0	McClelland 2, Birrell, J.Carr	7,946	1		3		5	6	10	8	9		11						2		7	4			
22 (a) Sheffield W		L 0-2		20,684	1		3		5	6	10	8	9		11						2		7	4			
27 (a) Darlington		W 2-0	McClelland, Birrell	15,118	1		3	4		6	10	8	9		11		5	7			2						
Mar 6 (h) Hull C		D 3-3	J.Carr 2, McClelland	8,843	1		3	4		6	10	8	9		11		5	7			2						
13 (a) Nottingham F		L 0-1		10,675	1		3			6	10	8	9		11		4	7							2	5	
20 (h) Southampton		W 3-0	O.Williams 2, McClelland (pen)	8,111	1		3	4		6	10	8	9		11										2	5	7
27 (a) Barnsley		W 1-0	Camsell	8,361	1		3		5	6		8			11	10				9					2	4	7
Apr 2 (a) South Shields		D 2-2	Camsell 2	14,839	1		3		5	6	10	8			11					9					2	4	7
3 (h) Port Vale		W 3-1	Webster, J.Carr, Birrell	10,231	1		3		5	6	10	8	9		11										2	4	7
10 (a) Bradford C		L 0-2		12,581	1		3		5	6	10	8	9		11										2	4	7
17 (h) Derby C		L 1-2	McClelland	9,462	1		3		5	6	10	8	9		11		4								2		7
24 (a) Chelsea		W 1-0	McClelland	25,522			3		5	6	10	8	9		11			7	1						2	4	
May 1 (h) Clapton O		L 1-2	McClelland	7,788			3		5	6	10	8	9		11			7	1						2	4	
Apps					39	26	39	18	38	35	29	42	38	8	33	20	23	24	3	4	10	2	6	2	9	8	6
Goals						1			1		6	17	32	3	8	2		1		3			3				

FA Cup

Date	Opp	Res	Scorers	Att	Clough J	Holmes W	Freeman RV	McAllister W	Webster M	Ashman D	Carr J	Birrell W	McClelland J	Thompson N	Williams O	Cochrane AF	Ferguson RG	Jones GW	Gowland N	Camsell GH	Wilson J	Swales N	Williams JT	Good H	Bissett JT	Watson A	Cartwright P	Round
Jan 9 (h) Leeds U		W 5-1	McClelland 5	29,000	1	2	3	4	5	6	10	8	9		11			7										3
30 (a) Clapton O		L 2-4	McClelland, Birrell	24,247	1	2	3	6		5	10	8	9		11		4	7										4
Apps					2	2	2	2	1	2	2	2	2		2		1	2										
Goals												1	6															

1926-27
Division 2

Date		Opponent	Result / Scorers	Att.	Mathieson JA	Wilson J	Freeman RV	Miller J	Webster M	Ashman D	Pease WH	Birrell W	McClelland J	Carr J	Williams O	Ferguson RG	Smith J	Holmes W	Camsell GH	Twine F	Williams JT	McKay J
Aug	28 (a)	Chelsea	L 0-3	29,849	1	2	3	4	5	6	7	8	9	10	11							
	30 (a)	Southampton	L 1-2 Birrell	9,401	1	2	3	4	5	6	7	8	9	10	11							
Sep	4 (h)	Preston NE	L 0-2	13,496	1	2	3	4	5		7	8	9	10	11	6						
	11 (a)	South Shields	D 0-0	7,519	1		3		5	6	7	8	9	10	11	4	2					
	18 (h)	Hull C	W 2-0 Pease (pen), O.Williams	11,618	1		3	4		6	7	8		10	11		2	5	9			
	22 (h)	Bradford C	W 4-3 Pease 2, Camsell 2	11,993	1		3	4		6	7	8		10	11		2	5	9			
	25 (a)	Wolves	W 2-1 Camsell, J.Carr	14,434	1		3	4		6	7	8		10	11		2	5	9			
	29 (a)	Bradford C	W 1-0 Camsell	8,759	1		3	4		6	7	8		10	11		2	5	9			
Oct	2 (h)	Notts C	W 4-2 Camsell 3, Birrell	15,386	1	2	3	4		6	7	8		10	11			5	9			
	9 (a)	Clapton O	W 3-2 O.Williams 2, Pease	12,034	1		3			6	7	4	8	10	11		2	5	9			
	16 (a)	Nottingham F	L 3-4 Camsell, Pease 2 (1 pen)	11,262	1		3	4		6	7	8		10	11		2	5	9			
	23 (h)	Barnsley	W 5-1 Pease 2, J.Carr 2, Camsell	12,740	1		3	4		6	7	8		10	11	5	2		9			
	30 (a)	Darlington	W 4-1 Pease 2, Camsell, O.Williams	17,625	1		3	4		6	7	8		10	11	5			9	2		
Nov	6 (h)	Portsmouth	W 7-3 Camsell 4, Pease 2, J.Carr	8,680	1		3	4		6	7	8		10	11	5	2		9			
	13 (a)	Oldham A	L 1-2 Camsell	11,868	1		3	4		6	7	8		10	11	5	2		9			
	20 (h)	Fulham	W 6-1 Camsell 4 (1 pen), Birrell, Pease	15,752	1		3	4		6	7	8		10	11	5	2		9			
	27 (h)	Southampton	W 3-1 O.Williams, Camsell, Pease	19,520	1		3	4		6	7	8		10	11	5			9	2		
Dec	4 (h)	Blackpool	D 4-4 Camsell 2, Pease 2	19,456	1		3	4		6	7	8		10	11	5	2		9			
	18 (h)	Swansea T	W 7-1 Pease, McClelland 2, Camsell 4	27,805	1		3	4		6	7		8	10	11	5	2		9			
	25 (a)	Manchester C	W 5-3 Camsell 5	44,077	1		3	4		6	7	8		10	11	5	2		9			
	27 (h)	Manchester C	W 2-1 Camsell 2	*43,754	1		3	4		6	7	8		10	11	5	2		9			
Jan	1 (h)	Port Vale	W 5-2 Camsell 3, Pease, Smith (og)	26,163	1		3	4		6	7	8		10	11	5	2		9			
	15 (h)	Chelsea	D 0-0	23,964	1			4		6	7	8		10	11	5	3		9	2		
	22 (a)	Preston NE	D 2-2 Camsell, Pease	20,122	1			4		6	7	8		10	11	5	3		9	2		
Feb	5 (a)	Hull C	D 3-3 Camsell 2 (1 pen), Pease	24,110	1		3	4		6	7	8		10		5	2		9		11	
	8 (a)	Grimsby T	W 7-4 Camsell 3, Birrell 2, McClelland, J.T.Williams	10,288	1		3	4		6		8	7	10		5	2		9		11	
	12 (h)	Wolves	W 2-0 Camsell (pen), Birrell	26,974	1		3	4		6		8	7	10		5	2		9		11	
	23 (a)	Notts C	D 2-2 Camsell 2	12,042	1		3	4		6	7	8		10	11	5			9	2		
	26 (h)	Clapton O	W 6-0 Birrell 2, Camsell 2, Pease 2 (1 pen)	21,761	1		3	4		6	7	8		10	11	5			9	2		
Mar	5 (h)	Nottingham F	W 1-0 Birrell	33,354	1		3	4		6	7	8		10	11	5			9	2		
	12 (a)	Barnsley	D 1-1 Pease	23,599	1		3	4	5	6	7	8		10	11		2		9			
	16 (h)	South Shields	W 5-0 O.Williams, Birrell, Camsell 3	25,322	1			4		6	7	8		10	11	5	3		9	2		
	19 (a)	Darlington	W 4-1 O.Williams 2, Ashman, Birrell	31,982	1			4		6		7	9	8	11	5	3			2		10
	26 (a)	Portsmouth	W 1-0 Camsell	24,153	1			4		6		8	7	10	11	5	3		9	2		
Apr	2 (h)	Oldham A	W 3-1 McClelland, Camsell, O.Williams	22,554	1			4		6		8	7	10	11	5	3		9	2		
	9 (a)	Fulham	W 3-0 Birrell 2 (1 pen), Camsell	12,178	1			4		6		8	7			5	3		9	2	11	10
	15 (a)	Port Vale	L 1-3 Birrell	21,056	1			4		6		8	7		11	5	3		9	2		10
	16 (h)	Grimsby T	W 3-0 Camsell, McClelland, Birrell (pen)	22,503	1			4		6		8	7		11	5	3		9	2		10
	20 (a)	Reading	L 1-2 Birrell	12,836	1			4		6		8	7		11	5	3		9	2		10
	23 (a)	Blackpool	D 2-2 McKay, Camsell	12,657	1			4		6		8	7		11	5	3		9	2		10
	30 (h)	Reading	W 5-0 Camsell 3, J.Carr 2 (1 pen)	23,786	1			4		6		8	7	10	11	5	3		9	2		
May	7 (a)	Swansea T	W 1-0 Camsell	11,913	1			4		6		8	7		11	5	3		9	2		10
		*Ground attendance record		Apps	42	4	29	40	5	41	30	41	20	35	38	31	33	7	37	18	4	7
				Goals						1	23	16	5	6	9				59		1	1

1 own-goal

FA Cup

Date		Opponent	Result / Scorers	Att.	Mathieson JA	Wilson J	Freeman RV	Miller J	Webster M	Ashman D	Pease WH	Birrell W	McClelland J	Carr J	Williams O	Ferguson RG	Smith J	Holmes W	Camsell GH	Twine F	Williams JT	McKay J	Round
Jan	8 (h)	Leicester C	W 5-3 O.Williams, Pease, Birrell 2, Camsell	30,000	1			4		6	7	8		10	11	5	3		9	2			3
	29 (a)	Preston NE	W 3-0 Camsell 3	34,778	1		3	4		6	7	8		10	11	5			9	2			4
Feb	19 (a)	Millwall	L 2-3 O.Williams, Pease	44,250	1		3	4		6	7	8		10	11	5			9	2			5
				Apps	3		2	3		3	3	3		3	3	3	1		3	3			
				Goals							2	2			2				4				

1927-28
Division 1

Date	Opp	Res	Scorers	Att	Mathieson JA	Twine F	Smith J	Miller J	Ferguson RG	Ashman D	Pease WH	Birrell W	Camsell GH	Carr J	Williams O	McKay J	Kennedy F	Webster M	Peacock J	Freeman RV	McClelland J	Millar VM	Bruce RF	Jarvis S	Hall BAC
Aug 27 (a) Manchester U		L 0-3		44,957	1	2	3	4	5	6	7	8	9	10	11										
31 (h) Tottenham H		W 3-1	McKay, O.Williams, Camsell	29,113	1	2	3	4	5	6	7		9	10	11	8									
Sep 3 (h) Everton		W 4-2	Camsell 4	30,299	1	2	3	4	5	6	7		9	10	11	8									
10 (a) Cardiff C		D 1-1	Pease	23,033	1	2	3	4	5	6	7		9	10	11	8									
12 (a) Tottenham H		L 2-4	J.Carr, Camsell	19,219	1	2	3	4	5	6	7		9	10	11	8									
17 (h) Blackburn R		W 2-0	Ashman, Camsell	28,300	1	2	3	4	5	6	7	8	9	10			11								
24 (a) Bolton W		D 0-0		21,720	1	2	3	4		6	7	8	9	10	11			5							
Oct 1 (h) Sheffield W		D 3-3	Camsell 2, McKay	22,230	1	2	3	4	5	6	7	8	9			10	11								
8 (a) Aston Villa		L 1-5	Birrell	38,180	1	2	3	4	5	6	7	8	9	10	11										
15 (a) Birmingham		L 2-3	Camsell, Pease	17,143	1	2	3	4	5		7	8	9	10	11										
22 (h) Burnley		L 2-3	Pease 2	17,803	1		2	4	5		7	10	9		11				6	3	8				
29 (a) Bury		W 4-1	Pease 3, J.Carr	18,756	1	2	3	4			7		9	10	11			5	6		8				
Nov 5 (h) Sheffield U		W 3-0	McKay, Camsell 2	22,061	1	2	3	4			7		9		11	10		5	6		8				
12 (a) Arsenal		L 1-3	Camsell	25,921	1	2	3	4	5		7		9	10	11				6		8				
19 (h) Liverpool		D 1-1	Pease	18,741	1	2	3	4	5		7		9	10	11				6		8				
26 (a) West Ham U		W 5-4	O.Williams 2, Pease, Camsell 2	14,666	1	2	3	4	5		7		9	10	11				6		8				
Dec 3 (h) Portsmouth		W 5-1	McClelland, Camsell 2, O.Williams, J.Carr	18,163	1	2	3	4	5		7		9	10	11				6		8				
10 (a) Leicester C		D 3-3	Pease, Camsell 2	26,815	1	2	3	4	5		7		9	10	11				6		8				
17 (h) Derby C		D 3-3	Camsell, McClelland, Ferguson	15,235	1	2		4	5		7		9			10			6	3	8	11			
24 (a) Sunderland		L 0-1		23,633	1	2	3	4	5		7		9	10	11				6		8				
26 (h) Newcastle U		D 1-1	Pease	37,478	1	2	3	4	5		7		9	10	11				6		8				
27 (a) Newcastle U		D 3-3	Pease 2, Camsell	40,208	1		3	4	5		7		9		11	10			6	2	8				
31 (h) Manchester U		L 1-2	McClelland	19,652	1		3	4	5		7		9		11	10			6	2	8				
Jan 2 (h) Huddersfield T		W 3-1	Camsell 2, Pease	26,032	1	2	3		5	6	7		9	10	11				4		8				
7 (a) Everton		L 1-3	Peacock	46,432	1	2	3		5	6	7		9	10	11				4		8				
21 (h) Cardiff C		L 1-2	Camsell	21,728	1	2	3	4	5	6	7		9	10	11						8				
Feb 4 (h) Bolton W		L 2-5	Camsell 2	21,109	1	2	3	4	5	6	7		9	10	11								8		
11 (a) Sheffield W		W 3-2	Camsell, J.Carr, Bruce	15,631	1	2	3	4	5		7		9	10	11				6				8		
23 (a) Blackburn R		L 0-3		12,855	1	2	3	4	5		7		9	10	11				6		8				
25 (h) Birmingham		D 1-1	McClelland	18,329	1	2	3	4	5		7		9	10	11				6		8				
Mar 3 (a) Burnley		D 1-1	Camsell	18,209	1	2	3	4	5		7		9	10	11				6		8				
10 (h) Bury		W 6-1	Camsell 4, Pease 2	13,922	1	2	3	4			7		9	10	11			5	6		8				
17 (a) Sheffield U		L 1-4	Pease	26,328	1	2	3	4			7		9		11			5	6		8		10		
21 (h) Aston Villa		D 0-0		15,698	1	2	3	4	5		7		9		11				6		8		10		
31 (a) Liverpool		D 1-1	Millar	26,840	1	2	3	4	5		7		9	8					6			11	10		
Apr 7 (h) West Ham U		D 2-2	J.Carr, Ferguson	21,860	1	2	3	4	5		7		9	8					6			11	10		
10 (a) Huddersfield T		W 4-2	Millar, Pease, Hall, Bruce	29,034	1		3	4	5		7			8					6			11	10	2	9
14 (a) Portsmouth		L 1-4	Bruce (pen)	23,897	1		3	4	5		7			8					6			11	10	2	9
18 (h) Arsenal		D 2-2	Bruce, Camsell	16,731	1	2	3	4	5		7		9	8					6			11	10		
21 (a) Leicester C		D 1-1	Pease	18,854	1		3	4	5		7		9	8					6			11	10	2	
28 (a) Derby C		L 1-2	J.Carr	12,017	1		3	4	5		7		9	8					6			11	10	2	
May 5 (h) Sunderland		L 0-3		41,997	1		3	4	5		7		9	8					6				10	2	
Apps					42	34	41	40	35	15	41	7	40	32	31	9	8	5	32	4	19	8	12	5	2
Goals									2	1	19	1	33	6	4	3			1		4	2	4		1

FA Cup

Date	Opp	Res	Scorers	Att	Mathieson JA	Twine F	Smith J	Miller J	Ferguson RG	Ashman D	Pease WH	Birrell W	Camsell GH	Carr J	Williams O	McKay J	Kennedy F	Webster M	Peacock J	Freeman RV	McClelland J	Round
Jan 14 (h) South Shields		W 3-0	Camsell, Peacock 2	25,000	1	2	3	4	5	6			9	10	11				8		7	3
28 (a) Southport		W 3-0	Camsell 3	12,000	1	2	3	4	5	6	7		9	10	11				8			4
Feb 18 (a) Huddersfield T		L 0-4		55,200	1	2	3	4	5		7		9	10	11				6		8	5
Apps					3	3	3	3	3	2	2		3	3	3				3		2	
Goals													4						2			

1928-29
Division 2

Date	Opponent	Res	Scorers	Att	Mathieson JA	Jarvis S	Freeman RV	Miller J	Ferguson RG	Peacock J	Pease WH	Carr J	Camsell GH	Kennedy F	Millar WM	Williams O	McKay J	Webster M	Ashman D	Bruce RF	Smith J	Gowland N	Hall BAC	Emmerson GA	Gardner JR
Aug 25 (a)	Reading	W 3-2	Camsell 2, Peacock	20,925	1	2	3	4	5	6	7	8	9	10	11										
27 (a)	Tottenham H	W 5-2	Camsell, Pease 2, O.Williams, Kennedy	23,990	1	2	3	4	5	6	7	8	9	10		11									
Sep 1 (h)	Preston NE	L 2-3	Camsell 2	25,280	1	2	3	4	5	6	7	8	9	10		11									
8 (a)	Chelsea	L 0-2		48,775	1	2	3	4	5	6	7	8	9			11	10								
12 (h)	Hull C	D 1-1	Camsell	15,998	1	2	3	4		6		8	9		7	11	10	5							
15 (a)	Oldham A	W 3-1	Camsell, Millar 2	15,819	1	2	3	4				8	9		7	11		5	6	10					
22 (h)	Southampton	L 1-2	Pease	15,525	1	2	3	4		6	7	8	9			11		5		10					
29 (a)	Wolves	D 3-3	Camsell, O.Williams, Bruce	16,470	1	2	3	4	5	6	7	8	9			11				10					
Oct 6 (h)	Notts C	W 3-1	Pease 3	16,984	1	2		4	5	6	7	8	9			11				10	3				
13 (a)	Millwall	W 3-2	Kennedy (pen), Camsell, Hill (og)	30,373	1	2		4	5	6	7		9	8		11				10	3				
20 (h)	Blackpool	W 4-1	Camsell, Pease, Kennedy (pen), Williams	15,727	1	2		4	5	6	7		9	8		11				10	3				
27 (a)	Swansea T	L 0-2		12,026	1	2		4	5	6	7		9	8	11					10	3				
Nov 3 (h)	Bradford	W 5-3	Bruce, Kennedy 2 (1 pen), O.Williams, Pease	18,783	1	2		4	5	6	7		9	8		11				10	3				
10 (a)	Barnsley	D 2-2	Millar, Pease	9,635	1	2		4	5	6	7		9	8	11					10	3				
17 (h)	Stoke C	W 1-0	Camsell	15,620	1	2		4		6	7	8	9			11		5		10	3				
24 (a)	Clapton O	L 0-3		9,391		2		4	5	6	7			8	11					10	3		1	9	
Dec 1 (h)	West Brom A	D 1-1	Millar	15,075			2	4	5	6	7			8	11					10	3		1	9	
8 (a)	Nottingham F	D 1-1	Pease	8,837	1		2	4		6	7		9			11	8	5		10	3				
15 (h)	Bristol C	W 3-1	Camsell 2, Pease (pen)	9,541	1		2	4			7		9			11	8	5	6	10	3				
22 (a)	Grimsby T	W 4-1	Pease, Bruce 2, Camsell	10,984	1		2	4		6	7		9			11	8	5		10	3				
25 (h)	Port Vale	W 5-1	O.Williams 2, Bruce, Camsell, Pease	23,977	1		2	4		6	7	8	9			11		5		10	3				
26 (a)	Port Vale	W 3-2	Camsell 2, Pease	13,988	1		2	4		6	7		9			11	8	5		10	3				
29 (a)	Reading	D 0-0		16,963	1		2	4		6	7		9			11	8	5		10	3				
Jan 1 (h)	Tottenham H	W 3-0	Bruce 2, Camsell	25,145	1		2	4		6	7	8	9	11				5		10	3				
5 (a)	Preston NE	D 0-0		17,734	1		2	4		6	7		9	11			8	5		10	3				
19 (h)	Chelsea	L 4-5	Williams, Pease 2 (1 pen), Camsell	24,768	1		2	4	5	6	7	8	9			11				10	3				
Feb 2 (a)	Southampton	D 1-1	Pease	12,908	1	2				6	7	8	9	10		11		5	4		3				
9 (h)	Wolves	W 8-3	Bruce, Pease 4 (2 pens), Camsell 3	14,636	1	2		4		6	7	8	9			11		5		10	3				
16 (h)	Notts C	W 3-0	Camsell, Pease, Bruce	11,534	1	2		4		6	7	8	9			11		5		10	3				
20 (h)	Oldham A	W 1-0	Bruce	11,754	1	2		4		6		8	9			11		5		10	3			7	
23 (h)	Millwall	W 3-0	Emmerson 3	21,082	1	2		4		6		8	9			11		5		10	3			7	
Mar 2 (a)	Blackpool	L 0-3		10,440	1	2		4		6	7	8	9	10		11		5			3				
9 (h)	Swansea T	D 0-0		18,430	1		2	4		6		8	9			11		5		10	3			7	
16 (a)	Bradford	L 2-3	Camsell, Bruce	26,109	1		2	4		6	7	8	9			11		5		10	3				
23 (h)	Barnsley	W 1-0	Pease	17,050	1		2	4		6	7	8	9			11		5		10	3				
30 (a)	Stoke C	L 2-3	O.Williams, Pease	19,719	1		2	4		6	7	8	9			11		5		10	3				
Apr 1 (a)	Hull C	D 1-1	Camsell	19,740	1		2	4		6	7	8	9			11		5		10	3				
6 (h)	Clapton O	W 4-0	Camsell 3, J.Carr	16,140	1		3	4	2	6	7	8	9			11				10					
13 (a)	West Brom A	D 1-1	Pease	11,569	1		2	4		6	7	8	9			11		5		10	3				
20 (h)	Nottingham F	W 1-0	Pease (pen)	18,220	1		2	4		6	7	8	9			11				10	3				
27 (a)	Bristol C	W 1-0	Pease (pen)	18,234	1		2	4	5	6	7	8	9			11				10	3				
May 4 (h)	Grimsby T	W 3-0	Camsell 2, O.Williams	36,503	1		2	4	5	6		8	9			11				10	3			7	
Apps					40	22	28	40	19	40	36	29	40	15	8	33	8	25	3	35	33	2	2	4	
Goals										1	27	1	30	5	4	9				11				3	

1 own-goal

FA Cup

Date	Opponent	Res	Scorers	Att	Mathieson JA	Jarvis S	Freeman RV	Miller J	Ferguson RG	Peacock J	Pease WH	Carr J	Camsell GH	Kennedy F	Millar WM	Williams O	McKay J	Webster M	Ashman D	Bruce RF	Smith J	Gowland N	Hall BAC	Emmerson GA	Gardner JR	Round
Jan 12 (a)	Walsall	D 1-1	Camsell	14,980	1		2	4		6	7	8	9			11		5		10	3					3
21 (h)	Walsall	W 5-1	Camsell 2, Williams, Pease 2	14,917	1		2	4		6	7	8	9			11		5		10	3					R
26 (a)	West Brom A	L 0-1		33,446	1	2		4			7	8	9	11			10		6		3				5	4
Apps					3	1	2	3		2	3	3	3	1		2	1	2	1	2	3				1	
Goals											2		3			1										

1929-30
Division 1

Date	Match	Res	Scorers	Att	Mathieson JA	Freeman RV	Smith J	Miller J	Webster M	Macfarlane J	Pease WH	Carr J	Camsell GH	Bruce RF	Williams O	Cameron K	Ferguson RG	Ashman D	McKay J	Elkes JE	Peacock J	Hall BAC	Jarvis S	Muttitt E	Watson HL	Emmerson GA	Forrest W	Hillier EJG	Jennings J	Warren FW
Aug 31 (h)	Liverpool	W 5-0	Williams, Carr, Bruce 2, Camsell	28,286	1	2	3	4	5	6	7	8	9	10	11															
Sep 4 (h)	Sheffield U	W 3-1	Carr, Camsell 2	25,361	1	2	3	4	5	6	7	8	9	10	11															
Sep 7 (a)	West Ham U	L 3-5	Cameron 2, Camsell	22,760	1	2	3	4	5	6	7	8	9	10		11														
Sep 9 (a)	Sheffield U	W 3-1	Cameron, Camsell 2	14,303	1	2	3	4	5	6	7	8	9	10		11														
Sep 14 (h)	Manchester U	L 2-3	Pease, Bruce	26,428	1	2	3	4	5	6	7	8	9	10		11														
Sep 18 (a)	Bolton W	D 2-2	Camsell, Cameron	13,795	1			4	5	6	7	8	9	10		11	2	3												
Sep 21 (a)	Grimsby T	W 3-0	Williams, Camsell, Pease	15,863	1			4	5	6	7	8	9		11	10	2	3												
Sep 28 (h)	Leicester C	L 0-2		26,851	1			4	5	6	7	8	9		11	10	2	3												
Oct 5 (a)	Birmingham	D 1-1	Camsell	23,140	1			4	5	6	7	8	9		11		2	3	10											
Oct 12 (h)	Huddersfield T	L 1-3	Pease (pen)	24,231	1			4	5	6	7	8	9		11		2	3	10											
Oct 19 (a)	Everton	L 2-3	Pease, Cameron	30,657	1					6	7	8				11	2	3	10	5	4	9								
Oct 26 (h)	Derby C	W 4-0	Camsell 3, Pease	18,409	1					6	7	8	9			11	2	3	10	5	4									
Nov 2 (a)	Manchester C	L 1-3	Carr	33,302	1					6	7	8	9			11		3	10	5	4		2							
Nov 9 (h)	Sunderland	W 3-0	Pease 2 (1 pen), Camsell	29,953	1					6	7	8	9	10		11	2	3		5	4									
Nov 23 (h)	Aston Villa	L 2-3	Bruce, Elkes	16,051	1			4		6	7	8	9	10		11	2	3		5										
Nov 27 (a)	Arsenal	W 2-1	Camsell, Muttitt	28,326	1			4		6	7		9	10			2	3	8	5				11						
Nov 30 (a)	Leeds U	W 2-1	Bruce, Camsell	19,508	1			4	5	6	7		9	10			2	3	8					11						
Dec 7 (h)	Sheffield W	W 4-1	Bruce, Camsell 2, Webster	21,265	1				5	6	7		9	10			2	3	8					11	4					
Dec 14 (a)	Burnley	L 1-4	Bruce	8,671	1				5	6	7		9	10			2	3	8					11	4					
Dec 21 (h)	Portsmouth	W 2-0	Camsell, McKay	11,391	1			4	5	6	7		9	10			2	3	8					11						
Dec 25 (a)	Newcastle U	L 2-3	Pease, Bruce	38,922	1			4	5	6	7		9	10			2	3	8					11						
Dec 26 (h)	Newcastle U	D 2-2	Camsell, Bruce (pen)	40,538	1			4	5	6			9	10			2	3	8					11		7				
Dec 28 (h)	Liverpool	L 2-5	Elkes 2	23,982	1				5	6				10			2	3	8	9				11	4	7				
Jan 1 (a)	Blackburn R	L 0-7		24,370	1				5	6				10				3	8	9			2	11	4	7				
Jan 4 (h)	West Ham U	W 2-0	Camsell, Pease	17,767	1			4	5	6	7		9	10			2	3	8						11					
Jan 18 (a)	Manchester U	W 3-0	Muttitt, Pease, Camsell	21,028	1				5		7		9	10			2	3	8					11	4	6				
Feb 1 (a)	Leicester C	L 1-4	Camsell	19,057					5		7		9	10				3	8						4	6	2	1		11
Feb 8 (h)	Birmingham	W 5-1	Pease, Bruce, McKay, Hall, Watson	16,969	1						7			10				3	8	5		9			4	6	2			11
Feb 22 (h)	Everton	L 1-2	Jennings (pen)	17,730	1				5		7		9	10				3	8						4		2		6	11
Mar 1 (a)	Derby C	L 1-3	Warren	15,736	1			4	5	6	7		9	10				3	8								2			11
Mar 5 (h)	Grimsby T	L 1-5	Bruce (pen)	8,880	1		3	4	5	6	7	8	9	10													2			11
Mar 8 (h)	Manchester C	W 1-0	Warren	15,739	1				5	6	7		9	10				3	8						4		2			11
Mar 15 (a)	Sunderland	L 2-3	Warren, McKay	32,874	1				5	6	7		9	10				3	8						4		2			11
Mar 26 (a)	Huddersfield T	L 0-1		8,234	1				5		7		9					3	8		10	6			4		2			11
Mar 29 (a)	Aston Villa	L 2-4	Bruce, McKay	26,986	1				5	6	7		9	10				3	8			4					2			11
Apr 5 (h)	Leeds U	D 1-1	Camsell	14,136	1			4			7		9	10				3	8	5	6						2			11
Apr 9 (h)	Arsenal	D 1-1	Camsell	9,287	1			4			7		9	10				3	8	5	6						2			11
Apr 12 (a)	Sheffield W	L 0-1		23,087	1			4			7		9	10				3	8	5	6						2			11
Apr 19 (h)	Burnley	W 3-1	Camsell, McKay, Pease	5,370	1			4			7		9	10				3	8	5							2		6	11
Apr 21 (a)	Blackburn R	L 2-4	Warren, Camsell	18,146	1			4			7		9	10				3	8	5							2		6	11
Apr 26 (a)	Portsmouth	D 1-1	Camsell	16,446	1			4			7		9	10				3	8	5							2		6	11
May 3 (h)	Bolton W	W 3-1	Camsell 2, McKay	9,816	1			4			7		9	10				3	8	5							2		6	11
Apps					41	6	6	20	34	30	39	16	34	36	6	11	23	31	28	21	8	3	2	10	11	3	10	1	16	16
Goals									1		12	3	29	12	2	5			6	3		1		2	1				1	4

FA Cup

Date	Match	Res	Scorers	Att	Mathieson JA	Freeman RV	Smith J	Miller J	Webster M	Macfarlane J	Pease WH	Carr J	Camsell GH	Bruce RF	Williams O	Cameron K	Ferguson RG	Ashman D	McKay J	Elkes JE	Peacock J	Hall BAC	Jarvis S	Muttitt E	Watson HL	Emmerson GA	Forrest W	Hillier EJG	Jennings J	Warren FW	Round
Jan 11 (a)	Chesterfield	D 1-1	Bruce (pen)	16,656	1			4	5	6	7		9	10		11	2	3	8												3
Jan 15 (h)	Chesterfield	W 4-3	Camsell 2, Bruce 2	18,793	1			4	5	6	7	8	9	10			2	3						11							R
Jan 25 (h)	Charlton A	D 1-1	Muttitt	35,707	1			4	5	6	7	8	9	10			2	3						11							4
Jan 29 (a)	Charlton A	D 1-1	Bruce	24,884	1	2		4	5		7		9	10				3	8					11		6					R
Feb 3 (n†)	Charlton A	W 1-0*	McKay	16,676	1	2			5		7			10				3	8	9					4	6					2R
Feb 15 (h)	Arsenal	L 0-2		42,073	1	2			5		7			10				3	8	9					4	6			11		5
Apps					6	3		4	6	3	6	2	4	6		1	3	6	3	3				4	2	3			1		
Goals													2	4					1					1						

†Played at Maine Road, Manchester.   *After extra-time.

1930-31
Division 1

Date	Opponent	Result	Scorers	Att	Mathieson JA	Jennings J	Ferguson RG	Macfarlane J	Webster M	Forrest W	Pease WH	Scott WR	Camsell GH	Bruce RF	Warren FW	Freeman T	Elkes JE	Muttitt E	McKay J	Cameron K	Carr A	Holliday JW	Hillier EJG	Ashman D	McPhail DD	Jarvis S
Aug 30 (a)	Bolton W	L 0-3		14,946	1	2	3	4	5	6	7	8	9	10	11											
Sep 3 (h)	Manchester U	W 3-1	Camsell 2, Bruce	15,712	1	2	3	4	5	6	7	8	9	10	11											
6 (h)	Liverpool	D 3-3	Bruce, Warren, Pease	16,816	1	2	3	4	5	6	7	8	9	10	11											
8 (a)	West Ham U	W 3-0	Pease, Warren 2	13,597	1	2		4		6	7	8	9	10	11	3	5									
13 (a)	Blackpool	L 2-3	Warren, Bruce	20,050	1	2		4		6	7	8	9	10	11	3	5									
17 (h)	West Ham U	D 2-2	Camsell, Warren	14,748	1	2		4		6			9	10	11	3	5	7	8							
20 (a)	Huddersfield T	D 2-2	Webster, Warren	17,503	1	2		4	5	6	7		9	10	11	3			8							
27 (h)	Aston Villa	W 3-1	Pease, Bruce 2	19,260	1	2		4		6	7		9		11	3	5		8	10						
Oct 4 (a)	Chelsea	L 0-4		48,395	1	2		4		6	7		9		11	3	5		8	10						
11 (h)	Newcastle U	W 3-1	McKay, Pease, Camsell	24,827	1	2		4	5	6	7		9	10		3		11	8							
18 (h)	Sunderland	W 1-0	Forrest	30,307	1	2		4	5	6	7		9	10		3		11	8							
25 (a)	Leeds U	L 0-7		18,116	1	2		4	5	6	7		9	10		3			8	11						
Nov 1 (h)	Portsmouth	L 0-1		13,458	1	2		4		6	7		9	10		3	5		8	11						
8 (a)	Manchester C	L 2-4	Holliday 2	27,035	1	2		4		6	7					3		11	8	10	5	9				
15 (h)	Birmingham	D 1-1	Pease	11,883		2		4		6	7			10	11	3	5		8			9	1			
22 (a)	Arsenal	L 3-5	Bruce, Camsell, Warren	32,517		2		4		6	7		9	10	11	3	5		8				1			
29 (h)	Derby C	W 4-1	Camsell 2, McKay, Pease	13,987	1	2		4		6	7		9		11	3	5		8	10						
Dec 6 (a)	Leicester C	W 3-0	Warren, Cameron, Camsell	14,467	1	2		4		6	7		9		11	3	5		8	10						
13 (h)	Blackburn R	W 4-1	McKay 2, Cameron, Warren	16,119	1	2		4		6	7		9		11	3	5		8	10						
20 (a)	Sheffield U	L 2-4	Camsell, Warren	19,893	1	2		4	5	6	7		9		11	3			8	10						
26 (h)	Sheffield W	W 2-0	McKay, Warren	23,212	1	2		4		6	7		9		11	3	5		8	10						
27 (h)	Bolton W	W 3-0	Camsell 2, Warren	16,084	1	2		4		6	7		9		11	3	5		8	10						
29 (a)	Sheffield W	L 2-3	McKay, Camsell	18,530	1	2		4		6	7		9		11	3	5		8	10						
Jan 1 (h)	Grimsby T	W 2-1	Jennings (pen), Camsell	23,845	1	2		4		6	7		9		11	3	5		8	10						
3 (a)	Liverpool	L 1-3	Pease	21,133	1	2		4		6	7		9		11	3	5		8	10						
17 (h)	Blackpool	W 5-1	Jennings 2 (2 pens), Warren, Holliday, Bruce	16,060	1	2		4		6				8	11	3	5			10		9			7	
24 (h)	Huddersfield T	L 2-3	Scott, Muttitt	11,015	1	2		4		6		7	9	8		3	5	11		10						
31 (a)	Aston Villa	L 1-8	Camsell	15,947	1	2		4		6			9	10	11	3	5	7	8							
Feb 7 (h)	Chelsea	D 2-2	Camsell 2	16,443	1	2		4		6	7		9		11		5		8	10						3
14 (a)	Newcastle U	W 5-0	Warren, Cameron, Camsell 2, McKay	31,945	1	2		4		6	7		9		11		5		8	10						3
21 (a)	Sunderland	D 1-1	Camsell	31,183	1	2		4		6			9	7	11		5		8	10						3
28 (h)	Leeds U	W 5-0	Camsell 4, Warren	15,707	1	2		4		6	7		9		11		5		8	10						3
Mar 7 (a)	Portsmouth	L 0-1		11,422	1	2		4		6	7		9		11		5		8	10						3
14 (h)	Manchester C	W 4-1	Warren 2, Pease, Cameron	12,661	1	2		4		6	7		9	8	11		5			10						3
21 (a)	Birmingham	W 2-1	Pease, Camsell	20,311	1	2		4		6	7		9	8	11		5			10						3
28 (h)	Arsenal	L 2-5	Elkes, Cameron	23,476	1	2		4		6	7		9	8	11		5			10						3
Apr 3 (a)	Grimsby T	L 1-4	Camsell	19,821	1	2		4		6			9	8	11		5			10					7	3
4 (a)	Derby C	W 2-1	Camsell, Cameron	13,871	1	2		4		6			9	8	11		5			10					7	3
11 (h)	Leicester C	D 2-2	McPhail, Cameron	10,934	1	2		4		6			9	8	11		5			10					7	3
18 (a)	Blackburn R	W 5-4	Pease 2, Warren, Camsell 2	6,917		2		4	5	6	7		9	8	11					10			1	3		
25 (a)	Sheffield U	W 4-1	Pease, Bruce 2, Cameron	7,471		2		4	5	6	7		9	8	11					10			1	3		
May 2 (a)	Manchester U	D 4-4	Camsell 4	3,969	1	2		4	5	6	7		9		11				8	10				3		
	Apps				38	42	3	41	14	40	34	6	37	27	35	24	32	5	25	32	1	3	4	4	4	11
	Goals					3			1	1	12	1	32	9	18		1	1	7	8		3			1	

FA Cup

Date	Opponent	Result	Scorers	Att	Mathieson JA	Jennings J	Ferguson RG	Macfarlane J	Webster M	Forrest W	Pease WH	Scott WR	Camsell GH	Bruce RF	Warren FW	Freeman T	Elkes JE	Muttitt E	McKay J	Cameron K	Carr A	Holliday JW	Hillier EJG	Ashman D	McPhail DD	Jarvis S	Round
Jan 14 (h)	Bradford C	D 1-1	Warren	21,698	1	2		4		6	7		9	8	11	3	5			10							3
19 (a)	Bradford C	L 1-2	Barkas (og)	27,532	1	2		4		6			9	8		3	5	11		10					7		R
	Apps				2	2		2		2	1		2	2	1	2	2	1		2					1		
	Goals														1											

1 own-goal

1931-32
Division 1

Date	Match	Res	Scorers	Att	Mathieson JA	Jennings J	Jarvis S	Macfarlane J	Elkes JE	Forrest W	Pease WH	McKay J	Camsell GH	Cameron K	Warren FW	Ashman D	Freeman T	Brown WH	Bruce RF	Scott WR	Webster M	Holliday JW	Hillier EJG	Watson HL	Surtees J	Muttitt E	Marcroft EH	Williams JJ	Stuart RW	Carr A
Aug 29 (h)	Chelsea	L 0-2		24,510	1	2	3	4		5	6	7	8	9	10	11														
31 (a)	Leicester C	D 2-2	Pease, Warren	15,339	1					5	6	7	8	9	10	11	2	3	4											
Sep 5 (a)	West Ham U	W 2-0	Camsell, Cameron	23,129	1	2			5	6	7		9	10	11		3		4	8										
9 (h)	Liverpool	W 4-1	Bruce 2, Jennings (pen), Warren	15,042	1	2			5	6	7		9	10	11		3		4	8										
12 (h)	Sheffield W	W 4-0	Camsell, Forrest, Warren 2	24,050	1	2			5	6	7		9		11		3		4	10	8									
16 (a)	Liverpool	L 2-7	Camsell 2	20,854	1	2			5	6	7		9		11		3		4	10	8									
19 (a)	Bolton W	L 2-4	Camsell, Pease	14,180	1	2			5	6	7		9	11			3		10	8	4									
26 (h)	Derby C	W 5-2	Bruce 2, Scott, Camsell, Cameron	13,562	1	2		4	5	6	7		9	11			3		10	8										
Oct 3 (h)	Huddersfield T	W 1-0	Camsell	16,366	1	2		4	5	6	7		9		11		3		10	8										
10 (a)	Newcastle U	L 1-3	Pease	41,569	1	2		4	5	6	7			9	11		3		10	8										
17 (a)	Blackpool	W 2-1	Warren, Holliday	17,481	1	2			5	6	7				11		3		10	8	4	9								
24 (h)	Birmingham	W 2-0	Scott, Camsell	9,226	1				5	6			8	9	11		2	3	10	7	4									
31 (a)	Sunderland	D 0-0		28,387	1	2			5	6	7		9	11			3		10	8	4									
Nov 7 (h)	Manchester C	D 3-3	Cameron, Camsell, Scott	9,142	1	2			5	6	7		9	11			3		10	8	4									
14 (a)	Blackburn R	L 2-4	Camsell 2	8,795	1	2			5	6	7		9	11			3		10	8	4									
21 (h)	Portsmouth	L 0-1		11,136	1				5	6	7		9	11			2	3	10	8	4									
28 (a)	West Brom A	D 1-1	Cameron	17,856	1				5	6	7		9	11			2	3	10	8	4									
Dec 5 (h)	Sheffield U	W 4-3	Scott, Cameron 2, Bruce	11,385	1				5	6	7		9	11			2	3	10	8	4									
12 (a)	Everton	L 1-5	Cameron	33,182	1				5	6	7		9	11			2	3	10	8	4									
19 (h)	Arsenal	L 2-5	Pease, Bruce	17,083	1	2			6	5	7		9	11			3		10	8	4									
25 (a)	Aston Villa	L 1-7	Camsell	33,774	1				6	5	7		9	11			2	3	10	8	4									
26 (h)	Aston Villa	D 1-1	Cameron	28,006					6		7		9	11			2	3	10	8	5		1	4						
Jan 2 (a)	Chelsea	L 0-4		25,259					6		7		9	11			2	3		8	5		1	4	10					
16 (h)	West Ham U	W 3-2	Camsell, Bruce, Cameron	8,287	1	2			5	6	7		9	8				3	10		4					11				
25 (a)	Sheffield W	D 1-1	Marcroft	9,525	1	2			6				9	8				3	4	10	5					11	7			
30 (h)	Bolton W	W 3-1	Camsell 2, Pease	10,502	1	2			6		7		9	11			3	4	10		5					8				
Feb 6 (a)	Derby C	L 2-5	Camsell 2	11,917	1	2			6		7		9	11			3	4	10		5					8				
17 (a)	Huddersfield T	D 1-1	Bruce	9,491	1	2		4		6	7	8	9	11			3		10		5									
20 (h)	Newcastle U	W 2-1	Bruce, McKay	18,694	1	2		4		6	7	8	9	11			3		10		5									
27 (h)	Blackpool	L 0-3		11,371	1	2		4		6	7	8	9	11			3		10		5									
Mar 5 (a)	Birmingham	L 0-3		18,694	1	2		4	10	6		8	9	11			3		7		5									
12 (h)	Sunderland	L 0-1		21,591	1	2		4		6		8	9	11			3		10		5					7				
19 (a)	Manchester C	W 2-1	Camsell, Bruce	24,114		2			6	5		8	9	11			3		10		4		1					7		
25 (a)	Grimsby T	L 0-1		19,005		2			6	5		8	9	11			3		10		4		1					7		
26 (h)	Blackburn R	L 0-2		9,681		2			6	5		8		11			3		10		4	9	1					7		
28 (h)	Grimsby T	W 4-0	Camsell, Cameron, Bruce, McKay	8,373		2			6	5		8	9	11			3		10		4		1					7		
Apr 2 (a)	Portsmouth	L 0-2		9,949		2			6	5		8	9	11			3		10		4		1					7		
9 (h)	West Brom A	W 1-0	J.J.Williams	10,288		2			6	5	7	10	9	8			3				4		1					11		
16 (a)	Sheffield U	L 1-2	Camsell	10,728		2		4	5	6	7	10	9	8			3						1					11		
23 (h)	Everton	W 1-0	Bruce	10,728		2			6	5	7		9	8			3		10		4		1					11		
30 (a)	Arsenal	L 0-5		30,714						6	7	10		8			3				4	9	1					11	2	5
May 7 (h)	Leicester C	D 1-1	Cameron	5,410						6		8		11			3		10		4		1			9		7	2	5
	Apps				30	18	14	20	31	32	32	16	37	38	10	18	32	9	35	20	31	3	12	2	1	5	1	11	2	2
	Goals					1				1	5	2	20	11	5				12	4		1					1	1		

FA Cup

Date	Match	Res	Scorers	Att	Mathieson JA	Jennings J	Jarvis S	Macfarlane J	Elkes JE	Forrest W	Pease WH	McKay J	Camsell GH	Cameron K	Warren FW	Ashman D	Freeman T	Brown WH	Bruce RF	Scott WR	Webster M	Holliday JW	Hillier EJG	Watson HL	Surtees J	Muttitt E	Marcroft EH	Williams JJ	Stuart RW	Carr A	Round
Jan 9 (h)	Portsmouth	D 1-1	Bruce	22,949	1					5	6	7	9	11			2	3	10	8	4										3
13 (a)	Portsmouth	L 0-3		25,000	1	2		10	5	6	7		9	11			3			8	4											R
	Apps				2	1		1	2	2	2	1	2	2			2	1	1	2	2										
	Goals																		1											

1932-33
Division 1

Date		Opponent	Res	Scorers	Att	Mathieson JA	Jennings J	Freeman T	Webster M	Elkes JE	Macfarlane J	Pease WH	Martin GS	Blackmore HA	Bruce RF	Warren FW	Cameron K	Jarvis S	Forrest W	Williams JJ	Camsell GH	Brown WH	Rigby A	McKay J	Baxter RD	Hillier EJG	Gibson F	Stuart RW	Carr A	Griffiths TP	Martin J	Fenton M
Aug	27 (h)	Aston Villa	L 0-2		18,909	1	2	3	4	5	6	7	8	9	10	11																
	31 (a)	Newcastle U	L 1-5	Warren	35,109	1	2	3	4	5	6	7	8	9		11	10															
Sep	3 (a)	Manchester C	W 3-2	J.J.Williams, Cameron 2	20,211	1		3	4	5				10		11	8	2	6	7	9											
	10 (a)	Bolton W	L 3-4	Jarvis, Camsell, Cameron	12,035	1		3	4	5			10			11	8	2	6	7	9											
	17 (h)	Liverpool	L 0-1		11,371	1		3		5				10			8	2	6	7	9		4	11								
	24 (a)	Leicester C	D 1-1	Rigby	16,628	1		3		5	4			10				2	6	7	9		11		8							
Oct	1 (h)	Portsmouth	W 5-4	Camsell 2, Cameron 2, J.J.Williams	8,043	1		3	4	5				10			8	2	6	7	9		11									
	8 (a)	Chelsea	L 1-2	Camsell	18,181	1		3	4	5				10			8	2	6	7	9		11									
	15 (h)	Huddersfield T	D 1-1	Camsell	11,065	1	2	3	4	5				10	11	8			6	7	9											
	22 (h)	Sunderland	L 1-2	J.J.Williams	14,491	1	2	3	4	5				10	11	8			6	7	9											
	29 (a)	Birmingham	W 4-1	Camsell 2, J.J.Williams 2	9,090	1	2	3	4	5				8		11			6	7	9				10							
Nov	5 (h)	Derby C	L 0-3		11,964	1	2	3	4	5				8		11			6	7	9				10							
	12 (a)	Blackpool	L 1-3	Bruce	12,104		2			5	4			8	11		10	3	6	7	9					1						
	19 (h)	Everton	L 0-2		9,662		2	3		5				10		8			6	7	9	4					1					
	26 (a)	Arsenal	L 2-4	Camsell 2	37,748		2	3		5				9	10	11			6	7	8	4					1					
Dec	3 (h)	West Brom A	W 3-1	Blackmore 3	8,276		2	3		5				9	10	11			6	7	8	4					1					
	10 (a)	Sheffield W	L 1-2	Blackmore	10,754		2	3		5				9	10	11			6	7	8	4					1					
	17 (h)	Leeds U	L 0-1		9,341		2	3		5		7	10	9		11			6		8	4					1					
	24 (a)	Blackburn R	L 2-4	Blackmore, Baxter	8,303		2			5		7		9		11		3	6		8	4			10		1					
	27 (h)	Sheffield U	D 2-2	Pease, Camsell	13,566		2	3		5		7		8		11			6		9	4			10		1					
	31 (a)	Aston Villa	L 1-3	Baxter	22,309		2			5				9	8				6	11	7	4			10		1	3				
Jan	2 (h)	Newcastle U	L 2-3	Bruce, Baxter	20,218		2			5				9	8				6	11	7	4			10		1	3				
	7 (h)	Manchester C	W 2-0	Camsell, Blackmore	7,912		2	5						9		8			6	11	7	4			10		1	3				
	21 (h)	Bolton W	W 2-1	Blackmore	9,256		2							9	8				6	11	7	4			10		1	3		5		
Feb	1 (a)	Liverpool	W 3-1	Camsell 2, Blackmore	9,973		2							9	8				6	11	7	4			10		1	3	5			
	4 (h)	Leicester C	D 1-1	J.J.Williams	11,255		2							9	8				6	11	7	4			10		1	3	5			
	11 (a)	Portsmouth	L 0-2		11,759		2	5						9	8				6	11	7	4			10		1	3				
Mar	1 (h)	Chelsea	W 2-1	Camsell, Rigby	8,219		2	5						8				3	6	7	9	4	11		10		1					
	11 (h)	Birmingham	D 2-2	Morrall (og), Bruce	14,646		2							9	8			3	6	7		4	11		10		1			5		
	15 (a)	Huddersfield T	W 1-0	Young (og)	4,992		2					7		8				3	6			4	11		10		1			5		
	22 (a)	Sunderland	D 0-0		9,005		2							9	8			3	6	7		4	11		10		1			5		
	25 (h)	Blackpool	W 2-0	Baxter, Rigby	10,724		2							9	8			3	6	7		4	11		10		1			5		
	27 (a)	Sheffield U	L 0-2		6,404		2	5						9	8			3	6	7		4	11		10		1					
Apr	1 (a)	Everton	D 0-0		21,068		2					7		8		11	9	3	6			4			10		1			5		
	5 (a)	Derby C	D 2-2	Jennings (pen), Griffiths	6,587		2					7		8		11	9	3	6			4			10		1			5		
	8 (h)	Arsenal	L 3-4	Warren 2, Cameron	22,137		2					7		8		11	9	3	6			4			10		1			5		
	14 (a)	Wolves	L 0-2		28,992		2					7		8		11	9	3	6			4			10		1			5		
	15 (a)	West Brom A	W 1-0	Warren	17,511		2							8		11	9	3	6	7		4			10		1			5		
	17 (h)	Wolves	W 2-1	W.H.Brown, Baxter	16,255		2							8		11	9	3	6		7	4			10		1			5		
	22 (h)	Sheffield W	D 1-1	Bruce	10,640		2								8	11	9	3	6		7	4			10		1			5		
	29 (a)	Leeds U	W 1-0	Camsell	9,006		2							8	11		3	6	7	9	4			10		1			5		
May	6 (h)	Blackburn R	W 4-0	Camsell 2, Bruce, Fenton	7,340		2							8	11		3		7	9	4					1			5	6	10
		Apps				12	36	18	16	21	4	10	6	19	35	25	17	23	39	30	31	30	10	1	25	1	29	7	2	13	1	1
		Goals					1					1		9	5	4	6	1		6	17	1	3		5					1		1

2 own-goals

FA Cup

Date		Opponent	Res	Scorers	Att	Mathieson JA	Jennings J	Freeman T	Webster M	Elkes JE	Macfarlane J	Pease WH	Martin GS	Blackmore HA	Bruce RF	Warren FW	Cameron K	Jarvis S	Forrest W	Williams JJ	Camsell GH	Brown WH	Rigby A	McKay J	Baxter RD	Hillier EJG	Gibson F	Stuart RW	Carr A	Griffiths TP	Martin J	Fenton M	Round
Jan	14 (a)	Manchester U	W 4-1	J.J.Williams, Blackmore, Bruce 2	39,991		2	5						9	8				6	11	7	4			10		1	3					3
	28 (h)	Stoke C	W 4-1	Blackmore 2, Camsell, Baxter	29,457		2		5					9	8				6	11	7	4			10		1	3					4
Feb	18 (h)	Birmingham	D 0-0		27,705		2	5						9	8			3	6	11	7	4			10		1						5
	22 (a)	Birmingham	L 0-3		29,191		2	5						9		7		3	6	11	8	4			10		1						R
		Apps					4	3	1					4	3	1		2	4	4	4	4			4		4	2					
		Goals												3	2					1	1				1							

1933-34
Division 1

Date		Opponent	Res	Score	Scorers	Att	Gibson F	Jennings J	Jarvis S	Brown WH	Griffiths TP	Martin J	Williams JJ	Bruce RF	Camsell GH	Baxter RD	Warren FW	Fenton M	Cameron K	Stuart RW	Webster M	Ferguson C	McKay J	Weightman E	Forrest W	Chadwick C	Yorston BC	Hillier EJG	Smith J
Aug 26	(h)	Derby C	W	3-1	J.J.Williams, Camsell, Warren	14,577	1	2	3	4	5	6	7	8	9	10	11												
28	(a)	Leeds U	L	2-5	Camsell 2	10,896	1	2	3	4	5	6	7	8	9			10	11										
Sep 2	(a)	West Brom A	L	0-3		21,152	1	2	3	4	5	6	7	8	9		11	10											
9	(h)	Birmingham	L	0-3		11,501	1	2		4		6		8	9		11			3	5	7	10						
16	(a)	Sheffield W	L	0-3		12,429	1	2		4	5	6		8	9		11			3		7	10						
23	(h)	Manchester C	W	2-1	Bruce, Camsell	9,095	1	2		4	5	6	7	8	9	10	11			3									
30	(a)	Arsenal	L	0-6		28,293	1	2		4	5	6	7	8	9	10	11			3									
Oct 7	(h)	Everton	W	2-0	Warren, Bruce	10,985	1	2		4	5	6		8	9	10	11			3		7							
14	(a)	Chelsea	W	3-2	Camsell 2, Ferguson	16,878	1	2		4	5	6		8	9	10	11			3		7							
21	(h)	Liverpool	W	4-1	Camsell 2, Ferguson 2	10,899	1	2		4	5	6		8	9	10	11			3		7							
28	(a)	Tottenham H	L	0-2		35,800	1	2		4	5	6		8	9	10	11			3		7							
Nov 4	(h)	Stoke C	W	6-1	Camsell 2, Ferguson 2, Warren 2	6,969	1	2		4	5	6		8	9	10	11			3		7							
11	(a)	Aston Villa	L	0-3		27,740	1	2		4	5	6		8	9	10	11			3		7							
18	(h)	Sheffield U	W	10-3	Camsell 4, Ferguson, Warren, Bruce 3, Baxter	6,461	1	2		4	5	6		8	9	10	11			3		7							
25	(a)	Wolves	W	1-0	Camsell	22,708	1	2		4	5	6		8	9	10	11			3		7							
Dec 2	(h)	Sunderland	L	0-4		28,915	1	2		4	5			8	9	10	11			3		7		6					
9	(a)	Huddersfield T	L	1-2	Camsell	9,998	1	2		4	5	6		8	9	10	11			3		7							
16	(h)	Portsmouth	W	2-0	Warren, J.J.Williams	11,167	1	2		4	5		7	8	9	10	11			3					6				
23	(a)	Leicester C	W	2-1	Camsell, J.J.Williams	1,980	1	2		4	5		7	8	9	10	11			3					6				
25	(a)	Blackburn R	D	0-0		27,273	1	2		4	5	6	7	8	9	10	11			3									
26	(h)	Blackburn R	W	3-1	Camsell, Jennings, Bruce	19,203	1	2		4	5	6	7	8	9	10	11			3									
30	(a)	Derby C	L	0-2		17,387	1	2		4	5	10	7		9		11			3			8		6				
Jan 1	(h)	Leeds U	W	2-1	Baxter, Jennings (pen)	16,071	1	2		4	5		7		9	10	11			3			8		6				
6	(h)	West Brom A	W	3-0	Baxter, Bruce 2	13,927	1	2		4	5	11	7	8	9					3			10		6				
20	(a)	Birmingham	D	0-0		20,310	1	2		4	5	7			9	10				3		11	8		6				
Feb 3	(a)	Manchester C	L	2-5	Baxter 2	22,082	1	2		4	5		11		9	10		7		3			8		6				
7	(h)	Sheffield W	L	2-3	Camsell, Ferguson	9,069	1		2	4	5		11		9	10				3		7	8		6				
10	(h)	Arsenal	L	0-2		15,894	1		2	4	5		11	8	9					3		7	10		6				
17	(a)	Everton	D	1-1	Bruce	19,105	1	2		4	5		11	8	9					3		7	10		6				
24	(h)	Chelsea	D	2-2	Camsell, Jennings (pen)	12,962	1	2		4	5		11	8	9	10				3					6	7			
Mar 3	(a)	Liverpool	L	2-6	Yorston 2	25,946	1	2		4	5		11	10	9					3					6	7	8		
10	(h)	Tottenham H	D	1-1	Camsell	11,832	1	2			5	4	10		9		11			3					6	7	8		
17	(a)	Stoke C	L	0-2		20,623	1	2			5	4	7	10	9		11			3					6		8		
24	(h)	Aston Villa	L	1-2	Yorston	13,156	1	2			5	4	7	8		10	11			3					6		9		
30	(a)	Newcastle U	D	1-1	Yorston	35,142	1	2		4	5	6	7	8		10	11			3							9		
31	(h)	Sheffield U	L	1-3	Camsell	17,520	1	2		4	5			8		10	11			3							9		
Apr 2	(h)	Newcastle U	W	1-0	Warren	17,535		2		4		6	7	8	9	5	11			3							10	1	
7	(h)	Wolves	D	0-0		11,284		2		4	5	6	7		9	8	11			3							10	1	
14	(a)	Sunderland	L	0-2		12,204		2		4	5	6	7		9	8	11			3							10	1	
21	(h)	Huddersfield T	W	3-0	Baxter, Camsell, Yorston	11,042		2		4	5	6	7	8		10	11			3							9	1	
30	(a)	Portsmouth	L	1-4	Warren	13,546		2		4	5	6	7	8		10	11			3							9	1	
May 5	(h)	Leicester C	W	4-1	Yorston 2, Stuart, Warren	4,758				4	5	6	7	8			11			3			10				9	1	2
Apps							36	39	5	39	40	32	23	35	36	36	31	3	1	39	1	18	10	1	15	3	12	6	1
Goals								3					3	9	23	6	9			1		7					7		

FA Cup

Date		Opponent	Res	Score	Scorers	Att	Gibson F	Jennings J	Jarvis S	Brown WH	Griffiths TP	Martin J	Williams JJ	Bruce RF	Camsell GH	Baxter RD	Warren FW	Fenton M	Cameron K	Stuart RW	Webster M	Ferguson C	McKay J	Weightman E	Forrest W	Chadwick C	Yorston BC	Hillier EJG	Smith J	Round
Jan 13	(a)	Sunderland	D	1-1	Camsell	43,600	1	2		4	5	6	7	8	9		11			3			10							3
17	(h)	Sunderland	L	1-2	Ferguson	40,882	1	2		4	5		7	8	9	10				3		11			6					R
Apps							2	2		2	2	1	2	2	2	1	1			2		1	1		1					
Goals															1							1								

1934-35
Division 1

Date	Opponent	Res	Scorers	Att	Hillier EJG	Jennings J	Stuart RW	Brown WH	Griffiths TP	Martin J	Chadwick C	Bruce RF	Yorston BC	Baxter RD	Warren FW	Forrest W	Coleman E	Fenton M	Williams JJ	Camsell GH	Bell JN	Jarvis S	Birkett RJE	Gibson F
Aug 25 (a)	Leeds U	W 4-2	Yorston 3, Warren	15,949	1	2	3	4	5	6	7	8	9	10	11									
29 (h)	Portsmouth	D 1-1	Chadwick	17,977	1	2	3	4	5	6	7	8	9	10	11									
Sep 1 (h)	West Brom A	D 0-0		16,761	1	2	3	4	5		7	8	9	10	11	6								
5 (a)	Portsmouth	L 0-1		16,788	1	2	3	4	5		7	8	9	10	11	6								
8 (a)	Sheffield W	D 3-3	Baxter, Warren, Bruce	16,103	1	2	3	4	5		7	8	9	10	11	6								
15 (a)	Birmingham	L 0-1		15,477	1	2	3	4	5		7	8	9	10	11	6								
22 (a)	Stoke C	L 0-2		19,788	1	2	3	4				8	9	10	11	6	7							
29 (h)	Manchester C	L 1-2	Yorston	9,180	1	2	3	4				10	8	5	11	6	9	7						
Oct 6 (a)	Sunderland	D 1-1	Forrest	34,829	1	2	3	4	5			10	9		11	6	8	7						
13 (a)	Blackburn R	L 2-3	Coleman 2	12,429	1	2	3	4	5			10	9		11	6	8	7						
20 (h)	Leicester C	W 1-0	Baxter	12,363	1	2	3	4	5				9	10	11	6	8	7						
27 (a)	Derby C	L 0-2		15,561	1	2	3	4	5				9	10	11	6	8	7						
Nov 3 (h)	Preston NE	D 3-3	Fenton 3	6,572	1	2	3	4				10	9	5	11	6	8	7						
10 (a)	Tottenham H	L 1-3	Fenton	25,761	1	2	3	4	5				10			6	8	9	7	11				
17 (h)	Wolves	D 2-2	Baxter, Coleman	10,900	1	2	3	4					10	5		6	8	9	7	11				
24 (a)	Huddersfield T	L 1-3	Camsell	15,790	1	2	3	4			7			5	11	6	8	10		9				
Dec 1 (h)	Everton	W 3-2	Coleman 2, Fenton	12,914	1	2	3	4						5	11	6	10	8	7	9				
8 (a)	Grimsby T	D 2-2	Camsell 2	12,174	1	2	3		5					4	11	6	10	8	7	9				
15 (h)	Aston Villa	W 4-1	Fenton 2, Camsell 2	16,245	1	2	3		5					4	11	6	10	8	7	9				
22 (a)	Chelsea	L 1-2	Coleman	23,724	1	2	3		5					4	11	6	10	8	7	9				
26 (a)	Liverpool	D 2-2	Coleman, Camsell	45,936	1	2	3		5				7	4	11	6	10	8		9				
29 (h)	Leeds U	D 3-3	Fenton, Warren, Stuart	15,615	1	2	3		5					4	11	6	10	8	7	9				
Jan 1 (h)	Liverpool	W 2-0	Coleman 2	19,436	1	2	3		5					4	11	6	10	8	7	9				
5 (a)	West Brom A	L 3-6	Camsell 2 (1 pen), Coleman	19,599	1	2	3		5					4	11	6	10	8	7	9				
19 (h)	Sheffield W	W 5-3	Camsell, Warren 2, Martin, J.J.Williams	9,378	1	2	3	4	5	6					11		10	8	7	9				
Feb 2 (h)	Stoke C	W 2-0	Camsell 2	12,730	1	2	3	4	5	6					11		10	8	7	9				
6 (a)	Birmingham	L 2-4	Baxter, Jennings	5,729	1	2	3	4		6	7			5	11		10	8		9				
9 (a)	Manchester C	L 2-6	Camsell, Bruce	18,599	1	2	3	4		6	7	8		5	11		10			9				
16 (h)	Sunderland	D 0-0		17,416	1	2		4		6	7	8	9	5	11		10				3			
23 (h)	Blackburn R	D 3-3	Bruce, Warren, Baxter	9,108	1	2		4		6	7	8	9	5	11		10				3			
Mar 2 (a)	Leicester C	L 1-3	Chadwick	16,120	1		3	4	5		7	8		2	11	6	10			9				
9 (h)	Derby C	D 1-1	Camsell	13,642	1		3	4	5		7			6	11		10	8		9		2		
16 (a)	Preston NE	L 0-2		15,555	1		3	4		6				5	11		10	8		9		2	7	
23 (h)	Tottenham H	W 3-1	Coleman, Birkett 2	14,625	1		3	2	5	4		8		6	11		10			9			7	
30 (a)	Wolves	L 3-5	Warren, Coleman, Camsell	18,673	1		3	2	5	4		8		6	11		10			9			7	
Apr 6 (h)	Huddersfield T	W 2-1	Baxter (pen), Warren	12,570	1		3	2	5	4		8		6	11		10			9			7	
13 (a)	Everton	D 1-1	Birkett	15,214	1		3	2	5	4		8		6	11		10			9			7	
19 (a)	Arsenal	L 0-8		45,719	1	2	3	4	5			8		6	11		10		7	9				
20 (h)	Grimsby T	L 0-2		12,124	1	2	3	4	5					10	11	6	8		7	9				
22 (h)	Arsenal	L 0-1		29,171		2	3	4		6		8		5	11		10		7	9				1
27 (a)	Aston Villa	W 3-0	Yorston 2, Birkett	15,685		2	3	4		6			9	5	11		10			8			7	1
May 4 (h)	Chelsea	D 2-2	Warren, Yorston	17,505		2	3	4		6			9	5	11		10			8			7	1
Apps					39	35	40	35	29	16	12	22	19	39	39	24	36	21	14	26	2	4	7	3
Goals						1	1			1	2	3	7	6	9	1	12	8	1	14			4	

FA Cup

Date	Opponent	Res	Scorers	Att	Hillier EJG	Jennings J	Stuart RW	Brown WH	Griffiths TP	Martin J	Chadwick C	Bruce RF	Yorston BC	Baxter RD	Warren FW	Forrest W	Coleman E	Fenton M	Williams JJ	Camsell GH	Bell JN	Jarvis S	Birkett RJE	Gibson F	Round
Jan 12 (h)	Blackburn R	D 1-1	J.J.Williams	34,637	1	2	3		5					4	11	6	10	8	7	9					3
17 (a)	Blackburn R	L 0-1		32,783	1	2	3	4	5			8			11	6	10		7	9					R
Apps					2	2	2	1	2			1		1	2	2	2	1	2	2					
Goals																			1						

1935-36
Division 1

Date	Opponent	Res	Scorers	Att	Gibson F	Jennings J	Stuart RW	Brown WH	Baxter RD	Martin J	Birkett RJE	Yorston BC	Camsell GH	Coleman E	Warren FW	Griffiths TP	Fenton M	Chadwick C	Forrest W	Ferguson C	Cunliffe A	Weightman E	Ross AC	Parkin R	Hawkins GH	Higham N
Aug 31 (h)	Portsmouth	W 3-2	Camsell 2, Birkett	17,795	1	2	3	4	5	6	7	8	9	10	11											
Sep 4 (h)	Aston Villa	L 1-2	Martin	22,421	1		3	4	5	6	7	8	9	10		2	11									
7 (a)	Preston NE	W 5-0	Camsell, Chadwick, Birkett 2, Yorston	22,196	1	2	3	4	5	6	7	8	9	10				11								
9 (a)	Aston Villa	W 7-2	Coleman, Camsell 5, Birkett	19,109	1	2	3	4	5	6	7	8	9	10				11								
14 (h)	Brentford	D 0-0		38,107	1	2	3	4	5	6	7	8	9	10				11								
18 (h)	Wolves	W 4-2	Baxter (pen), Birkett 2, Camsell	15,637	1	2	3	4	5	6	7	8	9	10				11								
21 (a)	Derby C	L 2-3	Birkett, Yorston	27,170	1		3	4	5	6	7	8	9	10		2		11								
28 (h)	Everton	W 6-1	Birkett 3, Yorston, Camsell 2	19,308	1		3	4	5		7	8	9	10	11	2			6							
Oct 5 (a)	Bolton W	L 1-3	Birkett	29,910	1		3	2	5	4	7	8	9	10	11				6							
12 (h)	Huddersfield T	W 4-2	Yorston 2, Coleman, Chadwick	25,547	1		3	4	5	6	7	8	9	10		2		11								
19 (h)	Leeds U	D 1-1	Coleman	12,256	1		3	4	5	6		8	9	10	11	2		7								
26 (a)	Grimsby T	L 0-1		12,108	1		3	4	5	6		8	9	10		2		11								
Nov 2 (h)	Liverpool	D 2-2	Camsell, Birkett	18,104	1		3	2	5	4	7	8	9				10	11	6							
9 (a)	Chelsea	L 1-2	Camsell	33,408	1		3	2	5	4	7	8	9	10				11	6							
16 (h)	Blackburn R	W 6-1	Yorston, Camsell, Birkett 2, Chadwick, Coleman	14,945	1		3	2	5	4	7	8	9	10				11	6							
23 (a)	Sunderland	L 1-2	Coleman	58,902	1		3	2	5	4	7	8	9	10				11	6							
30 (h)	Manchester C	W 2-0	Camsell, Birkett	19,438	1		3	2	5	4	7	8	9	10				11	6							
Dec 9 (a)	Arsenal	L 0-2		23,365	1		3	2	5	4	7	8	9	10				11	6							
14 (h)	Birmingham	L 0-2		15,061	1		3	2	5	4		8	9	10				11	6	7						
21 (a)	Stoke C	D 1-1	Birkett	8,486	1		3	2	5	4	7	8	9	10				11	6							
26 (a)	West Brom A	L 2-5	Yorston, Camsell	25,968	1		3	2	5	4	7	8	9	10				11	6							
28 (h)	Portsmouth	L 0-1		21,320	1		3	2	5	4		8	9	10				7	6		11					
Jan 1 (h)	West Brom A	W 3-1	Camsell 3 (1 pen)	22,379	1		3	2	5	4		8	9	10				7	6		11					
4 (h)	Preston NE	W 2-0	Chadwick, Yorston	17,245	1		3	2	5	4		8	9				10	7	6		11					
18 (a)	Brentford	L 0-1		27,779	1			2	5		7	8	9				10		6		11		3	4		
29 (h)	Derby C	L 0-3		7,206	1			2	5		7		9	10			8		6		11		3	4		
Feb 1 (a)	Everton	L 2-5	Chadwick 2	26,602	1			2	5			8		10			9	7	6		11		3	4		
8 (h)	Bolton W	D 0-0		18,377	1			2	5	4	7	8	9	10					6		11		3			
19 (a)	Huddersfield T	L 1-4	Birkett	4,366	1		3	2	5		7	4	9	10					6		11				8	
22 (a)	Leeds U	W 1-0	Yorston	21,055	1		2	4	5		7	8	9	10					6		11		3			
Mar 4 (h)	Chelsea	W 4-1	Coleman, Cunliffe, Yorston, Camsell	7,968	1		3	2	5	4	7	8	9	10					6		11					
7 (a)	Manchester C	L 0-6		20,094	1		2		5	4	7	8	9	10					6		11		3			
14 (h)	Grimsby T	W 5-1	Camsell 2, Cunliffe 2, Yorston	14,174	1		3	2	5	4	7	8	9	10					6		11					
21 (a)	Blackburn R	D 2-2	Birkett, Camsell	13,779	1		3	2	5	4	7	10	9						6		11					8
28 (h)	Sunderland	W 6-0	Cunliffe, Birkett 2, Camsell, Yorston (pen), Higham	29,990	1		3	2	5	4	7	10	9						6		11					8
Apr 4 (a)	Liverpool	D 2-2	Baxter, Yorston	22,223	1		3	2	5	4	7	10	9						6		11					8
11 (h)	Arsenal	D 2-2	Birkett, Coleman	31,006	1		3	2	5	4	7	8	9	10					6		11					
13 (a)	Sheffield W	W 5-0	Camsell 4, Birkett	18,621	1		3	2	5	4	7	8	9	10					6		11					
14 (a)	Sheffield W	D 0-0		21,157	1		3	2	5	4	7	8	9	10					6		11					
18 (a)	Birmingham	L 0-1		17,072	1	2	3	4	5		7	8	9	10					6		11					
25 (h)	Stoke C	D 0-0		8,613	1	2	3	4			7	8	9	10				11	6			5				
May 2 (a)	Wolves	L 0-4		14,639	1	2	3	4			7	9		10				11	6			5				8
Apps					42	8	38	41	39	34	36	42	38	37	4	6	6	23	32	1	19	2	6	3	1	4
Goals									2	1	22	13	28	7				6			4					1

FA Cup

Date	Opponent	Res	Scorers	Att	Gibson F	Jennings J	Stuart RW	Brown WH	Baxter RD	Martin J	Birkett RJE	Yorston BC	Camsell GH	Coleman E	Warren FW	Griffiths TP	Fenton M	Chadwick C	Forrest W	Ferguson C	Cunliffe A	Weightman E	Ross AC	Parkin R	Hawkins GH	Higham N	Round
Jan 11 (h)	Southampton	W 1-0	Cunliffe	29,550	1			2	5	4	7	8	9				10		6		11	3					3
25 (h)	Clapton O	W 3-0	Camsell 2, Cunliffe	34,470	1			2	5		7	4	9	10			8		6		11		3				4
Feb 15 (h)	Leicester C	W 2-1	Camsell, Forrest	42,214	1		3	2	5		7	4	9	10			8		6		11						5
29 (a)	Grimsby T	L 1-3	Camsell	21,000	1		3	2	5	4	7	10	9	8					6		11						6
Apps					4		2	4	4	2	4	4	4	3			3		4		4	1	1				
Goals													4						1		2						

1936-37
Division 1

Date	Opponent	Result	Scorers	Att	Ferguson R	Brown WH	Stuart RW	Martin J	Baxter RD	Forrest W	Birkett RJE	Yorston BC	Camsell GH	Coleman E	Cunliffe A	Jennings J	Chadwick C	Fenton M	Higham N	Cumming DS	Cochrane T	Laking GE	Ross AC	Gibson F	Parkin R	Mannion WJ	Bryan R	Shepherdson H
Aug 29 (h)	Manchester C	W 2-0	Birkett, Yorston	23,081	1	2	3	4	5	6	7	8	9	10	11													
31 (a)	Wolves	W 1-0	Chadwick	30,209	1	4	3		5	6		8		10	11	2	7	9										
Sep 5 (a)	Portsmouth	L 1-2	Yorston (pen)	22,387	1	2	3	4	5	6		8				11		7	9	10								
9 (h)	Wolves	W 1-0	Fenton	20,550	1	2	3	4	5	6	7	8					11	9	10									
12 (h)	Chelsea	W 2-0	Birkett, Chadwick	21,278	1	2	3	4	5	6	7	8					11	9	10									
19 (a)	Stoke C	L 2-6	Camsell 2	29,206	1	2	3	4	5	6	7	8	9	10			11											
26 (h)	Charlton A	D 1-1	Yorston	22,795	1	2	3	4	5	6	7	8	9	10			11											
Oct 3 (a)	Grimsby T	L 1-5	Cunliffe	13,073	1	2	3	4	5	6	7	8	9	10	11													
10 (h)	Liverpool	D 3-3	Coleman, Cochrane, Yorston	22,858		2	3	4	5	6	7	8	9	10						1	11							
17 (h)	Sunderland	D 5-5	Camsell 3, Coleman, Birkett	36,030		4	3		5	6	7	8	9	10						1	11	2						
24 (a)	Huddersfield T	L 0-2		20,357		4	3		5	6	7	8	9	10						1	11	2						
31 (h)	Everton	W 2-0	Fenton, Birkett	23,569		4	3		5	6	7		9					8	10	1	11	2						
Nov 7 (a)	Bolton W	W 3-1	Camsell 3	18,264		4	3		5	6	7		9					8	10	1	11	2						
14 (h)	Brentford	W 3-0	Yorston, James (og), Cochrane	23,064		4	3		5	6	7	10	9					8		1	11	2						
21 (a)	Arsenal	L 3-5	Camsell, Birkett, Yorston	44,829		4	3		5	6	7	10	9					8		1	11	2						
28 (h)	Preston NE	W 2-1	Camsell 2	20,308		4	3		5	6	7		9	10				8		1	11	2						
Dec 5 (a)	Sheffield W	L 0-1		11,289		4	3		5	6	7			10				9	8	1	11	2						
12 (h)	Manchester U	W 3-2	Fenton 3	11,790		4	3		5	6	7			10				9	8	1	11	2						
19 (h)	Derby C	W 2-0	Fenton 2	16,155		4	3	6	5		7			10				9	8	1	11	2						
25 (a)	Leeds U	L 0-5		30,647		4	3	6	5			10	9			7		8			11	2	1					
26 (a)	Manchester C	L 1-2	Fenton (pen)	56,227		2	3	4	5	6			9			7		8	10		11			1				
28 (h)	Leeds U	W 4-2	Camsell, Fenton (pen), Birkett 2	14,191		2	3	4	5	6	7		9					8	10	1	11							
Jan 1 (h)	West Brom A	W 4-1	Chadwick 2, Higham, Fenton	28,231		4	3		5	6	8						7	9	10	1	11	2						
2 (h)	Portsmouth	D 2-2	Fenton 2	25,185			3		5	6	7							9	10	1	11	2		4	8			
9 (a)	Chelsea	L 0-1		30,201		4	3		5	6	7		9					8	10	1	11	2						
23 (h)	Stoke C	W 1-0	Fenton	16,445		4	3		5	6	7	10						9	8	1	11	2						
30 (a)	Charlton A	D 2-2	Higham, John Oakes (og)	16,559		4	3	6	5		7	10						9	8	1	11	2						
Feb 6 (h)	Grimsby T	D 0-0		20,457		4	3		5	6	7	10						9	8	1	11	2						
13 (a)	Liverpool	W 2-0	Fenton 2	22,459		4	3	6	5	10	7							9	8	1	11	2						
24 (a)	Sunderland	L 1-4	Camsell	32,309		4	3	6	5	10			9		7				8	1	11	2						
27 (h)	Huddersfield T	W 5-0	Martin, Camsell, Fenton, Chadwick 2	15,932		4	3	6	5	10			9				7	8		1	11	2						
Mar 6 (a)	Everton	W 3-2	Fenton, Camsell 2	30,719		4	3	6	5		7		9		11			8	10	1		2						
13 (h)	Bolton W	W 2-0	Chadwick, Camsell	20,025		4	3	6	5				9			11	7	8	10	1		2						
20 (a)	Brentford	L 1-4	Fenton (pen)	23,872		4	3	6	5				9			11	7	8	10	1		2						
26 (h)	Birmingham	W 3-1	Cochrane, Camsell, Fenton	24,958		4	3		5	6			9				7	8	10	1	11	2						
27 (h)	Arsenal	D 1-1	Fenton	44,523		4	3	6	5	10			9				7	8		1	11	2						
29 (a)	Birmingham	D 0-0		28,624			3	6	5	10			9						8	1	11	2		4	7			
Apr 3 (a)	Preston NE	L 0-2		18,942			3	6	5		7							9	10	1	11	2		4	8			
10 (h)	Sheffield W	W 2-0	Fenton, Catlin (og)	16,477		4	3	6	5	10	7		9					8		1	11	2						
17 (a)	Manchester U	L 1-2	Cochrane	17,656		4	3	6	5	10	7		9					8		1	11	2						
24 (h)	Derby C	L 1-3	Fenton	18,447		4	3		5	6	7	10	9					8		1	11	2						
May 1 (a)	West Brom A	L 1-3	Yorston	7,022		4	3	6		10	7		9					8		1	11	2						5
Apps					8	39	42	25	37	38	28	21	23	12	8	1	17	35	26	32	30	26	5	2	3	2	1	1
Goals								1			7	7	18	2	1		7	22	2		4							

3 own-goals

FA Cup

Round

Date	Opponent	Result	Scorers	Att	Ferguson R	Brown WH	Stuart RW	Martin J	Baxter RD	Forrest W	Birkett RJE	Yorston BC	Camsell GH	Coleman E	Cunliffe A	Jennings J	Chadwick C	Fenton M	Higham N	Cumming DS	Cochrane T	Laking GE	Ross AC	Gibson F	Parkin R	Mannion WJ	Bryan R	Shepherdson H	
Jan 16 (a)	Wolves	L 1-6	Birkett	38,495		2	3	4	5	6	7		9					8	10	1	11								3
Apps						1	1	1	1	1	1		1					1	1	1	1							
Goals											1																	

1937-38
Division 1

Date		Opponent	Result	Scorers	Att	Cumming DS	Laking GE	Stuart RW	Brown WH	Baxter RD	Forrest W	Birkett RJE	Fenton M	Camsell GH	Yorston BC	Cochrane T	Feguson R	Chadwick C	Higham N	Nash FC	Martin J	Hardwick GFM	Milne JV	Mannion WJ	Wardle G	Shepherdson H	Fowler HN	Murphy DA
Aug	28 (a)	Sunderland	L 1-3	Yorston	56,717	1	2	3	4	5	6	7	8	9	10	11												
Sep	1 (a)	Birmingham	L 1-3	Yorston	19,297	1	2	3	4	5	6	7	8	9	10	11												
	4 (h)	Stoke C	W 2-1	Forrest, Fenton	23,652		2	3	4	5	6		8	9	10	11	1	7										
	8 (h)	Birmingham	D 1-1	Yorston	18,831		2	3	4	5	6		8	9	10	11	1	7										
	11 (a)	Portsmouth	W 2-0	Camsell 2	21,344	1	2	3	4	5	6		8	9	10	11	7											
	13 (a)	West Brom A	L 1-3	Yorston	8,254	1	2	3	4	5	6				10	11	7	8										
	18 (h)	Chelsea	W 4-3	Fenton, Birkett, Camsell, Chadwick	19,631	1	2	3	4	5	6	7	8	9	10			11										
	25 (a)	Charlton A	L 0-1		27,782	1	2	3	4	5	6	7	8	9	10			11										
Oct	2 (h)	Preston NE	W 2-1	Camsell, Fenton	25,050		2	3	4	5	6	7	8	9	10			11		1								
	9 (a)	Grimsby T	L 1-2	Fenton	10,569	1	2	3		5	6	7	8	9	10			11			4							
	16 (a)	Derby C	D 1-1	Bell (og)	15,267	1	2	3	4	5		10	7	9				11	8		6							
	23 (h)	Manchester C	W 4-0	Cochrane, Higham, Fenton 2	18,442		2	3	4	5	6		8	9		11		7	10	1								
	30 (a)	Arsenal	W 2-1	Cochrane, Brown	39,066		2	3	4	5	6		8	9		11		7	10	1								
Nov	6 (h)	Everton	L 1-2	Birkett	25,083		2	3	4	5	6		8	9		11		7	10	1								
	13 (a)	Brentford	D 3-3	Higham, Forrest, Fenton	25,682		2	3	4	5	10	7	9					11	8	1	6							
	20 (h)	Leicester C	W 4-2	Fenton 3, Reeday (og) †	18,426		2	3	4	5	10	7	9					11	8	1	6							
	27 (a)	Huddersfield T	L 0-3		14,020		2	3		5	6	7	8	9				11	10	1	4							
Dec	4 (h)	Blackpool	D 2-2	Fenton, Camsell	12,970	1	2	3		5	6	7	8	9	10			11			4							
	18 (h)	Bolton W	L 1-2	Camsell	21,407	1	2			5	6	7	8	9					10		4	3	11					
	25 (h)	Leeds U	L 3-5	Higham, Fenton, Camsell	37,020	1	2		4	5	6	7	8	9					10			3	11					
	27 (h)	Leeds U	W 2-0	Fenton (pen), Mannion	34,640		2		4	5	6	7	8	9						1		3	11	10				
Jan	1 (h)	Sunderland	W 2-1	Mannion, Milne	*45,854		2			5	6	7	8	9						1	4	3	11	10				
	15 (a)	Stoke C	L 0-3		14,103	1	2			5	6	7	8	9				11				3		10				
	26 (h)	Portsmouth	D 0-0		12,957	1	2		4	5	6			9		11						3		10	7			
	29 (a)	Chelsea	W 1-0	Mannion	27,081	1	2			5	6			9				8			4	3	7	10				
Feb	5 (h)	Charlton A	W 3-1	Fenton, Camsell, Milne	24,687	1	2	3		5	6		8	9				11			4		7	10				
	16 (a)	Preston NE	W 2-0	Yorston 2	13,416	1	2	3		5	6	7			9	10					4		11	8				
	19 (h)	Grimsby T	W 1-0	Betmead (og)	20,156		2	3		5	6	7			9	10				1	4		11	8				
	26 (h)	Derby C	W 4-2	Fenton 2, Cochrane, Milne	21,863	1	2	3		5	6		9			10					4		7	8				
Mar	9 (a)	Manchester C	W 6-1	Cochrane 4‡, Fenton 2	16,396	1	2	3	4	5	6		9		10	11							7	8				
	12 (h)	Arsenal	W 2-1	Fenton 2	*46,747	1	2	3		5	6		9		10	11					4		7	8				
	19 (a)	Everton	D 2-2	Yorston, Higham	28,808	1	2	3			6				10	11			9		4		7	8		5		
	23 (a)	Wolves	W 1-0	Mannion	22,327	1	2	3	4		6		9		10	11							7	8		5		
	26 (h)	Brentford	L 0-1		29,339	1	2		4		6		9		10	11						3	7	8		5		
Apr	2 (a)	Leicester C	W 1-0	Cochrane	17,759	1	2	3		5	6		9		10	11							7	8			3	
	9 (h)	Huddersfield T	L 0-1		20,901		2	3	4	5	6		9			11		7	10	1				8				
	15 (h)	Liverpool	D 1-1	Cochrane	29,843	1	2	3	4	5	6		9		10	11							7	8				
	16 (a)	Blackpool	L 2-4	Yorston, Cochrane	29,822	1	2	3		5	6		9		10	11					4		7	8				
	18 (a)	Liverpool	D 1-1	Forrest	32,010	1	2	3	4	5	6		9		10	11							7	8				
	23 (h)	Wolves	L 0-3		26,085	1	2	3	4	5	6	7	9		10	11								8				
	30 (a)	Bolton W	L 1-3	Camsell	12,164	1	2						10	9		11		7						8		5	3	6
May	7 (h)	West Brom A	W 4-1	Fenton 4	12,905	1	2	3	4	5			9		10	11							7	8				6
					Apps	28	42	32	29	38	40	22	36	24	25	26	2	19	13	12	16	8	19	22	1	4	2	2
					Goals				1		3	2	24	9	8	10		1	4				3	4				

†Some sources credit Chadwick, Birkett, Fenton 2.   *Ground attendance record
‡Some sources credit Yorston with one goal, club credit Cochrane.

3 own-goals

FA Cup

Date		Opponent	Result	Scorers	Att	Cumming DS	Laking GE	Stuart RW	Brown WH	Baxter RD	Forrest W	Birkett RJE	Fenton M	Camsell GH	Yorston BC	Cochrane T	Feguson R	Chadwick C	Higham N	Nash FC	Martin J	Hardwick GFM	Milne JV	Mannion WJ	Wardle G	Shepherdson H	Fowler HN	Murphy DA	Round
Jan	8 (h)	Stockport C	W 2-0	Fenton 2 (1 pen)	34,757	1	2			5	6	7	8	9							4	3	11	10					3
	22 (a)	Nottingham F	W 3-1	Mannion, Camsell, Milne	39,055	1	2		4	5	6	7	8	9								3	11	10					4
Feb	12 (a)	York C	L 0-1		23,860	1	2	3		5	6	7	8	9							4		11	10					5
					Apps	3	3	1	1	3	3	3	3	3							2	2	3	3					
					Goals								2	1									1	1					

1938-39
Division 1

Date	Opponent	Result	Scorers	Att	Cumming DS	Laking GE	Stuart RW	Brown WH	Baxter RD	Forrest W	Milne JV	Mannion WJ	Fenton M	Yorston BC	Cochrane T	McKenzie D	Fowler HN	Higham N	Martin J	Shepherdson H	Camsell GH	Scrimshaw CT	Chadwick C	Nash FC	Murphy DA	Armes S	Butler T
Aug 27 (h) Manchester U	W 3-1	Fenton, Mannion, Cochrane	25,359	1	2	3	4	5	6	7	8	9	10	11												
31 (h) Aston Villa	D 1-1	Fenton	29,281	1	2	3		5	6	7	8	9	10	11	4											
Sep 3 (a) Stoke C	W 3-1	Mannion, Fenton, Yorston	23,475	1	2	3		5	6	7	8	9	10	11	4											
10 (h) Chelsea	D 1-1	Yorston	28,359	1	2	3		5	6	7	8	9	10	11	4											
14 (a) Liverpool	L 1-3	Fenton	25,535	1	2			5	6	7		9	10	11	4	3	8									
17 (a) Preston NE	L 1-3	Fenton (pen)	23,746	1	2				6	7	8	9	10	11	4	3			5							
24 (h) Charlton A	W 4-0	Laking, Milne, Fenton 2	20,227	1	2					7	8	9	10	11	4	3			6	5						
Oct 1 (a) Bolton W	L 1-4	Yorston	28,505	1	2		4	5		7	8	9	10	11		3			6							
8 (h) Leeds U	L 1-2	Fenton	23,009	1	2		4	5	6	7	10	8		11		3				9						
15 (h) Grimsby T	W 3-2	Yorston 2, Camsell	21,720	1			2	5	6	7	8		10	11	4					9	3					
22 (a) Sunderland	W 2-1	Camsell, Yorston (pen)	39,440	1			2	5	6	7	8		10	11	4					9	3					
29 (h) Wolves	W 1-0	Cochrane	24,624	1			2	5	6	7	8		10	11	4					9	3					
Nov 5 (a) Everton	L 0-4		35,683	1			2	5	6	7		8	10	11	4					9	3					
12 (h) Huddersfield T	W 4-1	Fenton 3, Yorston	19,630	1			2	5	6	7	8	9	10	11	4						3					
19 (a) Portsmouth	D 1-1	Yorston	21,463	1			2	5	6	7	8	9	10	11	4						3					
26 (h) Arsenal	D 1-1	Higham	29,047	1			2	5	6	7		9	10	11	4		8				3					
Dec 3 (a) Brentford	L 1-2	Fenton	21,746	1			2	5	6	7	8	9	10	11	4						3					
10 (h) Blackpool	W 9-2	Chadwick 2, Mannion 4, Fenton 3	17,166	1		3	2	5	6	7	8	9	10		4							11				
17 (a) Derby C	W 4-1	Fenton 2 (1 pen), Yorston, Chadwick	17,168	1		3	2	5	6	7	8	9	10		4							11				
24 (a) Manchester U	D 1-1	Chadwick	33,235	1	2	3	4	5	6	7	8	9	10									11				
26 (a) Birmingham	L 1-2	Fenton	17,953	1		3	4	5	6	7	8	9	10						2			11				
27 (h) Birmingham	D 2-2	Fenton, Yorston	33,534	1		3	4	5	6	7	8	9	10						2			11				
31 (h) Stoke C	W 5-1	Chadwick 2, Fenton, Mannion, Milne	20,092			3	2	5	6	7	8	9	10				4					11	1			
Jan 2 (h) Liverpool	W 3-0	Fenton 2, Milne	25,309			3	2	5		7	8	9	10				4					11	1	6		
14 (a) Chelsea	L 2-4	Higham, Camsell	26,750	1	2			5	4	7			10				8			9	3	11		6		
25 (h) Preston NE	D 2-2	Fenton, Higham	9,262	1		3	2	5	4	7	8	9			11		10							6		
28 (a) Charlton A	L 0-3		23,473	1	2	3	4		5	7	8	9			11			10						6		
Feb 4 (h) Bolton W	L 1-2	Fenton	16,416	1		3		2			10	11	8	9				4	5					6	7	
11 (a) Leeds U	W 1-0	Mannion	18,273	1		3	2	5	6		10	8	9	11	4							7				
18 (a) Grimsby T	W 2-0	Fenton, Chadwick	11,717	1		3	2	5	6		10	8	9	11	4							7				
25 (h) Sunderland	W 3-0	Fenton 2, Chadwick	23,882	1		3	2	5	6		10	8	9	11	4							7				
Mar 8 (a) Wolves	L 1-6	Fenton	20,938	1		3	2	5	6		10	8	9	11	4							7				
11 (h) Everton	D 4-4	Chadwick, Yorston, Milne, Fenton	20,014	1		3	2	5	6	11	8	9	10		4							7				
18 (a) Huddersfield T	W 1-0	Camsell	16,011	1		3	2	5		11	8		10		4					9		7		6		
29 (h) Portsmouth	W 8-2	Camsell 2, Chadwick, Mannion 3, Forrest, Yorston	6,116	1		3	2		6	11	8		10		4				5	9		7				
Apr 1 (a) Arsenal	W 2-1	Mannion, Camsell	34,669	1		3	2		6	11	8		10		4				5	9		7				
8 (h) Brentford	W 3-1	Camsell 2, Chadwick	18,191			3	2	5	6	11	8		10		4					9		7	1			
10 (h) Leicester C	W 3-2	Camsell, Mannion, McKenzie	19,764			3	2			11	8		10		4				5	9		7	1	6		
11 (a) Leicester C	L 3-5	Fenton 2, Mannion	12,143	1		3	2				8	9	10		4			5				11		6	7	
15 (a) Blackpool	L 0-4		13,733	1		3	2	5	6		8	9	10	11				4							7	
22 (h) Derby C	W 2-0	Fenton 2 (1 pen)	13,673	1		3	2	5	6	7	8	9		11				10				4				
May 6 (a) Aston Villa	D 1-1	Fenton (pen)	20,149	1		3	2	5	6	11	8	9	10		4											7
Apps				38	25	16	34	33	37	40	38	33	33	24	28	5	6	5	9	11	9	19	4	10	3	2
Goals					1				1	4	14	34	12	2	1		3			10		11				

FA Cup

Date	Opponent	Result	Scorers	Att	Cumming DS	Laking GE	Stuart RW	Brown WH	Baxter RD	Forrest W	Milne JV	Mannion WJ	Fenton M	Yorston BC	Cochrane T	McKenzie D	Fowler HN	Higham N	Martin J	Shepherdson H	Camsell GH	Scrimshaw CT	Chadwick C	Nash FC	Murphy DA	Armes S	Butler T	Round
Jan 7 (h) Bolton W	D 0-0		32,790	1		3	2	5	6	7	8	9	10				4					11					3
11 (a) Bolton W	D 0-0‡		16,981	1		3	2	5	4	7	8	9	10						6			11					R
16 (n†) Bolton W	W 1-0	Fenton	25,577	1		3	2	5	4	7	8	9							10			11	6				2R
21 (h) Sunderland	L 0-2		*51,080	1		3	2	5	4	7	8	9							10			11	6				4
Apps				4		4	4	4	4	4	4	4	2				1		2			4	3				
Goals												1														

‡After extra-time. †Played at Elland Road, Leeds.   *Ground attendance record

1939-40
Division 1

				Att	Cummings DS	Laking GE	Stuart RW	McKenzie D	Baxter RD	Forrest W	Chadwick C	Yorston BC	Fenton M	Mannion WJ	Milne JV	Camsell GH	Murphy DA	Miller D
Aug 26 (a)	Aston Villa	L 0-2		32,427	1	2	3	4	5	6	7	8	9	10	11			
30 (a)	Liverpool	L 1-4	Fenton	16,762	1	2	3	4	5	6	11		9	8	7	10		
Sep 2 (h)	Stoke C	D 2-2	Fenton 2	12,298	1	2	3	4	5		7	10	9	8			6	11
			Apps		3	3	3	3	3	2	3	2	3	3	2	1	1	1
			Goals										3					

North Eastern Regional League

				Att	Cummings	Laking	Stuart	McKenzie	Baxter	Forrest	Chadwick	Yorston	Fenton	Mannion	Milne	Camsell	Murphy DA	Miller	Brown	Martin	Armes	Hardwick	Shepherdson	Heywood	Fowler	Murphy TE	Copping	Murphy GJ	Robinson	McMahon	Stobbart	Ainsworth
Oct 21 (a)	York C	W 3-1	Fenton 2 (1 pen), Camsell	4,500	1		3	4		5	11		9	8		10			2	6	7											
28 (h)	Huddersfield T	D 2-2	Mannion, Fenton	5,000	1		2			6	11		9	8		10		4				7	3	5								
Nov 11 (a)	Bradford	L 0-3		5,000			3			6	7		9	8			11	4	5						1	2	10					
25 (h)	Newcastle U	L 1-2	Camsell	4,000	1		3				11		10	8		9	2	4						5			7	6				
Dec 2 (a)	Hull C	L 0-3		3,000	1		2				6	11	9				10	4	5		3						7	8				
9 (h)	Halifax T	W 3-1	Fenton, Forrest, Camsell	1,200	1		3			10		11	8			9		4	6				5				7		2			
16 (h)	Darlington	W 8-1	Mannion 2, Camsell, Chadwick, Fenton 4	1,000	1		3			6		11	10	8		9		4	5								7		2			
23 (a)	Leeds U	L 1-3	T.E.Murphy	4,500	1		3			6		11	10	8		9		4								2	7		5			
Jan 6 (h)	Bradford C	W 3-0	Fenton, Mannion, Chadwick	2,000	1		3			10		11	9	8				4	6			2					7		5			
Feb 24 (a)	Huddersfield T	L 2-4	McMahon, Fenton	2,835	1		3			10			8			9		4	6							2	7		5	11		
Mar 2 (h)	Hartlepools U	W 2-0	Fenton, McMahon		1		3			6			9				7	4				2				10		8	5	11		
9 (h)	Bradford	D 3-3	Fenton 2, T.E.Murphy		1		3			6			9	8	7			4				2				10			5	11		
23 (a)	Newcastle U	W 5-3	Fenton 3, Forrest 2	9,410	1		3			10			9	8				4	6							2	7		5	11		
25 (a)	Darlington	L 0-8		5,497	1					10			9	8				4	6			3	2				7		5	11		
30 (a)	Hull C	L 2-3	Fenton 2	1,600	1		3			10			9	8	11			4	6							2	7		5			
Apr 6 (h)	Halifax T	D 1-1	G.Murphy	4,000	1		3			6			9	8	11			4								2	10	7	5			
13 (h)	Leeds U	D 1-1	Fenton	1,200	1		3			6			9				7	4					5			2	10			11	8	
May 18 (a)	Bradford C	W 4-1	Fenton 2, Stobbart, Mannion	1,028	1					6			8				7	2								3	10		5	11	9	4
25 (a)	Hartlepools U	L 1-2	Fenton	1,000	1					6			8	11	7		2	4								3	10		5		9	
Jun 5 (h)	York C	W 6-1	Stobbart 4, T.E.Murphy, Camsell	1,500	1					6			8	11	7		2	4								3	10		5		9	
			Apps		19		16	1		19	9		19	12	8	10		2	16	17	2	3	8	1	10	18	1	3	14	7	4	1
			Goals							3	2		22	5		5										3		1		2	5	

League North Cup

				Att	Cummings	Laking	Stuart	McKenzie	Baxter	Forrest	Chadwick	Yorston	Fenton	Mannion	Milne	Camsell	Murphy DA	Miller	Brown	Martin	Armes	Hardwick	Shepherdson	Heywood	Fowler	Murphy TE	Copping	Murphy GJ	Robinson	McMahon	Stobbart	Ainsworth	Round
Apr 20 (h)	Grimsby T	W 4-1	Fenton, Milne, D.A.Murphy, T.E.Murphy	7,987	1		3		5	6			9	8	7	11	2	4								10							1/1
27 (a)	Grimsby T	L 1-3	Fenton	4,000	1		3		5	6			9		7	11	2	4								10				8			1/2
May 4 (h)	Newcastle U	D 2-2	Stobbart, Fenton	10,229	1		3		5	6			9		7	11	2	4								10					8		2/1
11 (a)	Newcastle U	L 1-2	Fenton	15,300	1					10	11		9		7	6	2	4								3	8		5				2/2
			Apps		4		3		3	4	1		4	1	4	4	4	4								4	1		1	1	1		
			Goals										4		1		1									1					1		

Guest players:
W.Ainsworth, W.Copping (Leeds United), A.E.Heywood (Sunderland), H.McMahon (Sunderland).

1940-41
Football League North

Date		Opponent	Result	Scorers	Att	Cumming DS	Brown WH	Wilson A	Busby M	Forrest W	Meek J	Monro AD	Robinson J	Stobbart GC	Murphy TE	Simpson R	Gorman J	Martin J	Camsell GH	Mould W	Peppitt S	Ormston A	Smith H	Baker F	Fenton M	Mannion WJ	Shepherdson H	Butler F	Hardisty JRE	Clayton S	Johnson A	Hardwick GFM	Gillies J	Murphy DA	Cochrane T	McCabe JJ
Aug	31 (a)	York C	L 3-4	Simpson 2, Stobbart	2,700	1	2	3	4	5	6	7	8	9	10	11																				
Sep	7 (h)	York C	W 2-1	Stobbart 2	2,300	1	2		4	6		7		9	10	11	3		8	5																
	14 (a)	Newcastle U	L 0-3		5,700	1	2		4	6				9	10	11	3				5	7	8													
	21 (h)	Newcastle U	W 3-2	Robinson 2 (1 pen), Stobbart	3,300	1	2		4	6			8	9	10	7	3			5									11							
	28 (a)	Grimsby T	W 3-1	T.E.Murphy, Stobbart 2	1,500	1	2		4	6			10	9	8	11	3		7	5																
Oct	5 (h)	Sheffield W	W 5-4	Stobbart 4, Simpson	2,300	1	2		4	10			8	9	8	11	3	6		5	7															
	12 (a)	Bradford	W 2-0	Danskin (og), Stobbart	1,768	1	2		4	10			8	9	8	11	3	6		5	7															
	19 (h)	Bradford	W 6-2	Fenton 2, Stobbart 2, Simpson, Peppitt	3,000		2		4	6				9		11	3	5			7		1		8	10										
	26 (h)	Chesterfield	L 0-3		2,500	1	2		4					9	8	11		6			5	7					10									
Nov	2 (a)	Sheffield W	L 3-6	Simpson, Stobbart, Shepherdson	1,500	1	2		4					9	8			6			7						3	5								
	9 (a)	Leeds U	L 1-2	Stobbart	1,500	1	2			6				9	8	11	3			5	7								4							
	16 (h)	York C	W 6-4	Stobbart 3, Simpson, Robinson, Clayton	1,700		2			6			10	9		7	3				5		1			8			4	11						
	23 (a)	Bradford C	L 2-3	Baker, Ormston	1,468	1	2			6				9		7	3				5	10		11					4	8						
Dec	7 (h)	Doncaster R	D 2-2	Stobbart, Robinson	1,000	1	2			6			10	9		11	3			7	5					8			4							
	14 (h)	Grimsby T	W 2-1	Stobbart, Forrest	700	1	2		6	10				9		11	3				5					8			4							
	25 (a)	Newcastle U	W 3-1	Fenton 2, Stobbart	4,000	1				6			8	7		11	3				5				9	10			4		2					
	28 (a)	Doncaster R	L 0-5		3,313	1				6			8	7	11					5					9	10			4		2	3				
Feb	1 (a)	Newcastle U	L 2-6	Stobbart, T.E.Murphy	4,000	1	6							9	10	7	3			5						8			4		2		11			
	8 (h)	Newcastle U	W 4-3	Forrest, Gillies, Stobbart, Busby	2,000	1			6	10				9			3			5	7					8			4		2		11			
Apr	5 (a)	Hull C	W 8-0	Simpson, Cochrane, Stobbart, Camsell 5	2,000	1								8		7	3	5	9							10			4		2				11	6
	19 (a)	Barnsley	L 2-3	Stobbart 2		1				6				9		7	3														2				10	
	26 (h)	Barnsley	W 3-2	Simpson, Forrest, Russell	1,500	1			4	10				9		7		6										5			2				11	
May	3 (a)	Halifax T	L 2-4	Camsell 2		1			4					8		7	3	6	9								10		5		2				11	
	24 (a)	York C	W 4-2	Forrest 3, Cochrane	2,000	1				10				9		7		6											4		2				11	8
			Apps			21	15	1	13	19	1	2	5	24	13	22	18	13	7	13	6	2	3	2	4	9	1	4	10	2	9	1	2		5	2
			Goals						1	6			4	26	2	8			7		1	1		1	4			1				1		1	2

1 own-goal

War Cup

Date		Opponent	Result	Scorers	Att	Cumming DS	Brown WH	Wilson A	Busby M	Forrest W	Meek J	Monro AD	Robinson J	Stobbart GC	Murphy TE	Simpson R	Gorman J	Martin J	Camsell GH	Mould W	Peppitt S	Ormston A	Smith H	Baker F	Fenton M	Mannion WJ	Shepherdson H	Butler F	Hardisty JRE	Clayton S	Johnson A	Hardwick GFM	Gillies J	Murphy DA	Cochrane T	McCabe JJ
Feb	15 (a)	Huddersfield T	D 2-2	Gillies 2	3,000				4	6				8		7	3	5					1		9	10				2			11			
Mar	1 (h)	Huddersfield T	W 4-2	Fenton 3, Busby (pen)	5,221		2		6	5				8		11	3					7	1		9	10			4							
	8 (h)	Leeds U	W 2-0	Fenton 2	5,800	1	2			6				8		11	3	5				7			9	10			4							
	15 (h)	Leeds U	D 2-2	Stobbart, Mannion (pen)	5,600	1	2			4				8		11	3	5				7			9	10							6			
	22 (h)	Newcastle U	L 0-1		12,799	1				6				8		7	3	5							9	10	2		4				11			
	29 (a)	Newcastle U	L 0-3		12,397	1			4	6				8			3	5				7			9	10	2									11
			Apps			4	3		3	6				6		5	6	5				4	2		6	6	2		3		1		1	2		1
			Goals						1					1											5	1							2			

West Riding Cup

Date		Opponent	Result	Scorers	Att	Cumming DS	Brown WH	Wilson A	Busby M	Forrest W	Meek J	Monro AD	Robinson J	Stobbart GC	Murphy TE	Simpson R	Gorman J	Martin J	Camsell GH	Mould W	Peppitt S	Ormston A	Smith H	Baker F	Fenton M	Mannion WJ	Shepherdson H	Butler F	Hardisty JRE	Clayton S	Johnson A	Hardwick GFM	Gillies J	Murphy DA	Cochrane T	McCabe JJ
Jan	11 (h)	Bradford C	W 8-2	Peppitt 4, Stobbart, Mannion, Busby, Forrest	1,000	1			6	10				9		11	3				5	7				8			4		2					
	18 (h)	Bradford	W 5-3	Hardisty, Busby, Simpson, Stobbart, Forrest		1			6	10				9		11	3				5	7				8			4		2					
May	17 (h)	Leeds U	W 3-2	Nevins 2, Stobbart	3,400	1			6	10				9		7	3	5											4		2					
			Apps			3			3	3				3		3	3	1			2	2				2			3		3					
			Goals						2	2				3		1					4					1			1							

In the Football League North R.W.Stuart played number 3 against Chesterfield (h); A.W.Hepworth played number 10 against Sheffield Wednesday (a); H.McMahon played number 11 against Sheffield Wednesday (a); S.Pearson played number 10 against Leeds United (a); J.O.Spuhler played number 7 against Grimsby Town (h); H.Ferrier played number 3 against Newcastle United (a); J.W.Russell played number 10 against Hull City (a) and number 8 against Barnsley (a & h, scoring once); R.S.Woffinden played number 4 against Barnsley (a); R.E.Gilbraith played number 5 against Barnsley (a) and York City (a); E.Bray played number 11 against Barnsley (a); H.N.Fowler played number 3 against Barnsley (h) and York City (a). In the West Riding Cup J.W.Russell played number 8 and L.Nevins played number 11 against Leeds United (h), scoring twice.

Guest players:
F.Baker (Stoke City), E.Bray (Barnsley), M.Busby (Liverpool), F.Butler (Smith's Dock), S.Clayton (Notts County), T.Cochrane (Bradford), H.Ferrier (Barnsley), J.Gillies (Clyde), J.Gorman (Sunderland), J.R.E.Hardisty (Bishop Auckland), A.Johnson (Norwich City), H.McMahon (Sunderland), J.Meek (Swansea Town), A.D.Monro (Blackpool), W.Mould (Stoke City), L.Nevins (Newcastle United), A.Ormston (Stoke City), S.C.Pearson (Manchester United), S.Peppitt (Stoke City), J.Robinson (Sheffield Wednesday), J.W.Russell (Norwich City), R.Simpson (Darlington), J.O.Spuhler (Sunderland), A.Wilson (South Bank East End), R.S.Woffenden (Barnsley).

1941-42
League North (First Championship)

Player columns (left to right): Cumming DS, Johnson A, Ferrier H, McCabe JJ, Martin J, Forrest W, Simpson R, Mannion WJ, Camsell GH, Robinson J, Cochrane T, Fowler HN, Murphy DA, Stobbart GC, Kinnear D, Shepherdson H, Boyes W, Sherwood HW, Brown WH, Stuart RW, Kirk J, Hardisty JRE, Warburton A, Wright RCA, Kelly TW, Towers J, Knight G, Arran R, Blenkinsopp TW, Reid JDJ, Weston RP

Date	V	Opponent	Res	Score	Scorers	Att	Cum	Joh	Fer	McC	Mar	For	Sim	Man	Cam	Rob	Coc	Fow	Mur	Sto	Kin	She	Boy	Sher	Bro	Stu	Kirk	Har	War	Wri	Kel	Tow	Kni	Arr	Ble	Reid	Wes
Aug 30	(h)	Huddersfield T	W	3-1	Mannion, Camsell, Robinson	3,600	1	2	3	4	5	6	7	8	9	10	11																				
Sep 6	(a)	Huddersfield T	W	4-2	Robinson, Cochrane, Camsell 2	2,623	1	2	3	4	5	6	7	8	9	10	11																				
13	(a)	York C	L	5-9	Robinson 2, Stobbart, Camsell 2	3,600	1		3	4			7		9	10	11	2	6	8		5															
20	(h)	York C	W	5-2	Robinson 3, Kinnear, Camsell	4,900	1	2	3	4	5	6	7		9	8	11				10																
27	(h)	Gateshead	D	1-1	Robinson	5,900	1	2	3	4	5	6	7	8	9	10	11																				
Oct 4	(a)	Gateshead	L	1-4	Camsell	7,000	1		3	4	5	6	7	8	9	10						2	11														
11	(a)	Sunderland	D	4-4	Robinson (pen), Forrest, Stobbart 2	10,000	1	2	3	4	6	10	7			8				9		5	11														
18	(h)	Sunderland	D	2-2	Stobbart, Simpson	10,000	1			4	5		7	8			10			9		6	11	2	3												
25	(h)	Bradford	L	0-2		4,000	1			4	5		7	8						9		10				3	2	6									
Nov 1	(h)	Bradford	L	0-1		4,000	1	2	3	4			7		5	8						6		9					11		10						
8	(a)	Leeds U	W	3-2	Kinnear 2, Warburton	2,000	1		3	4	5	10	7				11		2		9								8	6							
15	(h)	Leeds U	L	1-2	Warburton	3,300	1		3		4	10	7				11				9	5				2			8	6							
22	(a)	Barnsley	L	1-3	Towers	3,000	1	5			6	10	7		9				2										4	8							
29	(h)	Barnsley	W	3-2	Cochrane, Forrest, Kinnear	2,000	1		3		4	6	7		9		11		10					2					8								
Dec 6	(h)	Newcastle U	L	0-7		3,000	1			4	3	6			9		11		8					2						5	10						
13	(a)	Newcastle U	L	4-7	Towers, Simpson, McCabe, Reid	8,920		2		4		6	7				11							3								8	10	1		5	9
20	(a)	Bradford C	L	1-5	Towers	1,603				4		6	7	8							2			3								11	10	1		5	9
25	(h)	Bradford C	W	6-0	Dawson 4, Towers, Reid (pen)	3,000				4			7	8										3								11	10	1	2	5	6
					Apps		15	8	11	15	14	13	17	9	9	8	10	2	3	5	5	4	2	4	1	2	7	1	3	2	2	5	4	3	3	3	1
					Goals					1		2	2	1	7	9	2			4	4								2			4				2	

League Cup (Qualifying Competition, also included in Second Championship analysis)

Date	V	Opponent	Res	Score	Scorers	Att	Cum	Joh	Fer	McC	Mar	For	Sim	Man	Cam	Rob	Coc	Fow	Mur	Sto	Kin	She	Boy	Sher	Bro	Stu	Kirk	Har	War	Wri	Kel	Tow	Kni	Arr	Ble	Reid	Wes
Dec 27	(a)	Sunderland	L	0-6		9,000	1		3	4		5	7	8	9																	11	10		2		6
Jan 3	(a)	Sunderland	W	3-0	Taylor, Stobbart 2	5,000	1	2				6					11	4	7													10					
10	(a)	Bradford	D	1-1	Laking	2,000	1					6	7				11	3	9													10					
17	(h)	Bradford	L	1-2	Dawson					4		6					11		7			2										10	3				
31	(h)	York C	D	3-3	Cochrane 2, Towers	2,000		2			5	6	7				11	3														10	5				
Feb 14	(a)	Gateshead	W	3-1	Taylor 2, Dawson	2,500		2				3	6	7			11		9													10	5				
21	(h)	Newcastle U	W	4-1	Taylor 3 (1 pen), Cochrane	2,600		2				3	6	8			11		7													10	5				
28	(a)	Newcastle U	D	1-1	Taylor	7,400						2	6	7			11		9													10					
Mar 14	(h)	Gateshead	W	7-1	Stobbart 4, Cochrane 2, Dawson	3,500		2				4	6	7			11	3	9													10	5				
21	(a)	York C	D	1-1	Stobbart	4,058			3			4	6	7	10		11		9														5				
					Apps		3	5	2	2	6	10	7	2	2		9	1	3	8								1				9	1		6		1
					Goals							5					7															1					

League North (Second Championship)

Date	V	Opponent	Res	Score	Scorers	Att	Cum	Joh	Fer	McC	Mar	For	Sim	Man	Cam	Rob	Coc	Fow	Mur	Sto	Kin	She	Boy	Sher	Bro	Stu	Kirk	Har	War	Wri	Kel	Tow	Kni	Arr	Ble	Reid	Wes
Mar 28	(a)	Sunderland	W	2-1	Camsell, Stobbart	3,500			3		4	6	7	10			11		9			5															
Apr 4	(h)	Bradford	W	3-2	Taylor 3 (1 pen)	5,600			3		2	6	7		8		11		9														5				
6	(a)	Bradford	L	0-2		6,000					6	10	7				11		9														4				
11	(h)	Newcastle U	L	2-3	Dawson 2	3,000		2			3	6	7				11		9														5				
18	(a)	Newcastle U	L	1-3	Towers	4,500					6						11		9					2		4						10					
25	(h)	Leeds U	L	2-3	Dawson (pen), Johnson	2,500					5	6					11		9													10					
May 9	(a)	Leeds U	W	2-1	Forrest, Dawson	2,000	2	3			5	6	7		9		11															10					
16	(a)	York C	L	1-4	Camsell	4,011	2				5	6	7		9		11															10					
					Apps		3	3			7	8	6		4		8		6			1		1		1						5	3				
					Goals			1				1			2				1													1					

In the League North (First Championship) T.Butler played number 5 against Huddersfield Town (a); G.Stephenson played number 11 against Bradford (h); T.Mulroy played number 3 against Barnsley (a); H.Gray played number 11 against Barnsley (a); R.B.Morris played number 5 against Barnsley (h); D.McKerrell played number 7 against Newcastle United (h); T.Dawson played number 9 against Bradford City (h), scoring four goals. In the League Cup (Qualifying Competition) J.Denmark played number 5 against Sunderland (h); T.Dawson played number 9 against Sunderland (h), Bradford (h), scoring once, and York City (h), number 4 against Gateshead (a), scoring once, and Newcastle United (h & a), number 8 against Gateshead (h), scoring once, and York City (h); G.F.M.Hardwick played number 3 against Sunderland (h) and Newcastle United (a); P.T.Taylor played number 8 against Sunderland (h), scoring once, Bradford (a & h), York City (h), Gateshead (a), scoring twice, and Newcastle United (h) and number 9 against Newcastle United (h), scoring three goals; G.E.Laking played number 2 against Bradford (a), scoring once, and York City (a); R.E.Gilbraith played number 4 against Bradford (a) and York City (h) and number 5 against Bradford (h); M.Y.Middleton played number 1 against York City (h & a), Gateshead (a & h) and Newcastle United (h & a); R.D.Baxter played number 5 against Newcastle United (a); J.Yeats played number 5 against Bradford (a); H.Smith played number 1 against Bradford (h); In the League North (Second Championship) T.Dawson played number 8 against Sunderland (a), Bradford (a), Newcastle United (h, scoring twice, & a), York City (a) and Leeds United (a), scoring once, and number 4 against Bradford (h) and Leeds United (h), scoring once; P.T.Taylor played number 10 against Bradford (h), scoring three goals; G.E.Laking played number 2 against Bradford (a); R.E.Gilbraith played number 4 against Newcastle United (h) and Leeds United (a); M.Y.Middleton played number 1 against all Second Championship opponents; R.D.Baxter played number 5 against Bradford (a) and Newcastle United (a); W.B.Price played number 4 against York City (a) and number 3 against Leeds United (h); G.Hepplewhite played number 2 against Sunderland (a) and number 2 against Leeds United (h); R.G.Jones played number 3 against Bradford (a); D.R.Graham played number 3 against York City (a); W.K.McLean played number 3 against Newcastle United (a); S.Rickaby played number 7 against Newcastle United (a); R.J.E.Birkett played number 7 against Leeds United (h); T.Johnson played number 8 against Leeds United (h).

Guest Players
R.Arran (South Bank Juniors), R.J.E.Birkett (Newcastle United), T.W.Blenkinsopp (Grimsby Town), W.Boyes (Everton), T.Cochrane (Bradford), T.Dawson (Charlton Athletic), J.Denmark (Newcastle United), H.Ferrier (Barnsley), D.R.Graham (Leicester City), H.Gray (Barnsley), J.R.E.Hardisty (Bishop Auckland), G.Hepplewhite (Huddersfield Town), A.Johnson (Norwich City), R.G.Jones (York City), T.W.Kelly (Darlington), D.Kinnear (East Fife), J.Kirk (Clyde), G.Knight (Burnley), D.McKerrell (East Fife), W.K.McLean (South Bank Juniors), M.Y.Middleton (Plymouth Argyle), T.Mulroy (South Bank), W.B.Price (Tranmere Rovers), J.D.J.Reid (Stockport County), S.Rickaby (South Bank Juniors), J.Robinson (Sheffield Wednesday), J.W.Russell (Sunderland), A.W.Sherwood (Reading), R.Simpson (Darlington), G.Stephenson, P.T.Taylor (Preston North End), J.Towers (Darlington), A.Warburton (Queen's Park Rangers), R.P.Weston (Plymouth Argyle), R.C.A.Wright (Charlton Athletic).

1942-43

League North (First Championship)

Date		Opponent	Result	Scorers	Att	Middleton MY	Johnson A	Stuart RW	Hardisty JRE	Park W	Forrest W	Owen W	Dawson T	Stobbart GC	Towers J	Simpson R	Burchell GS	Wharton G	Martin J	Shepherdson H	Kearney SF	Murphy DA	Brown WH	Brown RCA	Wilson K	Warburton A	Nicholson WE	Sargent F	Osborne F	Douglass PG	Harrington DJA	McMahon H	Gilbraith RE	Franklin JL	Connor J	Rudkin TW
Aug 29	(a)	Leeds U	W 1-0	Simpson	3,000	1	2	3	4	5	6	7	8	9	10	11																				
Sep 5	(h)	Leeds U	W 2-0	Simpson, Dawson	3,500	1		3	4	5	6	7		9	10	11			2	8																
" 12	(a)	Bradford	D 0-0		3,500	1	2	3		5	6		8	9	10	11			4	7																
" 19	(h)	Bradford	D 2-2	Simpson, Owen	4,000	1	2	3	4			7		9	10	11				8	6	5														
" 26	(a)	York C	D 2-2	Dawson, Stobbart	3,448	1	2	3	4	5		7	8	9	10	11						6														
Oct 3	(h)	York C	L 2-3	Dawson, Kearney	3,500	1			4	5	6		8		10	11	2	3	7		9															
" 10	(h)	Bradford C	L 2-3	Wharton, Kearney	3,000	1		3	4	5			8		10	7	2	6			9	11														
" 17	(a)	Bradford C	W 3-2	Dawson, Stobbart, Wharton	2,000	1		3		5			8	9	10	11	2	6	7				4													
" 24	(h)	Huddersfield T	D 2-2	Simpson, Stobbart	2,500	1	2				6		8	9	10	7				5							3	4	11							
" 31	(a)	Huddersfield T	L 1-4	Simpson	3,155	1	2			5	6		8		10	7		4	3	9									11							
Nov 7	(a)	Sunderland	L 1-4	Wharton (pen)	8,500	1		2	4	5	6			9	10	11		3	7										8							
" 14	(h)	Sunderland	L 3-4	Wharton 2 (1 pen), Stobbart	5,500	1		3	4	5			8	9	10	7	2	6	11																	
" 21	(a)	Newcastle U	L 0-3		7,000	1		2	4		6		8	9	10	11		5								3	7									
" 28	(h)	Newcastle U	L 1-6	Hardisty	3,500	1			4	5	6		2			7		3															8	9	10	11
Dec 5	(a)	Gateshead	L 0-5		2,000	1		6	5			4		8	7			2								3								9	10	11
" 12	(h)	Gateshead	L 2-3	Stobbart 2		1		4	5	6			9			7	3	2	8															10	11	
" 19	(h)	Sunderland	L 2-7	Stobbart, Dawson (pen)	2,000	1	3		5			4	9	8				2						6				7						10	11	
" 25	(a)	Sunderland	W 4-0	Harrington, Stobbart, Wilson 2		1				2	9	6	7										3		5	11					10				4	8
Apps						18	6	11	12	14	10	4	16	11	16	17	5	11	13	1	4	2	2	3	3	1	2	2	1	2	5	4	1	1
Goals									1			1	5	8		5		5			2				2					1			

League Cup (Qualifying Competition)

Date		Opponent	Result	Scorers	Att	Middleton MY	Johnson A	Stuart RW	Hardisty JRE	Park W	Forrest W	Owen W	Dawson T	Stobbart GC	Towers J	Simpson R	Burchell GS	Wharton G	Martin J	Shepherdson H	Kearney SF	Murphy DA	Brown WH	Brown RCA	Wilson K	Warburton A	Nicholson WE	Sargent F	Osborne F	Douglass PG	Harrington DJA	McMahon H	Gilbraith RE	Franklin JL	Connor J	Rudkin TW
Dec 26	(a)	Newcastle U	L 2-3	Stobbart, Wilson	13,300	1				6		2	9	8	7					3		5	11							10	4					
Jan 2	(h)	Newcastle U	L 3-7	Stobbart, Franklin, Dawson	2,300	1	2		5			8	9		7	4				6										11		10				
" 9	(h)	Sunderland	W 4-1	Franklin, Carr 2, Stobbart	2,700	1		3				4	9		7		6	2				5								11		8				
" 16	(a)	Sunderland	L 0-7		6,000	1						4	9	10			6					2	5			7				11		8	3			
" 23	(h)	Gateshead	L 2-3	Wharton, Rudkin	3,500	1			6			9		10		8	4					2	5			7				11				3		11
" 30	(a)	Gateshead	L 0-6		3,400	1			6			9		10	7	4	2		3		5									8						11
Feb 6	(h)	Huddersfield T	L 1-2	Dawson	2,000				3	6	8					9	4	2			5	11		7				10								
" 13	(a)	Huddersfield T	L 0-5		3,544	1	2	3			4			7		6						11	9					10		8						
" 20	(h)	York C	L 1-5	Warburton	2,700		3					7	10			4	6						2	9				11		8						
" 27	(a)	York C	L 0-6		5,241		3		6					10			4						11	9						8						
Apps						7	4		6	3		8	5	6	5	5	8	2		3	2	7	4	3		3		7		1	7	2	2		
Goals												2	3										1							2		1	

League North (Second Championship)

Date		Opponent	Result	Scorers	Att	Middleton MY	Johnson A	Stuart RW	Hardisty JRE	Park W	Forrest W	Owen W	Dawson T	Stobbart GC	Towers J	Simpson R	Burchell GS	Wharton G	Martin J	Shepherdson H	Kearney SF	Murphy DA	Brown WH	Brown RCA	Wilson K	Warburton A	Nicholson WE	Sargent F	Osborne F	Douglass PG	Harrington DJA	McMahon H	Gilbraith RE	Franklin JL	Connor J	Rudkin TW
Mar 6	(a)	Leeds U	L 2-3	Franklin, Laking	2,000													4					11	10										8		
" 13	(h)	Leeds U	L 2-3	Bowers, Laking	2,500		3									10	5						11	4										8		
" 20	(a)	Sunderland	L 0-8		4,000		3					7				4	2																	8		
" 27	(h)	Sunderland	W 1-0	Gorman (og)	2,100	1				6					11		2																4	8		
Apr 3	(h)	Newcastle U	W 2-1	Wharton, Towers	3,000	1				6					11	10	2																4	8		
" 10	(a)	Newcastle U	L 0-4		7,000	1				6				9	11		2																4	8		
" 17	(a)	Halifax T	W 4-2	Bowers 3, Dicks	3,000	1								8	3			11													10			4		
" 24	(h)	Halifax T	W 7-3	Farrington 3, Johnson, Wharton, Bowers 2	2,000	1								11			8	6	2														4	6		
Apps						5	2			3		2		5	5		5	8	1				3	2							1	4	6		
Goals														1			2														1		

1 own-goal

In the League Cup (Qualifying Competition) G.F.M.Hardwick played number 3 against Newcastle United (h); E.M.Carr played number 10 against Sunderland (h); R.Arran played number 1 against Huddersfield Town (h) and York City (a); J.A.Dent played number 5 against Huddersfield Town (a) and York City (h & a); G.E.Laking played number 2 against York City (a); R.C.R.Craddock played number 1 against York City (h); E.Goldsborough played number 7 against York City (a).
In the League North (Second Championship) R.Arran played number 1 against Leeds United (a & h) and Sunderland (a); J.A.Dent played number 5 against Sunderland (a) and Halifax Town (a & h); G.E.Laking played number 2 against Leeds United (a & h), scoring once in both games; J.W.French played number 6 against Leeds United (a & h) and Sunderland (a), number 3 against Sunderland (h), Newcastle United (h) and Halifax Town (h); P.Bowers played number 9 against Leeds United (h), scoring once, Sunderland (a) and Halifax Town (a, scoring three goals, & h, scoring twice); T.Johnson played number 10 against Sunderland (a), Newcastle United (a) and Halifax Town (h), scoring once, number 9 against Sunderland (h) and Newcastle United (h); W.Cassidy played number 5 against Sunderland (h) and Newcastle United (h & a), number 2 against Halifax Town (a) and number four against Halifax Town (h); R.Farrington played number 7 against Sunderland (h), Newcastle United (h & a) and Halifax Town (h), scoring three goals; H.Hirst played number 3 against Leeds United (a); G.A.Mordue played number 5 against Leeds United (a); F.Buckley played number 7 against Leeds United (a); J.Oliver played number 9 against Leeds United (a); S.Rickaby played number 7 against Leeds United (h); T.O.Farrage played number 11 against Sunderland (a); J.J.Carey played number 10 against Sunderland (h); A.Livingstone played number 3 against Newcastle United (a); R.W.Dicks played number 7 against Halifax Town (a), scoring once.

Guest Players
R.Arran (South Bank Juniors), F.Buckley (Oldham Athletic), G.S.Burchell (Romford), J.J.Carey (Manchester United), E.M.Carr (Arsenal), W.Cassidy (Gateshead), J.Connor (Bolton Wanderers), T.Dawson (Charlton Athletic), R.W.Dicks (Dulwich Hamlet), T.O.Farrage (Birmingham), R.Farrington (Bradford City), J.R.E.Hardisty (Bishop Auckland), H.Hirst (Bradford), A.Johnson (Norwich City), T.Johnson (Gateshead), S.F.Kearney (Accrington Stanley), A.Livingstone (Gateshead), H.McMahon (Sunderland), M.Y.Middleton (Plymouth Argyle), G.A.Mordue, W.E.Nicholson (Tottenham Hotspur), J.Oliver (Burnley), F.Osborne (Aston Villa), W.Owen (Everton), W.Park (Blackpool), S.Rickaby (South Bank Juniors), T.W.Rudkin (Grimsby Town), F.Sargent (Tottenham Hotspur), R.Simpson (Darlington), J.Towers (Darlington), A.Warburton (Queen's Park Rangers), G.Wharton (Portsmouth), R.C.A.Wright (Charlton Athletic).

1943-44
League North (First Championship)

Date		Opponent	Result	Scorers	Att	Cumming DS	Martin J	Stuart RW	Brunskill N	Birse CV	Wright RCA	Farrington R	Murphy TE	Lyon TK	Barber E	Wilson K	Dicks RW	Skinner G	Crack FW	Blenkinsopp TW	Parlane J	Laking GE	Gilbraith RE	Harrington DJA	Stobbart GC	Middleton MY	French JW	Brown WH	Robinson JN	Forrest W	Hodgson S	Shepherdson H	Hardisty JRE	Oakes J	Towers J	Stevens RF
Aug 18 (a)		Hartlepools U	L 0-1		1,500	1	2	3	4	5	6	7	8	9	10	11																				
Sep 4 (h)		Hartlepools U	W 3-2	Wright (pen), Skinner, Farrington	5,000	1	2	3	4	5	6	11		9	10			7	8																	
11 (h)		Darlington	L 2-6	Lyon 2	7,024	1		3	4	5				9	10			7	8	11																
18 (a)		Darlington	D 3-3	Lyon 3 (1 pen)	3,000	1	6	3	4	5		7			10			11	9	2	8															
25 (a)		Leeds U	L 0-3		3,000	1		5	3	4			8	10							6	2	7	11												
Oct 2 (h)		Leeds U	D 3-3	Stobbart 2, Dicks	2,500	1	2	3	4				10				7	11	5	8		6		6	9											
9 (h)		Bradford	L 1-8	Stobbart	3,000	1	2	3	4	5		7	10				11			8		6		6	9											
16 (a)		Bradford	D 1-1	Dicks	4,596		5	3	8			7	10				11				2	4			1	6										
23 (h)		Gateshead	W 3-0	Murphy, Parlane, Stobbart	2,000		5	3				7	10				11		8		4		9	1	6	2										
30 (h)		Gateshead	L 3-5	Stobbart 2, Farrington	3,000		5	3	2			7	10						8		4	11	9	1	6											
Nov 6 (h)		York C	D 1-1	Parlane	3,500			3	2				10				7	11	5	8	4		9	1	6											
13 (a)		York C	L 3-5	Stobbart 2, Murphy	5,036		4	3	8				10		11	7			2		9	1	6							5						
20 (h)		Hartlepools U	L 1-3	Stobbart	4,000		4	3	8	5			10		11	7					9	1	6							2						
27 (a)		Hartlepools U	W 4-3	Farrington 2, Forrest, Stobbart	6,000		5	3	2			7	10				11		8		4		9	1						6						
Dec 4 (h)		Newcastle U	D 1-1	Parlane	3,000			3	2			7	8				11				9		6		1						10	4	5			
11 (a)		Newcastle U	D 1-1	Parlane	8,000			3	2				10	8			11		5	9		6		1								4				
18 (a)		Sunderland	L 1-6	Parlane	4,000	3			2			11					7		5		4	9	1							6						
25 (h)		Sunderland	W 4-0	Hardisty, Hodgson, Stobbart 2	9,000		3			2		7					11		5	10		6		9	1						4		8			
				Apps		7	14	16	16	5	4	12	14	5	2	3	14	2	5	7	11	3	12	2	10	11	6	1	2	2	4	1	1			
				Goals							1	4	2	5			2	1			5				12					1	1	1			

League Cup (Qualifying Competition)

Date		Opponent	Result	Scorers	Att	Cumming DS	Martin J	Stuart RW	Brunskill N	Birse CV	Wright RCA	Farrington R	Murphy TE	Lyon TK	Barber E	Wilson K	Dicks RW	Skinner G	Crack FW	Blenkinsopp TW	Parlane J	Laking GE	Gilbraith RE	Harrington DJA	Stobbart GC	Middleton MY	French JW	Brown WH	Robinson JN	Forrest W	Hodgson S	Shepherdson H	Hardisty JRE	Oakes J	Towers J	Stevens RF
Dec 27 (h)		Hartlepools U	D 1-1	Stobbart (pen)	8,500			3	2		6		7				11		5	10		4		9	1							8				
Jan 1 (a)		Hartlepools U	D 1-1	Stobbart	7,000	7	2					8					11		5	10	6		9	1	3					4						
8 (a)		Gateshead	L 1-2	Dicks	2,500	7	3	2									11		5	9	6		1	8					10	4						
15 (h)		Gateshead	W 4-2	Oakes 2, Parlane, Brunskill	4,500	11	3	8												9	6		7	1		2			4	5			10			
22 (h)		Darlington	L 0-1		6,000	11		2											5	8			7	1	3					4			9	10		
29 (a)		Darlington	D 0-0		10,591	5		2					7							8			1	3			10	4					9	6	11	
Feb 5 (h)		Newcastle U	W 2-1	Parlane, Stevens	5,000	5							7							8			1	2			10	4					9	6	11	
12 (a)		Newcastle U	L 1-4	Stobbart	12,000	2						8				11			6		9	1	3				4					7	10		
19 (a)		Sunderland	L 0-3		3,000			2				8				11			6		9	1	3				4					7	10		
26 (h)		Sunderland	L 4-5	Oakes, Gallagher, Murphy, Wilson	3,000			2				10		11			5	9	4		1	3									7	6				
				Apps		7	4	7	1			3	2	1	7		5	8	7		6	10	8	1		3	8	1	1	7	6	2				
				Goals			1					1					1	1			2				3							3		1		

League North (Second Championship)

Date		Opponent	Result	Scorers	Att	Cumming DS	Martin J	Stuart RW	Brunskill N	Birse CV	Wright RCA	Farrington R	Murphy TE	Lyon TK	Barber E	Wilson K	Dicks RW	Skinner G	Crack FW	Blenkinsopp TW	Parlane J	Laking GE	Gilbraith RE	Harrington DJA	Stobbart GC	Middleton MY	French JW	Brown WH	Robinson JN	Forrest W	Hodgson S	Shepherdson H	Hardisty JRE	Oakes J	Towers J	Stevens RF
Mar 4 (a)		Sunderland	L 1-4	Gallagher	1,000					2		10				11		5			4		9	1	3								7	6		
11 (h)		Sunderland	L 2-3	Oakes 2	3,000				2	6						11		5	9			1	3					4				10	7			
18 (a)		Gateshead	L 1-2	Hodgson	2,000	2						10				11			7		6	9	1	3				4					7			
25 (h)		Gateshead	W 4-1	Stobbart 2, Hodgson, Parlane	2,000	2										11			8		6	9	1	3				4					7	10		
29 (a)		Sunderland	D 3-3	Wilson, Martin, J.Bell (og)	2,000	7		2								11			4		9	1		3									6			
Apr 1 (a)		Darlington	W 3-2	Parlane 2, Oakes	6,000	3		2								11		5	8		6	9	1					4					7	10		
8 (h)		Darlington	L 1-4	Parlane	3,500	3		2								11		5	8		6	9	1					4					7	10		
10 (a)		Darlington	L 2-3	Martin, Stevens	5,536	1	4	2								11		5			9		3										7	6		10
15 (a)		Hartlepools U	W 6-2	Stobbart 5 (1 pen), Warburton	4,000											11		2			4	10	9										7	6		
22 (h)		Hartlepools U	L 0-5		2,000											11		2			4	7		3										6		
May 6 (h)		Sunderland	W 4-2	Harrington 2, Stobbart, McGorrighan	2,500			2								7					4	11	9	1		3								6		
				Apps		1	6		6		2		2			10	1		7	5		9	2	10	8	6		2		5			1	7	9	1	
				Goals		2										1					4		2	8						2				3	1		

1 own-goal

In the League North (First Championship) F.M.Evans played number 2 against Darlington (h); R.Walton played number 6 against Darlington (h); J.F.Stephen played number 9 against Bradford (a); A.W.Kerr played number 7 against Newcastle United (a); R.A.Fallaize played number 9 against Leeds United (a) and number 8 against Sunderland (a); J.L.Franklin played number 10 against Sunderland (a); In the League Cup (Qualifying Competition) E.C.Steele played number 6 against Darlington (h); G.F.M.Hardwick played number 3 against Newcastle United (h); W.Cassidy played number 5 against Newcastle United (a) and Sunderland (a); D.E.Gallagher played number 8 against Sunderland (h). In the League North (Second Championship) D.E.Gallagher played number 8 against Sunderland (a, 4 Mar) (h, 6 May), number 5 against Gateshead (a & h), Sunderland (a, 29 Mar) (h, 6 May) and Hartlepools United (a & h); J.L.Franklin played number 8 against Gateshead (a) and number 10 against Sunderland (h, 6 May); F.O.McGorrighan played number 8 against Sunderland (a, 29 Mar), Hartlepools United (h) and Sunderland (h, 6 May), scoring once; G.Warburton played number 10 against

Sunderland (a, 29 Mar) and Hartlepools United (h) and number 8 against Darlington (a) and Hartlepools United (a), scoring once; W.C.Davies played number 1 against Hartlepools United (a & h); L.Hubble played number 3 against Hartlepools United (a); A.Weir played number 9 against Hartlepools United (h).

Guest Players
E.Barber (Everton), C.V.Birse (Hibernian), T.W.Blenkinsopp (Grimsby Town), N.Brunskill (Barnsley), W.Cassidy (Gateshead), F.W.Crack (Grimsby Town), F.M.Evans (Tottenham Hotspur), R.A.Fallaize (Leeds United), R.Farrington (Bradford City), S.Hodgson (Grimsby Town), L.Hubble (Newcastle United), A.W.Kerr (Aston Villa), T.K.Lyon (Chesterfield), M.Y.Middleton (Plymouth Argyle), J.Oakes (Huddersfield Town), J.Parlane (Rangers), G.Skinner (Tottenham Hotspur), E.C.Steele (Stockport County), J.F.Stephen (Bradford), R.F.Stevens, J.Towers (Darlington), R.Walton (Leicester City), G.Warburton (Chester), A.Weir (Glentoran), R.C.A.Wright (Charlton Athletic).

1944-45

League North (First Championship)

Date	Opponent	Result	Scorers	Att	Middleton MY	Hardwick GFM	Kinsell TH	Brown WH	Shepherdson H	Gilbraith RE	Stuart RW	Dixon JT	Stobbart GC	McCorrighan FO	Wilson K	French JW	Blenkinsopp TW	Gallagher DE	Martin J	Moody J	Heweston K	Murphy TE	Long HR	Harrington DJA	Warburton G	Johnson T	Robinson R	Bowie JD	Franklin JL	Cumming DS	Wainwright EF	Bell HD	Forrest W	McArthur WJ	Harnby DR
Aug 26 (a)	Sunderland	D 0-0		15,000	1	2	3	4	5	6	7	8	9	10	11																				
Sep 2 (h)	Sunderland	L 1-5	Moody	3,000	1						2	8	9	10	11	3	4	5	6	7															
9 (h)	Gateshead	W 4-1	Stuart (pen), Dixon, Long 2	4,000	1	2	3				6	8	9				5			7	4	10	11												
16 (a)	Gateshead	D 5-5	Stobbart 4, Warburton	2,000	1						2		9	8	11	3			5	7	4			6	10										
23 (h)	Leeds U	W 3-2	Moody 2, Dixon	4,500	1		3				2	10	9	8	11				5	7	4			6											
30 (a)	Leeds U	L 2-4	Knight (og), Moody	8,000	1						3	10	9	8	11		5		6	7	4														
Oct 7 (a)	Newcastle U	W 1-0	Bowie	14,000	1						2	8	9	11		3				7				6		4	5	10							
14 (h)	Newcastle U	L 2-8	Murphy, McGorrighan	5,000	1						2		9	8		3				7	4	11		6			5								
21 (h)	Bradford C	L 2-3	Wilson, Stuart (pen)	3,000	1						2		9	8	11	3			5	7	4					6			10						
28 (a)	Bradford C	L 0-2		4,300	1						2		9			3			5	7	4			11	10		6		8						
Nov 4 (a)	Hartlepools U	W 3-2	Harrington, Stobbart 2	6,000	1			2			3	8	9			6				7	4			11		10	5								
11 (h)	Hartlepools U	L 0-3		3,349	1	3		4			2		9							7	6			11		10	5	8							
18 (h)	Huddersfield T	L 0-1		6,700					5		3		9			2				7						6	4	11		1	8	10			
25 (a)	Huddersfield T	L 1-5	Wainwright	7,532							3		9			2				11							5			1	8		4	6	
Dec 2 (a)	York C	L 1-5	Stobbart	4,941	1						3		9													10		8						6	2
9 (h)	York C	W 4-3	Deans, Nevins, Stobbart 2	4,000	1					4	3		9										10					8					5		2
16 (h)	Darlington	D 3-3	Fenton 2, Long	8,000	1					4	3		8						5				11										6		2
23 (a)	Darlington	L 2-5	Stobbart, Fenton	8,097	1						3		7															8	10				6		
				Apps	16	3	3	3	2	3	18	7	18	8	6	9	3	1	7	13	9	2	3	7	2	6	7	6	3	2	2	1	4	2	3
				Goals							2	2	10	1	1					4		1	3	1	1			1			1				

1 own-goal

League Cup (Qualifying Competition)

Date	Opponent	Result	Scorers	Att	Middleton MY	Hardwick GFM	Kinsell TH	Brown WH	Shepherdson H	Gilbraith RE	Stuart RW	Dixon JT	Stobbart GC	McCorrighan FO	Wilson K	French JW	Blenkinsopp TW	Gallagher DE	Martin J	Moody J	Heweston K	Murphy TE	Long HR	Harrington DJA	Warburton G	Johnson T	Robinson R	Bowie JD	Franklin JL	Cumming DS	Wainwright EF	Bell HD	Forrest W	McArthur WJ	Harnby DR
Dec 26 (h)	Hartlepools U	D 0-0		9,600	1						3		9			4				7				11					8				6		2
30 (a)	Hartlepools U	L 4-6	Fenton, Stobbart 2, Johnson	8,000	1						2		9			4	5									11							6		
Jan 6 (a)	Newcastle U	L 1-5	Rowley	20,000	1						3		7			2										6		10			8				
13 (h)	Newcastle U	W 5-3	Stobbart 4, Long	5,000	1						3		9			2							11			6		10			8		4		
20 (a)	Sunderland	L 3-4	Stobbart 2, Larner	5,300	1					4	3		9			2								11		6							5		
Feb 3 (h)	Darlington	L 0-1		8,000	1			2			3		9										11			6					8		4		
10 (a)	Darlington	L 4-6	Stobbart 3, Wilson	7,344	1						3		9		11	4										10							6		2
17 (h)	Gateshead	L 2-3	Wass, Stobbart	4,000	1						3		9		11						4					10					8		6		2
24 (a)	Gateshead	W 2-1	Stobbart, Stuart (pen)	6,000	1				5		3		9		11						4					6		10							
Mar 17 (h)	Sunderland	W 2-1	Stobbart 2	9,000	1				5		3		9		11											4		10			8		6		
				Apps	10			1	2	1	10		10		4	6	1			1	2		2	2		9		4	1		5		8		3
				Goals							1		15		1								1			1									

League North (Second Championship)

Date	Opponent	Result	Scorers	Att	Middleton MY	Hardwick GFM	Kinsell TH	Brown WH	Shepherdson H	Gilbraith RE	Stuart RW	Dixon JT	Stobbart GC	McCorrighan FO	Wilson K	French JW	Blenkinsopp TW	Gallagher DE	Martin J	Moody J	Heweston K	Murphy TE	Long HR	Harrington DJA	Warburton G	Johnson T	Robinson R	Bowie JD	Franklin JL	Cumming DS	Wainwright EF	Bell HD	Forrest W	McArthur WJ	Harnby DR
Mar 3 (a)	Darlington	L 0-1		4,697	1						3		9		11						4					6									
10 (h)	Newcastle U	L 1-5	Wainwright	5,000	1						3		9		11	7										4					8		5		
24 (h)	Hartlepools U	L 0-3		4,132	1						3		9		11											8							4		
31 (h)	Hartlepools U	L 1-3	Stobbart (pen)	3,000	1						2		9		11											8							6		
Apr 2 (h)	Gateshead	W 3-1	Wass, Johnson, J.N.Robinson	5,000	1						2										4					8							6		
7 (a)	Bradford	L 1-3	Stobbart	6,000	1						3		9		11	5					4								8				6		
14 (h)	Bradford	W 1-0	Stobbart	4,000					5		2		9		11						4					6					8				
21 (h)	Huddersfield T	W 2-1	Stobbart, Fenton	6,000							3		9													6							5		
28 (a)	Huddersfield T	L 0-1		2,007		3					2		9													6					8		5		
May 5 (h)	Newcastle U	D 1-1	Stobbart	4,000				4	5		3		9													6									
12 (a)	Newcastle U	L 0-11		7,000				4			3		9													6							5		
19 (h)	Hartlepools U	L 1-2	Stobbart	2,500							2		9													6				1			5		
				Apps	6	1		2	2		12		11		6	2					4					11			1	1	3		9		
				Goals									6													1					1				

In the League North (First Championship) G.E.Laking played number 2 against Leeds United (a); D.Miller played number 10 against Newcastle United (h); A.W.Kerr played number 7 against Huddersfield Town (a); A.G.Sutherland played number 10 against Huddersfield Town (a); W.H.G.Deans played number 11 against York City (a), Darlington (a) and number 7 against York City (h) and Darlington (h); L.Nevins played number 11 against York City (h); M.Fenton played number 9 against Darlington (h & a); K.H.Thompson played number 2 against Darlington (a); J.N.Robinson played number 5 against Darlington (a); I.Methley played number 4 against York City (a); R.Bicknell played number 5 against York City (a); L.Porter played number 7 against York City (a); W.Adams played number 6 against York City (h); J.D.Short played number 10 against Darlington (h); J.R.E.Hardisty played number 4 against Darlington (a). **In the League Cup (Qualifying Competition)** J.R.E.Hardisty played number 8 against Hartlepools United (a); M.Fenton played number 10 against Hartlepools United (h & a) and number 9 against Newcastle United (a); K.H.Thompson played number 2 against Gateshead (a); J.N.Robinson played number 5 against Hartlepools United (h) and Newcastle United (h) and number 3 against Hartlepools United (a); W.Wass played number 7 against Sunderland (h) and Gateshead (h & a); L.J.Forster played number 7 against Sunderland (a) and Darlington (h & a); C.Ferguson played number 7 against Hartlepools United (a) and number 4 against Newcastle United (a); T.Cross played number 5 against Newcastle United (a); G.A.Rowley played number 11 against Newcastle United (a); R.Simpson played number 7 against Newcastle United (h); J.T.T.Shreeve played number 2 against Sunderland (h); W.Temple played number 8 against Sunderland (a); L.Larner played number 10 against Sunderland (a) and Darlington (h); A.Chilton played number 5 against Darlington (h); J.Lilley played number 8 against Darlington (a); R.D.Sales played number 5 against Darlington (a) and Gateshead (h); J.Stevenson played number 7 against Gateshead (a). **In the League North (Second Championship)** M.Fenton played number 9 against Huddersfield Town (h) and number 10 against Huddersfield Town (a); K.H.Thompson played number 2 against Darlington (a), Newcastle United (h, twice & a), Hartlepools United (a), Bradford (a) and Huddersfield Town (h); J.N.Robinson played number 3 against Hartlepools United (h, twice), Gateshead (h) and Bradford (h); W.Wass played number 7 against Darlington (a), Hartlepools United (h, twice & a), Gateshead (h), Bradford (a & h) and Huddersfield Town (h & a); R.D.Sales played number 5 against Darlington (a), Hartlepools United (a & h, 31 Mar) and Gateshead (h); J.Stevenson played number 8 against Darlington (a); T.Stenson played number 10 against Darlington (a), Newcastle United (h, 10 Mar), Hartlepools United (a & h, 31 Mar) and Bradford (h & a); W.Borrowman played number 6 against Newcastle United (h, 10 Mar) and Hartlepools United (a); W.H.Johnson played number 8 against Hartlepools United (a) and number 4 against Hartlepools United (h, 19 May); L.Mahon played number 4 against Hartlepools United (h, 31 Mar); F.C.Nash played number 1 against Huddersfield Town (a), Newcastle United (h, 5 May & a) and Hartlepools United (h, 19 May); J.J.McCabe played number 4 against Huddersfield Town (h); P.C.Baines played number 10 against Huddersfield Town (h); W.C.Davies played number 1 against Huddersfield Town (h); C.Woollett played number 11 against Gateshead (h), Huddersfield Town (h & a), Newcastle United (h, 5 May & a) and Hartlepools United (h, 19 May); L.F.Howe played number 4 against Huddersfield Town (a); J.Sinclair played number 7 against Hartlepools United (h, 19 May); J.Sloan played number 8 against Hartlepools United (h, 19 May); J.Davison played number 10 against Hartlepools United (h, 19 May).

1945-46
Football League North

Date		Opponent	Res	Score	Scorers	Att	Cumming DS	Laking GE	Stuart RW	French JW	Jameson P	Johnson T	Wass W	Stobbart GC	Fenton M	Dews G	Chadwick C	Hardwick GFM	Heweston K	Shepherdson H	Wainwright E	McCabe JJ	Barclay R	Price AJW	Robinson R	Spuhler JO	Gordon J	Murphy TE	Maddison J	Watson R	Douglas JS	Bell HD	Mannion WJ	Butler T	Bambrough N	Bowes W	Hepple G
Aug	25 (a)	Manchester C	L	1-2	Stobbart	19,188	1	2	3	4	5	6	7	8	9	10	11																				
Sep	1 (h)	Manchester C	D	2-2	Stuart (pen), Stobbart	12,856	1	2	6			10	7	9				11	3	4	5	8															
	8 (h)	Newcastle U	L	0-6		16,419	1	2	3			11	7			10		6	4			5	8	9													
	12 (h)	Manchester U	W	2-1	Dews 2	6,506	1	2				10	7							4			3														
	15 (h)	Newcastle U	D	1-1	Stobbart	32,211	1	2				6	7	9		10		3				4									5	8					
	22 (a)	Sheffield W	L	1-2	Stuart (pen)	20,334	1		2			4		7	9	10		3				8									5	11					
	29 (h)	Sheffield W	W	2-0	Butler, Wass	12,506	1	2	3				7	9		10			4												5	8		11			
Oct	6 (h)	Huddersfield T	L	2-8	Stobbart 2	14,654	1	3	2					9		10		6														8		11	4	7	
	13 (a)	Huddersfield T	L	0-7		10,436	1		2		6			9		10		3													5	8		11	4	7	
	20 (h)	Chesterfield	L	0-1		12,446	1	2	3		6	11		9		10					5							7				4	8				
	27 (h)	Chesterfield	L	0-4		15,368	1	2	3				7	9		10					5										4	8		11			6
Nov	3 (h)	Barnsley	L	2-5	Stuart (pen), Spuhler	10,121	1	2	3				11	9		10					5					7						8					6
	10 (h)	Barnsley	D	2-2	Fenton 2	14,362	1		2		6		11	9	10			3		5						7					4	8					
	17 (a)	Everton	D	1-1	Spuhler	23,248	1		2		6		11	9	10			3	4							7					5	8					
	24 (h)	Everton	D	0-0		18,197	1		2				11	9	10			3		5						7	4				6	8					
Dec	1 (h)	Bolton W	W	1-0	Stobbart	16,666	1		2					9		10		3		5		4			3	7					6	8					11
	8 (a)	Bolton W	L	1-2	Spuhler	16,812	1		2				11	9				3		5		4				7	8				6	10					
	15 (h)	Preston NE	L	0-1		14,976	1		2				11	9	10			3		5						7	4				6	8					
	22 (a)	Preston NE	W	1-0	Spuhler	8,000	1		2					9	8			3		5					11	7					6	4					10
	25 (a)	Leeds U	L	0-1		12,217	1		2					9	8	10		3		5					11	7	6					4					
	26 (h)	Leeds U	W	4-1	Murphy, Fenton, Dews, Stobbart	23,019	1		2					7	9	8		3		5					11		6	10				4					
	29 (a)	Manchester U	L	1-4	Maddison	18,937	1		2				6	9	8	10									3			7	11		5	4					
Jan	1 (h)	Sunderland	W	1-0	Robinson	29,157	1	2	3					9	8	10		5							11	7	6					4					
	12 (a)	Sheffield U	W	7-2	Fenton 5, Murphy, Maddison	18,565	1	3						9	10											7	6	8	11		5	4					
	19 (h)	Sheffield U	L	3-4	Dews, Fenton, Spuhler (pen)	23,473	1	3		5				9	10				4							7	6	8	11								
Feb	2 (a)	Burnley	L	1-8	Stobbart	9,806	1		2			7	9						6								8			11	5						10
	16 (a)	Stoke C	W	4-1	Spuhler, Murphy, Stobbart 2	9,123	1	2	3					9		10				5						7	6	8			11	4					
	23 (a)	Grimsby T	D	1-1	Spuhler	8,739	1	2						9	10			3		5						7	6	8			11	4					
Mar	2 (h)	Grimsby T	W	3-1	Spuhler, Murphy 2	14,198	1	2						9	10			5							3	7	6	8			11	4					
	9 (h)	Blackpool	W	4-2	Fenton 2, Spuhler, Dews	23,000	1							9	10			3							2	7	6	8			11	5	4				
	16 (a)	Blackpool	L	1-3	Gordon	10,000	1							9	10			3							2	7	6	8	11			5	4				
	23 (a)	Liverpool	W	2-1	Fenton 2	30,000	1							9	10			3							2	7	6	8	11			5	4				
	30 (h)	Liverpool	L	2-5	Harley (og), Hardwick (pen)	25,000	1							9	10			3		6					2	7		8	11			5	4				
Apr	6 (h)	Bury	W	3-0	Spuhler, Murphy, Fenton	20,000			3					9	10					5					2	7	6	11				4	8				
	10 (h)	Burnley	W	2-1	Murphy, Fenton	19,358			3					9	10					5		6			2	7		11				4	8				
	13 (a)	Bury	D	1-1	Fenton	10,000	1		3					9	10	11									2	7	6				5	4	8				
	19 (a)	Blackburn R	D	3-3	Spuhler, Gordon, Dews	10,000	1							9	10			3		5					2	7	6	11				4	8				
	20 (h)	Bradford	W	3-0	Murphy, Dews 2	20,000	1							9	10			3							2	7	6	11				4	8				
	22 (h)	Blackburn R	W	5-1	Murphy 3, Fenton, Spuhler	24,000	1							9	10			3		5					2	7	6	8	11			4					
	27 (a)	Bradford	D	1-1	Chadwick	7,143	1							9	10	11	3								2	7	6	8				4					
May	1 (h)	Stoke C	W	3-1	Dews, Fenton 2	27,952	1							9	10	11	3					6			2							4	8				
	4 (a)	Sunderland	W	1-0	Fenton	32,000	1		3					9	10	11	5								2	7	6	8				4					
		Apps					38	16	27	2	2	10	7	25	30	37	6	27	5	18	2	9	1	1	21	27	21	19	6	5	22	36	6	5	2	2	5
		Goals							3				1	10	20	9	1	1							1	12	2	11	2					1			

1 own-goal

FA Cup

Date		Opponent	Res	Score	Scorers	Att	Cumming DS	Laking GE	Stuart RW	French JW	Jameson P	Johnson T	Wass W	Stobbart GC	Fenton M	Dews G	Chadwick C	Hardwick GFM	Heweston K	Shepherdson H	Wainwright E	McCabe JJ	Barclay R	Price AJW	Robinson R	Spuhler JO	Gordon J	Murphy TE	Maddison J	Watson R	Douglas JS	Bell HD	Mannion WJ	Butler T	Bambrough N	Bowes W	Hepple G	Round
Jan	5 (a)	Leeds U	D	4-4	Murphy, Fenton, Dews 2	18,000	1	2						9	10	11	5								3	7		8			6	4						3/1
	9 (h)	Leeds U	W	7-2	Gordon, Hardwick (pen), Fenton 3, Spuhler, Douglas	24,000	1							9	10		5								3	7	6	8				11	4					3/2
	26 (a)	Blackpool	L	2-3	Suart (og), Spuhler	17,160	1		2					9	10		5								3	7	6	8				11	4					4/1
	30 (h)	Blackpool	W	3-2	Fenton 2, Spuhler	46,556	1		2				11	9	10		5								3	7	6	8					4					4/2
Feb	4 (n*)	Blackpool	W	1-0	Hardwick (pen)	30,000	1						11	9	10		5								3	7	6	8					4					R
	9 (a)	Bolton W	L	0-1		43,550	1	2						9	10		5								3	7	6	8	11				4					5/1
	13 (h)	Bolton W	D	1-1	Fenton	51,612	1	2						9	10		5								3	7	6	8	11				4					5/2
		Apps					7	4	2					2	7	7	1	7							7	6	7	2			3	7						
		Goals													7	2		2								3	1	1				1						

*Played at Elland Road, Leeds.

1 own-goal

In the Football League North S.Jones played number 6 against Sheffield Wednesday (a); H.Wallbanks played number 6 against Sheffield Wednesday (h); R.B.Morris played number 5 against Huddersfield Town (h); J.Brown played number 4 against Barnsley (h); K.Wilson played number 11 against Newcastle United (a); W.H.Brown played number 4 against Barnsley (h), Burnley (a) and number 2 against Sheffield United (a & h); G.Wharton played number 5 against Manchester United (h); R.Atwell played number 6 against Manchester United (h); A.Herd played number 8 against Manchester United (h); J.C.McCormack played number 9 against Manchester United (a); J.Mullen played number 11 against Manchester United (h); J.N.Robinson played number 3 against Burnley (a); F.C.Nash played number 1 against Bury (h) and Burnley (h); N.F.Malan played number 1 against Liverpool (a & h); H.Mattinson played number 5 against Bradford (h & a) and Stoke City (h). **In the FA Cup** W.H.Brown played number 2 against Leeds United (h).

Guest Players

R.Attwell (West Ham United), N.Bambrough, R.Barclay (Preston North End), T.Butler (Oldham Athletic), A.Herd (Manchester City), T.Johnson (Gateshead), J.C.McCormack (Gateshead), J.Mullen (Wolverhampton Wanderers), A.J.W.Price (Hartlepools United), E.Wainwright (Everton), H.Wallbanks (Fulham), G.Wharton (Portsmouth), R.Watson (Vale of Leven).

NB — Records show that both J.S.Douglas (20 games) and P.Douglass (2 games) played for Middlesbrough this season but all reports name Douglas and do not differentiate between the players.

1946-47
Division 1

Date	Opponent	Res	Score	Scorers	Att	Cumming DS	Robinson R	Hardwick GFM	Bell HD	Shepherdson H	Gordon J	Spuhler JO	Mannion WJ	Fenton M	Dews G	Walker RG	Stuart RW	Murphy TE	Linwood AB	Laking GE	Robinson JN	McCabe JJ	Douglas JS	Nash FC	Mattinson H	Dobbie H	Maddison J	Gallacher C	Briggs W	McCormack JC	Malan NF	Hepple G
Aug 31 (a) Aston Villa		W	1-0	Mannion	49,246	1	2	3	4	5	6	7	8	9	10	11																
Sep 4 (a) Liverpool		W	1-0	Hughes (og)	34,140	1	2	3	4	5	6	7	8	9	10	11																
Sep 7 (h) Stoke C		W	5-4	Fenton 4, Mannion	43,685	1	2	3	4	5	6	7	8	9	10	11																
Sep 14 (a*) Manchester U		L	0-1		65,279	1	2	5	4		6	7	8	9		11	3	10														
Sep 21 (a) Preston NE		W	2-0	Hardwick (pen), Mannion	40,317	1	2	5	4				8	9		11	3	7	10													
Sep 28 (a) Sheffield U		L	1-2	Spuhler	36,931	1	3		4		6	7		9	10	11					8	2	5									
Oct 5 (h) Chelsea		W	3-2	Fenton, Mannion 2	44,082	1	2	3	4		6	7	8	9	10	11					5											
Oct 9 (h) Liverpool		D	2-2	Fenton, Dews	37,382	1	2	3	4			7	8	9	10	11					5	6										
Oct 12 (a) Bolton W		D	1-1	Fenton	32,000	1	2	3	4			7	8	9	10	11					5	6										
Oct 19 (a) Derby C		D	1-1	Spuhler	28,849	1	2	3	4			7	8		10	11			9		5	6										
Oct 26 (h) Huddersfield T		W	4-1	Fenton, Walker 2, Mannion	36,694	1	2	3	4			8	7		10	11			9		5	6										
Nov 2 (a) Wolves		W	4-2	Dews 2, Linwood, Walker	45,622	1	2	3	4			8	7		10	11			9		5	6										
Nov 9 (h) Sunderland		L	1-3	Walker	40,219	1	2	3	4		6	8	7		10	11			9		5											
Nov 16 (a) Blackburn R		W	2-1	Walker, Dews	23,797	1	2	3	4		6	8	7		10	11			9		5											
Nov 23 (h) Portsmouth		D	3-3	Mannion 3	31,824	1	2	3	4		6	10	7	8		11			9		5											
Nov 30 (a) Everton		L	1-2	Fenton	48,997	1	2	5			6	7	10	9	8	11	3				4											
Dec 7 (h) Arsenal		W	2-0	Fenton, Gordon	30,357	1	2	5			6	7	10	9	8	11	3				4											
Dec 14 (a) Blackpool		W	5-0	Mannion, Fenton, Spuhler 2, Murphy	14,571	1	2	5			6	7	10	9		11	3	8			4											
Dec 21 (h) Brentford		W	2-0	Spuhler 2	28,750	1	2	5			6	7	10	9		11	3	8			4											
Dec 25 (a) Leeds U		D	3-3	Spuhler 2, Fenton	28,942	1	2	5			6	7	10	9		11	3	8			4											
Dec 26 (h) Leeds U		W	3-0	Fenton 2, Walker	45,336	1	2	5			6	7	10	9		11	3	8			4											
Dec 28 (h) Aston Villa		L	1-2	Mannion	41,299	1	2	5			6	7	10	9		11	3	8			4											
Jan 1 (h) Grimsby T		W	3-0	Mannion 2, Dews	39,947	1	2	3	4		6	7	10	9	8	11					5											
Jan 4 (a) Stoke C		L	1-3	Fenton	34,057	1	2		4		6	7	10	9	8	11	3				5											
Jan 18 (h) Manchester U		L	2-4	Fenton, Mannion	37,556	1	2	5	4		6	7	10	9		11	3	8														
Jan 29 (a) Preston NE		W	1-0	Scott (og)	15,911	1	2	3	8		6	7	10	9		11					4				5							
Feb 1 (h) Sheffield U		L	2-4	Forbes (og), Dobbie	31,784	1	2	5	8		6	7	10			11					4				5	9						
Feb 15 (h) Bolton W		W	3-1	Mannion, Spuhler, Dews	31,437	1	2	3	4			7	8	9	10	11					5	6										
Feb 22 (h) Derby C		W	1-0	Mannion (pen)	32,612	1	2	3	4		6	7	8	9	10	11					5											
Mar 8 (h) Wolves		D	1-1	Dobbie	37,003	1	2	3	4		6	7	10	9							5					8	11					
Mar 15 (a) Sunderland		L	0-1		39,521	1	2	3	4		6	7	10	9		11					5					8						
Mar 22 (h) Blackburn R		L	0-1		31,001	1	2	3			6	7	10	8		11					4				5	9						
Mar 29 (a) Portsmouth		L	1-3	Fenton	30,502	1	2	3	4		6	10	7			11			9		5							8				
Apr 4 (a) Charlton A		D	3-3	Fenton, Linwood 2	38,402	1	2		4		6	10	7	8		11	3		9		5											
Apr 5 (h) Everton		W	4-0	Walker 2, Mannion 2	27,106	1	2		4		6	10	7	8		11	3		9		5											
Apr 7 (h) Charlton A		L	1-2	Dews	36,903	1	2		4		6	10	7	8		11	3		9		5											
Apr 12 (a) Arsenal		L	0-4		44,230	1	2				6	8	7	10		11	3		9		5											
Apr 19 (a) Blackpool		L	1-2	Spuhler	28,849	1		3	4		6	7	10	9	8	11	2				5											
Apr 26 (a) Brentford		D	0-0		19,020		2	5	4		6	7	10	9		11	3	8						1								
May 3 (a) Grimsby T		L	0-4		22,482		2				6	8		9	10	11	3				5	4							1	7		
May 10 (a) Chelsea		L	0-2		16,328		2				6	7		9	10	11	3				5	4								8	1	
May 17 (a) Huddersfield T		L	1-3	Dews	16,328				4		7	8			10	11	3				2	5								9	1	6
Apps						37	40	33	31	3	36	32	37	40	27	41	20	8	14	1	15	27	2	2	3	4	1	1	1	3	2	1
Goals								1			1	10	18	18	8	8		1	3							2						

*Played at Maine Road, Manchester (Old Trafford bomb-damaged).

3 own-goals

FA Cup

Date	Opponent	Res	Score	Scorers	Att	Cumming DS	Robinson R	Hardwick GFM	Bell HD	Shepherdson H	Gordon J	Spuhler JO	Mannion WJ	Fenton M	Dews G	Walker RG	Stuart RW	Murphy TE	Linwood AB	Laking GE	Robinson JN	McCabe JJ	Round
Jan 11 (a) Queen's Park R		D	1-1	Fenton	24,549	1	2	5			6	7	10	9	8	11	3				4		3
Jan 15 (h) Queen's Park R		W	3-1	Fenton 2, Mannion	31,270	1	2	5	4		6	7	10	9	8	11	3						R
Jan 25 (h) Chesterfield		W	2-1	Spuhler 2	42,250	1	3	5	4		8	7	10	9		11	2				6		4
Feb 8 (a) Nottingham F		D	2-2	Mannion, Spuhler	34,000	1	2	5			6	7	8	9	10	11	3				4		5
Feb 12 (h) Nottingham F		W	6-2	Spuhler, Mannion 3 (1 pen), Fenton 2	26,907	1	2	5			6	7	8	9	10	11	3				4		R
Mar 1 (h) Burnley		D	1-1	Walker	†53,025	1	2	3	4		6	7	8	9	10	11					5		6
Mar 4 (a) Burnley		L	0-1		49,244	1	2	3	4		6	7	8	9		11			10		5		R
Apps						7	7	7	4		7	7	7	7	5	7	5		1		6		
Goals												4	5	5		1						

†Ground attendance record

1947-48
Division 1

Date	Opponent	Res	Score & Scorers	Att	Goodfellow DO	Robinson R	Hardwick GFM	Bell HD	Whitaker W	Gordon J	McCormack JC	Dews G	Fenton M	Mannion WJ	Dicks RW	Stuart RW	Spuhler JO	Walker RG	Nash FC	McCabe JJ	Murphy TE	Briggs W	Robinson JN	Dobbie H	Hepple G	Hodgson JP	Rickaby S	Reagan CM	Anderson JR	Johnston CP
Aug 23(h)	Manchester U	D	2-2 Fenton 2	39,554	1	2	3	4	5	6	7	8	9	10	11															
25(a)	Sheffield U	D	1-1 Hardwick	33,274	1		3	4	5	6		8	10	9	11	2	7													
30(a)	Preston NE	L	1-2 Spuhler	31,326	1		3	4	5	6			8	9	10	11	2	7												
Sep 3(h)	Sheffield U	W	3-0 McCormack, Fenton 2	35,312	1		3	4	5	6	8		9	10		7	2	11												
6(h)	Stoke C	W	2-1 McCormack 2	38,146	1		3	4	5	6	8		9	10		7	2	11												
10(a)	Wolves	W	3-1 Fenton, Dicks, Brice (og)	49,961	1		3	4	5	6		8	9	10		7	2	11												
13(a)	Burnley	L	0-3	34,944			3	4	5	6	7	8	9	10	11	2			1											
20(h)	Portsmouth	L	1-2 Fenton	29,590	1	3			5	6	8		9			11	2	7		4	10									
27(a)	Bolton W	W	3-1 McCormack 3	30,641		3		4	5	6	8		9	10	11	2	7					1								
Oct 4(h)	Liverpool	W	3-1 Fenton 2, Spuhler	41,140	1	3		4	5	6		8	9	10		2	7	11												
11(a)	Everton	L	0-1	38,686	1	3		4	5	6		8	9	10		2	7	11												
18(a)	Chelsea	L	2-4 Walker 2	48,398	1	3		4	5	6	8	10	9			2	7	11												
25(h)	Huddersfield T	W	1-0 Fenton	36,142	1	2	3	4	5	6	8		9	10			7	11												
Nov 1(a)	Derby C	L	2-4 Fenton, Walker	32,976	1	2	3	4	5	6	8		9	10			7	11												
8(h)	Manchester C	W	2-1 Fenton 2	36,548	1	2	3	4	5	6	8		9	10			7	11												
15(a)	Grimsby T	W	5-0 Fenton, McCormack 2, Walker, Spuhler	14,812	1	2	3	4	5	6	8		9	10			7	11												
22(h)	Blackpool	W	4-0 McCormack 2, Fenton, Spuhler	38,936	1	2	3	4	5	6	8		9	10			7	11												
29(a)	Blackburn R	W	7-1 McCormack 3, Walker 2, Fenton 2	26,506	1	2	3	4	5	6	8		9	10			7	11												
Dec 6(h)	Sunderland	D	2-2 McCormack, Spuhler	45,145	1	2	3	4	5	6	8		9	10			7	11												
13(a)	Aston Villa	D	1-1 McCormack	49,188	1	2	3	4	5	6	8		9	10			7	11												
20(a*)	Manchester U	L	1-2 Fenton	47,879	1	2	3	4	5	6	8		9	10			7	11												
25(a)	Charlton A	L	0-1	25,822	1	2	3	4	5	6	8		9	10			7	11												
27(h)	Charlton A	L	1-2 Spuhler	38,454	1	2	3	4	5	6	8		9	10			7	11												
Jan 1(h)	Wolves	L	2-4 Walker, Fenton	38,150	1		3	4	5	6	8		9	10			7	11					2							
3(h)	Preston NE	D	1-1 Walker	37,375	1	2	3	4	5	6	8				10		7	11						9						
17(a)	Stoke C	W	4-2 Mannion, Spuhler, Walker, Fenton	29,436	1	2	3	4		6			9	10			7	11		5				8						
31(h)	Burnley	L	1-2 Spuhler	36,208	1	2	3	4		6	8		9	10			7	11		5										
Feb 14(h)	Bolton W	W	4-1 Fenton, Dobbie, Spuhler, Walker	24,234	1	2	3	4		6			9		10		7	11		5				8						
21(a)	Liverpool	W	1-0 Fenton	36,133	1	2	3	4		6			9	10	8		7	11		5										
28(a)	Everton	L	1-2 Spuhler	46,364	1	2	3		5	6			9	10			7	11		4				8						
Mar 6(h)	Chelsea	D	0-0	28,174	1	2	3		5	6	8		9	10			7	11		4										
13(a)	Huddersfield T	L	1-2 Fenton	23,588	1		2	4	5	6	8		9	10			7	11							3					
20(h)	Derby C	D	1-1 Fenton (pen)	24,814		2		4	5				9	10	11		8								6	1	3	7		
26(a)	Arsenal	L	0-7	57,557		2	3		5	4			9		10		8	11							6			7	1	
27(a)	Manchester C	L	0-2	42,297	1	2	3	8	5	4			9		10		7	11							6					
29(h)	Arsenal	D	1-1 Spuhler	38,249	1	2	3	4	5				9	10	8		7	11							6					
Apr 3(h)	Grimsby T	W	4-1 Walker, Fenton 3	24,130	1	2	3	4	5				9	10	8			11							6			7		
10(a)	Blackpool	L	0-1	16,330	1	2		4	5				9	10	8		7	11							6		3			
14(a)	Portsmouth	L	1-6 Fenton (pen)	23,890	1	2		4	5				9	10	8		7	11							6		3			
17(h)	Blackburn R	D	1-1 Fenton	22,033		3		4	5				9	10	8		7	11							6	1	2			
24(a)	Sunderland	L	0-3	51,581	1		3		5				9	10	8		7	11							6		2	4		
May 1(h)	Aston Villa	L	1-3 Dicks (pen)	20,892		3			5					10	8			11						9	6	1	2	7		4
	Apps				36	35	30	36	37	35	26	6	40	35	22	11	35	35	1	7	1	1	1	5	11	3	6	4	1	2
	Goals						1				15		28	1	2		11	11						1						

*Played at Maine Road, Manchester (Old Trafford bomb-damaged).

1 own-goal

FA Cup

Date	Opponent	Res	Score & Scorers	Att	Goodfellow DO	Robinson R	Hardwick GFM	Bell HD	Whitaker W	Gordon J	McCormack JC	Dews G	Fenton M	Mannion WJ	Dicks RW	Stuart RW	Spuhler JO	Walker RG	Nash FC	McCabe JJ	Murphy TE	Briggs W	Robinson JN	Dobbie H	Hepple G	Hodgson JP	Rickaby S	Reagan CM	Anderson JR	Johnston CP	Round
Jan 10(a)	Hull C	W	3-1 Dobbie 2, Mannion	40,179	1	2	3	4		6	8			10			7	11		5				9							3
24(a)	Brentford	W	2-1 Spuhler, McCormack	34,500	1	2	3	4		6	8		9	10			7	11		5											4
Feb 7(h)	Derby C	L	1-2 Spuhler	43,708	1	2	3	4		6			9	10	8		7	11		5											5
	Apps				3	3	3	3		3	2		2	3	1		3	3		3				1							
	Goals										1			1			2							2							

1948-49
Division 1

Date		Opponent	Res	Scorers	Att	Ugolini R	Blenkinsopp TW	Hardwick GFM	Bell HD	Whitaker W	Gordon J	Spuhler JO	Johnston CP	McCormack JC	Dicks RW	Walker RG	Robinson R	Fenton M	Dobbie H	Hepple G	Hodgson JP	Reagan CM	McCrae A	Rickaby S	Mannion WJ	Donaldson A	Hartnett JB
Aug	21 (a)	Chelsea	L 0-1		60,981	1	2	3	4	5	6	7	8	9	10	11											
	25 (a)	Birmingham C	D 0-0		37,864	1	6	3	4	5		7		8	10	11	2	9									
	28 (h)	Everton	W 1-0	Fenton (pen)	35,960	1	6	3	4	5		7		8	10	11	2	9									
Sep	1 (h)	Birmingham C	D 1-1	Dobbie (pen)	34,016	1	6	3	4	5		7		8	10	11	2		9								
	4 (a)	Preston NE	L 1-6	Spuhler	36,468	1	6	3	4	5		7		8	10	11	2	9									
	8 (a)	Portsmouth	L 0-1		33,275	1	6			5	4	7			10	11	2	9	8	3							
	11 (h)	Burnley	W 4-1	Fenton, Dicks, Dobbie 2	28,903	1	6			5	4	7			10	11	2	9	8	3							
	15 (h)	Portsmouth	D 1-1	Fenton	33,247	1	6	3		5	4	7			10	11	2	9	8								
	18 (a)	Stoke C	L 0-3		28,931	1	6	3		5	4	7			10	11	2	9	8								
	25 (h)	Charlton A	L 2-4	Spuhler, Fenton	33,723		6			5	4	7			10	11	2	9	8	3	1						
Oct	2 (a)	Manchester C	L 0-1		45,146	1	10	3	4	5	6			8	7	11	2	9									
	9 (a)	Wolves	W 3-0	Fenton 2, Spuhler	38,544	1	10	3	4	5	6	8			7	11	2	9									
	16 (h)	Bolton W	W 5-0	Fenton 3, Spuhler, Reagan	28,628	1	10	3	4	5	6	8				11	2	9				7					
	23 (a)	Liverpool	L 0-4		57,561	1	10	3	4	5	6	8				11	2	9				7					
	30 (h)	Blackpool	W 1-0	Gordon	44,780	1	10	3	4	5	6	8				11	2	9				7					
Nov	6 (a)	Derby C	L 0-2		34,456	1	8	3	4	5	6	7				11	2	9					10				
	13 (h)	Arsenal	L 0-1		35,852	1	8	3	4	5	6	7				11	2	9					10				
	20 (a)	Huddersfield T	D 0-0		16,413	1	8	3	4	5	6	7				11	2	9					10				
	27 (h)	Manchester U	L 1-4	McCrae	31,435	1	4	3		5	6	8				11	2	9				7	10				
Dec	4 (a)	Sheffield U	L 0-1		30,793	1	4	3		5	6	8			7	11	2	9	10								
	11 (h)	Aston Villa	W 6-0	Fenton 3, Walker 2, Dicks	21,184	1	4	3		5	6	8			7	11	2	9	10								
	18 (h)	Chelsea	D 1-1	Spuhler	23,464	1	4	3		5	6	8		9	7	11	2						10				
	25 (a)	Sunderland	L 0-1		43,692	1	4	3		5	6	8			7	11	2	9	10								
	26 (h)	Sunderland	D 0-0		43,455	1	10	3	4	5	6	7				11	2	9	8								
Jan	1 (a)	Everton	L 1-3	Spuhler	39,445	1	2		4	5	6	7				11	3	9	8				10				
	15 (h)	Preston NE	W 1-0	Walker	37,702	1	6	3	4	5	10	7				11	2	9							8		
	22 (a)	Burnley	D 0-0		36,506	1	6	3	4	5	10	7				11	2	9							8		
Feb	19 (a)	Charlton A	L 0-2		42,739	1	6	3		5	4	7		10		11	2								8	9	
	26 (h)	Manchester C	L 0-1		37,073		6	3		5	4	7				11	2		8		1				10	9	
Mar	5 (h)	Wolves	D 4-4	Mannion 2, Hartnett, Donaldson	27,663			3	4	5	6	7					2				1		10		8	9	11
	12 (a)	Bolton W	L 1-4	Mannion	28,783	1		3	4	5	6	7					2						10		8	9	11
	19 (h)	Huddersfield T	W 1-0	Donaldson	33,279	1	5	3	4		6				7		2						10		8	9	11
Apr	2 (h)	Derby C	W 1-0	Donaldson	38,842	1	5	3	4		6				7		2						10		8	9	11
	9 (a)	Arsenal	D 1-1	Mannion	51,540	1	5	3	4		6				7		2						10		8	9	11
	15 (a)	Newcastle U	L 0-1		64,381	1	5	3	4		6	7					2						10		8	9	11
	16 (h)	Liverpool	L 0-1		32,308	1	5	3	4		6						2	9				7	10		8		11
	18 (h)	Newcastle U	W 3-2	McCrae, Hardwick 2 (2 pens)	44,037	1	5	3	4		6					11	2					7	10		8	9	
	23 (a)	Blackpool	D 1-1	Donaldson	23,128	1	5	3	4		6						2					7	10		8	9	11
	27 (h)	Stoke C	D 1-1	Donaldson	40,329	1	5	3	4		6						2					7	10		8	9	11
	30 (h)	Sheffield U	W 3-1	Hartnett 3	34,261	1	5	3	4		6						2					7	10		8	9	11
May	2 (a*)	Manchester U	L 0-1		22,889	1	5	3	4		6						2					7	10		8	9	11
	7 (a)	Aston Villa	D 1-1	Donaldson	38,051	1	5	3	4		6						2					7	10		8	9	11
				Apps		39	40	39	30	30	38	31	1	8	19	30	41	24	11	3	3	11	20	1	17	14	12
				Goals			2			1	6			2	3			12	3			1	2		4	6	4

*Played at Maine Road, Manchester (Old Trafford bomb-damaged).

FA Cup

Date		Opponent	Res	Scorers	Att	Ugolini R	Blenkinsopp TW	Hardwick GFM	Bell HD	Whitaker W	Gordon J	Spuhler JO	Johnston CP	McCormack JC	Dicks RW	Walker RG	Robinson R	Fenton M	Dobbie H	Hepple G	Hodgson JP	Reagan CM	McCrae A	Rickaby S	Mannion WJ	Donaldson A	Hartnett JB	Round
Jan	8 (a)	Brentford	L 2-3	Walker, Spuhler	30,000	1	10	3	4	5	6	8				11	2	9				7						3
				Apps		1	1	1	1	1	1	1				1	1	1				1						
				Goals								1				1												

1949-50
Division 1

Date	Opponent	Result	Scorers	Att.	Ugolini R	Robinson R	Hardwick GFM	Bell HD	Blenkinsopp TW	Gordon J	Spuhler JO	McKennan PS	McCrae A	Mannion WJ	Hartnett JB	Dicks RW	Hepple G	Walker RG	Rickaby S	Whittaker W	Brown J	Linacre W	Desmond P	Dobbie H	Woodward T	Reagan CM	Fenton M	Hodgson JP	Fitzsimmons AG	Delapenha LL
Aug 20 (h)	Everton	L 0-1		41,722	1	2	3	4	5	6	7	8	9	10	11															
22 (a)	Blackpool	D 1-1	Bell	28,243	1	2	3	4	5	6	7	8	9	10		11														
27 (a)	Huddersfield T	D 2-2	McCrae, McKennan	22,711	1	2		4	5	6		8	9	10			7	3	11											
31 (h)	Blackpool	W 2-0	McKennan 2 (1 pen)	47,870	1	2		4				8	9	10			6	3	11	5										
Sep 3 (h)	Portsmouth	L 1-5	McKennan (pen)	41,974	1	2		4			7	8	9	10			6	3	11	5										
7 (h)	Fulham	L 1-2	Spuhler	36,702	1	2		4			7	8	9	10				11	3	5	6									
10 (a)	Wolves	L 1-3	McCrae	50,424	1	2	3	4		6		8	9	10	11			7		5										
17 (h)	Aston Villa	L 0-2		30,525	1	2	3	4		6		8	9	10	11			7		5										
24 (a)	Charlton A	W 3-0	McKennan 2, McCrae	33,379	1	2	3	4		6		9	11	8				5		7	10									
Oct 1 (h)	Manchester C	D 0-0		38,515	1	2	3	4		6		9		8				5		7	10									
8 (a)	Liverpool	L 0-2		49,569	1	2	3		5	4	7	8	10			6		11					9							
15 (h)	Arsenal	D 1-1	McKennan	36,221	1	2	3		5	4	7	8	10			6							9	11						
22 (a)	Bolton W	W 2-1	Mannion, Woodward	30,095	1	2	3		5	4		9	8	10		6								11	7					
29 (h)	Birmingham C	W 1-0	Woodward	33,214	1	2	3		5	4		9	8	10		6								11	7					
Nov 5 (a)	Derby C	L 0-1		24,920	1	2	3		5	4		9	8	10		6								11	7					
12 (h)	West Brom A	W 3-0	McKennan, Mannion, Woodward	28,408	1	2	3		5	4		9	10	8		6		11							7					
19 (a)	Manchester U	L 0-2		44,646	1	2		4	5	6		9	10	8		3		11							7					
26 (h)	Chelsea	W 2-1	McCrae, Walker	24,815	1		3	4	5	6		9	10	8		2		11							7					
Dec 3 (a)	Stoke C	L 0-1		17,475	1		3	4		6		9	10	8		2		11		5		7								
10 (h)	Burnley	W 4-1	Linacre, McCrae 2, Walker	26,369	1		3	4		6		9	10	8		2		11		5		7								
17 (a)	Everton	L 1-3	Mannion	25,864	1		3	4		6		9	10	8		2		11		5		7								
24 (h)	Huddersfield T	W 3-0	McKennan 2 (1 pen), Walker	33,424	1		3	4		6		9	10	8		2		11		5		7								
26 (a)	Newcastle U	W 1-0	McCrae	61,184	1		3	4		6		9	10	8		2		11		5		7								
27 (h)	Newcastle U	W 1-0	McKennan	*53,802	1		3	4		6		9	10	8		2		11		5		7								
31 (a)	Portsmouth	D 1-1	McKennan	32,644	1		3	4		6		9	10	8		2		11		5		7								
Jan 14 (h)	Wolves	W 2-0	Walker, Spuhler	41,155	1			4	3	6	9		8	10		2		11		5		7								
21 (a)	Aston Villa	L 0-4		32,387	1			4	3	6		8		10		2		11		5					7	9				
Feb 4 (h)	Charlton A	W 1-0	Woodward	26,772		2		4	3	6		8		10						5		7	9	11			1			
18 (a)	Manchester C	W 1-0	Woodward	59,714	1	2		4	3	6		9	10	8						5		7								
25 (h)	Liverpool	W 4-1	McKennan 2, McCrae, Walker	31,804	1	2		4	3	6		9	10	8				11		5		7								
Mar 8 (a)	Arsenal	D 1-1	McCrae	34,464	1	2		4	3	6		9	10	8				11		5		7								
11 (h)	Manchester U	L 2-3	Walker, Woodward	46,702	1	2		4	3	6		9	10	8				11		5		7								
25 (h)	Derby C	W 3-1	McCrae, Mannion, McKennan	30,298	1		3	4		6	7	9	10	8		2				5		11								
29 (a)	Chelsea	L 1-2	Mannion	15,513	1		3	4	2	6	7	9	10	8						5		11								
Apr 1 (a)	West Brom A	W 3-0	Reagan 2, McCrae	32,972	1			4	2			9	10	11	3					5	6				7	8				
7 (a)	Sunderland	L 0-2		62,487	1			4	2			9	10	11	3					5	6				7	8				
8 (h)	Bolton W	W 2-0	Spuhler 2	21,764	1	2		4	3	6	9		10	8	11					5					7					
10 (h)	Sunderland	W 2-0	Bell, Reagan	44,260	1	2		4	3	6	9		10	8	11					5					7					
15 (a)	Birmingham C	D 0-0		31,579	1	2		4	3	6	9		10		11					5					7	8				
22 (h)	Stoke C	W 2-0	McCrae, Mannion (pen)	27,225	1	2		4	3		9		10	8	11					5	6				7					
29 (a)	Burnley	L 2-3	McCrae, Whitaker	12,367	1	2		4	3		9		10	8	11					5	6				7					
May 6 (a)	Fulham	W 2-1	Gordon, McCrae	21,031	1	2		4	3	6	7	9	10	11						5										8
	*Ground attendance record	Apps			41	28	22	34	19	38	20	33	36	38	11	22	11	22	3	29	5	19	2	3	12	8	1	1	3	1
		Goals						2		1	4	15	14	6				6		1		1			6	3				

FA Cup

Date	Opponent	Result	Scorers	Att.	Ugolini R	Robinson R	Hardwick GFM	Bell HD	Blenkinsopp TW	Gordon J	Spuhler JO	McKennan PS	McCrae A	Mannion WJ	Hartnett JB	Dicks RW	Hepple G	Walker RG	Rickaby S	Whittaker W	Brown J	Linacre W	Desmond P	Dobbie H	Woodward T	Reagan CM	Fenton M	Hodgson JP	Fitzsimmons AG	Delapenha LL	Round
Jan 7 (a)	Aston Villa	D 2-2	Linacre, McKennan	49,564	1		3	4		6		9	10	8		2		11		5		7									3
11 (h)	Aston Villa	D 0-0‡		49,850	1		3	4		6		9	10	8		2		11		5		7									R
16 (n†)	Aston Villa	W 3-0	McCrae 2, Mannion	43,011	1			4	3	6	9		10	8		2		11		5		7									2R
28 (a)	Chesterfield	L 2-3	Walker, Spuhler	27,500	1		3	4		6	9	8	10			2		11		5		7									4
		Apps			4		3	4	1	4	2	3	4	3		4		4		4		4									
		Goals									1	1	2	1				1				1									

‡After extra-time. †Played at Elland Road, Leeds.

1950-51
Division 1

Date	Opponent	Res	Scorers	Att	Ugolini R	Robinson R	Hardwick GFM	Bell HD	Whitaker W	Gordon J	Delapenha LL	Mannion WJ	Spuhler JO	McCrae A	Walker RG	Dicks RW	Woodward T	Hepple G	Reagan CM	Donaldson A	Hartnett JB	Blenkinsopp TW	Auld WB	McKennan PS	Linacre W	Brown J	Fitzsimons AG
Aug 19 (a)	Portsmouth	D 1-1	Mannion	43,773	1	2	3	4	5	6	7	8	9	10	11												
23 (h)	Everton	W 4-0	McCrae 3, Spuhler	41,478	1	2	3	4	5	6	7	8	9	10	11												
26 (h)	Chelsea	W 3-0	McCrae, Mannion, Walker	41,573	1	2	3	4	5	6	7	8	9	10	11												
30 (a)	Everton	L 2-3	Spuhler 2	43,459	1		3	4	5	6	7	8	9	10	11	2											
Sep 2 (a)	Burnley	L 1-3	Hardwick	29,779	1		3	4	5	6		8	9	10	11	2	7										
6 (h)	West Brom A	W 2-1	Spuhler, McCrae	28,829	1			4	5	6	7	8	9	10		2	11	3									
9 (h)	Arsenal	W 2-1	Spuhler, Delapenha	46,119	1	2		4	5	6	7	8	9	10		3	11										
13 (a)	West Brom A	W 3-2	Spuhler, Walker, McCrae	31,530	1	2		4	5	6	7	8	9	10	11	3											
16 (a)	Sheffield W	W 1-0	Walker	46,958	1	2		4	5	6	7	8	9	10	11	3											
23 (h)	Manchester U	L 1-2	Delapenha	48,051	1	2		4	5	6	7	8	9	10	11	3											
30 (h)	Huddersfield T	W 8-0	Mannion 3 (1 pen), Spuhler, McCrae 3, Walker	32,401	1	2	3	4	5	6	7	8	9	10	11												
Oct 7 (a)	Wolves	W 4-3	McCrae 2, Walker (pen), Spuhler	39,477	1	2	3	4	5	6		8	9	10	11					7							
14 (h)	Sunderland	D 1-1	McCrae	52,764	1	2	3	4	5		7	8	9	10	11	6											
21 (a)	Liverpool	D 0-0		47,426	1	2	3	4	5		7	8	9	10	11	6											
28 (h)	Fulham	D 1-1	Mannion	34,117	1	2	3	4	5	6		8	9	10	11		7										
Nov 4 (a)	Aston Villa	W 1-0	Bell	36,542	1	2	3	4	5	6	7	8		10				11		9							
11 (h)	Derby C	D 1-1	McCrae	36,943	1			4	5	6	8	10	7	11		2		3		9							
18 (a)	Bolton W	W 2-0	Spuhler, McCrae	37,296	1	2		4	5	6	7	8	9	10	11	3											
25 (h)	Blackpool	W 4-3	McCrae 3, Spuhler	40,487	1	2		4	5	6	7	8	9	10		3	11										
Dec 2 (a)	Tottenham H	D 3-3	Hartnett, Mannion, Delapenha	61,148	1	2		4	5	6	7	8	9	10		3					11						
9 (a)	Charlton A	W 7-3	Walker, Donaldson, Mannion 2, McCrae 2, E.Croker(og)*	34,050	1	2		4	5	6	7	8		10	11	3				9							
16 (h)	Portsmouth	W 3-1	Mannion 2 (2 pens), Delapenha	27,163	1	2		4	5	6	7	8		10	11	3				9							
23 (a)	Chelsea	D 1-1	Delapenha	35,323	1	2		4	5	6	7	8	9	10	11	3											
25 (h)	Newcastle U	W 2-1	Spuhler, Walker	41,318	1	2		4	5	6		8	10	7	11	3				9							
30 (h)	Burnley	D 3-3	McCrae, Mannion†, Delapenha	34,349	1	2		4	5	6	7	8	9	10	11	3											
Jan 13 (a)	Arsenal	L 1-3	L.Compton (og)	63,038	1	2		4	5	6	7	8	9	10		3					11						
20 (h)	Sheffield W	W 2-1	Dicks, Auld	34,031	1	2		4		6		8	9		7	3	10						5	11			
Feb 3 (a)	Manchester U	L 0-1		46,454	1	9		4	5	6		8	10			11	2	7	3								
17 (a)	Huddersfield T	W 3-2	Mannion 2 (1 pen), Delapenha	23,533	1	2		4	5	6	7	8		10	11	3				9							
Mar 3 (a)	Sunderland	L 1-2	Spuhler	57,958	1	2		4	5	6	7	10	9		11	3				8							
10 (h)	Liverpool	D 1-1	McKennan	29,247	1			4		6	7	10	9	8		2		3				5		11			
17 (a)	Fulham	L 0-2		29,446	1			4		6	7	10		8		2		3				5		9	11		
23 (h)	Stoke C	W 1-0	McKennan	36,200	1			4		6	7	8		10		2		3				5		9	11		
24 (h)	Aston Villa	W 2-1	Linacre, Delapenha	28,580	1			4		6	7	10		8		2		3				5		9	11		
26 (a)	Stoke C	L 0-2		19,000	1			4		6	7	10	9			2		3				5		8	11		
31 (a)	Derby C	L 0-6		16,788	1	2		4		6	7	10	9	8		3						5			11		
Apr 7 (h)	Bolton W	D 1-1	Bell	24,423	1	2		4			7	8	9		11	3						5				6	10
11 (h)	Wolves	L 1-2	McCrae	29,767	1	2		4			7		9	10	11	3						5				6	8
14 (a)	Blackpool	L 1-2	McKennan	16,300	1	2		4			7			10	11	3						5		9		6	8
21 (h)	Tottenham H	D 1-1	Spuhler	36,689	1	2		4			7		9	10	11	3						5				6	8
28 (a)	Charlton A	L 0-3		35,935	1	2		4			7		9	10	11	3						5				6	8
May 5 (a)	Newcastle U	L 0-1		35,935	1	2		4	5		7		9	10	11	3										6	8
Apps					42	33	11	42	32	34	40	35	35	32	29	35	7	7	1	7	2	12	2	7	5	6	6
Goals							1	2			8	14	13	21	7	1				1	1		1	3	1		

*Some sources credit Delapenha, club credit E.Croker (og).

†Some sources credit Spuhler, club credit Mannion.

2 own-goals

FA Cup

Round

Date	Opponent	Res	Scorers	Att	Ugolini R	Robinson R	Hardwick GFM	Bell HD	Whitaker W	Gordon J	Delapenha LL	Mannion WJ	Spuhler JO	McCrae A	Walker RG	Dicks RW
Jan 6 (a)	Leeds U	L 0-1		45,483	1	2		4	5	6	7	8	9	10	11	3
Apps					1	1		1	1	1	1	1	1	1	1	1
Goals																

Round 3

1951-52
Division 1

Date	Opponent	Result	Scorers	Att	Ugolini R	Robinson R	Dicks RW	Bell HD	Blenkinsopp TW	Gordon J	Linacre W	Mannion WJ	Mochan N	McCrae A	Walker RG	Delpenha LL	Whitaker W	Fitzsimons AG	Patterson RL	Spuhler JO	Aitken GB	Hartnett JB	Lawrie S	Barnard RS	Corbett R	Russell ET	Mulholland FG	Bilcliff R	Norris OP	Hodgson JP
Aug 18 (h)	Tottenham H	W 2-1	Farley (og), Bell	44,004	1	2	3	4	5	6	7	8	9	10	11															
22 (a)	Manchester U	L 2-4	Mochan 2	39,176	1	2	3	4	5	6	7	10	9			11		8												
25 (a)	Preston NE	W 1-0	Delapenha	37,389	1	2	3	4		6	7	10	9			11	5	8												
29 (h)	Manchester U	L 1-4	Delapenha (pen)	44,434	1	2	3	4		6	7	10	9			11	5	8												
Sep 1 (h)	Burnley	W 5-0	Mannion 2, Delapenha, Mochan, Walker	31,711	1	2	3	4		6		8	9		11	7	5			10										
3 (a)	Bolton W	L 1-3	Mochan	33,811	1	2	3	4		6		8	9		11	7	5			10										
8 (a)	Charlton A	L 3-4	Walker (pen), Mannion, Fitzsimons	26,999	1	2	6	4	3			8	9		11	7	5	7		10										
15 (h)	Fulham	W 2-0	McCrae, Mochan	23,626	1	2	6	4	3			8	9	10	11		5	7												
22 (a)	Huddersfield T	L 0-1		27,995	1	2	6	4	3			8	9	10	11		5	7												
29 (a)	West Brom A	W 3-2	Delapenha (pen), Mochan 2	28,830	1	2	6	4	3			8	9	10		7	5			11										
Oct 6 (h)	Chelsea	D 0-0		30,010	1	2		4	6	3		8	9	10		7	5			11										
13 (a)	Portsmouth	L 4-5	Fitzsimons, Mochan, Delapenha (pen), McCrae	34,633	1	2	6	4	3			10	9	11		7	5	8												
20 (h)	Liverpool	D 3-3	Mannion, Spuhler, Delpenha (pen)	26,126	1	2	6	4	3			8	9	10		7	5			11										
27 (a)	Blackpool	D 2-2	Spuhler, Mochan	23,195	1		3	4	2	6	7		9	10			5	8		11										
Nov 3 (h)	Arsenal	L 0-3		35,408	1	2	3	4		6		8	9	10	11				5				7							
10 (a)	Manchester C	L 1-2	Fitzsimons	47,522	1	2	3	4	5	6		10	9			7		8		11										
17 (h)	Derby C	D 0-0		25,656	1	2	3	4	5	6		10	9			7		8		11										
24 (a)	Aston Villa	L 0-2		25,415	1	2	3	4	5	6		10	9			7		8		11										
Dec 1 (h)	Sunderland	L 0-2		36,629	1	3	6	4			7	8	9			11	5			10					2					
8 (a)	Wolves	L 0-4		23,800	1	3	6	4	2			10	9			7	5	8		11										
15 (a)	Tottenham H	L 1-3	Delapenha (pen)	37,781	1	2	6	4			7	10	9			11	5	8							3					
22 (h)	Preston NE	L 2-5	Mannion, Delapenha (pen)	16,899	1		6	4			7	10	9			11	5	8						2	3					
26 (h)	Stoke C	W 3-0	Mannion, McCrae, Walker	29,515	1	2		4	6			8	9	10	11	7	5								3					
29 (a)	Burnley	L 1-7	Mochan	26,057	1	2	6					8	9	10	11	7	5								3	4				
Jan 5 (h)	Charlton A	W 2-1	Delpenha, Spuhler	24,672	1	2		4				8		10		11	5	7		9					3	6				
19 (a)	Fulham	L 0-6		28,941	1	2		4				8	9			11		7		10					3	5	6			
26 (h)	Huddersfield T	W 2-1	Spuhler, Mannion	22,876	1							8		10		11	5	7		9				2	3	4	6			
Feb 9 (h)	West Brom A	L 0-1		21,604	1							8	9			11	5	7		10				2	3	4	6			
16 (a)	Chelsea	L 0-5		37,805	1	11						8	9			7	5			10				2	3	4	6			
Mar 1 (h)	Portsmouth	W 2-1	Mannion 2 (1 pen)	26,599	1			4	3	6		8		10		11	5			9		7	2							
8 (a)	Liverpool	D 1-1	Mannion	41,945	1			4	3	6		8		10		11	5			9		7			2					
15 (h)	Blackpool	W 1-0	Spuhler	33,094	1			4	3	6		8		10		11	5			9		7			2					
22 (a)	Arsenal	L 1-3	Walker	50,979	1			4	3	6	7	8		10	11		5			9					2					
29 (h)	Manchester C	D 2-2	Bell, McCrae	16,920	1			4	3	6		8		10		11	5			9		7			2					
Apr 5 (a)	Derby C	L 1-3	Mochan	10,567	1	2		4	3	6		8	9	10		11	5			7										
11 (a)	Newcastle U	W 2-0	Spuhler, McCrae	59,364	1			4	2	6		8		10		11				9	5				3				7	
12 (h)	Aston Villa	W 2-0	McCrae, Delapenha	36,448	1			4	2	6		8		10		11				9	5	7			3					
14 (h)	Newcastle U	W 2-1	Walker, Delapenha	37,670	1			4	2	6		8		10	7	11				9	5				3					
19 (a)	Sunderland	L 1-3	Spuhler	23,591	1			4	2	6		8		10		11				9	5	7			3					
23 (a)	Bolton W	W 2-0	Delapenha (pen), Mannion	23,591	1			4	2	6		8	9	10		11				7	5				3					
26 (h)	Wolves	W 4-0	Walker, Delapenha 2 (1 pen), Mochan	25,577	1			4		6		8	9		7	11				10	5				3			2		
May 3 (a)	Stoke C	L 2-3	Walker, Delapenha	11,554				4		6		8	9		7	11				10	5				3			2		1
Apps					41	20	27	38	21	30	7	39	29	24	27	33	29	16	1	25	7	5	2	6	16	5	5	6	2	1
Goals								2				11	12	6	7	15		3		7										

1 own-goal

FA Cup

Date	Opponent	Result	Scorers	Att	Ugolini R	Robinson R	Dicks RW	Bell HD	Blenkinsopp TW	Gordon J	Linacre W	Mannion WJ	Mochan N	McCrae A	Walker RG	Delpenha LL	Whitaker W	Fitzsimons AG	Patterson RL	Spuhler JO	Aitken GB	Hartnett JB	Lawrie S	Barnard RS	Corbett R	Russell ET	Mulholland FG	Bilcliff R	Norris OP	Hodgson JP	Round
Jan 12 (h)	Derby C	D 2-2	Mannion 2	35,850	1		2	4				8	9	10	11	7										3	5	6				3
16 (a)	Derby C	W 2-0	Delapenha 2	30,711	1		2	4				8		10	11	9		7								3	5	6				R
Feb 6 (h)	Doncaster R	L 1-4	Bell	41,560	1	11	2	4				8	9	10		7										3	5	6				4
Apps					3		3	3				3	1	2	2	3		1		2					1	3	3	3			
Goals								1				2				2														

1952-53
Division 1

Date	Opponent	Result	Scorers	Att.	Ugolini R	Robinson R	Corbett R	Bell HD	Whitaker W	Russell ET	Delapenha LL	Mannion WJ	Mochan N	Fitzsimons AG	Walker RG	Blenkinsopp TW	McCrae A	Lawrie S	Dicks RW	Gordon J	Spuhler JO	Rayment JW	Edwards WI	Bilcliff R	Aitken GB	Norris OP	Mulholland FG	Hodgson JP
Aug 23 (a)	Burnley	W 1-0	Mochan	27,386	1	2	3	4	5	6	7	8	9	10	11													
27 (h)	Cardiff C	W 3-0	Bell 2, Fitzsimons	42,159	1	2	3	4	5	6	7	8	9	10	11													
30 (h)	Preston NE	D 1-1	Mannion	36,412	1	2	3	4		6	7	8	9		11		5	10										
Sep 3 (a)	Cardiff C	D 1-1	McCrae	51,512	1	2	3	4		6		8	9		11		5	10	7									
6 (a)	Stoke C	L 0-1		32,062	1		3	4	5			8	9		11		10	7	2	6								
13 (h)	Manchester C	W 5-4	Spuhler 2, Mannion, Fitzsimons, Delapenha	30,924	1	2	3	4	5	6	7	8		10	11						9							
17 (a)	Sheffield W	L 0-2		41,388	1	2	3	4	5	6	7	8		10	11						9							
20 (a)	Liverpool	L 1-4	Mannion	40,750	1	2	3	4	5	6	11	8		10							9	7						
27 (h)	Bolton W	L 1-2	Mannion	26,679	1	2		4	5	6	7	8		10	11				3		9							
Oct 4 (h)	West Brom A	W 4-2	Fitzsimons, Delapenha, McCrae, Mochan	24,420	1	2			5	6	7	8	9		11		3	10		4								
11 (a)	Aston Villa	L 0-1		30,280	1	2			5	6	7	8			11		3	10		4	9							
18 (h)	Sunderland	L 1-2	McCrae	38,305	1	2	3	4			7	8			11		5	10		6	9							
25 (a)	Wolves	D 3-3	Edwards, Russell, Mannion	36,683	1	2		4		6		8			11	10	5		7	3			9					
Nov 1 (h)	Charlton A	W 1-0	Fitzsimons	28,745	1		3	4		6		8		10	11						7	9		2	5			
8 (a)	Arsenal	L 1-2	Walker	48,564	1		3	4		6		8		10	11						7			2	5	9		
15 (h)	Derby C	W 1-0	Walker (pen)	14,682	1		3	4	5			8			11		10			6	7			2		9		
22 (h)	Blackpool	D 1-1	Norris	19,934	1		3	4		6		8		10	11						7			2	5	9		
29 (h)	Chelsea	W 4-0	Mannion 2, Lawrie, Delapenha	19,683	1		3	4			6	8		10	11			7						2	5	9		
Dec 6 (a)	Manchester U	L 2-3	Mannion, Delapenha (pen)	29,619	1		3	4			6	8		10	11						7			2	5	9		
13 (h)	Portsmouth	W 3-2	Walker, Mannion, Fitzsimons	22,583	1		3	4			6	8		10	11						7			2	5	9		
20 (h)	Burnley	D 2-2	Mannion, Fitzsimons	19,155	1		3	4			6	8		10	11						7			2	5	9		
25 (a)	Tottenham H	L 1-7	Norris	36,102	1		3	4			6	8		10	11						7			2	5	9		
27 (h)	Tottenham H	L 0-2		23,265	1		3	4			6	8		10	11						7			2	5	9		
Jan 1 (h)	Sheffield W	D 2-2	McCrae, Delapenha	30,632	1	3		4	5		7	8		10	11		9			6				2				
3 (a)	Preston NE	L 0-3		29,139	1	3				6	7	8		10	11		9							2	5		4	
17 (h)	Stoke C	D 0-0		20,861	1	3	11		5			8	9				10		7	6				2			4	
24 (a)	Manchester C	L 1-5	Mannion	26,822	1	2	3		5			8	9	10			11			6	7						4	
Feb 7 (h)	Liverpool	L 2-3	Delapenha 2 (1 pen)	15,445		3		4	5		6	8		10	11						9	7		2				1
18 (a)	Bolton W	L 3-5	Rayment 2, Spuhler	15,041	1	3		4	5			8		10	11					6	9	7		2				
21 (a)	West Brom A	L 0-3		24,269	1	3		4	5			8		10	11						9	7		2			6	
Mar 3 (h)	Aston Villa	W 1-0	Walker (pen)	13,176	1	2		4	5			8		10	11					6	9	7					3	
7 (a)	Sunderland	D 1-1	Spuhler	38,237	1	2		4	5		8			10	11					6	9	7					3	
14 (h)	Wolves	D 1-1	Mannion	24,454	1	2		4	5			8		10	11					6	9	7					3	
21 (a)	Charlton A	L 0-2		22,204	1	2		4	5		7	8		10	11					6	9						3	
28 (h)	Arsenal	W 2-0	Fitzsimons, Spuhler	25,911	1	5	3	4			7	8		10	11						9			2			6	
Apr 3 (a)	Newcastle U	L 0-1		48,434	1		3	4			7	8		10	11						9			2	5		6	
4 (h)	Derby C	D 3-3	Edwards, Mannion 2	17,935	1		3	4			7	8		10	11								9	2	5		6	
6 (h)	Newcastle U	W 2-1	Mannion 2	37,926	1		3	4			7	8		10	11						9			2	5		6	
11 (h)	Blackpool	W 5-1	Mannion, Fitzsimons 2, Spuhler 2	38,847	1		3	4			7	8		10	11						9			2	5		6	
18 (a)	Chelsea	D 1-1	Fitzsimons	40,042	1		3	4			7	8		10	11						9			2	5		6	
25 (h)	Manchester U	W 5-0	Mannion 2, Delapenha, Spuhler, Fitzsimons	34,344	1		3	4			7	8		10	11						9			2	5		6	
May 2 (a)	Portsmouth	W 4-1	Bell, Spuhler 2, Delapenha	18,757	1		3	4			7	8		10	11						9			2	5		6	
Apps					41	24	29	37	17	24	30	41	9	35	31	6	10	9	10	10	19	9	7	28	10	9	16	1
Goals								3		1	9	18	2	11	4		4	1			10	2	2			3		

FA Cup

Date	Opponent	Result	Scorers	Att.	Ugolini R	Robinson R	Corbett R	Bell HD	Whitaker W	Russell ET	Delapenha LL	Mannion WJ	Mochan N	Fitzsimons AG	Walker RG	Blenkinsopp TW	McCrae A	Lawrie S	Dicks RW	Gordon J	Spuhler JO	Rayment JW	Edwards WI	Bilcliff R	Aitken GB	Norris OP	Mulholland FG	Hodgson JP	Round
Jan 10 (a)	Aston Villa	L 1-3	Fitzsimons	41,557	1		3				7	8		10	11					6				2	5	9	4		3
Apps					1		1				1	1		1	1					1				1	1	1	1		
Goals														1														

1953-54
Division 1

Date	Opponent	Res	Scorers	Att	Ugolini R	Robinson R	Corbett R	McMurray J	Dicks RW	Mulholland FG	Delapenha LL	Mannion WJ	McPherson K	Fitzsimons AG	Walker RG	Bilcliff R	Bell HD	Edwards WI	Spuhler JO	Gordon J	Rayment JW	Hepple G	Hartnett JB	Norris OP	Birbeck J	Lawrie S	O'Connell SPC	Stonehouse D	Barnard RS	Harris WC	Watkin TWS	Robinson JN
Aug 19 (h)	Cardiff C	D 0-0		33,726	1	2	3	4	5	6	7	8	9	10	11																	
22 (h)	Preston NE	L 0-4		32,891	1	2	3	4	5	6	7	8	9	10	11																	
26 (a)	Bolton W	L 2-3	Mannion, Delapenha	29,502	1		3		5	6	7	8	9	10	11	2	4															
29 (a)	Tottenham H	L 1-4	Delapenha	44,911	1		3		5	6	7	8	9	10	11	2	4															
Sep 2 (h)	Bolton W	W 3-2	Delapenha 2, Mannion	25,458	1		3		5	6	7	8		10	11	2	4	9														
5 (h)	Burnley	L 1-3	Edwards	32,957	1		3		5	6	7	8		10	11	2	4	9														
9 (a)	Manchester U	D 2-2	Fitzsimons, Delapenha	19,893	1	2	3		5	6	7	8		10	11		4		9													
12 (a)	Charlton A	L 1-8	Spuhler	23,790	1	2	3		5	6	7	8		10	11		4		9													
16 (h)	Manchester U	L 1-4	Delapenha (pen)	23,791	1	5	3			6	7	8	9	10	11	2	4															
19 (h)	Sheffield W	W 4-1	Mannion, Spuhler, Gannon (og), Delapenha	22,638	1	5	3				7	8		10	11	2	4		9	6												
26 (a)	Huddersfield T	L 1-2	Mannion	37,054	1	5					7	8		10	11	2	4		9	6		3										
Oct 3 (a)	West Brom A	L 1-2	Spuhler	36,865	1	5					7	8		10	11	2	4		9	6		3										
10 (h)	Sheffield U	W 2-0	Mannion 2	26,136	1	5					7	8		10	11	2	4		9	6		3										
17 (a)	Chelsea	D 1-1	Rayment	23,513	1	5						8		10		2	4		9	6	7	3	11									
24 (h)	Blackpool	L 0-1		39,416	1	5					7	8		10	11	2	4		9	6		3										
31 (a)	Portsmouth	W 2-0	Fitzsimons, McPherson	24,342	1	5					7	8	9	10		2	4			6		3	11									
Nov 7 (h)	Wolves	D 3-3	Fitzsimons, McPherson, Hartnett	24,284	1	5					7	8	9	10		2	4			6		3	11									
14 (a)	Aston Villa	L 3-5	McPherson, Delapenha, Rayment	20,735	1	5					8		9	10		2	4			6	7	3	11									
21 (h)	Manchester C	L 0-1		22,099	1	5	3		4			8	9	10		2					7		11		6							
28 (a)	Sunderland	W 2-0	Walker 2	41,538	1	5	3		2		10		9		11		4		8						6	7						
Dec 5 (h)	Arsenal	W 2-0	Spuhler 2	30,085	1	5	3		2		10	8			11		4		9						6	7						
12 (a)	Cardiff C	L 0-1		31,776	1	5	3		2		10		9		11		4		8						6	7						
19 (a)	Preston NE	L 0-1		18,909	1	5	3		2		10	8	9		11		4								6	7						
25 (h)	Newcastle U	L 2-3	Spuhler, Walker	28,138	1	5	3		2		10	8			11		4		9						6	7						
26 (a)	Newcastle U	W 3-2	Delapenha, Lawrie, O'Connell	43,750	1	5	3		2		10				11		4		9						6	7	8					
Jan 2 (h)	Tottenham H	W 3-0	Spuhler, Lawrie, O'Connell	35,141	1	5			2		7	8					4		9						6	11	10	3				
16 (a)	Burnley	L 0-5		23,481	1	5			2	4		8	9										11		6	7	10	3				
23 (h)	Charlton A	L 0-2		19,327	1	5			3	4		8		10	11	2			9						6	7						
Feb 6 (a)	Sheffield W	L 2-4	Delapenha 2	30,856	1				5	4	10	8			11				9						6	7		3	2			
13 (h)	Huddersfield T	L 0-3		18,717	1				5		7	8		10	11	2	4		9						6			3				
24 (h)	West Brom A	D 1-1	Delapenha (pen)	17,144	1	5	3		6		10	8					4	9			7		11		2							
27 (a)	Sheffield U	D 2-2	Delapenha, Mannion	29,029	1		3		5		10	8					4	9		6	7		11		2							
Mar 6 (h)	Chelsea	D 3-3	Spuhler, Delapenha 2	27,920	1	5			2		10	8					4	9			7							3		6	11	
13 (a)	Blackpool	D 0-0		20,334	1	5			3		10	8					4	9			7							2		6	11	
20 (h)	Portsmouth	D 2-2	Mannion, Harris	20,743	1		3		5		10	8					4	9			7							2		6	11	
27 (a)	Wolves	W 4-2	Watkin, McPherson 2, Delapenha	29,145	1		3		5		10	8	9				4									7		2		6	11	
Apr 3 (h)	Aston Villa	W 2-1	Mannion, McPherson	21,142	1		3		5		10	8	9				4									7		2		6	11	
10 (a)	Manchester C	L 2-5	Delapenha, Little (og)	28,445	1		3		5	6	10	8	9													7		2		4	11	
16 (h)	Liverpool	L 0-1		26,882	1	5	3			6	10	8							9							7		2		4	11	
17 (h)	Sunderland	D 0-0		38,762	1	5			3		10	8	9				4									7		2		6	11	
19 (a)	Liverpool	L 1-4	Watkin	22,174	1	5			3		10	8	9				4									7		2		6	11	
24 (a)	Arsenal	L 1-3	Delapenha	35,069	1	5			3	6	7	10	9				4				11							2				8
Apps					42	30	24	2	32	14	40	37	19	17	21	17	35	7	19	10	12	8	9	1	11	16	3	16	1	9	9	1
Goals											18	9	6	3	3		1	8			2		1			2	2			1	2	

2 own-goals

FA Cup

Date	Opponent	Res	Scorers	Att	Ugolini R	Robinson R	Corbett R	McMurray J	Dicks RW	Mulholland FG	Delapenha LL	Mannion WJ	McPherson K	Fitzsimons AG	Walker RG	Bilcliff R	Bell HD	Edwards WI	Spuhler JO	Gordon J	Rayment JW	Hepple G	Hartnett JB	Norris OP	Birbeck J	Lawrie S	O'Connell SPC	Stonehouse D	Barnard RS	Harris WC	Watkin TWS	Robinson JN	Round
Jan 9 (h)	Leicester C	D 0-0		38,701	1	5			3		7	8			11	2	4		9						6		10						3
14 (a)	Leicester C	L 2-3	Spuhler, Mannion	29,736	1	5			3		7	8				2	4		9						6	11	10						R
Apps					2	2			2		2	2			1	2	2		2						2	1	2						
Goals												1							1													

1954-55
Division 2

Date	Opponent	Res	Scorers	Att	Ugolini R	Dicks RW	Corbett R	Bell HD	Robinson R	Harris WC	Rayment JW	Delapenha LL	McPherson K	Robinson JN	Walker RG	Hodgson JP	Stonehouse D	McMurray J	Hartnett JB	Mulholland FG	Watkin TS	Fitzsimons AG	Mitchell AJ	Barnard RS	Birbeck J	Edwards WI	Brown TE	Scott JC	Wayman C	Whitaker W	Robertson WG	Phillips BJ	Cooper D
Aug 21 (a)	Plymouth A	D 2-2	McPherson, Delapenha	26,484	1	2	3	4	5	6	7	8	9	10	11																		
25 (h)	Ipswich T	L 0-1		23,357	1	2	3	4	5	6	7	8	9	10	11																		
28 (h)	Stoke C	L 1-2	Hartnett	17,980			3	4	5	6		8	9		11	1	2		7	10													
Sep 1 (a)	Ipswich T	L 1-6	Walker	19,830		3			5	4		8			11	1	2		7	6	9	10											
4 (a)	Rotherham U	L 0-3		17,022		5	3	4			7	8				1	2		11	6	9	10											
8 (h)	Nottingham F	L 1-4	McPherson	16,241	1	5	3	4				8	7	9				2		6		10	11										
11 (h)	Luton T	L 0-2		16,071	1	5	3	4				8	9							11		10	7	2	6								
15 (a)	Nottingham F	L 2-4	Delapenha, Edwards	11,049		5	3	4				8	7			1						10	11	2	6	9							
18 (a)	Hull C	L 0-1		26,485	1	6			5	4		7										10	11	2		9	3	8					
25 (h)	Lincoln C	W 2-1	Scott 2	23,706	1	6			5	4		7										10	11	2			3	8	9				
Oct 2 (a)	Bury	W 1-0	Delapenha	18,522	1	6			5	4		7										10	11	2			3	8	9				
9 (a)	Swansea T	L 0-2		24,399	1	6			5	4		7										10	11	2			3	8	9				
16 (h)	Notts C	W 2-0	Fitzsimons, Mitchell	20,585	1	6			5	4		7										10	11	2			3	8	9				
23 (a)	Derby C	W 2-1	Delapenha, Dicks	15,541	1	6			5	4		7										10	11	2			3	8	9				
30 (h)	West Ham U	W 6-0	Bond (og), Wayman 4, Mitchell	25,601	1	6			5	4		7										10	11	2			3	8	9				
Nov 6 (a)	Blackburn R	L 0-9		29,189	1	6			5	4		7										10	11	2			3	8	9				
13 (h)	Fulham	W 4-2	Scott, Wayman 2, Delapenha	21,734	1	6			5	4		7										10	11	2			3	8	9				
20 (a)	Port Vale	D 1-1	Wayman	16,753	1	6			5	4		7										10	11	2			3	8	9				
27 (h)	Doncaster R	W 3-1	Scott 2, Wayman	21,373	1	6			5	4		7										10	11	2			3	8	9				
Dec 4 (a)	Liverpool	L 1-3	Scott	26,750	1	6			5	4		7										10	11	2			3	8	9				
11 (h)	Bristol R	W 1-0	Hartnett	20,561	1	6			5	4		7							11			10		2			3	8	9				
18 (h)	Plymouth A	W 4-1	Scott 3, Delapenha	15,662	1	6			5	4		7							11			10		2			3	8	9				
25 (a)	Leeds U	D 1-1	Scott	26,344	1	6			5	4		7							11			10		2			3	8	9				
27 (h)	Leeds U	W 1-0	Wayman	45,271	1	6			5	4		7							11			10		2			3	8	9				
Jan 1 (a)	Stoke C	W 2-1	Scott, Delapenha	19,275	1	6				4		7							11			10		2			3	8	9	5			
15 (h)	Rotherham U	W 5-1	Scott, Delapenha, Mitchell 2, Wayman	12,320	1	6				4		7										10	11	2			3	8	9	5			
22 (a)	Luton T	L 0-2		13,372	1	6				4		7										10	11	2			3	8	9	5			
Feb 5 (h)	Hull C	L 1-2	Scott	32,619	1	6			5	4		7										10	11	2			3	8	9				
12 (h)	Lincoln C	D 3-3	Wayman 2, Harris	8,368	1	6			5	4		7										10	11	2			3	8	9				
26 (h)	Swansea T	W 4-2	Wayman, Kiley (og), Scott 2	20,867	1	6			5	4		7										10		2			3	8	9		11		
Mar 5 (a)	Notts C	W 3-1	Fitzsimons, Scott 2	22,354	1	6			5	4		7										10	11	2			3	8	9				
12 (h)	Derby C	W 3-1	Delapenha, Fitzsimons 2	20,103	1	6			5	4		7										10	11	2			3	8	9				
19 (a)	West Ham U	L 1-2	Mitchell	22,313	1	6			5	4		7										10	11	2			3	8	9				
26 (h)	Blackburn R	W 4-3	Wayman 2, Delapenha 2	19,426	1	6			5	4		7										10	11	2			3	8	9				
Apr 2 (a)	Fulham	W 2-1	Fitzsimons, Delapenha	17,770	1	6			5	4		7										10	11	2			3	8	9				
8 (h)	Birmingham C	L 2-5	Delapenha (pen), Dicks	32,519	1	6			5	4		7										10	11	2			3	8	9				
9 (h)	Port Vale	W 2-0	Wayman, Delapenha	17,795	1	6			5	4		7										10	11	2			3	8	9				
11 (a)	Birmingham C	L 0-3		23,657	1	6			5	4		7	8									10	11	2			3		9				
16 (a)	Doncaster R	L 1-3	Robertson	9,925	1	6				4			8									10	11	2			3		9		7	5	
23 (h)	Liverpool	L 1-2	McPherson	11,737	1	6	3			4			8									10	11	2					9		7	5	
27 (h)	Bury	D 1-1	McPherson	7,944	1		3		5	4			8									10	7	2					9		11	6	
30 (a)	Bristol R	D 2-2	McPherson, Robertson	14,553	1	6	3		5	4			9									10	7	2							11		8
	Apps				38	39	10	7	33	41	3	38	9	2	4	4	4	1	9	5	2	38	31	36	2	2	31	29	32	3	5	3	1
	Goals					2				1		15	5		1				2			5	5			1		16	16		2		

2 own-goals

FA Cup

Date	Opponent	Res	Scorers	Att	Ugolini R	Dicks RW	Corbett R	Bell HD	Robinson R	Harris WC	Rayment JW	Delapenha LL	McPherson K	Robinson JN	Walker RG	Hodgson JP	Stonehouse D	McMurray J	Hartnett JB	Mulholland FG	Watkin TS	Fitzsimons AG	Mitchell AJ	Barnard RS	Birbeck J	Edwards WI	Brown TE	Scott JC	Wayman C	Whitaker W	Robertson WG	Phillips BJ	Cooper D	Round
Jan 8 (h)	Notts C	L 1-4	Wayman	30,503	1	6				4		7							11			10		2			3	8	9	5				3
	Apps				1	1				1		1							1			1		1			1	1	1	1				
	Goals																												1				

1955-56
Division 2

Date	Opponent	Res	Scorers	Att	Ugolini R	Barnard RS	Stonehouse D	Harris WC	Robinson R	Dicks RW	Delapenha LL	Scott JC	Wayman C	Fitzsimons AG	Mitchell AJH	McPherson K	Bilcliff R	Clough BH	Day W	Phillips BJ	Taylor PT	Lawrie S	Peacock A	Corbett R	Cooper D	Mulholland FG	Birbeck J	McLean JD
Aug 20 (h)	Notts C	W 3-0	Delapenha, Fitzsimons 2	20,291	1	2	3	4	5	6	7	8	9	10	11													
25 (a)	Swansea T	L 1-2	Wayman	21,351	1	2	3	4	5	6	7	8	9	10	11													
27 (a)	Leeds U	L 0-2		22,535	1	2	3	4	5	6	7	8	9	10	11													
31 (h)	Swansea T	W 4-1	Fitzsimons 2, McPherson 2	22,417	1	2	3	4	5	6	7	8		10	11	9												
Sep 3 (h)	Fulham	D 1-1	Delapenha (pen)	26,275	1		3	4	5	6	7	8		10	11	9	2											
10 (a)	Bury	D 1-1	McPherson	12,278	1		3	4	5	6	7	8		10	11	9	2											
17 (h)	Barnsley	D 1-1	Fitzsimons	24,960	1		3	4	5	6	7	8		10	11		2	9										
24 (a)	Liverpool	D 1-1	Scott	35,213	1	2	3	4	5	6	7	8		10	11			9										
Oct 1 (a)	Bristol C	L 0-2		28,788	1	2	3	4	5	6	7	8		10	11			9										
8 (h)	Leicester C	W 4-3	Clough, Fitzsimons, Delapenha (pen), Harris	20,642	1	2	3	4	5	6	11	8		10				9	7									
15 (h)	Lincoln C	W 2-1	Delapenha, Clough	12,532	1	2	3	4	5	6	11	8		10				9	7									
22 (h)	Stoke C	L 1-3	Delapenha	22,394	1	2	3	4		6	11	8		10				9	7	5								
29 (a)	Hull C	D 2-2	Fitzsimons, Day	14,013		2	3	4	5	6	11		9	10		8			7		1							
Nov 5 (h)	Nottingham F	W 3-2	Wayman, Lawrie, McPherson	17,573		2	3	4	5	6			9	10		8			7		1	11						
12 (a)	Sheffield W	L 1-3	Fitzsimons	24,030		2	3	4	5	6	11	8	9	10					7		1							
19 (h)	Doncaster R	W 4-1	Scott, Fitzsimons 2, Wayman	15,360		2	3	4		6	11	8	9	10					7	5	1							
26 (a)	Bristol R	L 2-7	Wayman, Delapenha	23,716		2	3	4		6	11	8	9						7	5	1		10					
Dec 3 (h)	Blackburn R	W 1-0	Delapenha (pen)	16,827	1		3	4	5	6	11	8	9	10			2		7									
10 (a)	Plymouth A	L 0-4		12,651	1		3	4	5	6	11	8	9	10			2		7									
17 (a)	Notts C	L 0-5		9,693	1		3	4	5	6	7	8		10	11		2	9										
24 (h)	Leeds U	W 5-3	Scott, Wayman 2, Delapenha 2	19,416	1		3	4	5	6	7	8	9	10	11		2											
26 (h)	West Ham U	W 2-0	Mitchell, Wayman	22,001	1		3	4	5	6	7	8	9	10	11		2											
27 (h)	West Ham U	L 0-1		21,522	1		3	4	5	6		8		10	11		2	9	7									
31 (a)	Fulham	L 1-4	Wayman	18,470	1		3	4	5	6		8	9	10	11		2		7									
Jan 2 (h)	Port Vale	D 1-1	Fitzsimons	21,664	1		3	4	5	6		8	9	10	11		2		7									
14 (h)	Bury	L 1-3	Wayman	8,657	1			4	5	6		8	9	10	11		2		7					3				
21 (a)	Barnsley	W 4-0	Wayman 3, Betts (og)	15,934	1			4	5	6	7	8	9	10	11		2							3				
Feb 4 (h)	Liverpool	L 1-2		12,171	1			4	5	6	7	8	9	10	11		2							3				
11 (h)	Bristol C	W 2-1	Delapenha, Clough	15,412	1	2		4	5	6	11	8		10				9	7					3				
Mar 3 (a)	Stoke C	W 5-2	Delapenha, Scott 2, Fitzsimons, Day	20,135	1	2		4	5	6	11	8		10					7					3	9			
10 (h)	Plymouth A	L 1-2	Delapenha (pen)	17,278	1	2		4		6	11	8		10					7	5			9	3				
17 (a)	Nottingham F	W 4-2	Day, Peacock 2, McKinlay (og)	22,918	1	2		4	5		11	8		10					7				9	3		6		
24 (h)	Sheffield W	D 2-2	Scott 2	19,026	1	2		4	5		11	8		10					7				9	3		6		
31 (a)	Leicester C	D 1-1	Fitzsimons	28,450	1	2		4	5		11	8		10					7				9	3		6		
Apr 2 (h)	Rotherham U	L 0-1		20,803	1	2		4			11	8		10					7	5			9	3		6		
3 (a)	Rotherham U	L 1-2	Day	13,032	1	2		4				9	8	10	11				7	5				3		6		
7 (h)	Bristol R	L 0-1		12,536	1	2		4			10	9	11						7	5				3		6	8	
14 (a)	Blackburn R	L 1-2	Day	21,070	1		3	4		6	11		9	10			2		7	5								8
18 (h)	Lincoln C	W 4-2	McLean, Wayman, Delapenha 2	8,298	1		3	4		6	11		9	10			2		7	5								8
21 (h)	Hull C	W 5-1	Fitzsimons, Delapenha 2 (1 pen), Wayman, Day	11,190	1		3	4		6	11		9	10			2		7	5								8
28 (h)	Port Vale	L 2-3	Wayman, McLean	11,781	1		3	4		6	11		9	10			2		7	5								8
May 3 (a)	Doncaster R	W 1-0	Lawrie	5,670			3	4		6		8	9				2		7	5	1	11						10
Apps					36	23	30	42	30	36	35	36	23	40	19	5	19	9	25	12	6	5	6	12	1	3	3	6
Goals							1				17	7	15	14	1	4		3	6			2	2				2

2 own-goals

FA Cup

Date	Opponent	Res	Scorers	Att	Ugolini R	Barnard RS	Stonehouse D	Harris WC	Robinson R	Dicks RW	Delapenha LL	Scott JC	Wayman C	Fitzsimons AG	Mitchell AJH	McPherson K	Bilcliff R	Clough BH	Day W	Phillips BJ	Taylor PT	Lawrie S	Peacock A	Corbett R	Cooper D	Mulholland FG	Birbeck J	McLean JD	Round
Jan 7 (a)	Bradford	W 4-0	Scott 2, Delapenha, Wayman	18,524	1		3	4	5	6	7	8	9	10	11		2												3
28 (a)	Tottenham H	L 1-3	Scott	41,895	1			4	5	6	7	8	9	10	11		2							3					4
Apps					2		1	2	2	2	2	2	2	2	2		2							1					
Goals											1	3	1															

1956-57
Division 2

Date	Opp	Res	Score	Scorers	Att	Taylor PT	Bilcliff R	Stonehouse D	Harris WC	Robinson R	Dicks RW	Day W	Scott JC	Cooper D	Fitzsimons AG	Delapenha LL	Lawrie S	Clough BH	Barnard RS	McLean JD	Peacock A	Corbett R	Million E	Burbeck RT	Mulholland FG	Brown TE	Phillips BJ
Aug 18 (h) Stoke C		D	1-1	Harris	13,413	1	2	3	4	5	6		7	8	9	10	11										
21 (a) Bury		L	2-3	Clough 2	14,979	1	2	3	4	5	6		8		10	11	7	9									
25 (a) Barnsley		W	3-1	Clough 2, Delapenha	11,651	1	2		4	5	6		8		10	11	7	9	3								
29 (h) Bury		D	2-2	Delapenha, Clough	18,344	1	2		4	5	6		8		10	11	7	9	3								
Sep 1 (a) Leicester C		D	1-1	Clough	27,227	1		3	4	5	6		8		10	11		9	2	7							
4 (a) Grimsby T		L	2-3	Clough 2	20,505	1		3	4	5	6		8		10	11	7	9	2								
8 (h) Bristol R		W	3-2	Scott, Clough, Peacock	19,149	1		3	4	5	6	7	8			11		9	2		10						
12 (h) Grimsby T		W	2-1	Delapenha (pen), Clough	15,999	1		3	4	5	6	7	8			11		9	2		10						
15 (a) Notts C		L	1-2	Harris	10,190	1			4	5	6	7	8			11		9	2		10	3					
22 (h) Liverpool		D	1-1	Clough	21,912	1		3	4	5	6	7	8			11		9	2		10						
29 (a) Leyton O		L	1-3	Clough	17,146	1		3	4	5	6		8			7	11	9	2		10						
Oct 6 (h) Port Vale		W	3-1	Delapenha 2 (2 pens), Clough	18,586			3	4	5	6				10	7		9	2	8			1	11			
13 (a) Rotherham U		W	3-2	Clough, McLean, Burbeck	13,644			3	4	5	6				10	7		9	2	8			1	11			
20 (h) Bristol C		W	4-1	Clough 2, Delapenha, Harris	23,824			3	4	5	6				10	7		9	2	8			1	11			
27 (a) Swansea T		D	2-2	Dicks, McLean	17,552	1		3	4	5	6				10	7		9	2	8				11			
Nov 3 (h) Fulham		W	3-1	McLean, Clough, Burbeck	29,201	1		3	4	5	6				10	7		9	2	8				11			
10 (a) Nottingham F		W	4-0	Clough 3, Fitzsimons	20,862	1		3	4	5	6				10	7		9	2	8				11			
17 (h) West Ham U		W	3-1	Burbeck, Fitzsimons 2	31,513	1		3	4	5	6				10	7		9	2	8				11			
24 (a) Blackburn R		L	0-1		21,066	1		3	4	5	6		10			7		9	2	8				11			
Dec 1 (h) Lincoln C		W	3-0	Delapenha 2 (1 pen), Clough	24,598	1		3	4	5	6				10	7		9	2	8				11			
8 (a) Sheffield U		L	1-2	McLean	20,479	1		3	4	5	6				10	7		9	2	8				11			
15 (a) Stoke C		L	1-3	Fitzsimons	20,689	1		3	4	5	6		8		10	7		9	2					11			
22 (h) Barnsley		L	1-2	Dicks	11,147			3	4	5	6				10	7		9	2	8			1	11			
25 (h) Doncaster R		W	3-2	Clough 2, Harris	16,515	1		3	4	5	6				10	7		9	2	8				11			
26 (a) Doncaster R		L	1-2	Robinson	8,975	1		3	4	5		7	8		10			9	2					11	6		
29 (h) Leicester C		L	1-3	Fitzsimons	29,704	1		3	4	5	6		8		10	7		9	2					11			
Jan 12 (a) Bristol R		W	2-0	Scott, Clough	24,015	1			4	5	6	7	8		10			9	2					11		3	
19 (h) Notts C		D	0-0		23,085	1		3	4	5	6	7	8		10			9	2					11			
Feb 2 (h) Liverpool		W	2-1	Fitzsimons, Burbeck	38,890	1		3	4	5	6		8		10			9	2	7				11			
9 (h) Leyton O		L	1-2	Clough	27,315	1		3	4	5	6	7	8					9	2	10				11			
16 (a) Port Vale		L	1-2	Clough	12,064	1		3	4	5	6		8		10			9	2	7				11			
23 (h) Rotherham U		L	0-1		14,829	1			4	5	6	7			10			9	2	8				11		3	
Mar 2 (a) Bristol C		L	1-2	McLean	22,402	1	2		4		6	7			10			9		8				11		3	5
9 (h) Swansea T		W	6-2	Fitzsimons, Day, Harris, McLean, Clough 2	17,072	1	2	3	4		6	7			10			9		8				11			5
16 (a) Fulham		W	2-1	Clough, McLean	20,450	1	2	3	4		6	7			10			9		8				11			5
23 (h) Nottingham F		D	2-2	McLean, Clough	25,009	1	2		4	3	6	7			10			9		8				11			5
30 (a) West Ham U		D	1-1	Clough	15,166	1	2		4	3	6	7			10			9		8				11			5
Apr 6 (h) Blackburn R		W	2-1	Clough 2	20,716	1	2		4	3	6	7			10			9		8				11			5
13 (a) Lincoln C		D	1-1	McLean	8,601	1	2		4	3	6	7			10			9		8				11			5
20 (h) Sheffield U		W	3-1	Harris 2 (2 pens), Clough	21,075	1	2		4	3	6	7			10			9		8				11			5
22 (h) Huddersfield T		W	7-2	Clough 4, McLean, Fitzsimons, Harris (pen)	20,651	1	2		4	3	6	7			10			9		8				11			5
23 (a) Huddersfield T		W	1-0	Fitzsimons	13,818	1	2		4	3	6	7			10			9		8				11			5
Apps						38	21	22	42	39	41	17	19	3	36	26	4	41	30	29	4	1	4	31	1	3	10
Goals									8	1	2	1	2		9	8		38		10	1			4			

FA Cup

Date	Opp	Res	Score	Scorers	Att	Taylor PT	Bilcliff R	Stonehouse D	Harris WC	Robinson R	Dicks RW	Day W	Scott JC	Cooper D	Fitzsimons AG	Delapenha LL	Lawrie S	Clough BH	Barnard RS	McLean JD	Peacock A	Corbett R	Million E	Burbeck RT	Mulholland FG	Brown TE	Phillips BJ	Round
Jan 5 (h) Charlton A		D	1-1	Scott	32,863	1		3	4	5	6	7	8		10			9	2					11				3
10 (a) Charlton A		W	3-2	Day, Clough, Fitzsimons	22,613	1		3	4	5	6	7	8		10			9	2					11				R
26 (h) Aston Villa		L	2-3	Clough, Harris	42,396	1		3	4	5	6		8		10	7		9	2					11				4
Apps						3		3	3	3	3	2	3		3	1		3	3					3				
Goals									1			1	1		1			2										

1957-58
Division 2

Date		Result	Scorers	Att	Taylor PT	Bilcliff R	Robinson R	Harris WC	Phillips BJ	Dicks RW	Day W	McLean JD	Clough BH	Fitzsimons AG	Burbeck RT	Peacock A	Delapenha LL	Mulholland FG	Stonehouse D	Scott JC	Taylor CW	Henderson R	Holliday E	Brown TE	Birbeck J	Million E
Aug 24 (a) Stoke C		L 1-4	Clough	23,398	1	2	3	4	5	6	7	8	9	10	11											
28 (h) Rotherham U		D 2-2	Dicks, Burbeck	28,696	1	2	3	4	5	6	7	8	9	10	11											
31 (h) Bristol C		D 0-0		21,834	1	2	3	4	5	6	7	8	9		11	10										
Sep 5 (a) Rotherham U		W 4-1	Clough 2, McLean, Fitzsimons	13,195	1	2	3	4	5	6		8	9	10	11		7									
7 (a) Cardiff C		W 2-0	Clough 2	14,013	1	2	3	4	5	6		8	9	10	11		7									
11 (h) Doncaster R		W 5-0	Burbeck, Clough 4	24,758	1	2	3	4	5	6		8	9	10	11		7									
14 (h) Liverpool		D 2-2	Peacock, McLean	30,645	1	2	3	4	5	6		8	9		11	10	7									
18 (a) Doncaster R		L 2-3	McLean, Peacock	9,237	1	2	3	4	5	6	7	8			11	9	10									
21 (a) Barnsley		D 1-1	Peacock	11,577	1	2	3		5	6		8		10	11	9	7	4								
28 (a) Leyton O		L 0-4		18,487	1	2	3	4	5	6		8	9	10	11		7									
Oct 5 (h) Charlton A		W 2-0	Clough, Fitzsimons	28,123	1	2		4	5	6		8	9	10	11		7		3							
12 (h) Fulham		W 2-0	Clough 2	31,752	1	2		4	5	6		8	9	10	11		7		3							
19 (a) Swansea T		W 4-1	McLean 2, Burbeck, Clough	8,905	1	2			5	6		8	9	10	11		7	4	3							
26 (h) Derby C		W 3-2	Clough, Fitzsimons, McLean	30,531	1	2		4	5	6		8	9	10	11		7		3							
Nov 2 (a) Bristol R		L 0-5		20,390	1	2		4	5	6			9	10	11		7		3	8						
9 (h) Lincoln C		W 3-1	Clough 2, Burbeck	20,705	1	2		4	5	6		8	9	10	11		7		3							
16 (a) Notts C		L 0-2		13,800	1	2		4	5	6		8	9	10	11				3		7					
23 (h) Ipswich T		W 5-2	Clough 4, Day	20,522	1	2		4	5	6	7	8	9	10	11				3							
30 (a) Blackburn R		D 3-3	Woods (og), Day, Burbeck	29,248	1	2	3	4	5	6	7	8	9		11							10				
Dec 7 (h) Sheffield U		L 1-2	Henderson	22,207	1	2	3	4	5	6		8	9		11		7					10				
14 (a) West Ham U		L 1-2	Cantwell (og)	20,737	1	2	3	4	5	6	7		9	10					8				11			
21 (h) Stoke C		L 1-3	Clough	22,354	1	2		4	5	6	7		9	10				3	8				11			
25 (a) Huddersfield T		L 0-1		16,281	1	2		4	5										8				11	3	6	
26 (h) Huddersfield T		L 0-1		22,964	1	2			5	4	7	8	9	10									11	3	6	
28 (a) Bristol C		D 0-0		23,124	1	2		4	5		7	8	9			10							11	3	6	
Jan 11 (h) Cardiff C		W 4-1	Peacock 3, Harris (pen)	23,115	1	2		4	5		7	8	9			10							11	3	6	
18 (a) Liverpool		W 2-0	Clough, Burbeck	39,246	1	2		4	5			8	9		7	10							11	3	6	
Feb 1 (h) Barnsley		W 3-1	Clough, Peacock 2	19,498	1	2		4	5			8	9		7	10							11	3	6	
15 (a) Charlton A		L 2-6	Clough 2	26,198	1	2		4	5		7	8	9			10							11	3	6	
22 (a) Ipswich T		D 1-1	Clough	17,768	1	2		4	5			8	9		7	10							11	3	6	
Mar 1 (h) Swansea T		W 2-1	Clough 2	23,312		2		4	5				9	8	7	10							11	3	6	1
8 (a) Derby C		L 1-2	Clough	17,419		2		4	5		7		9			10						8	11	3	6	1
15 (h) Bristol R		W 4-3	Peacock 2, Clough 2	21,274		2	3	4	5		7	8	9			10							11		6	1
19 (h) Leyton O		W 2-0	Peacock 2	20,346		2	3	4	5			8	9			10	7						11		6	1
22 (a) Lincoln C		W 3-2	Holliday, McLean, Clough	8,901		2	3	4	5			8	9			10	7						11		6	1
29 (h) Notts C		W 3-1	Clough 2, Peacock	14,879		2	3	4	5		7	8	9			10							11		6	1
Apr 4 (a) Grimsby T		L 1-4	Harris (pen)	17,579		2	3	4	5		7	8	9			10							11		6	1
7 (h) Grimsby T		W 5-1	Clough 3, Peacock, Harris (pen)	22,546		2	3	4	5		7	8	9			10							11		6	1
12 (h) Blackburn R		L 2-3	Clough 2	31,771		2	3	4	5			8	9			10	7						11		6	1
19 (a) Sheffield U		L 2-3	C.Taylor, Peacock	20,967		2	3	4	5				9			8	10				7		11		6	1
21 (a) Fulham		W 1-0	Clough	26,148	1		3	4		5			9			8	10			2	7		11			1
26 (h) West Ham U		L 1-3	Fitzsimons	30,526	1		3	4		5			9			8	10			2	7		11		6	
Apps					32	40	23	39	40	25	18	34	40	22	24	22	17	2	11	5	4	2	22	10	20	10
Goals								3		1	2	7	40	4	6	15					1	1	1			

2 own-goals

FA Cup

Date		Result	Scorers	Att	Taylor PT	Bilcliff R	Robinson R	Harris WC	Phillips BJ	Dicks RW	Day W	McLean JD	Clough BH	Fitzsimons AG	Burbeck RT	Peacock A	Delapenha LL	Mulholland FG	Stonehouse D	Scott JC	Taylor CW	Henderson R	Holliday E	Brown TE	Birbeck J	Million E	Round
Jan 4 (h) Derby C		W 5-0	Day, Holliday, Peacock 2, Clough	29,530	1	2		4	5		7	8	9			10							11	3	6			3
25 (a) Stoke C		L 1-3	Clough	43,756	1	2		4	5		7	8	9			10							11	3	6			4
Apps					2	2		2	2		2	2	2			2							2	2	2			
Goals											1		2			2							1				

1958-59
Division 2

Date	Opponent	Result	Scorers	Att	Taylor PT	Bilcliff R	Robinson R	Harris WC	Phillips BJ	Walley E	Day W	McLean JD	Clough BH	Peacock A	Holliday E	Stonehouse D	Burbeck RT	Rodgerson AR	Dicks RW	Scott JC	Fitzsimons AG	Taylor CW	Jordan BA	Million E	Fernie DW	Yeoman RI	McNeil M	Barnard BS	Birbeck J
Aug 23 (h)	Brighton & HA	W 9-0	Harris 2 (2 pens), Clough 5, Peacock 2	32,367	1	2	3	4	5	6	7	8	9	10	11														
25 (a)	Sheffield U	W 1-0	Clough	25,666	1		3	4	5	6		8	9	10	11	2	7												
30 (a)	Grimsby T	L 2-3	Clough, Day	21,327	1		3	4	5	6	7	8	9	10	11	2													
Sep 3 (h)	Sheffield U	D 0-0		42,866	1		3	4	5	6		8	9	10	11	2	7												
6 (h)	Liverpool	W 2-1	Clough 2	34,714	1		3	4	5	6		8	9	10	11	2	7												
11 (a)	Rotherham U	W 4-1	Rodgerson 2, Clough 2	12,089	1		3	4	5	6	7		9	10	11	2		8											
13 (a)	Stoke C	L 1-3	Clough	24,866	1		3	4	5	6	7		9	10	11	2		8											
17 (h)	Rotherham U	L 1-2	Clough	34,231	1		3	4	5	6	7		9	10	11	2		8											
20 (a)	Charlton A	L 0-1		19,407	1	2		4	5		7		9	10	11	3		8	6										
27 (h)	Bristol C	D 0-0		29,498	1	2		4	5		7		9			3	11		6	8	10								
Oct 4 (a)	Cardiff C	L 2-3	Phillips, Peacock	20,560	1	2		4	5			8	9	10		3	11		6			7							
11 (h)	Sunderland	D 0-0		37,223	1	2		4	5				9	10		3	11	8	6			7							
18 (a)	Lincoln C	D 1-1	Peacock	10,803	1	2		4	5				9	10		3	11		6		8	7							
25 (h)	Fulham	L 2-3	Clough 2	31,973	1	2	5	4			7	8	9	10		3	11		6										
Nov 1 (a)	Swansea T	L 2-5	Peacock, Holliday	15,741	1	2	5	4			7	8	9	10	11	3			6										
8 (h)	Scunthorpe U	W 6-1	Peacock 3, Clough 3	23,020	1		3	4	5			8	9	10	11	2					7		6						
15 (a)	Leyton O	L 2-5	Peacock 2	10,234	1		3	4	5				9	10	11	2	7				8		6						
22 (h)	Derby C	W 5-0	Holliday, Harris, Peacock, Scott, Davies (og)	16,773		2		4	5				9	10	11	3	7			8			6	1					
29 (a)	Bristol R	L 1-3	Clough	15,767		2		4	5				9	10	11	3	7			8			6	1					
Dec 6 (h)	Ipswich T	L 2-3	Clough, Burbeck	25,946		2		4	5				9	10		3	11				7		6	1	8				
13 (a)	Sheffield W	L 0-2		25,127		2			5		7		9	10		3	11			6				1	8	4			
20 (a)	Brighton & HA	W 6-4	Peacock 2, Clough 3, Bertolini (og)	21,063		2	3		5		7		9	10			11							1	8	4	6		
26 (h)	Barnsley	W 3-1	Clough 2, Peacock	31,720		2			5		7		9	10		3	11							1	8	4	6		
27 (a)	Barnsley	L 0-1		14,917		2			5		7		9	10		3	11							1	8	4	6		
Jan 1 (h)	Huddersfield T	W 3-1	Clough 2, Fernie	28,154		2		6	5		7		9	10		3	11							1	8	4			
31 (h)	Stoke C	D 0-0		19,077		2		6	5				9	10	11	3						7		1	8	4			
Feb 7 (h)	Charlton A	L 1-3	Peacock	16,210		2		6	5				9	10		3					11	7		1	8	4			
14 (a)	Bristol C	D 2-2	Harris (pen), Clough	18,336	1			6	5				9	10	11	3					7				8	4		2	
21 (a)	Cardiff C	D 1-1	Peacock	12,986	1			6	5				9	10	11	3	2				7				8	4		2	
28 (a)	Scunthorpe U	W 3-0	Clough 3	11,171	1				5				9	10	11	3					7				8	4		2	6
Mar 7 (h)	Lincoln C	L 1-2	Peacock	14,396	1				5				9	10	11	3					7				8	4		2	6
11 (h)	Grimsby T	W 1-0	Clough	12,019	1			4	5		7		9		11	2					10				8	6	3		
14 (a)	Fulham	L 2-3	Clough, Harris	26,800	1			4	5				9	10				11				7			8	6	3	2	
21 (h)	Swansea T	W 6-2	Clough 4, Fernie, Harris (pen)	15,272	1	2		4	5				9	10	11	3	7								8	6			
28 (a)	Sunderland	D 0-0		45,954	1	2		4	5		7		9	10	11	3									8	6			
30 (a)	Huddersfield T	L 1-5	Clough	14,671	1	2	5	4					9		11	3	7	10							8	6			
Apr 4 (h)	Leyton O	W 4-2	Peacock 2, Harris, Clough	20,683	1			4	5				9	10	11	3	7								8	6		2	
8 (a)	Liverpool	W 2-1	Holliday, Clough	36,288	1			4	5				9		11	3	7	10							8	6		2	
11 (h)	Derby C	W 3-0	Clough 2, Burbeck	19,911	1			4	5				9		11	3	7	10							8	6		2	
18 (h)	Bristol R	D 2-2	Burbeck, Clough	17,451	1			4	5				9		11	3	7	10							8	6		2	
22 (h)	Sheffield W	D 2-2	Holliday, Rodgerson	25,822				4					9		11	3	7	10						1	8	6	5	2	
25 (a)	Ipswich T	L 1-2	Burbeck	11,927				4					9		11	3	7	10						1	8	6	5	2	
Apps					30	21	14	36	37	8	14	11	42	34	29	39	26	11	8	4	10	6	5	12	23	22	7	11	2
Goals								7	1		1		43	19	4		4	3		1					2				

2 own-goals

FA Cup

Date	Opponent	Result	Scorers	Att	Taylor PT	Bilcliff R	Robinson R	Harris WC	Phillips BJ	Walley E	Day W	McLean JD	Clough BH	Peacock A	Holliday E	Stonehouse D	Burbeck RT	Rodgerson AR	Dicks RW	Scott JC	Fitzsimons AG	Taylor CW	Jordan BA	Million E	Fernie DW	Yeoman RI	McNeil M	Barnard BS	Birbeck J	Round
Jan 24 (h)	Birmingham C	L 0-1		36,587		2		6	5		7		9	10		3	11							1	8	4				3
Apps						1		1	1		1		1	1		1	1							1	1	1				
Goals																													

1959-60
Division 2

Date	Opponent	Result	Scorers	Att.	Taylor PT	Barnard RS	McNeil M	Harris WC	Phillips BJ	Yeoman RI	Day W	Fernie DW	Clough BH	Peacock A	Holliday E	Bilcliff R	McLean JD	Windross D	Burbeck RT	Wilkie D	Thomson KG	Million E	Waldock R	Stonehouse D	Taylor CW	Walker DH	Rodgerson AR	Appleby R
Aug 22 (h) Portsmouth	D 0-0			26,122	1	2	3	4	5	6	7	8	9	10	11													
26 (a) Cardiff C	L 0-2			23,052	1	2	3	4	5	6	7	8	9	10	11													
29 (a) Derby C	W 7-1	Peacock 4, Day, Holliday, Harris		19,537	1	2	3	4	5	6	7	8	9	10	11													
Sep 2 (h) Cardiff C	D 1-1	Harris (pen)		29,122	1	2	3	4	5	6	7	8	9	10	11													
5 (h) Plymouth A	W 6-2	Clough 4, Peacock 2		22,562	1		3	4	5	6	7	8	9	10	11	2												
9 (h) Hull C	W 4-0	Clough, Harris (pen), Yeoman, Day		28,368	1		3	4	5	6	7		9	10	11	2	8											
12 (a) Liverpool	W 2-1	Phillips, Harris		39,000	1		3	4	5	6	7	8	9	10	11	2												
14 (a) Hull C	D 3-3	Peacock 2, Clough		22,024	1		3	4	5	6	7	8	9	10	11	2												
19 (h) Charlton A	W 3-0	Clough 3		30,918	1	2	3	4	5	6	7	8	9	10	11													
26 (a) Bristol C	L 0-2			21,640	1	2	3	4	5	6	7	8	9	10	11													
Oct 3 (h) Scunthorpe U	W 3-1	Fernie, Clough 2		27,979	1		3	4	5	6	7	8	9	10	11	2												
10 (h) Sunderland	D 1-1	Holliday		47,297	1		3	4	5	6	7	8	9	10	11	2												
17 (a) Aston Villa	L 0-1			35,362	1		3	4	5	6	7	8				2	10	9	11									
24 (h) Lincoln C	W 3-2	McLean 2, Clough		24,007	1		3	4	5	6	7	8	9		11	2	10											
31 (a) Leyton O	L 0-5			15,600	1		3	4	5	6	7	8	9	10	11	2												
Nov 7 (h) Huddersfield T	W 1-0	Holliday		23,077	1		3	4		6		8	9	10	11	2				7	5							
14 (a) Ipswich T	L 0-1			12,975	1		3	4		6		8	9	10	11	2				7	5							
21 (h) Bristol R	W 5-1	Clough 3, Day, Harris		24,357	1		3	4		6	7	8	9	5	11	2	10											
28 (a) Swansea T	L 1-3	Holliday		13,889	1		3	4		6		8	9	5	11	2	10		7									
Dec 5 (h) Brighton & HA	W 4-1	Harris (pen), Clough 2, Holliday		19,677	1		3	4		6	7	8	9	5	11	2	10											
12 (a) Stoke C	W 5-2	Holliday, Day, Clough 3		15,195	1		3	4	5	6	7	8	9	10	11	2												
19 (a) Portsmouth	L 3-6	Clough, Harris (pen), Day		9,912	1		3	4		6	7	8	9	10	11	2					5							
26 (a) Rotherham U	W 2-0	Peacock, McLean		19,980	1		3	4		6		8	9	10	11	2	7				5							
28 (h) Rotherham U	W 3-0	Holliday, Harris (pen), Clough		36,184	1		3	4		6		8	9	10	11	2	7				5							
Jan 2 (h) Derby C	W 3-0	McLean, Clough 2		32,575	1		3	4		6		8	9	10	11	2	7				5							
16 (a) Plymouth A	D 2-2	Peacock, Clough		20,854	1		3	4		6		8	9	10	11	2	7				5							
23 (h) Liverpool	D 3-3	Clough 2, Harris (pen)		28,800			3	4		6		8	9	10	11	2	7				5	1						
Feb 6 (a) Charlton A	L 0-1			16,487	1		3	4		6		8	9		11	2	7				5		10					
13 (h) Bristol C	W 6-3	Clough 3, Harris (pen), McLean 2		17,871	1		3	4		6		8	9		11		7				5		10	2				
20 (a) Scunthorpe U	D 1-1	Haig (og)		10,817	1		3	4		6		8	9		11		7				5		10	2				
27 (a) Sunderland	D 2-2	Waldock, Harris (pen)		37,059	1		3	4		6		8	9		11		7				5		10	2				
Mar 5 (h) Aston Villa	L 0-1			39,432	1		3	4		6		8	9		11		7				5		10	2				
12 (a) Lincoln C	L 2-5	Clough 2		9,780	1		3	4		6		8	9	10	11						5			2	7			
19 (h) Swansea T	W 2-0	Waldock, Clough		15,719	1		3			4		8	9	10	11						5		7	2		6		
26 (a) Huddersfield T	L 0-2			13,887	1		3			4		8	9	10	11						5		7	2		6		
Apr 2 (h) Ipswich T	W 4-1	Peacock, Holliday, Clough 2		13,336			3			4			9	10	11				7		5	1		2		6	8	
9 (a) Bristol R	W 2-0	Clough, Holliday		15,847			3			4		8	9	10	11				7		5	1		2		6		
16 (h) Stoke C	W 1-0	Clough		17,394			3			4		8	9	10	11				7					2		6		1
18 (h) Sheffield U	L 1-2	Clough		18,713			3		5	4		8	9	10	11				7					2		6		1
19 (h) Sheffield U	D 0-0			13,667			3	8	5	4			9	10	11				7					2		6		1
23 (a) Brighton & HA	L 2-3	Jennings (og), Clough		17,526			3	8	5	4			9	10	11				7					2		6		1
30 (h) Leyton O	D 2-2	Peacock 2		13,044			3			4		8	9	10	11				7					2		6		1
Apps					34	6	42	35	19	42	19	39	41	35	41	22	16	1	9	2	18	3	8	14	1	9	1	5
Goals								11	1	1	5	1	39	13	8		6							2				

2 own-goals

FA Cup

Date	Opponent	Result	Scorers	Att.	Taylor PT	Barnard RS	McNeil M	Harris WC	Phillips BJ	Yeoman RI	Day W	Fernie DW	Clough BH	Peacock A	Holliday E	Bilcliff R	McLean JD	Windross D	Burbeck RT	Wilkie D	Thomson KG	Million E	Waldock R	Stonehouse D	Taylor CW	Walker DH	Rodgerson AR	Appleby R	Round
Jan 9 (a) Sheffield W	L 1-2	Clough		49,586	1		3	4		6		8	9	10	11				7		5			2					3
Apps					1		1	1		1		1	1	1	1				1		1			1					
Goals													1															

1960-61
Division 2

Date	Opponent	Res	Scorers	Att	Appleby R	Stonehouse D	McNeil M	Harris WC	Thomson KG	Yeoman RI	McLean JD	Fernie DW	Livingstone J	Peacock A	Holliday E	Clough BH	Waldock R	Windross D	Burbeck RT	Henderson A	Bilcliff R	Million E	Wilkie D	Walker DH	Rodgerson AR	Kaye A	Jones GE	Day W	Hamilton W	Horner W
Aug 20 (a)	Bristol R	W 3-2	Peacock 2, Holliday	20,093	1	2	3	4	5	6	7	8	9	10	11															
Aug 24 (h)	Derby C	L 1-2	McLean	18,348	1	2	3	4	5	6	7	8	9	10	11															
Aug 27 (h)	Liverpool	D 1-1	Peacock	21,236	1	2	3	4	5	6	7	8		10	11	9														
Aug 31 (a)	Derby C	L 0-1		19,019	1	2	3	4	5	6	8			10	11	9	7													
Sep 3 (a)	Rotherham U	W 2-1	Clough, Peacock	10,568	1	2	3	4	5	6	7			10		9		11	8											
Sep 10 (h)	Southampton	W 5-0	Windross, Clough 2, Peacock, Harris	16,760	1	2	3	4	5	6	7			10		9		8	11											
Sep 15 (a)	Scunthorpe U	D 1-1	Clough	13,852	1	2	3	4	5	6	7			10		9		11	8											
Sep 17 (a)	Leeds U	D 4-4	Henderson, Clough 2, McLean	17,799	1	2	3	4	5	6	7			10		9			11	8										
Sep 21 (h)	Scunthorpe U	L 1-3	Henderson	19,744	1		3	4	5	6	7			10		9			11	8	2									
Sep 24 (h)	Sunderland	W 1-0	Clough	27,458			3	4	5	6	7			10	11	9				8		1	2							
Oct 1 (h)	Brighton & HA	D 2-2	Clough, Henderson	15,700			3	4	5	6	7			10	11	9				8		1	2							
Oct 8 (a)	Plymouth A	D 3-3	Burbeck, Clough 2	19,894	1			4	5	6				10		9	7		11	8	2				3					
Oct 15 (h)	Norwich C	W 2-0	Henderson, Clough	14,737	1		3	4	5	6				10		9	7		11	8	2									
Oct 22 (a)	Charlton A	D 6-6	Clough 3, Burbeck 2, McLean	10,064	1		3	4	5	6	8			10		9	7		11		2									
Oct 29 (h)	Sheffield U	W 3-1	Harris (pen), Clough, McLean	23,070	1		3	4	5	6	8			10		9	7		11		2									
Nov 5 (a)	Stoke C	D 1-1	Harris (pen)	9,019	1		3	4	5	6				10		9	7		11		2						8			
Nov 12 (h)	Swansea T	W 3-1	Clough, Peacock 2	17,178	1		3	4	5	6	8			10		9	7		11		2									
Nov 19 (a)	Luton T	L 1-6	Waldock	12,579	1		3	4	5	6	8			10		9	7		11		2									
Nov 26 (h)	Lincoln C	D 1-1	Harris	13,053	1	2	3	4	5	6				10	11	9	8										7			
Dec 10 (h)	Huddersfield T	W 2-1	Harris (pen), Clough	9,948	1	2	3	4	5	6				10		9	8		11								7			
Dec 17 (h)	Bristol R	D 1-1	Kaye	11,759	1	2	3	4	5	6						9	8		11							10	7			
Dec 26 (h)	Leyton O	W 2-0	Clough, Kaye	15,996	1	2	3		5	4				10		9	8		11							6	7			
Dec 31 (a)	Liverpool	W 4-3	Molyneux (og), Peacock, Clough 2	34,645	1	2	3		5	4				10		9	8		11							6	7			
Jan 14 (h)	Rotherham U	D 2-2	Morgan (og), Clough	15,638		2	3		5	4				10		9	8		11			1				6	7			
Jan 21 (a)	Southampton	L 2-3	Harris (pen), Peacock	18,560			3	8	5	4				10		9			11			1		2		6	7			
Jan 28 (a)	Portsmouth	W 3-0	Clough 3	7,272			3	8	5	4				10		9			11			1		2		6	7			
Feb 4 (h)	Leeds U	W 3-0	Peacock, Clough 2	16,593			3	8	5	4				10		9			11			1		2		6	7			
Feb 11 (h)	Sunderland	L 0-2		53,254			3	8	5	4				10		9			11			1		2		6	7			
Feb 18 (a)	Brighton & HA	W 1-0	Peacock	16,286			3		5	4				10		9			11			1		2		6	7			
Feb 23 (h)	Plymouth A	W 3-1	Hamilton, Yeoman, Walker (pen)	16,606			3		5	4				10		9			11			1		2		6	7		8	
Mar 4 (a)	Norwich C	L 1-4	Kaye	25,610			3		5	4				10		9			11			1		2		6	7		8	
Mar 11 (h)	Charlton A	D 2-2	Peacock, McNeil	15,126			3		5	4				10		9			11			1		2		6	7		8	
Mar 14 (a)	Leyton O	D 1-1	Clough	11,658			3		5	4					11	9						1		2		8	7		10	6
Mar 18 (a)	Huddersfield T	L 0-1		11,788			3		5	4					11	9						1		2		8	7		10	6
Mar 25 (h)	Stoke C	W 1-0	Clough	8,736			3		5	4					11	9						1		2		10	7		8	6
Mar 31 (h)	Ipswich T	L 1-3	Peacock	22,239			3		5	4				10	11	9						1		2			7		8	6
Apr 1 (a)	Lincoln C	L 2-5	Clough, Peacock	5,115		2	3		5	4				10	11	9						1				6	7		8	
Apr 3 (h)	Ipswich T	W 3-1	Yeoman, Harris (pen), Clough	12,996		2	3	5		4	6			10	11	9	8					1					7			
Apr 8 (h)	Luton T	W 2-1	Clough 2	13,017		2	3	5		4	6			10	11	9	8					1					7			
Apr 15 (a)	Swansea T	L 2-3	Peacock, Clough	15,335		2	3	5		4	6			10	11	9	8					1					7			
Apr 22 (h)	Portsmouth	W 3-0	Waldock 2, Clough	9,339	1	2	3	5		4	6			10	11	9	8										7			
Apr 29 (a)	Sheffield U	L 1-4	McLean	18,868	1	2	3		5	4	6			10	11	9	8										7			
Apps					23	21	39	31	38	42	20	3	2	34	17	40	22	3	20	7	8	19	2	12	1	20	17	9	8	4
Goals						1		7		2	5			15	1	34	3	1	3	4				1					1	

2 own-goals

FA Cup

Date	Opponent	Res	Scorers	Att	Appleby R	Stonehouse D	McNeil M	Thomson KG	Yeoman RI	Peacock A	Clough BH	Waldock R	Burbeck RT	Kaye A	Jones GE	Round
Jan 7 (a)	Manchester U	L 0-3		49,184	1	2	3	5	4	10	9	8	11	6	7	3
Apps					1	1	1	1	1	1	1	1	1	1	1	
Goals																

League Cup

Date	Opponent	Res	Scorers	Att	Appleby R	McNeil M	Harris WC	Thomson KG	Yeoman RI	McLean JD	Peacock A	Holliday E	Clough BH	Waldock R	Bilcliff R	Round
Oct 3 (h)	Cardiff C	L 3-4	Clough 2, Peacock	15,695	1	3	4	5	6	8	10	11	9	7	2	1
Apps					1	1	1	1	1	1	1	1	1	1	1	
Goals											1		2			

1961-62
Division 2

Results

Date		Opponent	Res	Score	Scorers	Attendance
Aug	19 (h)	Derby C	L	3-4	Livingstone, Waldock 2	15,462
	26 (a)	Leyton O	L	0-2		9,269
	30 (h)	Rotherham U	W	5-1	Holliday, Peacock 4	11,919
Sep	2 (h)	Preston NE	W	1-0	McNeil	16,100
	9 (a)	Plymouth A	D	1-1	Day	16,213
	16 (h)	Huddersfield T	W	1-0	Peacock	14,003
	20 (h)	Luton T	L	2-4	Peacock, Kaye	15,878
	23 (a)	Swansea T	D	3-3	Livingstone 2, Kaye	14,730
	27 (a)	Luton T	L	2-3	Peacock 2	11,276
	30 (h)	Southampton	D	1-1	Kaye	13,880
Oct	7 (h)	Liverpool	W	2-0	White 2 (2 og's)	24,123
	14 (a)	Charlton A	L	0-1		12,156
	21 (h)	Bury	W	2-1	Peacock, Harris	15,188
	28 (a)	Brighton & HA	L	0-2		13,387
Nov	4 (h)	Scunthorpe U	L	1-2	Peacock	12,142
	11 (a)	Sunderland	L	1-2	Kaye (pen)	48,428
	18 (h)	Leeds U	L	1-3	Day	10,758
	25 (a)	Bristol R	W	2-0	Peacock, Harris	9,504
Dec	2 (h)	Stoke C	D	2-2	Peacock, Harris	21,066
	9 (a)	Norwich C	L	4-5	Peacock 3, Neal	14,928
	16 (a)	Derby C	L	2-3	Kaye, Neal	15,838
	23 (h)	Leyton O	L	2-3	Harris 2 (2 pens)	9,955
	26 (a)	Newcastle U	W	4-3	Peacock, Harris 3	21,038
Jan	13 (a)	Preston NE	L	3-4	Holliday 2, Peacock	10,912
	20 (h)	Plymouth A	D	1-1	Day	11,156
Feb	3 (a)	Huddersfield T	D	0-0		11,619
	10 (h)	Swansea T	L	1-3	Livingstone	11,220
	21 (a)	Southampton	W	3-1	Peacock, Burbeck, Weddle	13,535
	24 (a)	Liverpool	L	1-5	Livingstone	37,629
Mar	3 (h)	Charlton A	W	3-2	Thomson, Harris 2	13,193
	7 (h)	Newcastle U	W	3-0	Orritt 2, Harris	21,296
	10 (a)	Bury	L	1-2	Harris	9,418
	16 (h)	Brighton & HA	W	4-0	Burbeck 2, Orritt, Peacock	17,465
	23 (a)	Scunthorpe U	D	1-1	Harris	8,149
	31 (h)	Sunderland	L	0-1		35,666
Apr	3 (a)	Rotherham U	W	1-0	Gibson	6,037
	7 (a)	Leeds U	L	0-2		16,116
	14 (h)	Bristol R	W	5-0	Gibson 2, Burbeck, Harris (pen), Kaye	10,599
	21 (a)	Stoke C	L	0-2		8,379
	23 (a)	Walsall	W	2-1	Peacock 2	9,664
	24 (h)	Walsall	W	3-0	Peacock 2, Livingstone	18,238
	28 (h)	Norwich C	W	2-1	Kaye, Peacock	12,704

Appearances & Goals (shirt numbers by player)

Player columns: Appleby R, Jones GE, McNeil M, Yeoman RI, Thomson KG, Horner W, Day W, Harris WC, Livingstone J, Waldock R, Holliday E, Peacock A, McLean JD, Kaye A, Burbeck RT, Stonehouse D, Gates WL, Neal RM, Walker DH, Weddle DK, Hamilton W, Million E, Chapman N, Orritt B, Gibson IS

Date	App	Jon	McN	Yeo	Tho	Hor	Day	Har	Liv	Wal	Hol	Pea	McL	Kay	Bur	Sto	Gat	Nea	Wlk	Wed	Ham	Mil	Cha	Orr	Gib
Aug 19	1	2	3	4	5	6	7	8	9	10	11														
Aug 26	1	2	3	4	5	6	7	8	9		11	10													
Aug 30	1	2	3	4	5	6	7	8			10	11	9												
Sep 2	1	2	3	4	5	6	7	8			10	11	9												
Sep 9	1	2	3	4	5	6	7				10	11	9	8											
Sep 16	1	2	3	4	5	6	7		9	8	10	11													
Sep 20	1	2	3	4	5	6			11		9	8		10	7										
Sep 23	1		3	5	4		6		10		11	9		8	7	2									
Sep 27	1		3	4			6		10		11	9		8	7	2	5								
Sep 30	1			3	4		6		10		11	9		8	7	2	5								
Oct 7	1		3	4		10		7			11	9		8		2	5	6							
Oct 14	1		3	4		10		7			11	9		8		2	5	6							
Oct 21	1		3	4				7			11	9		8		2	5	6	10						
Oct 28	1		3	4				7			11	9		8		2	5	6	10						
Nov 4	1		3	4		10	7	8			11	9				2	5	6							
Nov 11	1		3	5	4			7			11	9		8		2		6			10				
Nov 18	1		3	4			7				11	9		8		2	5	6			10				
Nov 25		2	3	4	5			7	10		11	9		8				6					1		
Dec 2		2	3	4	5			7	10		11	9		8				6					1		
Dec 9		2	3	4	5			7	10	8	11	9						6					1		
Dec 16			3	4	5			7	10		11	9		8		2		6					1		
Dec 23	1		3	4	5			7	10		11	9		8		2		6							
Dec 26	1		3	6	4			7	10		11	9		8		2	5								
Jan 13	1		3	6	4	5	7	10			11	9		8		2									
Jan 20	1		3	6	4	5	7	10			11	9		8		2									
Feb 3	1		3	6	4	5	7	10			11	9		8								2			
Feb 10	1		3	6	4	5		7	10		11	9		8								2			
Feb 21	1		3	6	4	5						9		10	7	11	2			8					
Feb 24	1		3	6	4	5			10			9			11	2	7			8					
Mar 3	1		3	6	4			7	10		11	9				2	5							8	
Mar 7	1		3	6	4			7	10		11	9				2	5							8	
Mar 10	1		3	6	4			7	10		11	9				2	5							8	
Mar 16	1		3	6	4			7	10			9			11	2	5							8	
Mar 23	1		3	6	4			7	10		11	9				2	5							8	
Mar 31	1		3	6	4			7	10		11	9				2		5						8	
Apr 3	1		3	6	4			7	10		11					2		5						9	8
Apr 7	1		3	6	4			7	10			9				2		5						11	8
Apr 14	1		3	6	4			7	10					11	5	2								9	8
Apr 21	1		3	6	4			7	10					11	5	2								9	8
Apr 23	1		3	6	4			7			11	9				2		5						10	8
Apr 24	1		3	6	4			7	5		11	9				2								10	8
Apr 28	1		3	6	4			7			11	9		5		2								10	8
Apps	38	38	38	42	25	12	18	30	14	4	25	34	3	36	16	17	14	13	2	3	2	4	14	12	8
Goals		1		1		3	14	6	2	3	24		7	4			2			1				3	3

2 own-goals

FA Cup

Date		Opponent	Res	Score	Scorers	Attendance				Round
Jan	10 (h)	Cardiff C	W	1-0	Peacock	29,260				3
	27 (a)	Shrewsbury T	D	2-2	Peacock 2	14,534				4
	31 (h)	Shrewsbury T	W	5-1	Harris, Holliday 2, Peacock, Kaye	34,751				R
Feb	17 (a)	Blackburn R	L	1-2	Burbeck	39,714				

Date	App	Jon	McN	Yeo	Tho	Hor	Day	Har	Liv	Wal	Hol	Pea	McL	Kay	Bur	Sto	Gat
Jan 10	1		3	6	4	5	7	10			11	9		8		2	
Jan 27	1		3	6	4			7	10		11	9		8		2	5
Jan 31	1		3	6	4			7	10		11	9		8		2	5
Feb 17	1		3	6	4	5		7	10			9		8	11	2	
Apps	4		4	4	4	2		4	4		3	4		4	1	4	2
Goals								1			2	4		1	1		

League Cup

Date		Opponent	Res	Score	Scorers	Attendance			Round
Sep	13 (a)	Tranmere R	W	6-3	Day, Peacock 3, Burbeck 2	9,077			1
Oct	4 (h)	Crewe A	W	3-1	Kaye 2, Peacock	9,830			2
Nov	15 (a)	Norwich C	L	2-3	Holliday, Allcock (og)	15,242			

Date	App	Jon	McN	Yeo	Tho	Hor	Day	Har	Hol	Pea	McL	Kay	Bur	Sto	Gat	Mil
Sep 13	1	2	3	4	5	6	7			9	8	10	11			
Oct 4	1		3	4		6	7		11	9		8		2	5	10
Nov 15	1		3	4	5	6		7	11	9		8		2		10
Apps	3	2	3	3	1	3	2	1	2	3	1	3	1	2	1	2
Goals							1		1	4		2	2			

1 own-goal

1962-63
Division 2

					Att	Appleby R	Chapman N	Jones GE	Yeoman RI	Thomson KG	Neal RM	Kaye A	Gibson IS	Peacock A	Orritt B	Burbeck RT	Harris WC	Lightening AD	Horner W	McNeil M	Livingstone J	Gates WL	Hume RM	Nurse MTG	Emmerson M	Povey W	Knowles CB	Bryan PA	Stonehouse D	Walker DH
Aug 18	(a) Sunderland	L	1-3	Burbeck	48,106	1	2	3	4	5	6	7	8	9	10	11														
22	(h) Newcastle U	W	4-2	Peacock, Gibson, Kaye (pen), Burbeck	30,841	1	2	3	4	5	6	7	8	9	10	11														
25	(h) Huddersfield T	L	0-5		18,470	1	2	3	4	5	6	7	8	9			11	10												
29	(a) Newcastle U	L	1-6	Gibson	41,550			3	4	5		7	8	9			11	10	1	6	2									
Sep 1	(a) Cardiff C	W	2-1	Kaye 2 (1 pen)	18,940	1		3	4			7	8	9	10					6	2		11							
4	(a) Walsall	L	0-1		10,691	1		3	4			7	8	9	10					6	2		11							
7	(h) Portsmouth	W	4-2	Peacock, Gibson 2, McNeil	15,958	1		3	4			7	8	9	10					6	2		11							
12	(h) Walsall	L	2-3	Kaye (pen), Livingstone	18,436	1		3	4			7	8	9	10					6	2	11		5						
15	(a) Preston NE	W	1-0	Peacock	14,070		6	3	4			7		9	10			1	8	2			11	5						
22	(h) Plymouth A	W	3-0	Peacock 2, Kaye	17,812			3	4			7	8	9	10			1		6	2		11	5						
29	(a) Grimsby T	W	4-3	Orritt, Peacock 2, Kaye (pen)	11,857		2		4			7	8	9	10			1		6	3		11	5						
Oct 6	(a) Leeds u	W	3-2	Gibson, Hume, Peacock	28,222	1		3	4		6	7	8	9	10					2			11	5						
13	(h) Swansea T	D	2-2	Neal, Hume	19,718	1		3	4		6	7	8	9	10					2			11	5						
20	(a) Chelsea	L	2-3	Orritt, Kaye (pen)	32,551			3	4		6	7	8	9	10			1		2			11	5						
27	(h) Luton T	L	0-2		13,835		2	3	4		6	7	8	9	10			1					11	5						
Nov 3	(a) Southampton	L	0-6		14,956			3	4		6	7	8	9	10			1		2			11	5						
10	(h) Scunthorpe U	W	4-3	Peacock 2, Burbeck, Hume	10,738			3	4		6	7	8	9	10					2			11	5		1				
17	(a) Bury	L	0-1		10,131			3	4		6	7	8	9	10					2			11	5		1				
24	(h) Rotherham U	W	2-1	Neal, Hume	12,478			3	4		6	7	8	9	10					2			11	5		1				
Dec 1	(a) Charlton A	W	4-3	Peacock 3, Gibson	12,562			3	4		6	7	8	9	10					2			11	5		1				
8	(h) Stoke C	D	2-2	Peacock, Hume	12,004			3	4		6	7		9	8	10				2			11	5		1				
15	(h) Sunderland	D	3-3	Horner, Kaye, Orritt	43,509			3	4			7	8	9	10				6	2			11	5		1				
29	(a) Norwich C	W	4-3	Gibson 2, Orritt, Peacock	13,039	1		3	4			7	8	9	10				6	2				5	11					
Feb 9	(a) Plymouth A	W	5-4	Kaye, Reeves (og), Peacock 2, Gibson	12,612	1		3	4			7	8	9					6	2			11	5	10					
16	(h) Grimsby T	L	0-1		17,804	1		3	4			7	8	9	10				6	2				5	11					
Mar 2	(a) Swansea T	D	1-1	Peacock	9,686			3	4		6	7	8	9	10	11		1		2				5						
9	(h) Chelsea	W	1-0	Kaye (pen)	24,781			3	4			7	8	9	10	11		1	6	2				5						
23	(h) Southampton	L	1-2	Peacock	15,416			3	4			7	8	9		11	10		1	6	2			5						
25	(a) Luton T	L	3-4	Peacock 2, Orritt	6,431		2	3	4			7	8	9	10			1		6				5	11						
29	(a) Scunthorpe U	D	1-1	Kaye (pen)	7,474		2	3	4			7	8	9			10	1		6				5	11						
Apr 6	(h) Bury	D	0-0		8,888			3	4			7	8	9	11		10	1		6		2		5						
12	(h) Derby C	W	5-1	Harris 2, Peacock 2, Gibson	11,116			3	4			7	8	9	6		10	1	4				11	5			2			
13	(a) Rotherham U	L	1-4	Horner	8,059			3	2			7	8	9	6		10	1	4				11	5						
15	(a) Derby C	D	3-3	Orritt, Moore (og), Gibson	13,253	1		3	4				8	9	10				6				11	5	7		2			
20	(h) Charlton A	W	2-1	Peacock, Wakeham (og)	9,223	1		3	4			7	8	9	10				6				11	5			2			
27	(h) Stoke C	W	1-0	Peacock	25,746	1		3	4			7	8	9	10				6				11	5			2			
29	(a) Huddersfield T	D	0-0		14,000	1		3	4			7	8	9	10				6				11	5			2			
May 6	(h) Leeds U	W	2-1	Peacock, Orritt	17,465	1			4			7	8	9	10				6	3			11	5			2			
11	(h) Cardiff C	W	3-2	Peacock 2, Horner	9,423	1			4			7	8	9	10				6	3			11	5			2			
15	(h) Preston NE	W	2-0	Peacock, Kaye	11,553	1			4			7	8	9	10				6	3			11	5			2			
18	(a) Portsmouth	D	1-1	Kaye (pen)	11,605	1			4			7	8	9	10				6	3			11	5			2			
21	(h) Norwich C	W	6-2	Metcalfe (og), Gibson, Kaye (pen), Orritt, Peacock 2	7,626	1			4			7	8	9	10				6	3			11	5			2			
Apps						17	8	36	42	3	20	40	39	40	35	13	15	15	25	32	4	2	19	32	10	6	9			
Goals											2	14	12	31	8	3	2		3	1	1		5							

4 own-goals

FA Cup

					Att			Jones GE	Yeoman RI			Kaye A	Gibson IS	Peacock A	Orritt B	Burbeck RT	Harris WC	Lightening AD	Horner W	McNeil M			Hume RM	Nurse MTG							Round
Mar 5	(a) Blackburn R	D	1-1	Orritt	16,375			3	4			7	8	9	10	11			6	2				5	1						3
11	(h) Blackburn R	W	3-1	Peacock 2, Kaye (pen)	39,595			3	4			7	8	9	10	11			6	2				5	1						R
16	(h) Leeds U	L	0-2		39,672			3	4			7	8	9	10	11			6	2				5	1						4
Apps								3	3			3	3	3	3	3			3	3				3	3					
Goals												1		2	1														

League Cup

					Att	Appleby R	Chapman N	Jones GE	Yeoman RI	Thomson KG	Neal RM	Kaye A	Gibson IS	Peacock A	Orritt B	Burbeck RT	Harris WC	Lightening AD	Horner W	McNeil M	Livingstone J	Gates WL	Hume RM	Nurse MTG	Emmerson M	Povey W	Knowles CB				Round
Sep 24	(a) Hull C	D	2-2	Burbeck 2	10,640			3	4	5		7	8	9	10	11		1		6	2										2
Oct 8	(h) Hull C	D	1-1*	Gibson	15,612	2		3	4		6	7	8		10			1		9	5	11									R
10	(a) Hull C	L	0-3		11,960	2			4		6			7	8				5	11						9	3	10			2R
Apps						2	2	3	3	2	2	1	2	2	1	3	1	1	1	2	2					1	1	1		
Goals													1			2													

*After extra-time

1963-64
Division 2

Date	Opponent	Result	Scorers	Att	Connachan ED	Knowles CB	Jones GE	Orritt B	Nurse MTG	Horner W	Kaye A	Gibson IS	Peacock A	Harris WC	Braithwaite RM	Yeoman RI	Horsfield A	Kirk H	McNeil M	Gates WL	Ratcliffe D	Chapman N	Townsend J	Appleby R	Spraggon F	Rodgerson AR
Aug 24 (h)	Plymouth A	W 5-0	Gibson, Horner*, Peacock 2, Harris	18,744	1	2	3	4	5	6	7	8	9	10	11											
26 (h)	Newcastle U	W 3-0	Gibson, Kaye 2	37,803	1	2	3	4	5	6	7	8	9	10	11											
31 (a)	Charlton A	W 4-2	Braithwaite 2, Kaye, Gibson	13,345	1	2	3	4	5	6	7	8	9	10	11											
Sep 4 (a)	Newcastle U	L 0-2		56,918	1	2	3	4	5	6	7	8	9	10	11											
7 (h)	Grimsby T	W 6-0	Harris 2, Gibson 2, Kaye, Horsfield	22,458	1	2	3	11	5	6	7	8		10		4	9									
9 (h)	Rotherham U	D 2-2	Kaye (pen), Harris	30,013	1	2	3	9	5	6	7	8		10		4	11									
14 (a)	Preston NE	D 2-2	Jones, Gibson	15,499	1	2	11	4	5	6	7	8		10			9		3							
17 (a)	Rotherham U	L 1-2	Gibson	12,572	1	2	11	4	5	6	7	8		10					3	9						
21 (h)	Leyton O	W 2-0	Gibson 2	23,282	1	2	11	4	5	6	7	8	9	10						3						
28 (a)	Swansea T	L 1-2	Harris	10,519	1	2	3	4	5	6	7	8	9	10							11					
Oct 5 (h)	Southampton	W 1-0	Peacock	19,892	1	2	3	4	5	6	7	8	9	10							11					
9 (a)	Leeds U	L 0-2		37,019	1	2	3	9	5	6	7	8		10		4					11					
12 (h)	Portsmouth	W 3-1	Harris, Orritt, Gibson	17,388	1	2	3	9	5	6	7	8		10		4					11					
19 (a)	Scunthorpe U	L 0-1		7,347	1	2	3	9	5	6	7	8		10		4					11					
26 (h)	Sunderland	W 2-0	Orritt 2	43,905	1	2	3	9	5	6	7	8		10		4					11					
Nov 2 (a)	Cardiff C	D 1-1	Orritt	13,455	1	2	3	9	5	6	7	8		10		4					11					
9 (h)	Swindon T	D 1-1	Harris	26,476	1	2	3	9	5	6	7	8		10		4					11					
23 (h)	Bury	W 2-0	Gibson, Orritt	15,815	1	2	3	9		6	7	8		10		4				5	11					
30 (a)	Northampton T	L 2-3	Kaye, Gibson	10,346	1	2	3	9		6	7	8		10		4				5	11					
Dec 7 (h)	Norwich C	L 0-1		15,592	1		3	9	5	6	7	8		10		4					11	2				
14 (a)	Plymouth A	L 0-2		8,559	1	2	3	9	5		7	8		10		4		6			11					
21 (h)	Charlton A	L 2-3	Nurse, Braithwaite	11,917	1	2	3	4	5	6	7	8			11		9			10						
26 (h)	Derby C	W 3-0	Orritt, Braithwaite, Ratcliffe	18,422	1	2	3	4	5	6	10	8			11		9				7					
28 (h)	Derby C	D 2-2	Ratcliffe, Horsfield	11,506	1	2	3	4	5	6		8		10	11		9				7					
Jan 11 (a)	Grimsby T	L 1-3	Peacock	6,681	1	2	3	4	5	6	10	8	9		11						7					
18 (h)	Preston NE	W 3-0	Peacock, Kaye, Harris	14,985	1			6	5		7	8	9	10	11	4			3			2				
Feb 1 (a)	Leyton O	L 2-3	Horsfield 2	8,367	1			6	5		7	8		10	11	4	9		3			2				
8 (h)	Swansea T	W 2-1	Horsfield, Kaye	12,668	1			6			7	8			11	4	9		3	5	10	2				
15 (a)	Southampton	D 2-2	Harris, Braithwaite	14,978	1			9	5		7	8		10	11	6			3			2	4			
22 (a)	Portsmouth	L 0-1		12,081	1			9	5		10	8			11	6			3		7	2	4			
29 (h)	Manchester C	D 2-2	Gates, Harris	12,763	1			6	5		7	8		10	11				3	9		2	4			
Mar 7 (a)	Sunderland	D 0-0		46,855	1	2		6	5		7	8			11	4			3	9	10					
14 (h)	Leeds U	L 1-3	Horsfield	15,987	1	2		6	5		7	8			11	4	9		3		10					
17 (a)	Manchester C	L 0-1		8,053		2		6			7	8	10		11	4	9		3	5				1		
21 (h)	Swindon T	L 0-2		13,810	1	2		6			7	8	10		11	4	9		3	5						
28 (a)	Scunthorpe U	W 2-0	Harris, Gates	8,839	1			6	5			8		10	11	4			3	9	7	2				
30 (h)	Huddersfield T	D 1-1	Gates	9,871	1			6	5			8		10	11				3	9	7	2	4			
31 (a)	Huddersfield T	L 0-1		6,148	1		3		5		7	8		10					2	9	11		4		6	
Apr 4 (a)	Bury	D 1-1	Gibson	9,220	1		3		5		7	8		10					2	9	11		4		6	
10 (h)	Northampton T	W 1-0	Branston (og)	9,220	1		3		5		7	8		10					2	9	11		4		6	
15 (a)	Norwich C	D 1-1	Braithwaite	13,135	1		3		5			8		10	11					9	7	2	4		6	
24 (h)	Cardiff C	W 3-1	Gibson, Horsfield 2	8,472	1		7		5			8		10	11		9		3			2	4		6	
		Apps			41	28	29	37	37	27	36	42	9	34	22	20	12	1	20	14	25	9	13	1	5	
		Goals					1	6	1	1	8	14	5	11	6		8			3	2					

*Some sources credit Williams (og), club credit Horner.

1 own-goal

FA Cup

Date	Opponent	Result	Scorers	Att	Connachan ED	Knowles CB	Jones GE	Orritt B	Nurse MTG	Horner W	Kaye A	Gibson IS	Peacock A	Harris WC	Braithwaite RM	Yeoman RI	Horsfield A	Kirk H	McNeil M	Gates WL	Ratcliffe D	Chapman N	Townsend J	Appleby R	Spraggon F	Rodgerson AR	Round
Jan 4 (a)	Brentford	L 1-2	Kaye	16,070	1	2	3	4	5	6	8	10	9		11						7						3
		Apps			1	1	1	1	1	1	1	1	1		1						1						
		Goals									1																

League Cup

Date	Opponent	Result	Scorers	Att	Connachan ED	Knowles CB	Jones GE	Orritt B	Nurse MTG	Horner W	Kaye A	Gibson IS	Peacock A	Harris WC	Braithwaite RM	Yeoman RI	Horsfield A	Kirk H	McNeil M	Gates WL	Ratcliffe D	Chapman N	Townsend J	Appleby R	Spraggon F	Rodgerson AR	Round
Sep 25 (a)	Bradford	D 2-2	Peacock 2	9,273	1	2	11	4	5	6	7	8	9						3				10				2
Oct 2 (h)	Bradford	L 2-3	Peacock, Harris	11,991	1		3	4	5		7	8	9	10	11							2	6				R
		Apps			2	1	2	2	2	1	2	2	2	1	1				1			1	2				
		Goals											3	1													

1964-65
Division 2

Date	Opponent	Res	Score	Scorers	Att	Connachan ED	Gates WL	Jones GE	Townsend J	Nurse MTG	Orritt B	Kaye A	Gibson IS	Horsfield A	Irvine JD	Braithwaite RM	Harris WC	Ratcliffe D	Horner W	Bryan PA	Spraggon F	Masson DS	Chapman N	Appleby R	Davidson I	Le Flem RP
Aug 22 (a)	Southampton	W	3-0	Braithwaite 2, Horsfield	18,855	1	2	3	4	5	6	7	8	9	10	11										
24 (h)	Northampton T	W	1-0	Horsfield	27,122	1	2	3	4	5	6	7	8	9	10	11										
29 (h)	Huddersfield T	D	0-0		23,152	1	2	3	4	5	6	7	8	9	10	11										
Sep 1 (a)	Northampton T	D	1-1	Horsfield	17,028	1	2	3	4	5	6	7	8	9	10	11										
5 (a)	Coventry C	L	0-3		36,086	1	2	3	4	5	6	7	8	9	10	11										
7 (h)	Bolton W	W	5-2	Harris 2, Kaye (pen), Townsend, Irvine	22,670	1	2	3	4	5	6	7	8		9		10	11								
12 (h)	Cardiff C	D	0-0		22,770	1	2	3	4	5	6	7	8		9		10	11								
16 (a)	Bolton W	L	2-4	Harris, Gibson	13,912	1		3	4	5	6	7	8		9		10	11	2							
19 (a)	Preston NE	L	3-4	Kaye (pen), Irvine 2	15,726	1	2	3	4	5	6	7	8	9	10	11										
26 (h)	Ipswich T	L	2-4	Bolton (og), Horsfield	15,593	1		3	4	5	6	7	8	9	10	11					2					
Oct 3 (a)	Plymouth A	L	0-1		18,382	1		3	10	5		7	8		9	11		4	2		6					
6 (a)	Charlton A	W	2-0	Irvine, Horner (pen)	11,837	1		3	10	5			8		9	11	7	4	2		6					
10 (h)	Bury	D	3-3	Irvine, Bunner (og), Nurse	11,772	1		3	10	5			8		9	11	7	4	2		6					
17 (a)	Crystal P	L	1-3	Irvine	18,055	1	2	3		5	10		8		9	11	7	4			6					
24 (h)	Norwich C	W	2-0	Kaye, Irvine	10,061	1	2	3	6	5		7	8		9	11		4				10				
31 (a)	Rotherham U	W	3-2	Braithwaite 2, Irvine	10,552	1	2	3	6	5		7	8		9	11		4				10				
Nov 7 (h)	Swansea T	W	4-0	Masson, Townsend 2, Kaye	11,855	1	2	3	6	5		7	8		9	11		4				10				
14 (a)	Derby C	D	3-3	Horner, Gibson, Irvine	11,933	1	2	3	6	5		7	8		9			4	11			10				
21 (h)	Swindon T	W	4-1	Nurse, Gibson, Masson 2	14,948	1		3	6	5	4	7	8		9	11						10	2			
28 (a)	Portsmouth	L	1-2	Irvine	10,653	1		3	6	5	4	7	8		9	11			2			10				
Dec 5 (h)	Manchester C	L	0-1		13,873	1		3	6	5	4	7	8		9	11			2			10				
12 (h)	Southampton	W	4-1	Irvine, Masson, Kaye (pen), Townsend	12,499	1			4	5	3	7	8		9	11			2		6	10				
26 (h)	Newcastle U	L	0-2		38,194	1		3	4	5	6	7	8		9	11			2			10				
28 (a)	Newcastle U	L	1-2	Kaye	54,750	1		3	4	5		7	8		9	11	10	2			6					
Jan 2 (h)	Coventry C	L	2-3	Gibson, Nurse	15,714	1		3	4	5		7	8		9						6	10	2			
15 (a)	Cardiff C	L	1-6	Irvine	9,490	1		3	4	5		7	8	9	10	11		2	6							
23 (h)	Preston NE	D	1-1	Townsend	12,466	1	2	3	4	5		7	8		9	11			6			10				
Feb 6 (a)	Ipswich T	L	2-5	Irvine, Nurse	11,071	1	2	3	4	5			8		9	11		7	6			10				
13 (h)	Plymouth A	L	1-3	Irvine	10,165	1	2	3	4	5		7	8	9	10	11		4								
23 (a)	Bury	L	2-3	Gibson, Horsfield	6,143		2	3	7	5			8	9	10			11	4					1	6	
27 (h)	Crystal P	D	0-0		12,071		2	3		5			8	9	10			11	4					1	6	7
Mar 6 (a)	Manchester C	D	1-1	Irvine	14,231		2	3	10	5			8		9			11	4					1	6	7
13 (h)	Rotherham U	L	3-5	Nurse (pen), Le Flem, Irvine	10,972		2	3	10	5			8		9			11	4					1	6	7
20 (a)	Swansea T	W	2-1	Irvine, Nurse	9,366	1	2	3	4	5	9		8		10			11							6	7
27 (h)	Derby C	L	1-2	Gibson	12,719	1	2	3	4	5	9		8		10			11							6	7
30 (a)	Huddersfield T	L	0-1		13,215	1	2	3	10	5		7	8		9	11			4						6	
Apr 3 (a)	Swindon T	W	1-0	Jones	13,862	1	2	3		5	9	7	8		10	11			4						6	
9 (h)	Portsmouth	W	4-1	Orritt, Gibson, Irvine 2	10,533	1	2	3		5	9	7	8		10	11			4						6	
16 (a)	Leyton O	D	1-1	Gibson	11,200	1	2	3		5	9	7	8		10	11			4						6	
17 (a)	Norwich C	L	0-2		12,228	1	2	3	4	5		7	8	9	10	11									6	
19 (h)	Leyton O	W	2-0	Horner, Irvine	11,749	1	2	3	6	5		7	8		9	11			4			10				
24 (h)	Charlton A	L	1-2	Nurse	8,627	1	2	3	6	5		7	8		9	11			4			10				
Apps						38	29	41	37	41	22	32	41	11	42	26	6	26	23	4	7	14	2	4	11	5
Goals							1		5	6	2	6	8	5	20	4	3		3			4				1

2 own-goals

FA Cup

Date	Opponent	Res	Score	Scorers	Att	Connachan ED	Gates WL	Jones GE	Townsend J	Nurse MTG	Orritt B	Kaye A	Gibson IS	Horsfield A	Irvine JD	Braithwaite RM	Harris WC	Ratcliffe D	Horner W	Bryan PA	Spraggon F	Masson DS	Chapman N	Appleby R	Davidson I	Le Flem RP	Round
Jan 9 (h)	Oldham A	W	6-2	Horsfield 2, Irvine 3, Kaye	17,178	1		3	4	5		7	8	9	10			11	6				2				3
30 (a)	Charlton A	D	1-1	Nurse	17,982	1	2	3	4	5		7	8		9			11	6			10					4
Feb 1 (h)	Charlton A	W	2-1	Gibson, Masson	30,460	1	2	3	4	5		7	8		9			11	6			10					R
20 (h)	Leicester C	L	0-3		31,099		2	3	6	5		7	8	9	10			11	4				1				5
Apps						3	3	4	4	4		4	4	2	4			4	4			2	1	1		
Goals										1		1	1	2	3							1				

League Cup

Date	Opponent	Res	Score	Scorers	Att	Connachan ED	Gates WL	Jones GE	Townsend J	Nurse MTG	Orritt B	Kaye A	Gibson IS	Horsfield A	Irvine JD	Braithwaite RM	Harris WC	Ratcliffe D	Horner W	Bryan PA	Spraggon F	Masson DS	Chapman N	Appleby R	Davidson I	Le Flem RP	Round
Sep 23 (a)	Charlton A	L	1-2	Irvine	8,625	1		3	4	5	6	7		9	11	8		2				10					2
Apps						1		1	1	1	1	1		1	1	1		1				1				
Goals															1											

1965-66
Division 2

Date	Opp	R	Score	Scorers	Att	Connachan ED	Gates WL	Jones GE	Horner W	Nurse MTG	Davidson I	Holliday E	Gibson IS	Horsfield A	Ratcliffe D	Braithwaite RM	Orritt B	Le Flem RP	Rooks R	Townsend J	Irvine JD	Chapman N	Garbett TG	Appleby R	McMordie A	Downing DG	Marshall SK	Spraggon F	Masson DS	Anderson S	McPartland D	Smith RA	Butler G	Lawson J
Aug 21 (h) Manchester C		D	1-1	Nurse	17,982	1	2	3	4	5	6	7	8	9	10	11																		
25 (a) Birmingham C		D	1-1	Orritt	16,772	1	2	3	4	5	6	7	8	9				10	11															
28 (a) Huddersfield T		L	0-6		14,772	1	2	3	4	10	6	7	8	9					11	5														
31 (h) Birmingham C		D	1-1	Orritt	17,300	1	2	3			6	7	8					9	11	5	4	10												
Sep 4 (h) Crystal P		D	2-2	Irvine, Rooks	10,269	1	2	3			6	7	8					9	11	5	4	10												
7 (a) Ipswich T		L	1-2	Gibson	15,478	1		3	4		6		8		7	11			5		10		2		9									
11 (a) Preston NE		D	1-1	Irvine	15,024			3	4		6		8		7	11	12		5		10		2*	1	9									
14 (h) Ipswich T		W	3-2	Ratcliffe, Garbett, Irvine	15,221		2	3	4		6		8		7	11			5		10		9	1										
18 (h) Charlton A		D	2-2	Braithwaite, Horner	13,476		2	3	4		6		8		7	11	12		5		10			1*	9									
25 (a) Plymouth A		D	2-2	Orritt, Holliday	11,955	1	2	3	4		6	7	8			11	9		5						10									
Oct 9 (h) Rotherham U		W	4-0	Horner, McMordie, Gibson, Irvine	13,152	1	2	3	4		6	7	8			11			5		9				10									
16 (a) Wolves		L	0-3		20,927	1	2	3	4		6	7	8			11			5		10				9									
22 (h) Norwich C		L	0-1		10,897	1	2	3	4		6	11	8*						5		9							7	10	12				
26 (h) Portsmouth		W	5-2	Harris (og), Rooks (pen), Horsfield, Holliday, Irvine	9,582	1	2	3				11		8	7			4	5		9				10					6				
30 (a) Bury		L	0-2		8,070	1	2	3			6	11		8	7			4	5						10					12	9*			
Nov 6 (h) Southampton		D	0-0		11,555	1		3			6	11		9	7			4	5		10		2		8									
13 (a) Derby C		L	0-5		12,019	1	2	3			6	11		9	7			4	5		10				8									
20 (h) Cardiff C		L	3-4	McMordie, Holliday, Anderson	11,898	1	2	3			6	11	10		7				5		9				8					4				
Dec 4 (h) Coventry C		D	1-1	Irvine	12,024	1*	2	3				11	10		7		12		5		9				8				6	4				
11 (a) Bristol C		D	2-2	Irvine, Holliday	16,086		2	3			6	11	10	7*					5	12	9				8					4	1			
18 (h) Wolves		W	3-1	Rooks, Gibson, Horsfield	13,419		2	3			6	11	10	9					5	7					8					4	1			
27 (h) Leyton O		W	2-1	McMordie, Horsfield	21,107		2	3			6	11	10	9					5	7					8					4	1			
Jan 1 (a) Rotherham U		L	1-4	Anderson	10,922		2	3	12		6	11*	10	9					5	7					8					4	1			
8 (h) Derby C		D	0-0		11,897		2	3					10	9	11				5	7					8				6	4	1			
29 (a) Manchester C		L	1-3	Townsend	25,278		2	3			6		8						5	7			9			11	10			4	1			
Feb 5 (h) Huddersfield T		L	1-3	Downing	13,485		2	3			6	7							5	4	9					10	11			8	1			
19 (a) Crystal P		D	1-1	Irvine	13,902	5		3	4				8			11					9					10	2	7		6	1			
26 (h) Preston NE		W	2-1	Singleton (og), Irvine	13,229	5		3	4				8			11					9					10	2	7		6	1			
Mar 5 (h) Bristol C		W	4-2	Irvine 2, Gibson, Rooks	13,744	5		3	4*				8			11					9					10	2	7		6	1	12		
8 (a) Carlisle U		L	1-2	Irvine	13,459	5		3					8			11					9					10	2	7		6	1	4		
12 (a) Charlton A		L	0-1		11,482	5*		3					8			11					9	12				10	2	7		6	1	4		
19 (h) Plymouth A		L	0-1		12,284			3					8			11					9					10	2	7	6	4	1	5		
25 (a) Portsmouth		L	1-4	Gibson	10,640			3	2			11	8	9					5	4						10		7		6	1			
Apr 2 (a) Southampton		L	1-3	Irvine	13,687			3	4		6		8			11					9	7				10	2				1	5		
9 (h) Bury		W	1-0	Braithwaite	12,983			3	4				8			11					9	7				10	2			6	1	5		
11 (a) Bolton W		L	0-6		11,948			3	4				8			11					9	7				10				6	1	5	2	
12 (h) Bolton W		D	1-1	Gibson	11,384			3	4			7	8						5		10	9		1						6			2	11
18 (a) Leyton O		W	3-2	Irvine 2, Rooks (pen)	2,286			3	4			7	8						5		10	9		1						6			2	11
23 (h) Carlisle U		L	0-2		15,564			3	4			7	8						5		10	9		1						6			2	11
27 (h) Norwich C		W	2-1	McMordie, Downing	7,849			3	4		6		8								9			1	10	7						5	2	11
30 (a) Coventry C		L	1-2	Gibson	19,747			3	4		6		8								9			1	10	7						5	2	11
May 3 (a) Cardiff C		L	3-5	Rooks 3 (1 pen)	12,935		11		4		6		8						5		9			1	10	7				2				
Apps						16	28	42	24	3	27	23	38	12	14	16	9	4	37	15	31	11	7	9	17	13	2	5	1	21	17	9	6	5
Sub apps							1											3		2								1	1		1			
Goals									2	1		4	7	3	1	2	3		8	1	15		1		4	2			2				

2 own-goals

FA Cup

Date	Opp	R	Score	Scorers	Att	Connachan ED	Gates WL	Jones GE	Horner W	Nurse MTG	Davidson I	Holliday E	Gibson IS	Horsfield A	Ratcliffe D	Braithwaite RM	Orritt B	Le Flem RP	Rooks R	Townsend J	Irvine JD	Chapman N	Garbett TG	Appleby R	McMordie A	Downing DG	Marshall SK	Spraggon F	Masson DS	Anderson S	McPartland D	Smith RA	Butler G	Lawson J	Round
Jan 22 (a) Tottenham H		L	0-4		37,349		2	3			6	10	9	7		11			5						8					4	1				3
Apps							1	1			1	1	1	1		1			1						1					1	1				
Goals																																		

League Cup

Date	Opp	R	Score	Scorers	Att	Connachan ED	Gates WL	Jones GE	Horner W	Nurse MTG	Davidson I	Holliday E	Gibson IS	Horsfield A	Ratcliffe D	Braithwaite RM	Orritt B	Le Flem RP	Rooks R	Townsend J	Irvine JD	Chapman N	Garbett TG	Appleby R	McMordie A	Downing DG	Marshall SK	Spraggon F	Masson DS	Anderson S	McPartland D	Smith RA	Butler G	Lawson J	Round
Sep 22 (a) Colchester U		W	4-2	Horner, Irvine 2, McMordie	7,777	1	2	3	4		6	7	8			11			5		9				10											2
Oct 13 (h) Millwall		D	0-0		12,927	1	2	3	4		6	7	8			11			5		9				10											3
18 (a) Millwall		L	1-3*	Gibson	12,888	1	2	3	4		6	7	8					9	5	11					10											R
Apps						3	3	3	3		3	3	3			2		1	3	1	3				3										
Goals									1				1								2				1										

*After extra-time

1966-67
Division 3

Player columns (left→right): Appleby R, Gates WL, Jones GE, Davidson I, Rooks R, Horner W, Chadwick DE, Masson DS, O'Rourke J, Irvine JD, Lawson J, Chapman N, McPartland D, Braithwaite RM, McMordie A, Butler G, Horsfield A, Smith RA, Hickton J, Lugg R, Whigham W, Downing DG, Spraggon F

Date	Opponent	Res	Scorers	Att	App	Gat	Jon	Dav	Roo	Hor	Cha(DE)	Mas	O'R	Irv	Law	Cha(N)	McP	Bra	McM	But	Hor(A)	Smi	Hic	Lug	Whi	Dow	Spr
Aug 20 (a)	Colchester U	W 3-2	Lawson, O'Rourke 2	4,382	1	2	3	4	5*	6	7	8	9	10	11	12											
27 (h)	Bristol R	L 1-2	Irvine	10,658	1	5	3	4		6	7	8	9	10	11	2											
Sep 3 (a)	Oxford U	D 1-1	Masson (pen)	6,668		5	3	4		6	7	8	9	10		2	1	11									
6 (a)	Queen's Park R	L 0-4		8,807		5	3	4		6	7	8	9	10		2	1	11									
10 (h)	Oldham A	L 0-2		8,932		2	3	4	5	6	7		9*	10			1	11	8	12							
17 (a)	Scunthorpe U	L 2-3	Horsfield 2	4,053	9		3	4	5*	6	7			10	11		1		2	8	12						
24 (h)	Workington	W 3-2	Hickton (pen), Horsfield 2	8,813			3	4		6	7		9	10	11		1		2	8			5				
26 (h)	Queen's Park R	D 2-2	Horsfield, O'Rourke	13,091			3			6			9	10	11		1		7	2	8	4	5				
Oct 1 (a)	Gillingham	L 1-5	Horsfield	5,789			3		9	6		10		11*			1		7	2	8	4	5	12			
8 (a)	Watford	L 0-2		6,677	5*	6		4	9		7		11	10				12		3	8		2		1		
15 (h)	Swindon T	W 4-0	O'Rourke 3, Irvine	8,126			6		5	4	7		9	10						3	8		2		1	11	
17 (h)	Swansea T	W 4-1	Horner, O'Rourke, Horsfield, Downing	12,471			6		5	4	7		9	10						3	8		2		1	11	
22 (a)	Reading	D 0-0		6,485			6		5	4	7		9	10						3	8		2		1	11	
29 (h)	Doncaster R	W 2-0	Horner, Horsfield	12,082	12		6		5	4	7		9	10*						3	8		2		1	11	
Nov 5 (a)	Mansfield T	W 5-4	O'Rourke 2, Downing 2, Hickton	6,379			6		5	4	7		9						10	3	8		2		1	11	
12 (h)	Grimsby T	L 0-1		14,164			6		5	4	7		9						8	3	10		2		1	11	
15 (a)	Swansea T	D 4-4	O'Rourke 2, Downing, Hickton	4,297			6		5	4	7		9						2	3	8		10		1	11	
19 (a)	Walsall	L 1-2	Horsfield	8,967			6		5	4	7		9						2	3	8		10		1	11	
Dec 3 (a)	Torquay U	L 1-2	Hickton	4,701			6		5	4	7		9						2	3	8		10		1	11	
10 (h)	Brighton & HA	W 1-0	O'Rourke	9,585			6		5	4	7		9						2	3			10		1	11	8
17 (h)	Colchester U	W 4-0	O'Rourke 2, Horsfield 2	8,819			6		5	4	7		9	10						3	8		2		1	11	
26 (a)	Darlington	W 3-0	Downing, O'Rourke, Chadwick	18,144	12		6		5*	4	7		9	10						3	8		2		1	11	
27 (h)	Darlington	W 4-0	Hickton (pen), Horsfield 2, Lawson	25,213	5		6			4	7		9*	12	10					3	8		2		1	11	
31 (a)	Bristol R	D 2-2	Horsfield, Chadwick	10,645	5		6			4	7		9		10					3	8		2		1	11	
Jan 14 (a)	Oldham A	W 1-0	Horsfield	12,659	2		6		5	4	7					1			9	3	8		10	11			
21 (h)	Scunthorpe U	W 2-1	Gates, Horsfield	19,005		5	6			4	7				10	1			9	3	8		2	11			
Feb 4 (a)	Workington	W 2-1	Hickton, Lugg	4,246	2		6		5*	4	7				12				9	3	8		10	11	1		
11 (h)	Gillingham	D 1-1	Horsfield	18,945		5	6			4	7				10				9	3	8		2		1	11	
18 (a)	Bournemouth	D 1-1	Butler	5,479		5	6			4	7				10				9	3	8		2		1	11	
25 (h)	Watford	W 3-0	Downing 2, Horsfield	22,059		5	6			7	4		9						10	3	8		2		1	11	
Mar 4 (a)	Swindon T	L 1-4	O'Rourke	14,370		5	6			7	4		9						10	3	8		2		1	11	
11 (h)	Bournemouth	W 3-1	Hickton, Jones, Downing	15,644		5	6			4	7		9						10	3		2	8		1	11	
18 (h)	Reading	D 2-2	O'Rourke, Horsfield	17,569		5	6			4	7	8	9							3	10		2		1	11	
25 (a)	Doncaster R	W 4-0	O'Rourke, Horsfield 3	9,628		5	6			4	7	8	9							3	10		2		1	11	
27 (h)	Shrewsbury T	W 1-0	Hickton	23,452		5	6			4	7	8*	9	12						3	10		2		1	11	
29 (a)	Shrewsbury T	L 0-1		6,497		5	6			4	7		9		10*				12	3	8		2		1	11	
Apr 1 (h)	Mansfield T	W 1-0	Edwards (og)	23,226		5	6			4	7		9						10	3	8		2		1	11	
8 (a)	Grimsby T	L 1-2	O'Rourke	4,905		5	12			4	7		9		10*					3	8		2		1	11	
10 (a)	Leyton O	L 0-2		5,772		5	6			4	7	8	9							3	10		2		1	11	
15 (h)	Walsall	L 0-2		18,090		5	6			4	7		9						10	3	8		2		1	11	
22 (a)	Peterborough U	W 2-1	O'Rourke, Rooks	6,458		2*	12		5	6	7	4	9						8	3			10		1	11	
24 (h)	Leyton O	W 3-1	O'Rourke 2, Hickton (pen)	15,184			3		5	6	7	4	9						10	2			8		1	11	
29 (h)	Torquay U	W 4-0	Hickton 3, O'Rourke	27,160			3		5	6	7	4	9						10	2*	12		8		1	11	
May 6 (a)	Brighton & HA	D 1-1	O'Rourke	12,692			3		5	6	7	4	9						10	2*	12		8		1	11	
13 (h)	Peterborough U	W 2-1	Hickton 2	32,503			3		5	6	7	4	9						10	2			8		1	11	
16 (h)	Oxford U	W 4-1	O'Rourke 3, Hickton	39,683			3		5	6	7	4	9						10	2			8		1	11	
Apps					2	25	40	8	26	42	44	19	39	17	17	7	9	3	19	41	33	2	40	4	35	33	1
Sub apps						2		2								1	2	2	1	1	2	1		1			
Goals						1	1		1	2	2	1	27	2	2					1	22		15	1		8	

1 own-goal

FA Cup

Date	Opponent	Res	Scorers	Att	App	Jon	Roo	Hor	Cha(DE)	O'R	Irv	Law	Cha(N)	McM	But	Hor(A)	Hic	Lug	Whi	Dow	Round
Nov 26 (a)	Chester	W 5-2	O'Rourke 3, Downing, Hickton	7,607		6	5	4	7	9*				2	3	8	10	12	1	11	1
Jan 7 (h)	York C	D 1-1	Hickton	20,573	12	6	5	4	7	9*	10				3	8	2		1	11	2
11 (a)	York C	D 0-0*		14,531		6	5	4	7			10		9	3	8	2		1	11	R
16 (n†)	York C	W 4-1	Lawson, Jackson (og), Lugg, Horsfield	21,347	5	6		4	7			10	1	9	3	8	2	11			2R
28 (a)	Mansfield T	L 0-2		17,332	2	6	5	4	7			11		9	3	8	10		1		3
Apps					2	5	4	5	5	2	1	4	1	3	5	5	5	1	4	3	
Sub apps					1													1			
Goals										3		1				1	2	1		1	

*After extra-time.   †Played at St James' Park, Newcastle.

1 own-goal

League Cup

Date	Opponent	Res	Scorers	Att	App	Gat	Jon	Dav	Hor	Cha(DE)	Mas	O'R	Irv	Law	Cha(N)	McP	But	Hor(A)	Round
Aug 24 (h)	York C	D 0-0		9,758	1	5	3	4	6	7	8	9	10	11	2				1
29 (a)	York C	L 1-2	Chadwick	4,970		5	3	4		7	8	9		11	2	1	10	6	R
Apps					1	2	2	2	1	2	2	2	1	2	2	1	1	1	
Sub apps																			
Goals										1									

1967-68
Division 2

Date	Opponent	Res	Scorers	Att	McPartland D	Butler G	Jones GE	Masson DS	Rooks R	Horner W	Chadwick DE	Hickton J	O'Rourke J	McMordie A	Downing DG	Gates WL	Spraggon F	Crossan JA	Lugg RJ	Smith D	Lawson J	Horsfield A	Worthington PR	Kear MP	Whigham WM	Allen M	McNeill AA	Wilson FP	Laidlaw JD	Smith RA	Short M	Webb SJ
Aug 19 (h)	Ipswich T	L 0-2		25,916	1	2	3	4	5	6	7	8	9	10	11																	
26 (a)	Carlisle U	D 2-2	Jones, O'Rourke	12,389	1	2	3		5			7	8	9			4	6	10	11												
29 (h)	Birmingham C	D 1-1	Rooks	25,814	1	2	3	4	5			7	8	9		11*	6		10	12												
Sep 2 (h)	Blackburn R	D 0-0		23,757	1	2	3	4		6	7	8	9	12		5			10	11*												
5 (a)	Bristol C	D 0-0		13,216	1	2	3	7	5	6	11	8	9				4		10													
9 (a)	Blackpool	L 0-3		24,346	1	2	3	7	5	6	11	8	9				4		10													
16 (h)	Millwall	L 0-1		23,446	1	3	6	4	5		7	2	9	8				10			11*12											
23 (a)	Hull C	W 2-0	Lawson, O'Rourke	17,727	1		6		5*	4		2	12	8		3		10	7		11	9										
26 (a)	Birmingham C	L 1-6	Crossan	28,885	1					6		2	9	8		5		4			11	10	3	7								
30 (h)	Aston Villa	D 1-1	Hickton	20,534		3	4	5	6	11*	9	8				2	10						12	7	1							
Oct 7 (a)	Charlton A	D 2-2	Kear, O'Rourke	14,798		3		5	4		8	9	10			2	6			11				7	1							
14 (a)	Plymouth A	W 5-0	Hickton 3, Crossan, O'Rourke	18,025		3	12	5	4*		8	9				2	6	10						7	1							
24 (a)	Cardiff C	L 0-3		10,441		3		5	4	11	8	9				2	6	10						7	1							
28 (h)	Portsmouth	W 1-0	Hickton	18,180		3	4	5		11	8					2	6	9					10	7	1							
Nov 4 (a)	Norwich C	L 1-2	Horsfield	12,429		3	4	5		11	8	9				2*	6	10					12	7	1							
11 (h)	Rotherham U	D 1-1	Hickton (pen)	16,519		3	4	5		11	2	9					6	10					8	7	1							
18 (a)	Queen's Park R	D 1-1	Hickton	17,557		3		5	4	11	2	9	8				6	10						7	1							
25 (h)	Preston NE	W 5-0	Hickton, O'Rourke, Masson, Rooks, Kear	14,359		3	8	5	4	11	2	9					6	10						7	1							
Dec 2 (a)	Derby C	W 4-2	O'Rourke 3, Hickton	20,381		3		5	4	11	2	9	8				6	10						7	1							
9 (h)	Crystal P	W 3-0	Kear, McMordie, Crossan	16,654		3		5	4	11	2	9	8				6	10					12	7*	1							
16 (h)	Ipswich T	W 2-1	Hickton 2 (1 pen)	12,724		3			4	11	2	9	8			5	6	10						7	1							
23 (a)	Carlisle U	W 4-0	O'Rourke 3, Kear	27,952		3		5	4	11	2	9	8				6	10						7	1							
26 (a)	Bolton W	L 0-2		16,076		3		5	4	11	2	9	8			6*	10						12	7	1							
30 (h)	Bolton W	L 1-2	Hickton	29,217		3		5	4	11	2	9	8					10						7	1	6						
Jan 6 (a)	Blackburn R	L 0-3		14,420		3		5	4	11*	2	9	8				6	10					12	7	1							
13 (h)	Blackpool	D 0-0		19,728		3	12	5	4	11	2	9	8				6	10*						7	1							
20 (a)	Millwall	L 0-4		12,139		3			4	11*	2	9	8			5	6	10			12			7	1							
Feb 3 (h)	Hull C	W 2-1	Hickton 2 (1 pen)	16,028		3	4		2			9		10	11	5	6						8	7	1							
10 (a)	Aston Villa	W 1-0	Horsfield	22,724		2	4					9				5	6	10				8	3	7	1	11						
24 (h)	Charlton A	D 1-1	Hickton	13,414		3	4				10	9			11	5	6							7	1	8	2					
Mar 2 (a)	Plymouth A	W 1-0	Horsfield	9,040		3			4	12	2		8	11*	5	6	10					9		7	1							
9 (h)	Cardiff C	L 2-3	Crossan, Hickton	15,582		3			4	12	2		8		5	6	11					10		7	1			9*				
23 (a)	Portsmouth	L 0-2		18,197		3	4*	5	12	7	2		8	11	6	10						9			1							
30 (h)	Norwich C	W 2-0	Kear, Hickton	10,181		3	4*	5			8	9	11	2	6	10						12	7	1							
Apr 6 (a)	Rotherham U	W 1-0	Rooks	15,399		3		5			11	9	8			6						10	7	1	4			2			
13 (h)	Queen's Park R	W 3-1	Hickton 2, Horsfield	20,849		3		5			11	9	8			6						10	7	1	4			2			
15 (h)	Huddersfield T	W 3-2	Hickton 2 (1 pen), Horsfield	15,065		3		5			11	9	8			6						10	7	1	4			2			
16 (a)	Huddersfield T	L 0-1		12,709		3		5	4		9	8				6						11	10	7	1			2			
20 (a)	Preston NE	D 0-0		15,229		3		5	12		11	9	8			6						10	7	1	4*			2			
27 (h)	Derby C	D 2-2	Hickton 2	13,123		3		5	4		11	9	8			6						10	7					2	1		
May 4 (a)	Crystal P	W 3-1	Hickton, Crossan, Horsfield	9,679		3*		5			11	9	8			6	8					10	7	1	12			2			
11 (h)	Bristol C	W 2-1	Webb 2	12,684		3		5			7	10			8		6	4	11				1					2			9
Apps					9	7	41	16	33	26	34	42	24	29	7	20	32	32	5	1	3	16	2	32	32	5	2	1	1	8	1	1
Sub apps							2			2	2			1	1				1	1	4	3				1						
Goals							1	1	3			24	11	1				5			1	6		5							2

FA Cup

Date	Opponent	Res	Scorers	Att	McPartland D	Butler G	Jones GE	Masson DS	Rooks R	Horner W	Chadwick DE	Hickton J	O'Rourke J	McMordie A	Downing DG	Gates WL	Spraggon F	Crossan JA	Lugg RJ	Smith D	Lawson J	Horsfield A	Worthington PR	Kear MP	Whigham WM	Allen M	McNeill AA	Wilson FP	Laidlaw JD	Smith RA	Short M	Webb SJ	Round
Jan 27 (h)	Hull C	D 1-1	Crossan	28,509		3	4		2		8	9*				5	6	10			11			12	7	1								3
31 (a)	Hull C	D 2-2*	Horsfield 2	33,916		3	4		2			9		12	11*	5	6	10				8			7	1								R
Feb 7 (nt)	Hull C	W 1-0	Downing	16,524		3	4		2			9			11	5	6	10				8			7	1								2R
17 (h)	Bristol C	D 1-1	Parr (og)	29,086		3	4*		2			9			11	5	6	10				8		12	7	1								4
20 (a)	Bristol C	L 1-2	Hickton	21,771		3	4			12	10				11	5	6	8*				9	2		7	1								R
Apps						5	5		4		5	1			4	5	5	5			1	4	1		5	5							
Sub apps									1			1								1			1									
Goals									1			1			1			1				2										

*After extra-time. †Played at Bootham Crescent, York.

1 own-goal

League Cup

Date	Opponent	Res	Scorers	Att	McPartland D	Butler G	Jones GE	Masson DS	Rooks R	Horner W	Chadwick DE	Hickton J	O'Rourke J	McMordie A	Downing DG	Gates WL	Spraggon F	Crossan JA	Lugg RJ	Smith D	Lawson J	Horsfield A	Worthington PR	Kear MP	Whigham WM	Allen M	McNeill AA	Wilson FP	Laidlaw JD	Smith RA	Short M	Webb SJ	Round
Aug 22 (h)	Barnsley	W 4-1	Hickton 3, Smith	15,968	1	2	3		5	4	7	8	9				6		10	11														1
Sep 13 (h)	Chelsea	W 2-1	McMordie, Smith	30,417	1	3	6	4	5	12	7	2	9	8*			10		11															2
Oct 11 (a)	Blackburn R	L 2-3	Hickton (pen), O'Rourke	10,442		3		5	4	11*	8	9				2	6	10	12					7	1									3
Apps					2	2	3	1	3	2	3	3	3	1		1	2	2	1	2				1	1							
Sub apps									1										1													
Goals										4	1	1						2														

1968-69
Division 2

Date	Match	Res	Scorers	Att	Whigham WM	Smith RA	Jones GE	McNeill AA	Rooks R	Spraggon F	Kear MP	McMordie A	Hickton J	Horsfield A	Crossan JA	Downing DG	Lugg RJ	Horner W	Gates WL	Myton B	Webb SJ	Chadwick DE	Kinnell G	Short M	Allen M	Moody A	Smith G	Laidlaw JD	Maddren WD	Mills DJ
Aug 10 (h)	Preston NE	W 2-1	Hickton 2 (1 pen)	19,014	1	2	3	4*	5	6	7	8	9	10	11	12														
14 (a)	Norwich C	W 2-0	Horsfield, Downing	19,431	1	2	3		5	6	7	8	9	10	11	4														
17 (a)	Portsmouth	L 0-3		24,273	1	2	3		5	6	7	8	9	10	11	4														
20 (h)	Crystal P	W 4-0	Horsfield 2, Crossan, Lugg	21,622	1	2	3		5	6		8	9	10	11	4	7													
24 (h)	Carlisle U	W 1-0	Hickton	22,392	1	2	3		5	6		8	9	10	11	4	7													
27 (h)	Huddersfield T	D 1-1	McMordie	25,422	1	2	3		5	6		8	9	10	11	4	7													
31 (h)	Hull C	L 0-3		16,838	1	2	3		5	6	7	8	9	10	4			11												
Sep 7 (a)	Cardiff C	L 0-2		14,225	1	2	3				7	8	9	10		11		4	6											
14 (h)	Birmingham C	W 3-1	Hickton, Gates 2	17,398	1	2	3		5			8	10	9	6	11	7		4											
21 (a)	Bury	W 3-2	Horsfield 2, Webb	7,471	1	2	3		5	6		8		10	11		7		4		9									
28 (h)	Charlton A	W 1-0	Downing	21,628	1	2	3		5	6		8		10	11		7		4		9									
Oct 5 (h)	Derby C	D 0-0		28,636	1	2	3		5	6		8		10	11		7		4		9									
8 (a)	Huddersfield T	L 0-3		14,799	1	2	3		5	6		8*	9	10	11		7		4		12									
12 (a)	Sheffield U	W 3-1	Chadwick, Kear, Downing	18,334	1	2	3		5	6	7	12	9		11	4					8	10*								
19 (h)	Fulham	W 2-0	McMordie, Downing	23,238	1	2	3		5			12	9	10	11*	4	7				8	6								
26 (a)	Oxford U	W 4-2	Downing, Horsfield 2, Rooks (pen)	11,209	1	2	3		5			12	9	10	11	4	7*				8	6								
Nov 9 (a)	Millwall	L 0-2		22,019	1		3		5	2			9	10	11	4	7				8	6								
16 (h)	Bolton W	D 0-0		18,458	1	2	3		5			8*	9	10	11	4	7				12	6								
23 (a)	Aston Villa	L 0-1		15,281	1	2	3		5			12	9	10*	11	4	7				8	6								
30 (h)	Blackburn R	W 2-0	Coddington (og), Downing	16,423	1	2	3		5				9	10	11	4	7				8	6								
Dec 3 (a)	Bristol C	W 4-1	Hickton 2 (1 pen), Downing, McMordie	18,038	1	2	3		5			8	9	10	11	4	7					6								
7 (a)	Blackpool	D 1-1	Rooks	13,356		2	3		5				9	10	11	4	7					6	1	8						
21 (h)	Fulham	W 3-0	Downing, Hickton 2	13,333	1	2	3		5				9*	10	11	4	7				8	6						12		
26 (h)	Derby C	L 2-3	Hickton 2 (1 pen)	34,481	1	2	3		5				9	10	11	4	7				8	6								
Jan 11 (a)	Bristol C	L 0-2		13,696	1	2	3		5				9	10	11	4*	7				8	6						12		
18 (h)	Millwall	D 1-1	Kinnell	17,153	1		3		5				9	10	11	4	7				8	6	2							
24 (h)	Oxford U	W 2-0	Crossan, Hickton	23,030	1		3		5	6			9	10	11*		7			12					2	4				
28 (h)	Sheffield U	W 3-1	Hickton, Webb 2	24,784	1		3		5	6			9	10	11		7				8				2	4				
Feb 1 (a)	Bolton W	D 0-0		7,658	1		3		5	6			9	10	11		7				8				2	4				
22 (h)	Blackpool	W 2-1	Hickton (pen), Webb	18,707	1		3		5	6			9	10	11		7				8				2	4				
Mar 1 (a)	Preston NE	W 2-1	Hickton, Lugg	12,520	1		3		5	6			9	10	11		7				8				2	4				
4 (h)	Aston Villa	D 0-0		29,824	1		3		5	6			9	10	11		7*			12	8				2	4				
8 (h)	Portsmouth	W 1-0	Crossan	23,982	1		3		5	6			9	10	11				7		8				2	4				
15 (a)	Carlisle U	L 0-3		13,920	1				5	6	7*		9	10	11						8	12			2	4	3			
22 (h)	Hull C	W 5-3	Hickton 4, McMordie	18,330	1	2	3		5	6		8	9	10	11		7		4											
25 (a)	Blackburn R	D 1-1	Downing	7,193	1	2	3		5	6		8	9	10	11	4	7													
29 (h)	Cardiff C	D 0-0		24,470	1	2	3		5	6		8*	9	10	11	4	7			12										
Apr 4 (a)	Crystal P	D 0-0		43,781	1	2	3		5	6*		8	9	10	11	4	7			12										
5 (a)	Charlton A	L 0-2		23,930	1				5	6		8*		10	11		7								2	3	9	4	12	
8 (h)	Norwich C	D 0-0		19,366	1	2*	3		5	6		8		10	11		7			12							4	9		
12 (h)	Bury	L 2-3	Maddren, McMordie	10,417	1					6		8			11								5	3		2	4	9	10	
19 (a)	Birmingham C	L 1-3	McMordie	25,899	1	2	3		5		7	10			4		11				8*	6						9	12	
Apps					41	27	38	1	40	38	16	39	34	23	22	30	21	1	17	3	11	15	12	1	3	10	15	3	1	
Sub apps										2		3				3			1		3		1		1		1	1	1	
Goals							2		1			6	18	7	3	9	2		2		4	1	1						1	

1 own-goal

FA Cup

Date	Match	Res	Scorers	Att	Whigham WM	Smith RA	Jones GE	McNeill AA	Rooks R	Spraggon F	Kear MP	McMordie A	Hickton J	Horsfield A	Crossan JA	Downing DG	Lugg RJ	Horner W	Gates WL	Myton B	Webb SJ	Chadwick DE	Kinnell G	Short M	Allen M	Moody A	Smith G	Laidlaw JD	Maddren WD	Mills DJ	Round
Jan 4 (h)	Millwall	D 1-1	Allen	26,960			3		5	4		10	8	12	11				2		7	6	1		9*							3
6 (a)	Millwall	L 0-1		22,230		2	3		5	6		10	8		12	11	4				7		1		9*							R
Apps						1	2		2	2		2	2		1	1			2		2	1	2		2						
Sub apps														1		1														
Goals																									1					

League Cup

Date	Match	Res	Scorers	Att	Whigham WM	Smith RA	Jones GE	McNeill AA	Rooks R	Spraggon F	Kear MP	McMordie A	Hickton J	Horsfield A	Crossan JA	Downing DG	Lugg RJ	Horner W	Gates WL	Myton B	Webb SJ	Chadwick DE	Kinnell G	Short M	Allen M	Moody A	Smith G	Laidlaw JD	Maddren WD	Mills DJ	Round
Sep 4 (a)	Bristol C	L 0-1		14,218	1	2	3		5		7	8	9	10*	11	12		4	6													2
Apps					1	1	1		1		1	1	1	1	1			1	1												
Sub apps																1														
Goals																													

1969-70
Division 2

Date	Opponent	Res	Scorers	Att	Short M	Moody A	Jones GE	Smith G	Gates WL	Spraggon F	McMordie A	Kear MP	Laidlaw JD	Hickton J	Chadwick DE	Smith RA	Downing DG	Lugg RJ	Webb SJ	Mills DJ	Myton B	McIlmoyle H	Allen M	Whigham WM	Murray A	Crossan JA	Maddren WD
Aug 9 (a)	Sheffield U	L 0-3		14,707	1	2	3	4	5	6	7	8	9	10	11												
12 (h)	Millwall	W 3-1	Hickton, McMordie, Laidlaw	16,221	1		3	4	5	6	7	8	9	10	11	2											
16 (h)	Leicester C	W 2-1	Laidlaw, Hickton	22,159	1		3	4	5	6	7	8	9	10	11	2											
18 (a)	Millwall	D 1-1	Hickton	12,641	1		3	4*	5	6	7	8	9	10		2		11	12								
23 (a)	Carlisle U	L 0-1		12,578	1		3	4	5	6	7	8	9	10	11	2											
27 (a)	Cardiff C	L 0-1		21,623	1		3	4	5	6	7	8	9	10	11	2											
30 (h)	Aston Villa	W 1-0	Hickton	19,438	1	2	3	4	5	6	7	8*	9	10	11		12										
Sep 6 (a)	Blackburn R	L 0-4		12,120	1		3	4	5	6	7	8	9	10		2		11									
13 (h)	Bristol C	W 2-0	Downing, R.A.Smith	14,513	1		3	4	5	6	8			10		2		11	7		9						
16 (h)	Swindon T	D 0-0		15,632	1		3	4	5	6	8*			10		2		11	7	12	9						
20 (a)	Oxford U	D 1-1	McMordie	9,496	1		3	4	5	6	8			10		2		12	7	9*	11						
27 (h)	Blackpool	L 0-2		20,268	1		3	4	5	6	8			10	7	2		11			9						
Oct 4 (a)	Queen's Park R	L 0-4		21,421	1		3	4	5	6	8		9	10		2	7						11				
8 (a)	Leicester C	L 1-2	Downing	26,528	1		3	4	5	6	8			10		2	7					9	11				
11 (h)	Bolton W	W 4-0	Hickton 2, McIlmoyle 2	14,020			3	4	5	6	8			10		2	7					9	11	1			
18 (a)	Huddersfield T	D 0-0		12,269			3	4	5	6			8	10		2	7					9	11	1			
25 (h)	Watford	W 3-1	Hickton, McIlmoyle, Laidlaw	15,402			3	4	5	6			8	10		2	7					9	11*	1	12		
Nov 1 (a)	Preston NE	W 1-0	Hickton (pen)	13,075			3	4	5	6			8	10		2	7					9	11	1			
8 (h)	Charlton A	W 2-0	Hickton, Downing	15,196			3	4	5	6	12		8	10		2	7					9	11*	1			
15 (h)	Hull C	W 1-0	Hickton	14,235			3	4	5	6	12		8	10		2	7*					9	11	1			
22 (a)	Portsmouth	W 3-2	Hickton, McIlmoyle, Laidlaw	15,621			3	4	5	6	12		8	10		2	7					9	11*	1			
Dec 13 (a)	Bristol C	D 0-0		15,290			3	4	5	6			8	10		2	7					9	11	1			
16 (h)	Birmingham C	W 4-2	Hickton 2, Laidlaw, Spraggon	17,020			3	4	5	6			8	10*		2	7					9	11	1	12		
26 (h)	Carlisle U	L 0-2		29,703		2	3	4	5	6			8	10			7					9	11*	1		12	
Jan 10 (h)	Oxford U	W 2-0	Hickton 2	16,922			3	4	5	6	11*		8	10		2	7					9		1		12	
13 (h)	Blackburn R	W 4-1	Gates, Mills, Murray, Downing	21,950			3	4	5	6	11*			10		2	7			12		9		1	8		
17 (a)	Blackpool	D 1-1	Laidlaw	15,154			3	4	5	6	12		11	10		2	7					9		1	8*		
31 (h)	Queen's Park R	W 1-0	Downing	25,821			3	4	5	6	8		11	10		2	7					9		1			
Feb 11 (h)	Bolton W	L 1-2	Laidlaw	9,928			3	4	5	6	8		11	10		2	7					9		1			
28 (h)	Preston NE	D 1-1	Hickton	25,050			3	4		6	8		11	10		2	7*		12			9		1			5
Mar 3 (a)	Charlton A	W 2-0	Laidlaw, Hickton	9,805			3	4		6	8		11	10		2	7					9		1			5
7 (h)	Portsmouth	W 2-1	Laidlaw, Hickton (pen)	22,498			3	4		6	8*		11	10		2	7		12			9		1			5
11 (a)	Norwich C	L 0-2		10,390			3	4		6	8		11	10		2	7					9		1			5
14 (a)	Birmingham C	D 0-0		17,974			3	4		6			11	10		2	8					9		1	7		5
17 (h)	Sheffield U	W 1-0	Hickton	25,026			3	4		6			11	10		2	8					9		1	7		5
21 (a)	Norwich C	D 0-0		24,514			3	4		6*			11	10		2	8		12			9		1	7		5
27 (a)	Watford	W 3-2	Hickton 2, McMordie	22,486			3	4			8		11	10		2	7					9	6	1			5
28 (a)	Hull C	L 2-3	Laidlaw, Hickton	17,434			3	4			8		11	10		2	7		12			9	6	1			5*
31 (h)	Huddersfield T	D 1-1	Hickton (pen)	27,519			3	4*			8		11	10		2	7		12			9	6	1			5
Apr 4 (h)	Cardiff C	W 2-1	McIlmoyle, Laidlaw	13,859		5	3	4			8		11	10		2	7		6			9		1			
8 (a)	Aston Villa	L 0-2		22,805			3	4	5				11*	10		2	7		6	12		9		1			
14 (a)	Swindon T	W 3-0	McIlmoyle, Mills, Hickton	16,668		4	3		5	6	8			10		2	7			11		9		1			
Apps					14	5	42	41	31	37	28	8	35	42	7	39	32	4	5	1	4	29	15	28	5		10
Sub apps											4						2	1	4	4					2	2	
Goals								1	1	3			11	24		1	5			2		6			1		

FA Cup

Date	Opponent	Res	Scorers	Att	Jones GE	Smith G	Gates WL	Spraggon F	McMordie A	Laidlaw JD	Hickton J	Smith RA	Downing DG	McIlmoyle H	Whigham WM	Murray A	Crossan JA	Round
Jan 3 (h)	West Ham U	W 2-1	McIlmoyle, Downing	32,585	3	4	5	6	8		10	2	7	9	1		11	3
24 (h)	York C	W 4-1	McMordie, G.Smith, Hickton (pen), Laidlaw	32,283	3	4	5	6	8	11	10	2	7	9	1			R
Feb 7 (a)	Carlisle U	W 2-1	Hickton, Downing	27,599	3	4	5	6	8	11	10	2	7	9	1			4
21 (h)	Manchester U	D 1-1	Hickton	40,040	3	4	5	6	8	11	10	2	7	9	1			5
25 (a)	Manchester U	L 1-2	Hickton	63,418	3	4	5	6	8	11	10	2	7	9	1			R
Apps					5	5	5	5	4		5	5	5	5	5	5	1	
Sub apps																		
Goals						1			1	1	4		2	1				

League Cup

Date	Opponent	Res	Scorers	Att	Short M	Jones GE	Smith G	Gates WL	Spraggon F	McMordie A	Kear MP	Laidlaw JD	Hickton J	Chadwick DE	Smith RA	Round
Sep 3 (a)	Manchester U	L 0-1		38,939	1	3	4	5	6	7	8	9	10	11	2	2
Apps					1	1	1	1	1	1	1	1	1	1	1	
Sub apps																
Goals																

1970-71
Division 2

Date	Opponent	Result	Scorers	Att	Whigham WM	Smith RA	Jones GE	Smith G	Gates WL	Spraggon F	Mills DJ	McMordie A	Maddren WD	Hickton J	Laidlaw JD	Downing DG	McIlmoyle H	Allen M	Myton B	Moody A	Webb SJ	Charlton H	Vincent JV	Burluraux D	Murray A
Aug 15 (h)	Carlisle U	W 2-1	Laidlaw, Hickton	21,228	1	2	3	4	5	6	7	8	9*	10	11	12									
22 (a)	Hull C	L 0-1		20,929	1	2	3	4	5	6	7	8		10	11		9								
29 (h)	Oxford U	L 0-2		17,548	1	2*	3	4	5	6	7	8		10	11	12	9								
Sep 1 (a)	Birmingham C	W 1-0	Hickton	27,769	1			4		6		12	5	10	11*		9	2	3	7	8				
5 (a)	Luton T	L 0-1		16,018	1		3		12	6			5	10	7		9*	2	11	4	8				
12 (h)	Blackburn R	D 1-1	McIlmoyle	15,083	1		3	4		6			5	10	8	7	9	2	11						
19 (a)	Sheffield U	D 1-1	Hickton	19,780	1		3	4	5	6		8	2	10	11	7	9								
26 (h)	Queen's Park R	W 6-2	Hickton 3 (1 pen), McIlmoyle 2, Downing	16,788	1		3	4	5	6	12	8	2	10	11	7	9*								
30 (a)	Leicester C	L 2-3	Hickton 2	26,260	1		3	4	5	6		8	2	10	11	7	9								
Oct 3 (a)	Cardiff C	W 4-3	Hickton, McIlmoyle, Laidlaw, Maddren	20,925	1		3	4	5	6		8	2	10	11	7	9								
10 (h)	Portsmouth	W 3-2	McIlmoyle 2, Hickton	18,775	1		3	4	5	6	7	8	2	10	11		9								
17 (a)	Carlisle U	L 0-1		15,863	1		3	4	5	6	12	8	2	10	11		9	7*							
20 (h)	Bristol C	W 1-0	Hickton	16,651	1		3	4	5	6	7	8*	2	10	11		9			12					
24 (a)	Swindon T	L 0-3		15,434	1		3	4	5	6	7		2	10			9	11		8					
31 (h)	Watford	D 2-2	Laidlaw, Downing	16,018	1	2	3	4		6			5	10	11	7	9				8				
Nov 7 (a)	Orient	D 0-0		6,690	1	2	3		4	6			5	10	11	7	9				8				
14 (a)	Charlton A	W 3-0	Hickton, Downing, McIlmoyle	14,247	1	2*	3		4	6	12		5	10	11	7	9				8				
21 (a)	Sheffield W	L 2-3	Downing, McIlmoyle	15,421	1	2	3		4	6	12		5	10	11	7	9					8*			
28 (h)	Millwall	W 1-0	Hickton	13,036	1	2	3		4	6	8	12	5*	10	11	7	9								
Dec 5 (a)	Norwich C	D 1-1	Downing	13,073	1	2	3	8	5	6				10	11	7	9			4					
12 (h)	Bolton W	W 1-0	Hickton	12,873	1	2	3	8	5	6		12		10	11	7	9			4*					
19 (h)	Hull C	W 1-0	Hickton	17,957	1	2	3	4	5	6	12	8		10	11	7*	9								
26 (a)	Sunderland	D 2-2	Hickton 2	42,617	1	2	3	4	5	6		8		10	11	7	9								
Jan 9 (h)	Leicester C	W 1-0	Hickton	30,682	1	2	3		5	6		8		10	11	7	9			4					
16 (a)	Bristol C	W 2-0	Hickton, Downing	10,535	1	2	3		5	6		8		10	11	7	9			4					
30 (a)	Millwall	L 0-1		10,180	1	2	3		5			8	6	10	11	7	9			4					
Feb 6 (h)	Norwich C	W 5-0	Downing, Hickton 2, McIlmoyle, Laidlaw	19,106	1	2	3		5			8	6	10	11	7	9			4					
13 (a)	Bolton W	W 3-0	Laidlaw, Downing 2	9,877	1	2	3		5			8	6	10	11	7	9			4					
20 (h)	Sheffield W	W 1-0	Hickton	25,916	1	2	3		5			8	6	10	11	7	9			4					
26 (a)	Watford	L 0-1		14,112	1	2	3		5		12	8	6	10	11	7	9			4*					
Mar 6 (h)	Swindon T	W 3-0	McIlmoyle, Maddren, Downing	20,813	1	2	3		5			8	6	10	11	7	9			4					
13 (a)	Charlton A	L 0-1		9,420	1	2	3		5			8*	6	10	11	7	9			4		12			
20 (h)	Orient	L 0-1		17,132	1	2	3		5	4	12		6	10	11	7	9*					8			
27 (h)	Luton T	W 2-1	McIlmoyle 2	19,585	1	2	3		5			8	6	9	4	7*	12					10	11		
Apr 3 (a)	Oxford U	D 2-2	Hickton, McMordie	7,517	1	2	3		5			7	6	9	4		8					10	11		
9 (a)	Blackburn R	D 1-1	Laidlaw	11,210	1	2	3		5		12	7	6	9	4	11	8					10*			
10 (h)	Sunderland	D 2-2	Laidlaw, Hickton	26,479	1	2	3		5			7	6	9	10	11	8			4					
13 (h)	Cardiff C	D 1-1	Downing	19,559	1	2	3		5			7	6	9	10	11	8			4					
17 (a)	Portsmouth	D 1-1	McIlmoyle	8,193	1	2	3		5		12	7	6	9	4	11*	8						10		
24 (h)	Sheffield U	D 1-1	Hickton	16,946	1	2	3		5		10*	7	6	9	4	11	8							12	
27 (h)	Birmingham C	D 0-0		12,802	1	2	3		5		10	8	6		4	11	9							7*	12
May 1 (a)	Queen's Park R	D 1-1	Mills	10,390	1		3		5		7	8	6	10		11	9	4		2					
	Apps				42	30	41	18	38	26	10	30	34	41	40	32	40	6	3	16	3	4	4	3	1
	Sub apps							1			9	3				2	1	1		1		1	2		
	Goals										1	1	2	25	7	11	13								

FA Cup

Date	Opponent	Result	Scorers	Att	Whigham WM	Smith RA	Jones GE	Smith G	Gates WL	Spraggon F	Mills DJ	McMordie A	Maddren WD	Hickton J	Laidlaw JD	Downing DG	McIlmoyle H	Allen M	Myton B	Moody A	Webb SJ	Charlton H	Vincent JV	Burluraux D	Murray A	Round
Jan 2 (a)	Manchester U	D 0-0		47,024	1	2	3		5	6		8		10	11	7	9			4						3
5 (h)	Manchester U	W 2-1	McIlmoyle, Downing	40,040	1	2	3		5	6		8		10	11	7	9			4						R
23 (a)	Everton	L 0-3		54,875	1	2	3		5	6		8		10	11	7	9			4						4
	Apps				3	3	3		3	3		3		3	3	3	3			3						
	Sub apps																									
	Goals															1	1									

League Cup

Date	Opponent	Result	Scorers	Att	Whigham WM	Smith RA	Jones GE	Smith G	Gates WL	Spraggon F	Mills DJ	McMordie A	Maddren WD	Hickton J	Laidlaw JD	Downing DG	McIlmoyle H	Allen M	Myton B	Moody A	Webb SJ	Charlton H	Vincent JV	Burluraux D	Murray A	Round
Sep 8 (a)	Oldham A	W 4-2	Laidlaw, McIlmoyle, Downing, Hickton	9,539	1		3	4		6			5	10	8	7	9	2	11							2
Oct 7 (a)	Chelsea	L 2-3	Hickton, Jones	28,597	1		3	4	5	6	12	8	2	10	11	7*	9									3
	Apps				2		2	2	1	2		1	2	2	2	2	2	2	1	1						
	Sub apps										1															
	Goals						1							2	1	1	1									

1971-72
Division 2

Date	Opponent	Res	Scorers	Att	Whigham WM	Maddren WD	Jones GE	Stiles NP	Boam SW	Spraggon F	Downing DG	Mills DJ	Hickton J	Vincent JV	Laidlaw JD	McMordie A	Craggs JE	Allen M	Gates WL	Burluraux D	Platt JA	Moody A	Smith RA	Stone JG	Lynch P	Armstrong D	Smith M
Aug 14 (a)	Portsmouth	L 1-2	Vincent	15,649	1	2	3	4	5	6	7	8	9	10	11*			12									
21 (h)	Queen's Park R	W 3-2	Hickton, Mills, Vincent	20,547	1	2	3	4	5	6	7	8	9	10		11											
28 (a)	Bristol C	L 1-2	Maddren	16,474	1	2	3	4	5	6	7	12	8	10	11*	9											
31 (h)	Sheffield W	W 2-1	Maddren, Hickton	23,963	1	9	3		5	6	11	7	10	8			2	4									
Sep 4 (h)	Fulham	W 2-0	Vincent, Maddren	20,228	1	9	3		5		11	7*	10	8			2	4	6	12							
11 (a)	Charlton A	W 2-0	Maddren 2	11,167	1	9	3	4	5		7		10	8	11		2		6								
18 (h)	Cardiff C	W 1-0	Gates	18,288	1	9	3		5		7		10	8*	11	12	2	4	6								
25 (a)	Luton T	L 2-3	Hickton, Maddren	13,001	1	9	3	4*	5		7		10	11	12	8	2		6								
29 (a)	Sunderland	L 1-4	Vincent	28,129	1	9	3	4	5		7		10	11		8	2		6								
Oct 2 (h)	Blackpool	W 1-0	Gates	18,671		9	3						10	11		8	2		6	7	1	4	5				
9 (a)	Oxford U	D 0-0		9,925		9	3						10	11	7	8	2		6		1	4	5				
16 (h)	Portsmouth	W 2-1	Hickton, Vincent	16,296		9	3		5				10	11	7	8	2		6		1	4					
19 (h)	Millwall	W 1-0	Hickton	20,383		9	3		5				10	11	7	8	2		6		1	4					
23 (h)	Watford	W 2-1	Craggs, Laidlaw	19,947		9	3		5				10	11	7	8	2		6		1	4					
30 (a)	Swindon T	W 1-0	Maddren	13,782		9	3		5				10	11	7	8	2		6		1	4					
Nov 6 (h)	Preston NE	L 0-1		21,907		9	3		5		12		10	11	7	8	2		6		1	4*					
13 (a)	Burnley	L 2-5	Laidlaw, Downing	15,720		9	3		5		10			11	7	8	2		6		1	4					
20 (h)	Orient	W 1-0	Hickton	13,288		9	3		5		12		10	11	7	8*	2		6		1	4					
27 (a)	Norwich C	L 0-2		21,303	12		3	7	5				10	11	9*	8	2		6		1	4					
Dec 4 (h)	Birmingham C	D 0-0		15,671	12		3	7	5		11		10		9	8	2		6		1	4*					
11 (a)	Hull C	L 3-4	Mills 2, Craggs	13,532		4	3	7	5		11	9	10			8	2		6		1						
18 (a)	Fulham	D 2-2	Stiles, Hickton	7,571		4	3	7*	5		11	9	10		12	8	2		6		1						
27 (h)	Carlisle U	D 2-2	Mills, Downing	24,796		4	3		5		11	9	10	7		8	2		6		1						
Jan 1 (a)	Cardiff C	L 0-1		12,758		4			5		11	9	10		7	8	2		6		1		3				
8 (h)	Bristol C	W 1-0	Downing	13,117		4			5		11	9	10		7	8	2		6		1		3				
22 (h)	Sunderland	W 2-0	Hickton 2	34,446		4	3	7*	5		11	9	10		12	8	2		6		1						
29 (a)	Millwall	L 0-1		14,127		4	3	7	5		11	9	10			8	2		6		1						
Feb 12 (a)	Watford	W 1-0	Hickton	8,109	6		3	4	5		11	9	10		7	8	2				1						
19 (h)	Swindon T	W 2-0	Downing, Mills	18,205		4	3	7	5		11	9	10			8	2		6		1						
Mar 4 (h)	Burnley	W 1-0	Dobson (og)	17,069		4	3	7	5		11	9	10	12		8	2		6*		1						
11 (h)	Oxford U	W 2-1	Mills 2	13,334		4	3	7	5			9	10	11		8	2		6		1						
14 (a)	Carlisle U	L 0-3		10,313	6		3	7		4		9	10	11	12	8	2		5*		1						
18 (a)	Queen's Park R	L 0-1		11,467	5		3	4		6	7		9*	10	11	8	2				1	12					
25 (h)	Charlton A	D 2-2	Hickton, McMordie	11,100		4	3	7	5	6	11	9	10			8	2				1						
31 (h)	Luton T	D 0-0		11,720		4	3	7*	5	6	12		10	11	9	8	2				1						
Apr 3 (a)	Blackpool	L 1-3	Vincent	13,726	6		3		5	4	12	9*	10	7		8	2				1					11	
8 (a)	Orient	D 1-1	McMordie	7,372	6			4	5	3		9	12	11*	7	8	2				1					10	
15 (h)	Norwich C	W 1-0	Spraggon	14,279	6			4*	5	3		9	10	12	7	8	2				1					11	
17 (a)	Preston NE	L 0-1		11,388	6				5	3	12	9	10	8	4	7*	2				1					11	
22 (a)	Birmingham C	D 1-1	Hickton	37,202	6			4	5	3		9	10	11	7	8	2				1						
26 (a)	Sheffield W	L 0-1		13,936	6			4	5	3	11	9	10*	8	7		2				1					12	
29 (h)	Hull C	W 3-0	McMordie, Vincent, Mills	9,539	6			7*	5	3		9	10			8	2				1	4				11	12
Apps					9	40	34	25	38	14	25	25	39	29	25	36	38	3	26	1	33	11	4	2		5	
Sub apps					2						4	1	1	2	4	1		1		1		1				1	1
Goals						7		1		1	4	8	12	7	2	3			2								

1 own-goal

FA Cup

Date	Opponent	Res	Scorers	Att	Whigham WM	Maddren WD	Jones GE	Stiles NP	Boam SW	Spraggon F	Downing DG	Mills DJ	Hickton J	Vincent JV	Laidlaw JD	McMordie A	Craggs JE	Allen M	Gates WL	Burluraux D	Platt JA	Round
Jan 15 (a)	Manchester C	D 1-1	Mills	42,620		4	3	7	5		11	9	10			8	2		6		1	3
18 (h)	Manchester C	W 1-0	Hickton	39,917		4	3	7*	5		11	9	10		12	8	2		6		1	R
Feb 5 (a)	Millwall	D 2-2	Hickton, Downing	23,579		4	3	7*	5		11	9	10		12	8	2		6		1	4
8 (h)	Millwall	W 2-1	Downing, Hickton (pen)	36,489	6		3	4	5		11	9	10		7	8	2				1	R
26 (a)	Manchester U	D 0-0		53,850		4	3	7	5		11	9	10			8	2		6		1	5
29 (h)	Manchester U	L 0-3		39,671		4	3	7	5		11	9	10			8	2		6		1	R
Apps					1	5	6	6	6		6	6	6		1	6	6		5		6	
Sub apps															2							
Goals											2	1	3									

League Cup

Date	Opponent	Res	Scorers	Att	Whigham WM	Maddren WD	Jones GE	Stiles NP	Boam SW	Spraggon F	Downing DG	Mills DJ	Hickton J	Vincent JV	Laidlaw JD	McMordie A	Craggs JE	Allen M	Gates WL	Round
Sep 8 (a)	York C	D 2-2	Downing, Hickton	11,041	1	9	3	4	5		7		10	8	11		2		6	2
14 (h)	York C	L 1-2	Craggs	21,021	1	9	3	4	5		7		10	8	11		2		6	R
Apps					2	2	2	2	2		2		2	2	2		2		2	
Sub apps																				
Goals											1		1				1			

1972-73
Division 2

Date	Opponent	Res	Score	Scorers	Att	Platt JA	Craggs JE	Spraggon F	Stiles NP	Boam SW	Maddren WD	McMordie A	Mills DJ	Smith M	Charlton H	Vincent JV	Moody A	Creamer PA	Jones GE	Hickton J	Armstrong D	Gates WL	Brine PK	Foggon A	Taylor B	Souness GJ
Aug 12 (h)	Sunderland	W	2-1	M.Smith 2	24,145	1	2*	3	4	5	6	7	8	9	10	11	12									
19 (a)	Oxford U	L	0-4		8,651	1	2	3	4	5	6	7*	8	9	10	11	12									
26 (h)	Fulham	L	1-2	McMordie	11,410	1	2			5	6	7	8	9*	10	11	4	3	12							
28 (a)	Orient	L	0-2		5,130	1	2		4	5	6		8	9		11	7*	3	12	10						
Sep 2 (a)	Queen's Park R	D	2-2	M.Smith, Hickton	10,601	1	2	12	4	5	6	7	8	9				3*	11	10						
9 (h)	Carlisle U	W	1-0	Mills	9,799	1	2	3	4	5	6	7	8	9					11	10						
16 (a)	Bristol C	D	1-1	McMordie	12,185	1	2	3	4	5	6	7	8	9					11	10						
19 (h)	Preston NE	D	0-0		9,679	1	2	3	4	5	6	7	8	9						10	11					
23 (h)	Hull C	W	1-0	Mills	9,180	1	2	3	4	5	6	7	8	9					11	10						
26 (a)	Burnley	D	0-0		12,398	1	2	3	4	5	6	7		9					11	10		8				
30 (a)	Blackpool	W	1-0	Boam	14,714	1	2	3	4	5	6	7		9					11	10		8				
Oct 7 (h)	Millwall	W	1-0	Maddren	10,863	1	2	3	4	5	6	7		9					11*	10		8	12			
14 (a)	Cardiff C	L	0-2		10,407	1	2	3		5	6	7*		9			4		11	10		8	12			
21 (h)	Huddersfield T	W	2-1	Craggs, Gates	9,907	1	2	3	4	5	6			9					11	8	10	7				
28 (a)	Aston Villa	D	1-1	Armstrong	30,345	1	2	3	4	5	6			9					11	8	10	7				
Nov 4 (h)	Burnley	D	3-3	Mills, McMordie, Hickton	18,127	1	2	3	4	5	6	8	9							10	11	7				
11 (a)	Preston NE	W	1-0	Hickton	10,015	1	2	3	4	5	6	11	9							8	10	7				
18 (a)	Sheffield W	L	1-2	Hickton (pen)	15,874	1		3	4*	5	6	11	9					2	12	8	10	7				
25 (h)	Swindon T	L	0-2		11,418	1	2	3	4	5	6	11*	9							8	10	7		12		
Dec 2 (a)	Brighton & HA	W	2-0	M.Smith, Hickton	11,116	1	2		4	5	6		10	9				3		8	11	7				
9 (h)	Nottingham F	D	0-0		10,326	1	2	4		5	6		10*	9				3		8	11	7		12		
16 (a)	Portsmouth	D	0-0		4,688	1	2			5	7	8	9					3		10	11	4	6			
23 (h)	Luton T	L	0-1		10,122	1	2		4	5		11	9	12				3		8	10	7*	6			
26 (h)	Hull C	L	1-3	McMordie	13,580	1	2		4	5		10	9	7*				3		8	11	12	6			
30 (h)	Oxford U	W	1-0	Foggon	9,069	1	2		4*	5	6	8	9	12				3		10		7		11		
Jan 6 (a)	Fulham	L	1-2	M.Smith	9,693	1	2		4	5	6		9	12				3		8		7		11	10*	
20 (h)	Queen's Park R	D	0-0		8,398	1	2	3		5	6	7	9							10	4	8		11		
27 (a)	Carlisle U	D	1-1	Gates	7,653	1	2	3		5	6	7	8						11	10	12	4		9*		
Feb 2 (h)	Blackpool	W	2-0	Mills 2	10,446	1	2	3		5	6	7	8	9*						10		4	12	11		
10 (h)	Bristol C	W	2-1	Hickton, Boam	8,511	1	2*	3		5	6	7	8	9						10		4	12	11		
17 (a)	Sunderland	L	0-4		26,040	1	2	3		5	6	7	8	9						10		4		11		
24 (h)	Portsmouth	W	3-0	Foggon, Stiles, Hickton	7,038	1	2	3	4	5	6		10*	8						9		7	12	11		
Mar 2 (a)	Millwall	L	0-1		11,473	1	2	3	4	5	6		8							9		7		10		11
10 (h)	Cardiff C	W	2-0	Brine, Foggon	7,686	1	2	3	4	5	6									9		7	8	10		11
17 (h)	Huddersfield T	D	1-1	M.Smith	7,193	1	2	3	4	5	6*			9					12			7	8	10		11
24 (h)	Aston Villa	D	1-1	Hickton	9,776	1	2	3	4	5				9*					12	8	6	7		11	10	
31 (a)	Swindon T	L	0-1		7,278	1	2	3	4	5				9						8		7		10	6	11
Apr 7 (h)	Brighton & HA	D	1-1	Foggon	6,816	1	2	3	4	5	6		8							9	10	7		11		
14 (a)	Nottingham F	W	3-1	Foggon 2, Hickton (pen)	9,258	1	2	3	4	5	6		8	12						9*	10	7		11		
21 (h)	Sheffield W	W	3-0	Gates, Hickton, Foggon	8,119	1	2	3	4	5	6		8							9	10	7		11		
23 (a)	Luton T	W	1-0	Maddren	6,177	1	4	3		5	6		8					2		9	10	7		11		
28 (h)	Orient	W	3-2	Hickton 3	7,939	1	2	3	4	5	6			8*					12	9	10	7		11		
Apps						42	41	33	32	40	40	26	37	19	3	4	2	6	18	36	19	32	5	12	4	11
Sub apps							1							5			2		3	2	1	1	4	3		
Goals							1		1	2	2	4	5	6						13	1	3	1	7		

FA Cup

Date	Opponent	Res	Score	Att	Platt JA	Craggs JE	Spraggon F	Stiles NP	Boam SW	Maddren WD	McMordie A	Mills DJ	Smith M	Charlton H	Vincent JV	Moody A	Creamer PA	Jones GE	Hickton J	Armstrong D	Gates WL	Brine PK	Foggon A	Taylor B	Souness GJ	Round
Jan 13 (a)	Plymouth A	L	0-1	15,361	1	2		4	5	6	7	9	12				3		8			11*	10			3
Apps					1	1		1	1	1	1	1					1		1			1	1			
Sub apps													1													
Goals																										

League Cup

Date	Opponent	Res	Score	Att	Platt JA	Craggs JE	Spraggon F	Stiles NP	Boam SW	Maddren WD	McMordie A	Mills DJ	Smith M	Charlton H	Vincent JV	Moody A	Creamer PA	Jones GE	Hickton J	Armstrong D	Gates WL	Brine PK	Foggon A	Taylor B	Souness GJ	Round
Sep 5 (h)	Wrexham	W	2-0	Mills 2 — 5,808	1	2	3	4*	5	6	7	8	9					11	10	12						2
Oct 3 (h)	Tottenham H	D	1-1	Hickton — 23,822	1	2	3	4	5	6	7*	9			12			11	10		8					3
11 (a)	Tottenham H	D	0-0*	— 19,256	1	2	3	4*	5	6	7	9						11	10		8	12				R
30 (a)	Tottenham H	L	1-2*	Hickton — 19,287	1	2	3		5	6	7*	9				12		11	8	10	4					2R
Apps					4	4	4	3	4	4	4	4	1					4	4	1	3					
Sub apps															1	1				1		1				
Goals												2							2							

*After extra-time

1973-74
Division 2

Date	Opponent	Res	Scorers	Att	Platt JA	Craggs JE	Spraggon F	Boam SW	Taylor B	Maddren WD	McMordie A	Mills DJ	Hickton J	Foggon A	Armstrong D	Smith M	Souness GJ	Murdoch RW	Charlton H	Poskett M	McAndrew A	Gates WL	Brine PK	Cochrane JK	Creamer PA	Cuff PJ
Aug 25 (a)	Portsmouth	W 1-0	Foggon	19,799	1	2	3	4	5	6	7	8	9*	10	11	12										
Sep 1 (h)	Fulham	L 0-2		14,977	1	2	3	4	5	6	7*	8	9	10	11	12										
8 (a)	Crystal P	W 3-2	Hickton, Mills, Taylor	17,554	1	2	3	4	5	6	7	8	9	10	11											
11 (h)	Carlisle U	W 1-0	Craggs	16,837	1	2	3	5	4*	6	7	8	9	10	11			12								
15 (h)	Aston Villa	D 0-0		14,742	1	2	3	5		6	7	8	9	10	11		4									
17 (a)	Orient	D 0-0		9,744	1	2	3	5		6	7	8	9	10	11		4									
22 (a)	Blackpool	D 0-0		14,784	1	2	3	5		6		8	9	10	11		4	7								
29 (h)	Bristol C	W 2-0	Murdoch, Armstrong	17,069	1	2	3	5		6		8	9	10	11		4	7								
Oct 2 (h)	Orient	W 3-2	Foggon, Hickton 2 (1 pen)	22,164	1	2	3	5		6		8*	9	10	11		4	7		12						
6 (a)	Swindon T	W 1-0	Murdoch	6,958	1	2	3	5		6			9	10	11	8	4	7								
13 (h)	Hull C	W 1-0	M.Smith	22,135	1	2	3	4		6			9	10	11	8*	4	7		12						
20 (h)	West Brom A	D 0-0		18,997	1	2	3	5		6		8	9*	10	11	12	4	7								
23 (a)	Carlisle U	D 1-1	Foggon	11,152	1	2	3	5		6		8	9	10	11		4	7								
27 (a)	Millwall	W 1-0	M.Smith	13,253	1	2	3	5		6			9	10	11	8	4	7								
Nov 3 (h)	Luton T	W 2-1	Foggon, Armstrong	22,590	1	2	3	5*		6		12	9	10	11	8	4	7								
10 (a)	Oxford U	W 2-0	Foggon, Murdoch	8,983	1	2	3	5		6		8	9	10	11		4	7								
17 (h)	Cardiff C	W 3-0	Mills, Craggs, M.Smith	18,034	1	2	3	5		6	7	8	9	10*	11	12	4									
24 (a)	Notts C	D 2-2	Hickton, Mills	16,314	1	2	3	5		6		8	9		11		4	7				10				
Dec 8 (a)	Sheffield W	D 2-2	Foggon, Mills	11,968	1	2		5		6		8	9	10	11		4	7						3		
11 (h)	Preston NE	W 3-0	Mills, Murdoch, Souness	23,980	1	2	3	5		6		8	9	10	11		4	7								
15 (h)	Nottingham F	W 1-0	Boam	16,764	1	2	3	5		6		8	9	10	11		4	7								
22 (a)	Bristol C	D 1-1	Mills	13,116	1		3	5		6		8	9	10	11		4	7						2		
26 (h)	Sunderland	W 2-1	Foggon, Boam	37,030	1		3	5		6		8	9*	10	11	12	4	7						2		
29 (h)	Crystal P	W 2-0	Foggon, Armstrong	26,115	1	2	3	5		6		8	9*	10	11	12	4	7								
Jan 12 (a)	Aston Villa	D 1-1	Craggs	26,906	1	2	3	5		6		8	9*	10	11		4	7				12				
19 (h)	Portsmouth	W 3-0	Foggon, M.Smith, Souness	22,134	1	2	3	5		6		8	9*	10	11	12	4	7								
Feb 2 (a)	Nottingham F	L 1-5	Foggon	18,799	1	2	3	5		6		8	9*	10	11	12	4	7								
9 (h)	Blackpool	D 0-0		21,913	1	2	3	5		6		8	9	10	11	12	4	7*								
16 (a)	Hull C	W 3-1	Hickton, Mills, Foggon	15,287	1	2	3	5		6*		8	9	10	11		4					12	7			
23 (a)	Swindon T	W 2-1	Hickton, Foggon	23,194	1	2	3	5		6		8	9	10	11		4	7*				12				
Mar 2 (a)	Sunderland	W 2-0	Mills, Foggon	41,658	1	2	3	5		6		8	9*	10	11		4	7				12				
9 (h)	Millwall	W 2-1	Mills, Spraggon	20,740	1	2	3	5		6		8	9	10	11		4	7								
16 (a)	West Brom A	W 4-0	Foggon, Hickton 2 (1 pen), Souness	24,178	1	2	3	5		6		8	9	10	11		4	7								
19 (a)	Fulham	W 4-0	Maddren 2, Souness, Boam	18,114	1	2	3	5		6		8	9	10	11	12	4	7*								
23 (h)	Oxford U	W 1-0	Armstrong	26,877	1	2	3	5		6		8	9	10	11		4	7*				12				
30 (a)	Luton T	W 1-0	Mills	19,812	1	2		5		6		8	9	10	11		4	7								3
Apr 6 (h)	Notts C	W 4-0	Hickton, Needham (og), Armstrong, Foggon	27,823	1	2	3	5		6		12	9	10	11	8		7			4*					
9 (h)	Bolton W	D 0-0		28,143		2		5		6		8	9	10*	11		4	7				12			1	3
13 (a)	Cardiff C	L 2-3	Maddren, Foggon	12,861	1	2	3	5		6				10	11	9	4	12					7*			
15 (h)	Bolton W	L 1-2	Boam	22,545			3	5		6		8	9*	10	11		4	7				12		2	1	
20 (h)	Sheffield W	W 8-0	Hickton, Mills, Murdoch, Souness 3, Foggon 2	25,287	1	2	3	5		6		8	9	10	11		4	7*	12							
27 (a)	Preston NE	W 4-2	Brine 2, Foggon, Hickton	16,177	1	2	3	5		6		8	9	10	11			7					4			
Apps					40	39	39	42	4	42	7	38	40	41	42	6	34	33			1	1	5	3	3	2
Sub apps										1	1					10	1	1		2	1	6				
Goals						3	1	4	1	3		11	11	19	5	4	7	5					2			

1 own-goal

FA Cup

Date	Opponent	Res	Scorers	Att	Platt JA	Craggs JE	Spraggon F	Boam SW	Taylor B	Maddren WD	McMordie A	Mills DJ	Hickton J	Foggon A	Armstrong D	Smith M	Souness GJ	Murdoch RW	Charlton H	Poskett M	McAndrew A	Gates WL	Brine PK	Cochrane JK	Creamer PA	Cuff PJ	Round
Jan 5 (a)	Grantham	W 2-0	Mills, Armstrong	6,573	1	2	3	5		6		8	9*	10	11		4	7				12					3
26 (a)	Wrexham	L 0-1		20,612	1	2	3	5		6		8	9*	10	11	12	4	7									4
Apps					2	2	2	2		2		2	2	2	2		2	2									
Sub apps																1						1					
Goals												1			1												

League Cup

Date	Opponent	Res	Scorers	Att	Platt JA	Craggs JE	Spraggon F	Boam SW	Taylor B	Maddren WD	McMordie A	Mills DJ	Hickton J	Foggon A	Armstrong D	Smith M	Souness GJ	Murdoch RW	Charlton H	Poskett M	McAndrew A	Gates WL	Brine PK	Cochrane JK	Creamer PA	Cuff PJ	Round
Oct 8 (a)	Manchester U	W 1-0	M.Smith	23,906	1	2	3	5		6			9	10	11	8	4	7									2
31 (a)	Stoke C	D 1-1	Brine	19,194	1	2	3	5		6				10	11	8	4	7					9				3
Nov 6 (h)	Stoke C	L 1-2*	Foggon	26,068	1	2	3	5		6		8	9	10	11			7			4						R
Apps					3	3	3	3		3		1	2	3	3	2	2	3			1		1				
Sub apps																											
Goals														1		1							1				

*After extra-time

1974-75
Division 1

Date	Opponent	Res	Scorers	Att	Platt JA	Craggs JE	Spraggon F	Maddren WD	Boam SW	Taylor B	Murdoch RW	Mills DJ	Hickton J	Foggon A	Armstrong D	Souness GJ	Smith M	Brine PK	Willey AS	Woof W	Charlton H	McAndrew A	Paterson T	Cooper T	Creamer PA
Aug 17 (a)	Birmingham C	W 3-0	Hickton, Foggon 2	32,105	1	2	3	4	5	6	7	8	9	10	11										
20 (h)	Carlisle U	L 0-2		28,719	1	2	3	6	5		7	8	9*	10	11	4	12								
24 (h)	Luton T	D 1-1	Mills	21,478	1	2	3	6	5		7	8	9	10	11	4									
27 (a)	Carlisle U	W 1-0	Armstrong	18,473	1	2	3	6	5		7	8	9	10	11	4									
31 (a)	Stoke C	D 1-1	Souness	23,475	1	2	3	6	5		7	8	9	10	11	4*	12								
Sep 7 (h)	Chelsea	D 1-1	Maddren	25,480	1	2	3	4	5	6	7	8	9	10*	11		12								
14 (a)	Sheffield U	L 0-1		22,519	1	2		4	5	6	7	8	9	10	11		3								
21 (h)	Manchester C	W 3-0	Mills, Foggon 2	30,256	1	2		6	5	12	7	8	3	10	11	4*			9						
28 (a)	Tottenham H	W 2-1	Armstrong, Mills	23,282	1	2	3	6	5		7	8	9	10	11	4			9						
Oct 5 (h)	Wolves	W 2-1	Hickton, Willey	27,443	1	2	3	6	5		7*	8	9	10	11	4			12						
12 (a)	Liverpool	L 0-2		52,590	1	2	3	6	5		7	8	9	10	11	4									
16 (h)	Luton T	W 1-0	Foggon	10,464	1	2	3	6	5		7	8	9*	10	11	4			12						
19 (h)	Coventry C	D 4-4	Souness 2, Mills, Foggon	25,499	1	2	3	6	5		7	8	9*	10	11	4			12						
26 (a)	Derby C	W 3-2	Hickton, Foggon, Mills	24,036	1	2	3	6	5		7	8	9	10	11	4									
Nov 2 (a)	West Ham U	L 0-3		28,915	1	2	3	6	5		7	8*	9	10	11	4			12						
9 (h)	Newcastle U	D 0-0		38,380	1	2	3	6	5		7	8*	9	10	11	4	12								
16 (a)	Leeds U	D 2-2	Boam, M.Smith	45,488	1	2	3	6	5		7		9	10	11	4	8								
23 (h)	Queen's Park R	L 1-3	Foggon	27,530	1	2	3	6	5		7*		9	10	11	4	8			12					
30 (a)	Arsenal	L 0-2		25,283	1	2	3	6	5	12			9	10	11	4	8*			7					
Dec 7 (h)	Ipswich T	W 3-0	Souness 2, Foggon	23,735	1	2		6*	5				8	10	11	4	12	7	9		3				
10 (h)	Leicester C	W 3-0	Foggon 2, Willey	22,699	1	2	3	6*	5	12			8	10	11	4		7	9						
14 (h)	Birmingham C	W 3-0	Foggon, Hickton (pen), Page (og)	23,737	1	2	3	6	5		7		8	10	11	4	12					9*			
21 (a)	Burnley	D 1-1	Armstrong	17,637	1	2	3	6	5		7	8	9	10*	11	4			12						
26 (h)	Sheffield U	W 1-0	Armstrong	31,879	1	2	3	6	5		7	9	8	10*	11	4	12								
28 (a)	Everton	D 1-1	Maddren	41,105	1	2	3	6	5		7	9	8	10	11	4									
Jan 11 (a)	Ipswich T	L 0-2		24,720	1	2	3	6	5		7	8	9	10*	11	4			12						
18 (h)	Arsenal	D 0-0		27,996	1	2	3	6	5		7	8*	9	10	11	4			12						
Feb 1 (a)	Newcastle U	L 1-2	Hickton	42,514	1	2	3	6	5		7	8	9	10*	11	4			12						
8 (h)	West Ham U	D 0-0		29,179	1	2	3	6	5	12	4	8	9			11*		7	10						
22 (h)	Leeds U	L 0-1		39,500	1	2	3	6	5		7*	9	8	10	11	4		12							
25 (a)	Queen's Park R	D 0-0		18,487	1	2	3	6	5		7	9	8	10	11	4									
Mar 1 (h)	Stoke C	W 2-0	Hickton, Foggon	25,766	1	2	3	6	5		7	9	8	10	11	4									
15 (h)	Tottenham H	W 3-0	Hickton, Souness 2	25,637	1	2		6	5		7	9	8	10	11	4							3		
18 (a)	Everton	W 2-0	Mills, Armstrong	32,813	1	2		6	5		7	8		10	11	4			9				3		
22 (a)	Chelsea	W 2-1	Willey, Craggs	22,240	1	2		6	5		7	8		10	11	4			9				3		
28 (a)	Manchester C	L 1-2	Mills	37,772	1	2		6	5		7	8	9	10	11	4							3		
29 (h)	Burnley	W 2-0	Murdoch, Foggon	28,922	1	2	3	6	5		7	8	9	10	11	4									
Apr 5 (h)	Derby C	D 1-1	Mills	30,066	1	2		6	5		7	8	9*	10	11	4	12						3		
9 (a)	Leicester C	L 0-1		24,531	1	2		6	5		7*	8	9	10	11	4	12						3		
12 (a)	Wolves	L 0-2		21,066	1	2		6	5		7	8	9*	10	11	4			12				3		
19 (h)	Liverpool	W 1-0	Foggon	33,982	1	2		6	5		7	8	9	10	11	4							3		
26 (a)	Coventry C	W 2-0	Foggon, Hickton	18,121	1	2		6	5		7	8	9	10	11	4							3		
Apps					42	41	31	42	42	3	39	36	39	41	42	38	4	3	7	1	1	1	9		
Sub apps										4							6	4	9	1					
Goals						1		2	1		1	8	8	16	5	7	1		3						

1 own-goal

FA Cup

Date	Opponent	Res	Scorers	Att	Platt JA	Craggs JE	Spraggon F	Maddren WD	Boam SW	Taylor B	Murdoch RW	Mills DJ	Hickton J	Foggon A	Armstrong D	Souness GJ	Smith M	Brine PK	Willey AS	Woof W	Charlton H	Round
Jan 4 (a)	Wycombe W	D 0-0		12,200	1	2	3	6	5			9	8	10*	11	4		7	12			3
7 (h)	Wycombe W	W 1-0	Armstrong (pen)	30,128	1	2	3	6	5			9	8	10*	11	4		12		7		R
25 (h)	Sunderland	W 3-1	Murdoch, Hickton 2 (2 pens)	39,400	1	2	3	6	5		7	9	8	10	11	4						4
Feb 15 (a)	Peterborough U	D 1-1	Mills	25,742	1	2	3	6	5		4	9	7	10	11			12	8*			5
18 (h)	Peterborough U	W 2-0	Foggon 2	34,303	1	2	3	6	5		7	9	8*	10	11	4		12				R
Mar 8 (a)	Birmingham C	L 0-1		47,260	1	2	3	6	5		7	9	8	10	11	4						6
Apps					6	6	6	6	6		4	6	6	6	6	5		1	1	1		
Sub apps																		2	2			
Goals											1	1	2	2	1							

League Cup

Date	Opponent	Res	Scorers	Att	Platt JA	Craggs JE	Spraggon F	Maddren WD	Boam SW	Taylor B	Murdoch RW	Mills DJ	Hickton J	Foggon A	Armstrong D	Souness GJ	Smith M	Brine PK	Willey AS	Woof W	Paterson T	Round
Sep 11 (a)	Tottenham H	W 4-0	M.Smith, Mills, Hickton (pen), Armstrong	15,216	1	2		4	5	6	7	8	3	10	11		9					2
Oct 8 (h)	Leicester C	W 1-0	Mills	23,901	1	2	3	6	5		7	8	9	10*	11	4			12			3
Nov 12 (a)	Liverpool	W 1-0	Maddren	24,906	1	2	3	6	5	12	7*		9	10	11	4		8				4
Dec 4 (h)	Manchester U	D 0-0		36,005	1		3	6	5				8	10	11	4	12		9	7	2*	5
18 (a)	Manchester U	L 0-3		49,501	1	2	3	6	5		7	9	8	10	11	4						R
Apps					5	4	4	5	5	1	4	3	5	5	5	4	2	1	1	1		
Sub apps								1									1	1				
Goals								1				2	1		1		1					

1975-76
Division 1

Player columns: Platt JA, Craggs JE, Cooper T, Souness GJ, Boam SW, Maddren WD, Murdoch RW, Mills DJ, Hickton J, Willey AS, Armstrong D, Brine PK, Taylor B, Foggon A, Spraggon F, Boersma P, Bailey IC, McAndrew A, Woof W, Smith M, Cuff PJ, Coleman EP, Ramage A

Date		Opponent	Result	Scorers	Att	Platt JA	Craggs JE	Cooper T	Souness GJ	Boam SW	Maddren WD	Murdoch RW	Mills DJ	Hickton J	Willey AS	Armstrong D	Brine PK	Taylor B	Foggon A	Spraggon F	Boersma P	Bailey IC	McAndrew A	Woof W	Smith M	Cuff PJ	Coleman EP	Ramage A
Aug 16	(a)	Tottenham H	L 0-1		25,502	1	2	3	4	5	6	7	8	9	10	11												
20	(a)	Newcastle U	D 1-1	Gowling (og)	41,417	1	2	3	4	5	6	7	8	9		11	10											
23	(h)	Wolves	W 1-0	Hickton	22,639	1	2	3	4		6	7	8	9*	12	11	10	5										
26	(h)	Birmingham C	W 2-0	Hickton, Mills	22,423	1	2	3	4		6*	7	8	9	12	11	10	5										
30	(a)	Burnley	L 1-4	Armstrong	17,066	1	2	3	4		6	7	8	9*	12	11	10	5										
Sep 6	(h)	Stoke C	W 3-0	Hickton, Mills 2	21,975	1	2	3	4	5	6	7	8	9	10*	11			12									
13	(a)	Manchester C	L 0-4		30,353	1	2	3	4	5	6	7	8	9	10*	11			12									
20	(h)	Queen's Park R	D 0-0		24,867	1	2	3	4	5	6		8	9	12	11	7*		10									
23	(a)	Coventry C	W 1-0	Mills	15,132	1	2		4	5	6		8	9		11	7		10	3								
27	(a)	Ipswich T	W 3-0	Foggon, Armstrong, Hickton (pen)	22,321	1	2	3	4	5	6		8	9		11	7		10									
Oct 4	(h)	Aston Villa	D 0-0		24,102	1		3	4	5	6	12	8	9		11	7*		10	2								
11	(a)	Leicester C	D 0-0		19,095	1	2	3	4	5	6		8	9		11	7		10									
18	(h)	West Ham U	W 3-0	Souness, Armstrong, Foggon	25,831	1	2	3	4	5	6	7	8	9		11			10									
25	(a)	Arsenal	L 1-2	Mills	23,606	1	2	3	4	5	6		8	9		11	7		10									
Nov 1	(h)	Liverpool	L 0-1		30,952	1	2	3	4	5	6	7	8	9		11			10*	12								
8	(a)	Norwich C	W 1-0	Souness	19,286	1	2	10	4		6		8	9		11	7		3									
15	(h)	Leeds U	D 0-0		32,959	1	2	10	4*	5	6	7	8	9		11			12	3								
22	(a)	West Ham U	L 1-2	Mills	26,944	1	2	10		5	6	4	8	9*		11	7		12	3								
29	(a)	Derby C	L 2-3	Boam, Craggs	27,745	1	2	3		5	6	4	8	10		11	7		9									
Dec 6	(h)	Manchester U	D 0-0		32,454	1	2	3		5	6	7	8	10	9	11				4								
13	(a)	Wolves	W 2-1	Armstrong, Mills	13,548	1	2	3		5	6	7	8	10	9	11				4								
20	(h)	Tottenham H	W 1-0	Hickton (pen)	22,046	1	2	10		5	6	7		8	9	11			12	4	3*							
26	(a)	Sheffield U	D 1-1	Foggon	28,593	1	2	3		5	6	7	8	10		11	12		9*	4								
27	(h)	Everton	D 1-1	Maddren	29,275	1	2	3		5	6	7	8	10		11			9	4								
Jan 10	(h)	Manchester C	W 1-0	Armstrong	22,358	1	2	10	12	5	6	7	8		9*	11				4	3							
17	(a†)	Stoke C	L 0-1		21,049	1	2	3	4	5	6			10	9	11	7		8									
31	(h)	Newcastle U	D 3-3	Mills, Keeley (og), Maddren	30,365	1		10	4	5	6	7	8			11					2	9	3					
Feb 7	(a)	Birmingham C	L 1-2	Mills	18,599	1	2	10	4	5	6	7*	8	12		11						9	3					
14	(h)	Burnley	D 1-1	Boam	17,856	1		10	4	5	6		8*	9	12	11					2	7	3					
21	(a)	Leeds U	W 2-0	Hickton 2	32,993	1	2	3	4	5	10		8	9		11						7*		6	12			
24	(h)	Coventry C	W 2-0	Boam, Souness	18,553	1	2	3	4	5	10		8	9		11						7*		6	12			
28	(h)	Arsenal	L 0-1		19,857	1	2	3	4	5	10		8	9		11						7*		6	12			
Mar 6	(a)	Liverpool	W 2-0	Cooper, Hickton	41,391	1	2	3	4	5	10		8	9		11						7		6				
13	(a)	Leicester C	L 0-1		17,634	1		3	4	5	10		8	9*	12	11					2	7		6				
20	(h)	Derby C	L 0-2		24,120	1		3	4	5	10		8	9		11			12	2*		7		6				
27	(a)	Manchester U	L 0-3		58,527	1	2		4	5	10		8	3		11	12					7*		6		9		
Apr 3	(h)	Ipswich T	W 2-0	Mills, Armstrong	14,764		2	3	4	5			8			11	7							6	9	10	1	
6	(h)	Norwich C	L 0-1		15,768	1	2	3	4	5	10*		8			11			12			7		6	9			
10	(a)	Queen's Park R	L 2-4	Boersma, Brine	24,342	1		3	4	5	10		8	2		11	7					9		6				
17	(h)	Sheffield U	W 3-0	McAndrew 3	16,889	1	2	3	4	5	6	7	8*			11						10	9	12				
19	(a)	Everton	L 1-3	Woof	18,204	1	2	3	4	5	6			8	11*	7						10	9	12				
24	(a)	Aston Villa	L 1-2	Hickton	33,241	1	2	10	4	5	6		8			11	7				3					9*	12	
		Apps				41	36	40	34	39	41	21	38	35	9	42	18	3	11	9	19	6	12	3	3	1	1	
		Sub apps							1			1		1	6		2		7	1				3	2		1	
		Goals					1	1	3	3	2		10	9		6	1		3		1		3	1				

†Played at Vale Park, Burslem. Stoke's ground storm-damaged.

2 own-goals

FA Cup

Date		Opponent	Result	Scorers	Att	Platt JA	Craggs JE	Cooper T	Souness GJ	Boam SW	Maddren WD	Murdoch RW	Mills DJ	Hickton J	Willey AS	Armstrong D	Brine PK	Taylor B	Foggon A	Spraggon F	Boersma P	Bailey IC	McAndrew A	Woof W	Smith M	Cuff PJ	Coleman EP	Ramage A	Round
Jan 3	(h)	Bury	D 0-0		20,728	1	2	3		5	7		8	9*		11			10		4	12	6						3
6	(a)	Bury	L 2-3	Brine, Hickton (pen)	11,488	1	2	9		5	6	7	8	10		11	4		12		3*								R
		Apps				2	2	2		2	2	1	2	2		2	1		1		1	1	1						
		Sub apps																	1			1							
		Goals											1			1													

League Cup

Date		Opponent	Result	Scorers	Att	Platt JA	Craggs JE	Cooper T	Souness GJ	Boam SW	Maddren WD	Murdoch RW	Mills DJ	Hickton J	Willey AS	Armstrong D	Brine PK	Taylor B	Foggon A	Spraggon F	Boersma P	Bailey IC	McAndrew A	Woof W	Smith M	Cuff PJ	Coleman EP	Ramage A	Round
Sep 9	(a)	Bury	W 2-1	Hickton, Mills	9,121	1	2	3	4	5	6	7	8	9	10	11													2
Oct 7	(h)	Derby C	W 1-0	Foggon	25,740	1	2	3	4	5	6	7	8	9*		11			10	12									3
Nov 11	(h)	Peterborough U	W 3-0	Boam, Hickton (pen), Armstrong	17,749	1	2	10	4	5	6	7	8	9		11			12	3									4
Dec 3	(a)	Burnley	W 2-0	Mills, Maddren	15,509	1	2	3		5	6	4	8	9	10	11*	7						12						5
Jan 13	(h)	Manchester C	W 1-0	Hickton	34,579	1	2	10	4	5	6	7	8	9*		11			12		3								SF/1
21	(a)	Manchester C	L 0-4		44,246	1	2	3	4	5	6	7*	10	9		11	8						12						SF/2
		Apps				6	6	6	5	6	6	6	6	6	2	6	2		1	1	1								
		Sub apps																	1	1			2						
		Goals							1	1			2	3		1			1										

1976-77
Division 1

Date	Opponent	Result	Scorers	Att	Platt JA	Craggs JE	Cooper T	Souness GJ	Boam SW	Maddren WD	McAndrew A	Mills DJ	Hedley G	Boersma P	Armstrong D	Hickton J	Woof W	Willey AS	Brine PK	Wood AEH	Cummins S	Cuff PJ	Ramage A	Bailey IC
Aug 21 (h)	Coventry C	W 1-0	McAndrew	17,694	1	2	3	4	5	6	7	8	9	10	11									
25 (a)	Derby C	D 0-0		23,344	1	2	3	4	5	6	7	8		10	11	9								
28 (a)	Tottenham H	D 0-0		21,721	1	2	3	4	5	6	7	8		10	11	9*	12							
Sep 4 (h)	Newcastle U	W 1-0	Mills	26,014	1	2	3	4	5	6	7	8		10*	11			9	12					
11 (h)	Sunderland	W 2-1	Willey 2	28,329	1	2	3	4	5	6	7	8		10*	11			9	12					
18 (a)	Manchester U	L 0-2		56,712	1	2	3	4	5	6	7	8		12	11			9	10*					
25 (h)	Leeds U	W 1-0	Willey	24,671	1	2	3	4	5	6	7	8		10	11	12		9*						
Oct 2 (a)	Liverpool	D 0-0		45,107	1	2	3	4	5	6	7	8		10	11	9*	12							
9 (h)	Norwich C	W 1-0	Souness	21,998	1	2	3	4	5	6	7	8		10	11			9*	12					
16 (a)	Birmingham C	L 1-3	Boersma	27,740	1	2	3	4	5	6	7	8		10	11			9						
23 (h)	West Brom A	W 1-0	Mills	22,643	1	2	3	4	5	6	7	8		10*	11			12	9					
30 (h)	Leicester C	L 0-1		24,288	1	2	3	4	5	6	7	8			11			10*	12	9				
Nov 6 (a)	Stoke C	L 1-3	Armstrong	16,068	1	2	3	4	5	6	7	8			11	12		10*	9					
20 (a)	Queen's Park R	L 0-3		16,037	1	2	3	4	5	6	7	8		10	11	12		9*						
27 (h)	Ipswich T	L 0-2		20,070	1	2	3	4	5	6	7	12		10	11			9	8*					
Dec 4 (a)	West Ham U	W 1-0	Boersma	20,453	1	2	3	4	5	6	7	8		10*	11	12		9						
7 (h)	Manchester C	D 0-0		18,484	1	2	3	4	5	6	7	8			11		10*	9	12					
18 (a)	Bristol C	W 2-1	Armstrong (pen), Brine	15,145	1	2	3	4	5	6	7	8		12	11			9	10*					
27 (h)	Aston Villa	W 3-2	Mills 3	31,451	1	2	3	4	5	6*	7	8			11		12	9	10					
29 (a)	Everton	D 2-2	Armstrong 2	28,169		2	3	4	5	6	7	8		12	11			9	10*		1			
Jan 1 (h)	Stoke C	D 0-0		20,987		2	3	4	5	6	7	8			11			9	10		1			
15 (h)	Derby C	W 2-0	George (og), Mills	17,914		2	3	4	5	6	7*	8			11	12		9	10		1			
22 (a)	Coventry C	D 1-1	Mills	12,893		2	3	4	5	6		8		7	11			9	10		1			
Feb 5 (h)	Tottenham H	W 2-0	Mills 2	21,231		2	3	4	5	6		8	9	7	11				10		1			
15 (h)	Arsenal	W 3-0	Brine, Armstrong, Mills	26,083		2	3	4	5	6		8		7	11	12		9	10*		1			
19 (a)	Sunderland	L 0-4		33,226		2	3	4	5	6	12	8		7*	11			9	10		1			
Mar 5 (h)	Leeds U	L 1-2	Wood	32,125		2	3		5		4	8		7	11		12	9*	10		1	6		
9 (a)	Norwich C	L 0-1		16,625		2	3	4	5		7	8		12	11			9*	10		1			
12 (h)	Liverpool	L 0-1		29,166		2	3	4	5		7	8	9		11		12		10*		1	6		
16 (a)	Leicester C	D 3-3	Craggs, Mills, Wood	13,483		2	3	4	5		7	8			11			9	10		1	6		
22 (h)	Birmingham C	D 2-2	Willey, Boam	16,439		2	3	4	5	6	7	8			11		12	10	9*		1			
26 (a)	Newcastle U	L 0-1		33,643		2	3	4	5	6	7	8			11		9	10			1			
Apr 2 (a)	West Brom A	L 1-2	Mills	18,519		2	3		5	6	7	8		4*	11		9	10			1		12	
5 (a)	Aston Villa	L 0-1		32,646		2	3		5	6	7	8			11			10	9		1		4	
9 (h)	Everton	D 2-2	Hedley, Mills	16,159		2	10		5	6	7	8	4		11			9*	12		1		3	
11 (a)	Manchester C	L 0-1		37,735		2*	3	4	5	6	7	8		10	11			9			1		12	
16 (h)	Queen's Park R	L 0-2		14,500		2	3	4	5	6	9	8	7	10*	11						1		12	
23 (a)	Ipswich T	W 1-0	Armstrong	23,348	1	2	3	4	5	6	7	8			11			9	10					
26 (h)	Manchester U	W 3-0	Armstrong 2, Mills	21,744	1	2	3	4	5	6	7	8			11		10	9						
30 (h)	West Ham U	D 1-1	Mills	16,360	1	2	3	4	5	6	7	8		12	11		10*	9						
May 7 (a)	Arsenal	D 1-1	Souness	23,911	1	2		4	5	6	7	8	10		11			9					3	
14 (h)	Bristol C	D 0-0		14,849	1	2		4	5	6	7	8	10	12	11			9*					3	
Apps					24	42	40	38	42	39	38	41	6	22	42	4	11	25	22	1	18	3	4	
Sub apps											1	1		6		5	1	7	4	1		1	3	
Goals						1		2	1		1	15	1	2	8			4	2	2				

1 own-goal

FA Cup

Date	Opponent	Result	Scorers	Att	Platt JA	Craggs JE	Cooper T	Souness GJ	Boam SW	Maddren WD	McAndrew A	Mills DJ	Hedley G	Boersma P	Armstrong D	Hickton J	Woof W	Willey AS	Brine PK	Wood AEH	Cummins S	Cuff PJ	Ramage A	Bailey IC	Round
Jan 8 (a)	Wimbledon	D 0-0		8,750		2	3	4	5	6	7	8			11			9	10		1				3
11 (h)	Wimbledon	W 1-0	Armstrong (pen)	22,485		2	3	4	5	6	7	8			11			9	10		1				R
29 (a)	Hereford U	W 4-0	Souness, Armstrong 2 (1 pen), Willey	22,163		2	3	4	5	6		8		7	11		12	9	10*		1				4
Feb 26 (h)	Arsenal	W 4-1	Mills 3, Armstrong	35,208		2	3	4*	5	6	12	8		7	11			9	10		1				5
Mar 19 (a)	Liverpool	L 0-2		55,881		2	3	4	5	6	7	8		12	11			9	10*		1				6
Apps						5	5	5	5	5	3	5		2	5			5	5		5				
Sub apps											1			1			1								
Goals								1				3			4			1							

League Cup

Date	Opponent	Result	Scorers	Att	Platt JA	Craggs JE	Cooper T	Souness GJ	Boam SW	Maddren WD	McAndrew A	Mills DJ	Hedley G	Boersma P	Armstrong D	Hickton J	Woof W	Willey AS	Brine PK	Wood AEH	Cummins S	Cuff PJ	Ramage A	Bailey IC	Round
Aug 31 (h)	Tottenham H	L 1-2	McAndrew	19,042	1	2	3	4	5	6	7	8	9*	10	11	12									2
Apps					1	1	1	1	1	1	1	1	1	1	1									
Sub apps																1								
Goals											1													

1977-78
Division 1

Date	V	Opponent	Result	Scorers	Att	Platt JA	Craggs JE	Cooper T	Souness GJ	Boam SW	Maddren WD	Mahoney JF	Mills DJ	Woof W	McAndrew A	Armstrong D	Hickton J	Brine PK	Ashcroft W	Hedley G	Bailey IC	Ramage A	Willey AS	Cuff PJ	Cummins S	Johnston CP	Brown DJ	Walsh A	Johnson PE	Shearer DJ	Bell IC
Aug 20	(h)	Liverpool	D 1-1	Armstrong	30,805	1	2	3	4	5	6	7	8	9*	10	11	12														
24	(a)	Norwich C	D 1-1	Souness	14,245	1	2	3	4*	5	6	7	8	9	10	11	12														
27	(h)	Newcastle U	W 2-0	Armstrong 2	26,902	1	2	3		5	6	7	8	9	10	11		4													
Sep 3	(a)	West Brom A	L 1-2	Mills	19,044	1	2	3		5	6	7	8		10	11			4*	9	12										
10	(h)	Birmingham C	L 1-2	Ashcroft	19,240	1	2	3	4	5		7	8		6	11			10*	9	12										
17	(a)	Coventry C	L 1-2	Mills	13,910	1	2		4	5		7	8		10	11			9		3	6									
24	(h)	Ipswich T	D 1-1	Mills	19,843	1	2*		4	5		7	8		10	11			9		3	6		12							
Oct 1	(a)	Derby C	L 1-4	Armstrong	21,040	1	2	3	4	5		7	8		10	11			9			6									
3	(h)	West Ham U	W 2-0	Mills 2	26,508	1	2	3	4	5		7	8		10	11			9			6									
8	(h)	Manchester U	W 2-1	Mills, Ashcroft	26,822	1	2	3	4	5		7	8		10	11			9			6									
15	(a)	Chelsea	D 0-0		21,091	1		3	4	5		7	8		10	11			9		2	6									
22	(h)	Leeds U	W 2-1	Souness 2	27,493	1		3	4	5		7	8		10	11			9		2	6									
29	(a)	Nottingham F	L 0-4		27,373	1	2		4	5		7	8		10	11	12		9*		3	6									
Nov 5	(h)	Queen's Park R	D 1-1	Hedley	18,215			3	4	5		7	8		10*	11			9	12	2	6		1							
12	(a)	Aston Villa	W 1-0	Cummins	31,837			3	4	5		7			10	11			9		2	6		1	8						
19	(h)	Wolves	D 0-0		18,464		2	3	4	5		7*	8		10	11			9	12		6		1							
26	(a)	Bristol C	L 1-4	Mills	20,536		2	3	4	5		7	8		10	11*			9			6		1	12						
Dec 3	(h)	Arsenal	L 0-1		17,412		2*	3		5		7	8		10	11			9	4		6		1	12						
10	(a)	Everton	L 0-3		38,647		2	3*	4	5		7	8		10	11	12		9			6		1							
17	(h)	Aston Villa	W 1-0	Hedley	14,999		2			5			7		10	11			9	4	3	6		1	8						
26	(a)	Leicester C	D 0-0		18,476		2		4						10	11		5	9	7	3	6		1	8						
27	(h)	Manchester C	L 0-2		27,319		2		4				12		10	11		5	9*	7	3	6		1	8						
31	(h)	Norwich C	D 2-2	Cummins, Armstrong	15,646		2		4			7			10	11		5	9		3	6		1	8						
Jan 2	(a)	Liverpool	L 0-2		49,305	1	2			5		4	7		10	11			9		3	6			8						
14	(a)	Newcastle U	W 4-2	Boam, Ashcroft 2, Cummins	34,460	1	2			5		4	7		10	11	12		9*		3	6			8						
21	(h)	West Brom A	W 1-0	Boam	19,172	1	2			5		4	7		10	11			9		3	6			8						
Feb 4	(a)	Birmingham C	W 2-1	Craggs, Mills	14,302	1	2			5		4	7		12	11			9		3	6			8	10*					
25	(h)	Derby C	W 3-1	Mills, Craggs, Mahoney	20,703	1	2			5		4	7		10	11			9		3	6			8						
Mar 4	(a)	Manchester U	D 0-0		46,332	1	2			5		4	7	12	10	11			9*		3	6			8						
18	(a)	Leeds U	L 0-5		25,158	1	2			5		4	7		10	11			9		3	6			8						
21	(a)	Ipswich T	D 1-1	Ashcroft	17,759	1	2			5		4			10	11	12		9		3	6			8	7*					
25	(h)	Manchester C	D 2-2	Cummins, Ashcroft	37,944	1	2			5		4	7		10	11			9		3	6			8						
27	(h)	Leicester C	L 0-1		15,534		2			5		4	7		10	11			9*		3	6			8	12	1				
29	(h)	Nottingham F	D 2-2	Mills, Cummins	25,445		2			5		4	7		10	11			9		3	6			8		1				
Apr 1	(a)	Queen's Park R	L 0-1		12,925		2			5		4	7		10*	11			9		3	6			8		1	12			
4	(h)	Chelsea	W 2-0	Shearer 2	15,268					5		4	7		10	11					2	6			8*		1	12	3	9	
8	(h)	Bristol C	W 2-0	Ramage, Cummins	14,667		2			5		4			10	11					3	6			8		1		9		
11	(a)	Coventry C	D 1-1	Armstrong	14,184		2			5		4			10	11					3	6			8	7	1		9		
15	(a)	Wolves	D 0-0		15,466		2			5		4			10	11			9		3						1	12	6	8*	7
22	(h)	Everton	D 0-0		15,969		2			5		4			10	11	12		9*	7	3				8		1		6		
25	(h)	West Ham U	L 1-2	Johnston	13,247		2			5			7		10	11	12		9		3*	6			8	4	1				
29	(a)	Arsenal	L 0-1		32,138		2			5		4	7	12	10	11			9		8*						1		3		
Apps						22	37	16	19	39	4	37	35	3	41	42	3	3	36	5	29	35		10	23	4	10		4	4	1
Sub apps														4			8			3	1				2	1		3			
Goals							2		3	2		1	10			6			6	2		1			6	1				2	

FA Cup

Date	V	Opponent	Result	Scorers	Att	Platt JA	Craggs JE	Cooper T	Souness GJ	Boam SW	Maddren WD	Mahoney JF	Mills DJ	Woof W	McAndrew A	Armstrong D	Hickton J	Brine PK	Ashcroft W	Hedley G	Bailey IC	Ramage A	Willey AS	Cuff PJ	Cummins S	Johnston CP	Brown DJ	Walsh A	Johnson PE	Shearer DJ	Bell IC	Round
Jan 7	(h)	Coventry C	W 3-0	Mills 2, McAndrew	18,015	1	2			5		4	7		10	11			9		3	6			8							3
28	(h)	Everton	W 3-2	Mahoney, Mills 2	33,652	1	2			5		4	7		10	11			9		3	6			8							4
Feb 27	(h)	Bolton W	W 2-0	Ashcroft, Cummins	36,662	1	2			5		4	7			11			9		3	6			8	10						5
Mar 11	(h)	Orient	D 0-0		33,426	1	2			5		4	7		10*	11			9		3	6			8	12						6
14	(a)	Orient	L 1-2	Armstrong	18,051	1	2			5		4	7		10	11			9		3	6			8*	12						R
Apps						5	5			5		5	5		4	5			5		5	5			5	1						
Sub apps																										2						
Goals												1	4		1	1			1						1						

League Cup

Date	V	Opponent	Result	Scorers	Att	Platt JA	Craggs JE	Cooper T	Souness GJ	Boam SW	Maddren WD	Mahoney JF	Mills DJ	Woof W	McAndrew A	Armstrong D	Hickton J	Brine PK	Ashcroft W	Hedley G	Bailey IC	Ramage A	Willey AS	Cuff PJ	Cummins S	Johnston CP	Brown DJ	Walsh A	Johnson PE	Shearer DJ	Bell IC	Round
Aug 30	(a)	Sunderland	D 2-2	Armstrong 2 (1 pen)	26,597	1*	2	3		5	6	7	8	9	10	11	12	4														2
Sep 13	(h)	Sunderland	W 1-0	Boam	29,572	1	2	3*	4	5		7	8	9	10	11					12	6										R
Oct 25	(a)	Everton	D 2-2	Woof, Mills	32,766	1		3	4	5		7	8	9	10	11	12				2*	6										3
31	(h)	Everton	L 1-2	Mills	28,409	1		3	4	5		7	8	9	10*	11	12				2	6										R
Apps						4	2	4	3	4	1	4	4	4	4	4		1			2	3										
Sub apps																	3				1											
Goals										1			2	1		2															

1978-79
Division 1

Date		Opponent	Res	Scorers	Att	Stewart JG	Craggs JE	Bailey IC	Mahoney JF	Boam SW	Ramage A	Mills DJ	McAndrew A	Ashcroft W	Woof W	Armstrong D	Hedley G	Proctor MG	Johnson PE	Johnston CP	Cummins S	Hodgson DJ	Burns ME	Cochrane GT	Shearer DJ	Platt JA	Janković B	Bell IC
Aug 19	(h)	Coventry C	L 1-2	Woof	17,918	1	2	3	4	5	6	7	8	9	10	11*	12											
	22 (a)	Birmingham C	W 3-1	Armstrong, Ashcroft, Mills	24,409	1	2	3	4	5	6		8	9	10	11			7									
	26 (a)	Southampton	L 1-2	Armstrong	20,691	1	2	3	4	5	6		8	9*	10	11			7	12								
Sep 2	(h)	Ipswich T	D 0-0		14,427	1	2	3	4	5	6		8	9	10	11			7									
	9 (a)	Everton	L 0-2		36,191	1	2	3	4	5	6		8	10	9	11			7									
	16 (h)	Queen's Park R	L 0-2		12,822	1	2			5	6		9	8	12	11			7*	3	4	10						
	23 (a)	Nottingham F	D 2-2	Mills, Armstrong	26,287	1	2		4	5	6	7	8*	9		11				3		10	12					
	30 (h)	Arsenal	L 2-3	Ashcroft, Mills	14,511	1	2		4	5	6	7	8	9*		11				3		10	12					
Oct 7	(a)	Manchester U	L 2-3	Mills, Burns	45,402	1	2	3	4	5	6	7	8	9		11							10					
	14 (h)	Norwich C	W 2-0	Peters (og), Mills	18,286	1	2	3	4	5		8	6	9		11							10	7				
	21 (h)	Wolves	W 2-0	Burns, Armstrong	19,029	1	2	3	4*	5		8	6	9		11							10	7	12			
	27 (a)	Aston Villa	W 2-0	Burns, Cochrane	32,614	1	2	3	4	5		8	6	9		11							10	7				
Nov 4	(h)	Bristol C	D 0-0		20,461	1	2	3	4	5		8	6			11			7			9	10					
	11 (a)	Coventry C	L 1-2	Burns	18,636	1	2	3	4	5		8	6	9*		11			12				10	7				
	18 (h)	Southampton	W 2-0	Burns, Mills	17,169	1	2	3	4	5		8	6			11						9	10	7				
	21 (a)	Ipswich T	L 1-2	Armstrong	17,818	1	2	3	4*	5		8	6	9		11			12				10	7				
	25 (a)	Liverpool	L 0-2		39,812	1	2	3	4	5		8	6*	12		11						9	10	7				
Dec 9	(a)	West Brom A	L 0-2		19,865	1	2	3	4	5	6			12		11		8*				10		9	7			
	16 (h)	Chelsea	W 7-2	Proctor, Burns 4, Armstrong, Cochrane	15,107	1	2		4	5	6		3			11		8				10	9	7				
	23 (a)	Leeds U	L 1-3	Proctor	27,146	1	2		4*	5	6		3	12		11		8				10	9	7				
	26 (h)	Bolton W	D 1-1	Cummins	20,125	1	2		4	5	6		3			11		8				10	9	7				
Jan 20	(a)	Queen's Park R	D 1-1	Hodgson	9,899	1	2*	3	4	5	6			9		11		8				10	12	7				
Feb 3	(h)	Nottingham F	L 1-3	Proctor	21,330	1			4	5	6			2		11		8		3		10	12	9*	7			
	10 (a)	Arsenal	D 0-0		28,371	1	2		4	5	6		7*			11		8		3		10	12	9				
	24 (a)	Norwich C	L 0-1		12,914	1	2		4	5	6*			9		11		8		3		10	12	7				
Mar 3	(a)	Wolves	W 3-1	Ashcroft, McAndrew, Shearer	18,782	1	2		4	5			6	9*		11		8		3			10	7	12			
	6 (h)	Everton	L 1-2	Armstrong (pen)	16,084	1	2		4	5			6	9		11		8		3			10*	7	12			
	10 (a)	Aston Villa	W 2-0	Proctor, Cochrane	16,558		2		4	5			6	9		11		8		3			10	7		1		
	13 (h)	Derby C	W 3-1	Boam, Armstrong, Burns	16,286		2		4	5			6	9		11		8		3			10	7		1		
	17 (a)	Bristol C	D 1-1	Armstrong	13,559		2		4	5			6	9		11		8		3			10*	7		1	12	
	24 (h)	Birmingham C	W 2-1	Burns, Ashcroft	15,013		2		4	5			6	9		11		8		3			10*	7		1	12	
	27 (h)	Manchester U	D 2-2	Armstrong (pen), Proctor	20,138		2		4	5			6	9*		11		8		3			10	7	12	1		
	31 (h)	Tottenham H	W 1-0	Proctor	19,172		2		4	5			6	9		11		8		3			10	7		1		
Apr 7	(a)	Tottenham H	W 2-1	Proctor, Ashcroft	21,580		2		4	5			6	9		11		8		3			10	7		1		
	10 (h)	Leeds U	W 1-0	Ashcroft	23,260		2		4	5			6	9*		11		8		3			10	7		1	12	
	14 (a)	Bolton W	D 0-0		22,621		2		4	5			6	9		11		8		3			10			1	7	
	17 (h)	Manchester C	W 2-0	Proctor, Burns	19,676		2	12	4	5			6			11		8		3			10	7		1	9*	
	21 (a)	Chelsea	L 1-2	Armstrong	13,413		2		4	5	6			9		11		8		3	12		10*	7		1		
	24 (a)	Manchester C	L 0-1		28,264		2				6		9	12		11		8		3			10*	7		1	4	
	28 (h)	West Brom A	D 1-1	Burns	18,063		2			4		5	6	9		11		8	3*				10	7		1	12	
May 5	(h)	Derby C	W 3-0	Cochrane, Proctor, Janković	18,151		2	3	4			6	5			11		8				10		7		1	9	
	11 (h)	Liverpool	L 0-1		32,214		2	3	4	5			6	9		11		8					7			1	10	
		Apps				27	41	18	40	40	14	17	38	33	4	42		31	21	1	11	13	31	18	2	15	4	1
		Sub apps							1								4	1	1	2	1	1	6	1	3		4	
		Goals								1		6	1	6	1	11		9			1	1	14	3	1		1	

1 own-goal

FA Cup

Date		Opponent	Res	Scorers	Att	Stewart JG	Craggs JE	Bailey IC	Mahoney JF	Boam SW	Ramage A	Mills DJ	McAndrew A	Ashcroft W	Woof W	Armstrong D	Hedley G	Proctor MG	Johnson PE	Johnston CP	Cummins S	Hodgson DJ	Burns ME	Cochrane GT	Shearer DJ	Platt JA	Janković B	Bell IC	Round
Jan 9	(h)	Crystal P	D 1-1	Ashcroft	21,447	1	2	3*	4	5			6	12		11		8				10	9	7					3
	15 (a)	Crystal P	L 0-1		23,361	1	2	3	4	5			6	12		11		8				10	9*	7					R
		Apps				2	2	2	2	2			2			2		2				2	2	2					
		Sub apps												2															
		Goals												1															

League Cup

Date		Opponent	Res	Scorers	Att	Stewart JG	Craggs JE	Bailey IC	Mahoney JF	Boam SW	Ramage A	Mills DJ	McAndrew A	Ashcroft W	Woof W	Armstrong D	Hedley G	Proctor MG	Johnson PE	Johnston CP	Cummins S	Hodgson DJ	Burns ME	Cochrane GT	Shearer DJ	Platt JA	Janković B	Bell IC	Round
Aug 29	(h)	Peterborough U	D 0-0		12,510	1	2	3	4	5	6		8	9	10*	11			7	12									2
Sep 5	(a)	Peterborough U	L 0-1*		8,093	1	2	3	4*	5	6		8	10	9	11			7	12									R
		Apps				2	2	2	2	2	2	2	1	2	1	2			2										
		Sub apps																		2									
		Goals																											

1979-80
Division 1

Player columns (left → right): Platt JA · Craggs JE · Bailey IC · Johnston CP · Ashcroft W · McAndrew A · Hodgson DJ · Proctor MG · Janković B · Burns ME · Armstrong D · Johnson PE · Cummins S · Hedley G · Nattrass I · Ramage A · Shearer DJ · Cochrane GT · Peters J · Bell IC · Woof W · Stewart JG · Angus MA · Askew W

Date	V	Opponent	Res	Scorers	Att	Pl	Cr	Ba	Jo	As	Mc	Ho	Pr	Ja	Bu	Ar	Jn	Cu	He	Na	Ra	Sh	Co	Pe	Be	Wo	St	An	Ak
Aug 18	(a)	Tottenham H	W 3-1	Armstrong, Burns, Janković	32,743	1	2*	3	4	5	6	7	8	9	10	11	12												
21	(h)	Manchester C	W 3-0	Johnston, Burns, Cummins	24,002	1	2	3	4	5	6	7	8	9*	10	11		12											
25	(h)	Crystal P	D 1-1	Cummins	24,506	1	2	3	4	5	6	7	8		10	11		9											
Sep 1	(a)	Manchester U	L 1-2	Johnston	51,015	1	2	3	4	5	6	7	8*	9	10	11			12										
8	(h)	Norwich C	W 1-0	Proctor	19,575	1	2	3	4	5	6	7	8	9		11		10											
15	(a)	Arsenal	L 0-2		30,341	1	2	3	4	5	6	7	8*	9	12	11			10										
22	(a)	Derby C	L 0-1		18,620	1	2	3	4	5*	6		8	9	7	11		10	12										
29	(h)	Aston Villa	D 0-0		16,017	1	2	3	4		6	7	8			11		10		5	9*	12							
Oct 6	(h)	West Brom A	W 2-1	Burns, Armstrong (pen)	16,312	1	2	3	4	5	6	7	8	9*	10	11						12							
10	(a)	Manchester C	L 0-1		29,384	1	2	3	4	5	6		8		10	11				9	7								
13	(a)	Stoke C	D 0-0		18,406	1	2	3	4	5*	6	9	8		10	11					12	7							
20	(h)	Wolves	W 1-0	Proctor	18,393	1	2	3	4	5	6	9*	8		10	11					12	7							
27	(a)	Ipswich T	L 0-1		18,343	1	2	3	4	5	6	9	8	12	10	11						7*							
Nov 3	(h)	Tottenham H	D 0-0		19,557	1	2		4	5	6	9	8	10	7*	11							12	3					
10	(a)	Everton	W 2-0	Johnston 2	25,155	1	2		4	5	6	9			10	11							7	3	8				
17	(a)	Bristol C	W 1-0	Armstrong	14,517	1	2		4	5	6	9			10	11					4		7	3	8				
24	(h)	Brighton & HA	D 1-1	Burns	16,010	1	2		7	5	6	9			10	11					4		12	3	8*				
Dec 1	(a)	Liverpool	L 0-4		39,885	1	2		4*	5	6	7	8		10	11				9			12	3					
8	(h)	Southampton	L 0-1		15,469	1	2			5*	6	9	8		10	11			12	4			7	3					
21	(h)	Bolton W	W 3-1	Armstrong, Craggs, Cochrane	11,789	1	2			5	6	9	8		10	11	3		4				7						
26	(h)	Leeds U	W 3-1	Janković 2, Armstrong	26,655	1	2			5	6	9	8		10	11	3		4				7						
29	(a)	Crystal P	W 2-1	Hedley, Hodgson	25,272	1	2			5	6	9	8		10	11*	3		4		12		7						
Jan 1	(a)	Coventry C	L 0-2		17,081	1	2			5	6	9	8		10	11	3		4		12			7*					
12	(h)	Manchester U	D 1-1	Armstrong	30,587	1	2				6	9	8		10	11	3		4	5			7						
Feb 9	(h)	Derby C	W 3-0	Burns, Ashcroft, Armstrong	15,587	1	2			5	6	9	8		10*	11	3		4	12			7						
16	(a)	Nottingham F	D 2-2	Burns 2	23,889	1	2			5	6	9	8		10	11	3		4				7						
23	(a)	Stoke C	L 1-3	Burns	15,953	1	2			5	6	9	8		10	11	3		4*	12			7						
27	(a)	Norwich C	D 0-0		13,666	1	2			5	6	9			10	11	3		4	8			7						
Mar 1	(a)	Wolves	W 2-0	Hodgson 2	21,820	1	2		4			9	8		10*	11	3		12		6	5	7						
11	(h)	Ipswich T	D 1-1	Ashcroft	18,690	1	2		4	12	6	9	8			11	3*		10			5	7						
14	(a)	West Brom A	D 0-0		15,875	1	2		4	10	6	9	8			11	3					5	7						
19	(a)	Aston Villa	W 2-0	Ashcroft, Armstrong	15,319	1	2		4	10	6	9	8			11	3					5	7						
22	(h)	Everton	W 2-1	Hodgson, McAndrew	17,587	1	2		4	9	6	10	8			11	3					5	7						
Apr 2	(a)	Leeds U	L 0-2		17,906	1	2		4	9	6	10	8			11	3					5	7						
5	(h)	Coventry C	L 1-2	Hodgson	15,258	1	2		4	10*		9	8	12		11	3				6	5	7						
8	(a)	Bolton W	D 2-2	Hodgson, Burns	10,613	1	2		4		6	9	8		10	11	3					5	7						
19	(a)	Brighton & HA	L 1-2	Burns	20,394		2		4	5	6	9	8		10	11	3*		12				7				1		
22	(h)	Bristol C	L 1-3	Armstrong	12,013		2	3	4	5*		9	8		10	11			12				7			6	1		
26	(h)	Nottingham F	D 0-0		17,021		2	3			6	9	8		10	11			4	5			7				1		
May 3	(a)	Southampton	L 1-4	Ramage	18,476		2	3	12		6	9	8	7*	10	11			4	5							1		
6	(h)	Liverpool	W 1-0	Shearer	24,458	1	2	3	7		6	9	8			11			4	5		10							
19	(h)	Arsenal	W 5-0	Johnston, Hodgson, Shearer, Armstrong 2	15,579		2	3	7*	5	6	9	8			11			4			10					1	12	
Apps						37	42	18	29	34	39	40	38	17	23	42	17	4	14	10	13	4	25	6	3	1	5	1	
Sub apps									1	1				2	1		1	1	6	3	3	1	4				1		
Goals							1		5	3	1	7	2	3	10	11		2	1		1	2	1						

FA Cup

Date	V	Opponent	Res	Scorers	Att	Pl	Cr	Ba	Jo	As	Mc	Ho	Pr	Ja	Bu	Ar	Jn	Cu	He	Na	Ra	Sh	Co	Pe	Be	Wo	St	An	Ak	Round
Jan 9	(a)	Portsmouth	D 1-1	Cochrane	31,743	1	2			5	6	9	8	10		11	3		4				7							3
14	(h)	Portsmouth	W 3-0	Cochrane, Johnson, Armstrong	22,551	1	2				6	9	8	10		11	3		4	5			7							R
26	(a)	Birmingham C	L 1-2	Hodgson	29,152	1	2			5	6	9	8	10*	12	11	3		4				7							4
Apps						3	3			2	3	3	3	2		3	3		3	1			3							
Sub apps															1														
Goals												1				1	1						2						

League Cup

Date	V	Opponent	Res	Scorers	Att	Pl	Cr	Ba	Jo	As	Mc	Ho	Pr	Ja	Bu	Ar	Jn	Cu	He	Na	Ra	Sh	Co	Pe	Be	Wo	St	An	Ak	Round
Aug 29	(a)	Derby C	W 1-0	Armstrong (pen)	15,205	1	2	3	4	5	6	7	8	9	10	11														2/1
Sep 4	(h)	Derby C	D 1-1	Janković	19,466	1	2	3	4	5	6	7		9	10	11		12	8*											2/2
25	(h)	Nottingham F	L 1-3	Armstrong	29,869	1	2	3	4	5		7	8	9*	10	11					6		12							3
Apps						3	3	3	3	3	2	3	2	3	3	3			1		1									
Sub apps																		1					1						
Goals														1		2													

1980-81
Division 1

Date	Opponent	Res	Scorers	Att	Platt JA	Craggs JE	Bailey IC	Johnston CP	Ashcroft W	McAndrew A	Shearer DJ	Hedley G	Hodgson DJ	Nattrass I	Armstrong D	Burns ME	Proctor MG	Janković B	Cochrane GT	Askew W	Angus MA	Stewart JG	Macdonald G	Bell IC	Blackburn C	Ross C	Woof W	Nobbs KA
Aug 16 (a)	Manchester U	L 0-3		54,394	1	2	3	4	5	6	7	8*	9	10	11	12												
19 (h)	Leeds U	W 3-0	Johnston, Nattrass, Armstrong	19,468	1	2	3	4	5	6	10	8	9	7	11													
23 (a)	Crystal P	L 2-5	Ashcroft, Johnston	17,192	1	2	3	4*	5	6	7	8	9	10	11	12												
30 (h)	Manchester C	D 2-2	Mackenzie (og), Janković	15,761	1	2	3	4*	5		10	8	9	6	11			7	12									
Sep 6 (h)	Nottingham F	D 0-0		17,119	1	2	3	4	5*	6		12	9				8	10	7	11								
13 (a)	Sunderland	W 1-0	Janković	32,745	1	2	3	4		6			9				8	10	7	11	5							
20 (h)	Arsenal	W 2-1	Proctor, Armstrong	14,860		2	3	4		6			9	12	11		8	10	7*		5	1						
27 (a)	Stoke C	L 0-1		11,847		2	3	4		6		12	9	7*	11		8	10			5	1						
Oct 4 (h)	Norwich C	W 6-1	McAndrew, Janković 2, Armstrong, Woods (og), Johnston	12,958	1	2	3	4		6	9		7		11		8	10			5							
7 (a)	Liverpool	L 2-4	Johnston, Janković	28,204	1	2	3	4	12	6	9		7*		11		8	10			5							
11 (a)	Tottenham H	L 2-3	Hodgson, Johnston	27,380	1	2	3	4	12	6	9*		7		11		8	10			5							
18 (h)	Southampton	D 1-1	Janković	15,858	1	2	3	4		6			9	12	11		8	10	7*		5							
21 (h)	Leicester C	W 1-0	Armstrong	13,114	1	2		4*	12	6			9	3	11	7	8	10			5							
25 (a)	West Brom A	L 0-3		15,907	1	2	3	4	12	6			9		11	7*	8	10			5							
Nov 1 (h)	Birmingham C	L 1-2	Janković	13,292	1	2	3	4		6	7		9		11		8	10			5							
8 (h)	Brighton & HA	W 1-0	Johnston	12,117	1	2		4	5	6			9	3	11		8	10	7									
12 (a)	Leeds U	L 1-2	Janković	17,382	1	2		4	5	6	12		9	3	11		8	10			7*							
15 (h)	Manchester U	D 1-1	Johnston	20,606	1		3	4	5*	6	10	12	9	2	11		8		7									
22 (h)	Wolves	W 2-0	Johnston, Shearer	13,562	1		3	4	5	6	10		9	2	11		8		7									
Dec 6 (h)	Aston Villa	W 2-1	Johnston, Shearer	15,721	1	2	3	4	5		10		9	6	11		8		7									
13 (a)	Leicester C	L 0-1		13,998	1	2	3	4	5		10		9	6	11		8		7									
20 (h)	Tottenham H	W 4-1	Hodgson 3, Johnston	15,990	1	2	3	4	5		10		9	6	11		8		7									
26 (a)	Coventry C	L 0-1		16,106	1	2	3	4*	5	12	10		9	6	11		8		7									
27 (h)	Everton	W 1-0	Ashcroft	20,181	1	2	3		5	4	10		9	6	11		8		7									
Jan 10 (a)	Wolves	L 0-3		16,253	1	2	3		5*	4	10		9	6	11		8		7	12								
17 (a)	Manchester C	L 2-3	Hodgson, McAndrew	30,774	1		3			4	10*		9	2	11		8	12	7		5		6					
31 (h)	Crystal P	W 2-0	Armstrong, McAndrew (pen)	16,099	1		3		5*	6	12	4	9	2	11		8	10	7									
Feb 7 (h)	Sunderland	W 1-0	Hedley	35,065	1		3		5	6		4	9	2	11		8	10	7									
17 (a)	Ipswich T	L 0-1		24,772	1	7	3	4	5	6	10		9	2	11		8											
21 (h)	Stoke C	W 3-1	Janković 2 (1 pen), Cochrane	15,142	1		3	4	5	6			9	2	11		8	10	7									
28 (a)	Arsenal	D 2-2	Armstrong, Shearer	24,504	1	12	3	4	5*	6	9			2	11		8	10	7									
Mar 3 (a)	Nottingham F	L 0-1		19,690	1	2	3				9	4			5	11	8	10*			6		12	7				
17 (a)	Norwich C	L 0-2		13,561	1		3	4	5	6*	10		9	2	11		8		7	12								
21 (a)	Southampton	L 0-1		20,651	1		3	12		6				2			8		7*	11	5		9	4				
28 (h)	West Brom A	W 2-1	Batson (og), Shearer	13,228	1		3	12		6	10		9	2*	11		8		7		5			4				
Apr 4 (a)	Birmingham C	L 1-2	I.C.Bell	12,472	1		3	12		6	10			2	11				4	5	9*	8		7				
11 (h)	Brighton & HA	W 1-0	Shearer	11,076	1		3			6	10			2	11		8		5		9	4		7				
18 (a)	Everton	L 1-4	Shearer	15,709	1		3	12		6	10			2*	11	7	4		5		9	8						
21 (h)	Coventry C	L 0-1		11,371	1		3			6	10				11	9*	8		7	12	5		4			2		
25 (a)	Aston Villa	L 0-3		38,018	1	2	3		5	6	9				11		8	10	7				4					
May 2 (h)	Ipswich T	W 2-1	Janković 2	15,503	1	2	3			6	9				11		8	10	7		5		4					
5 (h)	Liverpool	L 1-2	Shearer	19,102	1	2	3			6	9				11		8	10	7		5		4					
			Apps		40	28	39	27	22	36	29	8	32	29	39	4	38	21	24	4	20	2	6	5	1	5	2	1
			Sub apps			1			8	1	1	4				2		2		2			1	2		1		
			Goals					10	2	3	7	1	5	1	6		1	12	1					1				

3 own-goals

FA Cup

Date	Opponent	Res	Scorers	Att	Platt	Craggs	Bailey	Johnston	Ashcroft	McAndrew	Shearer	Hedley	Hodgson	Nattrass	Armstrong	Burns	Proctor	Janković	Cochrane	Askew	Angus	Round
Jan 3 (a)	Swansea C	W 5-0	Hodgson 2, Ashcroft, Angus, Cochrane	18,015	1	2	3		5	11	10		9	6			8		7		4	3
24 (h)	West Brom A	W 1-0	Bailey	28,285	1		3	4*	5	6	9			2	11		8	10	7	12		4
Feb 14 (h)	Burnley	W 2-1	Proctor, Janković	37,557	1		3	4	5	6			9	2	11		8	10	7			5
Mar 7 (h)	Wolves	D 1-1	Cochrane	36,382	1		3	4	5	6	12		9	2	11		8	10*	7			6
10 (a)	Wolves	L 1-3*	Hodgson	40,524	1		3	4	5	6	12		9	2	11		8	10	7*			R
			Apps		5	1	5	4	5	5	2		4	5	4		5	4	5		1	
			Sub apps								2									1		
			Goals				1		1				3				1	1	2		1	

*After extra-time

League Cup

Date	Opponent	Res	Scorers	Att	Platt	Craggs	Bailey	Johnston	Ashcroft	McAndrew	Shearer	Hedley	Hodgson	Nattrass	Armstrong	Burns	Proctor	Janković	Cochrane	Askew	Angus	Round
Aug 26 (h)	Ipswich T	W 3-1	Shearer 2, Proctor	14,430	1	2	3	4*	5		10	8	9	6	11			7	12			2/1
Sep 2 (a)	Ipswich T	L 0-3		15,027	1	2	3			6	10	8	9	5*	11			7	12		4	2/2
			Apps		2	2	2	1	1	1	2	2	2	2	2			2			1	
			Sub apps																2			
			Goals								2								1			

1981-82
Division 1

	Date	Opponent	Result	Scorers	Att	Platt JA	Craggs JE	Bolton J	Hedley G	Baxter MJ	Nattrass I	Woof W	Otto HM	Macdonald G	Shearer DJ	McAndrew A	Hodgson DJ	McCreesh A	Angus MA	Cochrane GT	Ross C	Bailey IC	Wood DT	Ashcroft W	Askew W	Thomson R	Bell S	Thomas D	Currie DN
Aug	29 (h)	Tottenham H	L 1-3	Otto	20,490	1	2	3	4	5	6	7	8	9	10*	11	12												
Sep	1 (a)	Liverpool	D 1-1	Shearer	31,963	1		3	4	5		7	8		10*	6	9		2	11	12								
	5 (a)	Brighton & HA	L 0-2		13,383	1		3	4	5		7*	8		10	6	9		2	11	12								
	12 (h)	Birmingham C	W 2-1	Otto, Hodgson	13,167	1	2	3		5			8	12	10*	6	9			7	4	11							
	19 (a)	Southampton	L 0-2		20,105	1	2	3		5			8	9		6				7	4	11*	10	12					
	22 (h)	Manchester U	L 0-2		19,895	1	2	3		5		7	8		10	6	9				4				11				
	26 (h)	Stoke C	W 3-2	Cochrane, Woof, Shearer	11,604	1	2	3		5		7			10	6	9			7	4*	11	12						
Oct	3 (a)	West Brom A	L 0-2		12,977	1	2	3		5		9*	8		10	6				7	4			12		11			
	10 (h)	Nottingham F	D 1-1	Gunn (og)	15,043	1	2	3		5		12	8		10	6			4	7				9		11*			
	17 (a)	Wolves	D 0-0		12,061	1	2	3		5		12	8		10	6			4	7				9*		11			
	21 (a)	Manchester U	L 0-1		38,342	1	2	3		5		9	8		10	6			4	7						11			
	24 (h)	Everton	L 0-2		13,423	1	2	3		5		9	8		10*	6	12		4	7						11			
	31 (a)	West Ham U	L 2-3	Woof, Thomson (pen)	27,604	1		3		5	2	9	8	12	10	6*				7	4					11			
Nov	7 (a)	Manchester C	L 2-3	Angus, Thomson	32,025	1	2			5	3	9	8		10	6				7	4					11			
	14 (h)	Sunderland	D 0-0		21,019	1		3		5	2	9	8*		10	6	12			7	4					11			
	21 (h)	Aston Villa	D 3-3	McAndrew (pen), Ashcroft 2	12,522	1		3		5	2	9*	8			11	6			7	4			10					12
	28 (a)	Coventry C	D 1-1	Woof	10,403	1		3		5	2	9*	8			11	6			7	4			10					12
Dec	5 (h)	Ipswich T	L 0-1		13,577	1		3		5	2	9*	8		10	6				7	4			12		11			
Jan	27 (a)	Tottenham H	L 0-1		22,819	1	2			5			8	12	10*	6	9			7	4	3				11			
	30 (h)	Southampton	L 0-1		12,693	1	2			5			8			6	9			7	4	3				11		10	
Feb	6 (a)	Birmingham C	D 0-0		10,715	1	2			5	6		8			11	9			7	4	3				10			
	13 (h)	Swansea C	D 1-1	McAndrew (pen)	11,209	1	2			5	6		8			11	10			7	4	3		9					
	16 (a)	Arsenal	L 0-2		13,738	1	2			5	6		8			11*	10			4	7	3		9		12			
	20 (a)	Stoke C	L 0-2		10,683	1	2			5	6		8			11	12			4	7	3	10	9*					
	27 (a)	Nottingham F	D 1-1	Hodgson	16,464	1				5	2		8		10	6	9			7	4	3				11			
Mar	6 (h)	Wolves	D 0-0		10,155	1				5	2		8		10*	6	9			7	4	3		12		11			
	9 (h)	West Brom A	W 1-0	Hodgson	9,403	1				5	2	12	8			6	9			7*	4	3		10		11			
	13 (a)	Everton	L 0-2		15,328	1		8		5	2					6	9			7	4	3		10		11			
	20 (h)	West Ham U	L 2-3	McAndrew (pen), Ashcroft	12,134	1	2			5			8			6	9			7	4	3		10		11			
	27 (h)	Manchester C	D 0-0		11,709	1				5	2	12	8		10					7	4	3	6	9		11*			
Apr	3 (a)	Sunderland	W 2-0	Ashcroft, Baxter	19,006	1	7			5	2	12	8				9				4	3	6	10*		11			
	6 (h)	Leeds U	D 0-0		15,471	1	7			5	2		8			4	9					3	6	10		11			
	10 (h)	Notts C	W 3-0	Wood, Bolton, Bailey	10,402	1	7			5	2		8	12		4	9*					3	6	10		11			
	13 (a)	Leeds U	D 1-1	Shearer	20,458	1	7			5	2		8		10	4	9					3	6			11			
	17 (a)	Aston Villa	L 0-2		21,098	1	7*			5	2		8	12	10	4	9					3	6			11			
	20 (h)	Brighton & HA	W 2-1	Otto, McAndrew (pen)	9,788	1				5	2		8	12		4	9			7		3	6	10		11*			
	24 (h)	Coventry C	D 0-0		10,968	1	2			5	6		8	12	10	4	9			7		3				11*			
May	1 (h)	Ipswich T	L 1-3	Thomas	17,924	1	2			5	6		8		10*		9			7	4	3				12		11	
	8 (h)	Arsenal	L 1-3	Baxter	9,565	1	2			4*			8	12			9			7		3	6	10		11			
	11 (a)	Notts C	W 1-0	Macdonald	6,707	1		3		5			8	9	10				2	7	4		6			11			
	15 (a)	Swansea C	W 2-1	Otto, Stanley (og)	12,961	1	2	6		5			8		10		9			7	4	3		12		11*			
	18 (h)	Liverpool	D 0-0		17,431	1	2	6		5			8		10		9				4	3		12	7*	11			
		Apps				42	23	27	3	40	27	17	40	4	20	39	31	2	14	22	22	26	11	14	6	18	1	13	
		Sub apps										6		4	4		3			3			7		2				1
		Goals						1		2		3	4	1	3	4	3		1	1		1		4		2		1	

2 own-goals

FA Cup

	Date	Opponent	Result	Scorers	Att	Platt JA	Craggs JE	Bolton J	Hedley G	Baxter MJ	Nattrass I	Woof W	Otto HM	Macdonald G	Shearer DJ	McAndrew A	Hodgson DJ	McCreesh A	Angus MA	Cochrane GT	Ross C	Bailey IC	Wood DT	Ashcroft W	Askew W	Thomson R	Bell S	Thomas D	Currie DN	Round
Jan	2 (a)	Queen's Park R	D 1-1	Thomson	12,100	1		3		5	2		8		10	6	9			7	4					11				3
	18 (h)	Queen's Park R	L 2-3*	Otto, Thomson (pen)	14,819	1		3		5	2	12	8		10*	6	9			7	4					11				R
		Apps				2		2		2	2		2		1	2	2			2	2					2				
		Sub apps										1																	
		Goals											1													2			

*After extra-time

League Cup

	Date	Opponent	Result	Scorers	Att	Platt JA	Craggs JE	Bolton J	Hedley G	Baxter MJ	Nattrass I	Woof W	Otto HM	Macdonald G	Shearer DJ	McAndrew A	Hodgson DJ	McCreesh A	Angus MA	Cochrane GT	Ross C	Bailey IC	Wood DT	Ashcroft W	Askew W	Thomson R	Bell S	Thomas D	Currie DN	Round
Oct	6 (h)	Plymouth A	W 2-1	Ashcroft, Thomson	8,201	1	2	3		5		12	8		10	6			4	7				9		11*				2/1
	27 (a)	Plymouth A	D 0-0		6,402	1		3		5	2	9*	8			12	6	10		7	4					11				2/2
Nov	10 (a)	Liverpool	L 1-4	Shearer	16,145	1	2	11		5	3	9	8		10	6			4	7										3
		Apps				3	2	3		3	2	2	3		2	3	1		3	3	1			1		2				
		Sub apps										1					1												
		Goals													1									1		1			

1982-83
Division 2

Date		Opp	Res	Scorers	Att	Platt JA	Ross C	Bolton J	Otto HM	Baxter MJ	Wood DT	Cochrane GT	Currie DN	Shearer DJ	Kennedy MF	Bell S	Macdonald G	Brownlie J	Mowbray AM	Ward PT	Hankin R	Nattrass I	Roberts A	Beattie TK	Sugrue P	O'Hanlon KG	Hamilton GJ
Aug	28(a)	Sheffield W	L 1-3	Shearer	18,881	1	2	3	4	5	6	7	8*	9	10	11	12										
Sep	4(h)	Burnley	L 1-4	Shearer	8,036	1	4	3	12	5	6	7*		9	8	11	10	2									
	8(a)	Newcastle U	D 1-1	Wood	27,984	1	4	3	12	5	6			9	10	11		2	7	8*							
	11(a)	Derby C	D 1-1	Bell	9,050	1	4	3	8	5	6			9*	10	11		2	7	12							
	18(h)	Fulham	L 1-4	Shearer	6,427	1	4	3	8	5	6		12	9	10	11		2*	7								
	25(a)	Crystal P	L 0-3		7,530	1	4	3	8	5	6			9	10	11*		2	7	12							
	28(h)	Grimsby T	L 1-4	Shearer	5,927	1	2	3	4*	5	6	12		8	10	11			7		9						
Oct	2(h)	Oldham A	D 1-1	Otto	5,615	1		3	4	5	6	8			10	11	12	2*	7		9						
	9(a)	Shrewsbury T	D 2-2	Bell, Otto	3,620	1		3	4	5	6	8			10	11		2			9	7					
	16(h)	Bolton W	W 1-0	Macdonald	5,521	1		3	4	5	6	8				11	9	2	7			10					
	23(h)	Queen's Park R	W 2-1	Nattrass (pen), Otto	7,892	1		3	4	5	6	8				11	9	2	7			10					
	30(a)	Rotherham U	D 1-1	Otto	8,135	1		3	4	5	6	8			10	11		2	7*		9		12				
Nov	6(h)	Barnsley	W 2-0	Shearer, Wood	11,787	1		3	9	4	6			11	7	10		2			8			5			
	13(a)	Charlton A	W 3-2	Shearer 2, Kennedy	10,807	1	12	3	9	4	6			11	7	10			2		8			5*			
	20(a)	Leeds U	D 0-0		18,482	1	5	3	9	4	6			11	7	10			2		8						
	27(h)	Blackburn R	L 1-5	Cochrane	10,821	1	5*	3	9	4	6	12		11	7	10			2		8						
Dec	4(h)	Wolves	L 0-4		11,856	1		3	9	4	6		7	2	10	11					8	5					
	11(h)	Chelsea	W 3-1	Otto, Wood, Shearer	8,836	1		3	9	4	6	12		7	10	11					2	8*	5				
	17(a)	Cambridge U	L 0-2		2,533	1		3*	6	5	7	12		9	11					2	10	4		8			
	27(h)	Leicester C	D 1-1	Bell (pen)	12,665	1		3	6	5	7			9	11					2	10	4		8			
	28(a)	Carlisle U	W 3-1	Bell 2, Sugrue	8,181	1		3	6	4	7	12		9	11					2	10*	5		8			
Jan	1(h)	Leeds U	D 0-0		17,057	1		3	6	4	5	12		10*	9	11				2		5		8			
	3(a)	Burnley	D 1-1	Shearer	9,205	1		3	6	4	5	12		10	9	11			2*			5		8			
	15(h)	Sheffield W	D 1-1	Bell	11,863			3	6*	4	5			9	10	11		2			12	5		8	1		
	22(a)	Fulham	L 0-1		8,431			3	6		5			9	4	11			2		10	5		8	1		
Feb	5(h)	Newcastle U	D 1-1	Baxter	25,184			3	7	5	6		12	10		11					9	2	4*	8	1		
	12(a)	Oldham A	L 0-3		6,002			3	7	4	6			9	2	11			12		10	5*		8	1		
	26(a)	Bolton W	L 1-3	Otto	5,598			3*	7	4	6		10		8	11			2			5		9	1	12	
Mar	5(a)	Queen's Park R	L 1-6	Kennedy (pen)	9,596				6	4	7			10	8	11				5		9	2	3	1		
	8(h)	Shrewsbury T	W 2-1	Kennedy, Hankin	7,496				6	4	3			10	8	11				5		9	2	7	1		
	12(h)	Rotherham U	D 1-1	Sugrue	8,875				6	4	3			10	8	11				5		9	2	7	1		
	19(a)	Barnsley	L 0-2		10,681				6	4	9			10	8	11				5			2	7	1		3
	26(h)	Charlton A	W 3-0	Bell, Baxter 2	7,057			3	6*	4	9		12	10	8	11				5			2	7	1		
Apr	2(h)	Carlisle U	W 1-0	Bell	9,965			3	6	4	9			10	8	11				5			2	7	1		
	5(a)	Leicester C	L 0-1		12,025			3	6*	4	9				8	11				5		12	2	7	1		10
	9(h)	Derby C	L 2-3	Kennedy 2 (1 pen)	9,078			3*	6	4	9			10	8	11				5			2	12	7	1	
	16(a)	Grimsby T	W 3-0	Sugrue, Hamilton, Otto	5,985				6	4	9			10	8	11				5			2	7	1		3
	23(h)	Wolves	D 0-0		10,315				6	4	9		12	10*	8	11				5			2	7	1		3
	30(a)	Blackburn R	D 1-1	Otto	4,803		7		6	4	9			10*	8	11	12			5			2		1		3
May	7(h)	Cambridge U	L 0-1		9,949				6	4	9				8	11	10			5	12		2*	7	1		3
	10(h)	Crystal P	W 2-0	Hamilton, Otto (pen)	10,014				6	4	9				8	11	10			5	12		2	7*	1		3
	14(a)	Chelsea	D 0-0		19,341				6	4	9		8			11	10			5	7		2		1		3
		Apps				23	10	32	40	41	42	7		4	29	38	42	6	12	25	11	19	29		3	22	19
		Sub apps					1		2				7	4				3		1	4	2		1	1		1
		Goals							9	3	3	1		9	5	8	1				1	1			3		2

FA Cup

Date		Opp	Res	Scorers	Att	Platt JA	Ross C	Bolton J	Otto HM	Baxter MJ	Wood DT	Cochrane GT	Currie DN	Shearer DJ	Kennedy MF	Bell S	Macdonald G	Brownlie J	Mowbray AM	Ward PT	Hankin R	Nattrass I	Roberts A	Beattie TK	Sugrue P	O'Hanlon KG	Hamilton GJ	Round
Jan	8(h)	Bishop's Stortford	D 2-2	Bell 2	13,207	1		3	6	4	7			9	2	11					10	5		8				3
	11(a)	Bishop's Stortford	W 2-1	Shearer 2	6,000	1			6	4	7			9	10	11		2		3		5		8				R
	29(h)	Notts C	W 2-0	Hankin, Beattie (pen)	17,114			3	6		7			10		11			2		9	4		5	8	1		4
Feb	19(h)	Arsenal	D 1-1	Otto	20,790		5*	6	4	7		10		8	11	12		3			2			9		1		5
	28(a)	Arsenal	L 2-3	Shearer 2	28,689			6	4	7				10	8	11				5		9	2			3	1	R
		Apps				2		3	5	4	5		1	4	4	5		1	3	1	3	5		1	5	3		
		Sub apps														1											
		Goals						1						4		2					1			1			

League Cup

Date		Opp	Res	Scorers	Att	Platt JA	Ross C	Bolton J	Otto HM	Baxter MJ	Wood DT	Cochrane GT	Currie DN	Shearer DJ	Kennedy MF	Bell S	Macdonald G	Brownlie J	Mowbray AM	Ward PT	Hankin R	Nattrass I	Roberts A	Beattie TK	Sugrue P	O'Hanlon KG	Hamilton GJ	Round
Oct	5(a)	Burnley	L 2-3	Otto, Cochrane	3,926	1		3	4*	5	6	8			10	11		2	7		9	12						2/1
	26(h)	Burnley	D 1-1	Hankin	10,389	1		3	4	5	6	8				11	12	2	7		9	10*						2/2
		Apps				2		2	2	2	2	2			1	2		2	2		2	1						
		Sub apps															1					1						
		Goals							1			1									1							

1983-84
Division 2

Date	Opponent	Res	Scorers	Att	O'Hanlon KG	Wood DT	Ward PT	Otto HM	Baxter MJ	Nattrass I	Roberts A	Macdonald G	Currie DN	Sugrue P	Bell S	Mowbray AM	Kennedy MF	Hamilton GJ	Crawford A	Pears S	Gill G
Aug 27 (a)	Portsmouth	W 1-0	Otto	17,817	1	2	3	4	5	6	7	8	9	10*	11	12					
Sep 3 (h)	Leeds U	D 2-2	Currie 2	12,773	1	2	3	4	5	6	7	11	9	10			8				
Sep 6 (h)	Newcastle U	W 3-2	Currie 2, Hamilton	19,807	1	2	3	4*	5	6	7	11	9	10			8	12			
Sep 10 (a)	Barnsley	W 2-0	Wood, Otto	10,039	1	2	3	9	5	6	7	11		10			8	4			
Sep 17 (h)	Grimsby T	D 1-1	Baxter	10,248	1	2	3	4	5	6	7*	11	9	10			8	12			
Sep 24 (a)	Chelsea	D 0-0		15,822	1	2	3	4	5	6		11	9	10	7		8*	12			
Sep 27 (a)	Fulham	L 1-2	Currie	6,452	1	2	8	4	5	6		11	9	10*	7	12			3		
Oct 1 (h)	Crystal P	L 1-3	Macdonald	8,925	1	2	3	4	5	6	7	11	9	10	8						
Oct 8 (h)	Blackburn R	L 1-2	Currie	7,062	1	2	8	4	5	6		11	9	10	7*	3	12				
Oct 15 (a)	Oldham A	L 1-2	Macdonald	3,965	1	2	3	4	5	6		11	9	10	7	8					
Oct 22 (a)	Manchester C	L 1-2	Roberts	24,466	1	2		4	5	6	7	11	9	10		3			8		
Oct 29 (h)	Shrewsbury T	W 4-0	Otto, Currie 2, Ward	6,372	1	2	7	4	5	6			9	10		3	8		11		
Nov 5 (h)	Cardiff C	W 2-0	Currie, Crawford	7,686		2	7	4	5	6			9	10		3	8		11	1	
Nov 12 (a)	Derby C	L 0-1		12,683		2	7	4	5	6			9	12	11*	3	8		10	1	
Nov 19 (a)	Cambridge U	D 0-0		2,819		2	7*	4	5	6			9	10		3	8	12	11	1	
Nov 26 (h)	Swansea C	W 1-0	Otto	6,804		2	4	9	5	6				10	7	3	8		11	1	
Dec 3 (a)	Charlton A	L 0-2		5,053		2		9	5	6			11	10	7	3	8	4		1	
Dec 10 (h)	Brighton & HA	D 0-0		6,037		2		9	5	6		12	11	10*	7	3	8	4		1	
Dec 17 (a)	Huddersfield T	D 2-2	Baxter, Sugrue	7,889	1	2		9	5	6			11	10	7	3	8	4			
Dec 26 (h)	Carlisle U	L 0-1		11,147	1	2		9	5	6		12	11	10	7	3	8	4*			
Dec 27 (a)	Sheffield W	W 2-0	Sugrue, Currie (pen)	25,188	1	2	4	9	5	6			11	10	7	3	8				
Dec 31 (a)	Leeds U	L 1-4	Currie (pen)	14,148	1	2	7	4	5	6		9	11	10	12	3*	8				
Jan 2 (h)	Chelsea	W 2-1	Hamilton, Currie	11,620	1	2	7	4	5	6		9	11	10		3	8				
Jan 14 (h)	Portsmouth	D 0-0		7,971	1	2	12	4	5	6		9	11*	10		3	8	7			
Jan 21 (a)	Grimsby T	D 0-0		7,342		2	12	4	5	6		9		10	11	3	8	7*		1	
Feb 4 (a)	Crystal P	L 0-1		5,819		2		4	5	6		9	11	10		3	8	7		1	
Feb 11 (h)	Barnsley	W 2-1	Currie 2 (1 pen)	7,480		2		4	5	6		9	11	10	12	3	8	7*		1	
Feb 25 (h)	Manchester C	D 0-0		9,343		2		4	5	6		9	11	10	12	3	8	7*		1	
Feb 28 (a)	Shrewsbury T	L 0-1		3,043		2		4	5	6		9	11	10		3	8	7		1	
Mar 3 (a)	Cardiff C	L 1-2	Macdonald	4,422		2		4	5	6		9	11	10	8	3		7*	12	1	
Mar 17 (a)	Newcastle U	L 1-3	Bell	30,421	1	2		4	5	6		9	11	10	8	3		7*	12		
Mar 20 (h)	Derby C	D 0-0		5,735	1	2	11	4	5	6		9	12	10*	7	3	8				
Mar 24 (h)	Fulham	L 0-2		5,415	1	2		4	5	6		9	12	10	7*	3	8	11			
Mar 31 (a)	Oldham A	W 3-2	Bell, Sugrue, Otto	5,615	1	2	4	9	5	6		12		10*	7	3	8	11			
Apr 7 (a)	Blackburn R	L 0-1		4,914	1	2	4	9	5	6		12	11		7	3	8	10*			
Apr 14 (h)	Cambridge U	D 1-1	Otto	5,121	1	2	4	9	5	6		12		10	7*	3	8	11			
Apr 20 (a)	Carlisle U	D 1-1	Mowbray	5,674	1	2	4	9	5	6			11	10		3	8	7*	12		
Apr 25 (h)	Sheffield W	W 2-0	Hamilton, Currie	12,362	1	2	4	8	5	6		12	9	10		3	7	11*			
Apr 27 (a)	Swansea C	L 1-2	Wood	3,632	1	2	4	8	5	6			9	10	12	3		7*			
May 5 (h)	Charlton A	W 1-0	Otto	4,720	1	2		9	5	6			11	10		3	8	4			7
May 7 (a)	Brighton & HA	L 0-3		9,168	1	2		9	5	6			11	10		3	8	4			7
May 12 (h)	Huddersfield T	D 0-0		5,687	1	2	11	9		6		12	5*	10		3	8	4			7
Apps					30	42	26	42	41	42	7	24	35	39	21	33	30	26	8	12	4
Sub apps							2					5	4	1	4	2		5	1		2
Goals						2	1	7	2		1	3	15	3	2	1		3	1		

FA Cup

Date	Opponent	Res	Scorers	Att	O'Hanlon KG	Wood DT	Ward PT	Otto HM	Baxter MJ	Nattrass I	Roberts A	Macdonald G	Currie DN	Sugrue P	Bell S	Mowbray AM	Kennedy MF	Hamilton GJ	Crawford A	Pears S	Gill G	Round
Jan 7 (h)	Arsenal	W 3-2	Macdonald, Sugrue, Baxter	17,813	1	2		4	5	6		9	11	10		3	8	7				3
Jan 31 (h)	Bournemouth	W 2-0	Sugrue 2	20,175		2		4	5	6		9		10	11	3	8	7		1		4
Feb 18 (a)	Notts C	L 0-1		17,487		2	12	4	5	6		9	11	10*		3	8	7		1		5
Apps					1	3		3	3	3		3	2	3	1	3	3	3		2		
Sub apps							1															
Goals									1			1		3								

League Cup

Date	Opponent	Res	Scorers	Att	O'Hanlon KG	Wood DT	Ward PT	Otto HM	Baxter MJ	Nattrass I	Roberts A	Macdonald G	Currie DN	Sugrue P	Bell S	Mowbray AM	Kennedy MF	Hamilton GJ	Crawford A	Pears S	Gill G	Round
Aug 30 (h)	Chesterfield	L 0-1		7,163	1	2	3	4	5	6	12	7	9	10	11*		8					1/1
Sep 13 (a)	Chesterfield	W 1-0*	Otto	3,980	1	2	3*	4	5	6	7	11	9	10	12		8					1/2
Apps					2	2	2	2	2	2	1	2	2	2	1		2					
Sub apps											1				1							
Goals								1														

*After extra-time. Lost 5-3 on penalties.

1984-85
Division 2

Date		Opponent	Result	Scorers	Att.	O'Hanlon KG	Wood DT	Ward PT	Buckley MJ	Mowbray AM	Nattrass I	Mills DJ	Hamilton GJ	Otto HM	Sugrue P	Currie DN	Gill G	Scott G	Bell S	Roberts A	McAndrew A	Saxby MW	Beagrie PS	Thomas MR	Kay J	Ripley SE	Kernaghan AN	Strong A	Laws B	Stephens A
Aug 25	(a)	Portsmouth	L 0-1		13,070	1	2	3	4	5	6	7	8	9	10	11														
Sep 1	(h)	Grimsby T	L 1-5	Currie	5,252	1	2		4	5	6	7	8	9	10*	11	3	12												
8	(a)	Notts C	L 2-3	Otto, Mills	4,911	1	2		4	5	6*	7	8	9	10	11	3		12											
15	(h)	Wolves	D 1-1	Mowbray	4,688	1	2	12	4	5	6*		8	9		10	3					11								
18	(h)	Wimbledon	L 2-4	Mills, Currie	4,277	1	2	3	4	5			8	9	12	10*	6					11								
22	(a)	Fulham	L 1-2	Mills (pen)	4,736	1	2	3	4	5			8	9		10	6					11								
29	(h)	Cardiff C	W 3-2	Currie 2, Mills	4,259	1		3	4	5			8	9	12	10	2				6*	11								
Oct 2	(a)	Oldham A	L 0-2		2,815	1		3	4	5			8	9		10	2			7*	6	11	12							
6	(h)	Charlton A	W 1-0	Currie (pen)	4,172	1		3	4	5			8	9		10	2			7	6	11								
13	(a)	Sheffield U	W 3-0	Currie (pen), Bell, Mills	10,733	1		3	4	5			8	9		10	2			7	6	11								
20	(h)	Manchester C	W 2-1	Mills 2	7,735	1		3	4	5			8	9	12	10	2*			7	6	11								
27	(a)	Leeds U	L 0-2		14,824	1		3	4	5			8	9	12	10	2*			7	6	11			1					
Nov 3	(a)	Huddersfield T	L 1-3	Currie	5,811	1		3	4	5	2			9		10			12	8*	6	11			1					
10	(h)	Barnsley	D 0-0		5,231	1		3	4		6		8	9		10	2			7	5	11			1					
17	(h)	Blackburn R	L 1-2	Mills	4,815	1			4	5	6		8	9		10	3			7	2	11			1					
24	(a)	Brighton & HA	W 2-1	Mills 2	9,089	1			4	5	6		8	9		10	2			7		11								
Dec 1	(h)	Crystal P	D 1-1	Mills	4,681	1			4	5	6		8	9	10		2			7		11								
8	(a)	Birmingham C	L 2-3	Currie (pen), Mills	8,004	1			4	5	6		8	9		10				7		11	3*	12						
14	(h)	Shrewsbury T	D 1-1	MacLaren (og)	4,044	1		3	4	5	6		8	9		10*				7		11		12						
22	(a)	Grimsby T	L 1-3	Otto	5,760	1	10	4			2		8	3	12	9*				7		6	5	11						
26	(a)	Carlisle U	W 3-0	Currie, Mills, Mowbray	4,423	1		11	4*	7	2		8	3		9	10			12		6	5							
Jan 1	(h)	Oxford U	L 0-1		6,760	1		11	4	7	2		8	3*		9	10			12		6	5							
12	(a)	Wolves	D 0-0		6,152	1			6	4	7		8	3		9	10					11	5			2				
19	(h)	Portsmouth	D 0-0		4,622	1		7	4	5	6		8	3*		9	10			12		11				2				
Feb 2	(a)	Cardiff C	L 1-2	Currie	2,564	1		7*	4	5	6		8	3		9	10			12		11				2				
5	(h)	Oldham A	L 1-2	Mowbray	3,477	1		3	4	5	6*		8			9	10					11	7			2	12			
9	(h)	Notts C	L 0-1		3,364	1		3	4	6			8			10				12	7	5			2*		9			
23	(a)	Huddersfield T	D 2-2	Otto, Mills	4,453	1		3		5	6	8	7	9		11*			12			4			2		10			
26	(a)	Barnsley	L 0-1		6,866	1		3		5		8	7	9		12			11*		6	4			2		10			
Mar 2	(h)	Leeds U	D 0-0		8,817	1			5	6			7	9		8			11			4			2		10	3		
9	(a)	Manchester C	L 0-1		22,399	1			5	6	12	2	9			8			11*	7	4						10	3		
16	(h)	Sheffield U	W 1-0	Kernaghan	5,204	1			5	6	8	11	9			12				7	4						10	3*	2	
22	(a)	Charlton A	L 0-1		3,741	1			5	6		11	9			12				7	4						10*	3	2	8
30	(h)	Wimbledon	D 1-1	Stephens	2,338	1			5	6	8	7	9			11					4							3	2	10
Apr 6	(h)	Carlisle U	L 1-2	Roberts	5,278	1			5	6	8*	7	9			11				12	4							3	2	10
8	(a)	Oxford U	L 0-1		11,108	1		3*	5	6		8	9			12			11	7	4								2	10
13	(h)	Fulham	W 2-0	Stephens, Bell	4,443	1		3	5	6		7	9						11	8	4								2	10
20	(a)	Blackburn R	L 0-3		8,216	1		3	5	6*		7	9			12			11	8	4						10		2	
27	(h)	Brighton & HA	W 2-1	Otto, Currie	4,415	1		3	5	6		7	9			11				8	4								2	10
May 4	(a)	Crystal P	L 1-2	Otto, Currie	4,900	1		3	5	6		7	9			11				8	4*		12						2	10
6	(h)	Birmingham C	D 0-0		7,840	1		3*	5	6		7	9			11				12	4		8						2	10
11	(a)	Shrewsbury T	W 2-0	Laws, Beagrie	5,348	1		3	5	6		7	9			11					4		8						2	10
		Apps				38	6	29	27	40	30	31	34	41	5	34	14	2	15	20	32	15	3	4	8		8	6	11	9
		Sub apps					1			1	2	1	2	5			2	9				4			1					
		Goals							3		14		4		11				2	1			1			1		1	2

1 own-goal

FA Cup

Date		Opponent	Result	Scorers	Att.	O'Hanlon	Wood	Ward	Buckley	Mowbray	Nattrass	Mills	Hamilton	Otto	Sugrue	Currie	Gill	Scott	Bell	Roberts	McAndrew	Saxby								Round
Jan 5	(h)	Darlington	D 0-0		19,084	1		6	4	7	2	8	3	9		10				11	5										3
8	(a)	Darlington	L 1-2	McAndrew	14,237	1		6	4	7	2	8	3*	9		10			12	11	5										R
		Apps				2		2	2	2	2	2	2	2		2				2	2									
		Sub apps																	1											
		Goals																			1									

League Cup

Date		Opponent	Result	Scorers	Att.	O'Hanlon	Wood	Ward	Buckley	Mowbray	Nattrass	Mills	Hamilton	Otto	Sugrue	Currie	Gill	Scott	Bell												Round
Aug 29	(a)	Bradford C	L 0-2		4,788	1	2	8	4	5	6	7	3	9	10*	11	12														1/1
Sep 4	(h)	Bradford C	D 2-2	Buckley, Sugrue	3,980	1	2		4*	5	6	7	8	9	10	11	3	12													1/2
		Apps				2	2	1	2	2	2	2	2	2	2	2	1													
		Sub apps															1	1												
		Goals						1					1																	

1985-86
Division 2

Date	Opponent	Result	Scorers	Att.	Pears S	Laws B	Corden S	Pallister GA	Mowbray AM	Nattrass I	Roberts A	O'Riordan DJ	Stephens A	McAndrew A	Rowell G	Currie DN	Ward PT	Beagrie PS	Hamilton GJ	Kernaghan AN	Heard TP	Gill G	Cook M	Slaven BJ	McManus CE	Cooper CT	Ripley SE	Kite PD	Turnbull LM
Aug 17 (a)	Wimbledon	L 0-3		2,844	1	2	3*	4	5	6	7	8	9	10	11	12													
24 (h)	Fulham	W 1-0	Stephens	5,368	1	2			5			8	9	4	10	11*	3	6	7	12									
27 (a)	Charlton A	L 0-2		4,045	1	2			5			8	9	4	10	12	3	6	7	11*									
31 (h)	Brighton & HA	L 0-1		5,520	1	2			5			8	9	4	10		3*	11	7	12	6								
Sep 7 (a)	Hull C	D 0-0		7,710	1	2			5			8	9	4	10	11*		6		12	3	7							
10 (h)	Stoke C	D 1-1	Rowell	4,189	1	2			5			8	9	4	10	11		6			3	7							
14 (h)	Norwich C	D 1-1	Rowell (pen)	5,462	1	2			5	6		8	9	4	10			11			3	7*	12						
21 (a)	Sheffield U	W 1-0	Rowell	10,535	1	2			5	6		8	9	4	10			11	7		3								
28 (h)	Barnsley	D 0-0		5,572	1	2			5	6		8	9	4	10			11*	7		3			12					
Oct 5 (h)	Crystal P	L 0-2		4,991	1	2			5*	6		8		4	10			11	7	9	3			12					
12 (a)	Leeds U	L 0-1		14,095	1	2			5	6		8	10	4	12			11*	7		3			9					
19 (h)	Bradford C	D 1-1	Slaven	6,130	1	2		6	5					4	10			11	7		3	8		9					
22 (a)	Sunderland	L 0-1		20,541	1	2		6	5			10		4	11	12			7		3	8*		9					
26 (a)	Grimsby T	L 2-3	Stephens, Laws	4,378	1	2		6	5			10		4	11	12			7		3	8*		9					
Nov 2 (h)	Blackburn R	D 0-0		5,140	1	2		6	5			10		4	11			8	7		3			9					
16 (h)	Oldham A	W 3-2	Currie, Heard, Rowell	4,234	1	2		6	5			4			10	11			7		3	8		9					
23 (a)	Millwall	L 0-3		3,188	1	2		6	5			4			10	12		11	7*		3	8		9					
30 (h)	Shrewsbury T	W 3-1	Rowell, Heard, McAndrew	4,061	1	2		6	4			5	10	3	11				7			8		9					
Dec 7 (a)	Stoke C	L 2-3	Stephens, O'Riordan	7,646	1	2		6	4			5	10	3	11*	12			7			8		9					
14 (h)	Wimbledon	W 1-0	Mowbray	4,531	1	2		6	4			5	10	3	11				7			8		9					
21 (a)	Fulham	W 3-0	Slaven, Rowell 2	3,513	1	2		6	4			5	10	3	11				7			8		9					
26 (a)	Carlisle U	L 0-1		4,238	1	2		6	4			5	10	3	11				7			8		9					
28 (h)	Sunderland	W 2-0	Mowbray, McAndrew	19,701	1	2		6	4			5	10	3	11				7			8		9					
Jan 1 (h)	Huddersfield T	L 0-1		8,487	1	2		6	4			5	10	3	11				7			8		9					
11 (a)	Norwich C	L 0-2		13,050	1	2		6	4			5	10	3	11				7			8		9					
18 (a)	Brighton & HA	D 3-3	Rowell 2, Slaven	10,098		2		6	4			5	10	3	11				7			8	1	9					
25 (a)	Portsmouth	L 0-1		10,768		2		6	4			5	10	3	11				7			8	1	9					
Feb 1 (h)	Charlton A	L 1-3	Rowell (pen)	4,465	1	2		6*	4			5	10	3	11	12			7			8		9					
Mar 4 (h)	Grimsby T	W 3-1	Slaven 2, Mowbray	4,412	1	2		6	4			3	10	9				11			8			7					
8 (a)	Crystal P	L 1-2	Slaven	4,863	1	2		6	4			3	5*	10	9			11			8			7		12			
15 (h)	Leeds U	D 2-2	Currie 2	6,899	1	2		6	4			3	10			9		11			8			7					
18 (h)	Sheffield U	L 1-2	O'Riordan	5,736	1	2		6	4			3	10			9		11			8*			7		12			
22 (h)	Hull C	L 1-2	Currie	6,227	1	2		6	4			3				9		11	7			8		10*		12			
25 (a)	Barnsley	D 0-0		3,827	1	2		6	4			3				9		11	7					10	8				
29 (a)	Huddersfield T	W 3-0	Hamilton 2, Slaven	5,585	1	2		6	4			3				9		11	7					10	8				
31 (h)	Carlisle U	L 1-3	Hamilton	7,603	1	2		6	4			3				9	12	11	7*					10	8				
Apr 5 (a)	Blackburn R	W 1-0	Hamilton	4,049	1	2		6	4			5		3		9		11	7					10	8				
12 (h)	Portsmouth	W 1-0	Mowbray	7,188	1	2		6	4			5	10	3				11	9		8			7					
19 (a)	Oldham A	L 0-1		4,193		2		6	4			5*	10	3		12		11	9		8			7			1		1
23 (a*)	Bradford C	L 1-2	Oliver (og)	3,426		2		6	4			12	10	3				11*	9		8					5	6		1
26 (h)	Millwall	W 3-0	Beagrie, Slaven (pen), Laws	5,484	1	2		6	4			5	9	3				11	7		8*			10			12		
May 3 (a)	Shrewsbury T	L 1-2	Stephens	6,695	1	2		6	4			5	9	3		12		11	7					10					8*
			Apps		38	42	1	28	35	19	1	41	26	34	27	21	3	21	33	2	25	9	3	32	2	9	7	2	1
			Sub apps						2							5		4		4			3		2	1		1		
			Goals			2			4			2	4	2	10	4		1	4		2			8					

*Played at Leeds Road, Huddersfield, due to fire damage at Bradford.

1 own-goal

FA Cup

Date	Opponent	Result	Scorers	Att.	Pears S	Laws B	Corden S	Pallister GA	Mowbray AM	Nattrass I	Roberts A	O'Riordan DJ	Stephens A	McAndrew A	Rowell G	Currie DN	Ward PT	Beagrie PS	Hamilton GJ	Kernaghan AN	Heard TP	Gill G	Cook M	Slaven BJ	McManus CE	Cooper CT	Ripley SE	Kite PD	Turnbull LM	Round
Jan 13 (h)	Southampton	L 1-3	O'Riordan	12,703	1	2		6	4			5	10*	3	11	12			7			8		9						3
			Apps		1	1		1	1			1	1	1	1				1			1		1						
			Sub apps													1														
			Goals									1																		

League Cup

Date	Opponent	Result	Scorers	Att.	Pears S	Laws B	Corden S	Pallister GA	Mowbray AM	Nattrass I	Roberts A	O'Riordan DJ	Stephens A	McAndrew A	Rowell G	Currie DN	Ward PT	Beagrie PS	Hamilton GJ	Kernaghan AN	Heard TP	Gill G	Cook M	Slaven BJ	McManus CE	Cooper CT	Ripley SE	Kite PD	Turnbull LM	Round
Aug 20 (a)	Mansfield T	L 0-2		3,179	1	2		6	5		7*	8	9	4	10	11	3			12										1/1
Sep 3 (h)	Mansfield T	D 4-4	Pollard (og), Currie, Rowell 2 (1 pen)	4,051	1	2			5			8	12	4	10	11	3	6	7*	9										1/2
			Apps		2	2		1	2		1	2	1	2	2	2	2	1	1	1										
			Sub apps										1							1										
			Goals												2	1														

1 own-goal

1986-87
Division 3

Date	Opponent	Res	Scorers	Att	Pears S	Laws B	Cooper CT	Mowbray AM	Gill G	Parkinson GA	Slaven BJ	Stephens A	Hamilton GJ	Kernaghan AN	Ripley SE	Turnbull LM	Pallister GA	Proudlock P	Coyle RP	Kerr PA	Hodgson DJ	Spriggs S	Rowell G
Aug 23(h†)	Port Vale	D 2-2	Stephens 2	3,690	1	2	3	4	5	6	7	8	9	10*	11	12							
30(a)	Wigan A	W 2-0	Turnbull, Mowbray	2,904	1	2	3	4	10	5	7		9		11	8	6						
Sep 6(h)	Bury	W 3-1	Stephens 2, Slaven	6,499	1	2	3	4	10	5	7	8	9		11		6						
13(a)	Gillingham	D 0-0		4,888	1	2	3	4	10	5	7	8	9		11		6						
17(a)	Bristol R	W 2-1	Slaven 2	3,768	1	2	3	4	10	5	7	8	9		11		6						
20(h)	Chesterfield	W 2-0	Mowbray, Laws	7,633	1	2	3	4	10	5	7*	8	9		11	12	6						
27(a)	Fulham	D 2-2	Laws, Hamilton	3,852	1	2	3	4	10	5	7	8	9		11		6						
30(h)	Swindon T	W 1-0	Laws	9,221	1	2	3	4	10	5	7	8	9		11		6						
Oct 4(a)	Rotherham U	W 4-1	Stephens 2, Laws 2	4,321	1	2	3	4	10	5	7	8	9		11		6						
11(h)	Blackpool	L 1-3	Stephens	11,470	1	2	3	4	10	5	7*	8	9	12	11		6						
18(h)	Walsall	W 3-1	Stephens 2, Laws	8,349	1	2	3	4	10	5	7	8	9		11		6						
21(a)	Notts C	L 0-1		4,405	1	2	3	4	10	5	7	8	9		11*	12	6						
25(a)	Bristol C	D 2-2	Slaven, Laws	8,800	1	2	3	4	10	5	7	8	9		11		6						
Nov 1(h)	Bournemouth	W 4-0	Stephens, Slaven, Hamilton, Ripley	10,702	1	2	3	4	10*	5	7	8	9		11	12	6						
4(h)	Bolton W	D 0-0		10,092	1	2	3	4	10	5	7	8	9*		11	12	6						
8(a)	Darlington	W 1-0	Stephens	9,947	1	2	3	4	10	5	7	8		9	11		6						
22(a)	Newport C	W 1-0	Mowbray	2,788	1	2	3	4	10	5	7	8	12	9*	11		6						
29(h)	Chester C	L 1-2	Slaven	9,376	1	2	3	4	10*	5	7	8	12	9	11		6						
Dec 13(h)	Doncaster R	W 1-0	Mowbray	8,100	1	2	3	4	10	5	7	8	9				6	11					
21(a)	Brentford	W 1-0	Slaven	5,504	1	2	3	4	10	5	7	8*	9		11		6	12					
26(h)	Carlisle U	W 1-0	Gill	14,216	1	2	3	4	10	5	7	8	9		11		6						
27(a)	Mansfield T	D 1-1	Proudlock	5,042	1	2	3	4	10	5	7		9		11		6	8*	12				
Jan 1(a)	York C	L 1-3	Mowbray	8,611	1	2	3	4	10	5	7	8	9		11		6						
3(h)	Newport C	W 2-0	Gill, Stephens	9,595	1	2	3	4	10	5	7	8	9		11		6						
24(a)	Bury	W 3-0	Slaven 2, Laws (pen)	3,485	1	2	3	4	10	5	7	8			11		6			9			
Feb 7(h)	Bristol R	W 1-0	Ripley	9,610	1	2*	3	4	10	5	7	8		12	11		6			9			
14(a)	Chesterfield	L 1-2	Slaven	4,085	1		3	4	10	5	7	8	2		11		6			9			
17(h)	Port Vale	D 0-0		3,263	1		3	4	10	5	7	8	2		11		6			9			
21(h)	Fulham	W 3-0	Slaven, Hamilton 2	9,361	1		3	4	10	5	7	8	2		11		6			9			
28(a)	Swindon T	L 0-1		11,341	1		3	4		5	7	8	2	10	11		6			9			
Mar 3(a)	Bournemouth	L 1-3	Slaven	13,835	1		3	4		5	7	8	2	10	12		6*			9	11		
7(h)	Bristol C	W 1-0	Mowbray	10,220	1		3	4	10	5	7	8	9				6		2		11		
14(a)	Walsall	L 0-1		7,332	1		3	4	10	5	7	8*	2	12	11		6			9			
17(h)	Notts C	W 2-0	Stephens, Slaven	9,845	1		3	4		5	7	8	10	2	11		6			9			
21(a)	Blackpool	W 1-0	Stephens	7,132	1		3	4	12	5	7	8	10	2*	11		6			9			
28(h)	Rotherham U	D 0-0		9,569	1		3	4	12	5	7	8	10	2*	11		6			9			
Apr 5(h)	Darlington	D 1-1	Slaven	11,969	1		3	4	10	5	7	8	9		11		6					2	
11(a)	Bolton W	W 1-0	Slaven	5,858	1		3	4		5	7	8	9		11		6			10		2	
18(h)	York C	W 3-1	Ripley, Stephens, Turnbull	10,546	1		3	4		5	7	8	9		11	12	6			10		2*	
20(a)	Carlisle U	W 1-0	Pallister	5,993	1		3	4		5	7	8	2		11	9	6			10			
25(h)	Brentford	W 2-0	Slaven, Turnbull	9,942	1		3	4		5	7	8	2		11	9	6			10			
28(h)	Gillingham	W 3-0	Stephens, Slaven, Turnbull	11,937	1		3	4		5	7*	8	2		11	9	6		12	10			
May 2(a)	Chester C	W 2-1	Mowbray, Hamilton	3,788	1		3	4		5	7	8	2		11	9	6			10			
4(h)	Mansfield T	W 1-0	Hamilton (pen)	13,545	1		3	4	12	5	7	8	2		11	9*	6			10			
6(h)	Wigan A	D 0-0		18,523	1		3	4		5	7	8	2		11	9	6			10			
9(a)	Doncaster R	W 2-0	Hamilton, Ripley	3,556	1		3	4	2	5	7	8	9*		11	12	6			10			
			Apps		46	26	46	46	33	46	46	44	41	10	43	7	44	2	1	20	2	3	
			Sub apps						3				2	3	1	7		1	2				
			Goals			8		7	2		17	16	7		4	4	1	1					

†Played at the Victoria Ground, Hartlepool.

FA Cup

Date	Opponent	Res	Scorers	Att	Pears S	Laws B	Cooper CT	Mowbray AM	Gill G	Parkinson GA	Slaven BJ	Stephens A	Hamilton GJ	Kernaghan AN	Ripley SE	Turnbull LM	Pallister GA	Proudlock P	Coyle RP	Kerr PA	Hodgson DJ	Spriggs S	Rowell G	Round
Nov 15(h)	Blackpool	W 3-0	Slaven 3	11,205	1	2	3	4	10	5	7	8	9		11		6							1
Dec 7(a)	Notts C	W 1-0	Hamilton	7,415	1	2	3	4	10	5	7	8	9		11		6							2
Jan 10(h)	Preston NE	L 0-1		15,458	1	2*	3	4	10	5	7		9	14	11		6			12	8†			3
			Apps		3	3	3	3	3	3	3	2	2	1	3		3			1				
			Sub apps										1							1				
			Goals								3	1											

League Cup

Date	Opponent	Res	Scorers	Att	Pears S	Laws B	Cooper CT	Mowbray AM	Gill G	Parkinson GA	Slaven BJ	Stephens A	Hamilton GJ	Kernaghan AN	Ripley SE	Turnbull LM	Pallister GA	Proudlock P	Coyle RP	Kerr PA	Hodgson DJ	Spriggs S	Rowell G	Round
Aug 26(a)	Hartlepool U	D 1-1	Slaven	2,356	1	2	3	4	6	5	7	8	9	12	11								10*	1/1
Sep 2(h)	Hartlepool U	W 2-0	Ripley, Hamilton	7,735	1	2	3	4	10	5	7	8*	9		11	12	6							1/2
23(h)	Birmingham C	D 2-2	Stephens, Ripley	9,412	1	2	3	4	10	5	7	8	9		11		6							2/1
Oct 7(a)	Birmingham C	L 2-3*	Laws 2 (1 pen)	4,978	1	2	3	4	10*	5	7	8	9	12	11		6							2/2
			Apps		4	4	4	4	4	4	4	4	4		4		3						1	
			Sub apps											2		1								
			Goals			2					1	1	1		2									

*After extra-time

1987-88
Division 2

Date	Opponent	Result	Scorers	Att	Pears S	Glover DV	Cooper CT	Mowbray AM	Parkinson GA	Pallister GA	Slaven BJ	Stephens A	Hamilton GJ	Kerr PA	Ripley SE	Kernaghan AN	Gill G	Proudlock P	Laws B	Burke MS	Poole K	Senior TJ
Aug 15 (h) Millwall	D 1-1	Stephens	11,471	1	2	3	4	5	6	7	8	9	10	11							
22 (a) Stoke C	L 0-1		9,345	1	2	3	4	5	6	7	8	9*	10	11	12						
29 (h) Oldham A	W 1-0	Slaven	10,551	1	2	3	4	5	6	7	8	9	10	11*	12						
Sep 1 (a) Crystal P	L 1-3	Slaven	6,671	1		3	4	5	6	7	8	9	10	11			2				
5 (h) Swindon T	L 2-3	Stephens, Slaven	9,344	1		3	4	5	6	7	8	9	10	11†	12		2*	14			
8 (a) Aston Villa	W 1-0	Kerr	12,665	1	2	3	4	5	6	7	8	9	10	11							
15 (h) Bournemouth	W 3-0	Hamilton 2, Slaven	9,660	1	2	3	4	5	6	7	8*	9	10	11	12						
19 (h) Leeds U	W 2-0	Pallister, Kerr	12,051	1	2	3	4	5	6	7	8*	9	10	11	12						
26 (a) Blackburn R	W 2-0	Kernaghan, Kerr	6,879	1	2	3	4	5	6	7		9	10	11	8						
29 (h) Reading	D 0-0		10,093	1	2	3	4	5	6	7		9	10	11	8						
Oct 3 (a) Bradford C	L 0-2		14,114	1	2	3	4	5	6	7	12	9*	10	11	8						
10 (a) Huddersfield T	W 4-1	Slaven 3, Laws	6,169	1	2	3	4	5	6	7		9	10	12	8*			11			
17 (h) West Brom A	W 2-1	Slaven, Cooper	10,684	1	2	3	4	5	6	7		9	10	12	8*			11			
20 (h) Ipswich T	W 3-1	Pallister, Slaven, Kernaghan	10,491	1	2	3	4	5	6	7		9	10	12	8			11*			
24 (a) Birmingham C	D 0-0		7,404	1	2	3	4	5	6	7		9	10	11	8*			12			
31 (h) Shrewsbury T	W 4-0	Slaven 3, Kernaghan	10,183	1	2	3	4	5	6*	7		9	10	11	8			12			
Nov 4 (h) Manchester C	D 1-1	Glover	18,434	1	2	3	4	5	6*	7		9	10	11	8			12			
7 (a) Sheffield U	W 2-0	Slaven, Ripley	11,278	1	2	3	4	5	6	7		9	10	11	8						
14 (h) Hull C	W 1-0	Ripley	15,709	1	2	3	4	5	6	7	12	9	10	11	8*						
21 (a) Plymouth A	W 1-0	Hamilton	9,428	1	2	3	4	5	6	7		9	10	11	8						
28 (h) Barnsley	W 2-0	Slaven, Kernaghan	12,732	1	2	3	4	5	6*	7		9	10	11	8			12			
Dec 5 (a) Leicester C	D 0-0		9,411	1	2	3	4		6	7	12	9	10	11	8*			5			
12 (h) Stoke C	W 2-0	Hamilton, Slaven	12,289	1	2	3	4	12	6	7		9	10	11*	8			5			
19 (a) Bournemouth	D 0-0		6,792	1	2	3	4		6	7*		9	10	11	8			5	12		
26 (h) Blackburn R	D 1-1	Slaven	23,536	1	2*	3	4	12	6	7		9	10	11	8			5†	14		
28 (a) Leeds U	L 0-2		34,186	1		3	4	12	6	7		9	10	11	8			5*	2		
Jan 1 (a) Oldham A	L 1-3	Kerr	8,181	1		3	4	5	6	7		9	10	11†	8	12	2*	14			
16 (a) Millwall	L 1-2		8,617	1	2	3	4	5	6	7		9	10		8		11		1		
23 (h) Crystal P	W 2-1	Mowbray, Glover (pen)	12,597	1	2	3	4	5	6	7		9	10		8		11				
Feb 6 (a) Swindon T	D 1-1	Mowbray	9,941	1	2	3	4	5	6	7*		9	10		8	12	11				
14 (h) Aston Villa	W 2-1	Kernaghan, Mowbray	16,957	1	2	3	4	5	6	7		9	10†		8*	14	11	12			
20 (a) Reading	D 0-0		6,446	1	2	3	4	5	6	7		9	10†		8*	14	11	12			
27 (h) Bradford C	L 1-2	Cooper	21,079	1	2	3	4	5	6	7*		9	10†		8	12	11	14			
Mar 5 (a) West Brom A	D 0-0		8,316	1	2	3	4	5*	6	7		9	10		8†		11	12	14		
12 (h) Huddersfield T	W 2-0	Glover (pen), Kerr	13,866	1	2	3	4	5	6	7			10		8		11				9
19 (a) Shrewsbury T	W 1-0	Glover (pen)	5,603	1	2	3	4	5	6	7			10*		8	12	11				
26 (h) Birmingham C	D 1-1	Pallister	15,465	1	2	3	4	5	6	7			10	12	8		11*				9
Apr 2 (h) Sheffield U	W 6-0	Senior 2, Ripley 3, Slaven	17,340	1	2	3	4		6	7			10		8*	12	5	11			9
4 (a) Hull C	D 0-0		10,758	1	2	3	4		6	7			10		8		5	11			9
9 (h) Manchester C	W 2-1	Ripley, Hamilton	19,443	1		3	4	2	6	7			10		8		5	11			9
23 (a) Ipswich T	L 0-4		12,773	1	2*	3	4		6	7		12	10		8		5	11			9
30 (h) Plymouth A	W 3-1	Ripley, Kernaghan, Hamilton	16,615	1	12	3	4	2	6	7		5	10	8	9		11*				
May 2 (a) Barnsley	W 3-0	Ripley, Slaven 2	13,240	1		3	4	2	6	7		5	10	8*	9		11	12			
7 (h) Leicester C	L 1-2	Slaven	27,645	1	12		4	2	6	7		5	10	8*	9†		3	11			14
Apps				43	36	43	44	35	44	44	8	40	43	40	24	2	24	8	1		5
Sub apps				2			3				3	1	1	3	11	1	1	5	8		1
Goals					4	2	3		3	21	2	6	5	8	6			1			2

Play-Offs

Date	Opponent	Result	Scorers	Att	Pears S	Glover DV	Cooper CT	Mowbray AM	Parkinson GA	Pallister GA	Slaven BJ	Stephens A	Hamilton GJ	Kerr PA	Ripley SE	Kernaghan AN	Gill G	Proudlock P	Laws B	Burke MS	Poole K	Senior TJ	Round
May 15 (a) Bradford C	L 1-2	Senior	16,017	1	11		4	2	6	7		5	10		8		3				9	SF/1
18 (h) Bradford C	W 2-0*	Slaven, Hamilton	25,868	1	11	3	4	2	6	7		5	10		8*	12		14			9†	SF/2
25 (h) Chelsea	W 2-0	Senior, Slaven	25,531	1	11	3	4	2	6	7		5	10		8						9	F/1
28 (a) Chelsea	L 0-1		40,550	1	11	3	4	2	6	7		5	10		8						9	F/2
Apps				4	4	3	4	4	4	4		4	4		4		1				4	
Sub apps																1		1				
Goals							2			1											2	

*After extra-time

FA Cup

Date	Opponent	Result	Scorers	Att	Pears S	Glover DV	Cooper CT	Mowbray AM	Parkinson GA	Pallister GA	Slaven BJ	Stephens A	Hamilton GJ	Kerr PA	Ripley SE	Kernaghan AN	Gill G	Proudlock P	Laws B	Burke MS	Poole K	Senior TJ	Round
Jan 9 (a) Sutton U	D 1-1	Pallister	5,600	1		3	4	5	6	7		9	10	11		8	2					3
12 (h) Sutton U	W 1-0*	Kerr	17,932		2	3	4	5	6	7		9*	10†		8	14	12	11	1			R
30 (a) Everton	D 1-1	Kerr	36,564	1	2	3	4	5	6	7		9	10		8		11					4
Feb 3 (h) Everton	D 2-2*	Mowbray, Kernaghan	25,235	1	2	3	4	5	6*	7		9	10		8	12	11					R
9 (a) Everton	L 1-2	Ripley	32,222	1	2†	3	4	5	6	7*		9	10		8	12	11	14				2R
Apps				4	4	5	5	5	5	5		5	5	4	1		4	1	1			
Sub apps															2	1		1	1			
Goals						1		1					2	1	1							

*After extra-time

League Cup

Date	Opponent	Result	Scorers	Att	Pears S	Glover DV	Cooper CT	Mowbray AM	Parkinson GA	Pallister GA	Slaven BJ	Stephens A	Hamilton GJ	Kerr PA	Ripley SE	Kernaghan AN	Gill G	Proudlock P	Laws B	Burke MS	Poole K	Senior TJ	Round
Aug 18 (a) Sunderland	L 0-1		15,770	1	2	3	4	5	6*	7	8	9	10	11	12							1/1
25 (h) Sunderland	W 2-0	Slaven, Mowbray	15,570	1	2	3	4	5	6	7	8	9	10*	11	12							1/2
Sep 23 (h) Aston Villa	L 0-1		11,424	1	2	3	4	5	6	7	8*	9	10	11	12							2/1
Oct 7 (a) Aston Villa	L 0-1		11,702	1	2	3	4	5	6	7		9	10	11	8*			12				2/2
Apps				4	4	4	4	4	4	4	3	4	4	4	1							
Sub apps															2	1		1				
Goals						1			1													

1988-89
Division 1

Player columns (left to right): Pears S, Parkinson GA, Cooper CT, Mowbray AM, Hamilton GJ, Kernaghan AN, Slaven BJ, Brennan MR, Senior TJ, Ripley SE, Glover DV, Gill G, Burke MS, Pallister GA, Kerr PA, Davenport P, Mohan N, Poole K, Proudlock P, Proctor MG, Barham MF

Date	Opponent	Result	Scorers	Att	Pears S	Parkinson GA	Cooper CT	Mowbray AM	Hamilton GJ	Kernaghan AN	Slaven BJ	Brennan MR	Senior TJ	Ripley SE	Glover DV	Gill G	Burke MS	Pallister GA	Kerr PA	Davenport P	Mohan N	Poole K	Proudlock P	Proctor MG	Barham MF
Aug 27 (a)	Derby C	L 0-1		19,432	1	2	3	4	5*	6	7	8	9†	10	11	12	14								
Sep 3 (h)	Norwich C	L 2-3	Mowbray, Burke	18,595	1	2	3	4	5	12	7	8	9*	10			11	6							
10 (a)	Manchester U	L 0-1		40,442	1	2	3	4	5	12	7	8	9				11	6		10*					
17 (h)	Wimbledon	W 1-0	Hamilton	17,709	1	2	3	4	5		7	8	9	11				6		10					
24 (a)	Tottenham H	L 2-3	Slaven, Mowbray	23,427	1	2	3	4	5		7	8	9	11				6		10					
Oct 1 (a)	Coventry C	W 4-3	Slaven 3, Burke	14,527	1	2	3		5	4	7	8			9		11	6		10					
8 (h)	West Ham U	W 1-0	Pallister	19,608	1	2	3	4	5	12	7	8		11	9*		14	6		10†					
22 (h)	Luton T	W 2-1	Slaven, Cooper	17,792	1	2	3	4	5	12	7	8		11	9*			6		10					
26 (a)	Newcastle U	L 0-3		23,927	1	2	3	4	5	12	7	8		11†	9		14	6		10*					
29 (h)	Millwall	W 4-2	Slaven, Ripley, Burke, Parkinson (pen)	19,788	1	2	3	4	5	12	7	8		11	9			6		10*					
Nov 5 (a)	Liverpool	L 0-3		39,489	1	2	3	4	5		7	8		11	9			6		10					
12 (h)	Queen's Park R	W 1-0	Brennan	20,565	1	2	3	4	5	12	7	8		11	9†		14	6		10*					
19 (a)	Arsenal	L 0-3		32,294	1	2	3	4	5†	12	7	8		11	9*		14	6		10					
26 (h)	Sheffield W	L 0-1		19,310	1	2	3	4	5*		7	8		11	9	12		6		10					
Dec 3 (a)	Nottingham F	D 2-2	Brennan, Ripley	17,742	1	2	3	4	5		7	8		11	9			6		10					
10 (h)	Aston Villa	D 3-3	Brennan, Hamilton, Mowbray	18,096	1	2	3	4	5	14	7*	8		11†	9	12		6		10					
17 (h)	Charlton A	D 0-0		16,065	1	2	3	4	5	12	7	8		11	9			6		10*					
26 (a)	Everton	L 1-2	Glover (pen)	32,651	1	2	3	4	5	12	7	8		11*	9†			6	14	10					
31 (a)	Norwich C	D 0-0		16,021	1	2	3	4	5		7	8		11	9			6		10					
Jan 2 (h)	Manchester U	W 1-0	Davenport	24,411	1	2*	3	4	5		7	8		11	9	12		6		10					
14 (a)	Southampton	W 3-1	Kerr, Slaven, Burke	13,157	1		3	4	5		7	8*				12	11	6	9	10	2				
21 (h)	Tottenham H	D 2-2	Cooper, Ripley	23,692	1	2	3	4	5		7	8*		11		12		6	9	10					
Feb 4 (h)	Coventry C	D 1-1	Slaven	17,352			3	4	5		7	8		11		12		6	9	10*	2	1			
18 (a)	Luton T	L 0-1		8,187		2	3	4	5	14	7	8*		11		12		6	9†	10		1			
21 (a)	Millwall	L 0-2		11,396		2	3	4	5	9	7			11				6	8	10		1			
26 (h)	Newcastle U	D 1-1	Slaven	24,385		2	3	4	5		7	8		11		12		6	9*	10		1			
Mar 11 (h)	Liverpool	L 0-4		25,197	1	2	3	4	5		7	8*			9			6	11	10			12		
18 (h)	Derby C	L 0-1		16,580	1	2	3	4	5		7			11	9			6	8	10					
25 (a)	Wimbledon	D 1-1	Slaven	5,275	1	2	3	4			7				9			6	8	10				5	11
27 (h)	Everton	D 3-3	Slaven, Parkinson (pen), Davenport	23,151	1	2	3	4		12	7				9*			6	8	10				5	11
Apr 1 (a)	Charlton A	L 0-2		6,696		2	3	4	14	12	7*				9			6	8	10		1		5	11†
8 (h)	Southampton	D 3-3	Hamilton, Slaven, Burke	16,983		2	3	4	9	12	7	8*					11	6	14	10†		1		5	
11 (a)	West Ham U	W 2-1	Slaven 2	16,217		2	3	4			7	8			9*	12	11	6		10		1		5	
15 (h)	Queen's Park R	D 0-0		10,347		2	3	4			7	8			9		11	6		10		1		5	
22 (h)	Nottingham F	L 3-4	Ripley, Slaven, Davenport	20,778		2	3*	4			7			11†	9	12		6	8	10		1		5	14
29 (a)	Aston Villa	D 1-1	Davenport	18,590		2		4	9	12	7	8		11*				6		10	3	1		5	
May 6 (h)	Arsenal	L 0-1		21,803		2		4	9	12	7	8*		11†				6		10	3	1		5	14
13 (a)	Sheffield W	L 0-1		20,582		2		4	9	12	7			11*				6	8	10	3	1		5	
Apps					26	36	35	37	35	5	36	25	4	36	8	6	21	37	18	23	5	12		10	3
Sub apps							1		1	18			4	2	8				2	1	1		1		1
Goals						2	2	3	3		15	3		4	1		5	1	1	4					

FA Cup

Date	Opponent	Result	Scorers	Att	Pears S	Parkinson GA	Cooper CT	Mowbray AM	Hamilton GJ	Kernaghan AN	Slaven BJ	Brennan MR	Senior TJ	Ripley SE	Glover DV	Gill G	Burke MS	Pallister GA	Kerr PA	Davenport P	Mohan N	Poole K	Proudlock P	Proctor MG	Barham MF	Round
Jan 7 (h)	Grimsby T	L 1-2	Slaven	19,190	1		3	4	5		7*	8		11	9			6		10	2		12			3
Apps					1		1	1	1		1	1		1	1			1		1	1					
Sub apps																							1			
Goals											1															

League Cup

Date	Opponent	Result	Scorers	Att	Pears S	Parkinson GA	Cooper CT	Mowbray AM	Hamilton GJ	Kernaghan AN	Slaven BJ	Brennan MR	Senior TJ	Ripley SE	Glover DV	Gill G	Burke MS	Pallister GA	Kerr PA	Davenport P	Mohan N	Poole K	Proudlock P	Proctor MG	Barham MF	Round
Sep 28 (h)	Tranmere R	D 0-0		12,084	1	2	3	4	5	12	7	8	9*	11				6		10						2/1
Oct 11 (a)	Tranmere R	L 0-1		8,617	1	2	3	4	5	12	7	8		11	9			6		10						2/2
Apps					2	2	2	2	2		2	2	1	2	1			2		2						
Sub apps										2																
Goals																										

1989-90
Division 2

Date	Opponent	Res	Scorers	Att	Poole K	Parkinson GA	Mohan NM	Mowbray AM	Putney TA	Pallister GA	Slaven BJ	Proctor MG	Davenport P	Kerr PA	Comfort A	Ripley SE	Kernaghan AN	Brennan MR	Burke MS	Coleman S	Gill G	Cooper CT	Pears S	McGee OE	Baird IJ	Phillips JN
Aug 19 (h) Wolves	W 4-2	Slaven 2, Proctor, Davenport	21,727	1	2	3	4	5	6	7	8	9	10*	11	12										
23 (a) Leeds U	L 1-2	Comfort	25,004	1	2	3	4	5	6	7	8	9		11	10										
27 (a) Sunderland	L 1-2	Slaven	21,569	1	2	3	4	5	6	7	8	9		11	10*	12									
Sep 2 (h) Sheffield U	D 3-3	Slaven 2, Comfort	17,897	1	2	3	4	6		7	8	9*		11	12			5	10						
9 (a) Barnsley	D 1-1	Burke	10,535	1	2	3	4	6†		7	8	12		11	9*			5	10	14					
16 (h) Bournemouth	W 2-1	Slaven, Proctor	16,077	1	2	3	4	6		7	8	12		11	9*			5	10†	14					
23 (a) Portsmouth	L 1-3	Slaven	7,305	1	2	3	4	6		7	8	12		11	9*			5	10†	14					
27 (h) Hull C	W 1-0	Proctor	16,382	1	2	3	4	6		7	8			11	9			5	10						
30 (a) Watford	L 0-1		10,102	1	2	3	4	6		7	8			11	9†			5	10*	12	14				
Oct 14 (h) Plymouth A	L 0-2		15,003	1		3	4	6		7	8	9*		11	12			5			2	10†	14		
18 (h) Brighton & HA	D 2-2	Mowbray, Parkinson (pen)	13,551	1	2		4	6		7*	8			11	9	12	10		5		3				
21 (a) Oldham A	L 0-2		6,835	1	2		4	6		7	8			11	9		10		5		3				
28 (h) West Brom A	D 0-0		14,076	1	2		4	6		7	8			11	9			5	10*	12	3				
30 (a) Port Vale	D 1-1	Kernaghan	7,708	1	2		4	6		7	8			11	9			5	10		3				
Nov 4 (a) Newcastle U	D 2-2	Proctor, Brennan	23,349	1	2		4	6		7	8			11*	9†	5	10		12	14	3				
11 (h) Swindon T	L 0-2		13,720	1	2	12	4	6		7	8			11		5	10		9†	14	3*				
18 (h) West Ham U	L 0-2		18,720	1	2	3	4	6		7	8			11	12	5	10		9*						
21 (a) Blackburn R	W 4-2	Kernaghan 3, Slaven	8,317	1	2	3	4	6		7	8			11		9	10		5						
25 (h) Oxford U	W 1-0	Slaven	13,756	1	2	3	4	6		7	8			11		9	10		5						
Dec 2 (a) Wolves	L 0-2		12,357	1	14	2†	4			7	8			11	9*	6	10		12	5	3				
9 (h) Leeds U	L 0-2		19,686	1	2		4	10		7	8			11	9	6*	12		5		3				
16 (h) Leicester C	W 4-1	Cooper 2, Slaven, Ripley	11,428		2		4	6		7	8			11	12†	9*	10	14	5		3	1			
26 (a) Bradford C	W 1-0	Slaven	10,008		2		4	6		7	8			11	12	9*	10		5		3	1			
30 (a) Ipswich T	L 0-3		14,290		2		4	6*		7	8			11	12	9	10		5		3	1			
Jan 1 (h) Stoke C	L 0-1		16,238		2		4			7	8			11	6	9*	10	12	5		3	1			
14 (h) Sunderland	W 3-0	Davenport, Slaven, Parkinson	17,698		2		4			7	8	9*		11	12	6	10		5		3	1			
20 (a) Sheffield U	L 0-1		15,950		2		4			7	8			11	6	9	10*		5		3	1	12		
Feb 3 (h) Portsmouth	W 2-0	Kerr, Slaven	15,295		2		4			7	8		10	11	6*		12		5		3	1		9	
10 (a) Bournemouth	D 2-2	Mowbray, Slaven	7,630		2	3	4			7	8		11*		6	12	10		5			1		9	
24 (a) Oxford U	L 1-3	Brennan	5,949		2	3	4			7	8		11*		6	12	10		5			1		9	
28 (a) Brighton & HA	L 0-1		5,504		2	3	4			7	8*		11		6	12	10		5			1		9	
Mar 3 (h) West Ham U	L 0-1		23,617		2		4			7	8*	12	11		6		10		5		3	1		9	
7 (h) Watford	L 1-2	Coleman	14,008		2		4	6		7	8		11				10		5		3	1		9	
10 (a) Hull C	D 0-0		6,602		2		4	6		7	8		11				10		5		3	1		9	
17 (h) Blackburn R	L 0-3		15,259		2		4†	6		7	8	12	11				10*	14	5			1		9	3
20 (a) Plymouth A	W 2-1	Baird, Brennan	7,185		2		4	6		7*	8	12	11				10		5			1		9	3
31 (h) Oldham A	W 1-0	Slaven	17,238		2		4	6†		7	8	12	11				10	14	5			1		9*	3
Apr 7 (a) West Brom A	D 0-0		9,458		2		4	6*		7	8	12	11				10		5			1		9	3
11 (h) Port Vale	L 2-3	Slaven, Davenport	14,973		2		4	6		7	8	12	11				10		5			1		9*	3
14 (a) Stoke C	D 0-0		8,636		2		4	6*		7	8	12	11				10		5			1		9	3
16 (h) Bradford C	W 2-0	Slaven, Baird	16,376		2		4	6		7	8	12	11				10*		5			1		9	3
21 (a) Leicester C	L 1-2	Slaven	9,203		2		4	6		7	8	12	11				10*		5			1		9	3
25 (h) Ipswich T	L 1-2	Baird	15,232		2		4	6		7*	8	12	11				10		5			1		9	3
28 (h) Swindon T	D 1-1	Slaven	9,532		2		4	6		7	8		11				10		5			1		9	3
May 2 (a) Barnsley	L 0-1		17,015		2		4	6		7	8	12	11				10		5*			1		9	3
5 (h) Newcastle U	W 4-1	Slaven 2, Baird 2	18,484		2		4	6		7	8		10	11					5			1		9	3
Apps				21	40	21	28	25	3	46	45	30	13	15	26	34	36	3	33	1	18	25	12	19	12
Sub apps				1	1					5	4			13	3	4	9	3		3		1			
Goals					2		2			21	4	3	1	2	1	4	3	1	1		2			5	

FA Cup

Date	Opponent	Res	Scorers	Att	Parkinson GA	Mowbray AM	Slaven BJ	Proctor MG	Kerr PA	Ripley SE	Kernaghan AN	Brennan MR	Coleman S	Cooper CT	Pears S	Round
Jan 6 (h) Everton	D 0-0		20,075	2	4	7	8*	11	12	6	9	10	5	3	1	3
10 (a) Everton	D 1-1*	Parkinson	24,352	2	4	7	8	11	12	6	9*	10	5	3	1	R
17 (a) Everton	L 0-1		23,866	2	4	7	8	11*	10	6	12	9	5	3	1	2R
Apps				3	3	3	3	3	1	3	2	3	3	3	3	
Sub apps									2		1					
Goals				1												

League Cup

Date	Opponent	Res	Scorers	Att	Poole K	Parkinson GA	Mohan NM	Mowbray AM	Putney TA	Slaven BJ	Proctor MG	Comfort A	Ripley SE	Kernaghan AN	Brennan MR	Coleman S	Cooper CT	Round
Sep 20 (h) Halifax T	W 4-0	Comfort, Slaven 2, Kernaghan	10,613	1	2	3	4	6	7	8	11		9	10	5		2/1
Oct 3 (a) Halifax T	W 1-0	Slaven	1,641	1	2	3	4	6*	7	8	11	12	9	10	5		2/2
25 (h) Wimbledon	D 1-1	Slaven	12,933	1	2		4	6	7	8	11		9	10	5	3	3
Nov 1 (a) Wimbledon	L 0-1		3,554	1	2		4	6	7	8	11		9	10	5	3	R
Apps				4	4	2	3	4	4	4	4		4	4	4	2	
Sub apps												1					
Goals									4		1		1				

1990-91
Division 2

Players (left to right): Pears S, Cooper CT, Phillips JN, Mowbray AM, Kernaghan AN, Wark J, Slaven BJ, Mustoe R, Baird IJ, Proctor MG, Hendrie JG, Ripley SE, Russell MC, Kerr PA, McGee OE, Putney TA, Coleman S, Parkinson GA, Walsh CD, Dibble AG, Arnold I, Pollock J, Poole K

Date	Opponent	Res	Scorers	Att	Pears	Cooper	Phillips	Mowbray	Kernaghan	Wark	Slaven	Mustoe	Baird	Proctor	Hendrie	Ripley	Russell	Kerr	McGee	Putney	Coleman	Parkinson	Walsh	Dibble	Arnold	Pollock	Poole
Aug 25 (h)	West Ham U	D 0-0		20,680	1	2	3	4	5	6	7	8	9	10	11												
Sep 1 (a)	Plymouth A	D 1-1	Slaven	6,266	1	2	3	4	5	6	7	8			11	9	10										
Sep 8 (h)	Notts C	W 1-0	Wark	17,380	1	2	3	4	5	6	7*	8	12		11	9	10										
Sep 15 (a)	Swindon T	W 3-1	Slaven 2, Mustoe	9,127	1	2	3	4	5	6	7	8	12		11	9	10*										
Sep 17 (a)	Port Vale	L 1-3	Russell	7,880	1	2	3	4	5	6	7*	8	12		11	9	10										
Sep 22 (h)	Oldham A	L 0-1		19,363	1	2	3	4	5	6	7	8	9		11	12	10*										
Sep 29 (h)	Leicester C	W 6-0	Phillips, Hendrie, Kerr 2, Slaven, Baird	16,174	1	2	3	4	5†	6	12	8	9		11	7*		10	14								
Oct 3 (a)	Newcastle U	D 0-0		17,023	1	2	3	4	5	6	7	8	9		11			10									
Oct 6 (a)	Watford	W 3-0	Mowbray, Baird 2	8,057	1	2	3	4	5	6	7	8	9		11			10									
Oct 13 (h)	Millwall	W 2-1	Rae (og), Hendrie	20,277	1	2	3	4	5	6	7	8	9		11			10									
Oct 20 (h)	Bristol R	L 1-2	Kerr	18,589	1	2	3	4	5	6*	7	8	9		11			10		12							
Oct 23 (a)	Wolves	L 0-1		17,285	1	2	3	4	5		7	8	9		11			6*	10	12							
Oct 27 (a)	Brighton & HA	W 4-2	Slaven 3, Baird	7,532	1	2	3	4	5	6	7	8	9		11†		14	10*		12							
Nov 3 (h)	Barnsley	W 1-0	Kerr	18,470	1	2	3	4	5		7	8	9*		11	12		10		6							
Nov 6 (a)	West Brom A	W 1-0	Slaven	10,521	1	2	3	4	5†		7	8	9		11	12		10		6*	14						
Nov 10 (h)	Charlton A	L 1-2	Baird	17,998	1	2	3	4	5		7*	8	9		11	12		10		6							
Nov 17 (a)	Portsmouth	W 3-0	Slaven, Baird, Stevens (og)	8,433	1	2	3	4	5	6	7	8*	9	14	11	12		10									
Nov 24 (a)	Oxford U	W 5-2	Baird 3 (2 pens), Slaven, Mustoe	5,262	1	2	3	4	5†	6	7	8	9	14	11	12		10*									
Dec 1 (h)	Hull C	W 3-0	Baird, Slaven, Kerr	17,024	1	2	3	4		6†	7	8	9*	14	11	12		10			5						
Dec 15 (a)	West Ham U	D 0-0		23,705	1	2		4		6	7	8	9		11*	12		10	3		5						
Dec 22 (h)	Blackburn R	L 0-1		17,206	1	2	3	4		6	7	8	9		11	12		10*			5						
Dec 26 (h)	Ipswich T	W 1-0	Baird	12,508	1	2	3	4			8	7	9	6	11	12		10*			5						
Dec 29 (h)	Bristol C	L 0-3		14,023	1	2	3	4			7	8	9	6	11	10					5						
Jan 1 (h)	Sheffield W	L 0-2		22,869	1	2	3	4			8	7	9	6*	11	12		10			5						
Jan 12 (h)	Plymouth A	D 0-0		14,198	1	2†	3	4			7	8*	9		11	12		10	14	6	5						
Jan 19 (a)	Notts C	L 2-3	Baird, Ripley	9,316	1		3	4			8	12	9		7	11*		10†		6	5	2	14				
Feb 2 (h)	Swindon T	W 2-0	Mustoe, Slaven	14,588	1		3	4			8	7	10	9	11*	12				6		2	5				
Feb 19 (a)	West Brom A	W 3-2	Slaven, Mustoe, Rees (og)	15,334			3	4			8	7	10	9						6	5	2	1				
Feb 23 (a)	Charlton A	W 1-0	Slaven	5,510			3	4			8	7	10†	9	14	11*		12		6	5	2	1				
Feb 26 (h)	Portsmouth	L 1-2	Parkinson (pen)	15,922			3	4			8	7	10	9		11*		12		6	5	2	1				
Mar 2 (a)	Hull C	D 0-0		6,828			3	4			8	7	10	9		11*		12		6	5	2	1				
Mar 9 (a)	Oxford U	D 0-0		14,029	3			4			8	7	10	9		11		12	2	6*			5	1			
Mar 12 (h)	Newcastle U	W 3-0	Slaven 2, Walsh	18,250			3	4	8†		7	10	9		11			12	2	6		5*	1	14			
Mar 16 (a)	Leicester C	L 3-4	Putney, Phillips, McGee	8,324			3	4			8	7	10*	9		11		12	2	6		5	1				
Mar 20 (a)	Millwall	D 2-2	Kerr, Mowbray	10,371			3	4			8	7	10	9		11		12	2	6		5*	1				
Mar 23 (h)	Watford	L 1-2	Baird	14,583			3	4	8†		7	10	9		11*		5	2	6			14	1	12			
Mar 30 (h)	Ipswich T	D 1-1	Mowbray	15,140		2	3	4			7	10	9	14	12	11			6†	5	8*		1				
Apr 1 (a)	Blackburn R	L 0-1		8,925		2	3	4			7	10	9	8	6	11				5			1				
Apr 6 (h)	Bristol C	W 2-1	Ripley 2	13,846			3		4		7*	10	9	8	6	11				5	2	12	1				
Apr 9 (h)	Port Vale	W 4-0	Baird, Ripley, Russell, Wark	15,053			3	4		14	12	10†	9	8	6*	11	7			5	2		1				
Apr 13 (a)	Sheffield W	L 0-2		30,598			3	4				12	10	9	8	6*	11	7		5	2		1				
Apr 20 (a)	Bristol R	L 0-2		5,722			3		14	4	12	10†	9	8	6	11	7*			5	2		1				
Apr 27 (h)	Wolves	W 2-0	Ripley, Hendrie	16,447		2	3		4		7	12		8	9	11	6*		10†	5			1		14		
May 4 (h)	Brighton & HA	W 2-0	Coleman, Ripley	18,054		2	3		4*		7	12	9	8	10†	11	14			6	5		1				
May 7 (a)	Oldham A	L 0-2		14,213		2	3		4		7		9	8	10	11				6	5		1				
May 11 (a)	Barnsley	L 0-1		14,494		2	3		4		7		9	8	10	11				6	5		1				
Apps					27	32	44	40	23	31	41	39	41	13	40	22	10	20	6	20	18	10	10	10	19		
Sub apps							1	1	5	2	3	5	1	17	1	4	2	3	1		3			2	1		
Goals							2	3		2	16	4	14		3	6	2	6	1	1	1	1	1				

3 own-goals

Play-Offs

Date	Opponent	Res	Scorers	Att	Pears	Cooper	Phillips	Mowbray	Kernaghan	Wark	Slaven	Mustoe	Baird	Proctor	Hendrie	Ripley	Russell	Kerr	McGee	Putney	Coleman	Parkinson	Walsh	Dibble	Round
May 19 (h)	Notts C	D 1-1	Phillips	22,343		2†	3	12	4		7	14	9	8	10†	11*				6	5		1		SF/1
May 22 (a)	Notts C	L 0-1		18,249			3	4	2		7*	10	9	8	11		12			6	5		1		SF/2
Apps						1	2	1	2		2	1	2	2	2	1				2	2		2		
Sub apps								1				1					1								
Goals							1																		

FA Cup

Date	Opponent	Res	Scorers	Att	Pears	Cooper	Phillips	Mowbray	Kernaghan	Wark	Slaven	Mustoe	Baird	Proctor	Hendrie	Ripley	Russell	Kerr	McGee	Putney	Coleman	Parkinson	Walsh	Round
Jan 5 (h)	Plymouth A	D 0-0		13,042	1	2	3†	4			7	8	9	6*	11	12		10	14	5				3
Jan 14 (a)	Plymouth A	W 2-1	Baird, Kerr	6,956	1		3	4			8	7*	9		12	11		10		6	5	2		R
Jan 26 (a)	Cambridge U	L 0-2		9,531			3	4			8	12	10	9	7	5				6		2	11*	4
Apps					2	1	3	3			2	2	3	1	2	2		2		2	2	2	1	
Sub apps												1				1		1						
Goals												1						1						

League Cup

Date	Opponent	Res	Scorers	Att	Pears	Cooper	Phillips	Mowbray	Kernaghan	Wark	Slaven	Mustoe	Baird	Proctor	Hendrie	Ripley	Russell	Kerr	McGee	Putney	Round
Aug 28 (h)	Tranmere R	D 1-1	Mowbray	10,667	1	2	3	4	5	6	7*	8	9		11	12	10				1/1
Sep 3 (a)	Tranmere R	W 2-1	Mustoe, Slaven	6,135	1	2	3	4	5	6	7	8	12		11	9*	10				1/2
Sep 25 (h)	Newcastle U	W 2-0	Mustoe 2	15,042	1	2	3	4	5	6		8	9		11	7		10			2/1
Oct 10 (a)	Newcastle U	L 0-1		12,778	1	2	3	4	5	6	7	8	9		11			10			2/2
Oct 30 (h)	Norwich C	W 2-0	Kerr, Hendrie	17,024	1	2	3	4	5		7	8	9		11			10		6	3
Nov 28 (a)	Aston Villa	L 2-3	Slaven 2	17,317	1	2	3	4	5*	6	7	8	9		11	12	10				4
Apps					6	6	6	6	6	5	5	5	6		6	2	2	4		1	
Sub apps													1			2					
Goals							1				3	3			1			1		1	

1991-92
Division 2

Date	Opponent	Result	Scorers	Att	Pears S	Parkinson GA	Phillips JN	Mowbray AM	Kernaghan AN	Falconer WH	Mustoe R	Proctor MG	Wilkinson P	Ripley SE	Hendrie JG	Slaven BJ	Fleming C	Shannon R	Hewitt J	Pollock J	Arnold I	Marwood B	Young MS	Mohan NM	Payton AP	Peake AM	Gittens J	Ironside I
Aug 17 (h)	Millwall	W 1-0	Mustoe	16,234	1	2	3	4	5	6	7	8	9	10	11													
21 (a)	Derby C	L 0-2		12,805	1	2	3	4	5	6	7*	8	9	10	11	12												
24 (a)	Ipswich T	L 1-2	Wilkinson	9,822	1	2†	3	4	5	6	7	8*	9	10	11	12	14											
27 (h)	Newcastle U	W 3-0	Wilkinson, Proctor, Falconer	16,970	1	2	3	4	5	6	7	8	9	10	11													
31 (h)	Portsmouth	W 2-0	Falconer, Slaven	12,320	1	2	3	4	5	6	7*	8	9	10	11	12												
Sep 4 (a)	Oxford U	W 2-1	Slaven 2	4,229	1	2	3	4	5	6	7	8	9	10*	11	12												
7 (a)	Watford	W 2-1	Wilkinson, Falconer	8,715	1	2	3	4	5	6	10	8	9		11	7												
14 (h)	Leicester C	W 3-0	Slaven, Wilkinson 2	16,633	1	2	3	4	5	6	10*	8	9	12	11	7												
17 (h)	Tranmere R	W 1-0	Falconer	16,550	1	2	3	4	5	6	12	8	9	10	11*	7												
21 (a)	Plymouth A	D 1-1	Wilkinson	5,280	1	2†	3	4	5	6	12	8*	9	10	11	7	14											
28 (h)	Sunderland	W 2-1	Slaven, Wilkinson	19,424	1	2	3	4	5		6	8	9	10	11	7												
Oct 5 (a)	Bristol R	L 1-2	Yates (og)	4,936	1	2	3	4	5		6†	8	9	10	11	7*	12	14										
12 (h)	Wolves	D 0-0		15,253	1	2	3	4	5	6		8	9	10†		7	12		11*	14								
19 (a)	Grimsby T	L 0-1		10,265	1	2	3	4	5	6		8	9			7			10	11								
26 (h)	Port Vale	W 1-0	Kernaghan	11,403	1	2	3	4	5	6		8*	9		11	7			12	10								
Nov 2 (h)	Southend U	D 1-1	Ripley	9,664	1	2†	3	4	5	6			9	10*	11	7	12		8			14						
5 (a)	Barnsley	L 1-2	Slaven	6,525	1	2*	3	4	5	6		8	9	10	11	7			12									
9 (a)	Brighton & HA	D 1-1	Slaven (pen)	8,270	1		3	4		6	14		9	10	11	12	2		8†	7*			5					
16 (h)	Charlton A	W 2-0	Mohan, Slaven	13,093	1		3	4		6		8	9		11	7	2			12			5	10*				
23 (h)	Bristol C	W 3-1	Payton, Slaven 2	12,928	1		3	4		6		8	9		11	7	2		12				5	10*				
30 (h)	Blackburn R	L 1-2	Slaven (pen)	15,541	1	14	3	4		6*		8	9		11	7	2†		12				5		10			
Dec 7 (h)	Swindon T	D 2-2	Wilkinson, Slaven	13,300	1		3	4		6		8	9	10		7	2		11*				5		12			
26 (a)	Newcastle U	W 1-0	Wilkinson	26,563	1		3	4		6		8	9			7	2		11*				5	12	10			
28 (a)	Portsmouth	L 0-4		12,324	1	14	3	4		6	12		9			7	2*		10†				5	8	11			
Jan 1 (h)	Derby C	D 1-1	Mohan	16,288	1	2	3	4		6*	11†		9	10		7			14				5	12	8			
11 (a)	Ipswich T	W 1-0	Payton	15,104	1	2	3	4		6			9	10*	11	7			8				5		12			
18 (a)	Millwall	L 0-2		8,125	1	2	3	4		6	12		9	10	11	7†							5		8*	14		
Feb 8 (a)	Port Vale	W 2-1	Hendrie, Mustoe	7,019	1	2	3	4		6	12		9	10	11	7*							5		8			
22 (h)	Blackburn R	D 0-0		19,353	1	2	3			6*	12		9	10†	11				14				5	8	7	4		
29 (a)	Swindon T	W 1-0	Kernaghan	10,379	1		3	4		6			9		11	7	2		10				5	8				
Mar 7 (h)	Cambridge U	D 1-1	Wilkinson	14,686	1	2†	3	4			12		9	10	11	7			8*				5	6	14			
14 (a)	Southend U	W 1-0	Slaven (pen)	7,272	1		3	4					9	10		7	2		8				5	6				
17 (h)	Cambridge U	D 0-0		7,318	1		3	4	11				9	10		7	2		8*				5	6	12			
21 (h)	Brighton & HA	W 4-0	Slaven 3 (1 pen), Hendrie	13,054	1		3	4	11				9*	10†	14	7	2		8				5	12	6			
28 (a)	Charlton A	D 0-0		8,250	1			4	3			8	9	10	11*	7	2						5	12	6			
Apr 1 (a)	Leicester C	L 1-2	Pollock	19,352	1			4	3	14			9	10	11*	7	2			8†			5	12	6			
4 (h)	Watford	L 1-2	Wilkinson	13,669	1			4	3	14			9	10	11	7*	2		8				5†	12	6			
7 (a)	Bristol C	D 1-1	Hendrie	12,814	1			4	11				9	10	12	7	2						5	8*	6			
10 (a)	Tranmere R	W 2-1	Proctor, Phillips	8,842	1		3	4†				8	9	10	11*	7	2						5	12	6	14		
13 (h)	Barnsley	L 0-1		12,743	1	14	3	4	7				9	10	11	12	2†		8*				5		6			
15 (h)	Oxford U	W 2-1	Ripley, Payton	11,928	1		3	8		14			9	10*	11	7	2						5	12	6†	4		
18 (h)	Plymouth A	W 2-1	Ripley, Falconer	15,086	1	14	3	8		6			9	12	11*	7†	2						5	10		4		
20 (a)	Sunderland	L 0-1		25,093	1		3	8		7†			9	10	11	12	2						5*	14	6	4		
25 (h)	Bristol R	W 2-1	Wilkinson 2	14,057	1		3	8					9	12	11*	7	2		14				5	10	6†	4		
28 (h)	Grimsby T	W 2-0	Phillips (pen), Wilkinson	18,570	1		3	8					9	12	11	7	2						5	10	6†	4		
May 2 (a)	Wolves	W 2-1	Gittens, Wilkinson	19,123			3	8					9	10	11†	7*	2		6				5	12	14		4	1
			Apps		45	23	43	17	38	25	28	27	46	36	38	28	23		21		3		27	8	20	9	1	1
			Sub apps			4					2	9			3		10	5	1	2	5	1		1	11	3	3	
			Goals				2		2	5	2	2	15	3	3	16				1				2	3		1	

1 own-goal

FA Cup

Date	Opponent	Result	Scorers	Att	Pears S	Parkinson GA	Phillips JN	Mowbray AM	Kernaghan AN	Falconer WH	Mustoe R	Proctor MG	Wilkinson P	Ripley SE	Hendrie JG	Slaven BJ	Fleming C	Shannon R	Hewitt J	Pollock J	Arnold I	Marwood B	Young MS	Mohan NM	Payton AP	Peake AM	Gittens J	Ironside I	Round
Jan 4 (h)	Manchester C	W 2-1	Kernaghan, Wilkinson	21,174	1	2	3		4		6*		9	7*	11	12			8				5	14	10				3
Feb 4 (a)	Sheffield W	W 2-1	Hendrie, Wilkinson	29,772	1	2	3		4		6	12	9	10	11*				7*				5	14	8				4
15 (a)	Portsmouth	D 1-1	Kernaghan	18,138	1	2	3		4		6	12	9	10†	11				7*				5	14	8				5
26 (h)	Portsmouth	L 2-4	Wilkinson 2	19,479	1	2	3				6		9	10	11	12				4			5	8*	7				R
			Apps		4	4	4		3		4		4	4	3	1			4				4	1	4				
			Sub apps									2								1		1		3					
			Goals						2				4		1														

League Cup

Date	Opponent	Result	Scorers	Att	Pears S	Parkinson GA	Phillips JN	Mowbray AM	Kernaghan AN	Falconer WH	Mustoe R	Proctor MG	Wilkinson P	Ripley SE	Hendrie JG	Slaven BJ	Fleming C	Shannon R	Hewitt J	Pollock J	Arnold I	Marwood B	Young MS	Mohan NM	Payton AP	Peake AM	Gittens J	Ironside I	Round
Sep 24 (h)	Bournemouth	D 1-1	Wilkinson	10,577	1	2	3	4	5	6*	12	8	9	10	11	7													2/1
Oct 8 (a)	Bournemouth	W 2-1*	Hendrie, Parkinson (pen)	5,528	1	2	3	4	5	6		8	9	10*	11	12		7†	14										2/2
29 (h)	Barnsley	W 1-0	Wilkinson	9,381	1	2	3	4	5	6			9		11	7	12		8		10*								3
Dec 3 (h)	Manchester C	W 2-1	Mustoe, Wilkinson	17,286	1		3	4		6		8	9	10		7	2		11				5						4
Jan 8 (a)	Peterborough U	D 0-0		15,302	1	2	3	4		6		8	9		11	7			10				5						5
Feb 12 (h)	Peterborough U	W 1-0	Ripley	21,973	1	2	3	4		6	7		9	10	11				8				5						R
Mar 4 (h)	Manchester U	D 0-0		25,572	1	2	3	4		6*	12		9	10	11	7			8				5						SF/1
11 (a)	Manchester U	L 1-2*	Slaven	45,875	1		3	4	14	6*	12		9	10	11†	7	2		8				5						SF/2
			Apps		8	6	8	3	8	1	7	4	8	7	7	6	2	1	6		1		5						
			Sub apps								1	1		2								1	1		1				
			Goals			1					1		3	1	1	1													

*After extra-time

1992-93
FA Premier League

Player columns: Pears S · Morris CB · Phillips JN · Kernaghan AN · Whyte D · Peake AM · Wright TE · Mustoe R · Wilkinson P · Hendrie JG · Falconer WH · Slaven BJ · Gittens J · Ironside I · Pollock J · Parkinson GA · Horne BS · Kavanagh GA · Proctor MG · Fleming C · Moore AT · Hignett CJ · Mohan NM · Kamara C · Marshall DW · Collett AA

Date		Opponent	Res	Scorers	Att	Pears	Morris	Phillips	Kernaghan	Whyte	Peake	Wright	Mustoe	Wilkinson	Hendrie	Falconer	Slaven	Gittens	Ironside	Pollock	Parkinson	Horne	Kavanagh	Proctor	Fleming	Moore	Hignett	Mohan	Kamara	Marshall	Collett
Aug 15	(a)	Coventry C	L 1-2	Wilkinson	12,681	1	2	3	4	5	6	7	8*	9	10	11	12														
19	(h)	Manchester C	W 2-0	Slaven 2	15,369		2	3	4	5	6		10*	12	9	11	8	7	1												
22	(h)	Leeds U	W 4-1	Wilkinson 2, Wright, Hendrie	18,649		2	3	4	5	6		10	14	9†	11	8	7*	1	12											
29	(a)	Southampton	L 1-2	Wilkinson	13,003		2	3	4	5	6		10	11	9		8	7	1												
Sep 1	(h)	Ipswich T	D 2-2	Kernaghan, Wilkinson	14,255			3	4	5	6	10	11	9			8	7	1†		2	12									
5	(h)	Sheffield U	W 2-0	Falconer, Wright	15,179		2	3	4	5	6	10	11	9			8	7	1												
12	(a)	Manchester C	W 1-0	Flitcroft (og)	25,244		2	3	4	5	6	10	7	9	11		8		1												
19	(a)	Queen's Park R	D 3-3	Kernaghan, Wright, Falconer	12,272		2	3	4	5		10	11	9	7	8	12		1	6*											
26	(a)	Aston Villa	L 2-3	Slaven, McGrath (og)	20,905		2	3	4	5	6		11	8	9		7		1	10											
Oct 3	(h)	Manchester U	D 1-1	Slaven	24,172	1	2	3		5	6		10	8	9	12	7	4	1	11*											
17	(a)	Tottenham H	D 2-2	Mustoe, Wilkinson	24,735	1	2	3	4	5		10	8	9			7*		6			11	12								
21	(a)	Nottingham F	L 0-1		17,846	1	2	3	4	5		10		9			7		6		8*	11	12								
24	(h)	Sheffield W	D 1-1	Wilkinson	18,414	1	2	3	4			11		9			7		6		10	8	5								
31	(a)	Norwich C	D 1-1	Wilkinson	14,449	1	12	3	4	5		7*		9	11	8			6		10	2									
Nov 7	(a)	Liverpool	L 1-4	Phillips (pen)	34,974	1	12	3	4*	5			7	9	11	8	14		6		10†	2									
21	(h)	Wimbledon	W 2-0	Hendrie, Morris	14,524	1	11	3*		5			6	9	10	7			4	8†	14	12	2								
28	(a)	Oldham A	L 1-4	Falconer	12,401	1				5			11	4	9	7			6	12	3	14	10†	2			8*				
Dec 5	(h)	Blackburn R	W 3-2	Hendrie 3	20,096	1		3		5		8		11	6*	9	7			12				14	2		10†	4			
11	(h)	Chelsea	D 0-0		15,599	1		3		5		8		11		9	7			6*			12		2		10	4			
19	(a)	Arsenal	D 1-1	Seaman (og)	23,197	1		3		5		8		11†	9		7		12	6			14		2		10*	4			
26	(a)	Everton	D 2-2	Hignett 2	24,391	1		3		5		8		11	9		7		12	6*					2		10	4			
28	(h)	Crystal P	L 0-1		21,123	1		3		5		8		11	9		7		12	6*			14		2†		10	4			
Jan 4	(h)	Queen's Park R	L 0-1		15,616	1		3				8	10*		9		11	12	5				7				4				
17	(a)	Aston Villa	L 1-5	Hignett	19,977	1		3	4†			8	10		9	11	6	5		12	7*						14	2			
26	(h)	Southampton	W 2-1	Mohan, Wilkinson	13,921	1	4	3				10	7		9	11	6			8					2		5				
30	(a)	Leeds U	L 0-3		30,344	1	4	3				10	7*		9	11	6			8					2		12	5			
Feb 6	(h)	Coventry C	L 0-2		14,008	1	2†	3				10	12		9	11*	6	7	5	14							8	4			
9	(a)	Sheffield U	L 0-2		15,184	1†			4			10*	9					7	6	14	8	3		12	2		11	5			
20	(h)	Nottingham F	L 1-2	Phillips	15,639	1	12	3	4			6	11		9			7	5		2*		14				8†	10			
27	(a)	Manchester U	L 0-3		36,251	1	2	3				4	6	11	8*	9	7			12							5	10			
Mar 2	(a)	Ipswich T	W 1-0	Wilkinson	15,430		2	3	4	6	5	11	8	9	7	12			1								10*				
9	(a)	Wimbledon	L 0-2		5,821	1	2	3	4	6	5	11*	8	9	7	10	12														
13	(h)	Liverpool	L 1-2	Nicol (og)	22,463		2	3	6*	5	12	8	9	7	10				1								11	4			
20	(a)	Blackburn R	D 1-1	Hendrie	14,041		2*	3	6	5	7	8	9	11	10				1								4	12			
22	(h)	Oldham A	L 2-3	Mohan, Hignett	12,290			3	6	5*	11	8†	9	7	10				1					2			14	4	12		
Apr 3	(a)	Chelsea	L 0-4		13,043			3	5	6		11	8	9	7	10			1					2			4*		12		
6	(h)	Arsenal	W 1-0	Hendrie	12,726	1		3	4		6			9	7					10		8		2			11	5			
10	(h)	Everton	L 1-2	Wilkinson	16,627	1		3	4	12	6			9	7					10		8*		2	14		11†	5			
12	(a)	Crystal P	L 1-4	Wilkinson	15,123	1		3	4		6			9	7					10		8		2			11	5			
20	(h)	Tottenham H	W 3-0	Wright 2, Wilkinson	14,472	1		3	4	5	6	8		9	7					10				2			11				
May 1	(a)	Sheffield W	W 3-2	Falconer, Pollock, Hendrie	25,949		5	3			6	10	11†	9	7	14				8*				2			4			12	1
8	(h)	Norwich C	D 3-3	Falconer, Wilkinson, Hendrie	15,155			3*	4	5	6		11	9	7	8								2	12	10†			14		1
Apps						26	22	40	22	34	33	34	21	41	31	22	13	13	11	17	4	3	6	6	22		18	18	3		2
Sub apps							3			1		2	2			1	6	5		1	5		1	4	5	2	2	3		2	3
Goals							1	2	2			5	1	14	9	5	4			1							4	2			

4 own-goals

FA Cup

Date		Opponent	Res	Scorers	Att	Pears	Morris	Phillips	Kernaghan	Whyte	Peake	Wright	Mustoe	Wilkinson	Hendrie	Falconer	Slaven	Gittens	Ironside	Pollock	Parkinson	Horne	Kavanagh	Proctor	Fleming	Moore	Hignett	Mohan	Kamara	Marshall	Collett	Round
Jan 13	(h)	Chelsea	W 2-1	Wright, Falconer	16,766	1		3				8	11	9	7	10			5	12	6†	14	2*				4					3
23	(a)	Nottingham F	D 1-1	Falconer	22,296	1	4	3				10	7	9	11	6				8			2				5					4
Feb 3	(h)	Nottingham F	L 0-3		20,514	1	4	3				10†	7	9	11	6	14			8*			12				2	5				R
Apps						3	2	3				3	3	3	3	3			1	2			3				3					
Sub apps																	1				1	1	1							
Goals												1				2														

League Cup

Date		Opponent	Res	Scorers	Att	Pears	Morris	Phillips	Kernaghan	Whyte	Peake	Wright	Mustoe	Wilkinson	Hendrie	Falconer	Slaven	Gittens	Ironside	Pollock	Parkinson	Horne	Kavanagh	Proctor	Fleming	Moore	Hignett	Mohan	Kamara	Marshall	Collett	Round
Sep 23	(a)	Newcastle U	D 0-0		25,814		2	3	4	5		10	11	9	7	8*	12		1	6												2/1
Oct 7	(h)	Newcastle U	L 1-3	Wilkinson	24,390		2	3	4	5	6†	10	8	9	11*		7	14	1	12												2/2
Apps							2	2	2	2	1	2	2	2	2	1	1		2	1											
Sub apps																	1	1		1										
Goals														1																

Middlesbrough Against Other League Clubs

Since September 1899, Middlesbrough have played 91 other Football League clubs. Some clubs, like Bradford, New Brighton Tower and Glossop have dropped out of the League. Some, like Leicester Fosse, Woolwich Arsenal and Burslem Port Vale have modified their names. Some clubs have totally changed their names from the original choice registered with the Football League. For example, Small Heath became Birmingham and then Birmingham City, Newton Heath became Manchester United etc. The names listed here are the names by which the clubs are currently known or were last known in the case of those who have dropped out of the League. Three points for a win started in 1981-82. Football League positions of clubs sharing the same number of points was originally decided on goal-average, but since season 1977 the Football League positions have been determined by goal-difference, although the new FA Premier League relied on most goals scored. Play-off games in 1987-88 against Bradford City and Chelsea and in 1990-91 against Notts County are not included.

		HOME					AWAY					
	P	W	D	L	F	A	W	D	L	F	A	Pts
AFC Bournemouth	8	4	0	0	12	2	0	3	1	4	6	14
Arsenal	92	20	13	13	69	55	5	12	29	44	112	76
Aston Villa	102	20	14	17	78	66	13	9	29	59	120	91
Barnsley	38	13	3	3	36	10	6	5	8	29	24	52
Birmingham City	78	15	14	10	54	44	7	12	20	44	72	71
Blackburn Rovers	90	18	11	16	74	61	9	12	24	55	104	82
Blackpool	52	17	4	5	62	31	6	10	10	31	42	61
Bolton Wanderers	86	21	10	12	82	52	6	10	27	52	97	76
Bradford	8	2	0	2	9	9	0	1	3	3	9	5
Bradford City	32	9	3	4	31	25	9	1	6	18	17	42
Brentford	12	4	1	1	10	2	1	2	3	6	10	15
Brighton & HA	30	9	5	1	35	10	6	3	6	24	25	44
Bristol City	54	21	5	1	52	15	4	11	12	24	44	69
Bristol Rovers	24	7	2	3	26	15	5	2	5	19	26	31
Burnley	46	12	7	4	54	28	2	7	14	21	59	42
Burton United	6	3	0	0	16	2	0	1	2	2	8	7
Bury	42	9	7	5	38	30	6	5	10	32	32	44
Cambridge United	6	0	2	1	2	3	0	2	1	2	2	4
Cardiff City	42	9	7	5	32	19	3	3	15	21	44	35
Carlisle United	28	7	1	6	15	15	4	4	6	14	17	32
Charlton Athletic	64	17	6	9	59	39	8	5	19	40	64	67
Chelsea	78	18	14	17	70	45	5	10	24	33	76	72
Chester City	2	0	0	1	1	2	1	0	0	2	1	3
Chesterfield	8	3	0	1	11	2	1	1	2	5	11	10
Colchester United	2	1	0	0	4	0	1	0	0	3	2	4
Coventry City	26	2	6	5	15	18	3	3	7	15	21	20
Crystal Palace	28	6	5	3	20	11	3	3	8	17	29	28
Darlington	8	3	1	0	12	4	4	0	0	10	1	16
Derby County	102	27	12	12	100	57	12	11	28	78	102	101
Doncaster Rovers	14	7	0	0	24	4	3	1	3	11	8	23
Everton	86	20	12	11	74	47	3	9	31	44	104	67
Fulham	40	11	2	7	39	24	8	3	9	30	31	47
Gainsborough Trinity	6	2	1	0	12	3	1	1	1	5	7	8
Gillingham	4	1	1	0	4	1	0	1	1	1	5	5
Glossop	4	1	1	0	7	2	0	0	2	0	3	3
Grimsby Town	52	17	3	6	54	27	7	3	16	45	56	57
Huddersfield Town	80	24	8	8	83	43	9	9	22	37	63	86
Hull City	36	13	2	3	36	14	3	9	6	22	26	46
Ipswich Town	42	9	5	7	36	28	5	2	14	19	40	43
Leeds United	62	16	9	6	55	31	7	6	18	35	72	63
Leicester City	56	15	5	8	58	35	4	11	13	34	46	57
Leyton Orient	36	12	2	4	41	19	3	6	9	15	35	38
Lincoln City	20	6	3	1	20	10	3	3	4	17	24	24
Liverpool	108	19	17	18	91	76	13	13	28	59	119	94
Loughborough Town	2	1	0	0	3	0	0	1	0	1	1	3
Luton Town	22	4	3	4	11	14	3	1	7	12	21	19
Manchester City	94	27	12	8	90	38	6	8	33	55	106	89
Manchester United	76	16	10	12	74	57	8	6	24	47	80	65
Mansfield Town	4	2	0	0	2	0	1	1	0	6	5	8

		HOME					AWAY					
	P	W	D	L	F	A	W	D	L	F	A	Pts
Millwall	26	10	2	1	23	8	2	2	9	8	23	32
New Brighton	4	2	0	0	7	3	0	1	1	2	4	5
Newcastle United	88	22	14	8	68	46	10	11	23	47	76	94
Newport County	2	1	0	0	2	0	1	0	0	1	0	6
Northampton Town	4	2	0	0	2	0	0	1	1	3	4	5
Norwich City	40	11	5	4	38	16	4	6	10	19	31	41
Nottingham Forest	50	11	10	4	41	27	5	8	12	36	46	50
Notts County	50	19	2	4	59	22	4	6	15	30	47	58
Oldham Athletic	44	11	5	6	33	24	4	4	14	17	42	43
Oxford United	22	8	1	2	15	6	4	4	3	18	17	33
Peterborough United	2	1	0	0	2	1	1	0	0	2	1	4
Plymouth Argyle	28	8	2	4	34	15	4	7	3	21	24	37
Portsmouth	82	26	10	5	96	48	10	7	24	48	74	94
Port Vale	28	10	2	2	36	12	3	4	7	17	26	35
Preston North End	80	23	10	7	74	43	12	9	19	49	64	89
Queen's Park Rangers	28	6	4	4	20	17	0	7	7	11	31	25
Reading	8	1	3	0	7	2	1	2	1	4	4	9
Rotherham United	30	5	4	6	32	20	9	1	5	29	24	36
Scunthorpe United	14	5	0	2	19	11	1	4	2	9	8	16
Sheffield United	86	23	8	12	92	52	10	9	24	42	74	89
Sheffield Wednesday	80	22	9	9	94	46	8	5	27	43	80	77
Shrewsbury Town	12	5	1	0	15	3	2	1	3	6	6	22
Southampton	32	7	5	4	27	14	3	3	10	21	34	30
Southend United	2	0	1	0	1	1	1	0	0	1	0	4
South Shields	6	1	1	1	7	3	1	2	0	3	2	7
Stockport County	8	3	1	0	13	1	3	1	0	7	3	14
Stoke City	80	25	10	5	78	33	9	8	23	43	71	88
Sunderland	106	24	12	17	83	69	6	14	33	46	98	90
Swansea City	34	12	3	2	49	21	4	4	9	27	38	41
Swindon Town	26	7	3	3	23	12	6	2	5	13	14	35
Torquay United	2	1	0	0	4	0	0	0	1	1	2	2
Tottenham Hotspur	54	18	6	3	58	25	7	5	15	47	66	62
Tranmere Rovers	2	1	0	0	1	0	1	0	0	2	1	6
Walsall	12	3	1	2	11	8	1	2	3	4	6	12
Watford	14	3	1	3	13	10	4	0	3	9	7	17
West Bromwich Albion	70	21	9	5	58	27	7	8	20	32	59	77
West Ham United	34	7	5	5	29	18	6	3	8	25	26	36
Wigan Athletic	2	0	1	0	0	0	1	0	0	2	0	4
Wimbledon	8	3	0	1	6	4	0	2	2	2	7	11
Wolverhampton W	72	21	11	4	71	36	13	7	16	49	70	89
Workington	2	1	0	0	3	2	1	0	0	2	1	4
York City	2	1	0	0	3	1	0	0	1	1	3	3

Middlesbrough have yet to play the following teams in the Football League: Crewe Alexandra, Exeter City, Hartlepool United, Hereford United, Rochdale, Scarborough, Wrexham and, of course, Wycombe Wanderers. There are several former League teams who they never played, including Accrington Stanley, Aldershot, Barrow, Southport and the most recently departed, Halifax Town.

Middlesbrough In Other Competitions

Anglo-Italian Cup

1969-70
May 2 v AS Roma (h) 1-0
Hickton
Whigham; R.A.Smith, Jones, G.Smith, Gates, Spraggon, McMordie, Laidlaw, McIlmoyle, Hickton, Mills.
Att: 14,196
May 8 v Lanerossi Vicenza (h) 2-0
Laidlaw, Hickton (pen)
Whigham; R.A.Smith(Webb), Jones, G.Smith, Gates, Spraggon, Downing, McMordie(Moody), McIlmoyle, Hickton, Laidlaw.
Att: 6,656
May 10 v AS Roma (a) 1-1
Downing
Whigham; R.A.Smith(Moody), Jones, G.Smith, Gates, Spraggon, Downing, Laidlaw, Webb, Hickton, McMordie.
May 24 v Lanerossi Vicenza (a) 2-2
Gates, McMordie
Whigham; R.A.Smith, Jones, G.Smith, Gates, Spraggon, Downing, McMordie, Hickton, Laidlaw, Mills.
Att: 2,000

	Apps	Subs	Gls
Downing DG	3	0	1
Gates WL	4	0	1
Hickton J	4	0	2
Jones GE	4	0	0
Laidlaw JD	4	0	1
McIlmoyle H	2	0	0
McMordie A	4	0	1
Mills DJ	2	0	0
Moody A	0	2	0
Smith G	4	0	0
Smith RA	4	0	0
Spraggon F	4	0	0
Webb SJ	1	1	0
Whigham W	4	0	0
	44	3	6

Summary	Pld	W	D	L	F	A	Pts
Home	2	2	0	0	3	0	7
Away	2	0	2	0	3	3	5
	4	2	2	0	6	3	12

Texaco Cup

Qualifying Rounds
1974-75
Aug 3 v Carlisle United (h) 0-1
Platt; Craggs, Spraggon, Souness, Boam, Maddren, Murdoch, Mills(M.Smith), Hickton, Foggon, Armstrong.
Att: 10,692
Aug 6 v Sunderland (a) 1-0
Armstrong
Platt; Craggs, Spraggon, Souness, Boam, Taylor, Brine(H.Charlton), Mills, Hickton, M.Smith, Armstrong.
Att: 22,828
Aug 10 v Newcastle United (a) 0-4
Platt; Craggs, J.Cochrane, Brine, Boam, Maddren, Murdoch, Mills, Hickton, M.Smith, Armstrong.
Att: 11,575

	Apps	Subs	Gls
Armstrong D	3	0	1
Boam SW	3	0	0
Brine PK	2	0	0
Charlton H	0	1	0
Cochrane JK	1	0	0
Craggs JE	3	0	0
Foggon A	1	0	0
Hickton J	3	0	0
Maddren WD	2	0	0
Mills DJ	3	0	0
Murdoch RW	2	0	0
Platt JA	3	0	0
Smith M	2	1	0
Souness GJ	2	0	0
Spraggon F	2	0	0
Taylor B	1	0	0
	33	2	1

Summary	Pld	W	D	L	F	A
Home	1	0	0	1	0	1
Away	2	1	0	1	1	4
	3	1	0	2	1	5

Anglo-Scottish Cup

Qualifying Rounds
1975-76
Aug 2 v Sunderland (h) 3-2
Souness, Craggs, Murdoch
Platt; Craggs, Bailey, Souness, Boam, Maddren, Murdoch, Mills, Hickton(Brine), Cooper, Armstrong.
Att: 12,849
Aug 5 v Carlisle United (h) 4-1
Willey 2, Hickton (pen), Bailey
Platt; Craggs, Bailey, Souness, Boam, Maddren, Murdoch, Mills, Hickton, Willey, Armstrong.
Att: 8,737
Aug 9 v Newcastle United (a) 2-2
Willey, Armstrong
Cuff; Craggs, Bailey, Souness, Boam, McAndrew, Brine, Mills(M.Smith), Willey, H.Charlton, Armstrong.
Att: 12,362
Quarter-final (lst leg)
Sep 16 v Aberdeen (h) 2-0
Hickton (pen), Mills
Platt; Craggs, Cooper, Souness, Boam, McAndrew, Murdoch(H.Charlton), Mills, Hickton, Foggon, Armstrong.
Att: 13,965
Quarter-final (2nd leg)
Oct 1 v Aberdeen (a) 5-2 (agg 7-2)
Hickton 2, Mills 2, Foggon
Platt(Cuff); Craggs, Cooper, Souness, Boam, Maddren, Brine, Mills, Hickton, Foggon(Murdoch), Armstrong.
Att: 9,200
Semi-final (1st leg)
Oct 21 v Mansfield Town (h) 3-0
Armstrong 2, Hickton
Platt; Craggs, Cooper, Souness, Boam, Maddren, Murdoch, Mills, Hickton, Foggon(Spraggon), Armstrong.
Att: 14,929
Semi-final (2nd leg)
Nov 3 v Mansfield Town (a) 2-0 (agg 5-0)
Murdoch, Souness
Platt; Craggs, Spraggon, Souness, Boam, Maddren, Murdoch(Brine), Mills, Hickton, Cooper, Armstrong.
Att: 7,110
Final (1st leg)
Nov 26 v Fulham (h) 1-0
Strong (og)
Platt; Craggs, Spraggon, Murdoch(Foggon), Boam, Maddren, Brine, Mills, Hickton, Cooper, Armstrong.
Att: 14,700
Final (2nd leg)
Dec 9 v Fulham (a) 0-0 (agg 1-0)
Platt; Craggs, Cooper, Boersma, Boam, Maddren, Murdoch, Mills, Willey, Hickton, Armstrong.
Att: 13,723

1976-77
Qualifying Rounds
Aug 7 v Hull City (a) 2-0
Souness, Boersma
Platt; Craggs, Bailey, Souness, Boam, Maddren, Boersma(Hickton), Mills, Hedley, Armstrong, Cooper.
Att: 6,837
Aug 10 v Sheffield United (a) 1-0
Souness
Cuff; Craggs, Bailey, Souness, Boam, Ramage, Boersma, Mills, Hedley, Armstrong, Cooper.
Att: 4,043
Aug 14 v Newcastle United (a) 0-3
Platt; Craggs, Bailey, Souness, Boam, Maddren, Brine, Mills, Hedley(Hickton), Armstrong, Cooper.
Att: 14,708

	App	Sub	Gls	Summary	Pld	W	D	L	F	A
Armstrong D	12	0	3	Home	5	5	0	0	13	3
Bailey IC	6	0	1	Away	7	4	2	1	12	4
Boam SW	12	0	0		12	9	2	1	25	7
Boersma P	3	0	1							
Brine PK	4	2	0							
Charlton H	1	1	0							
Cooper T	10	0	0							
Craggs JE	12	0	1							
Cuff PJ	2	1	0							
Foggon A	3	1	1	Ramage A	1	0	0			
Hedley G	3	0	0	Smith M	0	1	0			
Hickton J	8	2	5	Souness GJ	10	0	4			
McAndrew A	2	0	0	Spraggon F	2	1	0			
Maddren WD	9	0	0	Willey AS	3	0	3			
Mills DJ	12	0	3	Strong(Fulham)	0	0	1(og)			
Murdoch RW	7	1	2		132	10	25			
Platt JA	10	0	0							

Full Members Cup

1985-86
Oct 8 v Carlisle United (h) 2-0
O'Riordan, Saunders (og)
Pears; Laws, Heard, McAndrew, Mowbray, Nattrass, Hamilton,
O'Riordan, Currie, Rowell(Cook), Beagrie.
Att: 2,177
Northern Area semi-final
Nov 5 v Hull City (a) 1-3 (aet; 90 mins: 1-1)
Slaven
Pears; Laws, Heard, McAndrew(Cooper), O'Riordan, Hamilton,
Turnbull(Beagrie), Currie, Slaven, Kernaghan, Cook.
Att: 3,637

	Apps	Subs	Gls
Beagrie PS	1	1	0
Cook M	1	1	0
Cooper CT	0	1	0
Currie DN	2	0	0
Hamilton GJ	2	0	0
Heard TP	2	0	0
Kernaghan AN	1	0	0
Laws B	2	0	0
McAndrew A	2	0	0
Mowbray AM	1	0	0
Nattrass I	1	0	0
O'Riordan DJ	2	0	1
Pears S	2	0	0
Rowell G	1	0	0
Slaven BJ	1	0	1
Turnbull LM	1	0	0
Saunders (Carlisle)	0	0	1(og)
	22	3	3

Summary	Pld	W	D	L	F	A
Home	1	1	0	0	2	0
Away	1	0	0	1	1	3
	4	2	2	0	3	3

Peter Beagrie, went to Sheffield United.

Freight/Rover Trophy

1986-87
Preliminary Round
Nov 24 v Doncaster Rovers (h) 3-0
Proudlock 2, Turnbull
Pears; Laws, Cooper, Mowbray, Parkinson, Pallister, Slaven(Turnbull),
Proudlock, Hamilton(Kernaghan), Gill, Ripley.
Att: 3,977
Preliminary Round
Dec 2 v Chesterfield (a) 1-2
Stephens
Pears; Laws, Cooper, Mowbray, Parkinson, Pallister, Slaven, Stephens,
Hamilton, Gill, Ripley.
Att: 1,764
Round 1
Jan 21 v Halifax Town (a) 2-1
Kernaghan, Ripley
Pears; Kernaghan, Cooper, Mowbray, Parkinson, Pallister, Slaven, Kerr,
Hamilton, Gill, Ripley.
Att: 1,411
Round 2
Feb 10 v Rochdale (a) 0-0
Pears; Kernaghan(Coyle), Cooper, Mowbray, Parkinson, Pallister,
Slaven, Stephens, Kerr, Gill, Ripley(Hamilton).
Att: 2,615
(Middlesbrough won 4-3 with penalties from *Stephens, Cooper, Slaven
and Hamilton*)
Area semi-final
Mar 10 v Mansfield Town (h) 0-1
Pears; Coyle(Kerr), Cooper, Mowbray, Parkinson, Kernaghan, Slaven,
Stephens, Hamilton, Gill, Hodgson(Ripley).
Att: 11,754

	Apps	Subs	Gls
Cooper CT	5	0	1
Coyle RP	1	1	0
Gill G	5	0	0
Hamilton GJ	4	1	1
Hodgson DJ	1	0	0
Kernaghan AN	3	1	1
Kerr PA	2	1	0
Laws B	2	0	0
Mowbray AM	5	0	0
Pallister GA	4	0	0
Parkinson GA	5	0	0
Pears S	5	0	0
Proudlock P	1	0	2
Ripley SE	4	1	1
Slaven BJ	5	0	1
Stephens A	3	0	2
Turnbull LM	0	1	1
	55	6	10

Summary	Pld	W	D	L	F	A
Home	2	1	0	1	3	1
Away	3	2	0	1	7	6
	5	3	0	2	10	7

Simod Cup

1987-88
Round 1
Nov 10 v Ipswich Town (a) 0-1
Poole; Glover, Laws, Mowbray, Parkinson, Pallister, Slaven
(Proudlock), Kernaghan(Gill), Hamilton, Kerr, Ripley.
Att: 6,108

1988-89
Round 1
Dec 14 v Oldham Athletic (h) 1-0
Glover (pen)
Pears; Parkinson, Cooper, Mowbray, Hamilton, Pallister, Slaven,
Brennan, Glover, Davenport, Burke.
Att: 7,439
Round 2
Dec 21 v Portsmouth (h) 2-1 (aet)
Slaven, Glover
Pears; Parkinson, Cooper, Mowbray, Hamilton, Pallister, Slaven,
Brennan, Glover, Davenport, Ripley(Kerr).
Att: 6,853
Round 3
Jan 11 v Coventry City (h) 1-0
Davenport
Pears; Mohan, Cooper, Mowbray, Hamilton, Pallister, Slaven, Gill,
Kerr, Davenport, Ripley.
Att: 9,910

Round 4
Jan 28 v Crystal Palace (h) 2-3
Slaven, Cooper
Pears; Parkinson, Cooper, Mowbray, Hamilton, Pallister, Slaven, Brennan, Burke, Kernaghan, Ripley.
Att: 16,314

	Apps	Subs	Gls
Brennan MR	3	0	0
Burke MS	2	0	0
Cooper CT	4	0	1
Davenport P	3	0	1
Gill G	1	1	0
Glover DV	3	0	2
Hamilton GJ	5	0	0
Kernaghan AN	2	0	0
Kerr PA	2	1	0
Laws B	1	0	0
Mohan N	1	0	0
Mowbray AM	5	0	0
Pallister GA	5	0	0
Parkinson GA	4	0	0
Pears S	4	0	0
Poole K	1	0	0
Proudlock P	0	1	0
Ripley SE	4	0	0
Slaven BJ	5	0	2
	55	3	6

Summary	Pld	W	D	L	F	A
Home	4	3	0	1	5	3
Away	1	0	0	1	0	1
	5	3	0	2	5	4

Zenith Data Systems Cup

1989-90
Round 1
Nov 29 v Port Vale (h) 3-1
Slaven 2, Coleman
Poole; Mohan, Cooper, Mowbray, Coleman, Putney(Burke), Slaven, Proctor, Ripley, Brennan, Davenport.
Att: 6,691
Round 2
Dec 20 v Sheffield Wednesday (h) 4-1
Slaven 3, Kernaghan
Pears; Parkinson, Cooper, Mowbray, Coleman, Putney, Slaven, Proctor, Kernaghan, Brennan(Kerr), Davenport.
Att: 8,716
Northern semi-final
Jan 23 v Newcastle United (h) 1-0
Cooper
Pears; Parkinson, Cooper, Mowbray, Coleman, Ripley, Slaven, Proctor, Kerr, Brennan, Davenport(McGee)
Att: 16,948
Northern Final (1st leg)
Jan 30 v Aston Villa (a) 2-1
Slaven, Brennan
Pears; Parkinson, Mohan, Kerr, Coleman, Kernaghan, Slaven, Proctor, Ripley, Brennan, McGee.
Att: 16,547
Northern Final (2nd leg)
Feb 6 v Aston Villa (h) 2-1 (aet; 90 mins: 2-2) (agg 4-2)
Slaven, Kerr
Pears; Parkinson, Mohan, Mowbray, Coleman, Ripley(Davenport), Slaven, Proctor, Kernaghan, Putney(McGee), Kerr.
Att: 20,806
Final (at Wembley)
Mar 25 v Chelsea 0-1
Pears; Parkinson, Cooper, Kernaghan, Coleman, McGee, Slaven, Proctor, Ripley, Brennan, Davenport.
Att: 76,369

1990-91
Round 1
Nov 20 v Hull City (h) 3-1 (aet; 90 mins: 0-0)
Baird, Kerr, Ripley
Pears; Cooper(McGee), Phillips, Mowbray, Coleman, Proctor, Slaven, Mustoe, Baird, Kerr, Ripley.
Att: 8,926
Round 2
Dec 19 v Manchester City (a) 1-2
Hendrie
Pears; Cooper, McGee, Mowbray, Coleman, Wark(Proctor), Slaven, Mustoe, Baird, Kerr, Hendrie.
Att: 6,406

1991-92
Round 1
Oct 22 v Derby County 4-2 (aet; 90 mins: 2-2)

Mark Brennan, joined Manchester City.

Wilkinson 2, Phillips, Slaven
Pears; Parkinson(Fleming), Phillips, Mowbray, Kernaghan, Mustoe, Slaven, Proctor, Wilkinson, Marwood, Pollock(Arnold).
Att: 6,385
Round 2
Nov 26 v Tranmere Rovers (h) 0-1
Pears; Fleming, Phillips, Kernaghan, Mohan, Mustoe, Slaven, Proctor, Wilkinson, Ripley, Pollock(Young).
Att: 6,952

	Apps	Subs	Gls
Arnold, I	10	1	0
Baird, IJ	2		1
Brennan, MR	5		1
Burke, MS	0	1	0
Coleman, S	8		1
Cooper, CT	6		1
Davenport, P	4	1	0
Fleming, C	1	1	0
Hendrie, JG	1		1
Kernaghan, AN	6		1
Kerr, PA	5	1	2
McGee, OE	3	3	0
Marwood, B	1		0
Mohan, NM	4		0
Mowbray, AM	7		0
Mustoe, R	4		0
Parkinson, GA	6		0
Pears, S	9		0
Phillips, JN	3		1
Pollock, J	2		0
Poole, K	1		0
Proctor, MG	9	1	0
Putney, TA	3		0
Ripley, SE	7		1
Slaven, BJ	10		8
Wark, J	1		0
Wilkinson, P	2		2
Young, MS	0	1	0
Total	110	10	20

Summary	Pld	W	D	L	F	A
Home	7	6	0	1	17	7
Away	2	1	0	1	3	3
Neutral	1	0	0	1	0	1
	10	7	0	3	20	11

Middlesbrough in the FA Cup
1883-1899

MIDDLESBROUGH first entered the FA Cup competition in 1883 and Archie Pringle is credited with scoring the Club's first FA Cup goal, against Staveley, a Derbyshire mining side, in a physical game which saw several Middlesbrough men require subsequent hospital treatment.

Contemporary newspapers covered the games but the paucity of available information regarding such vital elements as team line-ups, goalscorers, attendances etc, was not always recorded and has now been lost to history — a football historian's nightmare.

1883-84
Round 1
Nov 10 v Staveley (h) 1-5
Pringle

1884-85
Round 2
Dec 6 v Newark (h) 4-1
Pringle 2, Borrie, Hardwick
Att: 2,000
Round 3
Bye
Round 4
Jan 24 v Old Etonians (a) 2-5
Borrie, Pringle

1885-86
Round 2
Nov 21 v Gainsborough Trinity (a) 2-1
Thompson, Wilson
Round 3
Dec 19 v Grimsby Town (h) 2-1
Pickstock, Borrie
Round 4
Bye
Round 5
Jan 23 v Redcar* (a) 1-2
Pickstock
* Redcar lost 2-0 (a) to Small Heath in the 6th round.

1886-87
Qualifying Round
Oct 30 v Bishop Auckland CI (a) 1-0
Borrie
Att: 3,000
Qualifying Round
Nov 20 v Lincoln City (h) 1-1
Borrie
Replay
Nov 27 v Lincoln City (a) 0-2

1887-88
Qualifying Round
Oct 8 v Hallam (h) 6-0
Scorers unknown
Round 1
Oct 15 v Whitburn (h) 4-0
Borrie, Other scorers unknown
Round 2
Nov 5 v South Bank (h) 4-1
Borrie 2, E.J.Wilson, Dennis
Round 3
Nov 26 v Sunderland (h) 2-2
McCrie, Dennis
Replay
Dec 3 v Sunderland (a) 2-4
Cochrane, Unknown
Tie awarded to Middlesbrough, Sunderland disqualified because of veiled professionalism.
Round 4
Bye
Round 5
Jan 7 v Old Foresters (h) 4-0
Dennis, Borrie, Fox, E.J.Wilson
Meeting held in London on 14 January to hear Old Foresters' complaint that the ground conditions affected the result of the game. Mr Jope, the referee, reported that in places the ground was covered in 'tan and sand', and therefore the conditions did not allow a 'fair battle to be waged'. The Association ruled that a replay was necessary and was to be played on 21 January at Middlesbrough and, if the ground was still unfit, the tie would be switched to Sheffield. On hearing that the replayed tie was scheduled for Middlesbrough, the Old Foresters scratched from the competition.

Round 6
Jan 28 v Crewe Alexandra (h) 0-2

1888-89
Qualifying Round
Oct 6 v Ecclesfield (h) 0-1

1889-90
Round 1
Sep 21 v Ecclesfield (h) 3-1
Taylor, Garland, Unknown
Round 2
Oct 5 v South Bank (h) 3-4
Dennis, Other scorers unknown
Att: 6,000

1890-91
Qualifying Round
Oct 4 v Scarborough (h) 11-0†
Johnston 3, Wilson, Allen, Petrie 2, Dennis 3, Stevenson
†Middlesbrough's record score
Qualifying Round
Oct 25 v St Augustines (a) 4-1
Kay (og), Allan 2, Unknown
Att: 2,000
South Bank protested on eligibility of some of 'Boro's players, who had played in some Scottish games during the close season. The Association ruled that the relevant players could still play in the English Cup.
Qualifying Round
Nov 15 v Darlington (h) 2-0
Allan, Theakston (og)
Darlington protested over Bell's registration, alleging that he had played in a Scottish five-a-side competition in June, the day after signing as a professional with Middlesbrough. The player, supported by an affidavit signed by the referee, claimed that the game had been played the week before his signing. Despite this the protest was upheld and the tie was awarded to Darlington.

1891-92
Round 1
Jan 16 v Luton Town (a) 3-0
Campbell, Bell, Black
Round 2
Jan 30 v Preston North End (h) 1-2
Scorer unknown

1892-93
Round 1
Jan 1 v Newcastle United (a) 3-2
Black, Blyth, McKnight
Round 2
Feb 4 v Wolverhampton Wanderers (a) 1-2 (aet)
Black

1893-94
Qualifying Round
Oct 14 v Leadgate Exiles (a) 4-2
Scorers unknown
Qualifying Round
Nov 4 v Gateshead NER (h) 2-1
Scorers unknown

Qualifying Round
Nov 25 v Tow Law (h) 3-0
Scorers unknown
Qualifying Round
Dec 16 v Willington Athletic (a) 4-1
Stewart, Dunkerley 2, Unknown
Round 1
Jan 27 v Newton Heath (a) 0-4

1894-95
Qualifying Round
Oct 6 v Rendel (h) 4-0
Scorers unknown
Qualifying Round
Oct 13 v Willington Athletic (h) 2-1
Davison, T.Morren
Att: 1,500
Qualifying Round
Nov 3 v Howden Rangers (h) 4-1
Bach, Other scorers unknown
Qualifying Round
Nov 24 v Darlington (a) 1-0
Scorer unknown
Qualifying Round
Dec 15 v Bishop Auckland (a) 3-1
Scorers unknown
Round 1
Feb 2 v Chesterfield (h) 4-0
Davison 2, Roger, Mullen
Round 2
Feb 16 v Sheffield Wednesday (a) 1-6
Nelmes

1895-96
Qualifying Round
Oct 12 v Jarrow (a) 3-0
A.Johnson, Adams, Mullen
Qualifying round
Nov 2 v Newcastle United (a) 1-4
Scorer unknown

1896-97
Qualifying Round
Dec 12 v Hebburn Argyle (a) 1-8
Scorer unknown

1897-98
Qualifying Round
Sep 25 v South Bank (a) 3-2
Scorers unknown
Qualifying Round
Oct 16 v Rendel (a) 1-0
Purvis
Qualifying Round
Oct 30 v Bishop Auckland (h) 3-1
Scorers unknown
Qualifying Round
Nov 20 v Hebburn Argyle (h) 2-0
Scorers unknown
Qualifying Round
Dec 11 v Newcastle United (h) 0-2

1898-99
Qualifying Round
Oct 29 v Hebburn Argyle (h) 0-1

	Summary					
	P	W	D	L	F	A
Home	26	17	2	7	70	29
Away	21	12	0	9	40	46
	47	29	2	16	110	75

Wilf Mannion is beaten by the Arsenal defence at Highbury in April 1949. But Mannion later scored to earn 'Boro a 1-1 draw as they battled against relegation.

First of many: an historic moment as Brian Clough scores his first goal for 'Boro as they beat Leicester City 4-3 in October 1955.

Friendly Matches as a League Club
1899-1993

Listed below are all games played by Middlesbrough under the general heading of 'Friendlies'. Included in this list are testimonial games, which are awarded to players who reach ten years' service with one club and are usually played at the end of a season. In days gone by these games were called benefit games but instead of playing an additional match outside the normal boundary of the League season, the club sanctioned a specific home League game and the net receipts were handed to the beneficiary. These games are not included in this list. Pre-season friendlies are used by a manager to assess the playing strengths and weaknesses of his playing squad in a competitive environment against other clubs but this was not always the case. For many years the pre-season games, usually two or three in number, took place within the confines of the club and 'the Reds' — the probable first team — played 'the Whites', the reserve side. More often than not the paying public witnessed these games with the turnstile money being donated to local charities. These matches are also excluded from this list. Line-ups, goalscorers and attendances are given where known.

1899-1900
Sep 7 v Kaffirs (South Africa) (h) 8-2
McNally, Osborne, Murphy, Pugh, Unknown 4
M.Hughes; T.W.Shaw, A.Ramsay, H.G.Allport, J.McNally, J.P.McCracken, G.Longstaffe, J.Callaghan, F.Osborne, Murphy, C.E.Pugh.
Att: 3,000
Dec 25 v Edinburgh St Bernard's (h) 2-1
Att: 6,000
Dec 26 v Hibernian (h) 3-4
Att: 4,000
Jan 1 v Tottenham Hotspur (h) 2-2
Jan 2 v Glossop (h) 1-2
M.Hughes; T.W.Shaw, J.P.McCracken, W.Todd(debut), L.Raisbeck, R.Page, J.Callaghan, T.J.Lamb, G.Reid, G.Madden, Murphy.
Att: 3,000
Jan 3 v London Casuals (h) 2-4
M.Hughes; T.W.Shaw, J.Jones, W.Todd, Dargue(debut), F.W.Bell, F.Osborne, McCallum(debut), S.Buckley, R.W.Evans, R.Eglington.
Att: 1,000
Apr 13 v Sunderland (h) 0-1
G.Smith; T.W.Shaw, McGregor(debut), Wheatley(debut), T.Linton, A.Ramsay, L.Raisbeck, T.J.Lamb, G.Reid, R.Pratt, Murphy.
Att: 4,000
Apr 16 v Clyde (h) 0-1
Att: 4,000

1900-01
Sep 5 v Newcastle United (h) 1-2
J.Frail; M.J.Dow, A.Ramsay, John Brown, W.Higgins, A.Davidson, M.Moran, W.Wardrope, A.Robertson, J.Eckford, C.Carrick.
Att: 4,000
Jan 2 v Everton (h) 1-6
Wilkie
G.Hodgson; J.Jones, T.Macfarlane, D.W.Smith, A.Jones, M.Moran, J.Wilkie, A.Thompson, A.McCowie, J.Eckford.
Att: 5,000
Apr 8 v Clyde (h) -
Young; M.Cochrane, A.Ramsay, J.Millar, Moore, A.Davidson, M.Moran, A.McCowie, Brown, J.Wilkie, C.Carrick.
Att: 2,000
Apr 30 v Sunderland (h) -
Probable: J.Frail; M.J.Dow, M.Cochrane, D.W.Smith, W.Higgins, A.Davidson, M.Moran, J.Brearley, A.Robertson, A.McCowie, W.Wardrope.

1901-02
Sep 2 v Newcastle United (h) 2-1
Att: 8,000
Sep 9 v Sunderland (h) 1-1
Wardrope
Oct 23 v Newcastle United (a) 1-4
Turner
J.Frail; M.J.Dow, A.Ramsay, D.W.Smith, Piercy, A.Davidson, M.Moran, J.Brearley, J.Cassidy, P.Turner, J.Tennant.
Att: 3,000
Dec 25 v Edinburgh St Bernard's (h) 3-2
Probable: J.Frail; M.J.Dow, A.Ramsay, J.Brearley, Piercy, Buchan, J.Crawford, J.Leslie, A.Thompson, P.Turner, J.Cassidy.
Att: 5,000
Dec 26 v Dundee (h) 3-0 (1-0)
Att: 5,000
Dec 30 v London Casuals (h) 1-2
Carrick
Young; Rhodes, Richley, Miller, Higgins, Barrie, M.Moran, R.Watson, A.Robertson, W.Wardrope, C.Carrick.
Att: 1,000
Jan 2 v Third Lanark (h) 3-2 (1-0)
Robertson, Brearley 2

J.Frail; M.J.Dow, A.Ramsay, Miller, D.W.Smith, Anderson, Murtha(Grangetown), W.Wardrope, J.Brearley, P.Turner, A.Robertson.
Apr 23 v Newcastle United (a) 1-2
Probable: R.G.Williamson; Smith, M.J.Dow, Miller, A.Jones, A.Davidson, M.Moran, R.Watson, A.Robertson, P.Turner, J.Tennant.
Att: 2,000
In aid of Ibrox Disaster Fund
Apr 30 v West Bromwich Albion (h) 1-1
Att: 6,150

1902-03
Sep 5 v Newcastle United (h) 1-2
Millar
Att: 4,000
Sep 8 v Hearts (h) 3-1
J.Muir, Turner, J.Robertson
R.Macfarlane; J.Hogg, A.Ramsay, W.Muir, D.W.Smith, A.Davidson, J.Robertson, W.Macaulay, A.Robertson, P.Turner, J.Muir.
Nov 19 v Newcastle United (h) 1-3
Thompson
R.Macfarlane; J.Hogg, Barrie, W.Hogg, D.W.Smith, Mille, Robertson, Richardson, A.Thompson, P.Turner, C.Carrick.
Att: 3,000
Dec 30 v Corinthians (h) 6-4
Godley, Macaulay, R.Watson, J.H.Gettins, Carrick 2
R.G.Williamson; J.Hogg, A.Ramsay, D.W.Smith, A.Davidson, R.Page, R.Watson, W.Macaulay, Gettins, W.Godley, C.Carrick.
Att: 1,000
Jan 1 v Manchester United (h) 0-1
R.G.Williamson; T.Craig, Skinner, Piercy, Miller, W.Muir, J.Robertson, A.Robertson, A.Thompson, P.Turner, J.Muir.
Att: 5,000
T.Craig was a triallist from Scotland. Harry Douglas was set to play for Middlesbrough at centre-half but United were a player short so he guested for them.
Feb 7 v Chesterfield (h) 1-2
Douglas
Probable: R.G.Williamson; T.Craig, A.Ramsay, W.Macaulay, A.Jones, A.Davidson, R.Watson, H.Douglas, R.Currie, J.Cassidy, Muir.
Feb 21 v Rangers (h) 1-1
Currie
Probable: R.Macfarlane; J.Hogg, A.Ramsay, D.W.Smith, A.Jones, A.Davidson, H.Douglas, P.Turner, R.Currie, W.Macaulay, C.Carrick.

1903-04
Sep 1 v Celtic (h) 1-0
White (pen)
R.G.Williamson; J.Hogg, A.Ramsay, D.W.Smith, S.Aitken, A.Davidson, E.Gettins, W.White, A.Brown, J.Cassidy, R.H.Atherton.
Att: 7,000
Oct 12 v Dundee (a) 2-2
Blackett, Cassidy
R.G.Williamson; J.Hogg, J.Blackett, D.W.Smith, A.Jones, A.Davidson, W.White, R.H.Atherton, A.Brown, J.Cassidy, C.Carrick.
Att: 5,000
Dec 1 v Manchester United (h) 0-1
Dec 25 v Leith Athletic (h) 5-1
Carrick 2, Millward 3
Davies; T.Craig, A.Ramsay, R.Piercy, F.Piercy, Harker, Hopkins, McNaughton, Millward, J.Suddick, C.Carrick.
Att: 1,000
Millward and Davies were triallists from Scotland.
Apr 4 v Dundee (h) 2-0
Brown, E.Gettins
Apr 27 v Darlington (a) 4-4
Brown, Cassidy 2, McGuigan
Probable: R.Macfarlane; J.Hogg, J.Blackett,

D.W.Smith, A.Jones, A.Davidson, A.McGuigan, R.H.Atherton, A.Brown, J.Cassidy, Roberts.
Apr 30 v West Bromwich Albion (h) 2-0
Scorers unknown
R.G.Williamson; J.Hogg, J.Blackett, S.Aitken, A.Jones, A.Davidson, R.H.Atherton, J.Suddick, A.Brown, J.Cassidy, L.Goodson.
Att: 3,400

1904-05
Sep 7 v Newcastle United (h) 2-1
Scorers unknown
R.G.Williamson; T.Craig, A.Ramsay, S.Aitken, R.Page, D.W.Smith, E.Gettins, R.H.Atherton, H.Astley, Buchanan, R.J.Roberts.
Andy Ramsay's Benefit
Feb 18 v Sunderland (h) 1-2
Phillipson
Probable: R.G.Williamson; G.T.Hedley, W.B.Agnew, Milton, Blyth, J.Cassidy, C.Hewitt, A.Common, T.Green, Phillipson, J.Thackeray.
Att: 1,000
Apr 3 v Newcastle United (h) 1-1
Phillipson
Att: 1,000
Apr 21 v Dundee (h) 2-0
Brown, Gettins
Att: 1,000
Apr 22 v Third Lanark (h) 1-1
Murray
Att: 1,000
Apr 30 v Newcastle United (h)
Phillipson
Att: 1,000

1905-06
Sep 6 v Sunderland (h) 4-0
Murray, Reid 3
Probable: R.G.Williamson; J.Hogg, D.McCallum, S.Aitken, Blyth, A.Davidson, T.Green, A.Common, G.Reid, W.Murray, J.Thackeray.
Att: 1,000
Jan 2 v Darlington (a) 6-2
J.Bell 3, Walker, Barker, Reid
W.B.Agnew, R.G.Williamson, G.T.Hedley also played.

1906-07
Apr 3 v Airdrieonians (h) –
Denmark Tour
May 8 v Danish University (a) 5-3
May 9 v Danish XI (a) 2-2
Tim Williamson did not go on the tour.

1907-08
Apr 29 v North Inverness XI (a) 5-0
Jun 10 v Prague (a) 4-2
Reported date
Denmark Tour
Jun v Denmark XI (a) 5-2
Bloomer 2, Hall 2, Cail

1908-09
Nov 18 v Newcastle United (a) 1-5
Scorer unknown
R.G.Williamson; D.McLeod, J.A.Groves, S.Aitken, H.Kent, F.J.Wilcox, A.Common, S.Bloomer, F.B.Pentland, T.Dixon, J.Thackeray.
Att: 1,000
In aid of Newcastle Royal Victoria Infirmary.
Dec 16 v Newcastle United (h) 1-2
Cail
R.G.Williamson; D.McLeod, J.A.Groves, T.Wilson, H.Kent, E.Verrill, W.A.Flint, T.Dixon, S.G.Cail, A.Common, Wood.
Att: 1,000
In aid of Medical Charities Fund.
Feb 6 v Oldham Athletic (h) 1-4

Feb 20 v Edinburgh St Bernard's (h) 4-0
Hall 2, Common, Verrill
Probable: R.G.Williamson; D.McLeod, T.Carrick,
S.Aitken, F.J.Wilcox, E.Verrill, F.B.Pentland,
S.Bloomer, J.H.Hall, A.Common, J.Thackeray.
Att: 2,000

1912-13
Mar 8 v Bradford City (h) 5-1
Carr (pen), Nichol, J.Cook 2, Elliott
H.Harrison; D.McLeod, J.M.Hisbent, G.Malcolm,
H.Cook, J.H.Haworth, J.Stirling, J.Carr,
G.W.Elliott, J.Cook, J.Nichol.
Att: 4,000
Apr 28 v Norwich City (a) 1-1

1913-14
Mar 21 v Celtic (a) 3-1
Tinsley 2, Elliott
Att: 10,000
Apr 29 v Darlington (a) 3-0
J.Carr 2, Elliott
Richard Jackson's Testimonial

1917-18
May 11 v Newcastle United (a) 3-3
Scorers unknown
Att: 4,000
War Fund Match

1918-19
Dec 18 v Rendel (a) 1-5
Dec 26 v South Shields (a) 4-2
Dec 27 v Rendel (h) 2-2
Jan 1 v Sunderland (a) 3-1
Jan 4 v Hartlepools United () -
Probable: R.G.Williamson; C.Dixon, J.Weir,
Robinson, W.Carr, G.Carr, T.Storey, J.Carr,
G.W.Elliott, J.Cook, W.Stage.
Apr 5 v Newcastle United (h) 4-1
Forshaw, Storey, G.Carr 2
R.G.Williamson; J.H.Haworth, C.Dixon,
S.Davidson, W.Ellerington, G.Malcolm, T.Storey,
G.Carr, J.Carr, Bertram(South Shields), R.Forshaw.
Att: 6,000
Apr 18 v Hartlepools United (h) 0-2
Apr 21 v Renton (h) 1-0
Apr 26 v Hartlepools United (a) 1-1
G.Carr
R.G.Williamson; W.V.Fox, C.Dixon, S.Davidson,
W.Carr, G.Malcolm, T.Storey, W.Stage, G.Carr,
Stewart, E.Lloyd.
Att: 2,000
May 3 v Newcastle United (a) 2-2
Stage, Lloyd
R.G.Williamson; Thwaites, C.Dixon, Robinson,
G.Carr, W.V.Fox, W.Stage, E.Lloyd, G.W.Elliott,
Alexander, W.Clarke.
Att: 15,000
Charity Match
Apr 21 v Newcastle United (h) 2-1
Att: 10,000
NE Counties Cup match

1920-21
Apr 4 v Raith Rovers (a) 0-3
Att: 9,000
Middlesbrough fielded many reserves
North Eastern Senior Championship Cup
Apr 20 v Newcastle United (h) 2-1
G.Carr 2
R.G.Williamson; J.Marshall, W.Holmes,
S.Davidson, W.Carr, P.Donaghy, Brown, G.Carr,
G.W.Elliott, R.Pender, T.Urwin.
Att: 12,000
Apr 27 v Sunderland 0-3
Probable: R.G.Williamson; J.Marshall, W.Holmes,
S.Davidson, W.Carr, P.Donaghy, Brown, W.Birrell,
E.W.Young, R.Pender, T.Urwin.
**North-Eastern Senior Championship Cup Final, at
Hartlepool.**

1921-22
May 3 v Hartlepools United (a) 2-2
Birrell, Elliott
Att: 1,000

1926-27
May 4 v Newcastle United (h) 0-0
J.A.Mathieson; F.Twine, J.Smith, J.Miller,
R.G.Ferguson, D.Ashman, J.McClelland, W.Birrell,
G.H.Camsell, J.Carr, O.Williams.
Att: 21,000
Charlie Cole's Benefit

Denmark Tour
May 21 v Danish XI (a) 2-4
Camsell 2
May 25 v Danish XI (a) 8-2
Camsell 5, Pease, McClelland, Opp own-goal

May 26 v Danish XI (a) 2-2
McClelland, O.Williams
Att: 25,000
1927-28
Oct 19 v Newcastle United (a) 5-2
Att: 3,350
McPherson's Testimonial

1929-30
Dec 30 v Corinthians (h) 1-0
Grieve; T.Freeman, J.Smith, W.H.Brown, A.Carr,
W.Forrest, D.D.McPhail, J.Peacock, B.A.C.Hall,
K.Cameron, O.Williams.
Att: 500

1930-31
Apr 27 v Hearts (a) 5-1
Camsell 4, Cameron
R.F.Bruce and J.A.Mathieson also played.
Att: 3,000
Bill Murray's Testimonial

1933-34
Oct 16 v Army XI (a) 2-4
Camsell, Warren
J.A.Mathieson; J.Smith, R.W.Stuart, W.H.Brown,
T.P.Griffiths, J.Martin, R.F.Bruce, J.McKay,
G.H.Camsell, J.J.Williams, F.W.Warren.
Jan 27 v Army XI (h) 2-2
Fenton 2
Probable: E.J.G.Hillier; S.Jarvis, R.W.Stuart,.
W.H.Brown, T.P.Griffiths, J.Martin, M.Fenton,
J.McKay, G.H.Camsell, McArthur, C.Ferguson.

1934-35
Sep 19 v South Bank (a) 1-3
McKay (pen)
E.J.G.Hillier; J.Smith, R.W.Stuart, E.Weightman,
W.Forrest, E.Coleman, R.F.Bruce, B.C.Yorston,
J.McKay, Rush.
Oct 17 v Newcastle United (a) 2-3
Camsell, Warren
E.J.G.Hillier; S.Jarvis, R.W.Stuart, W.H.Brown,
T.P.Griffiths, W.Forrest, G.H.Camsell, J.McKay,
B.C.Yorston, R.F.Bruce, F.W.Warren.
Att: 3,200
Gresford Colliery Disaster Fund

1935-36
May 4 v Norwich City (a) 3-1
Birkett, Coleman, Chadwick
F.W.Gibson; J.Jennings, R.W.Stuart, W.H.Brown,
W.Forrest, Murphy, R.J.E.Birkett, N.Higham,
B.C.Yorston, E.Coleman, C.Chadwick.
Att: 13,975
Norfolk and Norwich Hospital Cup

Norway Tour
May 12 v Oslo (a) 2-1 (2-0)
Cunliffe, Yorston
F.W.Gibson; J.Jennings, R.W.Stuart, W.H.Brown,
E.Weightman, W.Forrest, R.J.E.Birkett,
B.C.Yorston, G.H.Camsell, E.Coleman, A.Cunliffe.
May 14 v Fredrikstad (a) 1-1
Played at Fredrikstad
Camsell
E.Coleman, F.W.Gibson and R.J.E.Birkett also
played.
Norwegian champions
May 15 v Dammen (a) 3-2
Played at Oslo
Yorston 2, Birkett

1938-39
Aug 20 v Sunderland (a) 2-4
Yorston, Fenton
Probable: D.S.Cumming: G.E.Laking, R.W.Stuart,
W.H.Brown, R.D.Baxter, W.Forrest, J.V.Milne,
W.J.Mannion, M.Fenton, B.C.Yorston,
T.Cochrane.
Att: 10,871
FA Jubilee Fund
Nov 14 v Army XI (a) 9-0
Higham, Camsell 2, Chadwick 2, Cochrane
D.S.Cumming; G.E.Laking, C.T.Scrimshaw,
D.McKenzie, H.Shepherdson, Murphy,
C.Chadwick, N.Higham, G.H.Camsell,
B.C.Yorston, T.Cochrane.
Mar 25 v Hearts (h) 1-4
Camsell
D.S.Cumming; W.H.Brown, G.E.Laking,
D.McKenzie, R.D.Baxter, W.Forrest, C.Chadwick,
W.J.Mannion, G.H.Camsell, B.C.Yorston,
J.V.Milne.
Att: 15,500
Apr 26 v Scarborough (h) 2-3
Fenton 2 (1 pen)
F.C.Nash; H.N.Fowler, W.J.Mannion, R.D.Baxter,
H.Shepherdson and G.F.M.Hardwick also played.
Scarborough Hospital Shield

May 2 v South Bank (a) 6-1
Higham 3, G.Armes 2, Fenton
T.Butler, J.J.McCabe, H.Shepherdson and
Emmerson also played.
Jack Cottrell's Benefit
May 4 v Hartlepools United (a) 5-4
Fenton 2, Miller 2, T.E.Murphy
May 8 v Norwich City (a) 0-3
D.S.Cumming; W.H.Brown, R.W.Stuart,
D.McKenzie, R.D.Baxter, W.Forrest, T.Butler,
W.J.Mannion, B.C.Yorston, D.A.Miller, J.V.Milne.
Att: 4,000
Norwich Hospital Cup

1939-40
Oct 7 v Newcastle United (a) 2-3
Fenton 2
Att: 7,316
Oct 14 v Hartlepools United (h) 3-2
Camsell, Chadwick, Fenton
D.S.Cumming; W.H.Brown, R.W.Stuart, J.Martin,
H.Shepherdson, W.Forrest, S.Armes, W.J.Mannion,
M.Fenton, G.H.Camsell, C.Chadwick.
Att: 2,000
Nov 4 v Hartlepools United (a) 5-4
Fenton 2, Miller 2, Murphy
D.S.Cumming; R.W.Stuart, G.F.M.Hardwick,
W.H.Brown, J.Martin, W.Forrest, C.Chadwick,
W.J.Mannion, M.Fenton, D.Miller, T.E.Murphy.
Nov 18 v Stockton (h) 6-3
Camsell 3, Fenton 2, Chadwick
D.S.Cumming; W.H.Brown, G.F.M.Hardwick,
W.Forrest, J.Martin, W.J.Copping (guest), S.Armes,
W.J.Mannion, G.H.Camsell, M.Fenton,
C.Chadwick.
Dec 25 v Darlington (a) 5-1
Murphy, Camsell, Fenton 3
D.S.Cumming; H.N.Fowler, R.W.Stuart, W.H.Brown,
H.Shepherdson, W.Forrest, T.E.Murphy,
W.J.Mannion, G.H.Camsell, M.Fenton, C.Chadwick.
Dec 26 v Newcastle United (a) 1-1
Chadwick
D.S.Cumming; H.N.Fowler, R.W.Stuart,
W.H.Brown, Robinson, W.Forrest, T.E.Murphy,
W.J.Mannion, G.C.Stobbart, M.Fenton,
C.Chadwick.
Att: 6,500
Dec 30 v Barnsley (h) 4-2
Fenton 4
D.S.Cumming; H.N.Fowler, R.W.Stuart,
W.H.Brown, Robinson, W.Forrest, T.E.Murphy,
W.J.Mannion, G.H.Camsell, M.Fenton,
C.Chadwick.
Jan 1 v Newcastle United (h) 5-2
Fenton 3, Stobbart, Mannion
F.C.Nash; H.Shepherdson, R.W.Stuart, J.Martin,
Robinson, W.Forrest, T.E.Murphy, W.J.Mannion,
G.C.Stobbart, M.Fenton, C.Chadwick.
Att: 2,400
Apr 11 v Stockton (a) 1-2
Fenton
D.S.Cumming; H.N.Fowler, R.W.Stuart,
W.H.Brown, Robinson, W.Forrest, J.V.Milne,
M.Fenton, G.C.Stobbart, T.E.Murphy, McMahon.

1940-41
Apr 12 v Army XI (a) 8-1
McCabe 3, Camsell 2, Mannion 2, Fenton

1944-45
Victory Friendly Match
May 10 v Darlington (a) 3-5
Stobbart 2, Bowie
M.Middleton; Thompson, R.W.Stuart, W.H.Brown,
N.Robinson, Johnson, W.Wass, R.Bowie,
G.C.Stobbart, W.Forrest, Woollett.

1947-48
Apr 15 v Southend United (?) 3-0
Fenton, Dicks, Walker

1948-49
Jan 29 v Tottenham Hotspur (a) 1-4
McCrae
R.Ugolini; G.Hepple, G.F.M.Hardwick, H.D.Bell,
S.Rickaby, T.W.Blenkinsopp, J.O.Spuhler,
W.J.Mannion, A.Donaldson, A.McCrae, R.W.Dicks.
Att: 40,000
Feb 5 v Bolton Wanderers (h) 1-1
Donaldson
R.Ugolini; S.Rickaby, G.F.M.Hardwick, H.D.Bell,
W.Whitaker, T.W.Blenkinsopp, J.O.Spuhler,
W.J.Mannion, A.Donaldson, J.Gordon, R.G.Walker.
Att: 35,000
Feb 12 v Newcastle United (h) 3-3
Donaldson 2, Dicks
R.Ugolini; S.Rickaby, G.F.M.Hardwick, J.Gordon,
W.Whitaker, T.W.Blenkinsopp, C.M.Reagan,
W.J.Mannion, A.Donaldson, R.W.Dicks, R.G.Walker.
Att: 38,000

Mar 26 v Hearts (h) 4-0
Hardwick, Spuhler 2, Hartnett
R.Ugolini; R.Robinson, G.F.M.Hardwick,
H.D.Bell, T.W.Blenkinsopp, R.W.Dicks,
J.O.Spuhler, W.J.Mannion, J.C.McCormack,
A.McCrae, J.B.Hartnett.

1949-50
Feb 11 v Newcastle United (a) 2-3
Woodward 2
Probable: J.P.Hodgson; R.Robinson,
T.W.Blenkinsopp, H.D.Bell, W.Whitaker,
J.Gordon, W.Linacre, A.G.Fitzsimons,
P.S.McKennan, W.J.Mannion, T.Woodward.
Att: 17,000
Mar 4 v Blackburn Rovers (h) 5-0
Walker, Spuhler 3, Reagan
R.Ugolini; R.W.Dicks, G.F.M.Hardwick, H.D.Bell,
W.Whitaker, G.Hepple, C.M.Reagan,
A.G.Fitzsimons, J.O.Spuhler, W.J.Mannion,
R.G.Walker.
Att: 10,000

1950-51
Jan 27 v Barnsley (h) 2-1
Mannion, Delapenha
R.Ugolini; R.Robinson, R.W.Dicks, H.D.Bell,
T.W.Blenkinsopp, J.Brown, W.Linacre,
L.L.Delapenha, A.Donaldson, W.J.Mannion,
W.B.Auld.
Att: 15,000
Feb 10 v Southampton (a) 1-1
Mannion
R.Ugolini; R.W.Dicks, G.Hepple, H.D.Bell,
W.Whitaker, J.Brown, T.Woodward,
L.L.Delapenha, N.Robinson, W.J.Mannion,
J.B.Hartnett.
Att: 16,000
Feb 21 v Dutch XI (a) 1-4
Olympic Stadium, Amsterdam
Feb 24 v Everton (a) 1-1
Mannion
R.Ugolini; R.Robinson, G.Hepple, H.D.Bell,
W.Whitaker, J.Gordon, L.L.Delapenha,
P.S.McKennan, J.O.Spuhler, W.J.Mannion,
W.B.Auld.
Att: 16,000
Festival of Britain
May 12 v Partizan Belgrade (h) 2-3
Walker, Mochan
Att: 20,000

1951-52
Feb 23 v Notts County (h) 2-1
Bell, Mannion
Att: 12,000
Ireland Tour
May 8 v Glentoran (a) 3-0
McCrae, Mannion, Delapenha
R.Ugolini; T.W.Blenkinsopp, R.Corbett, H.D.Bell,
W.Whitaker, J.Gordon, L.L.Delapenha,
W.J.Mannion, J.O.Spuhler, A.McCrae, R.W.Dicks.
(Ugolini saved penalty)
May 9 v Glenavon (a) 3-0
Dicks, Delapenha, McCrae
May 11 v Cork (a) 5-1
Noonan 2 (2 og's), McCrae, Mannion, Delapenha
R.Ugolini; T.W.Blenkinsopp, R.Corbett, H.D.Bell,
W.Whitaker, E.T.Russell, L.L.Delanpenha,
W.J.Mannion, J.O.Spuhler, A.McCrae, N.Mochan.
Burke's Benefit
May 14 v Drumcondra (a) 6-1
Delapenha 2, Fitzsimons, McCrae 2, Spuhler

1952-53
Jan 31 v Aberdeen (h) 6-3
Mannion, Spuhler 4, Fitzsimons
R.Ugolini; R.W.Dicks, R.Corbett, H.D.Bell,
W.Whitaker, J.Gordon, L.L.Delapenha,
W.J.Mannion, J.O.Spuhler, A.McCrae,
A.G.Fitzsimons.
Att: 5,000
Feb 28 v Notts County (a) 1-4
Fitzsimons
Att: 7,095
Coronation Match
May 6 v Sunderland (a) 4-3
Fitzsimons 2, Walker, Edwards
Att: 5,896
Holland Tour
May 13 v Holland XI (at Rotterdam) (a) 2-2
Delapenha 2
Att: 38,000
May 19 v Holland 'B' (at Nijmegen) (a) 3-1
Fitzsimons 2, Delapenha
Att: 25,000
May 21 v Rapid Club of Vienna (a) 1-2
(Played in Amsterdam)
Delapenha
Att: 63,000
Flood disaster fund

1953-54
Feb 19 v Watford (a) 1-3
Rayment
Mar 16 v Falkirk (a) 1-2
Lawrie
Floodlit friendly, second half televised

1954-55
Jan 29 v Sheffield United (h) 4-1
Scott, Mitchell 2, J.Shaw (og)
J.P.Hodgson; R.S.Barnard, T.E.Brown,
W.C.Harris, R.Robinson, R.W.Dicks, S.Lawrie,
J.C.Scott, C.Wayman, A.G.Fitzsimons,
A.J.Mitchell.

1955-56
Nov 28 v Torquay United (a) 1-1
Delapenha

Floodlit Friendlies

1957-58
Oct 16 v Sunderland (h) 2-0
Fitzsimons, Clough
P.T.Taylor; R.Bilcliff, D.Stonehouse,
F.G.Mulholland, B.J.Phillips, R.W.Dicks,
L.L.Delapenha, J.D.McClean, B.H.Clough,
A.G.Fitzsimons, R.T.Burbeck.
Att: 27,273
Oct 30 v Newcastle United (h) 3-0
Fitzsimons, McLean, Peacock
P.T.Taylor; R.Bilcliff, D.Stonehouse, W.C.Harris,
B.J.Phillips, R.W.Dicks(capt), L.L.Delapenha,
J.D.McLean, A.Peacock, A.G.Fitzsimons,
R.T.Burbeck.
Att: 27,056
Nov 13 v FC Cologne (h) 1-2
Clough
Probable: P.T.Taylor; R.Bilcliff, D.Stonehouse,
F.G.Mulholland, B.J.Phillips, R.W.Dicks,
C.W.Taylor, A.G.Fitzsimons, B.H.Clough,
R.Henderson, R.T.Burbeck.
Att: 31,923
Nov 27 v Hibernian (h) 0-5
P.T.Taylor; R.Bilcliff, D.Stonehouse, W.C.Harris,
B.J.Phillips, R.W.Dicks, W.Day, J.D.McLean,
B.H.Clough, R.Henderson, R.T.Burbeck.
Att: 26,981
Dec 11 v Celtic (h) 6-1
Clough 4, Delapenha (pen), Scott
P.T.Taylor; R.Bilcliff, R.Robinson, W.C.Harris,
B.J.Phillips, R.W.Dicks, L.L.Delapenha, J.C.Scott,
B.H.Clough, A.G.Fitzsimons, E.Holliday.
Att: 14,062
Mar 27 v PSV Eindhoven (h) 3-3
Clough 3
E.Million; R.Bilcliff, R.Robinson, W.C.Harris,
B.J.Phillips, J.Birbeck, J.D.McLean, B.H.Clough,
A.Peacock, A.G.Fitzsimons, E.Holliday.
Att: 12,285
George Hardwick — chief coach at Eindhoven.
Apr 28 v Hull City (a) 3-1
Clough 2, Stonehouse
P.T.Taylor; R.Bilcliff, D.Stonehouse, W.C.Harris,
R.Robinson, R.W.Dicks, J.D.McLean,
A.G.Fitzsimons, B.H.Clough, A.Peacock,
E.Holliday.
Att: 5,172

1958-59
Oct 6 v Bela Vista (h) 4-0
Peacock 2, Scott 2
P.T.Taylor; R.Bilcliff, D.Stonehouse, W.C.Harris,
B.J.Phillips, R.W.Dicks, C.W.Taylor, J.C.Scott,
A.Peacock, A.R.Rodgerson, R.T.Burbeck.
Att: 15,944
Oct 22 v Munich 1860 (h) 2-2
Peacock, Burbeck
P.T.Taylor; R.Bilcliff, D.Stonehouse, W.C.Harris,
B.J.Phillips, R.W.Dicks, C.W.Taylor, A.G.Fitzsimons,
B.H.Clough, A.Peacock, R.T.Burbeck.
Att: 17,016
Dec 3 v Nimes Olympique (h) 3-0
Clough 2, Peacock
Att: 21,166
Feb 16 v 1. Vienna FC (h) 4-1
Holliday 2, Clough 2
P.T.Taylor; R.S.Barnard, D.Stonehouse, R.I.Yeoman,
B.J.Phillips, W.C.Harris, A.G.Fitzsimons,
D.W.Fernie, B.H.Clough, R.T.Burbeck, E.Holliday.
Att: 12,904

1959-60
Aug v Lille Olympique (a) 2-1
Scorers unknown
Friendship Cup
Nov 2 v Hibernian (a) 6-6
Peacock 2, Fernie 2, Clough, Harris
Att: 15,000
B.J.Phillips and P.T.Taylor also played.

Nov 9 v Hull City (h) 4-0
Yeoman, Clough, Day, Harris (pen)
Nov 12 v Hibernian (h) 3-4
Clough 2, Fernie
Probable: P.T.Taylor; R.Bilcliff, M.McNeil,
W.C.Harris, D.Wilkie, R.I.Yeoman, R.T.Burbeck,
D.W.Fernie, B.H.Clough, A.Peacock, E.Holliday.
Nov 23 v Army XI (h) 3-3
Fernie, Harris (pen), Clough
E.Million; R.Bilcliff, M.McNeil, W.C.Harris,
A.Peacock, R.I.Yeoman(D.H.Walker), R.T.Burbeck,
D.W.Fernie, B.H.Clough, J.D.McLean, E.Holliday.
Att: 9,191
Mar 14 v Peterborough United (a) 2-3
Peacock, Clough
P.T.Taylor; D.Stonehouse, G.E.Jones, R.I.Yeoman,
K.G.Thomson, D.H.Walker, R.T.Burbeck,
D.W.Fernie, B.H.Clough, A.Peacock, R.Waldock.
Att: 10,002
Mar 28 v Saarbrücken (h) 4-0
Holliday, Clough, Peacock, Rodgerson
E.Million also played.
Att: 7,849
May 2 v Fluminense (h) 2-3
Harris (pen), Clough
D.Windross; D.W.Fernie, A.Peacock, R.T.Burbeck,
E.Holliday, D.Stonehoue and M.McNeil also
played.
Att: 14,432
(Fluminense were Brazilian champions)
Switzerland/Germany Tour
May 8 v Bienne FC (a) 3-1
Peacock, Waldock, Alleman (og)
Att: 4,000
May 10 v Swiss 'B' (a) 2-0
Peacock, Fernie
Att: 4,000
May 12 v Bonn (a) 1-1
Rodgerson
(Abandoned after 74 minutes — thunderstorm)
May 14 v Fortuna Düsseldorf (a) 4-3
Waldock, Yeoman, Clough, Rodgerson
Att: 3,000

1960-61
Aug 14 v Lille Olympique (a) 2-1
Holliday, Peacock
R.Appleby; R.Bilcliff, M.McNeil, W.C.Harris,
K.G.Thomson, D.H.Walker, R.Waldock,
R.Henderson, B.H.Clough, A.Peacock,
R.T.Burbeck.
Friendship Cup
Oct 12 v Lille Olympique (h) 4-1
Waldock, Harris, Clough 2
R.Appleby; R.Bilcliff, M.McNeil, W.C.Harris,
K.G.Thomson, D.H.Walker, R.Waldock,
R.Henderson, B.H.Clough, A.Peacock,
R.T.Burbeck.
Att: 7,495
Friendship Cup
Oct 19 v Hibernian (a) 4-2
McLean, Henderson, Clough, Harris (pen)
R.Appleby; R.Bilcliff, G.E.Jones, W.C.Harris,
K.G.Thomson, R.I.Yeoman, R.Waldock,
J.D.McLean, B.H.Clough, R.Henderson,
R.T.Burbeck.
Nov 16 v Bonn (h) 5-0
Clough 3, Peacock 2
R.Appleby; R.Bilcliff, M.McNeil, W.C.Harris,
K.G.Thomson, R.I.Yeoman, R.Waldock,
J.D.McLean, B.H.Clough, A.Peacock, E.Holliday.
Att: 7,863
Dec 7 v Army XI (h) 2-1
Burbeck, Kaye
Att: 2,865

1961-62
Aug 5 v Arsenal (h) 2-1
Peacock 2
R.Appleby; G.E.Jones, M.McNeil, R.I.Yeoman,
K.G.Thomson, W.Horner, W.Day, W.C.Harris,
J.Livingstone, A.Peacock, E.Holliday.
Att: 8,865
Cock O' The North Trophy
Oct 11 v Sunderland (h) 2-0
Kaye, Holliday
R.Appleby; D.Stonehouse, G.E.Jones, R.I.Yeoman,
W.L.Gates, R.M.Neal, W.C.Harris, A.Kaye,
A.Peacock, W.Horner, E.Holliday.
Att: 24,733
Oct 16 v Newcastle United (a) 3-2
Peacock 2, Neal
R.Appleby; D.Stonehouse, G.E.Jones, R.I.Yeoman,
W.L.Gates, R.M.Neal, W.C.Harris, A.Kaye,
A.Peacock, D.H.Walker, E.Holliday.
Att: 10,154
Nov 1 v Sunderland (a) 2-2
Weddle, Peacock
R.Appleby; D.Stonehouse, G.E.Jones, R.I.Yeoman,
W.L.Gates, R.M.Neal, W.Day, A.Kaye, D.K.Weddle,
A.Peacock, E.Holliday.

Nov 8 v Newcastle United (h) 4-3
Peacock 2, Burbeck 2
R.Appleby; N.Chapman, D.Stonehouse,
R.I.Yeoman, W.L.Gates, R.M.Neal, W.Day, A.Kaye,
A.Peacock, R.T.Burbeck, W.Hamilton.
Att: 5,386
(Middlesbrough champions)

1962-63
Aug 11 v Bolton Wanderers (h) 0-2
R.Appleby; N.Chapman, G.E.Jones, R.I.Yeoman,
K.G.Thomson, R.M.Neal, A.Kaye, I.S.Gibson,
J.Livingstone, B.Orritt, R.T.Burbeck.
Att: 5,360

1963-64
Aug 13 v Mansfield Town (h) 4-0
Peacock 3, Gibson
R.Appleby; C.B.Knowles, G.E.Jones, B.Orritt,
M.T.G.Nurse, R.M.Neal, A.Kaye, I.S.Gibson,
A.Peacock, S.K.Marshall, R.M.Braithwaite.
Att: 8,300
Aug 17 v Peterborough United (a) 0-1
R.Appleby; N.Chapman, G.E.Jones, R.I.Yeoman,
M.T.G.Nurse, R.M.Neal, A.Kaye, A.Horsfield,
A.Peacock, W.C.Harris, R.M.Braithwaite.
Att: 8,364
Jan 25 v Newcastle United (a) 3-4
Gibson 2, Peacock
E.D.Connachan; N.Chapman, M.McNeil,
R.I.Yeoman, M.T.G.Nurse, B.Orritt, A.Kaye,
I.S.Gibson, A.Peacock, W.Horner, D.Ratcliffe.
Att: 14,455

1964-65
Aug 12 v Sunderland (h) 2-1
Garbett, Irvine
E.D.Connachan; W.L.Gates, G.E.Jones, J.Townsend,
M.T.G.Nurse, B.Orritt, D.Ratcliffe, I.S.Gibson,
T.G.Garbett, J.D.Irvine, R.M.Braithwaite.
Att: 16,451

1965-66
Aug 10 v Newcastle United (h) 2-0
Irvine, Horsfield
E.D.Connachan; W.L.Gates, G.E.Jones, W.Horner,
B.Orritt, J.Townsend, E.Holliday(D.Ratcliffe),
I.S.Gibson, T.G.Garbett(A.Horsfield), J.D.Irvine,
R.M.Braithwaite.
Att: 12,590
Aug 14 v Newcastle United (a) 2-3
Holliday 2
E.D.Connachan; W.L.Gates, G.E.Jones, W.Horner,
B.Orritt(R.A.Smith), J.Townsend(F.Spraggon),
E.Holliday(D.Ratcliffe), I.S.Gibson, A.Horsfield,
J.D.Irvine(D.S.Masson), R.M.Braithwaite(R.P.Le Flem).
Att: 13,534

1966-67
Aug 9 v FC Sparta (h) 2-0
O'Rourke, Eijkenbroeg (og)
R.Appleby; W.L.Gates, G.E.Jones, W.Horner,
R.Rooks, I.Davidson, D.E.Chadwick, D.S.Masson,
J.O'Rourke, J.D.Irvine, J.Lawson.
Att: 5,765
Aug 10 v Whitby (a) 4-2
Lugg, D.Smith, Horsfield 2
Middlesbrough fielded mainly reserve team
Aug 13 v Scarborough (a) 2-2
Horsfield, O'Rourke
D.McPartland; N.Chapman, G.E.Jones, I.Davidson,
W.L.Gates, W.Horner, D.S.Masson(R.A.Smith),
A.Horsfield, J.O'Rourke, J.Lawson,
A.McMordie(G.Butler).
Mar 4 v Hartlepools United (a) 1-0
Chadwick
Att: 2,926
Mar 14 v GAIS (Gothenburg) (h) 4-1
O'Rourke 4
W.Whigham(D.McPartland); W.L.Gates, G.Butler,
J.Hickton, R.Rooks, D.S.Masson, D.E.Chadwick,
J.D.Irvine, J.O'Rourke, A.McMordie(J.D.Laidlaw),
D.G.Downing.
Att: 8,127

1967-68
Aug 5 v Sunderland (a) 0-1
W.Whigham(D.McPartland); G.Butler, G.E.Jones,
D.S.Masson, R.Rooks, W.Horner,
D.E.Chadwick(A.A.McNeill), J.Hickton,
J.O'Rourke, R.Lugg, D.G.Downing.
Aug 8 v Newcastle United (h) 3-2
Hickton 3
D.McPartland; G.Butler(P.R.Worthington), G.E.Jones,
D.S.Masson, W.L.Gates, W.Horner, D.G.Downing,
J.Hickton, J.O'Rourke, R.Lugg(J.Lawson), D.Smith.
Att: 14,708

Aug 12 v Newcastle United (a) 0-2
D.McPartland(M.Short);
G.Butler(P.R.Worthington), G.E.Jones,
D.S.Masson, W.L.Gates(J.Hickton), W.Horner,
D.E.Chadwick, J.Lawson, J.O'Rourke
(A.McMordie), R.Lugg, D.Smith(D.G.Downing).
Att: 13,850
Apr 8 v Go Ahead Eagles (Deventer) (h) 1-3
Hickton
W.Whigham; R.A.Smith, G.E.Jones, M.Allen,
R.Rooks, F.Spraggon, M.P.Kear, A.McMordie,
J.Hickton, A.Horsfield, D.E.Chadwick.
Att: 6,004
Holland/Germany Tour
May 16 v Leeuwarden (a) 2-0
Hickton, Masson
W.Whigham; W.Horner, G.E.Jones, J.A.Crossan,
W.L.Gates, F.Spraggon, M.P.Kear,
A.Horsfield(S.Anderson), J.Hickton, A.McMordie,
D.E.Chadwick(D.S.Masson).
Att: 2,000
May 18 v Bremerhaven (a) 1-0
Horsfield
W.Whigham; W.Horner, F.Spraggon, R.Rooks,
W.L.Gates, D.S.Masson, M.P.Kear, A.McMordie,
J.Hickton, A.Horsfield, G.E.Jones.
Att: 1,000
(Gates sent off)

1968-69
Jul 30 v Sunderland (h) 0-1
W.Whigham; J.Hickton, A.Horsfield, Smith,
G.E.Jones, R.Rooks, F.Spraggon, J.A.Crossan,
A.A.McNeill, D.G.Downing, R.Lugg and S.J.Webb
all played.
Att: 13,502
Jul 31 v Watford (h) 5-0
Horsfield 2, Downing 2, Hickton
(Private friendly played at Hutton Road, agreed 30
minutes each half).
Aug 3 v Hearts (h) 4-3
Rooks, Hickton (pen), McMordie, Horsfield
W.Whigham; R.A.Smith, G.E.Jones, M.Allen,
R.Rooks, F.Spraggon, M.P.Kear, J.Hickton,
A.Horsfield, A.McMordie, D.G.Downing(R.Lugg).
Att: 7,150
Oct 21 v Hearts (a) 4-2
Laidlaw, Hickton 2, Chadwick
W.Whigham; F.Spraggon, G.E.Jones, J.A.Crossan,
R.Rooks, G.Kinnell, M.P.Kear, J.Hickton,
J.D.Laidlaw, D.E.Chadwick,
D.G.Downing(M.Allen).
Att: 6,500
Nov 11 v Bremerhaven (h) 1-1
Hickton
W.Whigham; R.A.Smith, G.E.Jones, M.Allen,
G.Kinnell, F.Spraggon(A.Horsfield), M.P.Kear,
J.Hickton, J.D.Laidlaw, J.A.Crossan, R.Lugg.
Att: 6,759

1969-70
Jul 26 v Sunderland (a) 0-0
M.Short; A.Moody, G.E.Jones, G.Smith, W.L.Gates,
F.Spraggon, M.P.Kear, A.McMordie, J.D.Laidlaw,
J.Hickton, D.E.Chadwick(D.G.Downing).
Jul 30 v Lincoln City (a) 2-0
Laidlaw, Jones
M.Short; A.Moody(M.Smith), G.E.Jones, G.Smith,
W.L.Gates, F.Spraggon(B.Myton), M.P.Kear,
A.McMordie(W.D.Maddren), J.D.Laidlaw
(D.J.Mills), J.Hickton, D.E.Chadwick.
Aug 2 v Burnley (a) 1-1
Laidlaw
M.Short; A.Moody(R.Lugg), G.E.Jones, G.Smith,
W.L.Gates, B.Myton, A.McMordie, M.P.Kear,
J.D.Laidlaw, J.Hickton, D.E.Chadwick.
Oct 20 v SC Cambuur (h) 3-0
Mills, McIlmoyle, Hickton
W.Whigham; R.A.Smith(A.Moody), G.E.Jones
(B.Myton), G.Smith, W.L.Gates, F.Spraggon,
A.Murray, D.J.Mills, H.McIlmoyle(D.E.Chadwick),
J.Hickton, D.Burluraux.
Att: 4,209
Nov 11 v All-Stars XI (h) 3-4
Hickton 2, Chadwick
W.Whigham; R.A.Smith, G.E.Jones, G.Smith,
W.L.Gates, F.Spraggon, D.E.Chadwick,
A.McMordie, J.D.Laidlaw, J.Hickton, A.Murray.
Att: 7,650
Gordon Jones' Testimonial
Nov 25 v VFR Neuess (h) 7-1
Hickton 3, Mills 3, Murray
W.Whigham; G.E.Jones, B.Myton, J.A.Crossan,
S.J.Webb, F.Spraggon, A.Murray, D.J.Mills,
W.D.Maddren, J.Hickton(M.P.Kear), A.McMordie.
Att: 1,177
Apr 22 v Go Ahead Eagles (Deventer) (a) 0-0
W.Whigham; R.A.Smith, G.E.Jones, A.Moody,
W.L.Gates, F.Spraggon, D.J.Mills, W.D.Maddren,
J.D.Laidlaw, J.Hickton, B.Myton.
Att: 4,000

Apr 25 v VFR Neuess (a) 0-1
W.Whigham; W.D.Maddren, B.Myton, A.Moody,
M.Allen, F.Spraggon, A.Murray, D.J.Mills,
S.J.Webb, J.Hickton, D.G.Downing.

1970-71
Aug 1 v Burnley (h) 2-2
McMordie, Maddren
W.Whigham; A.Moody(B.Myton), G.E.Jones, G.Smith,
W.L.Gates, F.Spraggon, D.G.Downing(D.J.Mills),
A.McMordie, W.D.Maddren, J.Hickton, J.D.Laidlaw.
Att: 8,333
Aug 5 v York City (a) 0-1
Att: 2,949
Aug 7 v Liverpool (h) 3-1
Mills 2, Laidlaw
W.Whigham; R.A.Smith, G.E.Jones, G.Smith,
W.L.Gates, F.Spraggon, D.J.Mills, A.McMordie,
W.D.Maddren, J.Hickton, J.D.Laidlaw(D.G.Downing).
Att: 13,120
Aug 8 v Mansfield Town (a) 0-3
W.Whigham(J.A.Platt); A.Moody, G.E.Jones
(B.Myton), G.Smith, M.Allen, F.Spraggon,
A.Murray, H.Charlton, D.G.Downing, J.Hickton,
D.Burluraux.
Att: 4,000
May 4 v Scarborough (a) 4-3
Downing, Stone, Murray, Vincent
Probable: W.Whigham; R.A.Smith, M.Allen,
A.Moody, W.L.Gates, W.D.Maddren, D.J.Mills,
J.V.Vincent, J.G.Stone, A.Murray, D.G.Downing.
(Scarborough's Player of the Year match)

1971-72
Jul 31 v Hibernian (a) 2-0
Laidlaw, Hickton
W.Whigham; W.D.Maddren, G.E.Jones,
N.P.Stiles(W.L.Gates), S.W.Boam, F.Spraggon,
D.G.Downing, D.J.Mills(A.McMordie), J.Hickton,
J.V.Vincent, J.D.Laidlaw.
Att: 15,000
Aug 4 v Hartlepools United (a) 2-2
Mills, Allen
Att: 1,560
Aug 7 v Hibernian (h) 4-2
Hickton 3, Laidlaw
W.Whigham(J.A.Platt); W.D.Maddren,
G.E.Jones(M.Allen), N.P.Stiles(W.L.Gates),
S.W.Boam, F.Spraggon, D.G.Downing, D.J.Mills,
J.Hickton, J.V.Vincent, J.D.Laidlaw(A.McMordie).
Att: 8,061
Aug 10 v Benfica (h) 1-1
Hickton
W.Whigham; M.Allen, G.E.Jones, N.P.Stiles
(A.McMordie), S.W.Boam, F.Spraggon,
D.G.Downing, D.J.Mills, J.Hickton, J.V.Vincent,
J.D.Laidlaw.
Att: 21,101

1972-73
Jul 31 v FC Groningen (h) 4-0
Mills 2, Hickton (pen), Smith (pen)
J.A.Platt; A.Moody(P.A.Creamer), F.Spraggon,
N.P.Stiles, S.W.Boam, W.D.Maddren, A.McMordie,
J.V.Vincent, D.J.Mills(M.Smith), J.Hickton,
D.Armstrong(H.Charlton).
Att: 3,700
(Hickton sent off for kicking opponent)
Aug 2 v Mansfield Town (a) 3-0
Mills, McMordie, Vincent
J.A.Platt; P.A.Creamer, F.Spraggon, A.Moody,
S.W.Boam, W.D.Maddren, A.McMordie, M.Smith,
D.J.Mills(P.K.Brine), H.Charlton, J.V.Vincent.
Aug 7 v Barnsley (a) 0-1
J.A.Platt; J.E.Craggs, F.Spraggon, N.P.Stiles,
S.W.Boam, W.D.Maddren, D.J.Mills, A.McMordie,
M.Smith(D.Armstrong), J.Hickton, J.V.Vincent.
May 7 v England XI (h) 7-5
Hickton 3, Foggon 2, Peters (og), Mills
J.A.Platt; J.E.Craggs, F.Spraggon, N.P.Stiles,
S.W.Boam, W.D.Maddren, T.Venables(Guest),
D.J.Mills, T.Hibbitt(guest), J.Hickton, A.Foggon.
Att: 10,674
Harold Shepherdson's Testimonial

1973-74
Jul 28 v Morton (a) 2-0
Mills 2
J.A.Platt; J.E.Craggs, F.Spraggon, S.W.Boam,
B.Taylor, W.D.Maddren, D.Armstrong,
A.McMordie, J.Hickton, D.J.Mills, A.Foggon.
Jul 30 v Hamilton Academical (a) 3-1
Craggs, Armstrong, Hickton
P.J.Cuff; J.E.Craggs(G.J.Souness), F.Spraggon
(P.A.Creamer), S.W.Boam, B.Taylor, N.P.Stiles,
W.D.Maddren, H.Charlton(A.McMordie),
D.Armstrong, J.Hickton, A.Foggon.
Att: 3,500

Aug 1 v Partick Thistle (a) 2-0
McMordie, Brine
J.A.Platt; J.E.Craggs, F.Spraggon, S.W.Boam,
B.Taylor, W.D.Maddren, A.McMordie(H.Charlton),
D.Armstrong, J.Hickton(P.K.Brine), M.Smith,
A.Foggon.
Aug 11 v Newcastle United (h) 1-3
Mills
J.A.Platt; J.E.Craggs, F.Spraggon, S.W.Boam,
B.Taylor, W.D.Maddren, A.McMordie, D.J.Mills,
J.Hickton, D.Armstrong(N.P.Stiles), A.Foggon.
Att: 12,272
Aug 16 v Shildon (a) 4-1
McGivern, M.Smith 2, Poskett
Aug 18 v York City (a) 1-2
Mills
J.A.Platt(P.J.Cuff); J.E.Craggs, G.J.Souness,
S.W.Boam, W.D.Maddren, W.L.Gates, N.P.Stiles,
A.McMordie, D.J.Mills, J.Hickton(M.Smith),
D.Armstrong.
Aug 20 v Grimsby Town (a) 2-1
Foggon, Hickton
J.A.Platt(P.J.Cuff); J.E.Craggs, F.Spraggon,
S.W.Boam(P.A.Creamer), B.Taylor, W.D.Maddren,
Frank McGivern(M.Smith), J.Hickton, D.J.Mills
(N.P.Stiles[W.L.Gates]), A.Foggon, D.Armstrong.
Att: 5,042
Mar 26 v Darlington (a) 4-0
Foggon 2, Mills, Boam
D.Armstrong; S.W.Boam, D.J.Mills, A.Foggon,
M.Smith, M.Poskett and P.J.Cuff all played.
Att: 5,000
Alan Sproates' Testimonial
May 1 v Aldershot (a) 0-1
J.A.Platt; J.E.Craggs, F.Spraggon, G.J.Souness,
S.W.Boam, W.D.Maddren, R.W.Murdoch,
D.J.Mills, J.Hickton, A.Foggon, D.Armstrong.
Att: 5,027
Richard Walden Testimonial
May 3 v Tunbridge Wells (a)
May 7 v Leeds U (h) 4-4
Mills, Foggon 3
J.A.Platt; J.E.Craggs, J.K.Cochrane, G.J.Souness,
S.W.Boam, W.L.Gates, R.W.Murdoch, D.J.Mills
(M.Smith), J.Hickton, A.Foggon, D.Armstrong.
Att: 31,643
Billy Gates' Testimonial
May 10 v Newcastle United (a) 3-5
Hickton, Foggon, M.Smith
J.A.Platt; J.E.Craggs, F.Spraggon(J.K.Cochrane),
G.J.Souness, S.W.Boam, J.Charlton(B.Taylor),
R.W.Murdoch(P.K.Brine), M.Smith, J.Hickton,
A.Foggon, D.Armstrong.
Att: 27,938
Tony Green Testimonial

Norway Tour
May 17 v Viking Stavanger (a) 3-1
M.Smith, Foggon, Boam
May 19 v SK Vard (a) 4-0
M.Smith 2, Hickton, Platt (pen)

1974-75
Jul 27 v Dunfermline Athletic (a) 1-2
Armstrong
J.A.Platt; J.E.Craggs, F.Spraggon, G.J.Souness,
S.W.Boam, W.D.Maddren(A.McAndrew),
R.W.Murdoch(A.McMordie), D.J.Mills,
J.Hickton(M.Smith), A.Foggon, D.Armstrong.
Att: 3,000
Apr 21 v SK Brann (a) –
Apr 29 v Viking Stavangar (a) 3-0
Hickton, Mills, Maddren
J.A.Platt; J.E.Craggs(P.K.Brine), F.Spraggon,
G.J.Souness(M.Smith), H.Charlton(S.W.Boam),
W.D.Maddren, R.W.Murdoch, D.J.Mills,
J.Hickton, A.Foggon(A.S.Willey), D.Armstrong.
Att: 2,000

Australia/New Zealand Tour
May 4 v Western Australia (a) 1-1
(Played at Perth)
Mills
J.A.Platt; J.E.Craggs(F.Spraggon), T.Cooper,
G.J.Souness, B.Taylor, W.D.Maddren,
R.W.Murdoch, D.J.Mills, J.Hickton(M.Smith),
A.Foggon, D.Armstrong.
Att: 6,000
May 7 v South Australia (a) 1-1
(Played at Adelaide)
Mills
J.A.Platt; J.E.Craggs, F.Spraggon, G.J.Souness,
S.W.Boam, W.D.Maddren, R.W.Murdoch,
M.Smith(P.K.Brine), D.J.Mills, T.Cooper,
D.Armstrong.
Att: 6,000

May 11 v Queensland (a) 4-0
(Played at Brisbane)
Maddren, Mills, Armstrong, J.Charlton
J.A.Platt; J.E.Craggs, T.Cooper, G.J.Souness,
S.W.Boam, W.D.Maddren, R.W.Murdoch,
D.J.Mills(J.Charlton), A.S.Willey(M.Smith),
A.Foggon(F.Spraggon), D.Armstrong.
Att: 7,000
May 14 v Balgownie (a) 5-3
(Played at Wollongong)
Murdoch 3 (2 pens), Boam, Souness
Att: 4,578
May 18 v Northern New South Wales (a) 8-0
(Played at Newcastle)
Mills 2, J.Charlton 2, Armstrong 2, Murdoch, Brine
J.A.Platt; J.E.Craggs, F.Spraggon, G.J.Souness
(P.K.Brine), S.W.Boam, W.D.Maddren(B.Taylor),
R.W.Murdoch(M.Smith), D.J.Mills(J.Charlton),
A.Foggon(A.S.Willey), T.Cooper, D.Armstrong.
Att: 10,500
May 19 v Christchurch (a) 2-0
(Played at Canterbury)
Cooper, Murdoch
J.A.Platt; J.E.Craggs, F.Spraggon, G.J.Souness,
S.W.Boam, W.D.Maddren, R.W.Murdoch,
D.J.Mills(J.Hickton), M.Smith(A.Foggon),
T.Cooper, D.Armstrong.
May 20 v Auckland (a) 5-1
Mills 3, Armstrong, Willey
P.J.Cuff; J.E.Craggs, F.Spraggon, G.J.Souness,
S.W.Boam, W.D.Maddren, R.W.Murdoch
(P.K.Brine), D.J.Mills, A.S.Willey(M.Smith),
T.Cooper(J.Hickton), D.Armstrong.
Att: 10,000
May 26 v Tahiti Select XI (a) 6-0
Mills 2, Craggs, Willey, Cooper, J.Charlton

1975-76
Oct 28 v Dinamo Zagreb (h) 2-2
Spraggon (pen), Hickton (pen)
J.A.Platt; J.E.Craggs, F.Spraggon, G.J.Souness,
S.W.Boam, W.D.Maddren, R.W.Murdoch, Cyril
Hewitt, J.Hickton, A.Foggon, T.Cooper.
Att: 9,393
Frank Spraggon's Testimonial
May 5 v SK Brann (a) 2-0
Souness, Maddren

1976-77
Finland Tour
Aug 3 v KuPS Palloseura (a) 2-1
Boersma, Craggs
J.A.Platt; J.E.Craggs, T.Cooper, G.J.Souness,
S.W.Boam, W.D.Maddren, P.Boersma, D.J.Mills,
J.Hickton, E.P.Coleman(R.W.Murdoch),
D.Armstrong.
Aug 4 v HJK (Helsinki) (a) 1-1
Hickton
J.A.Platt; J.E.Craggs, T.Cooper(I.C.Bailey),
G.J.Souness, S.W.Boam, W.D.Maddren, P.Boersma,
D.J.Mills, J.Hickton, R.W.Murdoch(Alex
McGarritty), D.Armstrong.
Aug 6 v Reipas Lahti (a) 3-0
Armstrong, Boersma, Maddren
D.J.Mills; D.Armstrong, A.McAndrew, G.J.Souness,
J.Hickton(W.Woof), W.D.Maddren(A.Ramage),
A.Walsh(I.C.Bell) all played.
Nov 13 v Hearts (h) 3-0
Brine, Cummins, Hickton
P.J.Cuff; J.E.Craggs, I.C.Bailey, P.K.Brine
(G.Hedley), S.W.Boam, A.Ramage, A.McAndrew,
D.J.Mills, S.Cummins, P.Boersma(J.Hickton),
Armstrong.
Att: 8,000
Apr 19 v Sunderland (h) 6-1
Hickton 3, Charlton, Hedley, Cummins
J.A.Platt(D.J.Brown); J.E.Craggs(P.K.Brine),
I.C.Bailey, G.J.Souness, S.W.Boam(A.McAndrew),
A.Ramage, H.Charlton(J.A.Platt), S.Cummins,
J.Hickton, A.E.H.Wood(G.Hedley),
D.Armstrong(A.Walsh).
Att: 10,500
John Hickton's Testimonial

1977-78
v Oslo (a) 1-0
Maddren
Aug 5 v Aberystwyth (a) 0-0
Aug 6 v Wrexham (a) 0-3
Att: 3,000
Aug 9 v Hearts (a) 0-1
J.A.Platt; J.E.Craggs, T.Cooper, G.J.Souness,
S.W.Boam, W.D.Maddren(A.Ramage), P.K.Brine
(G.Hedley), D.J.Mills, J.Hickton(W.Woof),
W.Askew, D.Armstrong.
Att: 8,000

May 9 v Scottish XI (h) 5-5
Ashcroft 3, Cummins, Armstrong (pen)
D.J.Brown; J.E.Craggs, I.C.Bailey, J.F.Mahoney,
S.W.Boam, A.Ramage, D.J.Mills, S.Cummins,
W.Ashcroft, M.E.Burns(Newcastle U, guest),
D.Armstrong.
Att: 18,000
Willie Maddren's Testimonial

1978-79
Aug 5 v Inverness Clachnacuddin (a) 4-0
Hedley 2, Armstrong (pen), McCrae (og)
J.G.Stewart(D.J.Brown); J.E.Craggs(P.E.Johnson),
I.C.Bailey, A.Ramage, S.W.Boam(M.G.Proctor),
A.McAndrew, G.Hedley, J.F.Mahoney
(C.P.Johnston), D.J.Shearer, S.Cummins,
D.Armstrong.
Aug 7 v Aberdeen (a) 2-3
Cummins, Hedley
Aug 8 v Hearts (a) 0-3
J.G.Stewart; I.C.Bailey, P.E.Johnson, J.F.Mahoney
(C.P.Johnston), S.W.Boam, A.Ramage,
G.Hedley(W.Woof), A.McAndrew, D.J.Shearer
(W.D.Maddren), S.Cummins(A.Walsh),
D.Armstrong.
Aug 11 v AFC Ajax (h) 1-0
Woof
J.G.Stewart; J.E.Craggs(P.E.Johnson), I.C.Bailey,
J.F.Mahoney(C.P.Johnston), S.W.Boam, A.Ramage
(M.G.Proctor), G.Hedley, A.McAndrew, W.Ashcroft
(D.J.Shearer), W.Woof, D.Armstrong.
Att: 9,527
Aug 16 v Huracán (h) 2-1
Woof, Ashcroft
J.G.Stewart; I.Stokoe(C.P.Johnston), I.C.Bailey,
J.F.Mahoney, S.W.Boam, A.Ramage, G.Hedley
(M.G.Proctor), D.J.Mills, W.Ashcroft, W.Woof,
D.Armstrong.
Att: 9,672
Dec 13 v Sheffield Wednesday (a) 3-0
Janković 2, Unknown
May 9 v Scottish XI (h) 5-5
Ashcroft 3, Cummins, Armstrong (pen)
D.J.Brown; J.E.Craggs, I.C.Bailey, J.F.Mahoney,
S.W.Boam, A.Ramage, D.J.Mills, S.Cummins,
W.Ashcroft, M.E.Burns (Newcastle U, guest),
D.Armstrong.
Willie Maddren's Testimonial
Aug 5 v Inverness Clachnacuddin (a) 4-0
Hedley 2, Armstrong (pen), McCrae (og)
J.G.Stewart(D.J.Brown); J.E.Craggs(P.E.Johnson),
I.C.Bailey, A.Ramage, S.W.Boam(M.G.Proctor),
A.McAndrew, G.Hedley, J.F.Mahoney
(C.P.Johnston), D.J.SHearer, S.Cummins,
D.Armstrong.
Aug 7 v Aberdeen (a) 2-3
Cummins, Hedley
Aug 8 v Hearts (a) 0-3
J.G.Stewart; I.C.Bailey, P.E.Johnson, J.F.Mahoney
(C.P.Johnston), S.W.Boam, A.Ramage, G.Hedley
(W.Woof), A.McAndrew, D.J.Shearer
(W.D.Maddren), S.Cummins(A.Walsh),
D.Armstrong.

1979-80
Aug 1 v Crook Town (a) 4-1
Cummins, Proctor, Hodgson, Janković
Nattrass also played.
Aug 4 v China (h) 2-0
Armstrong (pen), Ashcroft
J.A.Platt(J.G.Stewart), J.E.Craggs, I.C.Bailey,
I.Nattrass, W.Ashcroft, S.W.Boam, A.McAndrew,
D.J.Hodgson(G.T.Cochrane), M.G.Proctor,
B.Janković(S.Cummins), D.Armstrong.
Att: 8,605
Aug 10 v Gateshead (a) 9-1
*Burns 3, Janković 2, Johnston 2, Hodgson,
Armstrong.*
J.A.Platt; J.E.Craggs, I.C.Bailey, I.Nattrass,
W.Ashcroft, A.McAndrew, D.J.Hodgson,
M.G.Proctor, B.Janković, M.E.Burns(W.Woof),
D.Armstrong, C.P.Johnston (sub) — played.
Att: 450
Oct 16 v Tulsa Roughnecks (h) 4-0
Burns 3, Proctor
J.G.Stewart; J.E.Craggs, I.C.Bailey(J.Peters),
C.P.Johnston, A.Ramage, A.McAndrew
(M.A.Angus), G.T.Cochrane, M.G.Proctor,
D.J.Hodgson, M.E.Burns(G.Hedley), D.Armstrong.
Att: 4,114
Dec 12 v Army XI (a) 3-1
Hodgson, Woof 2
Japan Cup, Ohmiya Stadium
May 27 v Japan XI (a) 2-1
Hodgson 2
J.G.Stewart; J.E.Craggs, P.E.Johnson, G.Hedley,
W.Ashcroft, A.McAndrew, C.P.Johnston,
D.J.Shearer, D.J.Hodgson, W.Askew
(G.T.Cochrane), D.Armstrong.

May 29 v Argentinos Juniors (a) 4-0
Hodgson, Ashcroft, Janković, Woof
J.A.Platt; J.E.Craggs, P.E.Johnson, G.Hedley,
W.Ashcroft, A.McAndrew, G.T.Cochrane
(B.Janković), C.P.Johnston, D.J.Hodgson,
D.J.Shearer(W.Woof), D.Armstrong.
Japan Cup, National Stadium, Tokyo
May 31 v China (a) 3-1
Proctor, Shearer, Hedley
J.G.Stewart; J.E.Craggs, P.E.Johnson,
C.P.Johnston, W.Ashcroft(M.A.Angus),
A.McAndrew, G.T.Cochrane(B.Janković),
M.G.Proctor, D.J.Hodgson, D.J.Shearer, G.Hedley.
Jun 3 v RCD Español (a) 1-1
Johnston
J.A.Platt; J.E.Craggs, A.McAndrew, C.P.Johnston
(P.E.Johnson), W.Ashcroft, A.McAndrew,
M.G.Proctor, G.Hedley, D.J.Hodgson, D.J.Shearer,
D.Armstrong.
(Won 4-3 on penalties)

1980-81
Jul 27 v WAC Casablanca (a) 2-2
Shearer 2
J.A.Platt; J.E.Craggs, I.C.Bailey, C.P.Johnston,
G.Hedley(W.Ashcroft), A.McAndrew, D.J.Shearer
(M.G.Proctor), M.E.Burns(B.Janković),
D.J.Hodgson, I.Nattrass, D.Armstrong.
Jul 29 v Tetouan Cresta FC (a) 2-1
Shearer, Armstrong
J.G.Stewart; J.E.Craggs, I.C.Bailey(W.Ashcroft),
C.P.Johnston, A.McAndrew, I.Nattrass,
M.G.Proctor, M.E.Burns, D.J.Hodgson,
D.J.Shearer, D.Armstrong.
Aug 6 v Panathinaikos (a) 0-4
J.G.Stewart; J.E.Craggs, I.C.Bailey, C.P.Johnston,
W.Ashcroft(G.Hedley), A.McAndrew, I.Nattrass,
M.G.Proctor(B.Janković), D.J.Hodgson,
D.J.Shearer(M.E.Burns), D.Armstrong.
Att: 25,000
Aug 7 v Olympiakos (a) 2-2
Woof, Johnston
J.A.Platt; I.Nattrass(J.E.Craggs), I.C.Bailey,
C.P.Johnston, W.Ashcroft, A.McAndrew,
M.G.Proctor(G.Hedley), W.Woof, B.Janković,
D.J.Shearer, D.Armstrong.
Aug 9 v Olimpija Ljubljana (h) 4-1
Armstrong, Janković, Johnston, Hodgson
J.A.Platt; I.Nattrass, I.C.Bailey, C.P.Johnston,
W.Ashcroft, A.McAndrew, M.E.Burns,
M.G.Proctor, D.J.Hodgson, B.Janković,
D.Armstrong.
Att: 2,339
Oct 1 v Middlesbrough XI (1974) (h) 3-2
Janković, Nattrass, Shearer
J.G.Stewart; I.Nattrass, I.C.Bailey, C.P.Johnston,
M.A.Angus, A.McAndrew, D.J.Shearer,
M.G.Proctor, D.J.Hodgson, B.Janković, W.Askew
(G.Hedley).
Middlesbrough (1974)
Foggon, Armstrong (pen)
J.A.Platt; J.E.Craggs, F.Spraggon, A.McMordie,
S.W.Boam, W.D.Maddren(W.L.Gates),
R.W.Murdoch(Bobby Kerr, guest), S.Cummins,
J.Hickton, A.Foggon, D.Armstrong.
Att: 7,611
David Armstrong's Testimonial

1981-82
Aug 11 v Japan XI (h) 0-0
J.A.Platt; J.E.Craggs, J.Bolton, G.Hedley,
I.Nattrass, A.McAndrew, W.Woof, M.A.Angus
(C.Ross), W.Ashcroft, G.Macdonald, I.C.Bailey
(W.Askew).
Att: 4,200
Aug 17 v Shildon (a) 4-2
Shearer, Askew, Macdonald, McMahon
Squad: K.G.O'Hanlon; K.Nobbs, J.Peters, C.Ross,
M.A.Angus, P.Robinson, C.Blackburn,
M.Robinson, G.MacDonald, D.J.Shearer,
I.C.Bailey, W.Askew, A.McCreesh, McMahon,
Holyoek.
Aug 19 v Spennymoor United (a) 4-0
Hedley 2, Askew, Macdonald
J.A.Platt; J.E.Craggs, J.Bolton, G.Hedley,
I.Nattrass, A.McAndrew, G.T.Cochrane, H.M.Otto
(M.A.Angus), D.J.Shearer(G.Macdonald), W.Woof,
W.Askew.
Aug 22 v Sheffield Wednesday (a) 3-0
Macdonald, Cochrane, Holton (og)
J.A.Platt; J.E.Craggs, J.Bolton, G.Hedley(C.Ross),
M.J.Baxter, I.Nattrass, G.T.Cochrane(W.Ashcroft),
H.M.Otto, G.Macdonald, W.Woof, W.Askew
(I.C.Bailey).
Att: 4,139
Aug 24 v Queen of the South (a) 1-0
Nattrass (pen)
J.A.Platt; J.E.Craggs, J.Bolton, G.Hedley,
M.J.Baxter, I.Nattrass, W.Woof, H.Otto,
G.Macdonald, W.Ashcroft, A.McAndrew.
(Official opening of new floodlights)

Sep 8 v Sunderland (h) 1-2
Hodgson
George Best guested for Middlesbrough, Jim Platt
played at centre-forward from start of second half,
was replaced by Kelham O'Hanlon in goal.
Att: 7,425
Jim Platt's Testimonial
Nov 17 v Morton (a) 1-2
Hedley
K.G.O'Hanlon; G.Hedley, A.McAndrew, W.Woof,
R.Thomson, D.J.Hodgson and S.Bell all played.
Allan McGraw Testimonial
Dec 2 v Combined Services (a) 3-1
Hodgson, Ashcroft 2
Att: 2,854
Jan 23 v Sheffield Wednesday (a) 2-1
Thomson (pen), Hedley
J.A.Platt; J.E.Craggs, I.C.Bailey, C.Ross, I.Nattrass
(M.J.Baxter), A.McAndrew, G.T.Cochrane,
H.M.Otto, D.J.Hodgson, G.Macdonald,
R.Thomson(G.Hedley).
(Thomson missed penalty, Platt saved one)
May 20 v Cliftonville (a) 2-2
Largey (og), Armstrong
C.B.Knowles, D.Armstrong, J.A.Platt
(K.G.O'Hanlon) all played.
John Platt's Testimonial

1982-83
Aug 6 v Mansfield Town (h) 3-0
Otto, Shearer, Cochrane
J.A.Platt(K.G.O'Hanlon); J.Brownlie, J.Bolton,
H.M.Otto, M.J.Baxter(A.M.Mowbray), D.T.Wood
(M.A.Angus), G.T.Cochrane, C.Ross(S.Bell),
D.J.Hodgson(G.Macdonald), D.N.Currie
(D.J.Shearer), A.McAndrew.
(Private friendly, played at Ayresome Park)
Aug 9 v Berwick Rangers (a) 0-0
J.A.Platt(K.G.O'Hanlon); J.Brownlie, J.Bolton,
H.M.Otto, M.J.Baxter(A.M.Mowbray), D.T.Wood
(M.A.Angus), G.T.Cochrane(A.Roberts), C.Ross
(S.Bell), D.J.Shearer(G.Macdonald), D.N.Currie,
A.McAndrew.
Aug 12 v Linfield (a) 2-0
Ross, Shearer
J.A.Platt; J.Brownlie, J.Bolton, H.M.Otto(S.Bell),
M.J.Baxter, D.T.Wood, G.T.Cochrane, C.Ross,
D.J.Shearer, D.N.Currie(G.Macdonald),
A.McAndrew.
Aug 14 v Doncaster Rovers (h) 0-1
J.A.Platt(K.G.O'Hanlon); J.Brownlie, J.Bolton,
H.M.Otto(S.Bell), M.J.Baxter, D.T.Wood
(M.A.Angus), G.T.Cochrane(A.Roberts), C.Ross,
D.J.Shearer(M.Condon), G.Macdonald
(D.N.Currie), A.McAndrew.
(Private friendly)
Aug 18 v Spennymoor United (a) 4-0
Bell, Otto, Cochrane, Macdonald
J.A.Platt; C.Ross, J.Bolton, H.M.Otto, M.J.Baxter,
D.T.Wood, G.T.Cochrane, D.N.Currie
(G.Macdonald), A.McAndrew, J.Brownlie, S.Bell.
Nov 1 v Combined Services (a) –
Nov 16 v Newcastle United (h) 3-3
Hodgson 3
Att: 3,573
John Craggs' Testimonial
May 17 v England XI (h) 1-2
Sugrue
K.G.O'Hanlon(J.A.Platt); I.Nattrass (P.T.Ward),
G.J.Hamilton(C.B.Knowles), M.J.Baxter,
A.M.Mowbray, H.M.Otto, P.Sugrue,
M.F.M.Kennedy, D.T.Wood, G.Macdonald, S.Bell.
Att: 13,710
George Hardwick/Wilf Mannion Testimonial

1983-84
Jul 23 v Scarborough (a) 1-3
Att: 770
Aug 3 v Horden (a) 3-3
K.Spraggon, Angus, McMahon
Aug 8 v North Shields (a) 1-2
Gill
Aug 9 v ICI Wilton (a) 1-0
Kennedy
Aug 10 v Spennymoor United (a) 6-0
Currie 3, Hankin, Roberts, Hamilton
Currie; Hankin, Roberts, Macdonald, Hamilton all played.
Aug 12 v Darlington (a) 2-0
Wood, Currie
K.G.O'Hanlon; D.T.Wood, P.T.Ward, M.J.Baxter,
A.M.Mowbray, H.M.Otto, M.F.M.Kennedy,
D.N.Currie, G.Macdonald, S.Bell(G.Buckley),
A.Roberts(G.J.Hamilton).
Att: 1,623
Aug 15 v Hull City (a) 2-2
Currie 2
K.G.O'Hanlon; D.T.Wood, P.T.Ward, P.Sugrue,
M.J.Baxter, A.M.Mowbray, A.Roberts,
M.F.M.Kennedy(H.M.Otto), G.Macdonald
(R.Hankin), D.N.Currie, G.J.Hamilton.
Att: 2,857

Aug 19 v Sunderland (a) 0-4
K.G.O'Hanlon; A.M.Mowbray, P.T.Ward
(G.J.Hamilton), H.M.Otto, M.J.Baxter(P.Beagrie),
I.Nattrass, A.Roberts, M.F.M.Kennedy(S.McPhee),
D.N.Currie, G.Macdonald(R.Hankin), P.Sugrue.
Att: 5,006

1984-85
Aug 2 v Motherwell (a) 2-0
Mills 2
K.G.O'Hanlon; D.T.Wood, P.T.Ward,
A.M.Mowbray, G.Scott, I.Nattrass, P.Sugrue,
M.F.Buckley, S.Bell, H.M.Otto, D.J.Mills.
Aug 4 v Morton (a) 1-2
Currie
K.G.O'Hanlon; G.J.Hamilton, P.T.Ward,
G.S.Scott, A.M.Mowbray, D.T.Wood,
S.Bell(Roberts), D.J.Mills, H.M.Otto, D.N.Currie,
M.F.Buckley (P.S.Beagrie).
Aug 7 v Hibernian (a) 0-0
K.G.O'Hanlon; G.Gill, A.M.Mowbray, I.Nattrass,
G.Scott, A.Roberts, M.F.Buckley, H.M.Otto,
D.N.Currie(S.Bell), P.Sugrue, D.J.Mills.
Aug 14 v Sunderland (h) 0-1
K.G.O'Hanlon; D.T.Wood, G.Scott, M.F.Buckley,
A.M.Mowbray, I.Nattrass, A.Roberts(D.N.Currie),
D.J.Mills, H.M.Otto(P.T.Ward), P.Sugrue, S.Bell.
Att: 2,595
Aug 18 v Newcastle United (a) 2-2
Sugrue, Gill
K.G.O'Hanlon; D.T.Wood, G.J.Hamilton,
M.F.Buckley, A.M.Mowbray, G.Scott(G.Gill),
P.T.Ward, D.J.Mills, H.M.Otto, P.Sugrue(S.Bell),
D.N.Currie.
Att: 6,867

1985-86
Jul 30 v Billingham Synthonia (a) 0-1
S.Pears; B.Laws, A.M.Mowbray, I.Nattrass, G.Gill,
A.Roberts, G.J.Hamilton, A.McAndrew,
P.S.Beagrie, A.Stephens, G.Rowell.
Aug 3 v Lincoln City (a) 2-1
Rowell, Stephens
S.Pears; B.Laws, I.Nattrass, G.A.Pallister, G.Gill,
S.E.Ripley, D.J.O'Riordan, A.McAndrew,
P.S.Beagrie, A.Stephens, G.Rowell.
Att: 641
Aug 5 v Guisborough (a) 4-2
Corden, Roberts, Kernaghan, Hamilton
Aug 10 v Scarborough (a) 1-1
O'Riordan
S.Pears; B.Laws, G.A.Pallister, A.M.Mowbray,
G.Gill, S.E.Ripley, D.J.O'Riordan, A.McAndrew,
D.N.Currie, A.Stephens, G.Rowell.
Apr 28 v Newcastle United (h) 2-1
Duffield 2
P.D.Kite(P.Flear); G.A.Parkinson, M.Cook, G.Gill,
A.N.Kernaghan, C.Farnaby, S.E.Ripley(Craft),
D.J.Mills, D.N.Currie, P.Duffield, G.Rowell.
Att: 3,500
David Mills' Testimonial

1986-87
Jul 21 v Stockton (a) 3-0
Jul 29 v Billingham Town (a) 2-0
Hamilton 2
Aug 16 v Norton/Stockton Ancients (a) 4-0
Aug 18 v Billingham Synthonia (a) 3-0
Pallister, Rowell, Stephens

1987-88
Jul 21 v Norton/Stockton Ancients (a) 11-0
*Kerr 4, Stephens, Slaven 2, Hamilton,
Glover 2, Kernaghan*
Att: 1,500
Jul 23 v South Bank (a) 0-0
Jul 27 v Seattle Storm (h) 2-1
Kerr, Slaven
S.Pears; G.Gill(A.N.Kernaghan) C.T.Cooper
(D.V.Glover), A.M.Mowbray, G.A.Parkinson,
B.J.Slaven, A.Stephens, G.J.Hamilton, P.A.Kerr,
S.E.Ripley.
Att: 4,858
Jul 30 v Scunthorpe United 3-1
Proudlock 2, Hamilton
(Private Friendly played at Maiden Castle)
Aug 3 v Berwick Rangers (a) 2-0
Kernaghan 2
Aug 5 v Newcastle United (a) 1-1
Stephens
S.Pears(K.Poole); G.J.Hamilton(G.Gill),
C.T.Cooper, A.M.Mowbray, B.Laws
(G.A.Parkinson), D.V.Glover(N.M.Mohan),
B.J.Slaven, S.E.Ripley(A.N.Kernaghan), T.J.Senior,
P.A.Kerr, M.S.Burke.
(Private Friendly played at Benfield Road)
Apr 15 v Rochdale (a) 3-0
Senior, Slaven 2
Att: 843

North American Tour
Jun 3 v San Jose Earthquakes (a) 2-1
Kernaghan 2
Jun 8 v Calgary Kickers (a) 2-0
Kerr, Hamilton
Att: 2,700
Jun 11 v Seattle Storm (a) 1-2
Kernaghan
Jun 14 v Albany Capitals (a) 1-1
Burke

1988-89
Sweden Tour
Jul 30 v Saro (a) 2-1
Slaven, Brennan
S.Pears; G.A.Parkinson, A.M.Mowbray,
G.A.Pallister, C.T.Cooper, G.Gill, M.R.Brennan,
D.V.Glover, B.J.Slaven, S.E.Ripley, T.J.Senior.
Aug 1 v Munkedal (a) 4-1
Gill, Senior, Glover, Kernaghan
S.E.Ripley, G.A.Parkinson, A.N.Kernaghan also
played.
Aug 2 v Alingas (a) 2-0
Gill, Glover
B.J.Slaven, S.E.Ripley, M.S.Burke, M.R.Brennan,
G.A.Pallister, C.T.Cooper, A.N.Kernaghan,
N.M.Mohan (sub), M.Trotter (sub) and O.E.McGee
(sub) also played.
Aug 4 v Skara (a) 4-0
Cooper, Gill, Kernaghan 2
Aug 6 v Sodravingsif (a) 3-0
Slaven, Burke, Ripley
Aug 10 v Seattle Storm (h) 3-0
Slaven, Senior 2
K.Poole; G.A.Parkinson, C.T.Cooper,
A.M.Mowbray, G.J.Hamilton(D.V.Glover),
G.A.Pallister(A.N.Kernaghan), B.J.Slaven,
M.S.Burke(G.Gill), T.J.Senior, S.E.Ripley,
M.R.Brennan.
Att: 7,065
Aug 12 v Norton/Stockton Ancients (a) 5-1
Kernaghan 2, Hamilton, L.Tucker, Burke
Att: 1,500
Aug 17 v Hull City (a) 2-2
Ripley, Burke
S.Pears; G.A.Parkinson, C.T.Cooper,
A.M.Mowbray, G.J.Hamilton, D.V.Glover,
B.J.Slaven, M.S.Burke, T.J.Senior, S.E.Ripley,
M.R.Brennan.
Att: 1,214
Aug 20 v Shrewsbury Town (a) 1-0
Slaven
S.Pears; G.A.Parkinson, C.T.Cooper,
A.M.Mowbray, G.J.Hamilton, D.V.Glover,
B.J.Slaven, A.N.Kernaghan, T.J.Senior, S.E.Ripley,
M.R.Brennan.
Att: 1,379
Feb 16 v Sunderland (h) 1-1
Gill
(Private practice match behind closed doors)
Bermudan Tour
Mar 3 v Coventry City (a) 1-2
Davenport
Mar 7 v Bermudan XI (a) 3-0
Proudlock 2, Burke

1989-90
Jul 29 v Stockton (a) 5-1
Slaven, Davenport, Mowbray, Pallister, Burke
Att: 1,000
Jul 25 v Walsall 2-1
Slaven 2
(Private Friendly at Maiden Castle)
Jul 26 v Norton/Stockton Ancients (a) 5-0
Burke 2, Davenport, Fletcher, Mohan
Att: 1,500
Jul 28 v Billingham Synthonia (a) 6-0
Kerr 2, Proctor, Slaven, Burke, Pallister
K.Poole; P.Davenport, A.N.Kernaghan,
A.M.Mowbray, T.A.Putney, G.A.Pallister,
B.J.Slaven, M.R.Brennan, M.S.Burke, P.A.Kerr
(A.Comfort), M.G.Proctor.
Andrew Harbron's Testimonial
Jul 29 v Shildon (a) 1-3
A.Fletcher
Jones' Testimonial
Jul 31 v Carlisle United (a) 1-5
Mowbray
K.Poole; G.A.Parkinson, A.N.Kernaghan,
A.M.Mowbray, K.Wharton, G.A.Pallister, B.J.Slaven,
M.G.Proctor, M.S.Burke, P.A.Kerr, G.Agnew.
Att: 1,750
Aug 2 v Airdrieonians (a) 1-0
Kerr
K.Poole(S.Pears); M.G.Proctor, C.T.Cooper,
A.M.Mowbray, T.A.Putney, G.A.Pallister,
B.J.Slaven(S.E.Ripley), M.R.Brennan, P.Davenport,
P.A.Kerr, A.Comfort.

Aug 5 v St Mirren (a) 0-0
S.Pears; M.G.Proctor, C.T.Cooper
(A.N.Kernaghan), A.M.Mowbray, T.A.Putney,
G.A.Pallister, B.J.Slaven, M.R.Brennan, S.E.Ripley
(P.Davenport), P.A.Kerr, A.Comfort.
Aug 8 v Billingham Town (a) 1-2
Ripley
M.Coddington: O.E.McGee, M.Trotter,
N.M.Mohan, A.N.Kernaghan, G.Agnew, G.Gill,
M.R.Brennan, S.E.Ripley, A.Fletcher, M.S.Burke.
Aug 12 v Birmingham City (a) 2-1
Slaven, Davenport
K.Poole; M.G.Proctor(G.Parkinson), T.A.Putney,
A.M.Mowbray, A.N.Kernaghan, N.M.Mohan,
B.J.Slaven(S.E.Ripley), M.R.Brennan, P.Davenport,
P.A.Kerr, A.Comfort.
Aug 14 v York City (a) 2-2
Davenport 2
S.Pears; G.A.Parkinson, N.M.Mohan, A.M.Mowbray,
A.N.Kernaghan, M.G.Proctor, S.E.Ripley,
M.R.Brennan, P.Davenport, P.A.Kerr, A.Comfort.
Att: 1,183
Oct 10 v Green Howard Select XI (a) 5-2
(Gunner Thorpe Cup)
Jul 27 v Norton/Stockton Ancients (a) 5-1
Coleman, Baird, Ripley, Wark, Burke.
Att: 2,000
Jul 28 v North Shields (a) 0-0

1990-91
Aug 2 v South Bank (a) 2-1
D.Anderson, Tucker
Aug 3 v Newcastle Blue Star (a) 4-0
Ripley 2, Hendrie, Slaven
Aug 8 v Birmingham City (a) 2-0
Ripley, Mustoe
S.Pears; C.T.Cooper(G.A.Parkinson), J.N.Phillips,
A.M.Mowbray, S.Coleman(A.N.Kernaghan),
J.G.Hendrie, R.Mustoe, J.Wark, M.Russell,
I.J.Baird, S.E.Ripley (B.J.Slaven).
Att: 1,662
Aug 9 v Marske United (a) 3-0
Slaven 2, Kerr
Aug 11 v Mansfield Town (a) 2-3
Mustoe, Baird
S.Pears; C.T.Cooper, J.N.Phillips, A.M.Mowbray,
S.Coleman, M.Russell, B.J.Slaven, R.Mustoe,
I.J.Baird, S.E.Ripley, J.G.Hendrie.
Att: 1,397
Aug 15 v Crewe Alexandra (a) 2-2
Baird (pen), Russell
S.Pears(K.Poole); C.T.Cooper(G.A.Parkinson),
J.N.Phillips(O.E.McGee), A.M.Mowbray,
A.N.Kernaghan, J.Wark, B.J.Slaven(S.E.Ripley),
R.Mustoe, I.J.Baird(M.S.Burke), M.Russell
(P.A.Kerr), J.G.Hendrie.
Att: 1,030
Aug 16 v Billingham Town (a) 1-0
Fletcher
Aug 17 v St Mirren (a) 0-1
S.Pears; C.T.Cooper, O.E.McGee, A.M.Mowbray,
A.N.Kernaghan, J.Wark, B.J.Slaven, R.Mustoe,
I.J.Baird, M.Russell, J.G.Hendrie.
Att: 1,606
(Mainly reserve side)
Aug 18 v Guisborough Town (a) 2-2
Fletcher, D.Anderson
M.G.Proctor also played
Aug 20 v Hartlepool United (h) 4-2
Slaven 2, Baird, Proctor
(Played behind closed doors)
Mar 5 v Murton (a) 2-3
Mustoe, Arnold
(Official opening of Murton's new floodlights)

1991-92
Jul 26 v Norton (a) 4-0
Arnold 2, McGee, Kavanagh
Jul 27 v Marske United (a) 4-0
Jul 31 v Whitby Town (a) 7-0
Ripley 4, Hendrie, Slaven, Phillips
Aug 1 v Brandon (a) 2-2
Aug 2 v Portadown (a) 1-0
Slaven
S.Pears; C.Fleming, J.N.Phillips, A.M.Mowbray,
A.N.Kernaghan, G.A.Parkinson, B.J.Slaven,
M.G.Proctor, S.E.Ripley, R.Mustoe,
J.G.Hendrie(T.A.Putney).
Subs: N.M.Mohan, I.Arnold, M.Russell (all played)
Aug 4 v St Patrick's Athletic (a) 2-0
Arnold, Putney
I.Ironside(S.Pears); T.A.Putney, I.Arnold (sub) all
played.
Aug 6 v Crook Town (a) 6-0
Peverill 2, Pollock, Arnold, Russell, Ferguson
Aug 7 v Berwick Rangers (a) 2-0
Arnold, Young
Private Friendly played behind closed doors)
Aug 8 v Billingham Town (a) 2-0
Hamilton, unknown

Aug 10 v Walsall (a) 2-0
Falconer, Hendrie
S.Pears; G.A.Parkinson, J.N.Phillips,
A.N.Kernaghan, A.M.Mowbray, W.H.Falconer,
B.J.Slaven(I.Arnold[R.Mustoe]), M.G.Proctor,
P.Wilkinson, S.E.Ripley, J.G.Hendrie.
Att: 1,454
Aug 13 v Carlisle United (a) 3-2
Mustoe, Wilkinson 2
S.Pears; G.A.Parkinson, J.N.Phillips, N.M.Mohan,
A.N.Kernaghan, W.H.Falconer, R.Mustoe,
M.G.Proctor, P.Wilkinson, S.E.Ripley,
J.G.Hendrie.
Att: 1,528

1992-93
Jul 22 v Whitby (a) 3-1
Slaven, Wilkinson, Hendrie
S.Pears; G.A.Parkinson, P.Gilchrist,
A.N.Kernaghan, A.Todd, A.M.Peake, B.J.Slaven,
R.Mustoe, P.Wilkinson, J.G.Hendrie, A.Moore.
Att: 1,350
Jul 23 v Spennymoor United (a) 1-0
Phillips (pen)
S.Pears; G.A.Parkinson, J.N.Phillips,
A.N.Kernaghan, N.M.Mohan, M.G.Proctor,
B.J.Slaven, Unknown, P.Wilkinson, J.G.Hendrie,
T.Wright.
Jul 26 v Celtic (h) 1-1
Wilkinson
S.Pears; G.A.Parkinson, J.N.Phillips,
A.N.Kernaghan, N.M.Mohan, W.H.Falconer,
B.J.Slaven, M.G.Proctor, P.Wilkinson,
J.G.Hendrie, T.Wright.
Tony Mowbray's Testimonial
Att: 20,566
Jul 29 v York City (a) 2-2
Slaven, Falconer
S.Pears; G.A.Parkinson(A.N.Kernaghan),
J.N.Phillips, A.M.Peake, N.M.Mohan, J.Gittens,
R.Mustoe(M.O'Neill), A.P.Payton, P.Wilkinson
(B.J.Slaven), W.H.Falconer, T.Wright.
Aug 1 v Lincoln City (a) 1-5
Phillips
I.Ironside; G.A.Parkinson(N.M.Mohan),
J.N.Phillips(W.H.Falconer), A.N.Kernaghan,
R.Mustoe, J.Gittens, B.J.Slaven, M.G.Proctor,
P.Wilkinson, J.G.Hendrie, M.O'Neill(J.Pollock).
Aug 3 v Easington Colliery (a) 3-1
Aug 4 v Gillingham (a) 0-1
S.Pears; G.A.Parkinson, J.N.Phillips,
A.N.Kernaghan, J.Gittens, A.M.Peake(J.Pollock),
J.G.Hendrie(M.G.Proctor), A.P.Payton,
P.Wilkinson, W.H.Falconer, T.Wright(B.J.Slaven).
Aug 6 v Newcastle Blue Star 2-0
Newcastle Exhibition Superchallenge
Aug 8 v Newcastle United (a) 0-1
I.Ironside; G.A.Parkinson, J.N.Phillips,
A.N.Kernaghan(N.M.Mohan), J.Gittens, J.Pollock,
B.J.Slaven(M.O'Neill), J.G.Hendrie, P.Wilkinson,
R.Mustoe, T.Wright.
Aug 9 v Real Sociedad (a) 3-3
Hendrie, Falconer, Mustoe
I.Ironside; G.A.Parkinson, J.N.Phillips,
N.M.Mohan, W.H.Falconer, A.M.Peake(A.Todd),
A.P.Payton, P.Wilkinson, T.Wright(J.G.Hendrie),
M.G.Proctor, R.Mustoe.
(Lost 4-5 on penalties, Payton missed penalty)
Aug 10 v Billingham Synthonia (a) 0-0
Nov 2 v Billingham Town (a) 0-0
I.Ironside; W.H.Falconer, J.N.Phillips, R.Mustoe,
J.Pollock, B.J.Slaven, N.M.Mohan and C.Morris all
played.
(Official opening of new floodlights)

Abandoned Games

25 Dec 1912 v Bradford City (a) 0-1
(abandoned after 84 minutes – fading light)
Williamson; McLeod, Weir, Crosier, W.Carr, Malcolm,
Stirling, J.Carr, Elliott, Windridge, Nichol.
(Replayed on 4 February 1913)

3 Apr 1915 v Oldham Athletic (a) 4-1
(abandoned after 56 mins)
Tinsley 3 (1 pen), Urwin
Davies; Holmes, Walker, Davidson, Jackson, Malcolm, Storey,
Carr, A.N.Wilson, Tinsley, Urwin.
Match abandoned when Billy Cook, the Oldham Athletic full-
back, refused to leave the field after being sent off. The result
was ordered to stand.

4 Feb 1922 v Everton (a) 0-1
(abandoned after 57 mins – snowstorm)
Harrison; Holmes, Fox, S.Davidson, Ellerington, Pender,
Mordue, Birrell, Elliott, G.Carr, Urwin.
(Replayed on 1 March 1922)

16 Nov 1929 v Arsenal (a) 0-1
(abandoned after 55 minutes – fog)
Mathieson; Ferguson, Ashman, Miller, Elkes, Macfarlane,
Pease, J.Carr, Camsell, Bruce, O.Williams.
Att: 30,000
(Replayed on 27 November 1929)

10 Jan 1959 v Birmingham City (h) 1-1
(abandoned after 60 minutes – icy pitch)
Clough
Million; Bilcliff, Stonehouse, Yeoman, Phillips, Harris, Day,
Fernie, Clough, Peacock, Burbeck.
Att: 34,079
(Replayed on 24 January 1959)

24 Sep 1974 v Leicester City (h) 1-0
(abandoned after 29 minutes – floodlight failure)
Souness
Platt; Craggs, Hickton, Souness, Boam, Maddren, Murdoch,
Mills, Willey, Foggon, Armstrong.
(Replayed on 12 December 1974)

Brian Clough, robbed of a goal because the game against Birmingham City in January 1959 was abandoned.

Middlesbrough In The Northern League 1889-1899

THE Football League was formed in 1888 and, within a year, football in the North-East adopted the same rigid format as its parent body with the birth of the Northern League.

The founder members of the Northern League were Birtley, Bishop Auckland (then called Auckland Town), Darlington, Darlington St Augustine's, Elswick Rangers, Middlesbrough, Newcastle East End, Newcastle West End, South Bank and Stockton.

The first games in the League took place on Saturday, 7 September 1889, although Middlesbrough's first fixture was the following Saturday with a home game against Elswick Rangers.

Undoubtedly, the most dominant team of the Northern League's early days was Ironopolis of Middlesbrough. The infant club, formed in 1889, joined in the League's second season and won three consecutive championships, dropping only 12 points in three seasons.

In 1893, the Football League Second Division came into being and Ironopolis sought and gained entry — along with Liverpool — into the new League, leaving the door open for the other clubs in the Northern League to fight it out amongst themselves. Middlesbrough, with Ironopolis out of the way, came into prominence.

In May 1899 Middlesbrough followed the path of the now defunct Ironopolis and successfully gained entry into the Second Division, having spent ten seasons in the Northern League. All home games took place on the Linthorpe Road ground.

		HOME					AWAY						
	P	W	D	L	F	A	W	D	L	F	A	Pts	Pos
1889-1890	18	4	3	2	26	15	4	0	5	16	22	19	6th
1890-1891	14	6	1	0	21	4	2	2	3	12	13	19	2nd
1891-1892	16	6	0	2	18	10	7	0	1	15	3	26	2nd
1892-1893	10	4	0	1	12	5	0	0	5	5	12	8	4th
1893-1894	14	6	1	0	21	6	5	0	2	30	10	23	1st
1894-1895	18	7	2	0	39	5	5	3	1	19	12	29	1st
1895-1896	16	6	2	0	23	7	2	2	4	5	15	20	3rd
1896-1897	16	8	0	0	21	4	3	4	1	15	11	26	1st
1897-1898	16	5	2	1	28	10	4	2	2	14	12	22	2nd
1898-1899	16	5	1	2	21	10	2	3	3	8	17	18	3rd
	154	57	12	8	230	76	34	16	27	139	127	210	

200 or more appearances

† Includes play-off appearances in League total. * Still with the club at the end of 1992-93 season.

Player	Pos	Sns	Lge	FA	FL	Total		Player	Pos	Sns	Lge	FA	FL	Total
Tim Williamson	GK	1901-23	563	39	0	602		Micky Fenton	F	1932-50	240	29	0	269
Gordon Jones	FB	1960-73	457/5	40	26	523/5		Bobby Stuart	FB	1931-48	247	21	0	268
John Hickton	F	1966-77	395/20	37	26/4	458/24		Bob Baxter	CH	1932-39	247	19	0	266
John Craggs	FB	1971-82	408/1	33	31	472/1		Jimmy Mathieson	GK	1926-33	245	19	0	264
Jim Platt	GK	1971-83	401	34	33	468		Mark Proctor†	M	1978-93	210/21	14/3	13/2	237/26
George Camsell	CF	1925-39	418	35	0	453		Geoff Walker	OL	1946-55	240	19	3	259
Jackie Carr	IF	1910-30	421	28	0	449		Gary Hamilton†	D	1981-89	221/12	14	13	244/12
Dicky Robinson	FB	1946-59	390	26	0	416		Bobby Bruce	IF	1927-35	237	16	0	253
David Armstrong	OL	1970-81	357/2	29	27/1	413/3		Jimmy Gordon	WH	1946-54	231	22	0	253
Tony Mowbray†	D	1982-92	350/4	23	28/1	401/5		Alan Kernaghan†*	F/D	1984-93	168/41	8/4	22/7	198/52
David Mills	IF	1969-85	309/19	29	23/1	361/20		Gary Parkinson†*	FB	1986-93	198/8	17	20	235/8
Stuart Boam	CH	1971-79	322	29	27	378		Sam Aitken	WH	1903-10	227	15	0	242
Bill Harris	WH	1953-65	360	14	4	378		Johnny Spuhler	CF	1946-54	216	25	0	241
Wilf Mannion	IF	1936-54	341	27	11	368		Billy Pease	OR	1926-33	222	17	0	239
George Elliott	CF	1909-25	344	21	0	365		Alan Peacock	CF	1955-64	218	13	7	238
Bernie Slaven†	F	1985-93	292/21	16/3	26/2	334/26		Billy Birrell	IF	1920-28	225	10	0	235
Tony McAndrew	D	1973-86	311/2	23/1	15/2	349/5		Arthur Fitzsimons	IF	1949-59	223	8	2	231
Willie Maddren	D	1968-77	293/3	23	24	340/3		Ray Yeoman	WH	1958-63	210	10	7	227
Stephen Pears†*	GK	1983-93	292	23	26	341		Colin Cooper†	FB	1985-91	187/5	13	18	218/5
Rolando Ugolini	GK	1948-56	320	15	0	335		Brian Clough	CF	1955-61	213	8	1	222
Ronnie Dicks	WH	1947-58	316	18	0	334		Irving Nattrass	FB	1979-86	186/5	18	10/1	214/6
Billy Forrest	HB	1929-39	307	26	1	333		Billy Horner	WH	1960-69	184/3	17	12/1	213/4
Bill Gates	D	1961-74	277/6	26/1	18	321/7		Stewart Davidson	RH	1913-23	208	8	0	216
Frank Spraggon	WH	1963-76	277/3	23/1	18/1	318/5		Derrick Downing	WF	1965-72	172/11	22/1	5	199/12
Harry Bell	WH	1946-55	290	25	0	315		Willie Whigham	GK	1966-72	187	17	6	210
Stuart Ripley†	OL	1984-93	215/39	17/1	21/2	253/42		Jack Jennings	FB	1929-37	195	10	0	205
Maurice Webster	CH	1920-34	262	19	0	281		Graeme Souness	M	1972-78	174/2	13	15	202/2
Billy Brown	FB	1931-46	256	18	0	274		Andy Davidson	LH	1900-06	181	20	0	201
Eric McMordie	IF	1965-74	231/10	20/1	11	262/11		Thomas Urwin	WF	1914-24	192	8	-	200
Lindy Delapenha	F	1949-58	260	10	0	270								

50 or more Goals

Listed here are all players who have scored 50 or more goals in their Middlesbrough playing career. Only goals scored in the Football League and play-offs, FA Cup and League Cup are included in this analysis. A † indicates play-off details included in League statistics.

Player	Pos	Seasons	Lge	FA	LC	Total		Player	Pos	Seasons	Lge	FA	LC	Total
George Camsell	CF	1925-39	325	20	0	345		David Armstrong	OL	1970-81	59	8	6	73
George Elliott	CF	1909-25	203	10	0	213		Bill Harris	WH	1953-65	69	2	1	72
Brian Clough	CF	1955-61	197	5	2	204		Bobby Bruce	IF	1927-35	64	7	0	71
John Hickton	F	1966-77	159	13	13	185		Alf Common	CF	1905-10	58	7	0	65
Micky Fenton	F	1932-50	147	15	0	162		Billy Birrell	IF	1920-28	59	4	0	63
Alan Peacock	CF	1955-64	125	8	8	141		Steve Bloomer	IF	1905-09	59	3	0	62
Bernie Slaven†	F	1985-93	120	4	10	134		Andy Wilson	CF	1914-24	56	1	0	57
Wilf Mannion	IF	1936-54	99	11	0	110		Arthur Horsfield	F	1963-69	51	5	0	56
David Mills	IF	1969-85	90	10	8	108		Sammy Cail	IF	1906-13	52	3	0	55
Billy Pease	OR	1926-33	99	3	0	102		Benny Yorston	F	1933-39	54	0	0	54
Lindy Delapenha	F	1949-58	90	3	0	93		Geoff Walker	OL	1946-55	50	3	0	53
Johnny Spuhler	CF	1946-54	69	12	0	81		Arthur Fitzsimons	IF	1949-59	49	2	0	51
Jackie Carr	IF	1910-30	75	6	0	81		Freddy Warren	OL	1929-36	49	1	0	50

Hat-trick Heroes

	Lge	FA	LC	Tot			Lge	FA	LC	Tot
George Camsell	22	2	-	24		Alf Common	2	1	-	3
Brian Clough	17	-	-	17		Alex McCrae	3	-	-	3
George Elliott	11	2	-	13		Billy Pease	3	-	-	3
Micky Fenton	10	1	-	11		Sandy Robertson	1	1	-	2
Alan Peacock	6	-	1	7		George Carr	2	-	-	2
Bernie Slaven	5	1	-	6		Jacky Carr	-	2	-	2
Walter Tinsley	5	1	-	6		Cec McCormack	2	-	-	2
John Hickton	5	-	1	6		David Mills	1	1	-	2
Wilf Mannion	4	1	-	5		Charlie Wayman	2	-	-	2
John O'Rourke	4	1	-	5						
Jimmy McClelland	3	1	-	4		The following players have scored one				
Andy Wilson	3	-	-	3		hat-trick for the club: Ian Baird, Ralph				

Birkett, Billy Birrell, Harold Blackmore, Steve Bloomer, Jack Brearley, John Brown, Bobby Bruce, Mickey Burns, Sammy Cail, Joe Cassidy, Tommy Cochrane, Ian Dickson, George Emmerson, Tom Green, John Hall, Bill Harris, Jimmy Hartnett, John Hendrie, David Hodgson, Arthur Horsfield, Jim Irvine, Alan Kernaghan, Tony McAndrew, Joe Murphy, George Reid, Stuart Ripley, Dicky Rooks, Joe Scott, Graeme Souness, John Wilkie, Benny Yorston.

Leading Goalscorers
(1899-1993)

Listed below are the club's leading goalscorers. League, FA Cup, League Cup games and play-off matches are included in the analysis. *Division One leading goalscorer. † Division Two leading goalscorer.

Season	Leading goalscorer	Goals	Runner-up	Goals
DIVISION TWO				
1899-1900	Eddie Pugh	7	Tom Lamb	6
1900-01	Sandy Robertson	16	Willie Wardrope	14
1901-02	Jack Brearley	23	Joe Cassidy	16
DIVISION ONE				
1902-03	Sandy Robertson	8	Joe Cassidy	7
1903-04	Alex Brown	17	Joe Cassidy	12
1904-05	Harry Astley	5	Bob Atherton	4
			Alf Common	4
1905-06	Alf Common	24	Charlie Hewitt	11
1906-07	Steve Bloomer	20	Alf Common	13
1907-08	Steve Bloomer	12	Alf Common	9
	Sammy Cail	12	Freddy Wilcox	9
1908-09	John Hall	18	Steve Bloomer	14
1909-10	John Hall	12	Steve Bloomer	10
1910-11	George Elliott	10	Sammy Cail	9
1911-12	George Elliott	19	Sammy Cail	13
1912-13	George Elliott	25	Jackie Carr	19
1913-14	George Elliott	*31	Walter Tinsley	19
1914-15	Walter Tinsley	26	George Elliott	17
1919-20	George Elliott	34	Reuben Butler	11
1920-21	George Elliott	26	Alonzo Poulton	5
1921-22	Andy Wilson	32	George Carr	15
1922-23	George Elliott	23	Andy Wilson	12
1923-24	Andy Wilson	8	George Elliott	7
DIVISION TWO				
1924-25	Ian Dickson	7	George Elliott	5
	Owen Williams	7		
1925-26	Jimmy McClelland	38	Billy Birrell	18
1926-27	George Camsell	†63	Billy Pease	25
	(59 League goals — Division Two record)			
DIVISION ONE				
1927-28	George Camsell	37	Billy Pease	19
DIVISION TWO				
1928-29	George Camsell	33	Billy Pease	28
DIVISION ONE				
1929-30	George Camsell	31	Bobby Bruce	16
1930-31	George Camsell	32	Freddy Warren	19
1931-32	George Camsell	20	Bobby Bruce	13
1932-33	George Camsell	18	Harold Blackmore	12
1933-34	George Camsell	24	Freddy Warren	9
1934-35	George Camsell	14	Ernie Coleman	12
1935-36	George Camsell	32	Ralph Birkett	22
1936-37	Micky Fenton	22	George Camsell	18
1937-38	Micky Fenton	26	Tom Cochrane	10
			George Camsell	10
1938-39	Micky Fenton	35	Wilf Mannion	14
1946-47	Wilf Mannion	23	Johnny Spuhler	14
	Micky Fenton	23		
1947-48	Micky Fenton	29	Cec McCormack	16
1948-49	Micky Fenton	12	Johnny Spuhler	7
1949-50	Peter McKennan	16	Wilf Mannion	7
	Alex McCrae	16	Geoff Walker	7
1950-51	Alex McCrae	21	Wilf Mannion	13
1951-52	Lindy Delapenha	17	Neil Mochan	12
1952-53	Wilf Mannion	18	Arthur Fitzsimons	12
1953-54	Lindy Delapenha	18	Wilf Mannion	10
DIVISION TWO				
1954-55	Charlie Wayman	17	Joe Scott	16
1955-56	Lindy Delapenha	18	Charlie Wayman	16
1956-57	Brian Clough	40	Derek McLean	10
1957-58	Brian Clough	42	Alan Peacock	17
1958-59	Brian Clough	43	Alan Peacock	19
1959-60	Brian Clough	40	Alan Peacock	13
1960-61	Brian Clough	36	Alan Peacock	16
1961-62	Alan Peacock	32	Bill Harris	15
DIVISION TWO				
1962-63	Alan Peacock	33	Arthur Kaye	15
1963-64	Ian Gibson	14	Bill Harris	12
1964-65	Jim Irvine	24	Ian Gibson	9
1965-66	Jim Irvine	17	Dicky Rooks	8
DIVISION THREE				
1966-67	John O'Rourke	30	Arthur Horsfield	23
DIVISION TWO				
1967-68	John Hickton	29	John O'Rourke	12
1968-69	John Hickton	18	Derrick Downing	9
1969-70	John Hickton	28	Joe Laidlaw	12
1970-71	John Hickton	27	Hugh McIlmoyle	15
1971-72	John Hickton	16	David Mills	9
1972-73	John Hickton	15	Alan Foggon	7
			David Mills	7
1973-74	Alan Foggon	20	David Mills	12
DIVISION ONE				
1974-75	Alan Foggon	18	David Mills	11
1975-76	John Hickton	13	David Mills	12
1976-77	David Mills	18	David Armstrong	12
1977-78	David Mills	16	David Armstrong	9
1978-79	Micky Burns	14	David Armstrong	11
1979-80	David Armstrong	14	Micky Burns	10
1980-81	Bosco Jankovic	13	Craig Johnston	10
1981-82	Heine Otto	5	David Shearer	4
	Billy Ashcroft	5	Tony McAndrew	4
	Bobby Thomson	5		
DIVISION TWO				
1982-83	David Shearer	13	Heine Otto	11
1983-84	David Currie	15	Heine Otto	8
1984-85	David Mills	14	David Currie	11
1985-86	Gary Rowell	12	Bernie Slaven	8
DIVISION THREE				
1986-87	Bernie Slaven	21	Archie Stephens	17
DIVISION TWO				
1987-88	Bernie Slaven	24	Stuart Ripley	9
DIVISION ONE				
1988-89	Bernie Slaven	16	Mark Burke	5
DIVISION TWO				
1989-90	Bernie Slaven	25	Ian Baird	5
			Alan Kernaghan	5
1990-91	Bernie Slaven	19	Ian Baird	15
1991-92	Paul Wilkinson	22	Bernie Slaven	17
FA PREMIER LEAGUE				
1992-93	Paul Wilkinson	15	John Hendrie	9

Micky Fenton (left) and Brian Clough, two prolific 'Boro scorers.

Performance Analysis of all League Games

34 Games in Season (No of seasons – 6)

Home Analysis

Most wins in season 15
1901-02
Most draws in season 4
1899-1900, 1900-01
Most defeats in season 7
1904-05
Most goals scored in season 58
1901-02
Most goals conceded in season.................................24
1904-05

Fewest wins in season 8
1899-1900
Fewest draws in season 1
1901-02
Fewest defeats in season 1
1901-02
Fewest goals scored in season 21
1904-05
Fewest goals conceded in season 7
1901-02

Away Analysis

Most wins in season 8
1901-02
Most draws in season 9
1903-04
Most defeats in season 13
1899-1900
Most goals scored in season 32
1901-02
Most goals conceded in season.................................54
1899-1900

Fewest wins in season 0
1899-1900, 1903-04
Fewest draws in season 2
1902-03
Fewest defeats in season 5
1901-02
Fewest goals scored in season 11
1899-1900
Fewest goals conceded in season...............................17
1901-02

Seasonal Analysis

Most points won in season (2 pts for win) 51
1901-02
Fewest points won in season (2 pts for win) 24
1899-1900
Most wins in season 23
1901-02
Most draws in season 12
1903-04
Most defeats in season 18
1899-1900
Most goals scored in season 90
1901-02
Most goals conceded in season.................................69
1899-1900

Fewest wins in season 8
1899-1900
Fewest draws in season 5
1901-02, 1902-03
Fewest defeats in season 6
1901-02
Fewest goals scored in season 36
1904-05
Fewest goals conceded in season...............................24
1901-02

38 Games in Season (No of seasons – 11)

Home Analysis

Most wins in season 14
1913-14
Most draws in season 9
1912-13
Most defeats in season 7
1909-10
Most goals scored in season 55
1913-14
Most goals conceded in season.................................36
1909-10

Fewest wins in season 6
1912-13, 1988-89
Fewest draws in season 2
1906-07, 1907-08, 1908-09, 1913-14
Fewest defeats in season 2
1911-12
Fewest goals scored in season 28
1988-89
Fewest goals conceded in season...............................16
1907-08

Away Analysis

Most wins in season 5
1907-08, 1911-12, 1912-13, 1913-14
Most draws in season 7
1905-06, 1908-09
Most defeats in season 13
1912-13
Most goals scored in season 26
1912-13
Most goals conceded in season.................................50
1914-15

Fewest wins in season 0
1905-06
Fewest draws in season 1
1912-13
Fewest defeats in season 9
1907-08, 1908-09
Fewest goals scored in season 15
1905-06
Fewest goals conceded in season...............................29
1911-12

Seasonal Analysis

Most points won in season (2 pts for win) 43
1913-14
Most points won in season (3 pts for win) 39
1988-89
Fewest points won in season (2 pts for win) 31
1905-06
Fewest points won in season (3 pts for win) 39
1988-89

Most wins in season 19
1913-14
Most draws in season 12
1914-15, 1988-89
Most defeats in season 18
1909-10
Most goals scored in season 77
1913-14
Most goals conceded in season.................................74
1914-15

Fewest wins in season 9
1988-89
Fewest draws in season 5
1913-14
Fewest defeats in season 13
1914-15

Middlesbrough, 1905-06. Back row (left to right): Directors messrs A.McCallum, G.Pickard, D.Mullen and A.Barrett. Second row: Tinsley, Lieut-Col Poole (vice-chairman), Murray, Hewitt, Agnew, Frail, Hogg, Hedley, Aitken, Dr Bryan and Mr Allen (directors). Seated: Unknown, Atherton, McCallum, Cassidy, Henderson, R.W.Williams (chairman), Jones, Davidson, Smith, A.Mackie (manager), W.Allen. On ground: J.Bingley (trainer), Coxon, Bell, Thackeray, Common, Green, Reid, Barker, T.Coulson (assistant trainer).

Stephen Pears is in a tangle at Carrow Road on New Year's Eve 1988.

Wilf Mannion appeals for hands after Chelsea's Harris had robbed him of the ball at Ayresome Park in October 1951.

Teesside Mayor Alderman Len Poole invited Jack Charlton and his team to the Town Hall to celebrate promotion in 1974.

Fewest goals scored in season 44
1988-89
Fewest goals conceded in season.............................45
1911-12

42 Games in Season (No of seasons – 60)
Home Analysis
Most wins in season 18
1926-27
Most draws in season 10
1924-25
Most defeats in season 11
1923-24
Most goals scored in season 78
1926-27
Most goals conceded in season.............................35
1927-28, 1953-54, 1962-63

Fewest wins in season 5
1981-82
Fewest draws in season 1
1925-26, 1954-55
Fewest defeats in season 1
1926-27, 1936-37, 1968-69, 1971-72, 1973-74
Fewest goals scored in season 20
1981-82
Fewest goals conceded in season 8
1973-74

Away Analysis
Most wins in season 11
1973-74
Most draws in season 9
1924-25
Most defeats in season 18
1980-81
Most goals scored in season 44
1926-27
Most goals conceded in season.............................63
1951-52

Fewest wins in season 1
1923-24, 1948-49, 1963-64
Fewest draws in season 1
1925-26, 1980-81
Fewest defeats in season 3
1973-74
Fewest goals scored in season 9
1948-49
Fewest goals conceded in season...........................22
1973-74

Seasonal Analysis
Most points won in season (2 pts for win) 65
1973-74
Most points won in season (3 pts for win) 49
1983-84
Fewest points won in season (2 pts for win) 22
1923-24
Fewest points won in season (3 pts for win) 39
1981-82

Most wins in season 27
1926-27, 1973-74
Most draws in season 19
1924-25
Most defeats in season 27
1923-24
Most goals scored in season................................122
1926-27
Most goals conceded in season............................91
1953-54

Fewest wins in season 7
1923-24
Fewest draws in season 2
1925-26
Fewest defeats in season 4
1973-74

Fewest goals scored in season 34
1981-82
Fewest goals conceded in season.............................30
1973-74

44 Games in Season (No of seasons – 1)
Home Analysis
Most wins in season 15
1987-88
Most draws in season 4
1987-88
Most defeats in season 3
1987-88
Most goals scored in season 47
1987-88
Most goals conceded in season.............................16
1987-88

Fewest wins in season 15
1987-88
Fewest draws in season 4
1987-88
Fewest defeats in season 3
1987-88
Fewest goals scored in season 47
1987-88
Fewest goals conceded in season 16
1987-88

Away Analysis
Most wins in season 7
1987-88
Most draws in season 8
1987-88
Most defeats in season 7
1987-88
Most goals scored in season 19
1987-88
Most goals conceded in season.............................20
1987-88

Fewest wins in season 7
1987-88
Fewest draws in season 8
1987-88
Fewest defeats in season 7
1987-88
Fewest goals scored in season 19
1987-88
Fewest goals conceded in season...........................20
1987-88

Seasonal Analysis
Most points won in season (3 pts for win) 78
1987-88
Fewest points won in season (3 pts for win) 78
1987-88

Most wins in season 22
1987-88
Most draws in season 12
1987-88
Most defeats in season 10
1987-88
Most goals scored in season 66
1987-88
Most goals conceded in season.............................36
1987-88

Fewest wins in season 22
1987-88
Fewest draws in season 12
1987-88
Fewest defeats in season 10
1987-88
Fewest goals scored in season 66
1987-88
Fewest goals conceded in season.............................36
1987-88

46 Games in Season (No of seasons – 5)

Home Analysis

Most wins in season 16
1966-67, 1986-87
Most draws in season 6
1991-92
Most defeats in season 10
1989-90
Most goals scored in season 51
1966-67
Most goals conceded in season...........................29
1989-90

Fewest wins in season 10
1989-90
Fewest draws in season 3
1966-67, 1989-90
Fewest defeats in season 2
1986-87, 1991-92
Fewest goals scored in season 33
1989-90
Fewest goals conceded in season.........................11
1986-87

Away Analysis

Most wins in season 12
1986-87
Most draws in season 8
1989-90
Most defeats in season 12
1989-90
Most goals scored in season 36
1966-67
Most goals conceded in season...........................44
1966-67

Fewest wins in season 3
1989-90
Fewest draws in season 5
1986-87, 1990-91, 1991-92
Fewest defeats in season 6
1986-87
Fewest goals scored in season 19
1989-90
Fewest goals conceded in season.........................19
1986-87

Seasonal Analysis

Most points won in season (2 pts for win) 55
1966-67
Most points won in season (3 pts for win) 94
1986-87
Fewest points won in season (2 pts for win) 55
1966-67
Fewest points won in season (3 pts for win) 50
1989-90

Most wins in season 28
1986-87
Most draws in season 11
1989-90, 1991-92
Most defeats in season 17
1990-91
Most goals scored in season 87
1966-67
Most goals conceded in season...........................64
1966-67

Fewest wins in season 13
1989-90
Fewest draws in season 9
1986-87, 1990-91
Fewest defeats in season 8
1986-87
Fewest goals scored in season 52
1989-90
Fewest goals conceded in season.........................30
1986-87

All Games (No of Seasons – 83)

Home Analysis

Most wins in season 18
1926-27
Most draws in season 10
1924-25
Most defeats in season 11
1923-24
Most goals scored in season 78
1926-27
Most goals conceded in season...........................36
1909-10

Fewest wins in season 5
1981-82
Fewest draws in season 1
1901-02, 1925-26, 1954-55
Fewest defeats in season 1
1901-02, 1926-27, 1936-37, 1968-69, 1971-72, 1973-74
Fewest goals scored in season 20
1981-82
Fewest goals conceded in season.........................7
1901-02

Away Analysis

Most wins in season 12
1986-87
Most draws in season 9
1903-04, 1924-25
Most defeats in season 18
1980-81
Most goals scored in season 44
1926-27
Most goals conceded in season...........................63
1951-52

Fewest wins in season 0
1899-1900, 1903-04, 1905-06
Fewest draws in season 1
1912-13, 1925-26, 1980-81
Fewest defeats in season 3
1973-74
Fewest goals scored in season 9
1948-49
Fewest goals conceded in season.........................17
1901-02

Seasonal Analysis

Most points won in season (2 pts for win) 65
1973-74
Most points won in season (3 pts for win) 94
1986-87
Fewest points won in season (2 pts for win) 22
1923-24
Fewest points won in season (3 pts for win) 39
1981-82, 1988-89

Most wins in season 28
1986-87
Most draws in season 19
1924-25
Most defeats in season 27
1923-24
Most goals scored in season 122
1926-27
Most goals conceded in season...........................91
1953-54

Fewest wins in season 7
1923-24
Fewest draws in season 2
1925-26
Fewest defeats in season 4
1973-74
Fewest goals scored in season 34
1981-82
Fewest goals conceded in season.........................24
1901-02

Billy Ashcroft in action against Derby County in February 1980.

Another game against Derby, this time in August 1988. Bernie Slaven takes the ball through the Rams defence. Derby men are Mark Wright, Geraint Williams and Gary Micklewhite.

Stuart Boam (left) and Irving Nattrass (right) gave Middlesbrough great service.

Middlesbrough's Profit/Loss Account
1899-1993

The seasonal Profit/Loss figures listed below show how the club has fared financially since joining the Football League in 1899. Also listed are the club chairmen and team captains (at the start of each season) since that first season.

Season	Chairman	Team Captain	£ Profit	£ Loss
1899-1900	Alf Mattison	Peter McCracken	*176	
1900-1901	Alf Mattison	Bill Higgins	*433	
1901-1902	Robert Williams	Dave Smith	*824	
1902-1903	Robert Williams	Dave Smith	634	
1903-1904	Jack R Smiles	Joe Cassidy	*3,314	
1904-1905	Robert Williams	Bobby Atherton		*1,635.12
1905-1906	Robert Williams	Alf Common		588.56
1906-1907	Thomas Gibson-Poole	Alf Common	1,063.46	
1907-1908	Thomas Gibson-Poole	Sam Aitken	1,512.65	
1908-1909	Thomas Gibson-Poole	Sam Aitken		*1,674.81
1909-1910	Thomas Gibson-Poole	Sam Aitken	356.05	
1910-1911	Thomas Gibson-Poole/Phil Bach	Tim Williamson	*3,348.98	
1911-1912	Phil Bach	Tim Williamson	2,189.79	
1912-1913	Phil Bach	Tim Williamson		733.18
1913-1914	Phil Bach	George Elliott	*3,694.75	
1914-1915	Phil Bach	George Elliott		501.41
1918-1919	Phil Bach	George Elliott	1,646.61	
1919-1920	Phil Bach	George Elliott	*7,920.00	
1920-1921	Phil Bach	George Elliott	6,708.80	
1921-1922	Phil Bach	Stewart Davidson	643	
1922-1923	Phil Bach	Stewart Davidson		*7,198.30
1923-1924	Phil Bach	George Elliott		*8,586.57
1924-1925	Phil Bach/John G Pallister	Reg Freeman	1,146.52	
1925-1926	John G Pallister	Reg Freeman		760.87
1926-1927	John G Pallister	Billy Birrell	3,816.97	
1927-1928	John G Pallister	Billy Birrell	*8,166.17	
1928-1929	John G Pallister	Bob Ferguson	3,584.77	
1929-1930	John G Pallister	Bob Ferguson		7,228.85
1930-1931	John G Pallister	Jack Jennings	4,145.02	
1931-1932	Phil Bach	Jack Jennings		837.44
1932-1933	Phil Bach	Maurice Webster		*9,781.91
1933-1934	Phil Bach	Tom Griffiths	3,666.02	
1934-1935	Bill Kelly JP	Tom Griffiths		660.02
1935-1936	Bill Kelly JP	Tom Griffiths	*8,228.74	
1936-1937	Bill Kelly JP	Bob Baxter	7,211.96	
1937-1938	Bill Kelly JP	Bob Baxter	8,191.96	
1938-1939	Bill Kelly JP	Bob Baxter	7,405.50	
1945-1946	Bill Kelly JP	Bobby Stuart	1,483.00	
1946-1947	Bill Kelly JP	George Hardwick	*15,557.73	
1947-1948	Bill Kelly JP	George Hardwick	11,550	
1948-1949	Bill Kelly JP	George Hardwick		*15,959
1949-1950	Bill Kelly JP	George Hardwick	4,738	
1950-1951	Harry French	George Hardwick	*29,497.11	
1951-1952	Harry French	Jimmy Gordon		8,470.38
1952-1953	Harry French/Tommy Thomas	Bill Whitaker	9,745.94	
1953-1954	Stanley Gibson	Wilf Mannion		6,775.82
1954-1955	Stanley Gibson	Bill Harris		13,032.34
1955-1956	Stanley Gibson	Bill Harris	3,538.18	
1956-1957	Stanley Gibson	Ronnie Dicks	6,434	
1957-1958	Stanley Gibson	Ronnie Dicks	9,993	
1958-1959	Stanley Gibson	Brian Clough		7,123
1959-1960	Stanley Gibson	Brian Clough		7,122
1960-1961	Stanley Gibson	Ken Thomson		221
1961-1962	Stanley Gibson/Eric Thomas	Ken Thomson	14,985	
1962-1963	Eric Thomas	Ken Thomson		*47,697
1963-1964	Eric Thomas	Mel Nurse	6,934	
1964-1965	Eric Thomas	Mel Nurse		10,821
1965-1966	Eric Thomas	Ian Gibson		21,897
1966-1967	Eric Thomas	Gordon Jones	13,758	
1967-1968	Eric Thomas	Gordon Jones	*39,483	
1968-1969	Eric Thomas	Gordon Jones		31,206
1969-1970	Eric Thomas	Gordon Jones		5,401
1970-1971	Eric Thomas	Gordon Jones		4,878
1971-1972	Eric Thomas	Nobby Stiles		*55,402
1972-1973	George Winney	Nobby Stiles		27,099
1973-1974	Charles Amer	Stuart Boam		2,470
1974-1975	Charles Amer	Stuart Boam	*140,000	
1975-1976	Charles Amer	Stuart Boam	99,177	
1976-1977	Charles Amer	Stuart Boam	*142,196	
1977-1978	Charles Amer	Stuart Boam	3,800	
1978-1979	Charles Amer	Stuart Boam		29,017
1979-1980	Charles Amer	Tony McAndrew		40,020
1980-1981	Charles Amer	Tony McAndrew	*373,223	
1981-1982	Charles Amer/George Kitching	John Craggs		*307,718
1982-1983	George Kitching/Mike McCullagh	Jim Platt		16,987
1983-1984	Mike McCullagh	Irving Nattrass		*332,048
1984-1985	Mike McCullagh/Alf Duffield	Irving Nattrass		136,859
1985-1986	Alf Duffield/Colin Henderson	Brian Laws		
1986-1987	Colin Henderson	Tony Mowbray		
1987-1988	Colin Henderson	Tony Mowbray		
1988-1989	Colin Henderson	Tony Mowbray		
1989-1990	Colin Henderson	Tony Mowbray		
1990-1991	Colin Henderson	Tony Mowbray		
1991-1992	Colin Henderson	Tony Mowbray		
1992-1993	Colin Henderson/	Alan Kernaghan		

The club has not released any profit/loss accounts from season 1985-86 onwards.

*Indicates record Profit/Loss

Middlesbrough skipper George Hardwick leads out his team in August 1948.

The Substitutes

Substitutes were first allowed in Football League games from 1965-66 onwards but, during that first season, substitutions were permitted only for injured players. The introduction of substitutes then caught many a sports newspaper out for many a game was reported without the substitute being mentioned in the match report, whether he played or not. It was originally feared that the trend would spoil the game but the passing of time has proved its worth. Bryan Orritt holds the distinction of being Middlesbrough's first named substitute for a Football League match on 21 August 1965 against Manchester City at Ayresome Park. He was also the first Middlesbrough player to take to the field as a substitute when he replaced injured full back Neville Chapman at Deepdale on 11 September 1965, against Preston North End, the substitution being timed at 30 minutes into the game. Five players have appeared for the club only as substitute. The first was Pat Lynch, who substituted for David Mills after 60 minutes at Loftus Road against Queen's Park Rangers on 18 March 1972. The second was Malcolm Poskett, who replaced Malcolm Smith against Hull City after 78 minutes at Ayresome Park on 13 October 1973. Poskett was released by Jack Charlton at the end of the season, having played only 12 minutes of competitive football for the club. He went on to become a prolific goalscorer with Hartlepool United, Brighton, Watford and Carlisle United. The next player was Alan Walsh, he made three appearances as substitute in a Middlesbrough shirt during the 1977-78 season, before his transfer to Darlington where he became that club's all-time record goalscorer. He also enjoyed further scoring success at Bristol City. Michael Young was released by Newcastle United and was given a chance at Middlesbrough under Lennie Lawrence but made only one appearance as substitute. Alan Moore broke into the first team during the 1992-93 season, albeit as substitute, but he can hope to improve on this during the next few seasons. In 1986-87 two substitutes per game were permitted in FA Cup matches. This was extended into the Football League the following season and other matches with the second substitute normally wearing the number 14 shirt. Exclusively to the new Premier Division, goalkeeping substitutes were allowed from the start of the 1992-93 season and the first Middlesbrough goalkeeper named as a substitute was Ian Ironside in the opening game of the season, at Highfield Road against Coventry City on 15 August 1992. There are several instances where substitutes were named but, because of circumstances, they never appeared in the games they were named. To date, the players were Michael Hill (1967), Frank Harrison (1982), Craig Farnaby (1985), Ben Roberts and Nicky Peverell (both 1992). An asterisk (*) besides the player's name indicates the player was still with the club at the end of 1992-93 season.

Player	Pos	Seasons	Lge	FA	LC	Total
Alan Kernaghan*	D	1984-	40	4	7	51
Stuart Ripley	F	1984-92	39	1	2	42
Bernie Slaven	F	1985-93	20	3	4	27
Malcolm Smith	CF	1972-76	24	2	1	27
Alan Willey	F	1974-78	23	3	1	27
Mark Burke	F	1987-90	25	1		26
Mark Proctor	HB	1978-93	21	3	2	26
John Hickton	F	1966-77	20		4	24
Peter Brine	IF	1972-77	20	2	1	23
Billy Ashcroft	CF	1977-82	20	2		22
David Currie	CF	1982-86	19	1		20
David Mills	IF	1969-85	19		1	20
Billy Woof	F	1974-82	16	1	1	18
Terry Cochrane	WF	1978-83	15			15
Garry Macdonald	F	1980-85	13	1	1	15
Graeme Hedley	F	1976-81	14			14
Andy Payton	F	1991-92	11	3		14
Jamie Pollock*	M	1990-	11	1	2	14
Paul Kerr	F	1986-89	11	2		13
David Shearer	FG	1977-83	9	2	2	13
Derrick Downing	WF	1965-72	11	1		12
Alan Foggon	F	1972-76	10	1	1	12
Gary Hamilton	D	1982-89	12			12
Alan Roberts	OR	1983-84	10	1	1	12
Gary Gill	D	1983-89	8	1	2	11
Eric McMordie	IF	1965-74	10	1		11
Bosko Janković	F	1978-81	8		2	10
David Hodgson	F	1978-86	9			9
Lee Turnbull	F	1985-87	8		1	9
Stan Webb	CF	1967-71	9			9
Peter Beagrie	WF	1984-86	8			8
Curtis Fleming*	FB	1991-	7		1	8
Gary Parkinson	FB	1986-93	8			8
Paul Ward	D	1982-86	7	1		8
Ian Bailey	FB	1975-82	5	1	1	7
Stephen Bell	IF	1981-85	6		1	7
Phil Boersma	F	1975-77	6	1		7
Willie Falconer*	M	1991-	6		1	7
Bill Gates	D	1961-74	6	1		7
Arthur Horsfield	F	1963-69	5	2		7
Craig Johnston	F	1977-81	3	2	2	7
Joe Laidlaw	F	1967-72	5	2		7
Brian Laws	FB	1984-87	5	1	1	7
Robbie Mustoe*	M	1990-	6		1	7
Peter Davenport	IL	1988-90	6			6
Dean Glover	FB	1987-89	6			6
Jim Lawson	WF	1965-68	6			6
Irving Nattrass	FB	1979-86	5		1	6
Archie Stephens	IF	1984-88	5		1	6
Colin Cooper	FB	1974-78	5			5
Stan Cummins	F	1976-80	4		1	5
Gordon Jones	LB	1960-73	5			5
Graham Kavanagh*	M	1992-	4	1		5
Ray Lugg	F	1966-70	3		2	5
Tony McAndrew	D	1973-86	2	1	2	5
Frank Spraggon	FB	1963-76	3	1	1	5
Brian Taylor	HB	1972-76	4		1	5
Ian Baird	CF	1989-91	3		1	4
Mark Brennan	IR	1988-90	4			4
Micky Burns	F	1978-81	3	1		4
Simon Coleman	CH	1989-91	4			4
Jon Gittens	D	1992-93	3		1	4
John Hendrie*	WF	1990-	2	2		4
Billy Horner	WH	1960-60	3		1	4
Owen McGee	D	1989-92	3	1		4
Tony Mowbray	CH	1982-91	3		1	4
Alan Murray	IR	1969-71	4			4
Heine Otto	IF	1981-85	4			4
Alan Ramage	HB	1975-80	4			4
John Vincent	WF	1970-72	3		1	4
Mike Allen	HB	1967-72	3			3
Mick Angus	LH	1979-82	2	1		3
David Armstrong	OL	1970-81	2		1	3
Ian Arnold	F	1990-92	3			3
David Chadwick	WF	1966-70	2	1		3
Mitch Cook	IR	1985-86	3			3
Ronnie Coyle	FB	1986-87	2	1		3
Craig Hignett	IF	1992-	3			3
Willie Maddren	LH	1968-77	3			3
Dwight Marshall	F	1992-	3			3
Don Masson	IF	1964-68	3			3
Chris Morris*	FB	1992-	3			3
Bryan Orritt	F	1961-66	3			3
Andy Peake*	M	1991-	3			3
Trevor Putney	M	1989-91	3			3
Paul Sugrue	IF	1982-85	3			3
Alan Walsh	F	1977-78	3			3
Colin Walsh	M	1990-91	3			3
Billy Askew	WF	1980-82	2			2
Nev Chapman	FB	1961-67	2			2
Harry Charlton	WF	1970-75	2			2
Johnny Crossan	IF	1967-70	2			2
Ray Hankin	F	1982-83	2			2
John Hewitt	M	1991-92	2			2
Chris Kamara	D	1992-93	2			2
Mike Kear	WF	1967-70	2			2
Nicky Mohan*	D	1989-	2			2
Alan Moody	RB	1968-73	2			2
Alan Moore*	F	1992-	2			2
Bobby Murdoch	WH	1973-76	2			2
Paul Proudlock	F	1986-89	2			2
Alec Smith	FB	1965-72	2			2
Graeme Souness	WH	1972-78	2			2
Bobby Thomson	OL	1981-82	2			2
Jim Townsend	WH	1963-66	2			2
Tommy Wright*	F	1992-	2			2
Mark Barham	IF	1988-89	1			1
Kevin Beattie	HB	1982-83	1			1
Bobby Braithwaite	F	1963-67	1			1
Don Burluraux	WF	1970-72	1			1
Geoff Butler	FB	1965-67	1			1
John Craggs	FB	1971-82	1			1
Andy Crawford	F	1983-84	1			1
Peter Creamer	FB	1972-75			1	1
Brian Horne	GK	1992-93	1			1
Ian Ironside*	GK	1991-	1			1
Jim Irvine	F	1964-47	1			1
Peter Johnson	FB	1977-80	1			1
George Kinnell	LH	1968-69	1			1
Pat Lynch	F	1971-72	1			1
Hugh McIlmoyle	CF	1969-71	1			1
Allan McNeill	F	1967-69		1		1
Colin Ross	WH	1980-83	1			1
John O'Rourke	CF	1967-68	1			1
Malcolm Poskett	F	1973-74	1			1
Martin Russell	IF	1990-91	1			1
Trevor Senior	F	1987-88	1			1
Rab Shannon	M	1991-92	1			1
Dave Smith	OL	1967-68	1			1
John Wark	D	1990-91	1			1
Alf Wood	IF	1976-77	1			1
Derek Whyte*	D	1992-	1			1
Mike Young	F	1991-	1			1

John Wark (left) and Curtis Fleming (right).

Simon Coleman (left) and Derek Whyte (right).

Willie Falconer (left) and Alan Kernaghan (right).

Middlesbrough Players' Dismissals
(1899-1993)

League

15 Dec	1900	Bill Higgins	(h)	Birmingham
20 Mar	1915	Andy Wilson	(h)	Liverpool
17 Sep	1921	Andy Wilson	(h)	Tottenham Hotspur
7 Jan	1928	Jimmy McClelland	(a)	Everton
1 Nov	1930	John Holliday	(a)	Sunderland
29 Dec	1930	Freddy Warren	(a)	Sheffield Wednesday
7 Dec	1946	Dave Cumming	(h)	Arsenal
1 Dec	1951	Harry Bell	(h)	Sunderland
11 Nov	1961	Arthur Kaye	(a)	Sunderland
13 Oct	1962	Bryan Orritt	(h)	Swansea Town
7 Mar	1964	Jim Townsend	(a)	Sunderland
31 Mar	1964	Don Ratcliffe	(a)	Huddersfield Town
27 Mar	1965	Don Ratcliffe	(h)	Derby County
19 Apr	1965	Jim Irvine	(h)	Leyton Orient
3 Feb	1968	Bill Gates	(h)	Hull City
14 Aug	1968	John Hickton	(a)	Norwich City
14 Aug	1968	Eric McMordie	(a)	Norwich City
7 Sep	1968	Brian Myton*	(a)	Cardiff City
3 Apr	1972	John Vincent	(a)	Blackpool
23 Oct	1973	Graeme Souness	(a)	Carlisle United
22 Mar	1975	Terry Cooper	(a)	Chelsea
26 Mar	1977	Terry Cooper	(a)	Newcastle United
18 Mar	1978	David Mills	(a)	Leeds United
27 Oct	1978	Billy Ashcroft	(a)	Aston Villa
29 Dec	1979	Terry Cochrane	(a)	Crystal Palace
2 Apr	1980	Tony McAndrew	(a)	Leeds United
12 Nov	1980	John Craggs	(a)	Leeds United
22 Nov	1980	Tony McAndrew	(h)	Wolverhampton W
17 Jan	1981	David Hodgson	(a)	Manchester City
28 Sep	1982	Ray Hankin*	(h)	Grimsby Town
28 Sep	1982	Mick Kennedy	(h)	Grimsby Town
20 Nov	1982	Paul Ward	(a)	Leeds United
5 Apr	1983	Paul Sugrue	(a)	Leicester City
12 Nov	1983	Tony Mowbray	(a)	Derby County
12 Nov	1983	David Currie	(a)	Derby County
7 May	1984	Mick Kennedy	(a)	Brighton & HA
27 Oct	1984	Tony Mowbray	(a)	Leeds United
17 Nov	1984	David Currie	(h)	Blackburn Rovers
11 May	1985	Gary Hamilton	(a)	Shrewsbury Town
11 May	1985	Peter Beagrie	(a)	Shrewsbury Town
22 Oct	1985	Archie Stephens	(a)	Sunderland
3 May	1986	Gary Pallister	(a)	Shrewsbury Town
7 Mar	1987	David Hodgson†	(h)	Bristol City
2 Nov	1987	Gary Parkinson	(a)	Plymouth Argyle
28 Dec	1987	Stuart Ripley	(a)	Leeds United
23 Apr	1988	Colin Cooper	(a)	Ipswich Town
14 Jan	1989	Peter Davenport	(a)	Southampton
28 Sep	1991	John Hendrie	(h)	Sunderland
5 Oct	1991	Stuart Ripley	(a)	Bristol Rovers
14 Mar	1992	Jimmy Phillips	(a)	Southend United
2 May	1992	Nicky Mohan	(a)	Wolverhampton W
26 Jan	1993	Willie Falconer	(h)	Southampton
10 Apr	1993	Alan Kernaghan	(h)	Everton

FA Cup

16 Jan	1909	Jimmy Watson	(a)	Preston North End
29 Feb	1936	Ernie Coleman	(a)	Grimsby Town
3 Jan	1976	Phil Boersma	(h)	Bury

League Cup

27 Oct	1981	Bobby Thomson	(a)	Plymouth Argyle
18 Aug	1987	Dean Glover	(a)	Sunderland

Friendlies

18 May	1968	Bill Gates	(a)	Bremerhaven
31 Jul	1972	John Hickton	(h)	Groningen
7 Aug	1980	Billy Ashcroft	(h)	Olympiakos

*Players' League debut for Middlesbrough.
†Player on loan.

Tony Mowbray (left) and John Hendrie (right).

Jimmy Phillips (left, in action with Notts County's Chris Short) and Stuart Ripley (right).

Middlesbrough Debut Appearances
(1899-1993)

Listed below are debut details of all players who have played competitive football for Middlesbrough Football Club from 3 September 1899 to 8 May 1993. Where the player made his substitute or Cup debut before his full League debut these are also included here. The Height/Weight figures, where shown, are as accurate as possible and have been collated using Middlesbrough Football Club records, newspapers, various football yearbooks, etc.

Symbols used in this analysis: * = Scoring Debut; FA = FA Cup; LC = League Cup; ZDS = Zenith Data Systems Cup; FR = Freight/Rover Trophy; SC = Simod Cup; † = Abandoned season (1939-40); # = Sent off on debut.

Name	Ht	Wt	Date	Opposition	V	Res	Pos
Agnew WB	5ft 9in	12st	3 Sep 1904	Sheffield W	(h)	1-3	LB
Aitken A			3 Nov 1906	Liverpool	(h)	0-1	CH
Aitken GB	5ft 10in	12st 1lb	15 Sep 1951	Fulham	(h)	2-0	CH
Aitken S			14 Nov 1903	Newcastle U	(a)	1-2	RH
Allen M	5ft 11in	10st 10lb	30 Dec 1967	Bolton W	(h)	1-2	LH
Allport HG			2 Sep 1899	Lincoln C	(a)	0-3	RH
Anderson JR	5ft 11in	11st 4lb	26 Mar 1948	Arsenal	(a)	0-7	GK
Anderson S			20 Nov 1965	Cardiff C	(h)	3-4	RH
Angus MA	5ft 10in	12st 3lb	22 Apr 1980	Bristol C	(a)	1-3	LH
Appleby R	5ft 9.5in	11st 9lb	16 Apr 1960	Stoke C	(h)	1-0	GK
Armes S	5ft 7in	11st 1lb	4 Feb 1939	Bolton W	(h)	1-2	OR
Armstrong D	5ft 8in	11st	3 Apr 1972	Blackpool	(a)	1-3	OL
Arnold I			12 Mar 1991	Newcastle U	(h)	3-0	SU
Ashcroft W	6ft 1in	14st 4lb	3 Sep 1977	West Brom A	(a)	1-2	CF
Ashman D	5ft 10in	12st	1 Nov 1924	Coventry C	(a)	2-2	LH
Askew W	5ft 6.5in	10st 2lb	28 Mar 1981	West Brom A	(h)	2-1	OL
Astley H			3 Sep 1904	Sheffield W	(h)	1-3	OR
Atherton, RH	5ft 6in	11st 7lb	5 Sep 1903	Sheffield W	(a)	2-1	OL
Auld WB*			20 Jan 1951	Sheffield W	(h)	2-1	OL
Bailey IC	5ft 9in	10st 8lb	20 Dec 1975	Tottenham H	(h)	1-0	LB
Baird IJ	6ft	12st 9lb	3 Feb 1990	Portsmouth	(h)	2-0	CF
Barham MF	5ft 7in	11st	25 Mar 1989	Wimbledon	(a)	1-1	OL
Barker FM			15 Sep 1906	Sheffield W	(h)	1-2	RB
Barker WC	5ft 8.5in	11st 10lb	10 Feb 1906	Bury	(a)	1-1	RH
Barnard RS	5ft 11in	11st 2lb	1 Dec 1951	Sunderland	(h)	0-2	RB
Baxter MJ	6ft 1in	12st	29 Aug 1981	Tottenham H	(h)	1-3	CH
Baxter RD			29 Oct 1932	Birmingham	(a)	4-1	IL
Beagrie PS	5ft 8.5in	9st 10lb	2 Oct 1984	Oldham A	(a)	0-2	SU
			22 Dec 1984	Grimsby T	(a)	1-3	OL
Beaton S			19 Feb 1910	Chelsea	(a)	1-2	RH
Beattie TK			6 Nov 1982	Barnsley	(h)	2-0	CH
Bell FW			16 Sep 1899	New Brighton	(a)	1-1	LH
Bell HD	5ft 8in	11st 4lb	31 Aug 1946	Aston Villa	(a)	1-0	RH
Bell IC	5ft 9in	10st 10lb	15 Apr 1978	Wolves	(a)	0-0	OR
Bell James			22 Oct 1904	Notts C	(a)	0-0	IR
Bell Joseph N			10 Nov 1934	Tottenham H	(a)	1-3	OL
Bell S	5ft 7in	10st 4lb	30 Jan 1982	Southampton	(h)	0-1	IL
Best C			18 Mar 1911	Bury	(h)	2-1	OR
Bilcliff R	5ft 8.5in	12st 10lb	8 Mar 1952	Liverpool	(a)	1-1	RB
Birbeck J	5ft 8.5in	11st	28 Nov 1953	Sunderland	(a)	2-0	LH
Birkett RJE	5ft 9in	11st 7lb	16 Mar 1935	Preston NE	(a)	0-2	OR
Birrell W			5 Feb 1921	West Brom A	(a)	1-0	OR
Bissett JT	5ft11.5in	11st 12lb	30 Aug 1924	Barnsley	(h)	2-0	RB
Blackburn C	5ft 9in	10st 9lb	3 Mar 1981	Nottingham F	(a)	0-1	OR
Blackett J	5ft 11in	12st	19 Oct 1901	Arsenal	(a)	3-0	RB
Blackmore HA	5ft 10in	11st 7lb	27 Aug 1932	Aston Villa	(h)	0-2	CF
Blenkinsopp TW	5ft 11in	12st 8lb	21 Aug 1948	Chelsea	(a)	0-1	RB
Bloomer S			17 Mar 1906	Liverpool	(a)	1-6	IR
Boam SW	6ft 2in	13st 5lb	14 Aug 1971	Portsmouth	(a)	1-2	CH
Boardman H			26 Feb 1910	Tottenham H	(h)	4-3	RB
Boddington H			28 Mar 1904	Sheffield U	(h)	0-3	OL
Boersma P			6 Dec 1975	Manchester U	(h)	0-0	RH
Bolton J	5ft 11in	12st 2lb	29 Aug 1981	Tottenham H	(h)	1-3	LB
Bottrill WG	5ft 9in	10st 8lb	26 Dec 1922	Newcastle U	(h)	1-1	OR
Braithwaite RM	5ft 9in	10st 2lb	24 Aug 1963	Plymouth A	(h)	5-0	OL
Brawn WF	6ft 2.5in	13st 5lb	24 Mar 1906	Sheffield U	(h)	0-1	OR
Brearley J	5ft 6in	10st 7lb	27 Apr 1901	Grimsby T	(h)	0-0	IR
Brennan MR	5ft 9in	11st 1lb	27 Aug 1988	Derby C	(a)	0-1	IR
Briggs W	5ft 11in	12st 8lb	3 May 1947	Grimsby T	(a)	0-4	GK
Brine PK	5ft 10in	11st 3lb	20 Jan 1973	QPR	(h)	0-0	IR
Brown A	5ft 9.5in	12st 7lb	5 Sep 1903	Sheffield W	(a)	1-4	CF
Brown AS	5ft 9in	12st 6lb	4 Sep 1912	West Brom A	(a)	0-2	CF
Brown DJ	6ft 1in	12st 1lb	27 Mar 1978	Leicester C	(h)	0-1	GK
Brown James	5ft 9in	12st	1 Sep 1900	Lincoln C	(h)	2-0	OL
Brown John	5ft 8in	12st	8 Sep 1900	Manchester U	(a)	0-4	OL
Brown John R	5ft 7in	10st 12lb	6 Apr 1907	Bolton W	(a)	0-1	RB
Brown Joseph	5ft11.5in	11st 6lb	7 Sep 1949	Fulham	(h)	1-2	LH
Brown Thomas	5ft 11in	11st 6lb	23 Apr 1921	Chelsea	(h)	0-0	OR
Brown Thomas E	5ft 10in	11st 1lb	18 Sep 1954	Hull C	(a)	0-1	LB
Brown WH	5ft 10in		31 Aug 1931	Leicester C	(a)	2-2	RH
Brownlie JJ	5ft 11in	11st 10lb	4 Sep 1982	Burnley	(h)	1-4	RB
Bruce RF	5ft 7in	11st	4 Feb 1928	Bolton W	(a)	2-5	IR
Bryan PA	6ft .5in	10st 9lb	26 Sep 1964	Ipswich T	(h)	2-4	RB
Bryan R	5ft 4in	11st 4lb	29 Mar 1937	Birmingham	(a)	0-0	OR
Buckley MF	5ft 6in	10st 7lb	25 Aug 1984	Portsmouth	(a)	0-1	RH
Buckley S			27 Jan 1900	Chesterfield	(a)	0-7	CF
Burbeck RT	5ft 6in	10st 4lb	6 Oct 1956	Port Vale	(h)	3-1	OL
Burke MS	5ft 10in	11st 8lb	19 Dec 1987	Bournemouth	(a)	0-0	SU
			28 Dec 1987	Leeds U	(a)	0-2	RB
Burluraux D	5ft 10in	11st	27 Mar 1971	Luton T	(h)	2-1	OL
Burns ME*	5ft 7.5in	11st	7 Oct 1978	Manchester U	(a)	2-3	CF

Name	Ht	Wt	Date	Opposition	V	Res	Pos
Burton G			11 Dec 1909	Liverpool	(a)	0-0	CF
Butler G	5ft 8in	11st 5lb	11 Apr 1966	Bolton W	(a)	0-6	RB
Butler R	5ft 9in	11st 4lb	3 Sep 1919	Blackburn R	(h)	2-2	CF
Butler T	5ft 7.5in	10st 9lb	15 Apr 1939	Blackpool	(a)	0-4	OR
Butler W			28 Apr 1923	West Brom A	(a)	0-1	OR
Caig H	5ft 8in	11st	24 Apr 1915	Blackburn R	(a)	0-4	IR
Cail SG	5ft 8.5in	11st 2lb	2 Mar 1907	Aston Villa	(h)	1-0	CF
Callaghan J			9 Sep 1899	Birmingham	(h)	1-3	IR
Cameron K			7 Sep 1929	West Ham U	(a)	3-5	OL
Campbell A			1 Sep 1906	Everton	(h)	2-2	LB
Camsell GH	5ft 9in	11st 2lb	31 Oct 1925	Nottingham F	(h)	1-0	CF
Carr A			8 Nov 1930	Manchester C	(a)	2-4	CH
Carr G	5ft 9in	12st 4lb	1 Nov 1919	Aston Villa	(a)	3-5	LH
Carr H*			11 Feb 1911	Oldham A	(h)	1-2	CF
Carr J*	5ft 8.5in	11st 4lb	12 Jan 1911	Nottingham F	(h)	2-2	IR
Carr W	5ft 7.5in	11st 8lb	27 Apr 1911	Bradford C	(a)	0-1	CH
Carrick C	5ft 6in		24 Nov 1900	Arsenal	(a)	0-1	OL
Cartwright P			20 Mar 1925	Southampton	(h)	3-0	OR
Cassidy J*	5ft 9in	12st 4lb	7 Sep 1901	Stockport C	(a)	3-1	CF
Chadwick C	5ft 7in	9st 10lb	24 Feb 1934	Chelsea	(h)	2-2	OR
Chadwick DE	5ft 7in	9st 10lb	20 Aug 1966	Colchester U	(a)	3-2	OR
Chapman N	5ft 10in	11st 5lb	3 Feb 1962	Huddersfield T	(a)	0-0	RB
Charlton H	5ft 7in	9st 4lb	31 Oct 1970	Watford T	(h)	2-2	IR
Chipperfield F			30 Oct 1920	Bolton W	(a)	2-6	CH
Clark E			11 Nov 1899	Burton U	(h)	8-1	RB
Clark J			7 Apr 1900	Bolton W	(h)	0-3	IR
Clarke W	5ft 7in	10st	17 Jan 1920	Preston NE	(a)	1-3	OL
Clough BH	5ft 10in	11st 2lb	17 Sep 1955	Barnsley	(h)	1-1	CF
Clough J	6ft 1.5in	11st 8lb	10 Mar 1923	Arsenal	(a)	0-3	GK
Cochrane AF	5ft 5in	10st 7lb	10 Mar 1923	Arsenal	(a)	0-3	IL
Cochrane GT	5ft 7.5in	10st 9lb	14 Oct 1978	Norwich C	(h)	2-0	OR
Cochrane JK	5ft 9in	11st 11lb	8 Dec 1973	Sheffield W	(a)	2-2	LB
Cochrane M	5ft 8in	12st	30 Mar 1901	Arsenal	(h)	1-1	RB
Cochrane T	5ft 9in	12st 2lb	10 Oct 1936	Liverpool	(h)	3-3	OL
Coleman E	5ft 9in	12st 5lb	27 Sep 1934	Stoke C	(a)	0-2	OR
Coleman EP	5ft 11in	11st 9lb	24 Apr 1976	Aston Villa	(a)	1-2	CF
Coleman S	6ft	10st 8lb	30 Sep 1989	Watford	(a)	0-1	SU
			14 Oct 1989	Plymouth A	(h)	0-2	RB
Collett AA	5ft 11in	12st	1 May 1993	Sheffield W	(a)	3-2	GK
Comfort A	5ft 10in	11st 2lb	19 Aug 1989	Wolves	(h)	4-2	OL
Common A*	5ft 8in	13st	25 Feb 1905	Sheffield U	(a)	1-0	IR
Connachan ED	5ft 9.5in	12st 13lb	24 Aug 1963	Plymouth A	(h)	5-0	GK
Cook H	6ft 1in	11st 9lb	4 Oct 1913	Everton	(a)	0-2	CH
Cook J	5ft 7in	10st 9lb	24 Feb 1912	Arsenal	(a)	0-2	IL
Cook MC	5ft 10in	12st	14 Sep 1985	Norwich C	(h)	1-1	SU
			19 Oct 1985	Bradford C	(h)	1-1	IR
Cooper CT	5ft 10in	10st	8 Mar 1986	Crystal P	(a)	1-2	SU
			22 Mar 1986	Hull C	(h)	1-2	IL
Cooper D	5ft 11in	11st 3lb	30 Apr 1955	Bristol R	(a)	1-1	IR
Cooper T	5ft 8in	11st 3lb	9 Apr 1975	Leicester C	(a)	0-1	LB
Corbett R	5ft 8in	10st 7lb	15 Dec 1951	Tottenham H	(a)	1-3	LB
Corden S	5ft 8in	11st 2lb	17 Aug 1985	Wimbledon	(a)	0-3	LB
Cowan J			25 Nov 1899	Gainsborough T	(h)	0-0	RB
Coxon T			30 Sep 1905	Manchester C	(a)	0-4	OL
Coyle RP			7 Mar 1987	Bristol C	(h)	1-0	RB
Craggs JE	5ft 9in	12st 5lb	31 Aug 1971	Sheffield W	(h)	2-1	RB
Craig T			12 Nov 1904	Preston NE	(h)	1-1	LB
Crawford A	5ft 7in	10st 4lb	22 Oct 1983	Manchester C	(a)	1-2	IR
Crawford J	5ft 6in	11st 3lb	7 Dec 1901	Gainsborough T	(h)	3-1	OR
Creamer PA	6ft	11st 12lb	26 Aug 1972	Fulham	(h)	1-2	LB
Crosier J	5ft 8in	11st 8lb	4 Mar 1911	Manchester U	(h)	2-2	RH
Crossan JA	5ft 7in	11st 5lb	26 Aug 1967	Carlisle U	(a)	2-2	IL
Cuff PJ	6ft	12st 4lb	9 Apr 1974	Bolton W	(h)	0-0	GK
Cumming DS	5ft 10in	12st 8lb	10 Oct 1936	Liverpool	(h)	3-3	GK
Cummins S	5ft 5in	8st 12lb	27 Nov 1976	Ipswich T	(h)	0-2	IF
Cunliffe A	5ft 10in	10st 7lb	28 Dec 1935	Portsmouth	(a)	0-1	OL
Currie DN	6ft	11st 3lb	15 May 1982	Swansea C	(a)	2-1	SU
			28 Aug 1982	Sheffield W	(a)	1-3	IR
Currie R			14 Feb 1903	Newcastle U	(h)	1-0	CF
Curtis J	5ft 6.5in	11st 4lb	30 Aug 1919	Sheffield W	(a)	1-0	OR
Davenport P	5ft 11in	11st 3lb	29 Oct 1988	Millwall	(h)	4-2	IL
Davidson A	5ft 10in	12st 8lb	1 Sep 1900	Lincoln C	(h)	2-0	LH
Davidson I	6ft	11st	23 Feb 1965	Bury	(a)	2-3	LH
Davidson S	5ft 10in	12st	6 Sep 1913	Manchester C	(a)	1-1	RH
Davidson W			17 Dec 1910	Bradford C	(h)	3-2	OL
Davies AE	5ft 9in	11st 4lb	2 Jan 1915	West Brom A	(a)	0-1	OL
Davies B	6ft	11st 11lb	11 Feb 1911	Oldham A	(h)	1-2	GK
Davies WF			24 Dec 1904	Nottingham F	(a)	1-1	OR
Davison JW	5ft 9in	11st 9lb	29 Nov 1919	Chelsea	(a)	1-3	LH
Day W	5ft 9in	10st 2lb	8 Oct 1955	Leicester C	(h)	4-3	OR
Delapenha LL	5ft 8in	11st 2lb	6 May 1950	Fulham	(a)	2-1	IR

Mark Burke (left) flies through the air after a tackle by Norwich City's Ian Culverhouse. Alan Comfort (right) had to retire because of injury.

Craig Hignett (left) and Paul Kerr (right).

Name	Ht	Wt	Date	Opposition	V	Res	Pos
Desmond P			24 Sep 1949	Charlton A	(a)	3-0	IL
Dews G	5ft 9in	11st 10lb	31 Aug 1946	Aston Villa	(a)	1-0	IL
Dibble AG	6ft 2in	13st 7lb	19 Feb 1991	West Brom A	(h)	3-2	GK
Dickinson PE			18 Oct 1924	Hull C	(h)	0-1	OR
Dicks RW	5ft 8.5in	11st 2lb	23 Aug 1947	Manchester U	(h)	2-2	OL
Dickson IW	5ft 9.5in	13st	22 Dec 1923	Preston NE	(h)	1-2	CF
Dixon C	5ft 7in	11st 4lb	30 Aug 1919	Sheffield W	(a)	1-0	RB
Dixon T*			23 Nov 1907	Manchester C	(h)	2-0	IR
Dobbie H*	5ft 9in	11st 10lb	1 Feb 1947	Sheffield U	(h)	2-4	CF
Doig T			1 Dec 1900	Blackpool	(h)	3-1	RH
Donaghy P	5ft 9in	10st 5lb	24 May 1920	Bradford C	(a)	1-0	LH
Donaldson A	6ft	10st 12lb	9 Feb 1949	Charlton A	(a)	0-2	CF
Douglas H			7 Jan 1903	West Brom A	(a)	0-1	OR
Douglas JS	6ft 1in	12st	19 Oct 1946	Derby C	(a)	1-1	LH
Dow MJ	5ft 9in	10st 4lb	1 Sep 1900	Lincoln C	(h)	2-0	RB
Downing DG	5ft 9in	10st 4lb	21 Oct 1965	Norwich C	(h)	0-1	OR
Dowson F			15 Jan 1921	Sheffield U	(a)	1-1	IL
Duffy CF			7 Oct 1905	Bury	(h)	5-1	OL
Duguid W	5ft 7.5in	11st 3lb	1 Oct 1910	Tottenham H	(h)	2-0	RH
Eckford J	5ft 7in	11st 7lb	10 Nov 1900	Burton U	(a)	0-0	IL
Edwards WI	5ft 9in	11st	25 Oct 1952	Wolves	(a)	3-3	CF
Eglington R			16 Sep 1899	New Brighton	(a)	1-1	IL
Elkes AJE	6ft 1in	12st 6lb	12 Oct 1929	Huddersfield T	(h)	1-3	IL
Ellerington W	5ft 10in	12st	30 Aug 1919	Sheffield W	(a)	1-0	CH
Elliott GW	5ft 9in	11st 12lb	1 Sep 1909	Sheffield U	(h)	0-2	IR
Emmerson GA			20 Feb 1929	Oldham A	(h)	1-0	OR
Emmerson M	5ft 10in	11st 6lb	17 Nov 1962	Bury	(a)	0-1	GK
Evans RW			17 Feb 1900	Leicester C	(h)	0-1	IL
Eyre E	5ft 7.5in	12st	2 Sep 1911	Sunderland	(a)	0-1	OL
Falconer WH	6ft 1in	13st 2lb	12 Aug 1991	Millwall	(h)	1-0	LH
Featherstone T			9 Apr 1904	Bury	(a)	1-1	CF
Fenton M	5ft 9in	10st 7lb	6 May 1933	Blackburn R	(h)	4-0	IL
Ferguson C	5ft 8in	10st 8lb	9 Sep 1933	Birmingham	(h)	0-3	OR
Ferguson R	5ft 9in	10st 7lb	29 Aug 1936	Manchester C	(h)	2-0	GK
Ferguson RG	5ft 9.5in	11st	7 Feb 1925	Derby C	(a)	1-3	CH
Fernie DW	5ft 10in	11st 6lb	6 Dec 1958	Ipswich T	(h)	2-3	IR
Fitzsimons AG	5ft 7.5in	10st 11lb	1 Apr 1950	West Brom A	(a)	3-0	OR
Fleming C	5ft 10in	12st 2lb	24 Aug 1991	Ipswich T	(a)	1-2	SU
			9 Nov 1991	Brighton	(a)	1-1	RB
Flint WA			19 Feb 1910	Chelsea	(a)	1-2	OR
Foggon A	5ft 10in	13st	25 Nov 1972	Swindon T	(h)	0-2	SU
			30 Dec 1972	Oxford U	(h)	1-0	OL
Forrest W	5ft11.5in	12st 13lb	18 Jan 1930	Manchester U	(a)	3-0	LH
Fowler HN	5ft 8in	11st 9lb	2 Apr 1938	Leicester C	(a)	1-0	LB
Fox WV	5ft 9in	11st 6lb	30 Aug 1919	Sheffield W	(a)	1-0	LH
Frail J	5ft11.5in	13st 8lb	1 Sep 1900	Lincoln C	(h)	2-0	GK
Fraser A	5ft 6.5in	10st 10lb	5 Apr 1912	West Brom A	(h)	1-0	IR
Freeman RV	5ft 10in	12st 3lb	25 Aug 1923	Huddersfield T	(a)	0-1	RB
Freeman T			8 Sep 1930	West Ham U	(a)	3-0	LB
French JP			3 Jan 1925	Leicester C	(h)	1-5	LB
Gallacher C			29 Mar 1947	Portsmouth	(a)	1-3	IR
Gallagher J	5ft 8.5in	11st 8lb	9 Apr 1921	Manchester U	(h)	2-4	LB
Garbett TG	5ft 9in	11st 9lb	7 Sep 1965	Ipswich T	(a)	1-2	CF
Gardner JR			26 Jan 1929	West Brom A(FA)	(a)	0-1	CH
Gates WL	5ft 10in	11st 6lb	27 Sep 1961	Luton T	(a)	2-3	CH
Gettins E			5 Sep 1903	Sheffield W	(a)	1-4	OR
Gettins JH			2 Sep 1899	Lincoln C	(a)	0-3	CF
Gibson FW	6ft 2in	13st	19 Nov 1932	Everton	(h)	0-2	GK
Gibson IS	5ft 7in	10st 4lb	23 Mar 1962	Scunthorpe U	(a)	1-1	IR
Gibson RJ			3 Sep 1910	Everton	(h)	1-0	OR
Gill G	5ft 11in	10st 9lb	3 Mar 1984	Cardiff C	(a)	1-2	SU
			27 Apr 1984	Swansea C	(a)	1-2	OL
Gittens J	5ft 11in	12st 6lb	22 Feb 1992	Blackburn R	(h)	0-0	RH
Glover DV	5ft 10in	11st 11lb	15 Aug 1987	Millwall	(h)	1-1	RB
Godley W			26 Dec 1902	Wolves	(a)	0-2	CF
Good H	5ft 10in	12st	25 Oct 1924	Stoke C	(h)	1-0	CH
Goodfellow DO	6ft 1in	12st 7lb	23 Aug 1947	Manchester U	(h)	2-2	GK
Goodson L			20 Dec 1902	Sunderland	(a)	0-1	IL
Gordon D			12 Sep 1908	Manchester U	(a)	3-6	RB
Gordon J	5ft 7in	11st 1lb	31 Aug 1946	Aston Villa	(a)	1-0	LH
Gowland N	5ft 11in	12st	3 Oct 1925	Oldham A	(h)	2-1	GK
Gray RSM			14 Oct 1899	Leicester C	(a)	1-4	IL
Green T	5ft 9in	12st	11 Feb 1905	Manchester C	(a)	2-3	CF
Griffiths TP			11 Mar 1933	Birmingham	(h)	2-2	CH
Groves JA			4 Sep 1907	Birmingham	(h)	1-0	RB
Hall BAC	5ft 11in	12st 7lb	10 Apr 1928	Huddersfield T	(a)	4-2	CF
Hall JH			5 Sep 1908	Bradford C	(h)	1-0	CF
Hamilton GJ	5ft 9in	11st 2lb	26 Feb 1982	Bolton W	(a)	1-3	SU
			19 Mar 1982	Barnsley	(a)	0-2	LB
Hamilton W*		10st 2lb	23 Feb 1961	Plymouth A	(h)	3-1	IR
Hankin R#	6ft 2in	14st	27 Sep 1981	Grimsby T	(h)	1-4	CF
Hanlon E	5ft 8in	12st	8 Sep 1906	Arsenal	(a)	0-2	CF
Hardwick GFM	5ft 9.5in	11st 10lb	18 Dec 1937	Bolton W	(h)	1-1	LB
Harkins J	5ft 9in	11st 6lb	20 Oct 1906	Newcastle U	(h)	0-3	CH
Harris J			10 Mar 1923	Arsenal	(a)	0-3	RH
Harris WC	5ft 11in	11st 10lb	6 Mar 1954	Chelsea	(h)	3-3	LH
Harrison H	5ft 8in	11st 7lb	4 Oct 1919	Manchester U	(a)	1-1	GK
Hartnett JB	5ft 7in	11st 11lb	5 Mar 1949	Wolves	(h)	4-4	OL
Hasell AA	6ft	12st	12 Oct 1907	Everton	(h)	0-2	GK
Hastie J			28 Aug 1920	Oldham A	(h)	1-2	OR
Hawkins GH	5ft 9in	10st 7lb	19 Feb 1936	Huddersfield T	(a)	1-4	IR
Haworth JH	5ft 9in	12st 8lb	24 Feb 1912	Arsenal	(a)	0-2	LH
Healey R	5ft10.5in	12st 7lb	4 Apr 1914	Preston NE	(h)	4-1	IR
Heard TP	5ft 9in	11st 5lb	31 Aug 1985	Brighton	(h)	0-1	LH
Hedley George T			4 Nov 1905	Aston V	(a)	1-4	RB
Hedley Graeme	5ft 7in	8st 6lb	21 Aug 1976	Coventry C	(h)	1-0	CF
Henderson GH			4 Nov 1905	Aston Villa	(a)	1-4	RH
Henderson R	5ft 9in	11st	30 Nov 1957	Blackburn R	(a)	3-3	IL
Hendrie JG	5ft 7in	11st 4lb	25 Aug 1990	West Ham U	(h)	0-0	OL

Name	Ht	Wt	Date	Opposition	V	Res	Pos
Hepple G	5ft 9in	11st 12lb	17 May 1947	Huddersfield T	(a)	1-3	LH
Hewitt C			11 Feb 1905	Manchester C	(a)	2-3	OR
Hewitt J			5 Oct 1991	Bristol R	(a)	1-2	SU
Hick WM			8 Mar 1924	Blackburn R	(h)	2-0	CF
Hickling W			8 Sep 1906	Arsenal	(a)	0-2	LB
Hickton J*	6ft	11st 8lb	24 Sep 1966	Workington	(a)	3-2	CH
Higgins W	5ft 10in	12st 7lb	1 Sep 1900	Lincoln C	(h)	2-0	CH
Higham N	5ft 7.5in	9st 12lb	21 Mar 1936	Blackburn R	(a)	2-2	IR
Hignett CJ	5ft 10in	10st 8lb	28 Nov 1992	Oldham A	(a)	1-4	IR
Hillier EJG	5ft11.5in	11st 8lb	1 Feb 1930	Leicester C	(a)	1-4	GK
Hisbent JM			27 Sep 1913	Sunderland	(h)	0-2	RB
Hodgson DJ	5ft 10in	11st 8lb	23 Sep 1978	Nottingham F	(a)	2-2	SU
			4 Nov 1978	Bristol C	(h)	0-0	CF
			3 Mar 1987	Bournemouth	(a)	1-3	OL
Hodgson G			22 Dec 1900	Grimsby T	(a)	0-2	GK
Hodgson JP	6ft	11st 8lb	20 Mar 1948	Derby C	(h)	1-1	GK
Hogg J			13 Sep 1902	Sheffield W	(a)	0-2	RB
Holliday E	5ft 9in	11st	14 Dec 1957	West Ham U	(a)	1-2	OL
			21 Aug 1965	Manchester C	(h)	1-1	OR
Holliday JW	5ft 10in	12st 6lb	8 Nov 1930	Manchester C	(a)	2-4	CF
Holmes W			27 Feb 1915	Manchester C	(h)	1-0	RB
Honeyman JW	5ft 8in	11st 5lb	14 Oct 1919	Manchester U	(a)	1-1	LH
Horne BS	5ft 11in	13st 13lb	5 Sep 1992	Sheffield U	(h)	2-0	GK
Horner W			14 Mar 1961	Leyton O	(a)	1-1	LH
Horsfield A*	5ft11.5in	12st 11lb	7 Sep 1963	Grimsby T	(h)	6-0	CF
Howling E			1 Apr 1911	Aston Villa	(h)	0-1	GK
Hughes M			9 Sep 1899	Birmingham	(h)	1-3	GK
Hume RM			15 Sep 1962	Preston NE	(a)	1-0	OL
Hunter H			10 Mar 1906	Aston Villa	(h)	1-2	GK
Ironside I	6ft 2in	13st	2 May 1992	Wolves	(a)	2-1	GK
Irvine JD			22 Aug 1964	Southampton	(a)	3-0	IL
Jackson A	5ft 8in	11st 4lb	3 Sep 1910	Everton	(h)	1-0	CH
James WE	5ft 7.5in	11st 8lb	1 Apr 1911	Aston Villa	(h)	0-1	OL
Janković B	6ft 1in	13st	17 Mar 1979	Bristol C	(a)	1-1	SU
			14 Apr 1979	Bolton W	(a)	0-0	OR
Jarvis S	5ft 10in	11st 10lb	10 Apr 1928	Huddersfield T	(a)	4-2	RB
Jennings J	5ft 8in	11st 1lb	1 Feb 1930	Leicester C	(a)	1-4	RB
Jennings S			16 Apr 1920	Everton	(a)	2-5	CF
Johnson PE	5ft 9.5in	11st	4 Apr 1978	Chelsea	(h)	2-0	LB
Johnston Craig P	5ft 9in	10st 10lb	4 Feb 1978	Birmingham C	(a)	2-1	IL
Johnston C Pat			24 Apr 1948	Sunderland	(a)	0-3	RH
Jones A	5ft 7in	12st 6lb	7 Sep 1901	Stockport C	(a)	3-1	CH
Jones GE			21 Jan 1961	Southampton	(a)	2-3	RB
Jones GW	5ft 7in	11st	19 Sep 1925	Sheffield W	(h)	3-0	OR
Jones J			30 Dec 1899	Lincoln C	(h)	1-1	LB
Jones JL			20 Mar 1909	Manchester C	(h)	3-0	OL
Jordon BA	6ft	12st	8 Nov 1958	Scunthorpe U	(h)	6-1	LH
Kamara C	6ft 1in	12st	20 Feb 1993	Nottingham F	(h)	1-2	IL
Kavanagh GA	5ft 10in		21 Oct 1992	Nottingham F	(a)	0-1	IR
Kay J	5ft 10in	11st 6lb	12 Jan 1985	Wolves	(a)	0-0	RB
Kaye A	5ft 3.5in	9st 8lb	26 Nov 1960	Lincoln C	(h)	1-1	OR
Kear MP	5ft 9in	10st 4lb	26 Sep 1967	Birmingham C	(a)	1-6	OR
Kelly B	5ft 7in	12st	19 Nov 1910	Sheffield U	(h)	3-1	RB
Kennedy F			17 Sep 1927	Blackburn R	(h)	2-0	OL
Kennedy MFM	5ft 9.5in	11st 3lb	28 Aug 1982	Sheffield W	(h)	1-3	IR
Kent H	5ft10.5in	12st 6lb	12 Sep 1908	Manchester C	(a)	3-6	LH
Kernaghan AN	6ft 2in	12st 12lb	9 Feb 1985	Notts C	(h)	0-1	CF
Kerr PA	5ft 9in	11st 3lb	10 Jan 1987	Preston NE(FA)	(h)	0-1	CF
			24 Jan 1987	Bury	(a)	3-0	CF
Kinnell G			19 Oct 1968	Fulham	(h)	2-0	LH
Kirby F	5ft 9in	12st	4 Oct 1913	Everton	(a)	0-2	CF
Kirk HJ	5ft 9in	10st 9lb	9 Sep 1963	Rotherham U	(h)	2-2	OL
Kite PD	6ft 1in	14st 7lb	19 Apr 1986	Oldham A	(a)	0-1	GK
Knowles CB			15 Apr 1963	Derby C	(a)	3-3	RB
Laidlaw JD	5ft 8in	10st 12lb	9 Mar 1968	Cardiff C	(h)	2-3	CF
Laking GE	5ft 9in	10st 7lb	17 Oct 1936	Sunderland	(h)	5-5	RB
Lamb TJ			23 Sep 1899	Grimsby T	(h)	1-0	IR
Lawrie S	5ft 5in	9st 4lb	3 Nov 1951	Arsenal	(h)	0-3	OR
Laws B	5ft 10in	11st 5lb	16 Apr 1985	Sheffield U	(h)	1-0	RB
Lawson JJ	5ft 7.5in	10st	12 Apr 1966	Bolton W	(h)	1-1	OL
Layton AE			4 Nov 1911	Aston Villa	(a)	1-2	LB
Le Flem RP			27 Feb 1965	Crystal P	(h)	0-0	OR
Leonard HD			1 Apr 1911	Aston Villa	(h)	0-1	CF
Leslie J	5ft 6.5in	11st 4lb	12 Oct 1901	West Brom A	(h)	1-2	IR
Lightening AD	6ft 1in		29 Aug 1962	Newcastle U	(a)	1-6	GK
Linacre W	5ft 10in	11st 7lb	24 Sep 1949	Charlton A	(a)	3-0	OR
Linton T			24 Feb 1900	Luton T	(a)	1-1	CF
Linwood AB	5ft 8.5in	11st 8lb	21 Sep 1946	Preston NE	(h)	2-0	IL
Livingstone J	5ft 10in	11st 8lb	20 Aug 1960	Bristol C	(a)	3-2	CF
Lloyd E	5ft 8.5in	11st 8lb	6 Dec 1919	Liverpool	(h)	3-2	IL
Longstaffe G			2 Sep 1899	Lincoln C	(a)	0-3	IR
Lugg RJ	5ft 9in	10st 10lb	14 Jan 1967	Oldham A	(a)	1-0	OL
Lynch P	5ft 9in	11st 1lb	18 Mar 1972	QPR	(a)	0-1	SU
McAllister W	5ft 8.5in	11st 4lb	7 Feb 1925	Derby C	(a)	1-3	RH
McAndrew A*	6ft 1in	13st 1lb	3 Nov 1973	Luton T	(h)	2-1	RH
Macaulay W*			1 Sep 1902	Blackburn R	(a)	1-0	IR
			29 Sep 1984	Cardiff C	(h)	3-2	LH
Macdonald G	6ft	12st 1lb	8 Oct 1980	Brighton	(a)	1-0	OR
McCabe JJ	5ft 10in	10st 11lb	9 Oct 1946	Liverpool	(h)	2-2	LH
McCallum D			10 Dec 1904	Aston Villa	(a)	0-0	RB
McClelland J	6ft	12st 7lb	19 Mar 1925	Hull C	(a)	0-0	CF
McClure S			3 Sep 1910	Everton	(h)	1-0	IL
McCormack JC	5ft 7.5in	10st 12lb	3 May 1947	Grimsby T	(a)	0-4	OR
McCorquodale D			16 Dec 1899	Manchester U	(a)	0-2	OR
McCowie A			10 Nov 1900	Burton U	(a)	0-1	IL
McCracken JP			2 Sep 1899	Lincoln C	(a)	0-3	CH
McCrae A	6ft	11st 12lb	6 Nov 1948	Derby C	(a)	0-2	IL
McCulloch A	5ft 9in	11st 7lb	28 Sep 1907	Bolton W	(h)	0-1	CF
Macfarlane J	5ft 9in	11st 5lb	31 Aug 1929	Liverpool	(h)	5-0	LH

Name	Ht	Wt	Date	Opposition	V	Res	Pos
Macfarlane R			1 Sep 1902	Blackburn R	(a)	1-0	GK
Macfarlane T			11 Mar 1901	Port Vale	(a)	2-0	LB
McGee OE	5ft 7in	10st 7lb	3 Oct 1989	Halifax T(LC)	(a)	1-0	SU
			20 Jan 1990	Sheffield U	(a)	0-1	SU
			3 Feb 1990	Portsmouth	(h)	2-0	LB
McGuigan A			23 Apr 1904	Nottingham F	(a)	1-1	OR
McIlmoyle H	5ft 11in	11st 6lb	27 Sep 1969	Blackpool	(h)	0-2	CF
McKay J			19 Mar 1927	Darlington	(h)	4-1	IL
McKennan PS	5ft 11in	12st 4lb	20 Aug 1949	Everton	(h)	0-1	IR
McKenzie D	5ft 11in	11st 7lb	31 Aug 1938	Aston Villa	(h)	1-1	RH
McLean JD	5ft 8in	9st 6lb	7 Apr 1956	Bristol R	(h)	0-1	IR
McLeod D	5ft 8.5in	12st 10lb	10 Oct 1908	Notts C	(a)	0-2	RB
McManus CE	6ft 1in	13st	18 Jan 1985	Brighton	(a)	3-3	GK
McMordie A	5ft 7in	10st 4lb	25 Sep 1965	Plymouth A	(a)	2-2	IL
McMurray J	5ft 7in	10st 12lb	19 Aug 1953	Cardiff C	(h)	0-0	RH
McNally J			2 Sep 1899	Lincoln C	(a)	0-3	CH
McNeil M	5ft 11in	12st 2lb	20 Dec 1958	Brighton	(a)	6-4	RH
McNeill AA			10 Feb 1968	Aston Villa	(a)	1-0	OL
McPartland D	6ft	10st 10lb	11 Dec 1965	Bristol C	(a)	2-2	GK
McPhail DD			17 Jan 1931	Blackpool	(h)	5-1	OR
McPherson K*	5ft 11in	11st 13lb	31 Aug 1955	Swansea T	(h)	4-1	CF
McRobbie A	5ft 10in	12st 2lb	10 Feb 1912	Notts C	(h)	4-0	LB
Madden G			3 Feb 1900	Woolwich A	(h)	1-0	IL
Maddison JP	5ft 7.5in	10st 8lb	8 Mar 1947	Wolves	(h)	1-1	OL
Maddren WD*	6ft	12st 8lb	12 Apr 1969	Bury	(h)	2-3	CF
Mahoney JF	5ft 7.5in	11st 1lb	20 Aug 1977	Liverpool	(h)	1-1	OR
Maitland AE	5ft 8.5in	12st 3lb	25 Aug 1923	Huddersfield T	(a)	0-1	LB
Malan NF	5ft 8in	11st 2lb	6 May 1947	Chelsea	(a)	0-2	GK
Malcolm G	5ft 9.5in	11st 9lb	2 Nov 1912	Aston Villa	(a)	1-5	RH
Mannion WJ	5ft 6in	9st 7lb	2 Jan 1937	Portsmouth	(h)	2-2	IR
Marcroft EH*	5ft 7in	10st 4lb	25 Jan 1932	Sheffield W	(a)	1-1	OR
Marshall DW	5ft 11in	11st 8lb	3 Apr 1993	Chelsea	(a)	0-4	SU
Marshall J	5ft 9.5in	13st 12lb	22 Nov 1919	Chelsea	(h)	0-0	RB
Marshall SK	5ft 10in	10st 11lb	22 Oct 1965	Norwich C	(h)	0-1	IL
Martin GS	5ft 8.5in	11st 3lb	27 Aug 1932	Aston Villa	(h)	0-2	IR
Martin J			6 May 1933	Blackburn R	(h)	4-0	LH
Marwood B	5ft 7in	11st 6lb	19 Oct 1991	Grimsby T	(a)	0-1	OL
Masson DS	5ft 8in	10st 10lb	24 Oct 1964	Norwich C	(h)	2-0	IL
Mathieson JA			28 Aug 1926	Chelsea	(a)	0-3	GK
Mattinson H	6ft	12st 1lb	29 Jan 1947	Preston NE	(a)	1-0	CH
Millar J	5ft 7in	12st	1 Sep 1900	Lincoln C	(h)	2-0	RH
Millar WM			17 Dec 1927	Derby C	(h)	3-3	OL
Miller D†			2 Sep 1939	Stoke C	(a)	2-2	LH
Miller J			28 Aug 1926	Chelsea	(a)	0-3	RH
Million E	6ft	11st 8lb	6 Oct 1956	Port Vale	(h)	3-1	GK
Mills DJ	5ft 9in	11st	19 Apr 1969	Birmingham C	(a)	1-3	SU
			14 Apr 1970	Swindon T	(a)	3-0	OR
			25 Aug 1985	Portsmouth	(a)	0-1	IR
Milne JV	5ft 8in	11st	18 Dec 1937	Bolton W	(h)	1-2	OL
Mitchell AJ		10st 2lb	8 Sep 1954	Nottingham F	(h)	1-4	OL
Mochan N	5ft 8in	11st 4lb	18 Aug 1951	Tottenham H	(h)	2-1	CF
SC Mohan NM	6ft 2in	12st	11 Jan 1989	Coventry C	(h)	1-0	RB
			14 Jan 1989	Southampton	(a)	3-1	RB
Moody A	6ft	11st 4lb	18 Jan 1969	Millwall	(h)	1-1	RB
Moore AT	5ft 10in	11st	10 Apr 1993	Everton	(h)	1-2	SU
Moran M	5ft 5in	10st 7lb	1 Sep 1900	Lincoln C	(h)	2-0	OR
Mordue J			11 Sep 1920	Burnley	(a)	1-2	OR
Morris CB	5ft 10in	10st 8lb	15 Aug 1992	Coventry C	(a)	1-2	RB
Mowbray AM	6ft 1.5in	12st 2lb	8 Sep 1982	Newcastle U	(a)	1-1	OR
Muir J			1 Sep 1902	Blackburn R	(a)	1-0	OL
Muir W			4 Oct 1902	Bolton W	(h)	4-3	RH
Mulholland FG	5ft 10in	11st 1lb	5 Jan 1952	Charlton A	(a)	2-1	LH
Murdoch RW	5ft 9.5in	12st 6lb	22 Sep 1973	Blackpool	(a)	0-1	OR
Murphy DA	5ft 9in	10st 12lb	30 Apr 1937	Bolton W	(a)	1-3	LH
Murphy J*			11 Sep 1899	Burton S	(h)	8-1	IL
Murphy M*			9 Sep 1899	Small Heath	(h)	1-3	IL
Murphy TE	5ft4.75in	9st 12lb	14 Sep 1946	Manchester U	(a)	0-1	IL
Murray A	5ft 8in	10st 8lb	25 Oct 1969	Watford	(h)	3-1	SU
*			13 Jan 1970	Blackburn R	(h)	4-1	IR
Murray T			16 Sep 1905	Sheffield W	(a)	0-3	IL
Murray W	5ft 5in	10st 2lb	17 Apr 1922	Preston NE	(a)	1-1	OL
Mustoe R	5ft 10in	10st 8lb	25 Aug 1990	West Ham U	(h)	0-0	IR
Muttitt E*	5ft 7in	11st	27 Nov 1929	Arsenal	(a)	2-1	OL
Myton B#	5ft 9in	11st 3lb	7 Sep 1968	Cardiff C	(a)	0-2	LH
Nash FC	5ft 10in	12st 2lb	2 Oct 1937	Preston NE	(h)	2-1	GK
Nattrass I	5ft 11in	12st	15 Sep 1979	Arsenal	(a)	0-2	IL
Neal RM	6ft 1in	12st 7lb	7 Oct 1961	Liverpool	(h)	2-0	LH
Niblo TB*			14 Apr 1900	Loughborough	(a)	1-1	CF
Nichol J	5ft 8in	11st 7lb	3 Sep 1910	Everton	(h)	1-0	OL
Nobbs KA	5ft 10in	11st 10lb	21 Apr 1981	Coventry C	(h)	0-1	RB
Norris OP	5ft 8.5in	11st 2lb	11 Apr 1952	Newcastle U	(a)	2-0	CF
Nurse MTG	6ft	13st	29 Sep 1962	Grimsby T	(a)	4-3	CH
O'Connell SCP*	5ft 11in	13st	26 Dec 1953	Newcastle U	(a)	3-2	IR
O'Hagan C			22 Sep 1906	Bury	(a)	1-1	IL
O'Hanlon KG	6ft	12st	22 Jan 1983	Fulham	(a)	0-1	GK
O'Riordan DJ	6ft	12st	17 Aug 1985	Wimbledon	(a)	0-3	IR
O'Rourke J*	5ft 8.5in	10st 10lb	20 Aug 1966	Colchester U	(a)	3-2	CF
Orritt B	5ft10.5in	10st 10lb	3 Mar 1962	Charlton A	(h)	3-2	IR
Osborne F			4 Sep 1899	Port Vale	(a)	1-3	CF
Ostler J			14 Apr 1900	Loughborough	(a)	1-1	CH
Otto HM*	6ft	12st	29 Aug 1982	Tottenham H	(h)	1-3	IR
Page R			2 Sep 1899	Lincoln C	(a)	0-3	IL
Pallister GA	6ft 4in	13st	17 Aug 1985	Wimbledon	(a)	0-3	RH
Parkin R			18 Jan 1936	Brentford	(a)	0-1	RH
Parkinson GA	5ft 10in	11st 11lb	23 Aug 1986	Port Vale	(h)	2-2	LH
Patterson RL	6ft .5in	12st 10lb	8 Sep 1951	Charlton A	(a)	3-4	LB
Patterson T	5ft 10in	11st	14 Dec 1974	Birmingham C	(h)	3-0	CF
Payton AP*	5ft 9in	10st 6lb	23 Nov 1991	Bristol C	(h)	3-1	IL
Peacock A	6ft	11st	26 Nov 1955	Bristol R	(a)	2-7	IL

Name	Ht	Wt	Date	Opposition	V	Res	Pos
Peacock J	5ft 8in	11st 2lb	15 Oct 1927	Birmingham	(a)	2-3	LH
Peake AM	5ft 10in	12st 10lb	30 Nov 1991	Blackburn R	(a)	1-2	IL
Pears S	6ft 1in	11st 10lb	5 Nov 1983	Cardiff C	(h)	2-0	GK
Pease WH			28 Aug 1926	Chelsea	(a)	0-3	OR
Peggie J	5ft 8in	12st	19 Nov 1910	Sheffield U	(h)	3-1	CF
Pender R			3 Dec 1919	Newcastle U	(a)	0-0	LH
Pentland FB	5ft 9in	12st 4lb	5 Sep 1908	Bradford C	(h)	1-0	OR
Peters J	5ft 6in	10st 11lb	3 Nov 1979	Tottenham H	(h)	0-0	LB
Phillips BJ	5ft 11in	11st 1lb	26 Mar 1954	Blackburn R	(h)	4-3	CH
Phillips JN	6ft	11st 12lb	17 Mar 1990	Blackburn R	(h)	0-3	LB
Phillipson TF*			11 Feb 1905	Manchester C	(a)	2-3	IL
Piercy FR			14 Oct 1899	Leicester F	(a)	1-4	LH
Piercy HR			30 Dec 1899	Lincoln C	(h)	1-1	IR
Platt JA	6ft 1in	13st	2 Oct 1971	Blackpool	(h)	1-0	GK
LC Pollock J			8 Oct 1991	Bournemouth	(h)	2-1	SU
			12 Oct 1991	Wolves	(h)	0-0	OL
Poole K	5ft 10in	11st 11lb	16 Jan 1988	Millwall	(a)	1-2	GK
Poskett M	6ft	11st 2lb	13 Oct 1973	Hull C	(h)	1-0	SU
Poulton A			27 Mar 1920	Arsenal	(a)	1-2	IR
Povey W	5ft 8in	9st	29 Dec 1962	Norwich C	(a)	4-3	OL
Pratt R	5ft 9in	12st	16 Sep 1899	New Brighton	(a)	1-1	CF
Priest AE			22 Sep 1906	Bury	(a)	1-1	RB
Priest F			8 Sep 1906	Arsenal	(a)	0-2	CF
Proctor MG	5ft 10in	12st 8lb	22 Aug 1978	Birmingham C	(a)	3-1	OR
			25 Mar 1989	Wimbledon	(a)	1-1	CH
Proudlock P*	5ft 10in	11st	24 Nov 1986	Doncaster R(FR)	(h)	3-0	IR
			13 Dec 1986	Doncaster R	(h)	1-0	OL
Pugh CE			2 Sep 1899	Lincoln C	(a)	0-3	OL
Putney TA	5ft 7in	11st 10lb	19 Aug 1989	Wolves	(h)	4-2	CH
Raisbeck L			21 Oct 1899	Luton T	(h)	0-0	LH
Ramage A	6ft 2in	13st	24 Apr 1976	Aston Villa	(a)	1-2	SU
			5 Mar 1977	Leeds U	(a)	1-2	LH
Ramsay A	5ft 7in	12st	2 Sep 1899	Lincoln C	(a)	0-3	RB
Ratcliffe D	5ft 7.5in	10st 10lb	28 Sep 1963	Swansea T	(a)	1-2	OL
Ratcliffe E		11st 8lb	31 Mar 1906	Notts C	(a)	1-1	RB
Rayment JW*	5ft 8in	9st	20 Sep 1952	Liverpool	(a)	1-4	OR
Reagan CM	5ft 7.5in	11st 3lb	20 Mar 1948	Derby C	(h)	1-1	OR
Redfern J			9 Sep 1899	Birmingham	(h)	1-3	LH
Reid G*			11 Nov 1899	Burton U	(h)	8-1	CF
Reid GT	5ft 9in	12st 6lb	2 Sep 1905	Everton	(a)	1-4	IL
Rickaby S	5ft 10in	11st 12lb	20 Mar 1948	Derby C	(h)	1-1	LB
Rigby A	5ft 9in	11st 4lb	17 Sep 1932	Liverpool	(h)	0-1	OL
Ripley SE	6ft	13st 6lb	5 Feb 1985	Oldham A	(h)	1-2	SU
			25 Mar 1985	Barnsley	(a)	0-0	IR
Roberts A	5ft 9in	10st	30 Oct 1982	Rotherham U	(a)	1-1	SU
			27 Aug 1983	Portsmouth	(a)	1-0	OR
Roberts J			20 Oct 1906	Newcastle U	(h)	0-3	OL
Roberts RJ			2 Apr 1904	Liverpool	(h)	1-0	OL
Roberts WS			27 Oct 1906	Aston Villa	(a)	3-2	OL
Robertson A	5ft 9in	12st 7lb	1 Sep 1900	Lincoln C	(h)	2-0	CF
Robertson J			19 Oct 1901	Arsenal	(a)	3-0	OR
Robertson WG	5ft 7.5in	9st 12lb	26 Feb 1955	Swansea T	(h)	4-2	OL
Robinson J	5ft 10in	11st 3lb	24 Apr 1954	Arsenal	(a)	1-3	IR
Robinson JN	5ft 11in	11st 2lb	28 Sep 1946	Sheffield U	(a)	1-2	CH
Robinson R	5ft 10in	11st 8lb	31 Aug 1946	Aston Villa	(a)	1-0	RB
Rodgerson AR*	5ft 6in	10st 2lb	11 Sep 1958	Rotherham U	(h)	4-1	IR
Rooks R	5ft10.5in	13st 6lb	28 Aug 1965	Huddersfield T	(a)	0-6	CH
Ross AC	5ft 10in	10st 7lb	18 Jan 1936	Brentford	(a)	0-1	LB
Ross C	5ft 7in	11st	21 Mar 1981	Southampton	(a)	0-1	RH
Rowell G	5ft 10in	10st 3lb	17 Aug 1985	Wimbledon	(a)	0-3	OL
Russell ET	5ft 11in	11st 5lb	29 Dec 1951	Burnley	(a)	1-7	RB
Russell MC	5ft 9in	10st 5lb	28 Aug 1990	Tranmere R(LC)	(h)	1-1	IL
			1 Sep 1990	Plymouth A	(a)	1-1	IL
Saxby MW	6ft 2in	13st 10lb	2 Oct 1984	Oldham A	(a)	0-2	LH
Scott GS	5ft10.5in	12st 5lb	4 Sep 1984	Bradford C(LC)	(h)	2-2	LB
			8 Sep 1984	Notts C	(a)	2-3	LB
Scott JC	5ft 8in	10st 2lb	18 Sep 1954	Hull C	(a)	0-1	IR
Scott WR	5ft 7.5in	11st 3lb	30 Aug 1930	Bolton W	(a)	0-3	IR
Scrimshaw CT	5ft 8in	11st 7lb	15 Oct 1938	Grimsby T	(h)	3-2	LB
Senior TJ	6ft 1in	12st 8lb	26 Mar 1988	Birmingham C	(h)	1-1	CF
Shand H			1 Sep 1906	Everton	(h)	2-2	RH
Shannon R			5 Oct 1991	Bristol R	(a)	1-2	SU
Shaw TW			2 Sep 1899	Lincoln C	(a)	0-3	RB
Shearer DJ*	5ft 10in	12st	4 Apr 1978	Chelsea	(h)	2-0	CF
Shepherdson H	5ft 10in	11st 2lb	1 May 1937	West Brom A	(a)	3-1	CH
Short M	6ft 1in	12st	27 Apr 1968	Derby C	(h)	2-2	GK
Slade CH	5ft 7.5in	11st	21 Oct 1922	Birmingham	(h)	2-1	RH
Slaven BJ	5ft 11in	11st 10lb	12 Oct 1985	Leeds U	(a)	0-1	CF
Smith D	5ft 7.5in	11st 1lb	16 Sep 1967	Millwall	(h)	0-1	OL
Smith DW	5ft 11in	13st 6lb	26 Dec 1900	Barnsley	(h)	3-0	RH
Smith EE			26 Jan 1924	Everton	(h)	1-1	CH
Smith EG			2 Sep 1899	Lincoln C	(a)	0-3	GK
Smith G	5ft 7in	10st 8lb	24 Jan 1969	Oxford U	(h)	2-0	RH
Smith J			11 Sep 1926	South Shields	(a)	0-0	RB
Smith J			5 May 1933	Leiceter C	(h)	4-1	RB
Smith M	5ft 9in	11st 3lb	29 Apr 1972	Hull C	(h)	3-0	SU
*			12 Aug 1972	Sunderland	(h)	2-1	CF
Smith RA	5ft 9in	11st 8lb	87 Mar 1966	Carlisle U	(a)	1-2	RB
Souness GJ	5ft 11in	11st 3lb	6 Jan 1973	Fulham	(a)	1-2	IL
Spraggon F	5ft 9in	12st	31 Mar 1964	Huddersfield T	(a)	0-1	LH
Spriggs S	5ft 3in	10st 2lb	5 Apr 1987	Darlington	(h)	1-1	RB
Spuhler JO	5ft 9.5in	11st 2lb	31 Aug 1946	Aston Villa	(a)	1-0	OR
Stage W			6 Apr 1914	Burnley	(a)	2-1	OL
Stephens A	5ft 11in	12st 7lb	22 Mar 1985	Charlton A	(a)	0-1	IR
Stevenson AB			3 Nov 1923	Arsenal	(a)	1-2	OL
Stewart JG	6ft 1in	13st 8lb	19 Aug 1978	Coventry C	(h)	1-2	GK
Stiles NP	5ft 7in	10st 7lb	14 Aug 1971	Portsmouth	(a)	1-2	RH
Stirling J	5ft 8in	11st 4lb	2 Sep 1911	Sunderland	(a)	0-1	OR
Stone JG	6ft	12st 5lb	1 Jan 1972	Cardiff C	(a)	0-1	LB

Stephen Pears (left) and Alan Peacock (right).

Rolando Ugolini, 'Boro's Italian goalkeeper who made 335 senior appearances for the club between 1948-49 and 1955-56.

Darren Wood, made his debut against Southampton.

Name	Ht	Wt	Date	Opposition	V	Res	Pos
Stonehouse D	5ft 8.5in	11st	2 Jan 1954	Tottenham H	(h)	3-0	LB
Storey T	5ft 9in	11st 5lb	3 Jan 1914	Bradford C	(a)	3-2	OR
Stott J			23 Sep 1899	Grimsby T	(h)	1-0	LH
Strong AF	6ft 2in	10st 3lb	2 Mar 1985	Leeds U	(h)	0-0	LB
Stuart RW	5ft 8in	12st	30 Apr 1932	Arsenal	(a)	0-5	RB
Suddick J			30 Apr 1904	West Brom A	(h)	2-0	IR
Sugrue PA	5ft 7in	9st 10lb	17 Dec 1982	Cambridge U	(a)	0-2	IR
Surtees J	5ft 10in	11st	2 Jan 1932	Chelsea	(a)	0-4	IL
Swales N	5ft 8in	10st 9lb	19 Dec 1925	Clapton O	(a)	0-1	RH
Taylor B	5ft 11in	11st 9lb	16 Dec 1972	Portsmouth	(a)	0-0	LH
Taylor CW	5ft 6in	10st 1lb	16 Nov 1957	Notts C	(a)	0-2	OR
Taylor PT	6ft 1in	12st	29 Oct 1955	Hull C	(a)	2-2	GK
Tennant J*	5ft 5in	10st 7lb	7 Sep 1901	Stockport C	(a)	3-1	OL
Thackeray J			15 Oct 1904	Manchester C	(h)	0-1	OL
Thomas D	5ft 8in	10st 10lb	27 Mar 1982	Manchester C	(h)	0-0	OL
Thomas MR	6ft 1in	13st	27 Oct 1984	Leeds U	(a)	0-2	GK
Thompson A			11 Mar 1901	Port Vale	(a)	2-0	IR
Thompson N*	5ft 8in	11st 7lb	29 Aug 1925	Portsmouth	(a)	5-1	IL
Thompson WT*			9 Dec 1905	Bolton W	(h)	4-4	IL
Thomson KG	6ft 1in	12st 5lb	19 Dec 1959	Portsmouth	(a)	3-6	CH
Thomson R	5ft 10in	11st 6lb	26 Sep 1981	Stoke C	(h)	3-2	SU
			3 Oct 1981	West Brom A	(a)	0-2	RH
Tinsley W		11st 12lb	6 Dec 1913	Newcastle U	(h)	3-0	IL
Tomlin J			22 Sep 1906	Bury	(h)	1-1	CH
Townsend J	5ft 8in	11st 2lb	15 Feb 1964	Southampton	(a)	2-2	RH
Trechman OL			17 Feb 1906	Wolves	(a)	0-0	CF
Tucker WH*			13 Oct 1906	Preston NE	(a)	2-4	CF
Turnbull LM	6ft	11st 9lb	26 Apr 1986	Millwall	(h)	3-1	SU
			3 May 1986	Shrewsbury T	(a)	1-2	IR
Turner P			7 Sep 1901	Stockport C	(a)	3-1	IL
Twine F	5ft 11in	12st 4lb	30 Oct 1926	Darlington	(a)	4-1	RB
Tyldesley J			29 Sep 1906	Manchester C	(h)	2-3	RB
Ugolini R	5ft 9in	11st 12lb	21 Aug 1948	Chelsea	(a)	0-1	GK
Urquhart A			14 Dec 1907	Aston Villa	(a)	0-6	OR
Urwin J	5ft 7in	10st 10lb	1 Jan 1915	Sunderland	(h)	2-3	OL
Verrill E	5ft 8in	11st 4lb	23 Nov 1907	Manchester C	(h)	2-0	OR
Vincent JV	5ft 9in	11st 10lb	13 Mar 1970	Charlton A	(a)	0-1	SU
			20 Mar 1970	Orient	(h)	0-1	IR
Wainscoat WR*			22 Dec 1923	Preston NE	(h)	1-2	IL
Waldock R	5ft 8.5in	11st 10lb	6 Feb 1960	Charlton A	(a)	0-1	IL
Walker DH	5ft 9in	11st 6lb	19 Mar 1960	Swansea T	(h)	2-0	LH
Walker J	5ft 9in	13st	6 Sep 1913	Manchester C	(a)	1-1	RB
Walker RG	5ft6.25in	10st 12lb	31 Aug 1946	Aston Villa	(a)	1-0	OL
Walker RH			6 Mar 1906	Derby C	(a)	1-1	IL
Walley E	5ft 8.5in	12st 9lb	23 Aug 1958	Brighton	(h)	9-0	LH
Walsh A	6ft	12st 1lb	1 Apr 1978	Queens Park R	(a)	0-1	SU
Walsh CD	5ft 9in	10st 11lb	19 Jan 1991	Notts C	(a)	2-3	SU
			26 Jan 1991	Cambridge U(FA)	(a)	0-2	OL
			2 Feb 1991	Swindon T	(h)	2-0	CH
Wanless R			2 Sep 1899	Lincoln City	(a)	0-3	OR
Ward PT	5ft 11in	12st 5lb	8 Sep 1982	Newcastle U	(a)	1-1	IR
Wardle G	5ft 8in	10st 9lb	26 Jan 1938	Portsmouth	(h)	0-0	OR
Wardrope A			26 Nov 1910	Aston Villa	(a)	0-5	CH
Wardrope W	5ft 6in	10st 6lb	21 Apr 1900	Manchester U	(h)	2-0	OR
Wark J	5ft 10in	11st 7lb	25 Aug 1990	West Ham U	(h)	0-0	LH
Warren FW	5ft 7in		1 Feb 1930	Leicester C	(a)	1-4	OL
Watkin TWS	5ft 11in	11st 10lb	6 Mar 1954	Chelsea	(h)	3-3	OL
Watson A			13 Mar 1926	Nottingham F	(a)	0-1	CH
Watson HL			7 Dec 1929	Sheffield W	(h)	4-1	RH
Watson J			17 Apr 1907	Liverpool	(a)	4-2	LB
Watson R*			29 Mar 1902	Chesterfield	(h)	7-1	IR
Wayman C	5ft 6.5in	10st 10lb	25 Sep 1954	Lincoln C	(h)	2-1	CF
Webb SJ*			11 May 1968	Bristol C	(h)	2-1	CF
Webster M			1 May 1922	Huddersfield T	(a)	1-2	CH
Weddle DK			4 Nov 1961	Scunthorpe U	(h)	1-2	CF
Weightman E			11 Jan 1936	Southampton(FA)	(h)	1-0	LB
			25 Apr 1936	Stoke C	(h)	0-0	CH
Weir J	5ft 10in	13st 4lb	3 Sep 1910	Everton	(h)	1-0	LB
Whigham WM			8 Oct 1966	Watford	(a)	0-2	GK
Whitaker W	6ft	12st 4lb	23 Aug 1947	Manchester U	(h)	2-2	CH
White W			5 Sep 1903	Sheffield W	(a)	1-4	IR
Whyte D	5ft 11in	11st 5lb	15 Aug 1992	Coventry C	(a)	1-2	CH
Wilcox FJ			24 Mar 1906	Sheffield U	(h)	0-1	IL
Wilkie D	5ft 9in	11st 2lb	7 Nov 1959	Huddersfield T	(h)	1-0	CH
Wilkie J			1 Sep 1900	Lincoln C	(h)	1-0	IL
Wilkinson P	6ft	11st	17 Aug 1991	Millwall	(h)	1-0	CF
Willey AS	6ft	11st 4lb	21 Sep 1974	Manchester C	(h)	3-0	CF
Williams JJ			12 Mar 1932	Sunderland	(h)	0-1	OR
Williams JT			27 Sep 1924	South Shields	(a)	1-0	OL
Williams O			9 Mar 1924	West Brom A	(h)	0-1	OL
Williamson RG	5ft 9in	12st 8lb	19 Apr 1902	Bristol C	(h)	2-0	GK
Wilson A			1 Sep 1914	Sheffield W	(a)	1-3	OR
Wilson AN	5ft 8.5in	13st 6lb	2 Jan 1915	West Brom A	(a)	0-1	CF
Wilson FP	6ft 0.5in	12st 10lb	24 Feb 1968	Charlton A	(h)	1-1	RB
Wilson J			4 Apr 1925	Crystal P	(h)	0-0	RB
Wilson TT			4 Apr 1908	Bury	(a)	4-1	CH
Windridge JE	5ft 7.5in	11st 2lb	12 Dec 1911	Bolton W	(a)	0-1	IL
Windross D	5ft 9in	11st	17 Oct 1959	Aston Villa	(a)	0-1	CF
Wood AEH			30 Oct 1976	Leicester C	(h)	1-0	CF
Wood DT	5ft 10in	11st 8lb	19 Sep 1981	Southampton	(a)	0-2	IL
Woodward T	5ft 8in	11st 9lb	15 Oct 1949	Arsenal	(h)	1-1	OL
Woof W	5ft 10in	11st 8lb	23 Nov 1974	QPR	(h)	1-3	SU
			3 Apr 1976	Ipswich T	(h)	2-0	CF
Worrall WE			17 Mar 1906	Liverpool	(a)	1-6	GK
Worthington PR			26 Sep 1967	Birmingham C	(a)	1-6	LB
Wright TE	5ft 7in	9st 10lb	15 Aug 1992	Coventry C	(a)	1-2	OR
Wynn R*			13 Apr 1914	Tottenham H	(h)	6-0	OL
Yeoman RI	5ft 8.5in	12st	13 Dec 1958	Sheffield W	(a)	0-2	RH
Yorston BC*	5ft 5in		3 Mar 1934	Liverpool	(a)	2-6	IR
Young EW	5ft 11in	12st	23 Apr 1921	Chelsea	(h)	0-0	CF
Young MS			2 Nov 1991	Southend U	(h)	1-1	SU
Young RT			1 Jan 1909	Chelsea	(h)	1-4	LH

Middlesbrough Internationals

Appearances given here refer to caps won whilst with Middlesbrough. The number of caps won is shown in brackets after each player's name. The figures in brackets after results are goals scored by the player in that match. Before 1924 there was only one Ireland team, then the Republic of Ireland began separate matches. WCQ = World Cup Qualifier. WCF = World Cup Finals. ENC = Europe Nations' Cup ‡Cap awarded to player when Middlesbrough were in the Second Division. †Cap awarded to player when Middlesbrough were in the Third Division. *Another Middlesbrough player in same match.

England

Armstrong, David (1 cap)
31 May 1980 Australia   Sydney 2-1

Birkett, Ralph (1 cap)
19 Oct 1935 Northern Ireland   Belfast 3-1

Bloomer, Steve (2 caps)
18 Mar 1907* Wales   Fulham 1-1
6 Apr 1907* Scotland   Newcastle   1-1(1)

Camsell, George (9 caps)
9 May 1929* France†   Paris.......4-1(2)
11 May 1929* Belgium†   Brussels ....5-1(4)
19 Oct 1929* Northern Ireland   Belfast ....3-0(2)
20 Nov 1929 Wales   Chelsea ....6-0(3)
6 Dec 1934 France   Tottenham 4-1(2)
4 Dec 1935 Germany   Tottenham 3-0(2)
4 Apr 1936 Scotland   Wembley ...1-1(1)
6 May 1936 Austria   Vienna .....1-2(1)
9 May 1936 Belgium   Brussels ....2-3(1)

Carr, Jackie (2 caps)
25 Oct 1919 Ireland   Belfast 1-1
5 Mar 1923 Wales   Cardiff 2-2

Clough, Brian (2 caps)
17 Oct 1959* Wales†   Cardiff 1-1
28 Oct 1959* Sweden†   Wembley 2-3

Common, Alf (1 cap)
19 Mar 1906 Wales   Cardiff 1-0

Elliott, George (3 caps)
15 Feb 1913* Ireland   Belfast 1-2
14 Feb 1914 Ireland   Middlesbrough 0-3
15 Mar 1920 Wales   Highbury.....1-2

Fenton, Micky (1 cap)
9 Apr 1938* Scotland   Wembley 0-1

Hardwick, George (13 caps)
28 Sep 1946* Northern Ireland   Belfast 7-2
30 Sep 1946* Rep of Ireland   Dublin 1-0
13 Nov 1946* Wales   Maine Road...3-0
27 Nov 1946* Holland   Huddersfield 8-2
12 Apr 1947* Scotland   Wembley 1-1
3 May 1947* France   Highbury.....3-0
18 May 1947* Switzerland   Zurich........0-1
27 May 1947* Portugal   Lisbon 10-0
21 Sep 1947* Belgium   Brussels 5-2
18 Oct 1947* Wales   Cardiff 3-0
5 Nov 1947* Northern Ireland   Goodison Pk   2-2
19 Nov 1947* Sweden   Highbury.....4-2
10 Apr 1948* Scotland   Glasgow......2-0

Holliday, Eddie (3 caps)
17 Oct 1959* Wales†   Cardiff 1-1
28 Oct 1959* Sweden†   Wembley 2-3
18 Nov 1959 Northern Ireland†   Wembley 2-1

McNeil, Mick (9 caps)
8 Oct 1960 Northern Ireland†   Belfast 5-2
19 Oct 1960 Luxembourg†   Luxembourg   9-0
26 Oct 1960 Spain†   Wembley 4-2
23 Nov 1960 Wales†   Wembley 5-1
15 Apr 1961 Scotland†   Wembley 9-3
10 May 1961 Mexico†   Wembley 8-0
21 May 1961 Portugal†   Lisbon 1-1
24 May 1961 Italy†   Rome 3-2
28 Sep 1961 WCQ Luxembourg†   Highbury.....4-1

Mannion, Wilf (26 caps)
28 Sep 1946* Northern Ireland   Belfast .....7-2(3)
30 Sep 1946* Rep of Ireland   Dublin 1-0
13 Nov 1946* Wales   Maine Road 3-0(2)
27 Nov 1946* Holland   Huddersfield8-2(1)
12 Apr 1947* Scotland   Wembley ...1-1
3 May 1947* France   Highbury   3-0(1)
18 May 1947* Switzerland   Zurich........0-1
27 May 1947* Portugal   Lisbon 10-0
21 Sep 1947* Belgium   Brussels 5-2
18 Oct 1947* Wales   Cardiff 3-0
5 Nov 1947* Northern Ireland   Goodison Pk 2-2(1)
19 Nov 1947* Sweden   Highbury.....4-2
16 May 1948 Italy   Turin 4-0
18 May 1949 Norway   Oslo 4-1
22 May 1949 France   Paris 3-1
21 Sep 1949* Rep of Ireland   Goodison Pk   0-2
15 Apr 1950 WCQ Scotland   Glasgow......1-0
14 May 1950 Portugal   Lisbon 5-3
18 May 1950 Belgium   Brussels ...4-1 (1)
25 Jun 1950 WCF Chile   Rio de Janeiro2-0(1)
7 Oct 1950 Northern Ireland   Belfast 4-1
15 Nov 1950 Wales   Sunderland 4-2(1)
22 Nov 1950 Yugoslavia   Highbury.....2-2
14 Apr 1951 Scotland   Wembley 2-3
3 Oct 1951 France   Highbury.....2-2

Pallister, Gary (2 caps)
27 Apr 1988 Hungary†   Budapest 0-0
16 Nov 1988 Saudi Arabia   Riyadh 1-1

Peacock, Alan (4 caps)
2 Jun 1962 WCF Argentina†   Rancagua....3-1
7 Jun 1962 WCF Bulgaria†   Rancagua....0-0
20 Oct 1962 Northern Ireland†   Belfast 3-1
21 Nov 1962* Wales†   Wembley ....4-0(2)

Peacock, Joe (3 caps)
9 May 1929* France†   Paris 4-1
11 May 1929* Belgium†   Brussels 5-1
15 May 1929 Spain†   Madrid 3-4

Pease, Billy (1 cap)
12 Feb 1927 Wales†   Wrexham 3-3

Pentland, Fred (5 caps)
15 Mar 1909 Wales   City Gnd, Nottingham   2-0
3 Apr 1909 Scotland   Crystal Palace   2-0
29 May 1909 Hungary   Budapest 4-2
31 May 1909 Hungary   Budapest 8-2
1 Jun 1909 Austria   Vienna 8-1

Urwin, Tommy (2 caps)
21 May 1923 Sweden   Stockholm 4-2
24 May 1923 Sweden   Stockholm 3-1

Webster, Maurice (3 caps)
5 Apr 1930 Scotland   Glasgow......5-2
10 May 1930 Germany   Berlin 3-3
14 May 1930 Austria   Vienna 0-0

Williamson, Tim (7 caps)
25 Feb 1905 Ireland   Middlesbrough 1-1
11 Feb 1911 Ireland   Baseball Gnd, Derby   2-1
13 Mar 1911 Wales   Millwall.....3-0
1 Apr 1911 Scotland   Goodison Pk   1-1
11 Mar 1912 Wales   Wrexham 2-0
23 Mar 1912 Scotland   Glasgow......1-1
15 Feb 1913 Ireland   Belfast 1-2

Scotland

Aitken, Andy (3 caps)
4 Mar 1907 Wales   Wrexham 0-1
18 Mar 1907* England   Fulham 1-1
4 Apr 1908 England   Glasgow......1-1

Baxter, Bob (3 caps)
9 Nov 1938 Wales   Edinburgh 3-2
7 Dec 1938 Hungary   Glasgow......3-1
15 Apr 1939* England   Glasgow......1-2

Brown, Sandy (1 cap)
9 Apr 1904 England   Glasgow......0-1

Bruce, Bobby (1 cap)
29 Nov 1933 Austria   Glasgow......2-2

Cumming, Dave (1 cap)
9 Apr 1938* England   Wembley 1-0

Davidson, Stewart (1 cap)
9 Apr 1921* England   Glasgow......3-1

Marshall, John "Jock" (6 caps)
12 Feb 1921 Wales   Aberdeen 2-1
26 Feb 1921 Ireland   Belfast 2-0
9 Apr 1921* England   Glasgow......3-1
4 Feb 1922 Wales   Wrexham 1-2
4 Mar 1922 Ireland   Glasgow......2-1
8 Apr 1922* England   Villa Park 1-0

Milne, Jacky (2 caps)
9 Apr 1938* England   Wembley 1-0
15 Apr 1939* England   Glasgow......1-2

Souness, Graeme (3 caps)
30 Oct 1974 East Germany   Glasgow......3-0
20 Nov 1974 ENC Spain   Glasgow......1-2
16 Apr 1965 Sweden   Gothenburg 1-1(1)

Stewart, Jim (1 cap)
25 Oct 1978 ENC Norway   Glasgow......3-2

Watson, Jimmy (2 caps)
15 Mar 1909 Ireland   Glasgow......5-0
3 Apr 1909 England   Crystal Palace   0-2

Whyte, Derek (2 caps)
14 Oct 1992 Portugal   Glasgow......0-0
18 Nov 1992 Italy   Ibrox........0-0

Wilson, Andy (6 caps)
4 Feb 1922 Wales   Wrexham 1-2
4 Mar 1922 Ireland   Glasgow ...2-1(2)
8 Apr 1922* England   Villa Park   1-0(1)
3 Mar 1923 Ireland   Belfast ......1-0(1)
16 Mar 1923 Wales   Glasgow ...2-2(2)
14 Apr 1923 England   Glasgow ...2-2(1)

Wales

Atherton, Bobby (4 caps)
29 Feb 1904 England   Wrexham.....2-2
12 Mar 1904 Scotland   Dundee ....1-1(1)
21 Mar 1904 Ireland   Bangor.......0-1
8 Apr 1905 Ireland   Belfast .....2-2(1)

Davies, Albert (1 cap)
6 Mar 1905 Scotland   Wrexham.....3-1

Griffiths, Tom (6 caps)
25 May 1933 France   Paris.......1-1(1)
4 Oct 1933 Scotland   Cardiff 3-2
15 Nov 1933 England   Newcastle.....2-1
29 Sep 1934 England   Cardiff 0-4
27 Mar 1935 Northern Ireland   Wrexham 3-1
5 Oct 1935 England   Cardiff 1-1

Harris, Bill (6 caps)
6 May 1954 Austria   Vienna 0-2
19 May 1957 WCQ E Germany†   Leipzig 1-2
26 May 1957 Czechoslovakia†   Prague 0-2
25 Sep 1957 WCQ E Germany†   Cardiff 4-1
19 Oct 1957 England†   Cardiff 0-4
13 Nov 1957 Scotland†   Hampden Pk   1-1

Jones, Love (1 cap)
11 Apr 1910 Ireland   Wrexham.....4-1

Mahoney, John (13 caps)
6 Sep 1977 Kuwait   Wrexham 0-0
20 Sep 1977 Kuwait   Kuwait 0-0
12 Oct 1977 Scotland   Liverpool 0-2
16 Nov 1977 Czechoslovakia   Prague 0-1
18 Apr 1978 Iran   Tehran 1-0
13 May 1978 England(sub)   Cardiff 1-3
17 May 1978 Scotland   Glasgow......1-1
19 May 1978* Northern Ireland   Wrexham 1-0
2 May 1979 ENC West Germany   Wrexham 0-2
19 May 1979 Scotland   Cardiff 3-0
23 May 1979 England   Wembley 0-0
25 May 1979 Northern Ireland   Belfast 1-1
2 Jun 1979 ENC Malta   Valletta........2-0

Nurse, Mel (3 caps)
7 Nov 1962 ENC Hungary†   Budapest 1-3
21 Nov 1962* England†   Wembley 0-4
20 Nov 1963 Scotland†   Hampden Pk   1-2

Warren, Freddy (3 caps)
22 Apr 1931 Northern Ireland   Wrexham   3-2(1)
16 May 1932 England   Wrexham.....0-0
25 May 1933 France   Paris 1-1

Northern Ireland

Braithwaite, Bobby (7 caps)
15 Apr 1964 Wales†   Swansea 3-2
29 Apr 1964 Uruguay†   Belfast 3-0
3 Oct 1964 England†   Belfast 3-4
14 Oct 1964 Switzerland†   Belfast 1-0
14 Nov 1964 WCQ Switzerland†   Lausanne 1-2
25 Nov 1964 Scotland†   Glasgow......2-3
7 Apr 1965 Holland†   Rotterdam 0-0

Cochrane, Terry (19 caps)
25 Oct 1978 ENC Denmark   Copenhagen   0-4
29 Nov 1978 ENC Bulgaria   Sofia 2-0
7 Feb 1979 England   Wembley 0-4
2 May 1979 Bulgaria   Belfast 2-0
19 May 1979 England   Belfast 0-2
26 Mar 1980 WCQ Israel   Tel Aviv......0-0
20 May 1980 England(sub)   Wembley ...1-1(1)
23 May 1980* Wales(sub)   Cardiff 0-1
11 Jun 1980* Australia(sub)   Sydney 2-1
15 Jun 1980* Australia (Sub)   Melbourne 1-1
18 Jun 1980* Australia   Adelaide 2-1
15 Oct 1980 Sweden(sub)   Belfast 3-0
19 Nov 1980 WCQ Portugal(sub)   Lisbon 0-1
25 Mar 1981 WCQ Scotland   Glasgow......1-1
29 Apr 1981 WCQ Portugal   Belfast 1-0
19 May 1981 Scotland   Glasgow......0-2
3 Jun 1981* WCQ Sweden   Stockholm 0-1
23 Feb 1982 England(sub)   Wembley 0-4
24 Mar 1982* France   Paris 0-4
4 Jul 1982* WCF France   Madrid 1-4

Crossan, Johnny (1 cap)
21 Oct 1967 Scotland†   Belfast 1-0

McMordie, Eric (21 caps)
10 Sep 1968 Israel†   Jaffa 3-2
23 Oct 1968 WCQ Turkey†   Belfast .....4-1(1)
11 Dec 1968 WCQ Turkey†   Istanbul 3-0
3 May 1969 England†   Belfast 1-3
6 May 1969 Scotland†   Glasgow ...1-1(1)
10 May 1969 Wales†   Belfast 0-0
10 Sep 1969 WCQ USSR†   Belfast 0-0
18 Apr 1970 Scotland†   Belfast 0-1
21 Apr 1970 England†   Wembley 1-3
25 Apr 1970 Wales†   Swansea 0-1
3 Feb 1971 ENC Cyprus†   Nicosia 3-0
21 Apr 1971 ENC Cyprus†   Belfast 5-0
15 May 1971 England†   Belfast 0-1
18 May 1971 Scotland†   Glasgow 1-0
22 May 1971 Wales†   Belfast 1-0
13 Oct 1971 ENC USSR†   Belfast 1-1
16 Feb 1972 Spain†   Hull 1-1
20 May 1972 Scotland†   Glasgow 0-2
23 May 1972 England†   Wembley 1-0
27 May 1972 Wales†   Wrexham 1-0
18 Oct 1972 Bulgaria†   Sofia 0-3

Miller, Joe (3 caps)
2 May 1929 Wales†   Wrexham 2-2
23 Feb 1929 Scotland†   Belfast 3-7
19 Oct 1929* England   Belfast 0-3

Platt, Jim (20 caps)
24 Mar 1976 Israel(sub)   Tel Aviv 1-1
13 May 1978 Scotland   Glasgow 1-1
16 May 1978 England   Wembley 0-1
19 May 1978* Wales   Wrexham 1-1
16 May 1980 Scotland   Belfast 1-0
20 May 1980 England   Wembley 1-1
23 May 1980* Wales   Cardiff 1-0
11 Jun 1980* Australia   Sydney 2-1
15 Jun 1980* Australia   Melbourne....1-1
18 Jun 1980* Australia   Adelaide.....2-1
15 Oct 1980 WCQ Sweden   Belfast 3-0
19 Nov 1980 WCQ Portugal   Lisbon 1-0
24 Mar 1982* France   Paris 0-4
28 Apr 1982 Scotland   Belfast 1-1
27 May 1982 Wales(sub)   Wrexham 0-3
11 Jul 1982 WCF Austria   Madrid 2-2
13 Oct 1982 ENC Austria†   Vienna 0-2
17 Nov 1982 West Germany†   Belfast 1-0
15 Dec 1982 Albania†   Tiranë 0-0
30 Mar 1983 Turkey†   Belfast 2-1

Republic of Ireland

Desmond, Peter (4 caps)
8 Sep 1949* WCQ Finland   Dublin 3-0
21 Sep 1949* England   Goodison Pk 2-0
9 Oct 1949 WCQ Finland   Helsinki......1-1
13 Nov 1949 Sweden   Dublin 1-3

Fitzsimons, Arthur (25 caps)
8 Sep 1949* WCQ Finland   Dublin 3-0
10 May 1950 Belgium   Brussels 1-5
17 Oct 1951 West Germany   Dublin 3-2
4 May 1952 West Germany   Cologne 0-3
7 May 1952 Austria   Vienna 0-6
1 Jun 1952 Spain   Madrid 0-6
16 Nov 1952 France   Dublin 1-1
25 Mar 1953 Austria   Dublin 4-0
4 Oct 1953 WCQ France   Dublin 3-5
28 Oct 1953 Luxembourg   Dublin ....4-0(2)
25 Nov 1953 WCQ France   Paris 0-1
1 May 1955 Holland†   Dublin 1-0
25 May 1955 Norway†   Oslo 3-1
28 May 1955 West Germany†   Hamburg.....1-2
19 Oct 1955 Yugoslavia†   Dublin .....1-4(1)
27 Nov 1955 Spain†   Dublin 2-2
10 May 1956 Holland†   Rotterdam 4-1
3 Oct 1956 WCQ Denmark†   Dublin 2-1
25 Nov 1956 West Germany†   Dublin 3-0
8 May 1957 WCQ England†   Wembley 1-5
19 May 1957 WCQ England†   Dublin 1-1
2 Oct 1957 WCQ Denmark†   Copenhagen 2-0
11 May 1958 Poland†   Katowice 2-2
14 May 1958 Austria†   Vienna 1-3
5 Oct 1958 Poland   Dublin 2-2

Hartnett, Jimmy (2 caps)
12 Jun 1949 Spain   Dublin 1-4
7 Mar 1954 WCQ Luxembourg   Luxembourg 0-1

Kernaghan, Alan (6 caps)
9 Sep 1992 WCQ Latvia   Dublin 4-0
14 Oct 1992 WCQ Denmark   Copenhagen 0-0
28 Apr 1993 WCQ Denmark   Dublin 1-1
26 May 1993 WCQ Albania   Tiranë 2-1
9 Jun 1993 WCQ Latvia   Riga 2-0
16 Jun 1993 WCQ Lithuania   Vilnius 1-0

Morris, Chris (1 cap)
17 Feb 1993 Wales   Dublin 2-1

Slaven, Bernie (7 caps)
28 Mar 1990 Wales   Dublin .....1-0(1)
16 May 1990 Finland   Dublin 1-1

27 Nov 1990 Turkey (sub)   İzmir 0-0
2 Jun 1990 Malta   Valletta.......3-0
6 Feb 1991 Wales   Wrexham 2-0
1 May 1991 ENC Poland(sub)   Dublin 0-0
17 Feb 1993 Wales(sub)   Dublin 2-1

Under-23 Internationals

England

Armstrong, David (4)
19 Nov 1974 Portugal   Lisbon 3-2
21 Jan 1975 Wales   Wrexham 2-0
28 Oct 1975* Czechoslovakia   Selhurst Park 1-1
18 Nov 1975* Portugal   Selhurst Park 2-0

Clough, Brian (3)
26 Feb 1957 Scotland‡   Glasgow......1-1
19 May 1957 Bulgaria‡   Sofia.......1-2(1)
23 Apr 1958 Wales‡   Wrexham 1-2(1)

Holliday, Eddie (5)
23 Sep 1959 Hungary‡   Anfield 0-1
16 May 1960* Holland‡   Hillsborough 5-2
15 May 1960* East Germany‡   Berlin......4-1(2)
18 May 1960* Poland‡   Warsaw 3-2
22 May 1960 Israel‡   Tel Aviv......0-4

Jones, Gordon (9)
9 Nov 1961 Israel‡   Elland Road   7-1
29 Nov 1961 Holland‡   Rotterdam 5-2
28 Feb 1962 Scotland‡   Aberdeen 4-2
2 May 1962 Turkey‡   Southampton 4-1
7 Nov 1962* Belgium‡   Plymouth......6-1
28 Nov 1962* Greece‡   St Andrew's ..5-0
21 Mar 1963 Yugoslavia‡   Manchester ...0-0
13 Nov 1963 Wales‡   Bristol 1-1
27 Nov 1963 West Germany‡   Liverpool.....4-1

McNeil, Mick (9)
11 Nov 1959 France‡   Sunderland ...2-0
16 Mar 1960* Holland‡   Hillsborough 5-2
15 May 1960* East Germany‡   Berlin 4-1
18 May 1960* Poland‡   Warsaw 3-2
22 May 1960* Israel‡   Tel Aviv......0-4
2 Nov 1960 Italy‡   Newcastle.....1-1
28 Feb 1962 Scotland‡   Aberdeen 4-2
7 Nov 1962* Belgium‡   Plymouth......6-1
28 Nov 1962* Greece‡   St Andrew's ...5-0

Maddren, Willie (5)
7 Mar 1973 Czechoslovakia‡   Villa Park 1-0
13 Nov 1973 Denmark‡   Portsmouth ...1-1
13 Mar 1974* Scotland‡   Newcastle.....2-1
15 May 1974* Yugoslavia(sub)‡   Zrenjanin 0-1
19 May 1974* France‡   Valence 2-2

Mills, David (8)
13 Mar 1974* Scotland‡   Newcastle   2-1(1)
11 May 1974 Turkey‡   Ankara 0-0
(Abandoned at half-time, rain)
15 May 1974* Yugoslavia‡   Zrenjanin 0-1
19 May 1974* France‡   Valence 2-2
29 Oct 1974 Czechoslovakia   Selhurst Pk 3-1(1)
28 Oct 1975* Czechoslovakia   Trnava 1-1
18 Nov 1974 Portugal(sub)   Selhurst Pk 2-0(1)
10 Mar 1976 Hungary(sub)   Budapest 0-3

O'Rourke, John (1)
7 Jun 1967 Turkey†   Ankara.....3-0(1)

Scotland

Gibson, Ian (2)
4 Dec 1963 Wales‡   Wrexham.....1-3
24 May 1964 France‡   Nantes 2-0

Souness, Graeme (2)
13 Mar 1974* England‡   Newcastle.....0-2
18 Feb 1976 Holland   Breda 0-2

Northern Ireland

McMordie, Eric (1)
22 Feb 1967 Wales‡   Belfast 2-1
(Abandoned after 7¾ minutes, waterlogged pitch)

McNeill, Allan (1)
20 Mar 1968 Wales‡   Cardiff 1-0

Football League Representatives

Birkett, Ralph
30 Oct 1935* Scottish League   Glasgow......2-2
23 Sep 1936 Irish League   Belfast 2-3

Blenkinsopp, Tom
20 Sep 1948 *Irish League   Anfield 5-1

Camsell, George
30 Oct 1935* Scottish League   Ibrox ......2-2(1)

Carr, Jacky
4 Oct 1922 Irish League   Bolton 5-1
17 Feb 1923 Scottish League   Newcastle.....2-1
21 Sep 1927 Irish League   Newcastle.....9-1

Clough, Brian
8 Oct 1958 Scottish League   Ibrox 1-1 (1)
23 Sep 1959 Irish League   Windsor Pk 5-0(5)

Common, Alf
24 Mar 1906 Scottish League   Chelsea ....6-2(1)

Elliott, George
9 Feb 1914 Southern League   Millwall 3-1
24 Mar 1915 Scottish League   Glasgow ...4-0(1)
5 Apr 1919 Scottish League   Glasgow ...2-3(1)

Hardwick, George
19 Feb 1947* Irish League   Goodison Park 4-2
12 Mar 1947* Scottish League   Glasgow......3-1
17 Mar 1948* Scottish League   Newcastle.....1-1

Holliday, Eddie
4 Nov 1959 League of Ireland   Ewood Park...2-0

Mannion, Wilf
19 Feb 1947* Irish League   Goodison Park 4-2
12 Mar 1947* Scottish League   Glasgow ...3-1(2)
17 Mar 1948* Scottish League   Newcastle.....1-1
23 Mar 1949 Scottish League   Ibrox.........3-0
15 Feb 1950 League of Ireland   Molineux 7-0(3)
22 Mar 1950 Scottish League   Middlesbrough 3-1
4 Apr 1951 League of Ireland   Dublin 1-0

McNeil, Mick
22 Mar 1961 Scottish League   Ibrox.........2-3
10 Oct 1961 League of Ireland   Goodison Pk 9-1

Robinson, Dicky
30 Apr 1947 League of Ireland   Dublin 3-1
22 Oct 1947 Irish League   Windsor Pk ...4-3
20 Sep 1948* Irish League   Anfield 5-1
29 Nov 1950 Scottish League   Ibrox.........0-1
10 Oct 1951 League of Ireland   Goodison 9-1

Webster, Maurice
24 Sep 1930 Irish League   Belfast 2-2

Whitaker, Bill
26 Apr 1950 Irish League   Belfast 3-1

Williamson, Tim
12 Oct 1907 Irish League   Sunderland ...6-3
8 Oct 1910 Irish League   Belfast 6-2
17 Feb 1912 Scottish League   Middlesbrough 2-0
30 Sep 1912 Southern League   Manchester ...2-1
23 Oct 1912 Irish League   Belfast 0-0

Wartime Internationals

No caps were awarded to players who appeared for their countries in the unofficial wartime and Victory internationals.

England

Fenton, Micky (1)
20 Oct 1945 Wales   Hawthorns ...0-1

Hardwick, George (17)
16 Apr 1941 Wales   City Gnd, Nottingham   4-1
24 Oct 1942 Wales   Molineux.....1-2
17 Apr 1943 Scotland   Hampden Pk 4-0
8 May 1943 Wales   Cardiff 1-1
25 Sep 1943 Wales   Wembley 8-3
16 Oct 1943 Scotland   Manchester ...8-0
19 Feb 1944 Scotland   Wembley 6-2
16 Sep 1944 Wales   Anfield 2-2
14 Oct 1944* Scotland   Wembley 6-2
3 Feb 1945 Scotland   Villa Park 3-2
14 Apr 1945 Scotland   Hampden Pk 6-1
5 May 1945 Wales   Cardiff 3-2
26 May 1945 France   Wembley 2-2
19 Jan 1946 Belgium   Wembley 2-0
13 Apr 1946 Scotland   Hampden Pk 0-1
11 May 1946 Switzerland   Chelsea.......4-1
19 May 1946 France   Paris 1-2

Mannion, Wilf (4)
8 Feb 1941* Scotland   Newcastle.....2-3
3 May 1941 Scotland   Hampden Pk 3-1
4 Oct 1941 Scotland   Wembley 2-0
17 Jan 1942 Scotland   Wembley 3-0

Scotland

Baxter, Bob (4)
2 Dec 1939 England   Newcastle.....1-2
11 May 1940§ England   Hampden Pk 1-1
22 Apr 1944 England   Hampden Pk 2-3
14 Oct 1944* England   Wembley 2-6

Cumming, Dave (1)
14 Oct 1944 *England   Wembley 2-6

Milne, Jacky (1)
8 Feb 1941 *England   Newcastle.....3-2
§Listed as a Hearts player

England Trial Games

Birkett, Ralph
25 Mar 1936* Poss's v Prob's   Old Trafford 0-3

Camsell, George
17 Jan 1927* Rest v England   Stamford Bridge 3-7(1)
7 Feb 1927* Rest v England   Bolton .....3-2(2)
23 Jan 1928* Rest v England   Hawthorns ...1-5
8 Feb 1928 England v Rest   Middlesbrough 3-8(1)
12 Mar 1930* England v Rest   Anfield 1-6

Carr, Jacky
23 Jan 1928* England v Rest   Hawthorns ...5-1
8 Feb 1928 England v Rest   Middlesbrough 3-8
12 Feb 1923 England v South   Millwall 1-0
Cunliffe, Arthur
25 Mar 1936* Poss's v Prob's   Old Trafford   0-3
McNeil, Mick
5 May 1961 England v Young   Stamford Bdge 1-1
           England
Pease, Billy
17 Jan 1927* England v Rest   Stamford Bdge 7-3
7 Feb 1927* England v Rest   Bolton 2-3
Stuart, Bobby
25 Mar 1936* Poss's v Prob's   Old Trafford   0-3
13 Oct 1937 Poss's v Prob's   Goodison Pk   1-1
Webster, Maurice
12 Mar 1930* Rest v England   Anfield 6-1
Williams, Owen
11 Feb 1924 Rest v England   Tottenham ...0-1
Williamson, Tim
23 Jan 1911 Whites v Stripes   Tottenham ...4-1
First team is one the listed player turned out for.

England 'B' Players

Armstrong, David (2)
26 Mar 1980 Spain   Roker Park ...1-0
14 Oct 1980 USA   Old Trafford   1-0
Clough, Brian(1)
6 Feb 1957 Scotland   St Andrew's   4-1(1)
Mannion, Wilf
15 May 1949 Finland   Helsinki 4-0
22 Feb 1950 Holland   St James' Pk,
           Newcastle.....1-0
Mowbray, Tony (2)
16 May 1989* Switzerland   Winterthur ...2-0
22 May 1989* Norway   Stavanger 1-0
Pallister, Gary (3)
16 May 1989* Switzerland   Winterthur ...2-0
19 May 1989 Iceland   Reykjavik.....2-0
22 May 1989* Norway(sub)   Stavanger 1-0

Under-21 Internationals

England
Cooper, Colin (8)
13 Apr 1988 EC France   Besancon 2-4
5 Jun 1988 Mexico   Toulon.......2-1
7 Jun 1988* Russia   Toulon.......1-0
9 Jun 1988 Morocco   Toulon.......1-0
12 Jun 1988* France   Toulon.......2-4
13 Sep 1988* Denmark   Vicarage Rd..0-0
18 Oct 1988 EC Sweden   Highfield Rd   1-1
7 Feb 1989* Greece   Patras 0-1

Hodgson, David (6)
9 Sep 1980* Norway   The Dell 3-0
14 Oct 1980 EC Romania(sub)   Ploieşti 0-4
18 Nov 1980 EC Switzerland   Portman Rd 5-0(1)
25 Feb 1981* Rep of Ireland   Anfield 1-0
17 Mar 1982 EC Poland   Warsaw ....2-1(1)
21 Sep 1982 EC West Germany   Bramall Lane   3-1
Johnston, Craig (2)
25 Feb 1981* Rep of Ireland   Anfield 1-0
9 Sep 1980* Norway   The Dell 3-0
Proctor, Mark (2)
25 Feb 1981* Rep of Ireland(sub)   Anfield 1-0
31 May 1981 EC Switzerland   Neuenburg 0-0
Ripley, Stuart (8 caps)
7 Jun 1988* Russia   Toulon.......0-0
12 Jun 1988* France(sub)   Toulon.......2-4
13 Sep 1988* Denmark(sub)   Vicarage Rd..0-0
18 Oct 1988 EC Sweden(sub)   Highfield Rd   1-1
7 Feb 1989* Greece   Patras 0-1
7 Mar 1989 EC Albania   Shkoder ....2-1(1)
25 Apr 1989 EC Albania   Portman Rd   2-0
5 Sep 1989 Sweden   Uppsala   0-1

Scotland
Stewart, Jim (1)
28 Nov 1978 Portugal   Lisbon 3-0

FA Tour to South Africa (Test Matches)

Fenton, Micky
27 May 1939 Western Province   6-1(2)
10 Jun 1939 South Africa   6-1(2)
1 Jul 1939 South Africa   Johannesburg 2-1

Miscellaneous Representative Games Involving Middlesbrough Players

Birrell, Billy
22 Mar 1922 Home Scots v   Glasgow......1-1
           Anglo Scots

20 Mar 1923 Home Scots v   Glasgow......1-1
           Anglo Scots
Carr, Jackie
8 Mar 1922 Whites v Reds   Old Trafford   1-1
    (Benefit for John Robson's dependants)
Clough, Brian
30 Oct 1957 FA XI v Army   6-3(5)
Elliott, George
25 Feb 1920 The North v   Newcastle   3-5(1)
           England

Griffiths, Tom
11 May 1935 Wales XI v   Wrexham 10-2
           Ireland XI
Jennings, Jack
28 Sep 1931 FA XI v Sheffield   Hillsborough   0-1
           XI
     (Marsden Benefit Fund)
McMordie, A
Oct 1974 Sheffield W v   Hillsborough   5-0
           England XI
    (Testimonial for late Eric Taylor)
Maddren, Willie
Oct 1974 Sheffield W v   Hillsborough   5-0
           England XI
    (Testimonial for late Eric Taylor)
Mannion, Wilf
11 Oct 1941 Football Lge v   Bloomfield Rd
           Scottish Lge   ....3-2(1)
19 May 1948 England XI v   Zurich........5-1
           Switzerland 'B'
18 May 1950 England 'A' v   Brussels ....4-1(2)
           Belgium
Smith, Jock
13 Jan 1928 Home Scots v   Firhill Pk.....1-1
           Anglo Scots
Webster, Maurice
27 Apr 1925 Lancashire v   Turf Moor 3-4
           Yorkshire
First team is one the listed player turned out for.

Youth Internationals

England
Stephen Bell 1983
Steve Fenton 1969
Arthur Horsfield 1964
Gordon Jones 1960
Des McPartland 1966
Len Mole 1964
Alan Peacock 1956

Scotland
Tony McAndrew 1974

Under-19 International

England
Jamie Pollock

Brian Clough's shot is saved by the Swedish goalkeeper at Wembley in October 1959. Eddie Holliday was also in the England team, who lost 3-2.

The Transfer Trail

The 623 players listed below have played for Middlesbrough in the League and FA Cup since 2 September 1899 and the League Cup (under its various names) since its inception in 1960 to 8 May 1993. This list does not feature any player who played in the FA Cup from 1883 to May 1899 nor in the Northern Victory League covering the period November 1918 to May 1919. Also omitted are the games which took place between August 1939 and May 1946, when Middlesbrough took part in wartime football. Also excluded are friendly games, testimonials and benefit matches. It must be stressed that every possible effort has been taken over many years of diligent research to ascertain the data listed below, but many players, especially in the early days of the club's football League life, have scant information recorded against them, sometimes only a surname and an accompanying initial. For example, for many years it was believed that a player called Swan (or Swann) played for the club in the Football League circa 1902 but extensive research has failed to find any reference to this player's contribution, or indeed existence, in Middlesbrough Football Club's early League life and, as all club appearance records are accounted for this player's name is excluded from this list. Where exact details are incomplete the year is shown to indicate the approximate date of the player's career with the club (of course, many players played more games for the club's reserve side but the dates quoted here relate to first team activity). Also included here are details of loan appearances made by Middlesbrough players with other Football League clubs. (AM) indicates that some, if not all, of the appearances made by the player were as an amateur player.

Player	Birthplace	From	To
Agnew WB	Kilmarnock, 16 Dec 1880	Newcastle U, summer 1904	Kilmarnock, 1906
Aitken A	Ayr, 27 Apr 1877	Newcastle U, Oct 1906	Leicester F, Feb 1909
Aitken GB	Dalkeith, 13 Aug 1928	Edinburgh Thistles, Jun 1946	Workington, Jul 1953
Aitken S		Ayr U, 2 Sep 1903	Raith R, summer 1910
Allen M	South Shields, 30 Mar 1949	Wallsend Boys, May 1966	Brentford, Oct 1971
Allport HG		Ironopolis, 1894	1900
Anderson JR	Newcastle upon Tyne, 9 Nov 1924	13 Nov 1945	Blackhall CW, 1948
Anderson S	Hordern, 27 Feb 1934	Newcastle U, Nov 1965	Manager, 28 Apr 1966
Angus MA	Middlesbrough, 28 Oct 1960	Professional, Aug 1978	Scunthorpe U, Sep 1982 (loan) Released, Southend U, Aug 1983
Appleby R	Warkworth, 15 Jan 1940	Amble Welfare, 6 May 1957	Carlisle U, 10 Sep 1966
Armes S	New Seaham, 30 Mar 1908	Leeds U, 2 Feb 1939	Released, Apr 1946
Armstrong D	Durham, 26 Dec 1954	Professional, 31 Dec 1971	Southampton, 4 Aug 1981
Arnold, I	Durham City, 4 Jul 1972	Professional, Jan 1990	Released, 1992, Scarborough
Ashcroft W	Liverpool, 1 Oct 1952	Wrexham, 30 Aug 1977	Released, May 1982 FC Twente
Ashman D	Staindrop	Cockfield A, 5 May 1924	Queen's Park R, 9 May 1932
Askew W	Lumley 2 Oct 1959	Professional, Oct 1977	Released, May 1982 Gateshead
Astley H	1881	Millwall, summer 1904	Crystal P, 1905
Atherton RH	Wales	Hibs, 8 May 1903	Chelsea, May 1906
Auld WB	Bellshill, 9 Jul 1929	Bellshill A, Dec 1950	Berwick R, Jun 1952
Bailey IC	Middlesbrough, 20 Oct 1956	Professional, 18 Oct 1974	Doncaster R, Nov 1976(loan), Carlisle U, Feb 1977(loan), Bolton W, Nov 1981(loan), Sheffield W, 3 Aug 1982.
Baird, IJ	Rotherham, 1 Apr 1964	Leeds U, Feb 1990	Hearts, 31 Jul 1991
Barham MF	Folkestone, 12 Jul 1962	Huddersfield T, 2 Nov 1988	Released, summer 1989, West Brom A, Sep 1989
Barker FM		South Bank, summer 1906	1907
Barker WC	Linthorpe	South Bank, Jul 1905	Became assistant trainer, 1919
Barnard RS	Middlesbrough, 16 Apr 1933	Professional, 24 Apr 1950	Lincoln C, 30 Jun 1960
Baxter MJ	Birmingham, 30 Dec 1956	Preston NE, Aug 1981	Rejected contract, Portsmouth, 24 May 1984
Baxter RD	Gilmerton, 23 Jan 1911	Bruntonian Jrs, May 1931	Hearts, Aug 1945
Beagrie PS	North Ormesby, 28 Nov 1965	Juniors, Sep 1983	Sheffield U, 16 Aug 1986
Beaton S		Feb 1910	Huddersfield T, 1910
Beattie TK	Carlisle, 18 Dec 1953	Carlisle U, Nov 1982	Dispute, Aug 1983
Bell FW		Sep 1899	Released, 1900
Bell HD	Sunderland, 14 Oct 1924	Sunderland, Oct 1945	Darlington, Sep 1955
Bell IC	Middlesbrough, 14 Nov 1958	Professional, Dec 1976	Mansfield T, Jul 1981
Bell, James		Grangetown, Sep 1904	Eston U, 1905
Bell, Joseph N	30 Aug 1912	Amateur, 18 Sep 1934 Pro, 12 Oct 1934	West Ham U, May 1935
Bell S	Middlesbrough, 13 Mar 1965	Juniors May 1982	Contract cancelled, 1985, Portsmouth
Best C	Boosbeck, 1888	Eston U, 1910 (AM)	Hull C, 1911
Bilcliff R	Blaydon, 24 May 1931	Spennymoor Jrs, 14 May 1949	Hartlepools U, Jan 1961
Birbeck J	Gateshead, 15 Apr 1932	Evenwood T, 16 Apr 1953	Grimsby T, 30 Jun 1959
Birkett RJE	Ashford, 9 Jan 1913	Arsenal, 14 Mar 1935	Newcastle U, 30 Jul 1938
Birrell W	Anstruther, 13 Mar 1897	Raith R, Jan 1921	Raith R, Nov 1927
Bissett JT	Dundee	Rochdale, 5 May 1924	Lincoln C, 19 Jul 1926
Blackburn C	Dalton, 16 Jan 1961	Professional, 12 Dec 1979	Released, 1981
Blackett J	1875	Sunderland, Oct 1901	Luton T, 5 Jun 1905
Blackmore HA	Silverton, 13 May 1904	Bolton W, 10 Jun 1932	Bradford, 27 May 1933
Blenkinsopp TW	Whitton Park, 13 May 1920	Grimsby T, 11 May 1948	Barnsley, 7 Nov 1952
Bloomer S	Cradley Heath, 20 Jan 1875	Derby C, Apr 1906	Derby C, 23 Sep 1910
Boam SW	Kirkby-in-Stephen, 20 Jan 1948	Mansfield T, Jun 1971	Newcastle U, Aug 1979
Boardman H		Grangetown, Feb 1910	1910
Boddington H		Mar 1904	1904
Boersma P	Liverpool, 24 Sep 1949	Liverpool, Dec 1975	Luton T, Aug 1977
Bolton J	Barley Mow, 9 Feb 1955	Sunderland, Jul 1981	Sheffield U, Aug 1983
Bottrill WG	South Bank, 8 Jan 1903	Professional, 10 Oct 1921	Nelson, 2 Jun 1924
Braithwaite RM	Belfast, 24 Feb 1937	Linfield, 14 Jun 1963	Durban (SA), 27 Dec 1967
Brawn WF	Wellingborough, 1 Aug 1878	Aston V, Mar 1906	Chelsea, Jun 1907
Brearley J	Liverpool	Notts C, June 1901	Everton, summer 1902
Brennan MR	Rossendale, 4 Oct 1965	Ipswich T, July 1988	Manchester C, 25 Jul 1990
Briggs W	Middlesbrough, 29 Nov 1923	Cochranes, Apr 1947(AM) Pro, Jun 1947	Southport, Jun 1948
Brine PK	Greenwich, 18 Jul 1953	Winns W, Jul 1968	Retired, 1978
Brown Alexander	Beith, 7 Apr 1879	Portsmouth, Aug 1900	Luton T, 1905
Brown Arthur S	Gainsborough, 6 Apr 1885	Fulham, May 1912	1912
Brown DJ	Hartlepool, 28 Jan 1957	Horden CW, Feb 1977	Plymouth A, Aug 1979(loan), Oxford U, 11 Oct 1979
Brown James	Luton, 1880	Luton T, June 1900	1901
Brown John	Motherwell, 1876	Portsmouth, Aug 1900	1901
Brown John R	1885	South Bank, Mar 1907	Bristol C, 1908
Brown Joseph	Cramlington, 26 Apr 1929	Seaton Delaval, May 1946	Burnley, 23 Aug 1952
Brown Thomas	Middlesbrough, summer 1898	22 Apr 1921	Released, May 1922, Accrington S, May 1922
Brown Thomas E	Throckley, 8 Sep 1935	Juniors, 27 Apr 1953	Released, 30 Jun 1959
Brown WH	Choppington, 11 Mar 1909	West Stanley, Dec 1928	Hartlepools U, Jun 1946
Brownlie JJ	Calder Cruix, 11 Mar 1952	Newcastle U, Aug 1982	Released, May 1984, Hartlepool U
Bruce RF	Paisley, 20 Jan 1906	Aberdeen, 31 Jan 1928	Sheffield W, Oct 1935
Bryan PA	Birmingham, 22 Jun 1943	15 Aug 1961	Oldham A, Jul 1965
Bryan R	26 Jul 1916	Bishop Auckland, 6 May 1935	Agreement cancelled by mutual consent, 29 Sep 1938

Player	Birthplace	From	To
Buckley MJ	Manchester, 4 Nov 1953	Carlisle U, Aug 1984	Released, May 1985
Buckley S		Haverton Hill, Aug 1899	1900
Burbeck RT	Leicester, 27 Feb 1934	Leicester C, Oct 1956	Darlington, Jul 1963
Burke MS	Solihull, 12 Feb 1969	Aston V, Dec 1987	Darlington, 3 Oct 1990(loan), Wolves, 14 Mar 1991
Burluraux D	Skelton, 8 Jun 1951	Juniors, Jul 1968	York C, Dec 1971(loan), Darlington, Jul 1972
Burns ME	Preston, 8 Dec 1946	Cardiff C, 2 Oct 1978	Joined club staff, 1981
Burton G		Grangetown, Dec 1909	Cardiff C, 1910
Butler G	Middlesbrough, 29 Sep 1946	Professional, May 1964	Chelsea, Sep 1967
Butler R	Stillington, 10 Oct 1890	Professional, 20 Oct 1912	Oldham A, 10 May 1920
Butler T	Atherton, 28 Apr 1918	Oldham A, Mar 1939	Released, 1946 Accrington S
Butler W		Darlington, Apr 1923	1923
Caig H	Dalry 1894	Kilwinning, Jul 1913	1915
Cail SG	1888	Army, Mar 1907	Stalybridge Cel, 16 Jul 1913
Callaghan J		South Bank, summer 1899	Released, 1900
Cameron K	Hamilton, 1905	Preston NE, 16 Mar 1929	Bolton W, 12 Oct 1933
Campbell A		Aug 1906	Leeds C, 1909
Camsell GH	Framwelgate Moor, 27 Nov 1902	Durham C, 6 Oct 1925	Joined club staff, 1946
Carr A	Burradon	Percy Main, 6 May 1929	Mansfield T, 28 Jun 1934
Carr G	South Bank, 19 Jan 1899	Bradford, 14 Jun 1919	Leicester C, 19 Mar 1924
Carr H	South Bank	Feb 1911 (AM)	
Carr J	South Bank, 26 Nov 1891	South Bank, Dec 1910	Blackpool, 14 May 1930
Carr W	South Bank	South Bank, Apr 1911	1925
Carrick C	Stockton	Local, summer 1900	West Ham U, 1904
Cartwright P	Scarborough, 8 Feb 1908	March 1925	Bradford, 30 Mar 1926
Cassidy J	Motherwell	Manchester C, 7 May 1901	1906
Chadwick C	Bolton, 26 Jun 1914	Oldham A, Feb 1934	Hull C, 20 Sep 1946
Chadwick DE	Ooctamund, India, 19 Aug 1943	Southampton, Jul 1966	Halifax T, 24 Jun 1970
Chapman N	Cockfield, 15 Sep 1941	Juniors, Sep 1958	Darlington, Sep 1967
Charlton H	Gateshead, 22 Jun 1951	Redheugh BC, Jul 1968	Hartlepools U, Jan 1976(loan), Chesterfield, Mar 1976
Chipperfield F	Shiremoor	Lincoln C, 15 Jun 1920	Released, 13 Jun 1923 Ashington
Clark E		Nov 1899	Released 1900
Clark J	Dundee	Apr 1900	Scotland 1900
Clarke W	Jarrow, 14 Jul 1896	Durham C, summer 1919	Leeds U, 4 May 1921
Clough BH	Middlesbrough, 21 Mar 1935	Amateur, Nov 1951, Pro, May 1952	Sunderland, Jul 1961
Clough J	Murton, 13 May	Fatfield A, 23 Sep 1922	Bradford, 12 Jul 1926
Cochrane AF	Glasgow	Alloa A, 27 Feb 1923	Darlington, 21 Jul 1926
Cochrane GT	Killyleagh, 23 Jan 1953	Burnley, 15 Oct 1978	Gillingham, Oct 1983
Cochrane JK	Glasgow, 14 Jan 1954	Drumchapel Amateurs, 24 May 1971	Darlington, 14 Feb 1975
Cochrane M	Ireland	Leicester F, Mar 1901	Distillery, summer 1901
Cochrane T	Newcastle upon Tyne, 7 Oct 1908	Leeds U, 3 Oct 1936	Bradford, 14 May 1939
Coleman, Edward P	Middlesbrough, 23 Sep 1957	Professional, Sep 1975	Workington, Mar 1977
Coleman, Ernest	Hucknall, 4 Jan 1908	Arsenal, 10 Aug 1934	Norwich C, 11 Feb 1937
Coleman, S	Worksop, 13 Mar 1968	Mansfield T, Sep 1989	Derby C, 14 Aug 1991
Collett, AA	Middlesbrough, 23 Oct 1973	Juniors	
Comfort, A	Aldershot, 8 Dec 1964	Leyton O, Jul 1989	Retired, injury 1990
Common A	Millfield, 1880	Sunderland, 16 Feb 1905	Preston NE, 1910
Connachan ED	Preston Pans, 27 Aug 1935	Dunfermline A, 20 Aug 1963	Falkirk, 17 Nov 1966
Cook H	Middlesbrough	Local, Oct 1912	Killed during World War One
Cook J	Sunderland	South Bank, 4 Aug 1911	Notts C 1919
Cook MC	Scarborough, 15 Oct 1961	Darlington, 13 Sep 1985	Scarborough, Aug 1986
Cooper CT	Sedgefield, 28 Feb 1967	Juniors, Jun 1984	Millwall, 25 Jul 1991
Cooper D	Middlesbrough, 18 Oct 1936	Grangetown BC, 31 Oct 1953	Rotherham U, 17 Jan 1959
Cooper T	Castleford, 12 Jul 1944	Leeds U, 13 Mar 1975	Bristol C, Jul 1978
Corbett R	North Warbottle, 26 Mar 1922	Newcastle U, 13 Dec 1951	Northampton T, 15 Aug 1957
Corden S	Eston, 9 Jan 1967	Professional, Jun 1983	Broke leg, Aug 1985
Cowan J		Nov 1899	Released, 1900
Coxon T	Hanley, 10 Jun 1883	Stoke, Sep 1905	Southampton, May 1906
Coyle RP	Glasgow, 19 Aug 1961	Celtic, 11 Feb 1987(loan), Celtic, 7 Mar 1987	Rochdale, Aug 1987
Craggs JE	Flinthill, 31 Oct 1948	Newcastle U, Aug 1971	Released, May 1982, Newcastle U, Aug 1982
Craig T	Scotland	Scotland, Nov 1904	Falkirk 1905
Crawford A	Filey, 30 Jan 1959	Cardiff C, Oct 1983	Released, May 1984, Stockport C, Dec 1984
Crawford J	Leith	Derby C, 28 Nov 1901	Sunderland, 1903
Creamer PA	Hartlepool, 20 Sep 1953	Professional, Oct 1970	York C, Nov 1975(loan), Doncaster R, 4 Dec 1975
Crosier J	Middlesbrough, 4 Dec 1889	Mar 1911	Bradford
Crossan JA	Londonderry, 29 Nov 1938	Manchester C, 30 Aug 1967	Released, 6 May 1970, Tongren, Belgium
Cuff PJ	Middlesbrough, 19 Mar 1952	Professional, May 1969	Grimsby T, Sep 1971(loan), Millwall, 15 Jun 1978
Cumming DS	Aberdeen, 6 May 1910	Arbroath, 6 Oct 1936	Retired, 1947
Cummins S	Sedgefield, 6 Dec 1958	Professional, Dec 1976	Sunderland, 15 Nov 1979
Cunliffe A	Blackrod, 5 Feb 1909	Aston Villa, 27 Dec 1935	Burnley, 26 Apr 1937
Currie DN	Stockton, 27 Nov 1962	Professional, 1 Feb 1982	Darlington, 17 Jun 1986
Currie R	1888	Arthurlie, 4 Feb 1903	Bury, 1903
Curtis J	South Bank	Tottenham H, Aug 1919	1920
Davenport P	Birkenhead, 24 Mar 1961	Manchester U, Nov 1988	Sunderland, 15 Jul 1990
Davidson A	Ayr, 1878	Ayr U, summer 1900	Bury, 1906
Davidson I	East Lothian, 8 Sep 1937	Preston NE, 17 Feb 1965	Darlington, 5 Sep 1967
Davidson S	Aberdeen, 1 Jun 1889	Aberdeen, 17 Apr 1913	Aberdeen, May 1923
Davidson W		Dec 1910	Queen's Park, 1910-11
Davies AE		West Brom A, Dec 1914	Swindon T, 1914-15
Davies B	Middlesbrough	Shildon Feb 1911	Cardiff C, 1919
Davies WF		Dec 1904	1905
Davison JW	Byers Green	Local, 18 Oct 1919	Portsmouth, 17 May 1923
Day W	South Bank, 27 Dec 1936	South Bank Jrs, May 1955	Newcastle U, 10 Mar 1962
Delapenha LL	Kingston, Jamaica, 20 May 1927	Portsmouth, 28 Apr 1948	Mansfield T, 24 Jun 1958
Desmond P	Cork, 23 Nov 1926	Shelbourne, 11 May 1949	Southport, Jul 1950
Dews G	Ossett, 5 Jun 1921	Aug 1946	Plymouth A, 27 Oct 1947
Dibble, AG	Cwmbran, 8 May 1965	Manchester C, 20 Feb 1991 (loan)	
Dickinson PE		Willington A, Oct 1924	Released, 11 May 1925, Annfield Plain
Dicks RW	Kennington, 13 Apr 1924	Dulwich Hamlet, 15 Apr 1943 (AM) Professional, May 1943	Retired 1958
Dickson, IW	Maxwelltown	Aston Villa, 19 Dec 1923	Released, 1 May 1926
Dixon C	Middlesbrough	Darlington, Feb 1915	Hartlepools U, 1923
Dixon T		Bedlington U, Nov 1907	Watford, 1911
Dobbie H	Binchester, 20 Feb 1923	South Bank SP, Oct 1946	Plymouth A, 8 Mar 1950
Doig T		Nov 1900	1901
Donaghy P	Grangetown	Grangetown St Mary's, 20 Aug 1919	Bradford C, May 1923

Goalscoring legend George Camsell, pictured here in January 1927.

John Hendrie, signed from Leeds United in July 1990.

Player	Birthplace	From	To
Donaldson A	Newcastle upon Tyne, 22 Mar 1925	Newcastle U, 25 Jan 1949	Peterborough U, (Exeter C, 11 Sep 1953)
Douglas H	Hartlepool	South Bank, Jan 1903	1903
Douglas JS	West Hartlepool, 1 Dec 1917	Hartlepools U, 14 Sep 1945	Hartlepools U, Nov 1948
Dow MJ	Dundee 1873	Luton T, Aug 1900	1902
Downing DG	Doncaster, 3 Nov 1945	Frickley Colliery, 5 Feb 1965	Orient, 3 May 1972
Dowson F	North Ormesby	May 1920	Released, May 1922 Hartlepools U
Duffy CF	Jarrow, 1885	Jarrow, Oct 1905	Newcastle U, Aug 1906
Duguid W	Wishaw	Albion R, Sep 1910	1913
Eckford J	Kilcaldy, 1876	Luton T, Aug 1900	Raith R, Dec 1900
Edwards WI	Bowburn, 10 Dec 1933	Bowburn, 25 Mar 1952	Released, 1955
Eglington R		Thornaby, Sep 1899	Released, 1900
Elkes JE	Wellington St George's, 31 Dec 1895	Tottenham H, 26 Aug 1929	Watford, Aug 1933
Ellerington W	Sunderland	Darlington, 25 May 1919	Nelson, Jun 1924
Elliott GW	Sunderland, 7 Jan 1889	South Bank, May 1910	Retired, May 1925
Emmerson GA	Bishop Auckland, 1900	Jarrow, 24 Jan 1927	Cardiff C, 6 Jun 1930
Emmerson M	Sunniside, 23 Oct 1942	Juniors, 5 Nov 1959	Peterborough U, 19 Jul 1963
Evans RW		Bury, 1900	Released, 1900
Eyre E	Worksop	Aston Villa, Aug 1911	Birmingham, 3 Apr 1914
Falconer, WH	Aberdeen, 5 Apr 1966	Watford, 16 Aug 1991	
Featherstone T	Darlington	Local, Apr 1904	Bolton W, summer 1904
Fenton M	Stockton, 30 Oct 1913	South Bank EE, 6 Mar 1933	Joined club staff, 1948
Ferguson C	Dunfermline, 22 Nov 1910	Glasgow Benburb, 9 May 1932	Notts C, 8 May 1936
Ferguson R	Grangetown, 25 Jul 1917	Sunderland, 17 Aug 1935	York C, 27 May 1939
Ferguson RG	Glasgow	Sunderland, 30 Jan 1925	Crystal P, Sep 1932
Fernie DW	Kinglassie, 22 Nov 1930	Celtic, 1 Dec 1958	Celtic, 7 Oct 1960
Fitzsimons AG	Dublin, 16 Dec 1929	Shelbourne, 11 May 1949	Lincoln C, 16 Mar 1959
Fleming C	Manchester, 8 Oct 1968	St Patrick's A, 16 Aug 1991	
Flint WA	Eastwood, 21 Mar 1890	Hebburn Argyle, 1908	Notts C, 1910
Foggon A	West Pelton, 23 Feb 1950	Cardiff C, Oct 1972	Manchester U, 26 Jul 1976
Forrest W	Tranent, 28 Feb 1908	Edinburgh St Bernard's 16 Mar 1929	Darlington Manager, 1946
Fowler HN	Stockton, 3 Sep 1919	South Bank, Jun 1934	Hull C, 6 Sep 1946
Fox WV	Middlesbrough, 8 Jan 1898	Professional, 23 May 1919	Wolves, 6 Oct 1924
Frail J	Burslem, 1873	Chatham, 17 May 1900	Stockport C, 1 Nov 1905
Fraser A		Darlington, Apr 1911	Darlington 1913
Freeman RV	Birkenhead 1893	Oldham A, 14 May 1923	Rotherham U, May 1930
Freeman T	Brandon, 26 Jan 1907	Durham C, Oct 1929	Chester, 13 Jun 1933
French JP		Professional, 19 Feb 1924	Southend U, 1 May 1926
Gallacher C	Derry, 25 Apr 1922	Lochee Harps, 4 Jan 1947	Hull C, May 1947
Gallagher J	Dipton, 17 Feb 1897	Oldham A, 1921	Millwall, summer 1921
Garbett TG	Malton, 9 Sep 1945	Stockton, 14 Nov 1963	Watford, 6 Aug 1966
Gardner JR	Hartlepool, 1905	Hartlepools U, 21 Jun 1927	Aldershot, 5 May 1929
Gates WL	Ferryhill, 8 May 1944	Amateur, Sep 1961, Pro, Oct 1961	Retired, 30 Jun 1974
Gettins E		Gainsborough Tr, 2 May 1903	Released, May 1905, Reading
Gettins JH		1899 (AM)	
Gibson FW	Summerscoat, 18 Jun 1902	Hull C, 15 Nov 1932	Bradford C, 13 May 1937
Gibson IS	Newton Stewart, 30 Mar 1943	Bradford, 12 Mar 1962	Coventry C, 4 Jul 1966
Gibson RJ	Scotswood	Sep 1910	Newcastle U, 11 Aug 1911
Gill G	Middlesbrough, 28 Nov 1964	Professional, Dec 1982	Hull C, Dec 1983(loan), Darlington, Dec 1989
Gittens, J	Moseley, 22 Jan 1964	Southampton, 19 Feb 1992 (loan) Southampton, Jul 1992	Released, May 1993
Glover DV	Birmingham, 29 Dec 1963	Aston Villa, Jun 1987	Port Vale, 3 Feb 1989
Godley W		Local, Dec 1902	Stoke, 21 Apr 1904
Good H	Motherwell	Wishaw YMCA, 7 May 1924	Exeter C, 3 May 1926
Goodfellow DO	Shilbottle, 26 Jun 1917	Sheffield W, Jun 1947	Exeter C, 1948
Goodson L		Doncaster R, Dec 1902	1905
Gordon D	West Calder, 1885	St Mirren, May 1908	1908
Gordon J	Fauldhouse, 23 Oct 1915	Newcastle U, 20 Nov 1945	Joined club staff, 1953
Gowland N	Butterknowle, 1902	Chilton Colliery, 5 May 1924	Released, Stockport C, 1930
Gray RSM	Stirling, 27 Feb 1872	Bristol R, Oct 1899	Luton T, 1900
Green T	Rockferry, 25 Nov 1883	Stockport C, 8 Feb 1905	Queen's Park R, May 1906
Griffiths TP	Wrexham, 21 Feb 1906	Bolton W, 1 Mar 1933	Aston Villa, 6 Nov 1935
Groves JA	South Bank, July 1883	Sheffield U, 31 Aug 1907	Wingate A, 1912
Hall BAC	Sheffield, 29 Mar 1908	Doncaster R, 15 Mar 1928	Bradford C, 10 Jun 1930
Hall JH		Brighton, May 1908	Birmingham, 1910
Hamilton GJ	Glasgow, 27 Dec 1965	Professional, May 1983	Darlington, 19 Sep 1991(loan), retired, Mar 1992
Hamilton WM	Airdrie, 16 Feb 1938	Sheffield U, 19 Feb 1961	Hibs, 8 Jun 1962
Hankin R	Wallsend, 2 Feb 1956	Vancouver Whitecaps, Sep 1982	Peterborough U, Sep 1983
Hanlon E	Dundee	Darlington, Sep 1906	Barnsley, 1907
Hardwick GFM	Saltburn, 2 Feb 1920	South Bank EE, May 1937	Oldham A, 6 Nov 1950
Harkins J	Scotland	5 Sep 1906	Leeds C, 1907
Harris J	Glasgow, 19 Mar 1896	Partick Th, 1 Mar 1923	Newcastle U, 30 Sep 1925
Harris WC	Swansea, 31 Oct 1928	Hull C, 4 Mar 1954	Bradford C, Mar 1965(player-manager)
Harrison H	Redcar, 21 Nov 1893	Grangetown, May 1913	Darlington, 1924
Hartnett JB	Dublin, 21 Mar 1927	Dundalk, Jun 1948	Barry T, Sep 1952, (Hartlepools U, 13 Sep 1957)
Hasell AA	Bristol	Bolton W, Oct 1907	Swindon T, 1907
Hastie J		Plymouth A, 26 Sep 1919	Dundee
Hawkins GH	24 Nov 1915	4 Feb 1935	Watford, 4 Jun 1937
Haworth JH	Turton	Brighton, Feb 1912	1915
Healey R	Darlington 1890	Bishop Auck, (AM) Apr 1914	
Heard TP	Hull, 17 Mar 1960	Newcastle U, 30 Aug 1985(loan), Newcastle U, 27 Sep 1985	Hull C, 27 Mar 1986(loan), Hull C, 9 May 1986
Hedley, George T	County Durham, 1882	West Stanley, Oct 1905	Hearts, 19 Jan 1906
Hedley, Graeme	Easington, 1 Mar 1957	Professional, Mar 1975	Sheffield W, Feb 1978(loan), Darlington, Mar 1979(loan), York C, Oct 1981(loan), contract cancelled, Mar 1982
Henderson GH	Ladhope, 2 May 1880	Rangers, May 1905	Chelsea, 14 Apr 1906
Henderson R	Wallsend, 31 Mar 1937	Ashington, May 1957	Hull C, 23 Jun 1961
Hendrie JG	Lennoxtown, 24 Oct 1963	Leeds U, 5 Jul 1990	
Hepple G	Sunderland, 16 Sep 1925	North Sands, May 1947	Norwich C, 8 Jun 1954
Hewitt C	Oldham, 1885	West Hartlepool, 1905	Tottenham H, May 1906
Hewitt J	Aberdeen, 9 Feb 1963	Celtic, 27 Sep 1991 (loan)	
Hick WM	Beamish	South Shields, 4 Feb 1924	Southend U, 16 Mar 1925
Hickling W		Derby C, Sep 1906	Tottenham H, 1907
Hickton J	Brimington, 24 Sep 1944	Sheffield W, 23 Sep 1966	Hull C, Jan 1977(loan), contract cancelled, Fort Lauderdale, Apr 1978
Higgins W	Smethwick, 1874	Newcastle U, 4 May 1900	Manchester U, 27 Sep 1901
Higham N	Chorley, 14 Feb 1912	Everton, 4 May 1935	Southampton, 25 May 1939
Hignett, CJ	Whiston, 12 Jan 1970	Crewe Alexandra, Nov 1992	
Hillier EJG	Eastleigh, 10 Apr 1907	Cardiff C, 24 Jan 1930	Newport C, 17 Jun 1936

Player	Birthplace	From	To
Hisbent JM	Plymouth	Feb 1912	1915
Hodgson DJ	Gateshead, 1 Nov 1960	Professional, Aug 1978	Liverpool, Aug 1982
		Norwich C, Mar 1987 (loan)	
Hodgson G		Summer 1900	1901
Hodgson JP	Dawdon, 10 May 1922	Leeds U, 12 Mar 1948	Released, 1955
Hogg J		Hearts, Sep 1902	Luton T, Jun 1906
Holliday E	Barnsley, 17 Jun 1939	Juniors, 7 Aug 1956, Sheffield W, Jun 1965	Sheffield W, 17 Mar 1962, Hereford U, 1966
Holliday JW	Cockfield, 19 Dec 1908	Cockfield, 1930	Brentford, 2 May 1932
Holmes, W	Willington, 9 May	Willington A, Apr 1914(AM)	Released, 1928 Darlington
Honeyman JW	Middlesbrough, 29 Dec 1893	Cargo Fleet Works, Oct 1919	Dundee, 22 Sep 1920
Horne, BS	Billericay, 5 Oct 1967	Millwall, Aug 1992(loan)	
Horner W	Cassop, 7 Sep 1942	Professional, Sep 1959	Darlington, Jun 1969
Horsfield A	Newcastle upon Tyne, 5 Jul 1946	Professional, 5 Jul 1963	Newcastle U, 22 Jan 1969
Howling E		South Bank, Apr 1911 (AM)	Bristol C
Hughes M	Fauldhouse	Scotland, Jun 1899	1900
Hume RM	Kirkintilloch, 18 Mar 1941	Rangers, 14 Sep 1962	Aberdeen, 24 Jul 1963
Hunter H		Mar 1906	Apr 1906
Ironside, I	Sheffield, 8 Mar 1964	Scarborough, 16 Aug 1991	Scarborough, 5 Mar 1992 (loan)
Irvine JD	Whitburn, 17 Aug 1940	Dundee U, 26 May 1964	Hearts, 21 May 1967
Jackson A	Cambose Mount	Scotland, Aug 1910	Killed in action, World War One
James WE		Mar 1911	Portsmouth, 1912-13
Janković B	Sarajevo, 22 May 1951	Željezničar, Feb 1979	Released, summer 1981
Jarvis S	Sheffield,1905	Raith R, 11 Nov 1927	Darlington, 23 Jul 1936
Jennings J	Platt Bridge, 27 Aug 1902	Cardiff C, 29 Jan 1930	Preston NE, 22 Sep 1936
Jennings S	Cinderhill	Norwich C, 8 Apr 1920	Reading, Jun 1921
Johnson PE	Harrogate, 5 Oct 1958	Professional, 31 Oct 1976	Newcastle U, 31 Oct 1980
Johnston Craig P	Johannesburg, 8 Dec 1960	Professional, Feb 1978	Liverpool, Apr 1981
Johnston C Patrick	Dublin, 16 Jul 1924	Shelbourne, 15 Dec 1947	Grimsby T, 3 Feb 1949
Jones A		West Brom A, summer 1901	Luton T, 1906
Jones GW	Crook, 28 Jun	Everton, 12 Jun 1925	Southend U, 14 Jul 1926
Jones GE	Sedgefield, 6 Mar 1943	Professional, Mar 1960	Darlington, 1 Feb 1973
Jones James		Dec 1899	1905
Jones J Love		Stoke, 8 Mar 1908	Portsmouth, summer 1911
Jordon BA	Bentley, 31 Jan 1933	Rotherham U, 7 Nov 1958	York C, 14 Jul 1960
Kamara, C	Middlesbrough, 25 Dec 1957	Luton T, 19 Feb 1993 (loan)	
Kavanagh, GA	Dublin, 3 May 1973	Home Farm, 1991	
Kay J	Great Lumley, 29 Jan 1964	Wimbledon, 8 Jan 1985(loan)	
Kaye A	Barnsley, 9 May 1933	Blackpool, 24 Nov 1960	Colchester U, Jun 1965
Kear MP	Coleford, 27 May 1943	Nottingham F, Sep 1967	Contract cancelled, Apr 1970
Kelly B		Ashfield, Nov 1911	1911
Kennedy F	Radcliffe, 1904	Everton, 19 May 1927	Reading, 8 May 1929
Kennedy MFM	Salford, 9 Apr 1961	Huddersfield T, 24 Aug 1982	Portsmouth, 19 Jun 1984
Kent H		Brighton, May 1908	Watford, Aug 1909
Kernaghan AN	Otley, 25 Apr 1967	Professional, Mar 1985	Charlton A, 17 Jan 1991 (loan)
Kerr PA	Portsmouth, 9 Jun 1964	Aston Villa, 7 Jan 1987	Millwall, 28 Mar 1991
Kinnell G	Cowdenbeath, 22 Dec 1937	Sunderland, Oct 1968	Juventus, Australia 1969
Kirby F	Durham County	Durham C, Oct 1913	Bradford, 1914
Kirk HJ	Saltcoats, 25 Aug 1944	Ardeer A, May 1963	Third Lanark, summer 1964
Kite PD	Bristol, 26 Oct 1962	Southampton(loan), 27 Mar 1986	
Knowles CB	Fitzwilliam, 13 Jul 1944	Monckton CW, 26 Oct 1962	Tottenham H, May 1964
Laidlaw JD	Swalwell, 12 Jul 1950	Professional, Aug 1967	Carlisle U, 14 Jul 1972
Laking GE	Harthill, 17 Mar 1913	Wolves, 15 Oct 1936	1946-47
Lamb TJ		Newcastle U, Sep 1899	Willington A, 1900
Lawrie S	Dinnistown, 15 Dec 1934	Bedlay Jrs, Feb 1952	Charlton A, Nov 1956
Laws B	Wallsend, 14 Oct 1961	Huddersfield T, 13 Mar 1985	Nottingham F, 27 Jun 1988
Lawson JJ	Middlesbrough, 11 Dec 1947	South Bank, Dec 1964	Huddersfield T, 18 Jul 1968
Layton AE		Aston Villa, Nov 1911	1912
Le Flem RP	Bradford on Avon, 12 Jul 1942	Wolves, 26 Feb 1965	Leyton O, 9 Mar 1966
Leonard HD	Sunderland, 1886	Grimsby T, 11 Nov 1910	Newcastle U, Nov 1911
Leslie J		Sunderland, Oct 1901	Clyde, 1902
Lightening AD	Durban (SA), 1 Aug 1936	Coventry C, 29 Aug 1962	Released, May 1963, Durban City (SA)
Linacre W	Chesterfield, 10 Aug 1924	Manchester C, 20 Sep 1949	Goole Town, (Hartlepools U, Aug 1953)
Linton T		Stockton, Feb 1900	Released, 1900
Linwood AB	Drumsmudden, 13 Mar 1920	St Mirren, Jun 1946	Hibs, 2 Jun 1947
Livingstone J	Middlesbrough, 18 Jun 1942	Professional 25 Jan 1960	Carlisle U, 17 Nov 1962
Lloyd, E	Middlesbrough	Dec 1919	Bradford, 1920
Longstaffe G		Jun 1899	Released, 1900
Lugg RJ	Jarrow, 18 Jul 1948	Primrose FC, Jul 1965	Watford, Nov 1969
Lynch P	Belfast, 22 Jan 1950	Cliftonville, Jun 1970	Released, 1972, Kidderminster H
McAllister W	Glasgow	Brighton, 5 Jul 1924	Queen's Park R, 21 Oct 1926
McAndrew A	Lanark, 11 Apr 1956	Professional, Aug 1973	Chelsea, 2 Sep 1982
		Chelsea, 28 Sep 1984	Released, May 1986
Macaulay W		Summer 1902	Portsmouth, 1903
McCabe JJ	Draperstown, 17 Sep 1918	South Bank EE, 3 May 1937	Leeds U, 12 Mar 1948
McCallum D		Sunderland, Dec 1904	1905
McClelland J	Dysart	Southend U, 16 Mar 1925	Bolton W, 14 Mar 1928
McClure S		Grangetown, Sep 1910	Watford, 24 Aug 1911
McCormack JC	Newcastle upon Tyne, 15 Feb 1922	Gateshead, 19 Apr 1947	Barnsley, 25 Jul 1950, (Chelmsford C)
McCorquodale D		Scotland, Dec 1899	Returned to Scotland, Dec 1899
McCowie A		Arsenal, Nov 1900	1901
McCracken JP	1868	Nottingham F, summer 1899	Chesterfield, 1900
McCrae A	Stoneburn, 2 Jan 1920	Charlton A, 30 Oct 1948	Falkirk, 16 Mar 1953
McCreesh A	Billingham, 8 Sep 1962	Professional, Sep 1980	Contract cancelled, Mar 1982
McCulloch A	Scotland	Leith A, Feb 1907	Newcastle U, 19 Feb 1908
Macdonald G	Middlesbrough, 26 Mar 1962	Professional, March 1980	Released, Jul 1984, Carlisle U, Jul 1984
Macfarlane J	Bathgate	Celtic, 21 Jun 1929	Dunfermline, summer 1933
Macfarlane R	Greenock, 1875	Grimsby T, 1902	Aberdeen, 1908
Macfarlane T		Mar 1901	1901
McGee, OE	Middlesbrough, 29 Apr 1970	Jul 1988	Released, Feb 1991, Leicester C
McGuigan A		Liverpool, Jan 1903	Southport Central, Jun 1905
McIlmoyle H	Cambuslang, 29 Jan 1940	Carlisle U, 24 Sep 1969	Preston NE, Jul 1971
McKay J	Glasgow, 1 Nov 1898	Blackburn R, 10 Mar 1927	Bolton W, Jun 1936
McKennan PS	Airdrie, 16 Jul 1918	Brentford, 17 May 1949	Oldham A, 24 Jul 1951
McKenzie D	Glasgow, 10 Aug 1912	Brentford, 11 May 1938	Released, 1945
McLean JD	Brotton, 21 Dec 1932	Professional, Oct 1952	Hartlepools U, 12 Oct 1961
McLeod D	Stenhousemuir, Jun 1883	Celtic, Oct 1906	Retired 1914
McManus CE	Limavady, 14 Nov 1950	Bradford C, 17 Jan 1986 (loan)	
McMordie A	East Belfast, 12 Apr 1946	Professional, 7 Sep 1964	Sheffield W, 18 Oct 1974(loan), York C, May 1975

South African-born Craig Johnston, moved to Liverpool in April 1981.

Player	Birthplace	From	To
McMurray, J	Billingham, 5 Oct 1931	Billingham Synth, May 1949	Poole T, 11 Aug 1956
McNally J		Thornaby, Aug 1899	1900
McNeil M	Middlesbrough, 7 Feb 1940	Cargo Fleet Jrs, Jun 1954, Pro, 4 Jun 1957	Ipswich T, Jul 1964
McNeill AA	Belfast, 16 Aug 1945	Belfast Crusaders, Apr 1967	Huddersfield T, Nov 1968
McPartland D	Middlesbrough, 15 Oct 1947	Professional, Oct 1964	Carlisle U, 26 Jan 1968
McPhail DD	Dumbarton, 17 Feb 1911	Dumbarton, 3 Apr 1928	Released, Apr 1932
McPherson K	Hartlepool, 25 Mar 1929	Notts C, 1 Aug 1953	Coventry C, 8 Dec 1955
McRobbie A		Feb 1912	Swindon T, Apr 1913
Madden G	Loftus	Haverton Hill, Jan 1900	Released, 1900
Maddison JP	South Shields, 9 Nov 1924	Professional, 19 Dec 1945	Darlington, Aug 1949
Maddren WD	Billingham, 11 Jan 1951	Port Clarence, 19 Jun 1968	Retired, 1978, Manager, Jun 1984
Mahoney JF	Cardiff, 20 Sep 1946	Stoke C, Aug 1977	Swansea C, 23 Jul 1979
Maitland AE	Leith, 8 Oct 1896	South Shields, 21 Jun 1923	Newcastle U, Oct 1924
Malan NF	South Africa, 23 Nov 1923	Defos FC (SA), Oct 1945	Darlington, 28 Jul 1948
Malcolm G	Thornaby	Plymouth A, 29 Oct 1912	Darlington, 1915
Mannion WJ	South Bank, 16 May 1918	South Bank SP, Sep 1936(AM), Pro, 17 Sep 1936	Hull C, 24 Dec 1954
Marcroft EH	Rochdale, 1910	Great Harwood, 28 Dec 1931	Queen's Park R, 10 May 1932
Marshall, DW	Jamaica, 3 Oct 1965	Plymouth A, Apr 1993 (loan)	
Marshall J	Saltcoats	St Mirren, 18 Nov 1919	Llanelly, Apr 1923
Marshall SK	Goole, 20 Apr 1946	Goole T, 29 Jul 1963	Notts C, 24 Jun 1966
Martin GS	Bathgate, 14 Jul 1899	Everton, 6 May 1932	Luton T, 11 Aug 1933
Martin J	Sunderland, 6 Oct 1912	Horden CW, 23 Jan 1932	Released, 1946 Huddersfield T, trainer
Marwood, B	Seaham Harbour, 5 Feb 1960	Sheffield U, 18 Oct 1991 (loan)	
Masson DS	Banchory, 26 Aug 1946	Juniors, Sep 1963	Notts C, 7 Sep 1968
Mathieson JA	Methil, 10 May	Raith R, Jun 1926	Brentford, 17 May 1934
Mattinson H	Ireby, 20 Jul 1925	Professional, Nov 1945	Preston NE, 15 Mar 1949
Millar J	1877	Rangers, May 1900	Bradford C, summer 1903
Millar WM	Glasgow, 1902	Rhyl A, 16 Dec 1927	York C, summer 1929
Miller J	Belfast, 27 Apr	Aberdare A, 10 Apr 1926	Hibs, 13 Nov 1930
Million E	Ashington, 15 Mar 1938	Amble Jrs, 7 May 1956	Bristol R, 27 Jun 1962
Mills DJ	Whitby, 6 Dec 1951	Pro, Dec 1968, Newcastle U, Jun 1984	West Brom A, Jan 1979, released, summer 1985, Darlington, Aug 1986
Milne JV	Stirling, 25 Mar 1911	Arsenal, 14 Dec 1937	Dumbarton, 1941
Mitchell AJ	Stoke, 22 Jan 1922	Luton T, 7 Sep 1954	Southport, Aug 1956
Mochan N	Larbert, 6 Apr 1927	Morton, May 1951	Celtic, 7 May 1953
Mohan NM	Middlesbrough, 6 Oct 1970	Professional, Nov 1987	Hull C, 1991 (loan)
Moody A	Middlesbrough, 18 Jan 1951	Professional, 22 Jan 1968	Southend U, 10 Oct 1972
Moore, AT	Dublin, 25 Sep 1974	Rivermount, 1992	
Moran M	Glasgow, 1878	Sheffield U, August 1900	Scotland 1901
Mordue J	Edmondsley	Sunderland, May 1920	Hartlepools U, May 1922
Morris, CB	Newquay, 24 Dec 1963	Celtic, summer 1992	
Mowbray AM	Saltburn, 22 Nov 1963	Professional, Nov 1981	Celtic, 8 Nov 1991
Muir J		Leith A, Aug 1902	Summer 1903
Muir W		Hamilton A, Sep 1902	Bradford C, summer 1903
Mulholland FG	Belfast, 28 Oct 1927	Glentoran, 13 Oct 1951	Released, 30 Jun 1958
Murdoch RW	Bothwell, 17 Aug 1944	Celtic, Sep 1973	Juniors coach
Murphy DA	South Bank, 19 Jul 1917	South Bank SP, May 1935	Killed, Sep 1944
Murphy J	Ireland	Summer 1899	Released 1900
Murphy M		South Bank, 1899	Released, 1900
Murphy TE	South Bank, 25 Mar 1921	South Bank SP, 4 May 1939	Blackburn R, Dec 1947
Murray A	Newcastle upon Tyne, 5 Dec 1949	Professional, Sep 1967	York C, Feb 1972(loan), Brentford, Jun 1972
Murray T		Sep 1905	Aberdeen, 9 May 1907
Murray W	Bishop Auckland	Derby C, Jul 1921	Hearts, Jun 1923
Mustoe, R	Witney, 28 Aug 1968	Oxford U, 5 Jul 1990	
Muttitt E	Middlesbrough	South Bank, Apr 1929	Brentford, Oct 1932
Myton B	Strensall, 26 Sep 1950	Juniors, Sep 1967	Southend U, Nov 1971
Nash FC	South Bank, 30 Jun 1918	South Bank EE, Sep 1937	Southend U, Dec 1947
Nattrass I	Fishburn, 12 Dec 1952	Newcastle U, Jul 1979	Retired, 1986
Neal RM	Dinnington, 1 Oct 1933	Birmingham C, Oct 1961	Lincoln C, Aug 1963
Niblo, TB	Dunfermline, 24 Sep 1877	Newcastle U, Apr 1900	Transfer cancelled by League Returned to Newcastle U
Nichol J	Port Glasgow	Sep 1910	Liverpool, 1913
Nobbs KA	Bishop Auckland, 19 Sep 1961	Professional, Sep 1979	Released, May 1982, Halifax T, Sep 1982
Norris OP	Londonderry, 1 Apr 1929	Londonderry Jrs, Jun 1948	Bournemouth, Jul 1955, (Worcester C)
Nurse MTG	Swansea, 11 Oct 1937	Swansea T, 29 Sep 1962	Swindon T, 30 Aug 1965
O'Connell SCP	Carlisle, 11 Jan 1930	14 May 1953 (AM)	
O'Hagan C		Tottenham H, Jul 1906	Aberdeen, 1906
O'Hanlon KG	Saltburn, 16 May 1962	Professional, May 1980	Released, May 1985, Rotherham U, Aug 1985
O'Riordan DJ	Dublin, 14 May 1957	Carlisle U, 8 Aug 1985	Grimsby T, Aug 1986
O'Rourke J	Northampton, 11 Feb 1945	Luton T, Jul 1966	Ipswich T, Feb 1968
Orritt B	Cwm-y-Clo, 22 Feb 1937	Birmingham C, 1 Mar 1962	South Africa, 21 Mar 1966
Osborne F		Dykehead, 12 Aug 1899	Released 1900
Ostler J	Scotland	Newcastle U, Apr 1900	Transfer cancelled by League
Otto HM	Amsterdam, 24 Aug 1954	FC Twente, 25 Aug 1981	FC Den Haag, Jun 1985
Page R	1878	Grove Hill, 1898	Retired, 1906
Pallister GA	Ramsgate, 30 Jun 1965	Billingham T, Nov 1984	Darlington, 18 Oct 1985(loan), Manchester U, Aug 1989
Parkin R	Crook, 28 Jan 1911	Arsenal, 13 Jan 1936	Southampton, 17 Sep 1937
Parkinson GA	Thornaby, 10 Jan 1968	Jan 1986	Southend U, Oct 1992(loan), Bolton W, Apr 1993
Paterson T	Newcastle upon Tyne, 30 Mar 1954	Leicester C, Sep 1974	Bournemouth, Apr 1976
Patterson RL	Gateshead, 30 Oct 1929	Whitehall Jrs, 28 Jun 1949	Northampton T, 11 Jun 1952
Payton, AP	Burnley, 3 Oct 1967	Hull C, 22 Nov 1991	Celtic, Aug 1992
Peacock A	Middlesbrough, 29 Oct 1937	Lawson St School, Nov 1954	Leeds U, Feb 1964
Peacock J	Wigan, 15 Mar 1897	Everton, 17 May 1927	Sheffield W, 22 May 1930
Peake, AM	Market Harborough, 1 Nov 1961	Charlton A, 28 Nov 1991	
Pears S	Brandon, 22 Jan 1962	Manchester U(loan), Nov 1983 (signed 26 Jun 1985)	
Pease WH	Leeds, 30 Sep 1898	Northampton T, 18 May 1926	Luton T, Jan 1933
Peggie J		Hibs, Oct 1910	1911
Pender R	Dumbarton	Dumfermline A, 1 May 1919	St Johnstone, 11 Aug 1924
Pentland FB	Wolverhampton 1883	Queen's Park R, 17 Jun 1908	Halifax T 6 Feb 1913
Peters J	Wide Open, 7 Mar 1961	Professional, Mar 1979	Contract cancelled, Mar 1982, Blyth Spartans
Phillips BJ	Cadishead, 9 Nov 1931	Altrincham, 22 Jun 1954	Mansfield T, 21 Jun 1960
Phillips JN	Bolton, 8 Feb 1966	Oxford U, Mar 1990	
Phillipson TF	Stanhope, 1886	Bishop Auckland, Feb 1905	1905
Piercy FR		Jun 1899	West Ham U, 24 Jun 1904
Piercy HR		1899	

David Mills, spent two separate spells with Middlesbrough.

Player	Birthplace	From	To
Platt JA	Ballymoney, 26 Jan 1952	Ballymena U, 5 May 1970	Hartlepool U, Aug 1978(loan), Cardiff C, Nov 1978(loan), released, Apr 1983, Ireland
Pollock, J	Stockton, 16 Feb 1974	Professional, Dec 1991	
Poole K	Bromsgrove, 21 Jul 1963	Aston Villa, 20 Aug 1987	Hartlepool U, Mar 1991(loan), Leicester C, 30 Jul 1991
Poskett M	Middlesbrough, 19 Jul 1953	South Bank, Jul 1973	Hartlepool U, Jul 1974, (Whitby T)
Poulton A	Wolverhampton, 28 Mar 1890	Merthyr T, 19 Mar 1920	Bristol C, 27 Sep 1921
Povey W	Billingham, 11 Jan 1943	Juniors, May 1960	York C, Mar 1964
Pratt R	1876	South Bank, 26 May 1899	Released, 1900
Priest AE	Darlington, 1875	South Bank, Sep 1906	Sheffield U, 1907
Priest F		Sep 1906	1906
Proctor MG	Middlesbrough, 30 Jan 1961	Pro, Sep 1978, Sheffield W, 23 Mar 1989	Nottingham F, 1 Aug 1981, Tranmere R, Feb 1993(loan), released, May 1993
Proudlock P	Hartlepool, 25 Oct 1965	Hartlepools U, Nov 1986	Carlisle U, 23 Mar 1989
Pugh CE		St Augustine's 1899	1900
Putney, TA	Harold Hill, 11 Feb 1961	Ipswich T, Jul 1989	Watford, 15 Aug 1991
Raisbeck L		Third Lanark, 1900	
Ramage A	Guisborough, 29 Nov 1957	Professional, Nov 1975	Derby C, Aug 1980
Ramsay A	East Benhar, 1877	East Benhar, Aug 1900	Leyton, Jun 1905
Ratcliffe D	Newcastle-under-Lyme, 13 Nov 1934	Stoke C, Sep 1963	Darlington, Feb 1966
Ratcliffe E	Gee Cross 1880	Derby C, Mar 1906	
Rayment JW	West Hartlepool, 25 Sep 1934	Juniors, Oct 1951	Hartlepools U, Jul 1955
Reagan CM	York, 12 May 1924	Hull C, 12 Feb 1948	Shrewsbury T, 1 Aug 1951
Redfern J		Sep 1899	Released, 1900
Reid, George	Kilmarnock	West Brom A, Nov 1899	Millwall, 1900
Reid, George T	Blackland Mill, 1884	St Mirren, 20 May 1905	1906
Rickaby S	Stockton, 12 Mar 1924	South Bank, Jun 1946	West Brom A, Feb 1950
Rigby A	Chorlton, 7 Jun 1900	Blackburn R, 6 May 1932	Clapton O, 22 Aug 1933
Ripley SE	Middlesbrough, 20 Nov 1967	Apprentice, Nov 1985	Bolton W, Feb 1986(loan), Blackburn R, Jul 1992
Roberts A	Newcastle upon Tyne, 8 Dec 1964	Professional, Dec 1982	Darlington, 13 Sep 1985
Roberts J		Oct 1906	1906
Roberts RJ	Redditch, 1878	Newcastle U, Mar 1904	Crystal P, summer 1905
Roberts WS		Oct 1906	
Robertson A	Dundee 1878	Dundee, 18 May 1900	Manchester U, 1903
Robertson J		Oct 1901	Aberdeen, 23 Jun 1904
Robertson WG	Glasgow, 4 Nov 1936	Juniors, Nov 1953	Released, Jun 1959
Robinson J	Middlesbrough, 10 Feb 1934	Professional, Oct 1951	Hartlepools U, Jun 1959
Robinson JN	Middlesbrough, 15 Jan 1921	South Bank SP, 24 Jan 1946	Grimsby T, 1 Jun 1948
Robinson JW		Aug 1919	1920
Robinson R	Whitburn, 19 Jan 1927	Professional, Apr 1945	Barrow, Jun 1959
Rodgerson AR	Easington, 19 Mar 1939	Potter's Bar, May 1956	Cambridge U, 1964
Rooks R	Sunderland, 29 May 1940	Sunderland, Aug 1965	Bristol C, Jun 1969
Ross AC	York, 7 Oct 1916	Gainsborough Tr, Feb 1935	Bradford, Mar 1937
Ross C	Dailly, 29 Aug 1962	Ayr U BC, Sep 1980	Chesterfield, Mar 1983 (loan), Darlington, Aug 1983
Rowell G	Seaham, 6 Jun 1957	Norwich C, 16 Aug 1985	Released, Mar 1986, Brighton, Aug 1986
Russell ET	Cranwell, 15 Jul 1928	Wolves, 10 Dec 1951	Leicester C, Oct 1953
Russell, MC	Dublin, 27 Apr 1967	Scarborough, 15 Mar 1990	Portadown, 16 Aug 1991
Saxby MW	Mansfield, 12 Aug 1957	Newport C, 1 Oct 1984	Retired, Apr 1986
Scott GS	Birmingham, 31 Oct 1956	Charlton A, Sep 1984	Monthly contract cancelled Northampton T, Sep 1984
Scott JC	Fatfield, 9 Jan 1930	Luton T, Sep 1954	Hartlepools U Jan 1959
Scott WR	Willington Quay, 6 Dec 1907	Howden B Legion, May 1927	Brentford, May 1932
Scrimshaw CT	Heanor, 5 Apr 1911	Stoke C, Oct 1938	Released, 1945
Senior TJ	Dorchester, 28 Nov 1961	Watford, Mar 1988	Reading, 10 Oct 1988
Shand H	Scotland	Inverness Th, Aug 1906	Millwall, 1908
Shannon, R	Bellshill, 20 Apr 1966	Dundee, 18 Sep 1991 (loan)	
Shaw TW		Stockton, May 1899	Released, 1900
Shearer DJ	Caol, 16 Oct 1958	Inverness Clachnacuddin, Jan 1978	Wigan A, Mar 1980 (loan), Grimsby T, Jun 1983
Shepherdson H	Middlesbrough, 28 Oct 1918	South Bank EE, Dec 1934 (AM) Professional, May 1935	Southend U, May 1947
Short M	Middlesbrough, 29 Dec 1949	Juniors, Feb 1967	Oldham A, Jun 1970
Slade CH	Bristol, 1892	Huddersfield T, 16 Oct 1922	Darlington, 10 Sep 1925
Slaven BJ	Paisley 13 Nov 1960	Albion R, Oct 1985	Port Vale, Mar 1993
Smith, David	Thornaby, 8 Dec 1947	Professional, 21 Dec 1964	Lincoln C, Jul 1968
Smith, David W		Nottingham F, Dec 1900	Retired, 1907, became club director
Smith, Edward G		Aug 1899	1900
Smith, Ernest E	Donegal	Cardiff C, 22 Jan 1924	Watford, 4 Sep 1925
Smith G	Newcastle upon Tyne, 7 Oct 1945	Portsmouth, Jan 1969	Birmingham C, Mar 1971
Smith J	Dalbeattie, 7 Dec 1898	Ayr U, 3 Sep 1926	Cardiff C, 12 Sep 1930
Smith J	Hurlford	1933	Queen of South, 1935
Smith M	Stockton, 21 Sep 1953	Professional, Oct 1970	Bury, Oct 1975(loan), Blackpool, Jan 1976(loan), Burnley, Sep 1976
Smith RA	Billingham, 6 Feb 1944	Haverton Hill, 19 Dec 1961	Bangor C, 30 Jun 1972
Souness GJ	Edinburgh, 6 May 1953	Tottenham H, 30 Dec 1972	Liverpool, Jan 1978
Spraggon F	Marley Hill, 27 Oct 1945	Juniors, 5 Nov 1962	Released, Apr 1976 Minnesota Kicks
Spriggs S	Doncaster, 16 Feb 1956	Cambridge U, Mar 1987	Refused contract, Apr 1987
Spuhler, JO	Sunderland, 18 Sep 1917	Sunderland, 25 Oct 1945	Darlington, Jun 1954
Stage W		Apr 1914	Released, Apr 1914 Hibs
Stephens A	Liverpool, 19 May 1954	Bristol R, 16 Mar 1985	Carlisle U, 23 Dec 1987
Stevenson AB		Wigan, Oct 1923	Rhondda, summer 1924
Stewart JG	Kilwinning, 10 Mar 1954	Kilmarnock, May 1978	Rangers, 15 Mar 1981
Stiles NP	Manchester, 18 May 1942	Manchester U, 5 May 1971	Preston NE, 28 Aug 1973
Stirling J	Clydebank	Sep 1911	1914
Stone JG	Carlin Howe, 3 Mar 1953	South Bank Jrs, Mar 1970	York C, Jul 1972
Stonehouse D	Lingdale, 18 Nov 1932	Lingdale, May 1951	Hartlepools U, 30 Sep 1963
Storey T	Crook	Jan 1914	Port Vale, 1920
Stott J	Middlesbrough	Newcastle U, 14 Sep 1899	1900
Strong AF	Hartlepool, 17 Sep 1966	Juniors, Sep 1984	Released, Feb 1986
Stuart RW	Middlesbrough, 9 Oct 1913	South Bank Jrs, May 1928 (AM) Professional, Jan 1931	Plymouth A, Oct 1947
Suddick J		Apr 1904	Summer 1904
Sugrue PA	Coventry, 6 Nov 1960	Kansas C, Dec 1982	Portsmouth, Dec 1984
Surtees J	Newcastle upon Tyne, 1 Jul 1911	Percy Main, Mar 1930	Portsmouth, Jun 1932
Swales N	New Marske	Dec 1925	1926
Taylor B	Hodthorpe, 12 Feb 1954	Professional, Mar 1971	Doncaster R, Dec 1975
Taylor CW	Kirby Stephen, 20 Jan 1937	Penrith, Jan 1956	Aldershot, Jun 1960

Player	Birthplace	From	To
Taylor PT	Nottingham, 2 Jul 1928	Coventry C, Aug 1955	Port Vale, Jun 1961
Tennant J		Arsenal, Apr 1901	Apr 1902
Thackeray J	Hebburn, 1881	Hebburn Argyle, 1904	Bradford C, 1910
Thomas D	Kirkby, 5 Oct 1950	Vancouver Whitecaps, Mar 1982	Portsmouth, Jul 1982
Thomas MR	Senghenydd, 28 Nov 1959	Newcastle U, (loan), Oct 1984	
Thompson A		Mar 1901	Summer 1901
Thompson N	Forest Hall	South Shields, summer 1925	Barnsley, 1925
Thompson WT	South Bank	Grangetown, Jun 1905	Summer 1906
Thomson KG	Aberdeen, 25 Feb 1930	Stoke C, 11 Dec 1959	Hartlepools U, Oct 1962
Thomson R	Glasgow, 21 Mar 1955	Morton, 25 Sep 1981	Hibs, 31 Jul 1982
Tinsley W		Sunderland, Dec 1913	Nottingham F, May 1921
Tomlin J		Sunderland, Sep 1906	1907
Townsend J	Greenock, 2 Feb 1945	St Johnstone, Feb 1964	St Johnstone, Aug 1966
Trechman OL		W/Hartlepool, (AM) Feb 1906	
Tucker WH		Local, Oct 1906	1907
Turnbull LM	Stockton, 27 Sep 1967	Sep 1985	Aston Villa, Aug 1987
Turner P		Arsenal, Apr 1901	Apr 1902
Twine FW		Army 1927	Aldershot, summer 1928
Tyldesley J	Halesowen, 1882	Newcastle U, 21 Sep 1906	Leeds C, 1909
Ugolini R	Lucca, 4 Jun 1924	Celtic, May 1948	Wrexham, Jun1957
Urquhart A		Greenock Morton, Dec 1907	1908
Urwin T	Haswell, 5 Feb 1896	Shildon, Apr 1914	Newcastle U, Aug 1924
Verrill E	Staithes	South Bank, Feb 1908	Retired, 1915
Vincent JV	West Bromwich, 8 Feb 1947	Birmingham C, Mar 1971	Cardiff C, 10 Oct 1972
Wainscoat RW	Maltby, 28 Jul 1898	Barnsley, Dec 1923	Leeds U, 16 Mar 1925
Waldock R	Heanor, 6 Dec 1932	Plymouth A, Jan 1960	Gillingham, Oct 1961
Walker DH	Edinburgh, 10 Sep 1935	Leicester C, Oct 1959	Released, Grimsby T, Sep 1963
Walker J	Beith	Swindon T, Sep 1913	Reading T, 1921
Walker RG	Bradford, 29 Sep 1926	Bradford, 1 Jun 1946	Doncaster R, Dec 1954
Walker RH		Hearts, Jan 1906	Tottenham H, May 1906
Walley E	Caernarfon, 19 Apr 1934	Tottenham H, May 1958	Released, May 1960 Crystal P
Walsh A	Hartlepool, 9 Dec 1956	Horden CW, Dec 1976	Darlington, Oct 1978
Walsh, CD	Hamilton, 22 Jul 1962	Charlton A, 17 Jan 1991 (loan)	
Wanless R	Middlesbrough, 19 Jul 1876	Jun 1899	Released, 1900
Ward PT	Sedgefield, 15 Sep 1963	Professional, Nov 1982	Darlington, 13 Sep 1985
Wardle G	Kimbleworth, 24 Sep 1919	Durham BC, 1937	Exeter C, June 1939
Wardrope A	1887	Airdrie, Nov 1910	1911
Wardrope W	Motherwell, 1875	Newcastle U, summer 1900	Third Lanark, 1902
Wark, J	Glasgow, 4 Aug 1957	Ipswich T, Aug 1990	Released, Jul 1991, Ipswich T, Aug 1991
Warren FW	Cardiff, 23 Dec 1909	Cardiff C, 29 Jan 1930	Hearts, 9 May 1936
Watkin TWS	Grimsby, 21 Sep 1932	Gateshead, Mar 1954	Mansfield T, Jun 1955
Watson A	Ferryhill, 26 Dec 1903	Chilton, May 1925	1926
Watson HL	Springwell	Pelton Fell, May 1926	Brentford, May 1932
Watson J	Motherwell, 4 Oct 1877	Sunderland, Apr 1907	Retired, 1910
Watson R		South Bank, Sep 1902	W Arsenal, summer 1903
Wayman C	Bishop Auckland, 16 May 1921	Preston NE, 25 Sep 1954	Darlington, Dec 1956
Webb SJ	Middlesbrough, 6 Dec 1947	Juniors, Jul 1967	Carlisle U, Feb 1971
Webster, M	Blackpool, Nov 1899	Stalybridge Celtic, Mar 1922	Carlisle U, Jun 1935
Weddle DK	Newcastle upon Tyne, 27 Dec 1935	Cambridge C, Aug 1961	Darlington, Jun 1962
Weightman E	York, 4 May 1910	Scarborough, Mar 1933	Chesterfield, Oct 1936
Weir J	Benfoot Hill	Celtic, Sep 1910	Retired, 1920
Whigham WM	Airdrie, 9 Oct 1939	Falkirk, Oct 1966	Dumbarton, Aug 1974
Whitaker W	Chesterfield, 7 Oct 1923	Chesterfield, Jun 1947	Retired, summer 1955
White W	Braxburn	Dundee, Sep 1903	Aberdeen, 23 Jun 1904
Whyte, D	Glasgow, 31 Aug 1968	Celtic, Aug 1992	
Wilcox FJ	St Worburgh's	Birmingham, Mar 1906	Plymouth A, 1909
Wilkie D	Browney, 27 Jul 1939	Browney Jrs, Sep 1956	Hartlepools U, Sep 1961
Wilkie J	Govan	Rangers, Aug 1900	Rangers, 1901
Wilkinson, P	Louth, 30 Oct 1964	Watford, Aug 1991	
Willey AS	Houghton-le-Spring, 18 Oct 1956	Professional, Aug 1974	Contract cancelled, Feb 1978 Minnesota Kicks, 18 Oct 1978
Williams JJ	Rotherham, Jun 1902	Arsenal, 10 Mar 1932	Carlisle U, 3 Aug 1935
Williams, JT		Wrexham, May 1924	Clapton O, Jul 1928
Williams O	Ryhope, 23 Sep 1895	Clapton O, Feb 1924	Southend U, Aug 1930
Williamson RG	North Ormesby, 6 Jun 1884	Redcar Crusaders, Apr 1902	Retired, Apr 1923
Wilson Andrew N	New Mains, 14 Feb 1896	Cambuslang, 19 Feb 1914	Chelsea, Nov 1923
Wilson Archibald		Southend U, 7 Jul 1914	Killed in action, World War One
Wilson FP	Newcastle upon Tyne, 15 Sep 1947	Professional, Apr 1966	Gateshead, 1968
Wilson J	Chilton	Chilton CW, May 1924	Southend U, 1927
Wilson TT		Morpeth Harriers, Apr 1908	Hearts, 1909
Windridge JE	Sparkbrook, 21 Oct 1882	Chelsea, 2 Dec 1911	Birmingham, 8 Apr 1914
Windross D	Dunsdale, 12 May 1938	Blackett Hutton, May 1956	Brighton, Nov 1960
Wood AEH	Macclesfield, 25 Oct 1945	Hull C, Oct 1976	Walsall, Jul 1977
Wood DT	Scarborough, 9 Jun 1964	Professional, Jul 1981	Chelsea, Sep 1984
Woodward T	West Houghton, 8 Dec 1918	Bolton W, Oct 1949	Wigan A, Sep 1951
Woof W	Gateshead, 16 Aug 1956	Professional, Aug 1974	Peterborough U, Mar 1977(loan), Released, May 1982, Gateshead
Worrall WE	Shildon 1886	South Bank, 1905-06 (AM)	Sunderland, Nov 1905
Worthington PR	Halifax, 22 Apr 1947	Halifax T, Aug 1966	Notts C, 7 Sep 1968
Wright TE	Fife, 10 Jan 1966	Leicester C, Jul 1992	
Wynn R		Chester, Feb 1914	1914
Yeoman RI	Perth, 13 May 1934	Northampton T, Nov 1958	Darlington, Jun 1964
Yorston BC	Aberdeen, 14 Oct 1905	Sunderland, Mar 1934	Released, 1945
Young EW		Apr 1921	Darlington, summer 1921
Young, MS	Chester-Le-Street, 15 Apr 1973	Newcastle U, Jul 1991	Released, 1993
Young RT	Swinehill, 1886	West Ham U, Oct 1908	Everton, Jan 1910

Middlesbrough Career Records

The following is a full schedule of all players to have appeared in Football League, FA Cup and League Cup games for Middlesbrough. Excluded are wartime fixtures, abandoned matches, friendlies, tour games and testimonials, etc. A dagger (†) denotes the inclusion of play-off games in a players League statistics. An asterisk (*) denotes the player was still with the club at the end of the 1992-93 season. The years given are the first and last of the seasons played, irrespective of how many spells the player had with Middlesbrough. i.e. 1926-1936 is 1926-27 to 1935-36. The position given indicates that player's preferred role with the club (GK = goalkeeper, WH = wing-half etc).

Player	Pos	Seasons	League App	League Gls	FA Cup App	FA Cup Gls	FL Cup App	FL Cup Gls	TOTAL App	TOTAL Gls
AGNEW, William Barbour	LB	1904-1906	66	2	7	0	0	0	73	2
AITKEN, Andrew	CH	1906-1909	76	1	3	0	0	0	79	1
AITKEN, George Bruce	CH	1951-1953	17	0	1	0	0	0	18	0
AITKEN, Samuel	WH	1903-1910	227	6	15	0	0	0	242	6
ALLEN, Michael	HB	1967-1972	32/3	0	2	1	1	0	35/3	1
ALLPORT, Henry George	RH	1899-1900	31	0	1	0	0	0	32	0
ANDERSON, John Robert	GK	1947-1948	1	0	0	0	0	0	1	0
ANDERSON, Stanley	WH	1965-1966	21	2	1	0	0	0	22	2
ANGUS, Michael A	LH	1979-1982	35/2	1	1/1	0	4	0	40/3	1
APPLEBY, Robert	GK	1959-1967	99	0	6	0	5	0	110	0
ARMES, Samuel	OR	1938-1939	3	0	0	0	0	0	3	0
ARMSTRONG, David	OL	1970-1981	357/2	59	29	8	27/1	6	413/3	73
ARNOLD, Ian	F	1990-1992	0/3	0	0	0	0	0	0/3	0
ASHCROFT, William	CF	1977-1982	139/20	21	12/2	3	6	1	157/22	25
ASHMAN, Donald	WH	1924-1932	160	2	14	0	0	0	174	2
ASKEW, William	WF	1980-1982	10/2	0	0	0	0	0	10/2	0
ASTLEY, Henry 'Harry'	CF	1904-1905	14	4	2	1	0	0	16	5
ATHERTON, Robert H	WF	1903-1905	60	13	6	1	0	0	66	14
AULD, Walter Bottomley	OL	1950-1951	2	1	0	0	0	0	2	1
BAILEY, Ian Craig	FB	1975-1982	140/5	1	13/1	1	10/1	0	163/7	2
BAIRD, Ian John†	CF	1989-1991	62/3	19	3	1	5/1	0	70/4	20
BARHAM, Mark Francis	OR	1988-1989	3/1	0	0	0	0	0	3/1	0
BARKER, Frederick Malcolm	RB	1906-1907	1	0	0	0	0	0	1	0
BARKER, William Charles	HB	1905-1913	105	2	8	0	0	0	113	2
BARNARD, Raymond Scholey	RB	1951-1960	113	0	5	0	0	0	118	0
BAXTER, Michael John	CH	1981-1984	122	7	9	1	7	0	138	8
BAXTER, Robert Denholm	CH	1932-1939	247	19	19	1	0	0	266	20
BEAGRIE, Peter Sydney	WF	1984-1986	24/8	2	0	0	1	0	25/8	2
BEATON, Samuel	RH	1909-1910	2	0	0	0	0	0	2	0
BEATTIE, Thomas Kevin	HB	1982-1983	3/1	0	1	1	0	0	4/1	1
BELL, F William	LH	1899-1900	1	0	0	0	0	0	1	0
BELL, Henry Davey 'Harry'	WH	1946-1955	290	9	25	1	0	0	315	10
BELL, Ian Charles	IF	1977-1981	10	1	0	0	0	0	10	1
BELL, James 'Daisy'	IR	1904-1905	10	3	1	0	0	0	11	3
BELL, Joseph Nicholson	OL	1934-1935	2	0	0	0	0	0	2	0
BELL, Stephen	IF	1981-1985	79/6	12	6	2	2/1	0	87/7	14
BEST, Charles	IF	1910-1911	5	1	0	0	0	0	5	1
BILCLIFF, Raymond	RB	1951-1961	182	0	8	0	0	0	190	0
BIRBECK, Joseph	LH	1953-1959	38	0	4	0	0	0	42	0
BIRKETT, Ralph James Evans	WF	1934-1938	93	35	8	1	0	0	101	36
BIRRELL, William	IF	1920-1928	225	59	10	4	0	0	235	63
BISSETT, James Thompson	D	1924-1926	33	0	0	0	0	0	33	0
BLACKBURN, Colin	OR	1980-1981	1	0	0	0	0	0	1	0
BLACKETT, Joseph	FB	1901-1905	78	4	6	0	0	0	84	4
BLACKMORE, Harold Alfred	CF	1932-1933	19	9	4	3	0	0	23	12
BLENKINSOPP, Thomas William	D	1948-1952	98	0	2	0	0	0	100	0
BLOOMER, Stephen	IF	1905-1910	125	59	5	3	0	0	130	62
BOAM, Stuart William	CH	1971-1979	322	14	29	0	27	2	378	16
BOARDMAN, Harry	FB	1909-1910	4	0	0	0	0	0	4	0
BODDINGTON, Harold	OL	1903-1904	1	0	0	0	0	0	1	0
BOERSMA, Philip	F	1975-1977	41/6	3	3/1	0	1	0	45/7	3
BOLTON, Joseph	FB	1981-1983	59	1	5	0	5	0	69	1
BOTTRILL, Walter Gibson	OR	1922-1924	17	0	1	0	0	0	18	0
BRAITHWAITE, Robert Munn	F	1963-1967	67/1	12	1	0	3	0	71/1	12
BRAWN, William Frederick	OR	1905-1908	56	5	2	1	0	0	58	6
BREARLEY, John 'Jack'	IF	1900-1902	32	22	2	1	0	0	34	23
BRENNAN, Mark Robert	IR	1988-1990	61/4	6	4	0	6	0	71/4	6
BRIGGS, Walter	GK	1946-1948	2	0	0	0	0	0	2	0
BRINE, Peter Kenneth	IF	1972-1977	59/20	6	7/3	1	4/1	1	70/24	8
BROWN, Alexander	CF	1903-1905	44	15	5	5	0	0	49	20
BROWN, Arthur Samuel	CF	1912-1913	4	0	0	0	0	0	4	0
BROWN, David J	GK	1977-1978	10	0	0	0	0	0	10	0
BROWN, James	CH	1900-1901	4	0	0	0	0	0	4	0
BROWN, John	F	1900-1901	19	5	9	5	0	0	28	10
BROWN, John Robert	FB	1906-1908	25	0	1	0	0	0	26	0
BROWN, Joseph	LH	1949-1951	11	0	0	0	0	0	11	0
BROWN, Thomas	OR	1920-1923	5	0	0	0	0	0	5	0
BROWN, Thomas Edward	FB	1954-1958	44	0	3	0	0	0	47	0
BROWN, William Hutchinson	FB	1931-1946	256	2	18	0	0	0	274	2
BROWNLIE, John J	FB	1982-1983	12	0	1	0	2	0	15	0
BRUCE, Robert Frederick	IF	1927-1935	237	64	16	7	0	0	253	71
BRYAN, Peter Anthony	FB	1962-1965	4	0	0	0	1	0	5	0
BRYAN, Raymond	OR	1936-1937	1	0	0	0	0	0	1	0
BUCKLEY, Michael J	RH	1984-1985	27	0	2	0	2	1	31	1
BUCKLEY, Seth	CF	1899-1900	1	0	0	0	0	0	1	0
BURBECK, Ronald Thomas	WF	1956-1963	139	24	9	1	4	4	152	29
BURKE, Mark Stephen	F	1987-1990	32/25	6	2/1	0	3	0	37/26	6
BURLURAUX, Donald	WF	1970-1972	4/1	0	0	0	0	0	4/1	0

Player	Pos	Seasons	League App	League Gls	FA Cup App	FA Cup Gls	FL Cup App	FL Cup Gls	TOTAL App	TOTAL Gls
BURNS, Michael Edward	F	1978-1981	58/3	24	2/1	0	3	0	63/4	24
BURTON, George	CF	1909-1910	2	0	0	0	0	0	2	0
BUTLER, Geoffrey	FB	1965-1967	54/1	1	5	0	2	0	61/1	1
BUTLER, Reuben	F	1919-1920	27	11	1	0	0	0	28	11
BUTLER, Thomas	OR	1938-1939	2	0	0	0	0	0	2	0
BUTLER, William	OR	1922-1923	2	0	0	0	0	0	2	0
CAIG, Hugh	IR	1914-1915	1	0	0	0	0	0	1	0
CAIL, Samuel George	IF	1906-1913	136	52	7	3	0	0	143	55
CALLAGHAN, James	IR	1899-1900	2	0	0	0	0	0	2	0
CAMERON, Kenneth	WF	1929-1934	99	30	6	0	0	0	105	30
CAMPBELL, Alexander	FB	1906-1909	34	0	2	0	0	0	36	0
CAMSELL, George Henry	CF	1925-1939	418	325	35	20	0	0	453	345
CARR, Andrew	CH	1930-1933	5	0	0	0	0	0	5	0
CARR, George	IF	1919-1924	67	23	3	0	0	0	70	23
CARR, Henry 'Pep'	CF	1910-1911	3	3	0	0	0	0	3	3
CARR, John	IF	1910-1930	421	75	28	6	0	0	449	81
CARR, William 'Puddin'	CH	1910-1924	116	3	2	1	0	0	118	4
CARRICK, Christopher	F	1900-1904	26	6	6	4	0	0	32	10
CARTWRIGHT, Phillip	OR	1925-1926	6	0	0	0	0	0	6	0
CASSIDY, Joseph	F	1901-1906	126	33	9	0	0	0	135	33
CHADWICK, Clifton 'Cliff'	WF	1933-1939	93	27	4	0	0	0	97	27
CHADWICK, David E	WF	1966-1970	100/2	3	7/1	0	6	1	113/3	4
CHAPMAN, Neville	FB	1961-1967	51/2	0	2	0	5	0	58/2	0
CHARLTON, Harold 'Harry'	WF	1970-1975	8/2	0	1	0	1	0	10/2	0
CHIPPERFIELD, Francis 'Frank'	CH	1919-1920	1	0	0	0	0	0	1	0
CLARK, Ernest	RB	1899-1900	1	0	0	0	0	0	1	0
CLARK, Joseph	IR	1899-1900	1	0	0	0	0	0	1	0
CLARKE, Wallace	IF	1919-1921	8	0	1	0	0	0	9	0
CLOUGH, Brian Howard	CF	1955-1961	213	197	8	5	1	2	222	204
CLOUGH, John	GK	1922-1926	124	0	4	0	0	0	128	0
COCHRANE, Alexander Fraser	IF	1922-1926	67	8	1	0	0	0	68	8
COCHRANE, George Terence	WF	1978-1983	96/15	7	12	4	5	1	113/15	12
COCHRANE, James Kyle	LB	1973-1974	3	0	0	0	0	0	3	0
COCHRANE, Michael	FB	1900-1901	6	0	0	0	0	0	6	0
COCHRANE, Thomas	OL	1936-1939	80	16	1	0	0	0	81	16
COLEMAN, Edward P	CF	1975-1976	1	0	0	0	0	0	1	0
COLEMAN, Ernest	WF	1934-1937	85	21	5	0	0	0	90	21
COLEMAN, Simon†	CH	1989-1991	53/4	2	5	0	0	0	58/4	2
COLLETT, Andrew Alfred*	GK	1992-	2	0	0	0	0	0	2	0
COMFORT, Alan	OL	1990-1991	15	2	0	0	3	1	18	3
COMMON, Alfred	CF	1905-1910	168	58	10	7	0	0	178	65
CONNACHAN, Edward Devlin	GK	1963-1966	95	0	4	0	6	0	105	0
COOK, Henry 'Harry'	HB	1912-1915	23	0	2	0	0	0	25	0
COOK, John	F	1911-1915	52	3	2	0	0	0	54	3
COOK, Mitchell C	IR	1985-1986	3/3	0	0	0	0	0	3/3	0
COOPER, Colin Terence†	FB	1985-1991	187/5	6	13	0	18	0	218/5	6
COOPER, Douglas	F	1955-1957	5	0	0	0	0	0	5	0
COOPER, Terence	FB	1974-1978	105	1	7	0	11	0	123	1
CORBETT, Robert	FB	1951-1957	92	0	5	0	0	0	97	0
CORDEN, Stephen	FB	1985-1986	1	0	0	0	0	0	1	0
COWAN, James	FB	1899-1900	17	0	0	0	0	0	17	0
COXON, Thomas	OL	1905-1906	11	1	0	0	0	0	11	1
COYLE, Ronald Paul	FB	1986-1987	1/2	0	0/1	0	0	0	1/3	0
CRAGGS, John Edward	FB	1971-1982	408/1	12	33	0	31	1	472/1	13
CRAIG, Thomas	FB	1904-1905	2	0	0	0	0	0	2	0
CRAWFORD, Andrew	F	1983-1984	8/1	1	0	0	0	0	8/1	1
CRAWFORD, James	OR	1901-1904	24	1	2	0	0	0	26	1
CREAMER, Peter Anthony	FB	1972-1975	9	0	0	0	1/1	0	10/1	0
CROSIER, Joseph	RH	1910-1914	27	0	4	0	0	0	31	0
CROSSAN, John Anthony	IF	1967-1970	54/2	8	5	1	2	0	61/2	9
CUFF, Patrick Joseph	GK	1973-1978	31	0	5	0	0	0	36	0
CUMMING, David Scott	GK	1936-1947	135	0	22	0	0	0	157	0
CUMMINS, Stanley	F	1976-1980	39/5	9	7	1	0/1	0	46/6	10
CUNLIFFE, Arthur	OL	1935-1937	27	5	4	2	0	0	31	7
CURRIE, David Norman	CF	1982-1986	94/19	30	5/1	0	6	1	105/20	31
CURRIE, Robert	CF	1902-1903	3	1	0	0	0	0	3	1
CURTIS, John	OR	1919-1920	5	0	0	0	0	0	5	0
DAVENPORT, Peter	F	1988-1990	53/6	7	4	0	2	0	59/6	7
DAVIDSON, Andrew	LH	1900-1906	181	8	20	0	0	0	201	8
DAVIDSON, Ian	LH	1964-1967	46	0	1	0	5	0	52	0
DAVIDSON, Stewart	RH	1913-1923	208	4	8	0	0	0	216	4
DAVIDSON, William	OL	1910-1911	16	0	3	0	0	0	19	0
DAVIES, Albert E	OL	1914-1915	1	0	1	0	0	0	2	0
DAVIES, Benjamin	GK	1910-1915	31	0	0	0	0	0	31	0
DAVIES, William F	OR	1904-1905	10	0	2	0	0	0	12	0
DAVISON, John W	LH	1919-1920	1	0	0	0	0	0	1	0
DAY, William	F	1955-1962	120	18	9	2	2	1	131	21
DELAPENHA, Lloyd Lindberg 'Lindy'	F	1949-1958	260	90	10	3	0	0	270	93
DESMOND, Peter	IL	1949-1950	2	0	0	0	0	0	2	0
DEWS, George	F	1946-1948	33	8	6	0	0	0	39	8
DIBBLE, Andrew Gerald†	GK	1990-1991	21	0	0	0	0	0	21	0
DICKINSON, Peter E	OR	1924-1925	6	1	0	0	0	0	6	1
DICKS, Ronald William	WH	1947-1958	316	10	18	0	0	0	334	10
DICKSON, Ian W	CF	1923-1925	37	12	1	0	0	0	38	12
DIXON, Charles	RB	1919-1921	12	0	0	0	0	0	12	0
DIXON, Thomas	IR	1907-1911	27	8	2	1	0	0	29	9
DOBBIE, Harold	CF	1946-1950	23	6	1	2	0	0	24	8
DOIG, Thomas	RH	1900-1901	3	0	1	0	0	0	4	0
DONAGHY, Peter	HB	1919-1923	30	2	0	0	0	0	30	2

Player	Pos	Seasons	League App	League Gls	FA Cup App	FA Cup Gls	FL Cup App	FL Cup Gls	TOTAL App	TOTAL Gls
DONALDSON, Andrew	CF	1948-1951	21	7	0	0	0	0	21	7
DOUGLAS, Harry	OR	1902-1903	4	0	0	0	0	0	4	0
DOUGLAS, John Stuart	LH	1946-1947	2	0	0	0	0	0	2	0
DOW, M John	FB	1900-1902	34	0	7	0	0	0	41	0
DOWNING, Derrick George	WF	1965-1972	172/11	39	22/1	7	5	2	199/12	48
DOWSON, Francis 'Frank'	IL	1920-1921	7	2	0	0	0	0	7	2
DUFFY, Christopher Francis	OL	1905-1906	4	0	0	0	0	0	4	0
DUGUID, William	HB	1910-1913	23	0	1	0	0	0	24	0
ECKFORD, John	IF	1900-1901	4	0	3	0	0	0	7	0
EDWARDS, William Inman	CF	1952-1955	16	4	0	0	0	0	16	4
EGLINGTON, Robert	IL	1899-1900	5	2	1	1	0	0	6	3
ELKES, John E	F	1929-1933	105	4	8	0	0	0	113	4
ELLERINGTON, William	HB	1919-1924	127	0	4	0	0	0	131	0
ELLIOTT, George Washington	CF	1909-1925	344	203	21	10	0	0	365	213
EMMERSON, George Arthur	OR	1928-1930	7	3	0	0	0	0	7	3
EMMERSON, Morris	GK	1962-1963	10	0	3	0	0	0	13	0
EVANS, R W	IL	1899-1900	2	0	0	0	0	0	2	0
EYRE, Edmund 'Ninty'	OL	1911-1914	63	13	6	2	0	0	69	15
FALCONER, William Henry*	M	1991-	47/6	10	3	2	2/1	0	52/7	12
FEATHERSTONE, Thomas	CF	1903-1904	1	0	0	0	0	0	1	0
FENTON, Michael	F	1932-1950	240	147	29	15	0	0	269	162
FERGUSON, Charles	OR	1933-1936	19	7	1	1	0	0	20	8
FERGUSON, Robert	GK	1936-1938	10	0	0	0	0	0	10	0
FERGUSON, Robert G	HB	1924-1931	149	2	10	0	0	0	159	2
FERNIE, D William	IR	1958-1961	65	3	2	0	1	0	68	3
FITZSIMONS, Arthur Gerard	IF	1949-1959	223	49	8	2	0	0	231	51
FLEMING, Curtis*	FB	1991-	45/7	0	3	0	2/1	0	50/8	0
FLINT, William Arthur	OR	1909-1910	1	0	0	0	0	0	1	0
FOGGON, Alan	F	1972-1976	105/10	45	10/1	2	9/1	2	124/12	49
FORREST, William	HB	1929-1939	307	7	26	1	0	0	333	8
FOWLER, Henry Norman	LB	1937-1939	7	0	0	0	0	0	7	0
FOX, William Victor	FB	1919-1924	107	1	5	0	0	0	112	1
FRAIL, Joseph	GK	1900-1905	63	0	11	0	0	0	74	0
FRASER, Alexander	FB	1911-1913	5	0	0	0	0	0	5	0
FREEMAN, Reginald Victor	FB	1923-1930	178	0	8	0	0	0	186	0
FREEMAN, Thomas	FB	1930-1933	74	0	4	0	0	0	78	0
FRENCH, John Proctor	LB	1924-1925	1	0	0	0	0	0	1	0
GALLACHER, Constantine 'Con'	IR	1946-1947	1	0	0	0	0	0	1	0
GALLAGHER, James	LB	1920-1921	1	0	0	0	0	0	1	0
GARBETT, Terence G	CF	1965-1966	7	1	0	0	0	0	7	1
GARDNER, John Robert	CH	1928-1929	0	0	1	0	0	0	1	0
GATES, William Lazenby	D	1961-1974	277/6	12	26/1	0	18	0	321/7	12
GETTINS, Edward	OR	1903-1905	43	5	4	0	0	0	47	5
GETTINS, Joseph H	CF	1899-1903	10	1	0	0	0	0	10	1
GIBSON, Frederick William	GK	1932-1936	112	0	10	0	0	0	122	0
GIBSON, Ian Stewart	F	1961-1966	168	44	9	1	7	2	184	47
GIBSON, Robert J	OR	1910-1911	28	3	3	0	0	0	31	3
GILL, Gary	D	1983-1990	69/8	2	4/1	0	5/2	0	78/11	2
GITTENS, Jonathan	D	1992-1993	22/3	1	1	0	0/1	0	23/4	1
GLOVER, Dean Victor†	FB	1987-1989	48/6	5	5	0	4	0	57/6	5
GODLEY, William 'Snip'	F	1902-1904	2	0	0	0	0	0	2	0
GOOD, HUGH	HB	1924-1926	10	0	0	0	0	0	10	0
GOODFELLOW, Derek Ormond	GK	1947-1948	36	0	3	0	0	0	39	0
GOODSON, Leonard	OL	1902-1905	35	6	1	0	0	0	36	6
GORDON, David	RB	1908-1909	1	0	0	0	0	0	1	0
GORDON, James	WH	1946-1954	231	3	22	1	0	0	253	4
GOWLAND, Norman	GK	1925-1929	5	0	0	0	0	0	5	0
GRAY, Robert SM	IF	1899-1900	3	0	0	0	0	0	3	0
GREEN, Thomas	F	1904-1906	37	9	5	0	0	0	42	9
GRIFFITHS, Thomas Percival	CH	1932-1935	88	1	4	0	0	0	92	1
GROVES, James Albert	FB	1907-1910	27	2	0	0	0	0	27	2
HALL, Bertram Allan Couldwell	CF	1927-1930	7	2	0	0	0	0	7	2
HALL, John H	F	1908-1910	59	30	3	0	0	0	62	30
HAMILTON, Gary James†	D	1982-1989	221/12	25	14	1	13	1	248/12	27
HAMILTON, William Murdoch	IF	1960-1962	10	1	0	0	2	0	12	1
HANKIN, Raymond	F	1982-1983	19/2	1	3	1	2	1	24/2	3
HANLON, Edward	CH	1906-1907	1	0	0	0	0	0	1	0
HARDWICK, George Francis Moutrey	FB	1937-1950	143	5	23	2	0	0	166	7
HARKINS, John	LH	1906-1907	39	0	2	0	0	0	41	0
HARRIS, Joseph	WH	1922-1925	56	0	2	0	0	0	58	0
HARRIS, William Charles	WH	1953-1965	360	69	14	2	4	1	378	72
HARRISON, Henry	GK	1919-1922	20	0	0	0	0	0	20	0
HARTNETT, James Benedict	WF	1948-1955	48	8	1	0	0	0	49	8
HASELL, Albert A	GK	1907-1908	1	0	0	0	0	0	1	0
HASTIE, John	OR	1920-1921	1	0	0	0	0	0	1	0
HAWKINS, George Henry 'Harry'	IR	1935-1936	1	0	0	0	0	0	1	0
HAWORTH, John Houghton	LH	1911-1915	61	0	3	0	0	0	64	0
HEALEY, Richard	IF	1913-1915	4	2	0	0	0	0	4	2
HEARD, Timothy Patrick	IF	1985-1986	25	2	1	0	0	0	26	2
HEDLEY, George Thomas	RB	1905-1906	3	0	0	0	0	0	3	0
HEDLEY, Graeme	F	1976-1981	36/14	6	3	0	4	0	43/14	6
HENDERSON, George Hunter	RH	1905-1906	10	0	3	0	0	0	13	0
HENDERSON, Raymond	IF	1957-1961	9	5	0	0	0	0	9	5
HENDRIE, John Grattan†*	WF	1990-	111/2	15	8/2	1	15	2	134/4	18
HEPPLE, Gordon	FB	1946-1954	41	0	0	0	0	0	41	0
HEWITT, Charles	F	1904-1906	33	12	5	2	0	0	38	14
HEWITT, John	M	1991-1992	0/2	0	0	0	0	0	0/2	0
HICK, William Morris	F	1923-1925	16	7	1	0	0	0	17	7
HICKLING, William	LB	1906-1907	5	0	0	0	0	0	5	0

George Washington Elliott, who scored 213 goals in 365 League and Cup appearance for Middlesbrough between 1909 and 1925, pictured in 1948.

Gordon Jones made a remarkable 523/5 League and Cup appearances for Middlesbrough between 1960 and 1973.

Player	Pos	Seasons	League App	League Gls	FA Cup App	FA Cup Gls	FL Cup App	FL Cup Gls	TOTAL App	TOTAL Gls
HICKTON, John	F	1966-1977	395/20	159	37	13	26/4	13	458/24	185
HIGGINS, William	CH	1900-1901	24	1	5	3	0	0	29	4
HIGHAM, Norman	IF	1935-1939	49	10	1	0	0	0	50	10
HIGNETT, Craig John*	F	1992-	18/3	4	0	0	0	0	18/3	4
HILLIER, Ernest John Guy 'Joe'	GK	1929-1935	63	0	2	0	0	0	65	0
HISBENT, Joseph M	FB	1911-1915	44	0	3	0	0	0	47	0
HODGSON, David James	F	1978-1986	118/9	16	9	4	6	0	133/9	20
HODGSON, George	GK	1900-1901	4	0	0	0	0	0	4	0
HODGSON, John Percival	GK	1947-1955	13	0	0	0	0	0	13	0
HOGG, John	FB	1902-1906	90	0	10	0	0	0	100	0
HOLLIDAY, Edwin	WF	1957-1966	157	21	6	3	6	1	169	25
HOLLIDAY, John William	CF	1930-1932	6	4	0	0	0	0	6	4
HOLMES, Walter	FB	1914-1927	166	1	7	0	0	0	173	1
HONEYMAN, John William	LH	1919-1920	1	0	0	0	0	0	1	0
HORNE, Brian Simon	GK	1992-1993	3/1	0	0	0	0	0	3/1	0
HORNER, William 'Billy'	WH	1960-1969	184/3	11	17	0	12/1	1	213/4	12
HORSFIELD, Arthur	F	1963-1969	107/5	51	12/2	5	2	0	121/7	56
HOWLING, Edward	GK	1910-1911	1	0	0	0	0	0	1	0
HUGHES, Martin	GK	1899-1900	24	0	1	0	0	0	25	0
HUME, Robert Morgan	OL	1962-1963	19	5	0	0	2	0	21	5
HUNTER, Herbert	GK	1905-1906	3	0	0	0	0	0	3	0
IRONSIDE, Ian*	GK	1991-	12/1	0	0	0	2	0	14/1	0
IRVINE, James D	F	1964-1967	90/1	37	4	3	5	3	99/1	43
JACKSON, Andrew	CH	1910-1915	123	3	14	0	0	0	137	3
JAMES, William E	F	1910-1913	24	8	3	1	0	0	27	9
JANKOVIC, Bosko	F	1978-1981	42/8	16	7	1	3/2	1	52/10	18
JARVIS, Sydney	FB	1927-1935	86	1	4	0	0	0	90	1
JENNINGS, John 'Jack'	FB	1929-1937	195	10	10	0	0	0	205	10
JENNINGS, Samuel	F	1919-1920	10	2	0	0	0	0	10	2
JOHNSON, Peter E	FB	1977-1980	42/1	0	3	1	0	0	45/1	1
JOHNSTON, Christopher Patrick	RH	1947-1949	3	0	0	0	0	0	3	0
JOHNSTON, Craig Peter	F	1977-1981	61/3	16	5/2	0	4/2	0	70/7	16
JONES, Abraham	CH	1901-1906	140	9	9	0	0	0	149	9
JONES, George Wilfred	OR	1925-1926	24	1	2	0	0	0	26	1
JONES, Gordon Edward	FB	1960-1973	457/5	4	40	0	26	1	523/5	5
JONES, James	FB	1899-1905	7	0	2	0	0	0	9	0
JONES, John Love	OL	1908-1910	14	0	0	0	0	0	14	0
JORDAN, Brian Athol	LH	1958-1959	5	0	0	0	0	0	5	0
KAMARA, Christopher	D	1992-1993	3/2	0	0	0	0	0	3/2	0
KAVANAGH, Graham Anthony*	M	1992-	6/4	0	1/1	0	0	0	7/5	0
KAY, John	FB	1984-1985	8	0	0	0	0	0	8	0
KAYE, Arthur	WF	1960-1965	164	38	13	4	8	2	185	44
KEAR, Michael P	WF	1967-1970	56/2	6	5	0	3	0	64/2	6
KELLY, B	FB	1910-1911	4	0	0	0	0	0	4	0
KENNEDY, Frederick	IF	1927-1929	23	5	1	0	0	0	24	5
KENNEDY, Michael FM	M	1982-1984	68	5	7	0	4	0	79	5
KENT, Henry 'Harry'	HB	1908-1909	6	0	0	0	0	0	6	0
KERNAGHAN, Alan Nigel†*	F/D	1984-1989	168/41	15	8/4	3	22/7	1	198/52	19
KERR, Paul Andrew†	F	1986-1989	118/11	13	9/2	3	10	1	137/13	17
KINNELL, George	LH	1968-1969	12/1	1	1	0	0	0	13/1	1
KIRBY, Frederick	CF	1913-1914	2	0	0	0	0	0	2	0
KIRK, Harold J 'Harry'	OL	1963-1964	1	0	0	0	1	0	2	0
KITE, Philip D	GK	1985-1986	2	0	0	0	0	0	2	0
KNOWLES, Cyril Barry	FB	1962-1964	37	0	1	0	1	0	39	0
LAIDLAW, Joseph Dennis	F	1967-1972	104/5	20	9/2	1	5	1	118/7	22
LAKING, George Edward	FB	1936-1947	94	1	3	0	0	0	97	1
LAMB, Thomas John	IR	1899-1900	23	6	1	0	0	0	24	6
LAWRIE, Samuel	IF	1951-1957	36	5	1	0	0	0	37	5
LAWS, Brian†	FB	1984-1987	104/6	12	8/1	0	6/1	2	118/8	14
LAWSON, James J	WF	1965-1968	25/6	3	4	1	2	0	31/6	4
LAYTON, Arthur E	FB	1911-1912	7	0	1	0	0	0	8	0
LE FLEM, Richard Peter 'Flip'	WF	1964-1966	9	1	1	0	0	0	10	1
LEONARD, Henry Droxford 'Harry'	CF	1910-1912	13	3	0	0	0	0	13	3
LESLIE, James	IR	1901-1902	7	3	0	0	0	0	7	3
LIGHTENING, Arthur Douglas	GK	1962-1963	15	0	0	0	3	0	18	0
LINACRE, William	WF	1949-1950	31	2	4	1	0	0	35	3
LINTON, Thomas	CF	1899-1900	4	0	0	0	0	0	4	0
LINWOOD, Alexander Bryce	CF	1946-1947	14	3	1	0	0	0	15	3
LIVINGSTONE, Joseph	CF	1960-1963	20	7	0	0	2	0	22	7
LLOYD, Evan	IL	1919-1920	2	0	0	0	0	0	2	0
LONGSTAFFE, Geoffrey	OR	1899-1900	19	3	1	0	0	0	20	3
LUGG, Raymond J	F	1966-1970	34/3	3	2	1	1/2	0	37/5	4
LYNCH, Patrick	D	1971-1972	0/1	0	0	0	0	0	0/1	0
McALLISTER, William	RH	1924-1926	19	0	2	0	0	0	21	0
McANDREW, Anthony	D	1973-1986	311/2	15	23/1	2	15/2	1	349/5	18
MACAULAY, W	IF	1902-1903	21	2	0	0	0	0	21	2
McCABE, James Joseph	CH	1946-1948	34	0	8	0	0	0	42	0
McCALLUM, Donald	FB	1904-1906	25	0	2	0	0	0	27	0
McCLELLAND, James	CF	1924-1928	81	42	4	6	0	0	85	48
McCLURE, Samuel	IL	1910-1911	11	3	1	0	0	0	12	3
McCORMACK, James Cecil 'Cec'	F	1946-1949	37	15	2	1	0	0	39	16
McCORQUODALE, Douglas	CF	1899-1900	2	0	0	0	0	0	2	0
McCOWIE, Alexander	IF	1900-1901	16	5	4	2	0	0	20	7
McCRACKEN, James Peter	HB	1899-1900	33	0	1	0	0	0	34	0
McCRAE, Alexander	F	1948-1953	122	47	8	2	0	0	130	49
McCREESH, Andrew	FB	1981-1982	2	0	0	0	0	0	2	0
McCULLOCH, Alexander	CF	1907-1908	3	1	0	0	0	0	3	1
MACDONALD, Garry	F	1980-1985	40/13	5	4/1	1	2/1	0	46/15	6
MACFARLANE, John	HB	1929-1933	95	0	6	0	0	0	101	0
MACFARLANE, Robert 'Rab'	GK	1902-1903	18	0	1	0	0	0	19	0
MACFARLANE, Thomas	FB	1901-1902	2	0	1	0	0	0	3	0
McGEE, Owen Edward	D	1989-1992	18/3	1	0/1	0	0/1	0	18/5	1

Player	Pos	Seasons	League App	League Gls	FA Cup App	FA Cup Gls	FL Cup App	FL Cup Gls	TOTAL App	TOTAL Gls
McGUIGAN, Andrew	OR	1903-1904	1	0	0	0	0	0	1	0
McILMOYLE, Hugh	CF	1969-1971	69/1	19	8	2	2	1	79/1	22
McKAY, John	IF	1926-1934	104	19	5	1	0	0	109	20
McKENNAN, Peter Stewart	F	1949-1951	40	18	3	1	0	0	43	19
McKENZIE, Duncan	WH	1938-1939	28	1	0	0	0	0	28	1
McLEAN, James Derek	IF	1955-1962	119	30	3	0	1	0	123	30
McLEOD, Donald	FB	1908-1913	138	0	10	0	0	0	148	0
McMANUS, Charles Eric	GK	1985-1986	2	0	0	0	0	0	2	0
McMORDIE, Alexander 'Eric'	IF	1965-1974	231/10	22	20/1	1	11	2	262/11	25
McMURRAY, John	WH	1953-1955	3	0	0	0	0	0	3	0
McNALLY, John	CH	1899-1901	3	0	1	0	0	0	4	0
McNEIL, Michael	FB	1958-1964	178	3	9	0	6	0	193	3
McNEILL, Allan A	F	1967-1969	3	0	0/1	0	0	0	3/1	0
McPARTLAND, Desmond	GK	1965-1968	35	0	2	0	3	0	40	0
McPHAIL, Donald Douglas	OR	1930-1931	4	1	1	0	0	0	5	1
McPHERSON, Kenneth	CF	1953-1956	33	15	0	0	0	0	33	15
McROBBIE, Alan	LB	1911-1912	1	0	0	0	0	0	1	0
MADDEN, George	IF	1899-1900	3	0	0	0	0	0	3	0
MADDISON, James P	OL	1946-1947	1	0	0	0	0	0	1	0
MADDREN, William Dixon	D	1968-1977	293/3	19	23	0	24	2	340/3	21
MAHONEY, John F	WH	1977-1979	77	1	7	1	6	0	90	2
MAITLAND, Alfred Edward	LB	1923-1924	25	0	1	0	0	0	26	0
MALAN, Norman Frederick	GK	1946-1947	2	0	0	0	0	0	2	0
MALCOLM, George	LH	1912-1915	94	1	7	0	0	0	101	1
MANNION, Wilfred James	IF	1936-1954	341	99	27	11	0	0	368	110
MARCROFT, Edward Hallows	OR	1931-1932	1	1	0	0	0	0	1	1
MARSHALL, Dwight W*	F	1992-	0/3	0	0	0	0	0	0/3	0
MARSHALL, John	FB	1919-1923	116	0	5	0	0	0	121	0
MARSHALL, Stanley Kenneth	IL	1965-1966	2	0	0	0	0	0	2	0
MARTIN, George Scott	IF	1932-1933	6	0	0	0	0	0	6	0
MARTIN, John	WH	1932-1939	129	3	8	0	0	0	137	3
MARWOOD, Brian	M	1991-1992	3	0	0	0	1	0	4	0
MASSON, Donald Sanderson	IF	1964-1968	50/3	6	7	1	4	0	61/3	7
MATHIESON, James Adamson	GK	1926-1933	245	0	19	0	0	0	264	0
MATTINSON, Harold 'Harry'	CH	1946-1947	3	0	0	0	0	0	3	0
MILLAR, James	HB	1900-1903	19	0	3	0	0	0	22	0
MILLAR, William M	OL	1927-1929	16	6	0	0	0	0	16	6
MILLER, Joseph	WH	1926-1930	140	0	13	0	0	0	153	0
MILLION, Esmond	GK	1956-1962	52	0	1	0	0	0	53	0
MILLS, David John	IF	1969-1985	309/19	90	29	10	23/1	8	361/20	108
MILNE, John Vance	WF	1937-1939	59	7	7	0	0	0	66	7
MITCHELL, Albert James 'Bert'	OL	1954-1956	50	6	2	0	0	0	52	6
MOCHAN Neil	F	1951-1953	38	14	1	0	0	0	39	14
MOHAN, Nicholas Martin 'Nicky'*	D	1988-	71/2	4	7/1	0	7	0	85/3	4
MOODY, Alan	RB	1968-1973	44/2	0	3	0	0	0	47/2	0
MOORE, Alan Thomas*	F	1992-	0/2	0	0	0	0	0	0/2	0
MORAN, Martin	F	1900-1902	36	5	9	1	0	0	45	6
MORDUE, John 'Jacky'	WF	1920-1922	35	1	0	0	0	0	35	1
MORRIS, Christopher Brian*	FB	1992-	22/3	1	2	0	2	0	26/3	1
MOWBRAY, Anthony Mark†	D	1982-1992	350/4	26	23	1	28/1	1	401/5	28
MUIR, John	OL	1902-1904	13	0	0	0	0	0	13	0
MUIR, William	HB	1902-1904	4	0	0	0	0	0	4	0
MULHOLLAND, Francis Gerard	LH	1951-1958	46	0	4	0	0	0	50	0
MURDOCH, Robert White	WH	1973-1976	93/2	6	7	1	13	0	113/2	7
MURPHY, David Anthony	LH	1937-1938	12	0	3	0	0	0	15	0
MURPHY, Joseph	IL	1899-1900	6	5	0	0	0	0	6	5
MURPHY, Michael	IL	1899-1900	2	2	0	0	0	0	2	2
MURPHY, Thomas Edwin	IL	1946-1948	9	1	0	0	0	0	9	1
MURRAY, Alan	IR	1969-1971	6/4	1	0	0	0	0	6/4	1
MURRAY, Thomas	IF	1905-1907	12	2	0	0	0	0	12	2
MURRAY, William	OL	1921-1923	15	1	2	0	0	0	17	1
MUSTOE, Robbie*†	M	1990-	89/7	7	6	0	15/1	4	110/8	11
MUTTITT, Ernest	OL	1929-1932	20	3	5	1	0	0	25	4
MYTON, Brian	LH	1968-1971	10	0	0	0	2	0	12	0
NASH, Frank Cooper 'Paddy'	GK	1937-1948	19	0	0	0	0	0	19	0
NATTRASS, Irving	FB	1979-1986	186/5	2	18	0	10/1	0	214/6	2
NEAL, Richard Marshall	LH	1961-1963	33	4	2	0	3	0	38	4
NIBLO, Thomas Bruce	CF	1899-1900	3	2	0	0	0	0	3	2
NICHOL, James	WF	1910-1914	52	13	4	0	0	0	56	13
NOBBS, Keith Alan	FB	1980-1981	1	0	0	0	0	0	1	0
NORRIS, Oliver Plunkett 'Narker'	OR	1951-1954	12	3	1	0	0	0	13	3
NURSE, Melvyn Tudor George	CH	1962-1966	113	8	8	1	3	0	124	9
O'CONNELL, Seamus Cyril Patrick	IL	1953-1954	3	2	2	0	0	0	5	2
O'HAGAN, Charles	IF	1906-1907	5	1	0	0	0	0	5	1
O'HANLON, Kelham Gerrard	GK	1982-1985	87	0	6	0	4	0	97	0
O'RIORDAN, Donal Joseph	CH	1985-1986	41	2	1	1	2	0	44	3
O'ROURKE, John	CF	1966-1968	63/1	38	3	3	5	1	71/1	42
ORRITT, Bryan	F	1961-1966	115/3	22	4	1	6	0	125/3	23
OSBORNE, Fergus	IF	1899-1900	12	2	0	0	0	0	12	2
OSTLER, John	CH	1899-1900	3	0	0	0	0	0	3	0
OTTO, Heine M	IF	1981-1985	163/4	24	12	2	9	2	184/4	28
PAGE, Robert	HB	1899-1904	22	4	1	0	0	0	23	4
PALLISTER, Gary Andrew†	LH	1985-1990	160	5	10	1	10	1	180	7
PARKIN, Raymond	RH	1935-1937	6	0	0	0	0	0	6	0
PARKINSON, Gary Anthony†	D	1986-1993	198/8	5	17	1	20	1	235/8	7
PATERSON, Thomas	CF	1974-1975	1	0	0	0	0	0	1	0
PATTERSON, Ronald Lindsay	LB	1951-1952	1	0	0	0	0	0	1	0
PAYTON, Andrew Paul	F	1991-1992	8/11	3	1/3	0	0	0	9/14	3
PEACOCK, Alan	CF	1955-1964	218	125	13	8	7	8	238	141
PEACOCK, Joseph	LH	1927-1930	80	2	5	2	0	0	85	4
PEAKE, Andrew Michael*	M	1991-	53/3	0	7	0	1	0	61/3	0
PEARS, Stephen†*	GK	1983-	292	0	23	0	26	0	341	0

The great Wilf Mannion, 110 goals in 368 League and FA Cup games for Middlesbrough.

Bernie Slaven, 134 goals in 334/26 League and Cup games for Middlesbrough.

Player	Pos	Seasons	League App	League Gls	FA Cup App	FA Cup Gls	FL Cup App	FL Cup Gls	TOTAL App	TOTAL Gls
PEASE, William Harold	OR	1926-1933	222	99	17	3	0	0	239	102
PEGGIE, James	F	1910-1911	6	0	0	0	0	0	6	0
PENDER, Robert	HB	1919-1924	104	10	6	0	0	0	110	10
PENTLAND, Frederick Beaconsfield	F	1908-1911	92	11	4	0	0	0	96	11
PETERS, Jeffrey	LB	1979-1980	6	0	0	0	0	0	6	0
PHILLIPS, Bryan John	D	1954-1960	121	2	3	0	0	0	124	2
PHILLIPS, James Neil†*	LB	1989-	141	7	10	0	16	0	167	7
PHILLIPSON, Thomas F	IL	1904-1905	3	2	0	0	0	0	3	2
PIERCY, Frank R	LH	1899-1903	4	0	1	0	0	0	5	0
PIERCY, Henry Robert	WH	1899-1900	8	1	0	0	0	0	8	1
PLATT, James Archibald	GK	1971-1983	401	0	34	0	33	0	468	0
POLLOCK, Jamie*	M	1990-	38/11	2	6/1	0	7/2	0	51/14	2
POOLE, Kevin	GK	1987-1991	34	0	2	0	4	0	40	0
POSKETT, Malcolm	F	1973-1974	0/1	0	0	0	0	0	0/1	0
POULTON, Alonzo 'Jerry'	F	1919-1922	18	5	1	0	0	0	19	5
POVEY, William	IF	1962-1963	6	0	0	0	0	0	6	0
PRATT, Richard	IF	1899-1900	16	1	1	0	0	0	17	1
PRIEST, Alfred Ernest	FB	1906-1907	12	0	0	0	0	0	12	0
PRIEST, F	CF	1906-1907	1	0	0	0	0	0	1	0
PROCTOR, Mark Gerard†	M	1978-1993	210/21	18	14/3	1	13/2	1	237/26	20
PROUDLOCK, Paul	F	1986-1989	2/3	1	0	0	0	0	2/3	1
PUGH, Charles Edwin 'Eddie'	OL	1899-1900	31	7	1	0	0	0	32	7
PUTNEY, Trevor Anthony†	M	1989-1991	47/3	1	2	0	5	0	54/3	1
RAISBECK, Luke	CH	1899-1900	19	1	0	0	0	0	19	1
RAMAGE, Alan	HB	1975-1980	65/4	2	6	0	5	0	76/4	2
RAMSAY, Andrew	FB	1899-1904	124	1	12	0	0	0	136	1
RATCLIFFE, Donald	WH	1963-1966	65	3	6	0	0	0	71	3
RATCLIFFE, Emor 'Ernie'	FB	1905-1907	9	0	0	0	0	0	9	0
RAYMENT, Joseph Watson	WF	1952-1955	24	4	0	0	0	0	24	4
REAGAN, Charles Martin	OR	1947-1951	24	4	1	0	0	0	25	4
REDFERN J	LH	1899-1900	3	0	0	0	0	0	3	0
REID, George	CF	1899-1900	15	5	0	0	0	0	15	5
REID, George T	F	1905-1906	24	5	2	0	0	0	26	5
RICKABY, Stanley	FB	1947-1950	10	0	0	0	0	0	10	0
RIGBY, Arthur	OL	1932-1933	10	3	0	0	0	0	10	3
RIPLEY, Stuart Edward†	F	1984-1992	215/39	26	17/1	1	21/2	3	253/42	30
ROBERTS, Alan	OR	1983-1984	28/10	2	0/1	0	2/1	0	30/12	2
ROBERTS, J	OL	1906-1907	1	0	0	0	0	0	1	0
ROBERTS, Richard James	OL	1903-1905	23	5	0	0	0	0	23	5
ROBERTS, William S	OL	1906-1908	12	0	0	0	0	0	12	0
ROBERTSON, Alexander 'Sandy'	CF	1900-1903	48	24	8	8	0	0	56	32
ROBERTSON, James	OR	1901-1903	32	3	0	0	0	0	32	3
ROBERTSON, William George	OL	1954-1955	5	2	0	0	0	0	5	2
ROBINSON, John	IR	1953-1955	3	0	0	0	0	0	3	0
ROBINSON, Joseph Norman	CH	1946-1948	16	0	1	0	0	0	17	0
ROBINSON, John W	LH	1919-1920	1	0	0	0	0	0	1	0
ROBINSON, Richard	FB	1946-1959	390	1	26	0	0	0	416	1
RODGERSON, Alan Ralph	IF	1958-1964	13	3	0	0	1	0	14	3
ROOKS, Richard	CH	1965-1969	136	14	7	0	7	0	150	14
ROSS, Albert Cyril	FB	1935-1937	11	0	1	0	0	0	12	0
ROSS, Colin	WH	1980-1983	37/1	0	2	0	0	0	39/1	0
ROWELL, Gary	IF	1985-1987	27	10	1	0	2	2	30	12
RUSSELL, Edward Thomas	HB	1951-1953	29	1	3	0	0	0	32	1
RUSSELL, Martin Colin†	IF	1990-1991	10/2	2	0	0	2	0	12/2	2
SAXBY, Michael W	HB	1984-1985	15	0	2	0	0	0	17	0
SCOTT, Geoffrey C	LB	1984-1985	2	0	0	0	1	0	3	0
SCOTT, Joseph Cumpson	IF	1954-1958	93	26	6	4	0	0	99	30
SCOTT, William Reed	IF	1930-1932	26	5	2	0	0	0	28	5
SCRIMSHAW, Charles Thomas	LB	1938-1939	9	0	0	0	0	0	9	0
SENIOR, Trevor John†	F	1987-1988	13/1	4	0	0	1	0	14/1	4
SHAND, Hector	WH	1906-1907	2	0	0	0	0	0	2	0
SHANNON, Robert 'Rab'	M	1991-1992	0/1	0	0	0	1	0	1/1	0
SHAW, Thomas William	FB	1899-1900	12	0	1	0	0	0	13	0
SHEARER, David John	F	1977-1983	88/9	23	10/2	4	4/2	3	102/13	30
SHEPHERDSON, Harold	CH	1936-1947	17	0	0	0	0	0	17	0
SHORT, Maurice	GK	1967-1970	16	0	2	0	1	0	19	0
SLADE, Charles Howard	WH	1922-1925	68	2	2	0	0	0	70	2
SLAVEN, Bernard Joseph†	F	1985-1993	292/21	120	16/3	4	26/2	10	334/26	134
SMITH, David	OL	1967-1968	1/1	0	1	0	2	2	4/1	2
SMITH, David W	WH	1900-1905	108	12	6	0	0	0	114	12
SMITH, Edward George	GK	1899-1900	10	0	0	0	0	0	10	0
SMITH, Ernest Edwin	CH	1923-1925	21	0	0	0	0	0	21	0
SMITH, George	WH	1968-1971	74	0	5	1	3	0	82	1
SMITH, John	FB	1926-1930	113	0	10	0	0	0	123	0
SMITH, John	RB	1933-1934	1	0	0	0	0	0	1	0
SMITH, Malcolm	CF	1972-1976	32/24	11	0/2	0	5/1	2	37/27	13
SMITH, Robert Alexander	FB	1965-1972	119/2	1	9	0	3	0	131/2	1
SOUNESS, Graeme James	M	1972-1978	174/2	22	13	1	15	0	202/2	23
SPRAGGON, Frank	WH	1963-1976	277/3	3	23/1	0	18/1	0	318/5	3
SPRIGGS, Stephen	RB	1986-1987	3	0	0	0	0	0	3	0
SPUHLER, John Oswald	CF	1946-1954	216	69	25	12	0	0	241	81
STAGE, William 'Wit'	OL	1913-1914	3	0	0	0	0	0	3	0
STEPHENS, Arthur 'Archie'	IF	1984-1988	87/5	24	3	0	8/1	1	98/6	25
STEVENSON, Arthur Brown	OL	1923-1924	8	0	0	0	0	0	8	0
STEWART, James Garven	GK	1978-1980	34	0	2	0	2	0	38	0
STILES, Norbert Peter 'Nobby'	WH	1971-1973	57	2	7	0	5	0	69	2
STIRLING, John 'Jock'	WF	1937-1938	103	8	9	0	0	0	112	8
STONE, John G	LB	1971-1972	2	0	0	0	0	0	2	0
STONEHOUSE, Derek	FB	1953-1961	174	0	11	0	3	0	188	0
STOREY, Thomas	OR	1913-1920	33	1	0	0	0	0	33	1
STOTT, James	LH	1899-1900	1	0	0	0	0	0	1	0
STRONG, Andrew F	FB	1984-1985	6	0	0	0	0	0	6	0

Player	Pos	Seasons	League App	League Gls	FA Cup App	FA Cup Gls	FL Cup App	FL Cup Gls	TOTAL App	TOTAL Gls
STUART, Robert William	FB	1931-1948	247	2	21	0	0	0	268	2
SUDDICK, James	IR	1903-1904	1	1	0	0	0	0	1	1
SUGRUE, Paul A	IF	1982-1985	66/3	6	8	3	4	1	78/3	10
SURTEES, John	IL	1931-1932	1	0	0	0	0	0	1	0
SWALES, Norman	RH	1925-1926	2	0	0	0	0	0	2	0
TAYLOR, Brian	HB	1972-1976	14/4	1	0	0	1/1	0	15/5	1
TAYLOR, Carl Wilson	OR	1957-1960	11	1	0	0	0	0	11	1
TAYLOR, Peter Thomas	GK	1955-1961	140	0	6	0	0	0	146	0
TENNANT, James	OL	1901-1902	17	7	0	0	0	0	17	7
THACKERAY, James	OL	1904-1910	157	16	13	2	0	0	170	18
THOMAS, David	OL	1981-1982	13	1	0	0	0	0	13	1
THOMAS, Martin R	GK	1984-1985	4	0	0	0	0	0	4	0
THOMPSON, A	CF	1900-1903	7	3	1	0	0	0	8	3
THOMPSON, Norman	IL	1925-1926	8	3	0	0	0	0	8	3
THOMPSON, William T	IL	1905-1906	6	2	0	0	0	0	6	2
THOMSON, Kenneth Gordon	CH	1959-1963	84	1	4	0	2	0	90	1
THOMSON, Robert	OL	1981-1982	18/2	2	2	2	2	1	22/2	5
TINSLEY, Walter	IL	1913-1921	86	46	3	3	0	0	89	49
TOMLIN, John	CH	1906-1907	4	0	0	0	0	0	4	0
TOWNSEND, James	WH	1963-1966	65/2	6	4	0	1	0	70/2	6
TRECHMAN, Otto L	CF	1905-1906	1	0	0	0	0	0	1	0
TUCKER, William Henry	CF	1906-1907	4	1	0	0	0	0	4	1
TURNBULL, Lee Mark	F	1985-1987	8/8	4	0	0	0/1	0	8/9	4
TURNER, Peter	IL	1901-1902	23	6	2	0	0	0	25	6
TWINE, Frank	FB	1926-1928	52	0	6	0	0	0	58	0
TYLDESLEY, James	RB	1906-1907	23	0	2	0	0	0	25	0
UGOLINI, Rolando	GK	1948-1956	320	0	15	0	0	0	335	0
URQUHART, A	OR	1907-1908	4	0	0	0	0	0	4	0
URWIN, Thomas	WF	1914-1924	192	14	8	0	0	0	200	14
VERRILL, Edward	HB	1907-1915	181	4	11	0	0	0	192	4
VINCENT, John Victor	WF	1970-1972	37/3	7	0	0	2/1	0	39/4	7
WAINSCOAT, William Russell	IF	1923-1925	34	5	2	0	0	0	36	5
WALDOCK, Ronald	WF	1959-1962	34	7	1	0	0	0	35	7
WALKER, Donald Hunter	LH	1959-1962	23	1	1	0	1	0	25	1
WALKER, John	LB	1913-1921	106	0	3	0	0	0	109	0
WALKER, Robert Geoffrey	OL	1946-1955	240	50	19	3	0	0	259	53
WALKER, Robert H	IL	1905-1906	9	2	5	1	0	0	14	3
WALLEY, Ernest	LH	1958-1959	8	0	0	0	0	0	8	0
WALSH, Alan	F	1977-1978	0/3	0	0	0	0	0	0/3	0
WALSH, Colin D	M	1990-1991	10/3	1	1	0	0	0	11/3	1
WANLESS, Robert	OR	1899-1900	10	0	0	0	0	0	10	0
WARD, Paul Terence	D	1982-1986	69/7	1	3/1	0	5	0	77/8	1
WARDLE, George	OR	1937-1938	1	0	0	0	0	0	1	0
WARDROPE, Alexander	CH	1910-1911	10	0	1	0	0	0	11	0
WARDROPE, William	F	1899-1902	62	21	11	3	0	0	73	24
WARK, John	D	1990-1991	31/1	2	2	0	5	0	38/1	2
WARREN, Frederick Windsor	OL	1929-1936	160	49	4	1	0	0	164	50
WATKIN, Thomas William Steel	OL	1953-1955	11	2	0	0	0	0	11	2
WATSON, Arnold	WH	1925-1926	8	0	0	0	0	0	8	0
WATSON, Herbert Leonard	RH	1929-1932	13	1	2	0	0	0	15	1
WATSON, James	LB	1906-1910	103	0	4	0	0	0	107	0
WATSON, Robert	IR	1901-1903	16	5	1	0	0	0	17	5
WAYMAN, Charles	CF	1954-1956	55	31	3	2	0	0	58	33
WEBB, Stanley J	CF	1967-1971	20/9	6	0	0	0	0	20/9	6
WEBSTER, Maurice	CH	1920-1934	262	3	19	0	0	0	281	3
WEDDLE, Derek Keith	CH	1961-1962	3	1	0	0	0	0	3	1
WEIGHTMAN, Eric	D	1935-1936	2	0	1	0	0	0	3	0
WEIR, James	LB	1910-1915	113	0	12	0	0	0	125	0
WHIGHAM, William M	GK	1966-1972	187	0	17	0	6	0	210	0
WHITAKER, William	CH	1947-1955	177	1	7	0	0	0	184	1
WHITE, William	IR	1903-1904	7	0	0	0	0	0	7	0
WHYTE, Derek*	D	1992-	34/1	0	0	0	2	0	36/1	0
WILCOX, Frederick J	OR	1905-1910	106	12	4	0	0	0	110	12
WILKIE, Derrick	CH	1959-1961	4	0	0	0	0	0	4	0
WILKIE, John	IL	1900-1901	28	8	7	2	0	0	35	10
WILKINSON, Paul*	CF	1991-	87	29	7	4	10	4	104	37
WILLEY, Alan S	F	1974-1978	27/23	7	1/3	1	3/1	0	31/27	8
WILLIAMS, Jesse T	OL	1924-1928	37	8	1	0	0	0	38	8
WILLIAMS, Joseph Joshua	F	1931-1935	78	11	7	2	0	0	85	13
WILLIAMS, Owen	OL	1923-1930	184	40	10	4	0	0	194	44
WILLIAMSON, Reginald Garnet 'Tim'	GK	1901-1923	563	2	39	0	0	0	602	2
WILSON, Andrew Nesbit	CF	1914-1924	86	56	4	1	0	0	90	57
WILSON, Archibald	WF	1914-1915	21	4	2	0	0	0	23	4
WILSON, F Peter	RB	1967-1968	1	0	0	0	0	0	1	0
WILSON, John	RB	1924-1927	18	0	0	0	0	0	18	0
WILSON, Thomas T	F	1907-1910	10	0	0	0	0	0	10	0
WINDRIDGE, James Edward	IF	1911-1914	68	11	8	1	0	0	76	12
WINDROSS, Dennis	IR	1959-1961	4	1	0	0	0	0	4	1
WOOD, Alfred E H	IF	1976-1977	22/1	2	5	0	0	0	27/1	2
WOOD, Darren Terence	D	1981-1985	101	6	8	0	6	0	115	6
WOODWARD, Thomas	OL	1949-1951	19	6	0	0	0	0	19	6
WOOF, William	F	1974-1982	30/16	5	0/1	0	7/1	1	37/18	6
WORRALL, William Edward	GK	1905-1906	1	0	0	0	0	0	1	0
WORTHINGTON, Peter Robert	FB	1967-1968	2	0	1	0	0	0	3	0
WRIGHT, Thomas, Edward*	F	1992-	34/2	5	3	1	2	0	39/2	6
WYNN, Richard	OL	1913-1915	7	1	0	0	0	0	7	1
YEOMAN, Ramon Irvine 'Ray'	WH	1958-1963	210	3	10	0	7	0	227	3
YORSTON, Benjamin Collard	F	1933-1939	152	54	7	0	0	0	159	54
YOUNG, Ernest Wilson	CF	1920-1921	1	0	0	0	0	0	1	0
YOUNG, Michael Samuel	F	1991-1992	0/1	0	0	0	0	0	0/1	0
YOUNG, Robert T	CH	1908-1910	34	5	3	0	0	0	37	5

SUBSCRIBERS

1 Evening Gazette
2 ICI
3 Middlesbrough Football Club
4 Sandy Anderson
5 Colin Henderson
6 Lennie Lawrence
7 Keith Lamb
8 Les Bell
9 Albert Dicken
10 Brian Goodall
11 Mike McCullagh
12 Warwick Brindle
13 Ranald Allan
14 Eric Paylor
15 Stuart Garner
16 A B Hill
17 W Heeps
18 G R Oates
19 James Headley
20 Graham Appleyard
21 Chris Pyle
22 S Tweddle
23 James Scrimgour
24 David John Robinson
25 James William Livingstone
26 Stephen Richard Webb
27 Matt Reynolds
28 Grant Dickinson (Boro's Youngest Fan)
29 E Murphy
30 Wendy Shepherd
31 Alastair Brownlee
32 Dennis Moore
33 Nigel Fishburn
34 David J Jenkinson
35 Martin Dowey
36 Michael Baty
37 Ray Durent
38 Stuart A Wears
39 C J Lackenby
40 Simon Murphy
41 Howard Fleming
42 Yvonne Mason
43 Phillip Dent
44 Gillian Louise Smith
45 Kevin Roy
46 Paul Whitehead
47 Alyson Ruddock
48 Doreen Adams
49 Derek Ferguson
50 Paul Feeney
51 Billy McGee
52 Mr K J Quinn
53 J H Murray
54 Brian Appleton
55 Gary Finn
56 John Goodison
57 Paul Passman
58 James Clark
59 Simon McKeown
60 Emma Cannell
61 A Gibbons
62 Stan Denham
63 Graham Beulah
64 Ian Simpson
65 Rachel Sands
66 Colin Davidson
67 Mark Stinton
68 Sydney Summerfield
69 William Robert Smith
70 Garry & Diana Brogden
71 Graeme Burluraux
72 Neil Brown
73 Stephen Hill
74 Craig Turner
75 Graham R Bunn
76 Leslie G Harrison
77 Ray Smith
78 Neil R Chapman
79 R Lobley
80 Colin Forth
81 Ian David Leyden
82 Jeff Baker
83 T J Maggs
84 Paul James
85 A G Rowlands
86 Cliff B Holmes
87 Steven L Rayson
88 David L Gibb
89 Ian Davison
90 Julie Searle
91 Mark Anthony Smitheringale
92 Arnold Thwaites
93 David Cowen
94 Andrew Beane
95 T McCartney
96 Marc Bashford
97 D Blades
98 Allan Roberts
99 Paul Kapoor
100 Shaun Wilson
101 Jim Everall
102 David Stephenson
103 David Buck
104 Eric Harold Harris
105 Michael Boyer
106 Ted Brown
107 Stephen Livesey
108 Mr Russell Anthony Sullivan
109 Ben Clare
110 Paul Hardy
111 Gerard Eglington
112 K W Kitching
113 W A Hart
114 Raymond Dales
115 Dudley Graham
116 K Roberts
117 John Shaw
118 Bob Shaw
119 David Shaw
120 Jim McLaren
121 M Oliver
122 Stephen McDonagh
123 Charles Hayton
124 Darren Wong
125 Ian G Brown
126 Lee Wells
127 Michael A Ash
128 Andrew Maurice Lloyd
129 Mark Quigley
130 Tony Conroy
131 F T Whitfield
132 Cheryl & Peter Wells
133 Brian H Douglass
134 Wendy Anne Croshaw
135 Mrs E Hodgson (née Davison)
136 Stephen Riley
137 Colin Watson
138 Mike Cotton
139 Nigel Dotchin
140 S W Lindsay
141 Neil Millward
142 Lennie Downs
143 Paul Huskinson
144 D Young
145 Dorothy Cowell
146 Ian Veacock
147 Richard Bowen
148 Stewart Blair
149 Joseph Wardle
150 Denis Green
151 T Bryan Wilkinson
152 Richard Wilkinson
153 Denis E Jones
154 Christopher N Waites
155 Arthur McLay
156 Stuart Pearson
157 Jimmy Evans
158 Ken Atkinson
159 Damian Taylor
160 T S Myers
161 Dr J J McGrath
162 Dean Pankhurst
163 Iain Henry Thomson (Scotty)
164 Norman Pickthall
165 Mark Riley
166 Stuart Browne
167 Paul Michael Brooke
168 Peter Chambers
169 J Norman
170 Howard Boville
171 Michael Harvey
172 Ken Harrison
173 Christopher Hobaiter
174 Samuel Graham Smith
175 Philip Appleby
176 Alan Knox
177 E A Nobbs
178 John Lightfoot
179 Carl Erik Lindberg senior
180 Carl Erik Lindberg junior
181 Anthony Ford
182 Brian Day
183 Angela Patton
184 N A Keetley
185 Mr Nicholas Goldsbrough
186 Mr Andrew Whorlton
187 Mr Neil Stockton
188 Mr Stephen Millward
189 D G Sillars

190 Graeme Patton
191 Ted Leyshon
192 I Tombs
193 Andrew Davis
194 Michael Eric Smitheringale
195 Lee Patterson
196 Jonathan Ridley
197 Ron McCormick
198 Chris C Lilley
199 Steven Michael Wilcox
200 Kevin Stevens
201 T Anderson
202 K M Johnson
203 Bill Trewick
204 Simon Hurndall
205 R Tweddle
206 Simon Ditchburn
207 Mr J Scully
208 Alice Ferguson
209 Tony Hookey
210 John Harton
211 David Harton
212 Tony Fox
213 Colin Shaw
214 Andrew J Taylor
215 D C Swatman
216 D C R Swatman
217 D R Swatman
218 Ian James Hope
219 John Taylor
220 Joan L Dawson
221 Nick Miller
222 Jonathan P Gilby
223 R McLintock
224 Paul Rodgerson
225 Robert Ainscough
226 Dave Allan
227 S, R & J Knott
228 J W Thomas
229 R Dermont
230 Mrs Margaret French
231 Gareth Williams
232 Brian Ward
233 Brian G Garton
234 Michael Dallin
235 P Barnard
236 Nicola L Clark
237 Sidney Carr
238 Lee David McDonough
239 Michael Coleman
240 Peter Stage
241 Paul Wesson
242 Eric Lowe
243 John Taylor
244 Rachel Franks
245 Paul Flintoft
246 David Sayers
247 Trevor Braithwaite
248 George D Rawden
249 Phil Jeynes
250 Alasdair McWilliam
251 James Lockwood
252 Thomas L Dodsworth
253 Geoffrey Reynolds
254 Mark Baxtrem
255 Steve Roberts
256 Nicole M Weatherston
257 Christopher Fountain
258 David Smith

259 Terence Peter Wood
260 S M Smith
261 James W Fordham
262 Sarah Louise Hornsby
263 Alan Murray
264 Robert Boyes
265 Ian Parker
266 Peter Waterfield
267 Mark Wardle
268 S Coates
269 Bill Masters
270 Dr M J Ebdy
271 Justin Lithgo
272 Craig Emmerson
273 James & Mark Haddrill
274 Arthur Biggs
275 Terry French
276 Robert T Jackson
277 Christopher Chambers
278 Tim Metcalfe
279 John Evans
280 Denis Poole
281 David Moore
282 Chris Keeble
283 Craig Dempster
284 Trevor Eden
285 James Booth
286 Mark Davies
287 David James Partington
288 Michael Peter Nash
289 Paul Galloway
290 D A C O Dickson
291 R S Danieli
292 C Hearn
293 Philip Scott Chisem
294 Mark Cook
295 Graham Warr
296 David Golightly
297 Boro Programmes
298 Martin James Coulson
299 Edmund Moodie
300 Gordon Rees
301 Matthew & Tim Skipper
302 Richard Graham Peacock
      (Dicky)
303 Paul Watson
304 Fraser Scott Blunt
305 Brian Parker
306 Steven Lupton
307 Andrew Lowe
308 Clive Daniels
309 Eric N Emmerson
310 David I Sargeant
311 Mike Cheall
312 Stuart B Dick
313 Andrew Fisher
314 Christopher Fisher
315 Graeme Barrett Lewis
316 Edward Hunter
317 J E V Wells
318 Mick Collins
319 Paul Collins
320 Chris Jones
321 Sue Norgan
322 Caroline Walker
323 Matthew Whitfield
324 Vincent Walsh
325 Kevin Hobson
326 David McGurk

327 Stephen McGurk
328 Corey Joe Bell
329 Paul Blackburn
330 Mr R W McLinn
331 Ronald Taylor
332 Kenneth S Stephenson
333 Kevin Sweeney
334 Neil Errington
335 Nigel Gibb
336 Mr P E Kirby
337 Michael E Holder
338 Dr Brian T B Manners
339 Willy Østby
340 Mr G M Briggs
341 J A Harris
342 Mr Anthony Sullivan
343 Mike Young
344 Mr L Dixon
345 E P Yardley
346 E W Clutton
347 Phil Hollow
348 Julian Holmes
349 Glyn Jones
350 Colin Sillet
351 Christopher E C Hooker
352 Mr F C Beale
353 Harald Löhr
354 Mr L G Cooke
355 J A Retter
356 Paul Weaver
357 Nr Niall MacSweeney
358 Bjørn Langerud
359 Reiner Sawitzki
360 Mr Alan Jones
361 Mr David Walker
362 David Dickens
363 D Green
364 Christer Svensson
365 Colin Tustin
366 R Stocken
367 Göran Schönhult
368 Patricia Ramsey
369 John Taylor
370 Peter Riley
371 Burt Nicholson
372 Craig Richards
373 Paul Herman
374 Michael Greenup
375 T Donegan
376 A Dickinson
377 Miss Heather C Lewis
378 Mrs D Lax
379 David McGrory
380 Euan McGrory
381 T Balls